Analyzing Data and Making Decisions
Statistics for Business

Personalized Learning!

The *MyStatLab* Study Plan is based on your specific learning needs.

Auto-Graded Tests and Assignments

MyStatLab comes with two pre-loaded Sample Tests for each chapter so you can self-assess your understanding of the material.

Personalized Study Plan

A Study Plan is generated based on your results on Sample Tests and instructor assignments. You can clearly see which topics you have mastered and, more importantly, which topics you need to work on!

"I'm a visual learner so having the video lectures was helpful, and the homework allowed me to see which areas I was struggling in. The helpful hints for solving the homework questions were very helpful."

Practice Problems

Use the Study Plan exercises to get practice where you need it. To check how you're doing, click Results to get an overview of all your scores.

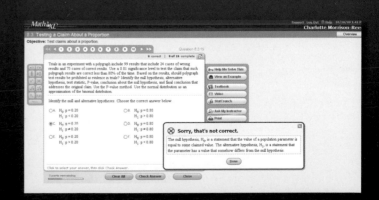

Save Time. Improve Results. www.mathxl.com

Unlimited Practice!

MyStatLab offers a wide variety of problems that let you practise to improve your understanding of the course material.

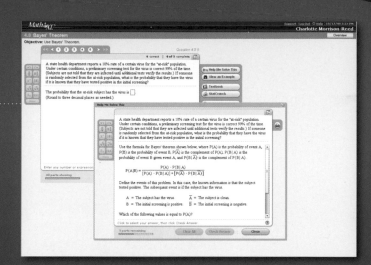

Help Me Solve This

Stuck on an exercise and don't know where to begin? Click the Help Me Solve This button to see a walkthrough that shows you how to set and solve the exercise.

eText

Pearson eText gives students access to the text whenever and wherever they have access to the internet. eText pages look exactly like the printed text, offering powerful new functionality for students and instructors. Users can create notes, highlight text in different colours, create book-marks, zoom, click hyperlinked words and phrases to view definitions, and choose single-page or two-page view.

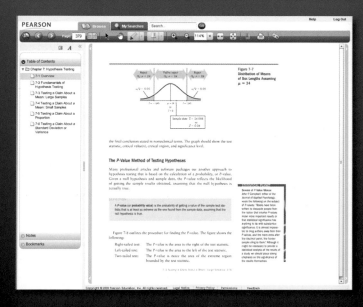

Similar Exercise

Once you have solved an exercise, *MyStatLab* allows you to practice similar exercises to reinforce concepts and prepare for mid-terms/finals.

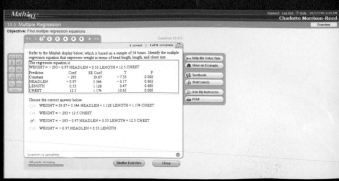

MyStatLab™

Save Time. Improve Results!

Use *MyStatLab* to prepare for tests and exams and to go to class ready to learn.

When you use *MyStatLab*, you don't just learn more about statistics—you learn how to learn.

More than three million students have used *MyStatLab* (and *MyMathLab*) at almost 2,000 institutions around the world.

We asked Canadian students what they thought about *MyStatLab*. Here are some of the things they had to say:

"I ended up with a 90% on my mid-term thanks to this program."

"The 'View an Example' was super helpful because it helped me go through the question and I was able to reiterate it when doing my homework. I got better grades because of this tool."

"I was able to use the examples during the homework exercises and apply them to other questions that I needed help in. I was able to get help when I needed by using the 'Help Me Solve This' button. Through the 'Results' feature I was able to keep track of my marks and I was able to see where I went wrong in them."

"I especially loved the tutorial (help section) within the homework."

"The interactiveness of the website makes it more motivating to do math."

"The videos saved my life!"

"This program helped me find out where my weaknesses are."

"You should make this program available for all courses!"

"I couldn't have passed the class without it!"

85% of students said they would recommend the program to another student or ask other professors to use it in class.

Save Time. Improve Results. www.mathxl.com

Second Edition

Analyzing Data and Making Decisions

Statistics for Business

Judith Skuce

Georgian College

Pearson Canada
Toronto

Library and Archives Canada Cataloguing in Publication

Skuce, Judith
    Analyzing data and making decisions / Judith Skuce.—2nd ed.

Includes index.
ISBN 978-0-13-245953-2

1. Commercial statistics—Textbooks.   2. Decision making—Statistical methods—Textbooks.   I. Title.

HF1017 S58 2011   519.5   C2009-906675-0

ISBN 978-0-13-245953-2

Vice President, Editorial Director: Gary Bennett
Editor-in-Chief: Nicole Lukach
Acquisitions Editor: Nick Durie
Sponsoring Editor: Carolin Sweig
Marketing Manager: Leigh-Anne Graham
Developmental Editor: John Lewis
Production Editors: Laura Neves, Cheryl Jackson
Copy Editor: Jennifer McIntyre
Proofreaders: Linda Jenkins, Susan Bindernagel
Production Coordinators: Lynn O'Rourke, Cheryl Jackson
Photo and Permissions Researcher: Sandy Cooke
Compositor: Integra
Art Director: Julia Hall
Cover and Interior Designer: Anthony Leung
Cover Image: Corbis Canada

For permission to reproduce copyrighted material, the publisher gratefully acknowledges the copyright holders listed on pages throughout this text and on this copyright page. Page 1, Jupiter Unlimited; page 25, Shutterstock; page 100, © Terrance Klassen/Alamy; page 152, Shutterstock; page 184, Shutterstock; page 224, Billy Lobo H. Shutterstock; page 259, Shutterstock; page 297, Shutterstock; page 325, Shutterstock; page 371, Shutterstock; page 399, Jupiter Unlimited; page 437, Jupiter Unlimited; page 477, Jupiter Unlimited; page 525, © David J. Green—Lifestyle/Alamy.

Statistics Canada information is used with the permission of Statistics Canada. Users are forbidden to copy the data and redisseminate them, in an original or modified form, for commercial purposes, without permission from Statistics Canada. Information on the availability of the wide range of data from Statistics Canada can be obtained from Statistics Canada's Regional Offices, its World Wide Web site at http://www.statcan.gc.ca, and its toll-free access number 1-800-263-1136.

1 2 3 4 5   14 13 12 11 10

Printed and bound in the United States of America.

*For my father, Glen Skuce, who taught me (among other things)
the value of hard work and high standards.*

About the Author

Judith Skuce earned a Bachelor of Mathematics from the University of Waterloo and a Master of Arts in Political Economy from the University of Toronto. She spent many years as an economic policy advisor and manager for several Canadian government departments before joining Georgian College in 1990. Judith teaches Statistics and Economics in the School of Business.

Brief Contents

Contents

Table of Guides

The following is a list of Guides used in this text.

Table of ⊠ Excel Instructions and Excel Templates

The following is a list of Excel instructions and templates used in this text. Note: Excel's Data Analysis Tools may need to be turned on. See Using Microsoft® Excel for Analyzing Data and Making Decisions on page xxx for more information.

Table of Examples

The following is a list of Examples used in this text.

A Note to Students: How to Get the Most Out of This Text

I wrote this book for you. I have taught many, many Statistics students over the years, and they have taught me where students need help. This text is full of features to help you learn. Here are some important tips:

1. *Read the text*. My students have told me the book is easy to read and understand. Sometimes a student says to me, "I don't know how to do this exercise." If I'm in a tutorial and can't spend much time with each student, I sometimes point out a section and an example the student can read to help them understand. Usually, when I come back a few minutes later, the student is happily doing the exercise that was previously a stumbling block. This book can help you!

2. *Do all of the exercises*. You can learn statistical techniques only if you practise them. Depending on the approach your instructor has chosen, you will find solutions to at least the odd-numbered exercises in the Study Plan of the MyStatLab that accompanies this text.

3. *Don't ignore MyStatLab as a learning tool,* even if your professor chooses not to use MyStatLab in your course evaluation. Start by taking the sample test for a chapter, and then use the Study Plan that guides you to areas where you need to do more work. From inside the Study Plan, you will have access to guided solutions and examples to help you learn.

4. *Rely on the Guides*. Guide to Technique and Guide to Decision Making features throughout the text will remind you of all the things you need to do and think about when performing certain tasks. The decision-making guides also point you to specific examples in the text (with page numbers). You can find the guides quickly by looking at the detailed table of contents, or the Table of Guides on page xviii.

5. *Refer to the Table of Examples*. On page xxi, you will find a list of all of the Examples in the book. If you need to look up how to do something, check there.

6. *Refer to the Table of Excel Instructions and Excel Templates*. On page xix, you will find a list of Excel instructions and descriptions of Excel templates. Use this list to quickly find what you need to know about Excel. Also, see Using Microsoft® Excel for Analyzing Data and Making Decisions (page xxx) if you have any questions about how to find Excel templates or data sets, or how to install Excel add-ins.

7. *Refer to the Guide to the Descriptive and Inferential Techniques of Analyzing Data and Making Decisions, inside the formula card at the front of the book.* This overall guide to all the descriptive and inferential techniques in the text will direct you to specific chapter(s) for reference. Then you can use the detailed table of contents to locate the correct technique for the decision you need to make. If you know what type of data you have (data types are explained at the beginning of Chapter 2) and what type of decision you have to make, chapter and section headings will lead you directly to the technique you should use.

Finally, keep at it. Persist, practise, get help when you are stuck on something, and keep working. I wish you the best of luck with the material in this text, and most of all, I hope that you will learn enough to confidently analyze data and make better decisions.

Preface

Many students (and professors) responded positively to the common-sense approach and plain language in the first edition of *Analyzing Data and Making Decisions*. The second edition retains the primary focus on decisions to be made, which motivates the discussion of statistical tools. Check the table of contents for most Statistics texts and you will see a list of tools, which isn't particularly useful if you are a student who hasn't yet learned how the tools are used. Check the table of contents of this text and you will see a list of decisions—a more natural organizing principle that is much easier for students to understand.

NEW TO THIS EDITION

Expanded Content   The content of the second edition is expanded with two new chapters:

- Chapter 11, Making Decisions with Three or More Samples, Quantitative Data—Analysis of Variance (ANOVA) covers Analysis of Variance techniques.
- Chapter 14, Analyzing Linear Relationships, Two or More Variables covers multiple regression, including the use of indicator variables.

Instructions, Add-Ins, and Templates for Excel 2007   The text provides detailed instructions for using Excel 2007, with many new and updated illustrations of menus and dialogue boxes. (Note that Excel 2003 instructions are still available in MyStatLab.) New and updated Excel add-ins and templates are also available in MyStatLab. As before, the add-ins are designed specifically for this text and are tied directly to the textbook content.

Integration with MyStatLab   MyStatLab content is now explicitly tied to the exercises in the text. Chapter Review

Exercises with red numbers are available for practice in MyStatLab and guided solutions are available. Furthermore, solutions to all of the odd-numbered Develop Your Skills and Chapter Review Exercises are now available to students through the MyStatLab Study Plan. Excel data files, add-ins, and templates are also included in the Study Plan (no more searching for lost CDs!). Instructor resources such as PowerPoint slides and full solutions are also available to professors through the Pearson Canada Inc. website (http://vig.pearsoned.ca).

New Design   The second edition has a fresh and streamlined design, aimed at highlighting important features such as the Guide to Technique and Guide to Decision Making boxes. Examples (which students often use for reference) now stand out clearly in the text. The annotations and Table of Examples remain as guideposts for students. As before, there is a list of Excel instructions and templates for quick reference. Note that the Guide to Decision Making features now indicate related example(s), which should help students who need more detailed guidance on a particular technique.

Updated and Reorganized Exercises   The second edition contains many new exercises, many of them based on items from the news or on Statistics Canada data. As well, the Chapter Review Exercises are now organized into four sections: *Warm-Up Exercises*, *Think and Decide* (which can be done without a computer), *Think and Decide Using Excel*, and *Test Your Knowledge* (containing capstone exercises).

ORGANIZATION

Part I provides a general overview of how data can be used to make better decisions. Part II covers the use of graphs, tables, and numbers to describe and summarize data. Part III introduces students to the building blocks of inferential statistics. Part IV applies these concepts to a series of hypothesis tests with associated confidence intervals. Part V discusses analyzing relationships and includes both simple linear and multiple regression.

This book could be used as a foundation for a number of different statistics courses. I have designed Chapter 1 as a basic building block for any selection of topics covered in the book.

I have included coverage of non-parametric methods for non-normal quantitative data and ranked data in this textbook. Some introductory courses do not cover these topics; while this omission may be a necessary one, it is also one that may leave some students thinking that all quantitative data are normal! It is possible to use the text without covering these topics and without losing continuity.

FEATURES

a) **This book is designed first as a learning tool.** I have presented a discussion of each new technique so that it flows naturally from the discussion that precedes it, which will allow students to make connections and build on previous knowledge.

I have included the following features to promote an ease of learning:

- **Introduction and Learning Objectives.** Each chapter begins with a list of learning objectives, which provide an overview of the chapter content. The Introduction provides context for the chapter material by describing a business problem or problems relevant to the chapter's theme.
- **Develop Your Skills Exercises.** At the end of every chapter section are questions designed to test and reinforce students' understanding of the material up to that point. I have developed the questions so that they are generally at the level of the examples I present in that section and provide immediate reinforcement of the material.
- **Chapter Review Exercises.** Every chapter has a set of exercises designed to test and reinforce students' understanding of all of the chapter content. These questions

require them to choose and apply the techniques in each chapter, but with no particular guidance about *which* technique to use. I have created these exercises so that in some instances they serve as building blocks for later discussions. All of the exercises are meaningful in the sense that they deal with realistic business problems or topics directly relevant to students' lives.

In the second edition, Chapter Review Exercises are organized into four sections: *Warm-Up Exercises, Think and Decide, Think and Decide Using Excel,* and *Test Your Knowledge.*

- **Guide to Technique and Guide to Decision Making.** The Guide to Technique boxes and Guide to Decision Making boxes summarize the steps involved in certain important statistical tasks. For example, in Chapter 2, I have included a Guide to Technique box that covers the comparison of histograms (see page 60). All of the hypothesis tests covered in this text are summarized in a Guide to Decision Making. These Guides summarize the type of data used and the type of decision involved in the test as well as all of the steps required to complete it. For an example see Guide to Decision Making: *Matched Pairs, Quantitative Data, Normal Differences— The t-Test to Decide About the Average Population Difference* (μ_D) These guides are listed in the detailed table of contents for easy reference.

GUIDE TO TECHNIQUE

Setting Up Appropriate Classes for a Frequency Distribution

When:
- summarizing data about one quantitative variable

Steps:
1. Identify maximum and minimum values, and the number of values in the data set, n.
2. Get some recommendations for class width.
   - If you are using Excel, use the Class Width Template to get some recommendations for class width.

GUIDE TO DECISION MAKING

Matched Pairs, Quantitative Data, Normal Differences—The t-Test to Decide About the Average Population Difference (μ_D)

When:
- matched pairs of quantitative data with normally distributed differences
- trying to make a decision about the average difference, μ_D, on the basis of $\bar{x}_D$, the average of the sample differences

Steps:
1. Specify H_0, the null hypothesis, which will be $\mu_D = 0$. Specify your hypotheses in words that reflect the context of the problem.

b) **This book is also designed as a reference tool.** Students will find the following features particularly helpful.

- **Chapter Summaries.** At the end of each chapter I have included a comprehensive summary of the chapter content. Students who have a firm grasp of what the chapter has covered will be able to use the summary for review and as a reference.

- **Meaningful Chapter and Section Headings.** Students sometimes struggle to figure out which technique to apply to a particular problem; it is my hope with this book that this decision will actually prove to be quite simple to make. I have created descriptive chapter and section headings that convey the information students need to choose the correct statistical technique. For example, instead of a traditional title such as "Chi-Square Tests," I use "Comparing Many Population Proportions" in Chapter 12. Students will find the listing of the first and second-level headings in the detailed table of contents in this text a useful reference. The new Guide to the Descriptive and Inferential Techniques of *Analyzing Data and Making Decisions,* located in the formula card at the beginning of the text, also provides an overview of all of the techniques described in the text.

- **Annotated Examples.** Every chapter has one or more examples that work through each of the statistical techniques I present. Each example also features a margin note, which describes what the example is about. Students will find the examples helpful references as they work through the Develop Your Skills and Chapter Review Exercises in each chapter. A list of the examples and their annotations can be found on p. xxi.

EXAMPLE 6.3B

Using the sampling distribution of $\hat{p}$ to make a decision about a population proportion

Suppose that the acceptable proportion of dented cans in the paint factory is 5%. Eleanor Bennett examines a random sample of 500 cans and finds that 6% of them are dented. What action should Eleanor take?

It is likely that the sample of 500 cans is not more than 5% of the total population of paint cans. Therefore, even though the sampling is done without replacement, it is still appropriate to use the binomial distribution as the underlying probability model. Check the conditions:

- $np = 500(0.05) = 25 \geq 10$
- $nq = 500(0.95) = 475 \geq 10$

- **Carefully Designed Statistical Tables.** Some of the tables in this text are presented using a non-standard approach so that they are easier for students to use and understand. For example, many books confine a normal table to one page and feature only the areas to the right of the mean. This design requires students to go through unnecessary mental hoops when doing normal probability calculations. In this book I have presented the table over two pages, which shows the areas to the left of the mean as well as to the right. Providing this additional information simplifies normal probability calculations for students and it means the presentation matches the way Excel calculates and displays normal probabilities.

c) **Computers should make statistical analysis easier, not harder.** Therefore, I have taken care to include several features that will ease students' introduction to using Excel for statistical analysis.

- **Excel Data Sets.** I have created a number of data sets in Excel, which will allow students to work through the statistical techniques presented in the book. I have included data sets to accompany specific examples, Develop Your Skills questions, chapter-section discussions, and Chapter Review Exercises. All of the data sets are available in the Study Plan in MyStatLab. Availability of a data set is highlighted with an Excel data set icon in the margin.

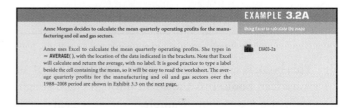

- **Excel Instructions.** Detailed instructions about how to use Excel appear throughout. I have included screen captures of Excel dialogue boxes so that students can clearly see how to use Excel functions (highlighted in red text) and add-ins. Each instance is highlighted with an Excel icon in the margin and detailed instructions are highlighted with a red line in the margin. The Excel instructions presume students have only a limited prior knowledge of Excel. A list of Excel instructions and templates follows this preface (p. xix).

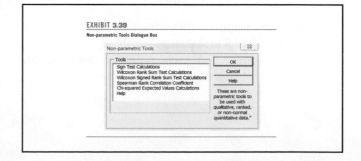

- **Excel Templates.** I have included Excel templates that automate the calculations required for the hypothesis tests and confidence intervals I have included in this textbook. You will find the templates in the Study Plan in MyStatlab. The templates are easy for students to use and feature cells that require input shaded in blue. The templates will remind students to check necessary conditions before proceeding with their calculations.

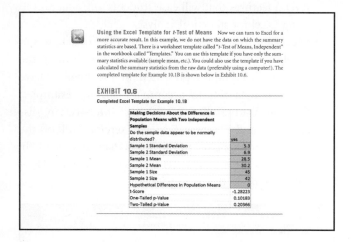

Using the Excel Template for *t*-Test of Means   Now we can turn to Excel for a more accurate result. In this example, we do not have the data on which the summary statistics are based. There is a worksheet template called "*t*-Test of Means, Independent" in the workbook called "Templates." You can use this template if you have only the summary statistics available (sample mean, etc.). You could also use the template if you have calculated the summary statistics from the raw data (preferably using a computer!). The completed template for Example 10.1B is shown below in Exhibit 10.6.

EXHIBIT 10.6

Completed Excel Template for Example 10.1B

Making Decisions About the Difference in Population Means with Two Independent Samples	
Do the sample data appear to be normally distributed?	yes
Sample 1 Standard Deviation	5.3
Sample 2 Standard Deviation	6.9
Sample 1 Mean	28.5
Sample 2 Mean	30.2
Sample 1 Size	45
Sample 2 Size	42
Hypothetical Difference in Population Means	0
t-Score	-1.28223
One-Tailed p-Value	0.10183
Two-Tailed p-Value	0.20366

d) **This book is not merely a Canadianized version of an American book.** It is Canadian through and through, featuring Canadian examples, measurements, and references.

Excel Add-ins

There are two distinct sets of Excel add-ins provided in MyStatLab. *Non-Parametric Tools* helps students calculate:

- counts of positive and negative differences for the Sign Test
- rank sums for the Wilcoxon Rank Sum Test, or the Wilcoxon Signed Rank Sum Test
- the Spearman Rank Correlation Coefficient
- Chi-square expected values for contingency tables

Multiple Regression Tools provides:

- models and summary measures for all possible regressions, with 2 to 8 explanatory variables
- regression prediction and confidence intervals, for models with 1 to 8 explanatory variables

SUPPLEMENTS

- **Instructor's Solutions Manual.** Full and detailed solutions are provided for all of the Develop Your Skills and Chapter Review Exercises in the book. The solutions are "teaching" solutions that justify choice of technique and approach.
- **PowerPoint® Slides.** Properly designed with appropriate animations, PowerPoint slides can be very helpful to illustrate concepts. I recommend that you preview the slides that accompany this book before they are used in class. The animations can be very helpful, but not if they come as a surprise to the professor! The time spent in preparing them for your needs will yield real rewards in student learning.
- **Instructor's Resource Manual.** The Instructor's Resource Manual provides more detailed background for the discussion in the text. For example, occasionally a student will ask a professor to prove that

$$s = \sqrt{\frac{\Sigma(x - \bar{x})^2}{n - 1}} = \sqrt{\frac{\Sigma x^2 - \dfrac{(\Sigma x)^2}{n}}{n - 1}}$$

The IRM contains a suggested approach to proving this formula.

Where appropriate, I provide further explanation for the approaches I use in this text. For example, in Chapter 10, I recommend the unequal variances approach to the *t*-test of means as the default. I have provided an explanation for this approach in Chapter 10 of the Instructor's Resource Manual.

- **Pearson Education Canada TestGen.** This powerful computerized testing package contains more than 600 multiple-choice, true/false, and short answer questions. Each question includes a correct answer, a skill and difficulty level rating, a chapter section reference, and a text page reference. This state-of-the-art software package in the Windows platform enables instructors to create tailor-made, error-free tests quickly and easily. The Custom Test allows instructors to create an exam, administer it traditionally or online, and evaluate and track students' results—all with the click of the mouse.

ACKNOWLEDGMENTS

Any textbook is built of a mind-boggling number of detailed elements. Getting them all down on the page with precision and style requires dedicated efforts from a whole team of people. I would like to thank all the people at Pearson Canada who helped me make this book a reality: Gary Bennett, Vice President, Editorial Director; Carolin Sweig, Sponsoring Editor; John Lewis, Developmental Editor; Laura Neves and Cheryl Jackson, Production Editors; Lynn O'Rourke and Cheryl Jackson, Production Coordinators; Anthony Leung, Designer; Jennifer McIntyre, Copy Editor; Melanie Christian, Technical Reviewer; Linda Jenkins and Susan Bindernagel, Proofreaders; and Sandy Cooke, Permissions Researcher.

As well, I want to again thank my friend and colleague Dan Phillips for updating the Excel add-ins and writing a whole new set for the second edition.

I would also like to thank all the professors who used or commented on the first edition. In particular, I would like to thank those who provided developmental reviews for the new chapters. Formal reviews were provided by:

- Veda Abu-Bakare, *Langara College*
- Randall Best, *Champlain College*
- Ulrieke Birner, *Kwantlen Polytechnic University*
- Melanie Christian, *St. Lawrence College*
- Michael Conte, *Durham College*
- Torben Drewes, *Trent University*
- Jim Graham, *Dawson College*
- Dave Kennedy, *Lethbridge College*
- Gerry Kowalchuk, *Lethbridge College*
- Eugene Li, *Langara College*
- Doug MacDormand, *Red Deer College*
- Don St. Jean, *George Brown College*
- Oded Tal, *Conestoga College*

Finally, as always, I would like to thank the students who have attended my statistics classes over the years. I continue to learn from them.

Judith Skuce
2009

Using Microsoft® Excel for Analyzing Data and Making Decisions

Throughout this text, Microsoft Excel is the software that illustrates how the computer can be used to do statistical analysis. When you are learning new techniques, it is useful to do some of the analysis and calculations by hand (with a calculator), and you will probably have to do calculations with only a calculator in test and exam situations. However, no one actually does much statistical analysis without the use of a computer. Using a computer is an integral part of the techniques discussed in this text.

WHY EXCEL?

The Microsoft® Office software suite is widely used, in business and elsewhere. You probably already have some experience with Excel, and it is highly likely that this software is available to you at the educational institution where you are studying. It is also quite likely that Excel will be available to you in your workplace. For reasons of familiarity and availability, Excel was chosen to illustrate computer-based approaches to analyzing data and making decisions. Some basic facility with Excel is assumed (basic formulas, and use of Excel functions).

Excel has a built-in set of **Data Analysis** tools, which are used throughout the text. The standard installation of Excel does not usually include the **Data Analysis** tools. Follow these steps to activate them.

In Excel:

1. Click on the **Office** button, and then click on **Excel Options**.

   Excel Options is at the bottom of the Office button menu, as shown in Exhibit 2.

2. Click on **Add-Ins**. This will activate a window showing active and inactive application add-ins. At the bottom of the window, there is an option to manage Excel add-ins (see the illustration in Exhibit 3).

   Click **Go** . . . , which will activate a window similar to what is shown in Exhibit 4 (it may not be exactly the same).

3. Put a tick mark beside **Analysis ToolPak**. Click **OK**. You may be asked for your installation disks for Excel.

   After you complete these steps, you will find **Data Analysis** available under the **Data** tab in the **Analysis** area. See Exhibit 5. Later in this text, you will be introduced to some of the **Data Analysis** tools.

While Excel is useful for an introductory course in statistics, it has some limitations. The MyStatLab that accompanies this text includes some additional Excel tools, described in following sections. As well, you should be aware that Excel does not always handle missing data correctly. You should always examine your data sets carefully, and adjust for missing data. Some of Excel's routines

EXHIBIT 1

The Office Button

EXHIBIT 2

Excel Options

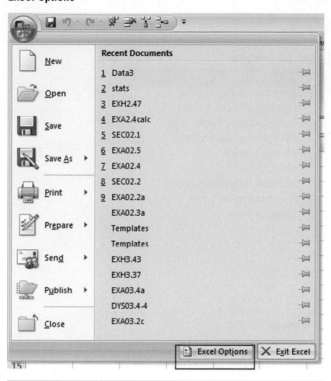

EXHIBIT 3

Manage Excel Add-Ins

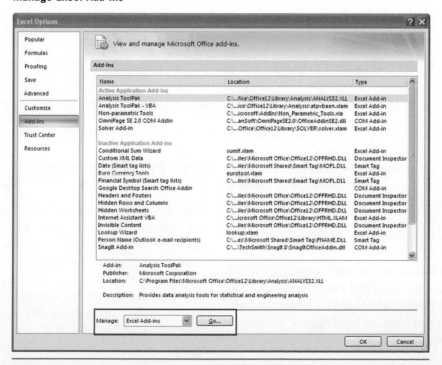

EXHIBIT 4

Add-Ins

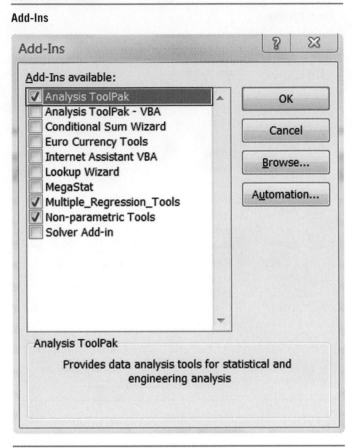

EXHIBIT 5

Data Analysis

produce unacceptable graphs (the histogram is one example). In any case where Excel's limitations could be a problem for the techniques covered here, advice is provided in the text. If you carry on in your study of statistics, you should consider learning how to use specialized statistical software.

Even if you choose to use another statistical analysis software package, the methods and concepts discussed in this book will still be helpful. Although your software output may look a little different from the Excel output described in the book, it will probably contain the same elements.

EXCEL TEMPLATES

The calculations required to analyze data or make decisions are repetitive. In some cases, Excel provides automatic functions to do some of the calculation required. In other cases, Excel formulas must be developed. A number of Excel templates with built-in formulas have been designed to assist you. The templates are provided in an Excel workbook called Excel Templates in the Study Plan in MyStatLab. When you open this workbook you will see the individual templates organized by worksheet (see the worksheet tabs to locate the template you want). You will find instructions for selecting and using the Excel Templates workbook in Chapters 2, 7, 8, 9, 10, 12, 13, and 14.

The templates contain some cells that require input from the user, and these cells are always shaded blue. Other cells contain formulas, and you should take care not to accidentally overwrite them. (The Excel worksheets are not protected, so that you can copy and paste the templates into the spreadsheets that contain the data you are analyzing, if you wish.) You can view the formulas, and if you have some experience with Excel, you should be able to see the direct correspondence between them and your manual calculations.

ADDITIONAL EXCEL ADD-INS

In the Study Plan in MyStatLab you will find files for additional add-ins for procedures not covered in the standard **Data Analysis** tools:

- **Non-Parametric Tools.** These add-ins provide calculations for non-parametric methods: the sign test, the Wilcoxon rank sum text, the Wilcoxon signed rank sum test, the Spearman rank correlation coefficient, and Chi-squared expected values. The add-ins automate calculations that would be time-consuming to do by hand for large data sets. The results of the calculations can then be input into the appropriate templates. Instructions for using the add-ins are included in the text, and there are also **Help** buttons to assist you.
- **Multiple Regression Tools.** These add-ins allow you to analyze and use linear relationships with one or more explanatory variables. They enable you to do all possible regressions for 2 to 8 explanatory variables, and create regression prediction and confidence intervals for models with 1 to 8 explanatory variables. Instructions for using add-ins are included in the text, and there are also **Help** buttons to assist you.

You may wish to install only one or both of the add-ins, depending on the material being covered in your course. When you see references to either of these add-ins in the text, you will need to install them.

The instructions for installing the add-ins are as follows.

1. Locate the files called **Non_Parametric_Tools_ver2** and **Multiple_Regression_Tools** in the Study Plan in MyStatLab and then copy the files to your computer, taking note of where you put them (or, you may choose to just download and install one of the add-ins). If you know where other Excel add-ins are located in your file system, put the files in the same directory (but the files can be located anywhere).
2. Start Excel and click on the Office button, and then click on **Excel Options** (see Exhibits 1 and 2 above).
3. Click on **Add-Ins**. This will activate a window showing active and inactive application add-ins. At the bottom of the window, there is an option to manage Excel add-ins (see Exhibit 3, above).
4. Click **Go . . .** , which will activate a window similar to Exhibit 4, above. If Non-parametric Tools and Multiple_Regression_Tools are included in the list of add-ins, tick the boxes next to them, click **OK**, and you are done! If the add-ins do not appear in the list, select Browse, locate and select the **Non_Parametric_Tools** and **Multiple_Regression_Tools** files (according to your note in Step 1), and click **OK**.
5. You will now be returned to the **Add-Ins** dialogue box. **Non-Parametric Tools** and **Multiple_Regression_Tools** should now appear in the "Add-Ins available:" list. Tick the boxes next to them and click **OK**.

Now that you are back to the usual view of Excel, you will find the non-parametric tools and multiple regression tools under the **Add-Ins** tab (see Exhibit 6). These tools are described in more detail in Chapters 9, 10, 12, 13, and 14.

EXHIBIT 6

Non Parametric Tools and Multiple Regression Tools

EXCEL DATA SETS

The data sets referenced in the text are available as Excel spreadsheets in the Study Plan in MyStatLab. Data set files have been created for examples and exercises in Chapters 1, 2, 3, 6, 7, 8, 9, 10, 11, 12, 13, and 14.

If a data set file is required to illustrate an example or for you to complete an exercise, you will find a data set icon in the margin with the file name. The file names have specific prefixes to help you identify them.

- The prefix "DYS" corresponds to the exercises in the Develop Your Skills sections (for example, DYS02-6).
- The prefix "CRE" corresponds to the Chapter Review Exercises (for example, CRE02-16).

- The prefix "EXA" corresponds to examples in the text. For example, if a data set is available for Example 2.2a, the file is labelled EXA02-2a.
- The prefix "SEC" is used when the data set is used in the general discussion in a particular section of the text. For example, a data set is introduced in Section 2.1, and it is labelled SEC02-1.

Sometimes the same data file is used in a number of exercises. As a result, the same data set can have a number of different file names, one for each of the locations where the data set is used. This labelling system is designed to make it very easy for you to find the corresponding Excel files.

Analyzing Data and Making Decisions
Statistics for Business

CHAPTER **1**

Using Data to Make Better Decisions

INTRODUCTION

Every day, in every walk of life, people make decisions and choices. Some decisions are relatively unimportant—such as what to eat for breakfast, what clothes to wear, and whether to take an umbrella when we leave home. Some decisions are more important—such as what post-secondary education to pursue, where to live, and how to manage our investments. We are likely to use data to make even relatively unimportant decisions. For instance, the weather forecast helps us decide what to wear and whether to take an umbrella. We probably gather more data before we make important decisions. For example, most students carefully research the alternatives before they choose a post-secondary educational institution.

In business, important decisions have to be made every day: Which of the candidates should be hired? Should a new product be launched? Should a new branch or factory be opened? Should one be closed? While we hear stories about larger-than-life executives who make such major decisions on gut feel, most of these choices are probably based on the analysis of relevant data. For example, the Starbucks Corporation, a leading coffee retailer, uses market research data to forecast sales and choose locations for its stores (you can read more

LEARNING OBJECTIVES

After mastering the material in this chapter, you will be able to:

1 Understand the approaches to gathering data.

2 Understand why sampling is necessary.

3 Recognize that there is art and science to summarizing and analyzing data.

4 Recognize that cause-and-effect conclusions must be drawn carefully.

5 Understand that clear and honest communication of results is necessary for them to be useful.

6 Be familiar with a framework for data-based decision making.

about this at the website **www.claritas.com/target-marketing/resources/case-study/starbucks.jsp**).

> **Why Do We Use Data to Make Decisions?**
> Using data to make decisions is better than guessing.

Collecting and analyzing data usually leads to a better understanding of the problem at hand, and a better decision about the solution, as you will see in the many examples in this text.

It is likely that you are reading this book because you are enrolled in a course in "statistics." By convention and tradition, we use this term to refer to techniques for analyzing data and making decisions. However, the word "statistics" is not very illuminating to most people, and is fear-inspiring to many. What you should know is that there is nothing to be afraid of. If you can develop the habit of looking at the data carefully before you make decisions, and if you master at least some of the techniques described in this book, you will make better decisions. This approach is not only *not scary,* it can be a real plus for your life and your career. And if you are thinking "not *my* career!" you are probably wrong. There is potential for using the techniques described in this book throughout the business world. An accountant doing an audit, a financial analyst deciding which stocks to recommend, a brand manager deciding on promotional strategies, a production manager assessing quality, a human resources expert recommending compensation plans—all of these people are using the tools of statistics to do their jobs better. Rather than resist the study of "statistics" because you've heard it's hard, realize that the tools you are going to learn about are essential to success in any business career.

The techniques involved in analyzing data and making decisions can also be fun. You might think of yourself as a data detective: you have to find the right data to help with the decision, and then you have to solve the mystery of what the data are telling you (or not telling you). It can be very satisfying to solve the mystery and arrive at the right decision.

This chapter provides you with a foundation for unravelling the mysteries of using data for decision making. Section 1.1 describes methods for getting the data you need. Section 1.2 describes the importance of sampling, and some of its challenges. Section 1.3 outlines the importance of analyzing the data that are collected, and Section 1.4 describes the kinds of conclusions that can (and cannot) be made from research studies. Section 1.5 stresses the importance of clearly communicating methods and conclusions. Section 1.6 provides a framework for a data-based decision-making approach, and describes how the material in this book relates to it.

1.1 GETTING THE DATA

Once you have understood the context of the problem at hand and identified the decision that is required, you will have to decide what data to collect. In some ways, this is the most important step in the process. Faulty data leads to faulty decisions.

There are two types of data that you might use to support decision making: data collected for your specific purpose are *primary data;* and data already collected for some other purpose are *secondary data.* Suppose you wanted to know if the average mark on the last statistics test you wrote was more than 60%. One way to find out would be to ask every student what mark he or she received on the test, and then calculate the average. In this case, you would be collecting primary data. Alternatively, if you could get access to the teacher's marks database, you could use this secondary data to calculate the class average.

Primary and Secondary Data

Primary data are data that are collected for your specific purpose. The advantage of primary data collection is that you can collect exactly the data you need, and as a result you are in a much better position to make decisions. As well, you can design data collection methods so that it is possible to draw conclusions about cause-and-effect relationships. This is discussed in more detail in Section 1.4.

> **Primary data** Data that are collected for your specific purpose.

Many manufacturing enterprises have sophisticated systems to monitor quality continually. These companies collect a range of primary data so that they can adjust production processes when products do not meet specifications. For example, the "**Six Sigma**" approach to quality control was first introduced by Motorola Inc. in the mid-1980s. It began as a process to control the number of defects in a manufacturing setting, but has since developed into a system for controlling quality in a wide range of industries, including financial services and healthcare. The Six Sigma process relies on primary data collection.

> BMO Financial Group appears to know the value of using statistical methods in business. The company first adopted Six Sigma methods in its Product Operations Group in 2005, resulting in fewer errors, less waste, and expected savings of $86 million over a five-year period. ("Six Sigma & Business Improvement Deployment Leader of the Year: Richard Lam, BMO Financial Group." The Global Six Sigma & Business Improvement Awards. **www.tgssa.com**.)

The disadvantage of primary data is that collecting it tends to be costly or difficult, as it usually involves designing and implementing some kind of survey. For example, if you tried to collect the data about marks on the last statistics test from your classmates, you might find it very time-consuming. To start with, you might not even know who the students in your class are. Even if you could identify them accurately, some of them might refuse to tell you their test mark, and some might lie about it.

Secondary data are data that were previously collected, not for your specific purpose. The advantage of secondary data is that it is usually cheaper to obtain than primary data. It may also be sufficient for your needs.

> **Secondary data** Data that were previously collected, not for your specific purpose.

EXAMPLE 1.1
Secondary data

Suppose you wanted to know how the gross margin for your pharmacy in Cranbrook compared with other pharmacies in British Columbia. One of the easiest ways to get this data is through Statistics Canada.

Exhibit 1.1 below shows the Statistics Canada data for pharmacies and personal care stores in British Columbia.

EXHIBIT 1.1

Statistics Canada Data for BC Pharmacies and Personal Care Stores

	2006 Operating Statistics (Annual)			
	$ thousands			%
	Operating Revenues	Cost of Goods Sold	Operating Expenses	Gross Margin
BC pharmacies and personal care stores	3,621,121	2,494,323	997,726	31.1

Source: Adapted from Statistics Canada website, **www40.statcan.ca/l01/cst01/trad38k-eng.htm**, accessed February 25, 2009.

There are many sources of secondary data about business activities in Canada. Most of these sources provide at least some of the available information on websites. Some useful sources are:

- Statistics Canada. This federal government agency collects all sorts of business information, and some of it is available for free. Libraries often house a selection of Statistics Canada publications. The website for Statistics Canada is **www.statcan. gc.ca/start-debut-eng.html**.
- Online databases, which can often be accessed through a library. There are four of particular interest:
  - Canadian Business & Current Affairs™ (CBCA) provides access to approximately 140 Canadian industry and professional periodicals and newsletters covering business and current affairs.
  - The ABI/INFORM® database provides content from business journals and international and scholarly content.
  - The Business Source® Complete online service provides access to a collection of scholarly journals and trade publications.
  - LexisNexis Academic® provides full-text documents from over 5,600 news, business, legal, medical, and reference publications.
- Industry Canada, available at **www.ic.gc.ca/eic/site/ic1.nsf/eng/h_00072.html**. The website provides access to a wide variety of economic and market research reports and statistics.
- Provincial government websites, which provide a range of business information.
- Business publications, for example
  - *Canadian Business* magazine **www.canadianbusiness.com/index.jsp**
  - *Maclean's* magazine **www2.macleans.ca/category/business**
  - *The Globe and Mail* Report on Business **www.theglobeandmail.com/report-on-business**

This is just a short list of general business information sources. Industry-specific trade publications can also provide data to help you analyze your specific industry sector. Many of these sources provide at least some data on websites. The ease of searching for information on the web, however, should not prevent you from pursuing other sources of data (including those in print form). As well, you must recognize that many web-based sources of "data" are misleading, incomplete, biased, or just plain wrong.

It takes some skill to navigate the wide array of information available (especially on the Internet), and to identify which data sources are both useful and reliable. Librarians are trained in these activities, and when you are doing research a good librarian can be your best resource.

DEVELOP YOUR SKILLS 1.1

1. Suppose you wanted to collect primary data about the music preferences of students at your school. How would you go about collecting it? What problems would you anticipate, and how would you solve them?

2. If you were trying to control quality at your bicycle manufacturing plant, what primary and secondary data could you use?

3. You are working in the bicycle manufacturing industry. You are interested in trends in household spending on bicycles and accessories. Find a secondary data source for this information.

4. Do you think data provided by government sources such as Statistics Canada are completely accurate and reliable? Do some research to see if your answer is correct.

5. Choose a Canadian industry of interest to you. Try to come up with three sources of secondary data about the industry.

1.2   SAMPLING

The data you require to make a good decision are often not readily available. Even if you have the resources to do primary research, you will not likely be able to gather all the data you want.

Why Sampling Is Necessary

As a business owner, you might be interested in characteristics of your current customers but not be able to survey all of them, either because you do not know how to contact them or because you cannot afford to. As a paint manufacturer, you might want to know that all of the cans coming off your production line contain the correct amount of paint, but you cannot (or cannot afford to) measure the paint level in all cans exactly. As a brewer, you might want to be sure that all of the beer you are producing is delicious, but if you drank all of it to check, you would have none left to sell!

Fortunately, you do not need all of the data in order to make reliable decisions. Many of the techniques described in this text allow you to make decisions on the basis of sample data. For example, you might be interested in whether your customers react differently to your products according to their ages. The complete collection of data—the ages of all of your current and potential customers and their product preferences—is described as *population data*. **Population data** are the complete collection of *all* of the data of interest. Because of cost and difficulty in surveying *all* of the elements in the population, we survey only some of them. **Sample data** are a subset of population data.

Exhibit 1.2 on the next page illustrates the difference between population data and sample data. Thousands of filled paint cans are coming off a paint-production line. For quality control, a sample of these cans is examined.

The reliability of the conclusions that can be drawn about population data on the basis of sample data depends on the type of sampling used: statistical or nonstatistical sampling.

Population data The complete collection of *all* of the data of interest.

Sample data A subset of population data.

Nonstatistical Sampling

Nonstatistical sampling is sometimes referred to as *nonprobability sampling*. In **nonstatistical sampling**, the elements of the population are chosen for the sample by convenience, or according to the researcher's judgment. There is no way to estimate the probability (likelihood, or chance) that any particular element from the population will be chosen for the sample.

With nonstatistical sampling, there is no way to measure the reliability of the sample results. Despite this, nonstatistical sampling can be useful. For example, although Statistics Canada uses statistical sampling for most of its data collection, it uses nonprobability sampling for testing questionnaires. Nonstatistical sampling can also legitimately be used to learn about emerging trends, or to test new product ideas. Focus groups are sometimes convened for these purposes.

Nonstatistical sampling The elements of the population are chosen for the sample by convenience, or according to the researcher's judgment; there is no way to estimate the probability that any particular element from the population will be chosen for the sample.

EXHIBIT 1.2

Population and Sample Data, Amount of Paint in 3-Litre Cans

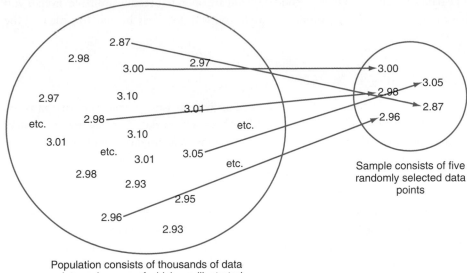

Sample consists of five randomly selected data points

Population consists of thousands of data points, only some of which are illustrated

EXAMPLE 1.2A

Nonstatistical sampling

A retail store might take a convenience sample by surveying the first 50 customers who come into the store.

This could provide useful information, particularly if there is reason to believe that all customers of the store are essentially the same. But since customers 51 and up will not be chosen in such a sampling approach, its results should be used with caution. The customers who arrive at the store early may have very different characteristics and preferences from other customers.

EXAMPLE 1.2B

Nonstatistical sampling

The websites for some of Canada's newspapers conduct online polls and report results. For example, on February 25, 2009, *The Globe and Mail* posed this question: Has the current economic situation caused you to rethink your career goals? (*Source:* "Poll Results," www.theglobeandmail.com, accessed February 25, 2009.)

The poll results: 1,472 votes of "yes" (44%), and 1,873 votes of "no" (56%).
The sampling approach here is nonstatistical, because responses were made by volunteers. Such a sample can be described as "self-selected," because the respondents

themselves choose to provide sample data. The poll results should never be interpreted as representative of the views of all Canadians. At best, such a poll indicates the views of those who visited the newspaper's website and took the time to respond to the poll. Such polls are best considered as entertainment.

Statistical Sampling

Statistical sampling is sometimes referred to as probability sampling. In **statistical sampling**, the elements of the population are chosen for the sample in a random fashion, with a known probability of inclusion. In this context, "random" does not mean "arbitrary" or "haphazard." It requires some thought and effort to select a random sample.

Statistical sampling The elements of the population are chosen for the sample in a random fashion, with a known probability of inclusion.

It is possible to make very reliable decisions about population data on the basis of data acquired through statistical sampling. The decision-making process is referred to as "inferential statistics." **Inferential statistics** is a set of techniques that allows reliable conclusions to be drawn about population data, on the basis of sample data. Usually, inferential statistics involves drawing some conclusion about, or estimating a population parameter on the basis of, a sample statistic. For example, you might want to know the average amount of paint in *all* of the paint cans you produce. This average is a population parameter. A **parameter** is a summary measure of the population data. A **sample statistic** is a summary measure of the sample data. You might take a random sample of 30 paint cans, measure the amount of paint in each can exactly, and calculate a sample average. This sample statistic will be the starting point for your conclusion about the population parameter. It would be too costly to measure the amount of paint in every can, and it isn't necessary. We can use the sample results to decide whether the paint filling line is working properly.

Inferential statistics A set of techniques that allow reliable conclusions to be drawn about population data, on the basis of sample data.

Parameter A summary measure of the population data.

Sample statistic A summary measure of the sample data.

Reliable statistical inference is possible only if the sample data are a good reflection of population data. While even the best sampling techniques cannot *guarantee* this, with statistical sampling we can estimate and control the possibility of error. It is this control that makes statistical sampling such a powerful aid to decision making.

There are many possible methods of statistical sampling. The particular sampling plan will depend on the type of data being collected, the costs involved, and the goals of the analysis or decision. The simplest of the possible methods is simple random sampling, and the inferential techniques discussed in this text all assume simple random sampling. The methods required to analyze data from more complex sampling plans (e.g., systematic sampling, stratified sampling, cluster sampling) are extensions of the foundation techniques based on simple random sampling.

Simple random sampling is a sampling process that ensures that each element of the population is equally likely to be selected. Suppose you wanted to collect some information about customer satisfaction with the delivery and installation service your store provides (for a fee) with the home theatre systems it sells. You have the budget for 10 interviews, and you want to talk with a random sample of customers. How would you select a simple random sample of 10 customers to interview?

Simple random sampling A sampling process that ensures that each element of the population is equally likely to be selected.

In order to conduct a true random sample, you must start with a list of the elements in the population. This list is called a **frame**. Because your technicians had to deliver the home theater systems, you probably have a list of the names and addresses of the customers of interest.

Frame A list of the elements in a population.

You could write all these customer names on slips of paper, put them into a container, mix them up, and then select 10 slips of paper. You would then interview the 10 randomly selected customers. However, this is a tedious process, and there is an easier way, particularly if the customer names are in a computer database. Random number generation software allows us to use computers to do the electronic equivalent of mixing up names in a hat and selecting some for a sample.

EXAMPLE **1.2C**

Random sampling with Excel

Suppose you have a list of the 60 customers who have bought home theatre systems in the last six months, and who also paid to have your store's technicians deliver and install the systems. You want to select a random sample of 10 of these customers for interviews about their service experience.

You can use Excel to do this. Begin by installing the **Data Analysis** tools of Excel (refer to the instructions on page xxx).

You can use Excel to generate a column of 60 random numbers beside the columns of customer names. Each name then has a randomly assigned random number tag that can be used to select a random sample. The process is as follows.

Click on the **Data** tab, then click on **Data Analysis**.

Then select **Random Number Generation**. This will activate the dialogue box illustrated in Exhibit 1.3 below.

EXHIBIT **1.3**

Random Number Generation in Excel

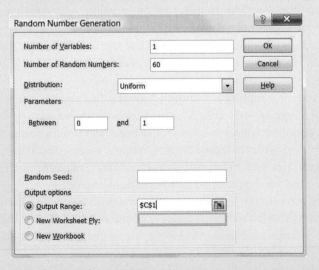

You must enter:

- **Number of Variables**, which in this case will be "1"
- **Number of Random Numbers**, which in this case will be "60." Remember, you have to create a random number for every element in the population (frame).
- **Distribution**, which should always be **Uniform** (this ensures that each digit is equally likely to appear)
- **Between** defaults to "0" and "1," which is fine
- **Output Range**, which is the top of the column next to the column containing the family names

The output you create will look something like the excerpt shown in Exhibit 1.4 below (your output may have different random numbers).

EXHIBIT 1.4

Excerpt of Excel Output for Random Number Generation (only the first 12 rows are shown)

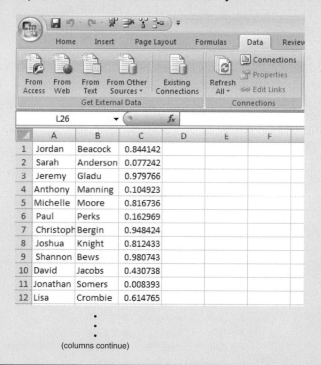

(columns continue)

The first two columns contain the first and last names of the customers who used the delivery and installation service (your population data), and the third column contains 60 random numbers between 0 and 1. Now you can use Excel to shuffle the customer names randomly, according to the random numbers in the third column.

Place your cursor on one of the cells in the column of random numbers. Then select the **Data** tab and **Sort**, which will activate the window shown in Exhibit 1.5 on the next page.

You want to sort by column C, which is the column of random numbers, so choose that column for **Sort by**. The default sort will be based on the values of the numbers, from smallest to largest, and these defaults are fine. When you click **OK**, Excel will

EXHIBIT 1.5

Sort Dialogue Box

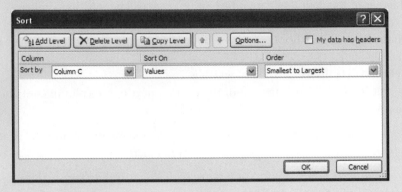

rearrange the population of customer names in a random way. An example of the output is shown in the excerpt below in Exhibit 1.6 (your output may have different customer names).

EXHIBIT 1.6

Excerpt of Excel Output, with Customer Names Sorted by Random Numbers

	A	B	C
1	Jonathan	Somers	0.008393
2	Andrea	Parulski	0.021546
3	Denise	Brown	0.0318
4	Tina	Brown	0.071657
5	Sarah	Anderson	0.077242
6	Colin	Sage	0.083346
7	Julie	Grainger	0.086673
8	Donnie	Schussler	0.090793
9	Vanessa	Ormsby	0.094943
10	Anthony	Manning	0.104923
11	Marc	Schalich	0.137516
12	Paul	Perks	0.162969
13	Tara	Alcott	0.165288
14	Sarah	Domchek	0.179052
15	Jennifer	Ansell	0.18955
16	Devon	Breau	0.220405
17	Shawn	Hellings	0.257149

(columns continue)

The names in the first two columns are equivalent to those you would pick out of a hat after you have electronically shuffled them around. If your sample size is 10, you would select the population elements corresponding to the first 10 names in the shuffled list, that is: Jonathan Somers, Andrea Parulski, Denise Brown, Tina Brown, Sarah Anderson, Colin Sage, Julie Grainger, Donnie Schussler, Vanessa Ormsby, Anthony Manning. (Note that these 10 names are shaded in for Exhibit 1.6, but they will not be in your Excel spreadsheet.) These are the names of a simple random sample of customers to interview about the delivery and installation service.

This discussion is designed to make you realize that taking a true random sample requires thought and effort. You may have enough information to create a true random sample if you are studying your own company. For example, you can take a random sample of employees or production output. You may also have sufficient data on hand to conduct a random sample of past customers. But you will never be able to conduct a true random sample of potential customers, because there is no way to know who they are.

Polling companies who conduct opinion polls of the population at large are also challenged to identify a true random sample. Polling companies generally gather data by telephone interviews, although online surveys are increasingly used. Of course, telephone surveys leave out anyone who does not have a phone. In Canada, over 98% of households have at least one phone number, and this small difference between the sampled population and the target population is usually not considered to be a significant problem. The telephone survey approach makes it difficult to survey those who do not answer their phones or will not respond to telephone surveys. Polling companies go to considerable trouble to overcome these difficulties so that they can make reliable statements about survey results.

Sampling and Nonsampling Error

Sampling error is the difference between the true value of the population parameter and the value of the corresponding sample statistic. Sampling error is expected. It would be unreasonable to expect the sample statistic to match the population parameter exactly. For example, if we managed to collect the test marks of a random sample of students, we would not expect the sample average mark to exactly match the true class average. Sampling error is something that we can estimate and control, as you will learn.

Nonsampling errors are other kinds of errors that can arise in the process of sampling a population. Suppose you plan to conduct a telephone survey of past customers about their product preferences. Here are some nonsampling errors that can occur.

1. Your survey frame may contain errors. Some customers may have been missed. Their phone numbers may have been incorrectly recorded or missing. Other information may not be correct. Such **coverage errors** arise because of inaccuracy or duplication in the survey frame.
2. Some of the customers you wish to speak to may never answer the phone. This causes **nonresponse error**, which arises when data cannot be collected for some elements of the sample.
3. There can be errors in acquiring the data. If the survey questions are biased or misleading, or difficult to understand, the customer being interviewed may not give

Sampling error The difference between the true value of the population parameter and the value of the corresponding sample statistic.

Nonsampling errors Other kinds of errors that can arise in the process of sampling a population.

Coverage errors Errors that arise because of inaccuracy or duplication in the survey frame.

Nonresponse error Error that arises when data cannot be collected for some elements of the sample.

Response errors Errors that arise because of problems with the survey collection instrument (e.g., the questionnaire), the interviewer (e.g., bias), the respondent (e.g., faulty memory), or the survey process (e.g., not ensuring that the respondent fits into the target group).

Processing errors Errors that occur when the data are being prepared for analysis.

Estimation errors Errors that arise because of incorrect use of statistical techniques, or calculation errors.

truthful or accurate answers. If the interviewer is not well trained, he or she may influence the survey responses. These **response errors** arise because of problems with the survey collection instrument (e.g., the questionnaire), the interviewer (e.g., bias), the respondent (e.g., faulty memory), or the survey process (e.g., taking answers from someone other than the intended respondent).

4. There can be errors in recording the data, even when data are collected with the help of a computer, and this can lead to biased results. **Processing errors** occur when the data are being prepared for analysis.

5. **Estimation errors** arise because of incorrect use of statistical techniques, or calculation errors.

It is important that you recognize that nonsampling errors can invalidate the conclusions drawn from the sample. You should be watchful for nonsampling errors when you examine research done by others, and you should take great care to avoid these errors when you are sampling. With some effort, you can greatly minimize the possibility of nonsampling error.

DEVELOP YOUR SKILLS 1.2

6. Nowadays, many companies use customer relationship management (CRM) software to keep track of customer sales information, financing arrangements, and product preferences. Is this sample or population data? See if you can find an article that describes how a particular company uses CRM data.

7. A restaurant owner decides to survey diners on Friday night, because he wants to collect a lot of data and Friday is always busy. Is this a statistical or a nonstatistical sample? Why? How much should the restaurant owner rely on the sample data?

8. "A new Ipsos-Reid survey conducted on behalf of Mosaik MasterCard finds that three-quarters (77%) of Canadian postsecondary students have at least one credit card. Of these students, 72% are currently carrying a balance, and 53% plan to pay it off entirely by their next statement due date." Are these population parameters or sample statistics? (*Source:* "School Credits of a Different Kind: The Mosaik MasterCard Back to School Student Survey on Credit Card Knowledge," **www.ipsos-na.com/news/pressrelease.cfm?id=2763**, accessed June 7, 2006.)

DYS01-9

9. As part of an employee satisfaction survey, a research team wants to conduct in-depth interviews with a random sample of 10 employees. The company's employee list is available in an Excel spreadsheet in the MyStatLab that accompanies this text. Use Excel to create a random sample of 10 employees.

10. Suppose Calgary Transit wants to do a survey to see if it can improve its services for people with disabilities. The organization decides to collect information through interviews of a random sample of riders. Outline some challenges Calgary Transit might face in gathering the data.

1.3 ANALYZING THE DATA

Once you collect the data you need, the information must be organized so that you can make sense of it. Raw (that is, unorganized) data usually do not tell us much.

EXAMPLE **1.3**

Analyzing the data

Suppose a Niagara region winery is interested in discovering if there is a difference between men's and women's average purchases from the winery. A random sample of 25 men and 28 women is selected, and their purchase amounts are collected. The data for purchases by men are as follows: $52.40, $20.67, $38.93, $51.32, $50.38, $46.80, $49.80, $43.19, $49.14, $22.96, $27.72, $15.71, $13.84, $24.27, $26.72, $10.58, $29.18, $31.15, $37.62, $31.61, $42.08, $31.56, $52.11, $34.98, $33.77. The data for purchases by women are: $46.32, $58.85, $47.82, $68.57, $13.80, $30.12, $37.30, $43.54, $24.73, $29.49, $67.55, $53.11, $13.17, $30.40, $49.42, $40.22, $53.99, $41.17, $28.36, $51.11, $34.76, $44.82, $58.00, $25.37, $67.25, $32.97, $31.09, $48.30.

EXA01-3

Just looking at these lists of numbers does not tell us much. We cannot easily see if there is a difference in the purchases made by men and women. Probably one of your instincts is to calculate the men's and women's average purchases. The average is an example of a numerical summary measure, and is discussed along with other numerical summary measures in Chapter 3. It is often helpful to create a graph to summarize data, and such graphs are discussed in Chapter 2 of this text. The techniques in Chapters 2 and 3 are part of a branch of statistics called "descriptive statistics." Once you master these, you will be able to produce graphs and summary statistics that help you see the data more clearly. Exhibit 1.7 shows some graphs that organize and display the winery purchase data for men and women, as well as a table with some summary statistics.

These graphs and summary measures have probably helped you understand the two data sets better. You can see that the average purchase by women is higher than the average purchase by men. You can also see that there is greater variability in the purchases by women than the purchases by men.

EXHIBIT **1.7**

Winery Purchase Data

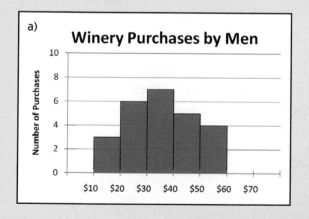

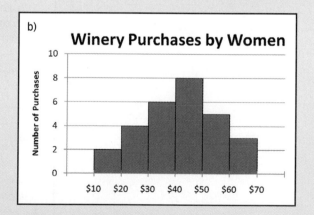

c)   **Summary Statistics for Winery Purchases**

Winery Purchases	Average Purchase	Lowest Purchase	Highest Purchase
By Men	$34.74	$10.58	$52.40
By Women	$41.84	$13.17	$68.57

Descriptive statistics A set of techniques to organize and summarize raw data.

Descriptive statistics are a set of techniques to organize and summarize raw data. As you explore the possibilities for summarizing and describing data, you will discover that there is both art and science involved. While there are many guidelines to help you, you will usually have to make choices about presenting data. Your goal should always be to represent the data truthfully. You should also be aware that some will choose to confuse or misrepresent data, and you should always be alert to these possibilities. Even if you do not become a statistician, you should be an informed and suitably skeptical consumer of statistical analysis done by others. You will learn more as you explore Chapters 2 and 3.

DEVELOP YOUR SKILLS 1.3

11. An advertisement claims that prices for electronic organizers have decreased by 125%. What do you think of this claim?

12. In the latter part of 2008, stock markets around the world declined significantly. Exhibit 1.8 shows two graphs depicting the Standard and Poor's Toronto Stock

EXHIBIT 1.8

S&P TSX Composite Index, January 2, 2007, to March 27, 2009

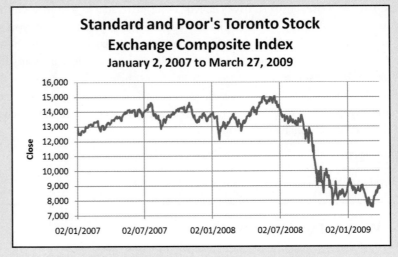

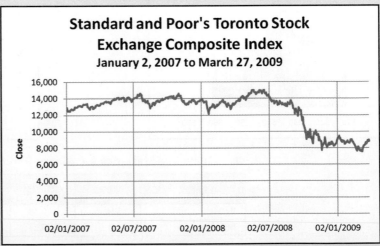

Source: "S&P/TSX Composite Index (Interi (^GSPTSE)," Yahoo Canada Finance, **http://ca.finance.yahoo. com/q/hp?s=%5EGSPTSE**, accessed March 28, 2009.

Exchange Composite Index for the period from January 2, 2007 to March 27, 2009. Which graph is the better representaion of the index during this time period, and why?

13. "[Student] Jane Woodsman has shown astonishing progress in academic achievement over the last semester. Jane's average grade has increased by a substantial 20%." Based on this statement, what is your impression of Jane Woodsman's academic success? (State your conclusion before you read any further.)

Now, here are the facts. Last semester, Jane's average grade was 13.8%. This semester, Jane's average grade is 20% higher, that is, 1.20(13.8%) = 16.6%. While Jane's grades have improved, she is still a long way from academic success. How would you rewrite the initial statement in this question so that it was more honest?

14. You are the national manager for a company that provides express oil changes at a number of locations, and you are concerned that the service level at one of these locations is not up to your standard. The location keeps records of its service completion times (from customer arrival to departure). You've asked to see these records, but the manager says he's too busy to send them to you. He also claims that the maximum wait time during the recent quarter has decreased by 50%, compared with the previous quarter. Would you be satisfied, or would you insist on seeing the records?

15. Consider the graph shown in Exhibit 1.9 below. Do you think it is a fair representation of sales over the period?

EXHIBIT 1.9

Annual Sales Graph

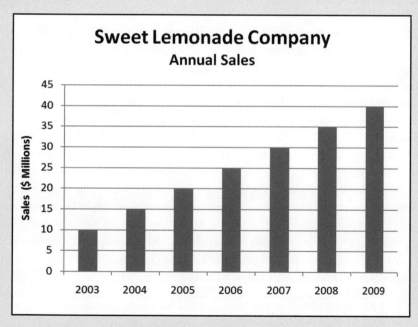

1.4   MAKING DECISIONS

After you have collected and analyzed the data, you will be in a position to make some decisions. The type of conclusion that you can draw depends on how the data were gathered.

Suppose a newspaper wants to know if its readers' average income has increased, compared with five years ago. This information could be very useful, because an attractive reader income profile helps to sell advertising. In this case, the decision to be made is a straightforward one: has readers' average income increased? By looking at the sample evidence, we can decide whether or not this appears to be the case, and you will learn reliable techniques to do this as you progress through this text. It is unlikely that the newspaper is particularly interested in *why* readers' average income has increased, if in fact it has.

Observational study The researcher observes what is already taking place.

This is an example of an observational study. In an **observational study**, the researcher observes what is already taking place. Many marketing studies are observational in nature. Companies collect data about their customers in order to understand them better.

Sometimes research is aimed at understanding cause and effect, that is, pinpointing *why* an observed change or difference has occurred. Example 1.4a illustrates.

EXAMPLE 1.4A

Cause and effect cannot be concluded from observational studies

Suppose that the vice-president of operations is interested in how training methods affect the number of worker errors. One way to study this would be to record the number of errors for a random sample of workers at two different plants—one where training has taken place, and one where it has not.

The first decision that must be made is whether the sample data provide evidence to suggest that the error rates differ between the two plants. Once you have mastered the techniques in this text, you will be able to make this decision.

But there is also a further question. If the error rates differ, is it because of the training program? The vice-president might be tempted to conclude that it is. But this further conclusion cannot be made on the basis of an observational study such as the one described here. Factors other than the training program could have caused the difference in the error rates. For example, the skills and experience of the workers could affect the number of errors. Choosing a random sample at each plant may result in these factors being about equal across the two samples. But there are other factors that will not be randomized. For example, the supervisor at one plant might be better at motivating workers to make fewer errors. Traffic conditions may be better at one plant, so that the workers arrive less tired and frustrated, and less prone to error. Because of these other possibilities, it is not possible to make a strong conclusion about the cause of the differences in error rates on the basis of this observational study.

Experimental study The researcher designs the study so that conclusions about causation can be drawn.

To make a stronger conclusion about the cause of any difference in error rates, the vice-president could conduct an experimental study. An **experimental study** is designed so that conclusions about causation can be drawn.

EXAMPLE 1.4B

Cause and effect may be concluded from experimental studies

Suppose an experimental study is designed as follows. A group of workers is randomly selected at a particular plant, and the numbers of errors made by the group are recorded over a period of time. The researcher then intervenes by putting the workers through a training program. The numbers of worker errors are recorded again after the training.

In this case, if the numbers of worker errors after the training are lower, it is easier to conclude that the training is the cause. However, even in this case, there could be other explanations. For example, the workers who took the training might have been motivated to pay particular attention and work carefully, simply because they were selected for the study. The results of the study might not generalize to the entire population of workers.

You can see from Example 1.4b that even experimental studies can have limitations, although generally they lead to stronger conclusions than observational studies. It is very important that you recognize what conclusions are justified—and what conclusions are *not* justified—from any particular research study. While statistical analysis can add to our understanding of the world, it cannot tell us everything.

This may surprise you. Many people expect that since statistical analysis involves data and mathematics (or at least arithmetic) and computers, the results should be very clear. This can sometimes be the case, but not always. The claim can be made that "using data to make decisions is better than guessing." This is true, but it does not imply that statistical techniques always lead to clear answers. Judgment is required to interpret the results of statistical analyses. In fact, judgment is required throughout the analysis, as you will see during your introduction to the techniques in this text. The ability to make good judgments develops with practice, experience, and reflection. This does not mean that anything goes, or that you can "prove" anything you want with statistics. Some conclusions and some choices are clearly unacceptable. In cases where judgment is required, you must be prepared to defend your choices objectively. And you should always critically evaluate the judgments made by others in their statistical analyses.

DEVELOP YOUR SKILLS 1.4

16. A study published in 2006 indicated that higher family incomes are associated with better physical, social/emotional, cognitive, and behavioural well-being among children (*Source:* "Study: Family Income and the Well-Being of Children," **www.statcan.ca/ Daily/English/060511/d060511c.htm**, accessed June 8, 2006). Barbara Arneil, a political science professor at the University of British Columbia, was quoted in a related article in *The Globe and Mail* as saying that the findings suggest the following: "If the outcomes for our kids are better with higher incomes, the goal should be to get both parents into the work force." (*Source:* "Well-Off Children Do Better on Tests, Study Finds," **www.theglobeandmail.com**, accessed May 15, 2006). Should you agree with Professor Arneil's conclusion?

17. A study of 10,000 people born in the UK in 1958 revealed that a man 6 feet in height was more likely to have a partner and children than was a man of average height (5 feet, 10 inches). Does this mean that women prefer to marry tall men?

18. An insurance company with a number of branch offices across the country has designed a diary system for salespeople, which is designed to increase their productivity. The diary system is colour-coded: green is for time spent with clients making sales calls, blue is for time spent supporting existing clients, and red is downtime (lunch, travelling, etc.). The idea is that the visual cue of the coded diary will focus the salesperson's attention on sales. A number of poor performers were selected and introduced to the diary system. Average sales increased by 11%. Can we conclude that the diary system caused the increase?

19. If you wanted to test the effectiveness of the diary colour-coding system described in the previous exercise, how would you design your study?

20. An ice cream store hired a mascot to entice people into the store to buy ice cream. During the period when the mascot was working, sales increased by 15%. Can we conclude that the mascot caused the increase in sales?

1.5 COMMUNICATION

This text focuses on introductory techniques for analyzing data and making decisions about population data on the basis of sample data. Once you master these techniques, you will be on your way to becoming a successful data detective. However, your detective work will be useful only if you learn to communicate your methods and conclusions clearly.

When reporting on your statistical analysis, you should completely describe the problem at hand, and the goal of any decisions to be made. You should also provide information about how the data were collected, organized, and summarized, usually showing both graphs and numbers. Describe the statistical techniques you used, as well as any judgments about areas of uncertainty. Finally, make a clear statement of conclusions or decisions, with justification. You may provide the technical detail in the body of the report or in an appendix, but it must always be presented so that an informed reader can assess the methods used and whether the conclusions are justified. How much of the technical detail is included in the body of the report depends on its intended reader: a report written for colleagues who are familiar with statistics would be written differently than a report for a supervisor with little understanding of statistics.

It is also important that you state your conclusions carefully, as Example 1.5 illustrates.

EXAMPLE 1.5

State conclusions carefully

Consider a study of a newspaper's readers' incomes. Here are three different ways the conclusion of the study might be expressed:

1. With a p-value of 0.0123, H_0 is rejected.
2. The average income of this newspaper's readers has increased over the last five years.
3. Sample evidence suggests that the average income of this newspaper's readers has increased over the last five years.

While statement 1 might be technically correct, it cannot be understood without reference to the study. But this is a minor point. The more important problem is that most people would have no idea what this statement means, even after referring to the study! It is important that you learn to state the results of your statistical analysis in language that can be easily understood by almost anyone. While you need to understand the specialized language of statistics, you should also learn to translate it for an audience without statistical knowledge. Bosses and clients are not impressed by fancy jargon; they are frustrated by it.

Statement 2 is much more promising, because anybody could read it and understand it. However, this statement has a major problem: it does not even hint at the fact that this conclusion is made on the basis of sample results. Even if the sampling and the analysis were done properly, there is still a chance that a rare and unrepresentative sample was taken. The conclusion could be completely wrong. However, the statement does not even hint at this possibility, and so it is simply not correct, unless you have somehow managed to collect all the relevant population data.

Statement 3 is the best of the three, by far. First of all, it is understandable. It also indicates that a sample has been taken, and it is not nearly as definitive as statement 2.

You might think that the differences between statement 2 and statement 3 are minor. The newspaper's employees are probably going to act and speak as if statement 2 were true, as they try to sell more newspaper ads, so why go to the bother of stating conclusions so carefully? The answer is quite simple: statement 2 is not truthful.

DEVELOP YOUR SKILLS 1.5

21. Think about the likely statistical knowledge of the intended reader of your statistical analysis in the following situations, and describe how much technical detail you would plan to include in the body of the report.

   a. The national manager of quality control wants a report on quality control measures at the plant where you work.
   b. The human resources department has asked you to analyze the educational levels of middle managers in the organization.
   c. Your boss has asked you to prepare a report on a new product's characteristics, which will be used in a consumer magazine article about the product.

22. Comment on the following statement about a study based on a random sample of past customers of your firm: "Study results prove that our products are more attractive to younger buyers, so we should target the under-35 market."

23. One of the mistakes that beginning statisticians often make is to focus their reports on themselves, instead of on the data being analyzed. Instead of talking about what "I" did, you should be talking about what the data show. Rewrite the following statement with focus on the data, not the analyst.

"I took a random sample of 30 paint cans off the line, and carefully measured the exact amount of paint in each can. The sample average was 3.012 litres, just a bit above the desired level of 3 litres. I plotted this on the control chart, and I noticed that this number was within control limits. So I concluded that there was no problem with the paint filling line."

24. Another mistake that beginning statisticians make is to use subjective language to describe results, thus influencing the reader's interpretation. The goal should be to let the data speak for themselves. Rewrite the following statement without the subjective flavour, and with the proper focus on the data. (Use your imagination to make the report more specific, if you wish.)

"After extensive and painstaking analysis, I am delighted to conclude that our study shows that the new training program dramatically increased worker productivity. You should not hesitate to expand the training program across the nation, as the analysis is crystal-clear."

25. "The study concludes that being tall increases your chances of being a CEO." Do you think that this conclusion could be valid? How would you rewrite this to be more truthful?

1.6   A FRAMEWORK FOR DATA-BASED DECISION MAKING

A general approach to data-based decision making is outlined below. It summarizes the discussion in this chapter.

Steps in Data-Based Decision Making

1. Understand the problem and its context as thoroughly as possible. Be clear about the goal of a good decision.

2. Think about what kind of data would help you make a better decision. See if helpful data are already available somewhere. Decide how to collect data if necessary, keeping in mind the kind of conclusion you want to be able to make.
3. Collect the data, if the benefit of making a better decision justifies the cost of collecting and analyzing the data.
4. Examine and summarize the data.
5. Analyze the data in the context of the decision that is required. This may require using the sample data to:
   • estimate some unknown quantity
   • test if a claim (hypothesis) seems to be true
   • build a model
6. Communicate the decision-making process. This requires:
   • a clear statement of the problem at hand, and the goal of the decision
   • a description of how the data were collected or located
   • a summary of the data
   • a description of the estimation, hypothesis test, or model-building process(es)
   • a statement of what decision should be made, with justification

All of the steps in this process are important. Below are some comments about how these steps relate to the material in this text.

Step 1   In the pages of this book, you will find regular encouragement to *think* carefully about the problem at hand and how to approach it. Learning to do this successfully takes practice.

Steps 2 and 3   Generally, in this book, the data will be provided for you and simple random sampling will be assumed. If you continue your study of statistics beyond your introductory course, you will at some point have to gain knowledge and experience concerning primary research and design of experiments.

Step 4   Part II of the book (Chapters 2 and 3) provides an introduction to the methods of descriptive statistics.

Step 5   Most of this book is focused on inferential statistics. In Part III (Chapters 4–6), the building blocks for inferential statistics are presented. Part IV (Chapters 7–12) introduces a range of techniques to use sample evidence to estimate unknown quantities or decide if a claim appears to be true. Part V (Chapters 13 and 14) introduces techniques to model the relationships between a quantitative variable and one or more explanatory variables.

Step 6   Throughout this text, there are Guides to Decision Making (see the detailed table of contents), which will help you with the technical side of the decision-making process. While this text does not focus on report writing, you may have an opportunity to develop your communication skills as you complete assignments associated with the course you are probably taking.

Chapter 1 has given you an overview of data-based decision making. The techniques you are about to learn are very powerful, but only if they are used correctly and wisely. You will be able to use this chapter as a reference when you are thinking about a business decision (or any other kind of decision) that you need to make.

Chapter Summary

1

Getting the Data

Primary data are data that are collected for your specific purpose. Secondary data are data that were previously collected not for your specific purpose. Some useful sources of secondary data about business activities in Canada are listed on page 4.

Sampling

Population data are the complete collection of *all* of the data of interest. Sample data are a subset of population data. The reliability of the conclusions that can be drawn about a population on the basis of sample data depends on the type of sampling used: statistical or nonstatistical sampling.

In nonstatistical sampling, the elements of the population are chosen for the sample by convenience, or according to the researcher's judgment. With nonstatistical sampling, there is no way to measure the reliability of the sample results. Despite this, nonstatistical sampling can be useful for testing questionnaires, learning about emerging trends, or testing new product ideas.

Statistical sampling is sometimes referred to as probability sampling. In statistical sampling, the elements of the population are chosen for the sample in a random fashion, with a known probability of inclusion. It is possible to make very reliable decisions about population data on the basis of data acquired through statistical sampling, using a set of techniques called inferential statistics. Usually, inferential statistics involves drawing some conclusion or estimating a population parameter on the basis of a sample statistic. A parameter is a summary measure of the population data. A statistic is a summary measure of the sample data.

The simplest method of statistical sampling is simple random sampling. Simple random sampling is a sampling process that ensures that each element of the population is equally likely to be selected. In order to conduct a true random sample, you must start with a list of the elements in a population, which is called a frame. It is possible to use random number generation software to randomly select elements from the population, as Example 1.2c on pages 8–11 illustrates.

Sampling error is the difference between the true value of the population parameter and the value of the corresponding sample statistic, which arises because we are examining only a subset of the population. Sampling error is expected, and is something that we can estimate and control. Nonsampling errors are other kinds of errors that can arise in the process of sampling a population. Nonsampling errors can invalidate the conclusions drawn from the sample.

Analyzing the Data

Once you collect the data you need, the information must be organized so that you can make sense of it. Raw (that is, unorganized) data usually do not tell us much. Descriptive statistics are techniques to organize and summarize raw data.

Making Decisions

In an observational study, the researcher observes what is already taking place. For example, many marketing studies are observational in nature. Companies collect data about their customers in order to better understand them.

Sometimes research is aimed at understanding cause and effect, that is, *why* an observed change or difference has occurred. Cause and effect cannot be concluded from observational studies. An experimental study is designed so that conclusions about causation can be drawn. Even experimental studies have their limitations in terms of establishing cause-and-effect relationships, particularly when human behaviour is being studied.

Judgment is required to interpret the results of statistical analyses. In cases where judgment is required, you must be prepared to defend your choices objectively. You should always critically evaluate the judgments made by others in their statistical analyses.

Communication

A report of any statistical analysis you do should completely describe the problem at hand, and the goal of any decisions to be made. It should also provide information about how the data were collected, organized, and summarized (usually with both graphs and numbers). The statistical techniques used and any judgments about areas of uncertainty should also be described. Finally, a clear statement of conclusions or decisions should be made, with justification.

The technical detail may be provided in the body of the report or in an appendix, but it must always be presented so that an informed reader can assess the methods used and whether the conclusions are justified. How much of the technical detail is included in the body of the report depends on its intended reader.

A Framework for Data-Based Decision Making

A general approach to data-based decision making is outlined in the box on pages 19–20.

Go to MyStatLab at **www.mathxl.com**. You can practise the exercises indicated with red in the Develop Your Skills and Chapter Review Exercises as often as you want, and guided solutions will help you find answers step by step. You'll find a personalized study plan available to you too!

CHAPTER REVIEW EXERCISES

WARM-UP EXERCISES

1. Why do businesses collect data before making major business decisions?

2. Why are business decisions made on the basis of only a limited amount of data? Can such decisions be reliable?

3. Is it valid to draw conclusions about population data on the basis of a convenience sample? Why or why not?

4. What numerical measure do students often rely on to summarize their performance in a particular semester?

5. Why is it important to communicate the results of your statistical analysis so that non-statisticians can understand?

THINK AND DECIDE

6. What are some of the difficulties in gathering data through personal interviews? As food for thought, watch some clips from a TV show segment called Talking to Americans (from *This Hour Has 22 Minutes*), in which Rick Mercer travelled to American cities and interviewed Americans about Canadian politics, geography, and weather. You will find some of these clips at **www.youtube.com.**

7. A poll conducted for Canwest News Service and Global Nation reported that 26% of Canadians either have made or plan to make changes in how their retirement funds are invested this year. (*Source:* "Most Canadians Holding Steady on Retirement Investments: Poll," *Canada.com*, **www.canada.com/Most+Canadians+holding+steady+retirement+ investments+Poll/1324814/story.html**, accessed February 25, 2009). The poll was conducted through an online survey of 1,003 Canadians. Why were only 1,003 Canadians surveyed? Are you surprised at the relatively low sample size, given the size of the Canadian population?

8. The Top 100 Employers list is compiled annually by Mediacorp Canada Inc. Mediacorp invites several thousand Canadian employers to complete an extensive application, and about a thousand apply. On the basis of the applications Mediacorp rates the employers, and publishes a book profiling the top 100. Do you think that this process is an effective way to identify Canada's "top 100" employers? You can find more details at **www.canadastop100. com/research.html.**

9. A BBC News article is titled "Short Workers Lose Small Fortune." The article says that each inch of height added USD $789 to annual pay. Professor Tim Judge from the University of Florida, who led the study described in the article, suggested that the reason for this was evolution. He is quoted as saying: "When humans evolved as a species and still lived in the jungles or the plain, they ascribed leader-like qualities to tall people because they thought they would be better able to protect them." What conclusions can be justified from this kind of a study, assuming it was done in a statistically correct manner? (*Source:* "Short Workers Lose Small Fortune," *BBC News,* **http://news.bbc.co.uk/2/hi/health/3200296.stm**, accessed February 25, 2009).

10. Your school has just approved a new policy that will make the campus entirely smoke-free. This means no smoking on the property at any time, starting at the beginning of the next semester. Because you smoke a pack a day, you are alarmed. You collect a sample of opinions about the new policy from students and staff near one of the designated smoking areas (where you spend a lot of time). You find that there are many people who share your alarm. You produce some graphs and tables, and write a report about your findings, which you take to the president of the school. She listens to your tale of woe but then tells you that your study is not representative of the views of all of the members of the school community. Where did you go wrong?

11. Many companies are building customer databases through loyalty programs. One example is the Optimum program of Shoppers Drug Mart Corporation. Customers collect Optimum points when they spend money at the stores. Each purchase is recorded, and so the company collects information about customer demographics and shopping patterns. These data can be used in a variety of ways to target marketing efforts. For example, flyer distribution can be limited to neighbourhoods where the flyers are most likely to have an impact. Do some research to identify other customer loyalty programs that allow companies to collect customer information.

12. An article published in September 2006 was called "No Booze? You May Lose: Why Drinkers Earn More Money Than Nondrinkers." (*Source:* "No Booze? You May Lose," Reason Foundation, **www.reason.org/pb44.pdf**, accessed February 25, 2009). Researchers reported that drinkers earn 10–14% more than people who do not drink. In an attempt to explain why this might be the case, the study suggests that drinkers are more social than non-drinkers, and that greater social networks lead to higher earnings. What kind of a study was this? Is it possible to draw a strong conclusion that drinking causes higher earnings on the basis of such a study?

13. In the early 1980s, Coca-Cola spent millions of dollars on taste tests and interviews with consumers to test a new flavour of Coke. "The data was unequivocal: Consumers preferred the new formula 8% more than Pepsi and an astonishing 20% more than the original Coca-Cola recipe." (*Source:* Ken Hunt, "Brand Surgery," *Report on Business*, November 2008, p. 36). Despite this, when the New Coke was launched, it was a disaster, because people were very loyal to the original Coke. Describe a question that researchers could have asked that would have indicated this potential problem.

14. In a study produced by the Conference Board of Canada about the impact of overtime on employee health, there is a section called "About the Study Data." This section describes in some detail the database on which the study relied. Why would the Conference Board include this kind of detail in their report?

15. A Statistics Canada study on commuting patterns in Canada reveals that the proportion of workers using a car to get to work fell from 80.7% in 2001 to 80% in 2006 (*Source:* Statistics

Canada, "Commuting Patterns and Places of Work of Canadians, 2006 Census," Catalogue no. 97-561, p. 10, **www12.statcan.gc.ca/english/census06/analysis/pow/pdf/97-561-XIE2006001.pdf**, accessed February 25, 2009). The report also noted than in 2006, more than 10 million Canadian workers drove their car to work, which is 714,900 more drivers than in 2001. These data were presented in a section of the report titled "The proportion of drivers is decreasing." Do you think this title accurately reflects the change in commuting patterns from 2001 to 2006?

THINK AND DECIDE USING EXCEL

16. Lotto 6/49 is a lottery in which players select six numbers from 1 to 49. Prizes vary according to how closely players' selections match the winning set of numbers. Many players do not actually select their six numbers; they rely instead on a "quick pick," where the numbers are selected (presumably randomly) for them. Use Excel to generate a quick pick for Lotto 6/49. Check to see if the numbers you selected would have won in the most recent draw (you can check at **www.olg.ca/lotteries/games/howtoplay.do?game=lotto649**). It is not recommended that you actually play the lottery. The probability of winning is quite low.

CRE01-17

17. A data set of marks is available in the file called CRE01-17. Select 10 random samples of size 10 from this data set. Using the **=AVERAGE** function in Excel, calculate the average mark from the population data, and calculate the sample average from each sample. Are the sample averages fairly close to the true population average?

18. Repeat exercise 17, but this time select 10 random samples of size 15 from the marks data set. Compare the sample averages you get from these 10 samples with the sample averages you got in exercise 17. Which averages are closer to the true population average? What do you expect the answer should be, and why?

19. Calculate the average of the sample averages from exercise 17. Is this average close to the population average? Calculate the average of the sample averages from exercise 18. Is this average close to the population average? Is it closer?

TEST YOUR KNOWLEDGE

20. The government of Ontario began collecting data on "key performance indicators" (KPI) for colleges in 1998. Data on graduate employment rates, graduate satisfaction, and employer satisfaction are collected by external service providers through telephone surveys (some 40,000 graduates, 10,000 employers, and 90,000 current students are surveyed). The data are used as a basis for distributing some of the colleges' funding.
    a. What are some of the difficulties that would be involved in collecting and interpreting these data?
    b. For the 1999–2000 year, 59% of the students surveyed (overall) indicated that they were very satisfied or satisfied with college services. In the 2000–2001 year, 66.8% of the students surveyed indicated that they were very satisfied or satisfied. This percentage has been above 66% for the entire period from 2000 to 2007 (the most recent data available at the time of publication). Do you think this means that the colleges all improved their services significantly between 1999–2000 and the following school year? (*Source:* Colleges Ontario, "Key Performance Indicators," **www.collegesontario.org/outcomes/key-performance-indicators.html**, accessed February 25, 2009).
    c. Go to the website mentioned in part b, and download the document called "2005 KPI Trends." What techniques are used to summarize the trends in key performance indicators?
    d. In the section on the "KPI Overview," in the document you downloaded for part c, read the section on the student satisfaction rate. What difficulties are there in comparing the data from 1999–2000 and the data from the subsequent years?

CHAPTER 2

Using Graphs and Tables to Describe Data

INTRODUCTION

As we saw in Chapter 1, once we collect data to help us analyze a situation and make a decision, we have to organize the data so that we can make sense of it. In Example 1.3 on page 13, the data on men's and women's purchases at a Niagara winery were difficult to assess when they were presented as two lists of numbers, but were easier to compare when they were summarized in graphs. When any researcher is analyzing a data set, one of the first steps is to create a graphical picture of the data. The type of graph depends on the type of data.

Section 2.1 begins with a description of the different types of data, in the context of a customer survey done by a drugstore owner. Understanding the distinctions among types of data will be crucially important as you learn more about statistical analysis, because you must be able to recognize the data type in order to choose the correct technique in descriptive or inferential statistics. In Section 2.2, you will explore a data set on quarterly operating profits. You will learn how to summarize these data using frequency distributions and histograms with Microsoft® Excel. Section 2.3 describes how to create tables, bar graphs, and pie charts for qualitative data. Section 2.4 describes how

LEARNING OBJECTIVES

After mastering the material in this chapter, you will be able to:

1 Distinguish among different types of data.

2 Create frequency distributions and histograms to summarize quantitative data.

3 Create tables, bar graphs, and pie charts to summarize qualitative data.

4 Create time-series graphs.

5 Create scatter diagrams for paired quantitative data.

6 Be aware of and avoid common errors that result in misleading graphs, and understand the factors that distinguish interesting from uninteresting graphs.

time-series data are graphed, and raises some interesting questions about such graphs. Section 2.5 discusses scatter diagrams of paired quantitative data. Finally, Section 2.6 discusses misleading and uninteresting graphs, and describes some common graphing errors. You should pay attention to these, to avoid either making them yourself or being misled when others make them.

2.1 TYPES OF DATA

Different methods are used to analyze data and make decisions, depending on the type of data involved. Understanding data types will be crucial to your ability to correctly identify the techniques you should use. The discussion that follows is therefore not just an exercise in learning new terms; it is critical to your learning.

SEC02-1

Suppose Lynda Parks surveys a random sample of the customers who shop at the drugstore she owns. The survey results contain data on the gender and age of each customer, how many times the customer has shopped at the store in the last month, and how the customer rates the store (on a scale of excellent, good, fair, and poor) in a number of areas (cleanliness, friendliness of staff, ease of locating products, speed of service). The survey results also contain data on the total amount of the customer's most recent purchase, and the customer's annual income. An excerpt (for just the first 10 customers of the sample) is shown below in Exhibit 2.1. You can view the entire set of survey results in an Excel worksheet called SEC02-1.

Variable A characteristic or quantity that can vary.

Each of the column headings in Exhibit 2.1 could be described as a **variable**, a characteristic or quantity that can vary. When we record the actual characteristics or

EXHIBIT 2.1

An Excerpt of Results from a Survey of Drugstore Customers

1 = Excellent, 2 = Good, 3 = Fair, 4 = Poor

Gender 0 = Male 1 = Female	Age	Number of Purchases Made at This Store in Past Month	Cleanliness Rating	Staff Friend- liness Rating	Ease of Locating Purchases Rating	Speed of Service Rating	Purchase Amount ($)	Annual Income ($)
0	24	3	1	1	1	3	30.68	42,400
1	30	1	2	1	1	3	22.49	65,200
1	29	4	2	1	1	2	29.89	47,150
0	36	4	3	3	1	2	13.31	41,500
1	52	3	4	2	3	3	27.19	53,900
0	37	3	2	2	2	2	29.25	51,850
0	42	3	2	2	1	4	26.00	62,200
1	30	4	2	1	1	3	34.82	44,150
1	35	1	2	1	1	3	28.50	56,300
1	38	5	1	2	3	3	29.34	46,500
↓	↓	↓	↓	↓	↓	↓	↓	↓

quantities for a particular variable, as was done for the sample of drugstore customers, we create a data set. We will use the data set illustrated in Exhibit 2.1 to distinguish among the different types of data.

Quantitative and Qualitative Data

One important distinction is whether the data are quantitative or qualitative. **Quantitative data** contain numerical information, for which arithmetical operations such as averaging are meaningful. Quantitative data are also sometimes called *numerical data,* and they may be referred to as *interval* or *ratio data* (two other data sub-types that are not important to our present work).

Qualitative data contain descriptive information, which may be recorded in words or numbers. If qualitative data are recorded as numbers, arithmetical operations such as averaging are not meaningful. The numbers in this case represent codes for the associated words. Qualitative data are also sometimes called *nominal* or *categorical data.*

Look at the data recorded in Exhibit 2.1. Are these quantitative or qualitative data? Your first answer might be "quantitative," because the table is full of numbers. But think carefully: what do the numbers mean? In column 1, the zeroes and ones are codes to represent "male" and "female." The data on gender of the customers are not quantitative data—they are qualitative data. The numbers assigned as codes could be changed, without losing any of the information. For example, we could just as easily have used 1 for male, and 2 for female. Or, in fact, we could have used 38 for male and 172 for female. The actual values of the numbers have no meaning in this context.

Consider the entire data set. The quantitative variables are:

• age
• number of purchases made at this store in the past month
• purchase amount
• annual income

The qualitative variables are:

• gender
• cleanliness rating
• staff friendliness rating
• ease of locating purchases rating
• speed of service rating

There is one more point to make about recognizing qualitative data. Often these data are summarized with counts or percentages. For example, the ratings for staff friendliness from the survey of drugstore customers might be presented in a table, as shown below in Exhibit 2.2.

Quantitative data Data containing numerical information, for which arithmetical operations such as averaging are meaningful.

Qualitative data Data containing descriptive information, which may be recorded in words or numbers (the numbers represent codes for the associated words; arithmetical operations such as averaging are not meaningful in this case).

EXHIBIT **2.2**

Summary Table for Staff Friendliness Ratings, Survey of Drugstore Customers

| | Staff Friendliness Ratings, Survey of Drugstore Customers | | | |
	Excellent	Good	Fair	Poor
Males	10	8	3	0
Females	5	15	7	2

The counts themselves are quantitative, but the underlying data are still qualitative in nature. When the data were collected, respondents indicated whether they thought the friendliness of staff was "excellent," "good," "fair," or "poor," and this is qualitative data.

Another example: it might be reported that 58% of the customers in the drugstore survey were female. Again, this percentage (or proportion) is a quantitative number, but the underlying data are still qualitative ("male" or "female"). Always think about what the raw data look like, and you should be able to distinguish correctly between quantitative and qualitative data.

Quantitative Data: Discrete or Continuous?

There are some other distinctions in data types. Sometimes it is important to determine whether quantitative variables are *discrete* or *continuous*. A **continuous variable** is a measurement variable that can take *any* possible value on a number line (possibly within upper and lower limits). A **discrete variable** can take on only certain identifiable values on a number line (possibly within upper and lower limits).

Which of the quantitative variables in the drugstore survey data are discrete, and which are continuous? The number of purchases made at the drugstore in the past month is an example of a discrete variable. This is a discrete variable because it can take on possible values of 0, 1, 2, 3, 4, 5, ... n, where n is some upper limit on the number of purchases. A value of 1.52 is not possible. Exhibit 2.3 below illustrates the possible values on a number line.

EXHIBIT 2.3

Possible Values of the Number of Purchases Made at the Drugstore in the Past Month

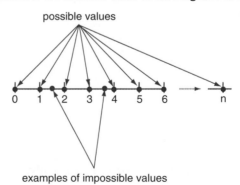

One way to identify a discrete variable is to realize that there are gaps in its possible values on a number line. Counts, by definition, are discrete random variables. Age is an interesting variable, because by convention, we speak of age in terms of the number of full years lived since birth. Although we are aging every second, we do not measure age with second-to-second accuracy. Age, as we use it, is really a counting variable (and therefore discrete), because we use it to count the number of full years lived since birth. It is useful to make a distinction here between "actual age" and "described age." Actual age is a continuous variable, and there are no gaps in the number line of possible values that actual age could take. Described age is a discrete variable because it can take on only

---

Sidebar:

Continuous variable A measurement variable that can take *any* possible value on a number line (possibly within upper and lower limits).

Discrete variable A variable that can take on only certain identifiable values on a number line (possibly within upper and lower limits).

some possible numbers, but this is really only a function of measuring conventions. We usually treat age data as if they were continuous, despite the measurement limitation. Purchase amounts and incomes, the other quantitative variables in the drugstore data set, are also normally treated as continuous data, although we do not measure these values beyond dollars and cents. It is not the limitations of our measuring devices but the theoretical possibilities that are important. Measurements such as height or weight are normally not measured beyond one or two decimal places, but no values on the relevant part of the number line are impossible, and so these are other examples of continuous variables.

Qualitative Data: Ranked or Unranked?

Some qualitative data are ranked. **Ranked data** are qualitative data that can be ordered according to size or quality. Ranked data are also sometimes called *ordinal* data. In the drugstore survey data, the ratings of cleanliness, staff friendliness, ease of locating products, and speed of service are examples of ranked data. We know that a rating of "excellent" is better than a rating of "good," for example, and so there is a natural order in the data.

Ranked data Qualitative data that can be ordered according to size or quality.

Cross-Sectional and Time-Series Data

Another distinction is between *cross-sectional* and *time-series data*. **Cross-sectional data** are all collected in the same time period. **Time-series data** are collected over successive points in time. The drugstore survey data are cross-sectional data, because they were all collected during the same time period. If the survey is repeated from year to year, then each variable could have time-series data associated with it. For example, suppose we collected the same data for 10 years. We could then calculate the average income of those surveyed each year, to create a time-series of average income data.

Cross-sectional data Data that are all collected in the same time period.

Time-series data Data that are collected over successive points in time.

DEVELOP YOUR SKILLS 2.1

1. Quality control is very important in manufacturing. Several times during the week, a paint company records the number of dented cans in a random sample of 30 paint cans from the filling line. What kind of data are these?

2. An investor is interested in a particular stock, and has collected its closing price every Friday for the last three years. What type of data are these?

3. A human resources (HR) manager wants to see if she can predict job success from a college graduate's final average grade. The manager collects data for a random sample of employees hired in the last two years. The employees' grades are in the personnel files (all are college graduates). The HR manager also asks each employee's supervisor to score the employee's performance, using a detailed questionnaire to arrive at a score from 0 (meaning the worst possible performance) to 100 (an outstanding performance). What kind of data are these? Do you see any difficulty with drawing conclusions based on such a study?

4. The owner of a local franchise of a national coffee store chain hires a student to do some market research. The owner asks the student to record the selling prices of different sizes of coffee at all the coffee stores within a 10-kilometre radius. What kind of data are these?

5. Your company has an extensive database on your customers. Among the information collected is the postal code for each customer's home address. What kind of data are these?

FREQUENCY DISTRIBUTIONS AND HISTOGRAMS FOR QUANTITATIVE DATA

In this section, we will discuss two important and related ways of summarizing quantitative data: the frequency distribution (a summary table), and its accompanying graph, the histogram. Both of these are best created with a computer. However, before we describe computer-based methods for frequency distributions and histograms, we will start with a simple method of organizing quantitative data by hand into a stem-and-leaf display. You may find this organizational method useful when you are working with small data sets. As well, a stem-and-leaf display provides an intuitive basis for summarizing quantitative data with frequency distributions and histograms.

Stem-and-Leaf Displays

A stem-and-leaf display can be used to organize a small data set quickly and easily. The display is created by breaking each number in the data set into two parts: the stem and the leaf. How many digits are in the stem and how many are in the leaf depend on the particular data set. Consider the data on the ages of the customers in the drugstore survey. The ages are as shown in Exhibit 2.4.

EXHIBIT 2.4

Survey of Drugstore Customers: Customer Ages (years)

24	30	29	36	52	37	42	30	35	38	25
54	33	40	63	33	33	26	34	38	31	31
36	42	73	35	36	33	41	85	30	32	30
32	74	39	31	30	66	28	67	29	32	32
82	58	41	39	59	54					

To create a stem-and-leaf display, we first identify the smallest and the largest data points. In this data set, the lowest age is 24 and the highest is 85. In this case, the data points have only two digits, so the stem will be the first digit and the leaf will be the second digit. We begin by setting up a column containing the stems, in order, for the entire range of the data set, as shown in Exhibit 2.5.

EXHIBIT 2.5

Stems for the Data Set of Customer Ages

```
2 |
3 |
4 |
5 |
6 |
7 |
8 |
```

EXHIBIT 2.6

Adding the Leaves in the Stem-and-Leaf Display (first column of the data set)

```
2 | 4
3 | 6  2
4 |
5 | 4
6 |
7 |
8 | 2
```

Then, working through the data set in some logical way (across the rows or down the columns), we record the second digit in the appropriate row of the display. Exhibit 2.6 illustrates how the stem-and-leaf display will look, once the first column of the data set is recorded.

Notice that the second digits are recorded as they are encountered in the data set. Do not try to order the stem-and-leaf display on the first pass. (Do a second stem-and-leaf display if ordering the data is something you want to accomplish by hand.) The completed stem-and-leaf display is shown in Exhibit 2.7.

EXHIBIT 2.7

Completed Stem-and-Leaf Display for Data Set of Customer Ages

```
2 | 4  9  6  8  9  5
3 | 6  2  0  3  9  6  5  1  9  3  6  0  7  3  3  0  4  5  8  0  8  1  2  2  1  0  2
4 | 2  0  1  2  1
5 | 4  8  2  9  4
6 | 3  6  7
7 | 4  3
8 | 2  5
```

This stem-and-leaf display has allowed us to organize the data quickly and easily. Now we have a much better sense of the ages of customers at the drugstore. Notice that all of the original data points can be recreated from the display, so no information is lost. The display also gives us a visual picture of the data. We can easily see, for example, that there are far more customers in their 30s than in the other age ranges. The stem-and-leaf display gives us a kind of preview of two important methods for summarizing quantitative data: the frequency distribution and the histogram.

Suppose we created a table corresponding to the stem-and-leaf display to summarize the data even further, as shown in Exhibit 2.8 on the next page. The new table has both lost and gained information, compared with the stem-and-leaf display. We can no longer recreate the original data from this table, but we know exactly how many customers are in their 30s (the count, or frequency, is 27). A table such as the one shown in Exhibit 2.8 is called a **frequency distribution**, which is a summary table that divides quantitative data into classes, and records the count (or frequency) of data points in each class.

Notice that this frequency distribution is not the only one we could have set up for this data set. The classes in the table correspond to our stem-and-leaf display, but we might have decided on other classes.

Frequency distribution A summary table that divides quantitative data into classes, and records the count (or frequency) of data points in each class.

EXHIBIT 2.8

Survey of Drugstore Customers

Customer Age	Number of Customers
20–29	6
30–39	27
40–49	5
50–59	5
60–69	3
70–79	2
80–89	2

Because the stem-and-leaf display provides a picture of the data, it is almost a bar graph. We could take this a step further and create a graph that corresponds to the stem-and-leaf display, replacing the leaf part of the display with bars of a corresponding length. The result would be as shown in Exhibit 2.9.

EXHIBIT 2.9

A Stem-and-Leaf Display Is Similar to a Bar Graph a) Stem-and-Leaf Display b) Bar Graph

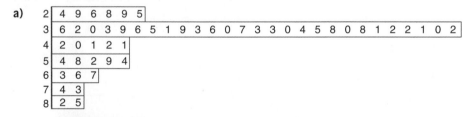

If we rotate this graph 90° counterclockwise, add information about frequencies, and provide some proper labels and a title, we get Exhibit 2.10. Such a graph is called a *histogram*. This is another standard way to represent quantitative data. Note that the histogram corresponds directly to the frequency distribution we created in Exhibit 2.8. A **histogram** is a graph of a frequency distribution, with lower class limits shown along the x-axis, and class frequencies shown along the y-axis. Each bar on the graph corresponds to

Histogram A graph of a frequency distribution, with lower class limits shown along the x-axis, and class frequencies shown along the y-axis.

EXHIBIT **2.10**

Histogram of Ages of Drugstore Customers

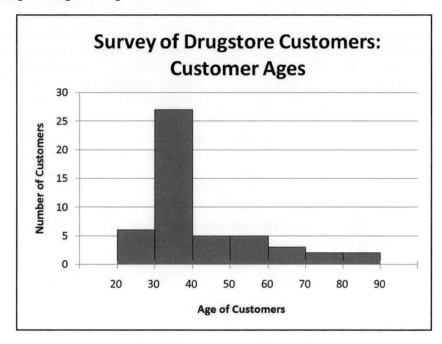

a class in the corresponding frequency distribution. The height of the bar corresponds to the frequency for the class. The width of the bar matches the width of the class.

Now that you have some idea of how summary tables and graphs can be used to summarize and represent data sets, we will discuss how Excel can be used to create frequency distributions and histograms. Remember, you can create a frequency distribution and a histogram without creating a stem-and-leaf display first. You will often find it useful to organize a data set with a stem-and-leaf display when you are working without a computer, but you will not need it when you are using Excel.

Frequency Distributions

Anne Morgan has a new job as a financial analyst for a wealthy investor. This investor, Mr. Big, is quite interested in the financial results of some Canadian industries. In particular, he is focused on quarterly operating profits for the sectors:

- Oil and Gas Extraction and Support Activities
- Manufacturing[1]

---

[1] The data presented on these industries are based on information from Statistics Canada: Statistics Canada, "Quarterly Balance Sheet and Income Statement, by North American Industry Classification System (NAICS), Quarterly," CANSIM Table 187-0001, **http://estat.statcan.gc.ca/Results/ OMNFA58.CSV**, accessed February 26, 2009. Statistics Canada, "Table 5-1, Oil and Gas Extraction and Support Activities—Balance Sheet and Income Statement" (table), *Quarterly Financial Statistics for Enterprises,* Catalogue no. 61-008-X, **www.statcan.gc.ca/pub/61-008-x/2008003/t019-eng.htm**, accessed February 26, 2009. Statistics Canada, "Table 9-1, Manufacturing—Balance Sheet and Income Statement" (table), *Quarterly Financial Statistics for Enterprises,* Catalogue no. 61-008-X, **www.statcan.gc.ca/pub/61-008-x/2008003/t015-eng.htm**, accessed February 26, 2009.

Mr. Big has asked Anne to summarize the quarterly operating profits of these industries over the last couple of decades or so. Mr. Big is interested in the amounts of quarterly profits and also their trends over time.

SEC02-2

The data set is in a file called SEC02-2, so you can examine it along with Anne. There are 83 data points for the quarterly operating profits of each sector! If Anne is going to compare these data sets effectively, she will have to summarize the data in some way. Anne decides to create a frequency distribution of quarterly operating profits for each sector.

Anne knows she can use Excel to create these frequency distributions, but first she has to decide how wide to make the classes in the frequency distribution. Deciding on the class width will simultaneously determine how many classes will be required to summarize the data.

The class-width decision is important, because if Anne uses too many classes, the data will not be summarized effectively. If she uses too few, the table may hide interesting characteristics in the data. Deciding on the class width requires some art as well as some science. In general, any frequency distribution should have somewhere between 5 and 20 classes, with larger data sets having more classes than smaller ones. Sometimes experimentation is needed to decide on the best number of classes (and class width). Some judgment is always required when class width is being decided.

Using the Class Width Template

Some help on deciding on class width is available in the Excel file called "Templates." The workbook contains a worksheet called "Class Width." Part of this worksheet is reproduced in Exhibit 2.11 below.

EXHIBIT 2.11

Class Width Template

COPY AND PASTE THIS WORKSHEET INTO THE WORKBOOK CONTAINING YOUR DATA. RIGHT-CLICK THE TAB AT THE BOTTOM OF THE SHEET, AND SELECT "Move or Copy", THEN FILL IN THE DIALOGUE BOX AS REQUIRED.		
Copy & paste the data to be analyzed into the first column of the spreadsheet, below (cells A3:A1002). Data sets of up to 1000 can be used. Be sure to paste values only, not formulas.	CLASS WIDTH TEMPLATE	
	The three rules generate suggested class widths. Use these suggestions as a basis for your judgement about an appropriate class width.	
	Recommendations for Class Width	
	Sturges' Rule	#NUM!
	Scott's Rule	#DIV/0!
	Freedman & Diacomis's Rule	#NUM!
	The other useful values shown below will help you to set up the classes for your frequency distribution.	
	Other Useful Values	
	Minimum Value	0.00
	Maximum Value	0.00
	n	0.00

Open both the Excel Templates workbook and the Excel workbook where your data reside. As you can see, the instructions for using the Class Width Template are right on the template. You should copy and paste the entire Class Width worksheet into the workbook where your data are located (right-click on the tab at the bottom of the Class Width worksheet, then fill in the dialogue box as required). Then copy and paste the data (values only) into the first column of the template (starting in cell A3).

There are some formulas built into the template that generate recommendations for class width. These formulas take into account the number of data points being analyzed and the variability in the data, and the resulting class width recommendations provide a general idea of appropriate class widths. Why three formulas? Because:

- No one formula can provide the best answer for all types of data sets.
- No formula can compete with your brain to make the final decision about class width. You have to make the final decision.

Remember, you have to use some judgment! It would not be reasonable to set up a class that was $1,508.20 wide, but a class width of $1,500 might be useful. Consider the recommendations as a starting point. Because it is relatively easy with a computer, experiment with class widths for any data set until you believe you have a histogram that faithfully represents the data.

The templates also calculate maximum and minimum values, and the number of data points in the data set. These will be helpful as you decide how to set up the classes for your frequency distribution.

If you do not have a computer available, you can get some guidance about class width by doing this calculation:

$$\text{Class width} = \frac{\text{maximum value} - \text{minimum value}}{\sqrt{n}}$$

where n is the number of data points in the data set.

Exhibit 2.12 on the next page shows the class width recommendations for the quarterly profits of the Canadian oil and gas extraction and support activities sector. The data are in millions of dollars, so keep that in mind as you read through the discussion. Class width recommendations are:

- 1,508.20
- 2,294.14
- 1,924.09

A good starting point for class width would be $2,000 (million), a nice round number in the ballpark of the class width recommendations shown above.

Just for comparison: without the computer, if Anne had used the manual calculation, the class width recommendation would have been:

$$\text{Class width} = \frac{\text{maximum value} - \text{minimum value}}{\sqrt{n}}$$

$$= \frac{11,228 - 105}{\sqrt{83}} = 1,220.9$$

EXHIBIT 2.12

Class Width Template for Oil and Gas Sector Data

	A	B	C
1	COPY AND PASTE THIS WORKSHEET INTO THE WORKBOOK CONTAINING YOUR DATA. RIGHT-CLICK THE TAB AT THE BOTTOM OF THE SHEET, AND SELECT "Move or Copy", THEN FILL IN THE DIALOGUE BOX AS REQUIRED.		
2	Copy & paste the data to be analyzed into the first column of the spreadsheet, below (cells A3:A1002). Data sets of up to 1000 can be used. Be sure to paste values only, not formulas.	CLASS WIDTH TEMPLATE	
3	906	The three rules generate suggested class widths. Use these suggestions as a basis for your judgement about an appropriate class width.	
4	822		
5	583	Recommendations for Class Width	
6	391	Sturges' Rule	1,508.20
7	854	Scott's Rule	2,294.14
8	752	Freedman & Diacomis's Rule	1,924.09
9	637		
10	655		
11	976	The other useful values shown below will help you to set up the classes for your frequency distribution.	
12	407		
13	1020	Other Useful Values	
14	1325	Minimum Value	105.00
15	692	Maximum Value	11,228.00
16	226	n	83.00
17	415		
18	286		

This might have led Anne to choose a class width of $1,000 or $1,500. You will get a chance to compare all three possible class widths in the Chapter Review Exercises.

Anne chooses a class width of $2,000 (this is actually $2 billion, since the data are in millions of dollars). Now she has to decide where the first class starts and the last class ends. This is where the additional information in the Class Width Template comes in handy.

The first class must be low enough to include the lowest value in the data set, which is $105. It is possible to make the first class 105 up to 2,105 (105 + 2,000 = 2,105), but this would be awkward. Remember, a frequency distribution is a communication tool, so it must be easy to understand. It is a good idea if the class limits are evenly divisible by the class width. The lower limit of the first class will be zero, and subsequent lower limits will be:

- 0 + 2,000 = 2,000
- 2,000 + 2,000 = 4,000
- 4,000 + 2,000 = 6,000

and so on.

The highest class must contain the highest value in the data set, which is $11,228. The lower limit of the highest class will be $10,000.

There are some other considerations for setting up classes for a frequency distribution.

1. The classes should not overlap. Each data point should clearly belong in only one class. Exhibit 2.13 illustrates.

EXHIBIT 2.13

Classes Should Not Overlap

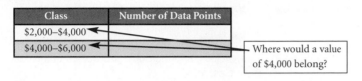

There are a number of ways to clarify class boundaries. The most general approach is illustrated in Exhibit 2.14.

EXHIBIT 2.14

Classes Do Not Overlap

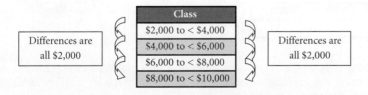

2. The classes should all be the same width, and open-ended classes (e.g., "> $10,000") should be avoided. Readers of the frequency distribution will expect regularity in the classes, and will be misled if classes are not the same width. It is easy to check whether the classes of a frequency distribution have the same width. Calculate the differences between adjacent lower limits (or upper limits). The differences should all be equal to one common class width. Exhibit 2.15 illustrates.

EXHIBIT 2.15

Class Widths Are All the Same

	Class
Differences are all $2,000	$2,000 to < $4,000
	$4,000 to < $6,000
	$6,000 to < $8,000
	$8,000 to < $10,000

Differences are all $2,000

The Guide to Technique on the next page should serve as a reference whenever you are setting up the classes of a frequency distribution.

Now that Anne has decided on the classes for the frequency distribution, she must organize the data on quarterly operating profits and count how many data points fall into each class. This is easy to do in Excel, using the **Histogram** tool.

GUIDE TO TECHNIQUE

Setting Up Appropriate Classes for a Frequency Distribution

When:

- summarizing data about one quantitative variable

Steps:

1. Identify maximum and minimum values, and the number of values in the data set, *n*.
2. Get some recommendations for class width.

   - If you are using Excel, use the Class Width Template to get some recommendations for class width.
   - If you are setting up the classes manually, use the class width formula to get a recommendation for class width, as follows:

   $$\text{Class width} = \frac{\text{maximum value} - \text{minimum value}}{\sqrt{n}}$$

3. Choose a class width that is within the range of values recommended by the Class Width Template, or close to the number produced by the manual class width formula. Choose a class width that is rounded to at least one or two fewer significant digits than the recommended class width values. For example, if a formula produces a recommended class width of 423.7, round to 400.
4. Set the lower limit of the first (lowest) class, and define the class. The lower limit must be evenly divisible by the class width. The first class must also include the minimum value in the data set. For example, if the lowest value in the data set were 1,800 and a class width of 400 were chosen, the lower limit of the first class would be 1,600 (and not 1,800) because 1,600 is evenly divisible by 400. The first class would be 1,600 to < 2,000, which includes the minimum value of 1,800.
5. Set the remaining classes, keeping the class width constant. The highest class should contain the maximum value in the data set. Suppose the class width was 400 and the minimum value was 1,800. If the highest value in the data set were 3,350, the classes would be as follows:

1,600 to < 2,000
2,000 to < 2,400
2,400 to < 2,800
2,800 to < 3,200
3,200 to < 3,600

6. Use your judgment to adjust class limits or widths in ways that make the data easy to understand. For example, when you are summarizing marks data, you would probably set up the classes so that it is possible to count how many people achieved a passing grade.
7. Some rules for classes:

   - There should be about 5 to 20 classes, with larger data sets having more classes than smaller data sets.
   - Classes should not overlap.
   - Classes should all be the same width. Open-ended classes should be avoided.

Click on **Data Analysis**[1] under the **Data** tab. You will see the **Data Analysis** dialogue box that is shown in Exhibit 2.16 below.

EXHIBIT **2.16**

Data Analysis Dialogue Box

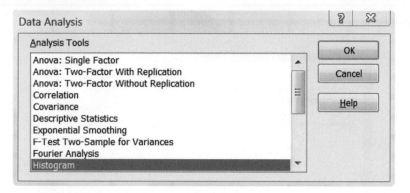

Click on **Histogram**, and **OK**.

The next dialogue box is shown in Exhibit 2.17 below.

EXHIBIT **2.17**

Histogram Dialogue Box

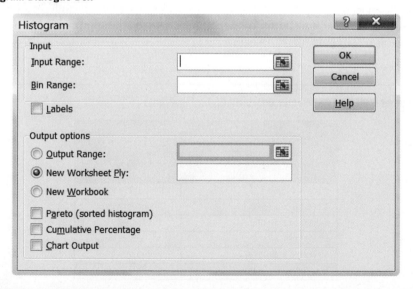

The dialogue box is filled in, as follows:

1. **Input Range** is the location of the data to be analyzed.
2. **Output Range** is the location of the output. The default location for the output is a new worksheet, but sometimes it is more convenient to have the Excel output on

---

[1] See the instructions for installing **Data Analysis** on page xxx at the beginning of the text.

the same worksheet as the data. Only one cell has to be identified in the output range: it is the cell that will be the upper left-hand corner of the output range, as illustrated in Exhibit 2.18 below. If cell A1 is identified as the output range, the Excel output will be placed below and to the right of cell A1.

EXHIBIT 2.18

Cell Identifying Output Range

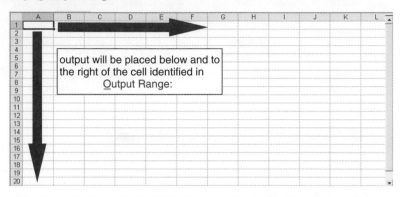

output will be placed below and to the right of the cell identified in Output Range:

3. **Bin Range** must also be filled in, if you want to control how the classes are set up (and you do—what Excel does automatically is not very useful). This requires you to type bin numbers into the worksheet. An **Excel bin number** is the upper included limit of a class.

Excel bin number The upper included limit of a class.

So, for example, the largest value in the first class ($0 to < $2,000) would be $1,999.99. For the quarterly operating profits of the oil and gas sector, the appropriate bin numbers would be as shown in Exhibit 2.19 below.

EXHIBIT 2.19

Bin Numbers, Oil and Gas Sector Quarterly Operating Profits

Canadian Oil and Gas Extraction and Support Activities Quarterly Operating Profits, I 1988 to III 2008	
Quarterly Operating Profits (Millions of Dollars)	Excel Bin Number
$0 to < $2,000	1,999.99
$2,000 to < $4,000	3,999.99
$4,000 to < $6,000	5,999.99
$6,000 to < $8,000	7,999.99
$8,000 to < $10,000	9,999.99
$10,000 to < $12,000	11,999.99

It is usually handy to type the required bin numbers onto the Class Width Template worksheet that you used to help you decide on class widths. Of course, you can do this by using Excel's auto completion feature, by dragging the fill handle down, after you have entered the first two bin numbers.

Exhibit 2.20 on the next page below shows the Class Width Template for the quarterly operating profits of the oil and gas sector, and the accompanying **Histogram** dialogue box from Excel.

EXHIBIT 2.20

Setting Up Excel Histogram Dialogue Box with Bin Numbers

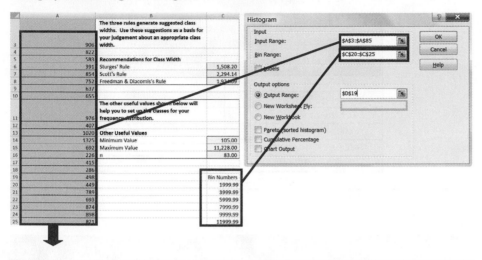

It is possible to include labels for the data being analyzed and the bin numbers. If you tick the **Labels** box, Excel will treat the first row in the selections of the input range and the bin range as labels. Remember to be consistent with both inputs (both must have labels, or neither should have labels).

In the dialogue box shown in Exhibit 2.20, the output range is set for the column right beside the bin numbers. This allows you to see if the bin numbers are what you expected. If they are not, you may have made an error completing the dialogue box.

The output created by Excel is reproduced in Exhibit 2.21 below.

EXHIBIT 2.21

Excel Histogram Output for Oil and Gas Sector Quarterly Operating Profits

Bin	Frequency
1999.99	44
3999.99	11
5999.99	11
7999.99	12
9999.99	4
More	1

As a communication tool, the frequency distribution produced in Excel leaves a lot to be desired. However, it does provide the counts (also called "frequencies") of data points in each class. With some typing, the Excel frequency distribution can become the more informative one shown in Exhibit 2.22 on the next page.

From this frequency distribution, we can see that quarterly operating profits for this sector are most often below $2 billion. We can also see that for a significant number of quarters over the last couple of decades, the quarterly operating profits have been in the $2 billion to $8 billion range. In five of the quarters, operating profits were above $8 billion.

EXHIBIT 2.22

Frequency Distribution for Quarterly Profits of Oil and Gas Sector

Canadian Oil and Gas Extraction and Support Activities Quarterly Operating Profits, I 1988 to III 2008	
Quarterly Operating Profits (Millions of Dollars)	Number of Quarters
$0 to < $2,000	44
$2,000 to < $4,000	11
$4,000 to < $6,000	11
$6,000 to < $8,000	12
$8,000 to < $10,000	4
$10,000 to < $12,000	1

EXAMPLE 2.2A

Setting up a frequency distribution with Excel

Anne must also set up a frequency distribution for the quarterly operating profits of the Canadian manufacturing sector.

EXA02-2a

First, Anne uses the Class Width Template to get a recommendation for class width. The results are shown in Exhibit 2.23.

EXHIBIT 2.23

Class Width Template for Canadian Manufacturing Quarterly Operating Profits

CLASS WIDTH TEMPLATE	
The three rules generate suggested class widths. Use these suggestions as a basis for your judgement about an appropriate class width.	
Recommendations for Class Width	
Sturges' Rule	1,871.58
Scott's Rule	2,753.43
Freedman & Diacomis's Rule	2,130.87
The other useful values shown below will help you to set up the classes for your frequency distribution.	
Other Useful Values	
Minimum Value	475.00
Maximum Value	14,278.00
n	83.00

Anne looks at the recommendations for class width, and considers $2,000 and $2,500 as possibilities. She also considers that she may be comparing quarterly operating profits of the oil and gas sector with the manufacturing sector. Using the same class width for both data sets will make the frequency distributions directly comparable. Anne decides to use a class width of $2,000 (million) for the manufacturing data.

For the minimum and maximum values in this data set, the appropriate classes are as shown in Exhibit 2.24 below.

EXHIBIT 2.24

Classes for Manufacturing Data

Canadian Manufacturing, Quarterly Operating Profits, I 1988 to III 2008	
Quarterly Operating Profits ($ Millions)	Number of Quarters
$0 to < $2,000	
$2,000 to < $4,000	
$4,000 to < $6,000	
$6,000 to < $8,000	
$8,000 to < $10,000	
$10,000 to < $12,000	
$12,000 to < $14,000	
$14,000 to < $16,000	

The Excel bin numbers corresponding to these class limits are shown in Exhibit 2.25 below. Anne types the bin numbers into the Excel spreadsheet, using the auto-fill feature.

EXHIBIT 2.25

Excel Bin Numbers for Classes for Manufacturing Data

Class Limits	Excel Bin Number
$0 to < $2,000	1,999.99
$2,000 to < $4,000	3,999.99
$4,000 to < $6,000	5,999.99
$6,000 to < $8,000	7,999.99
$8,000 to < $10,000	9,999.99
$10,000 to < $12,000	1,1999.99
$12,000 to < $14,000	1,3999.99
$14,000 to < $16,000	1,5999.99

Anne then uses the **Histogram** tool to produce the Excel results shown in Exhibit 2.26.

When proper titles, labels, and class descriptions are typed in, the frequency distribution is much more descriptive, as shown in Exhibit 2.27.

The frequency distribution illustrates that most often, quarterly operating profits have been above $6 billion but below $14 billion. Operating profits were at or above $14 billion only once during the period from the first quarter of 1988 to the third quarter of 2008.

EXHIBIT 2.26

Excel Histogram for Manufacturing Data

Bin	Frequency
1999.99	5
3999.99	7
5999.99	9
7999.99	11
9999.99	21
11999.99	16
13999.99	13
15999.99	1
More	0

EXHIBIT 2.27

Frequency Distribution for Manufacturing Data

Canadian Manufacturing, Quarterly Operating Profits, I 1988 to III 2008	
Quarterly Operating Profits ($ Millions)	**Number of Quarters**
$0 to < $2,000	5
$2,000 to < $4,000	7
$4,000 to < $6,000	9
$6,000 to < $8,000	11
$8,000 to < $10,000	21
$10,000 to < $12,000	16
$12,000 to < $14,000	13
$14,000 to < $16,000	1

Histograms

Frequency distributions are usually accompanied by a corresponding graph, which is called a "histogram." For example, the histogram for the oil and gas sector would look as shown in Exhibit 2.28.

It is easy to see from the histogram that for the majority of the quarters over the past couple of decades, the operating profits of the oil and gas sector have been less than $2 billion. It is also easy to see that for about 30 of those quarters, operating profits were above $2 billion but below $8 billion. In a very few quarters, the operating profits were above $8 billion.

There is a direct correspondence between the elements of the histogram and the frequency distribution. The titles are the same. The column headings in the frequency distribution are the axis labels on the graph.

You can use Excel to create an automatic histogram, and this is normally done at the same time that the frequency distribution is created. Unfortunately, Excel's automatic histogram is far from acceptable, and it requires a number of modifications.

EXHIBIT 2.28

Frequency Distribution and Histogram for Oil and Gas Data

Canadian Oil and Gas Extraction and Support Activities Quarterly Operating Profits, I 1988 to III 2008	
Quarterly Operating Profits (Millions of Dollars)	Number of Quarters
$0 to < $2,000	44
$2,000 to < $4,000	11
$4,000 to < $6,000	11
$6,000 to < $8,000	12
$8,000 to < $10,000	4
$10,000 to < $12,000	1

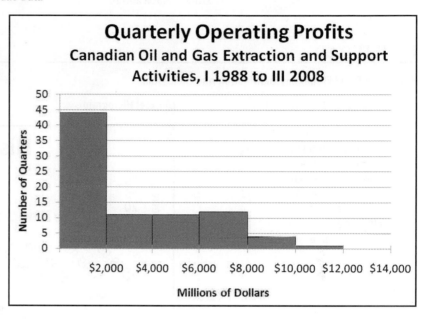

Not surprisingly, the Excel histogram is produced with the **Data Analysis** tool called **Histogram**, which we have already used to produce the frequency distribution for a data set. The Excel histogram is produced by ticking the **Chart Output** box in the **Histogram** dialogue box, as illustrated in Exhibit 2.29 below.

EXHIBIT 2.29

Creating a Chart with Histogram Dialogue Box

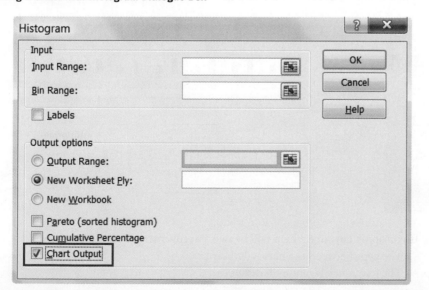

Of course, Excel's automatic histogram corresponds exactly to Excel's frequency distribution. The table and the graph produced by Excel look as shown below in Exhibits 2.30a and b.

EXHIBIT 2.30

Automatic Excel Frequency Distribution and Histogram

a) Excel Frequency Distribution

	Bin	Frequency
1999.999	1999.999	44
3999.999	3999.999	11
5999.999	5999.999	11
7999.999	7999.999	12
9999.999	9999.999	4
11999.999	12000	1
	More	0

b) Excel Histogram

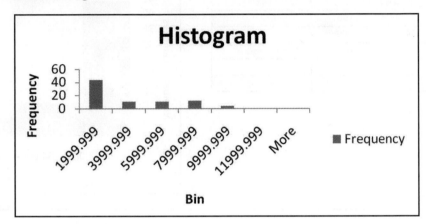

Adjusting Excel's Histogram You can change elements in Excel's automatically produced histogram by clicking or right-clicking on those elements. There are a number of formatting changes that must be applied to the automatic histogram in Excel.

1. Highlight the chart to activate **Chart Tools**. Click on **Design**, and then use the drop-down menu on **Chart Layouts** to illustrate the gallery of layouts possible.

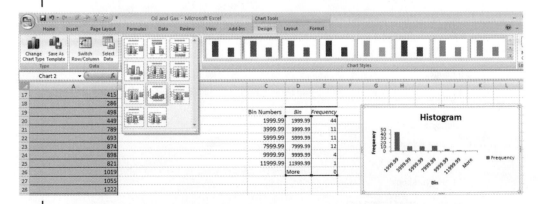

If you apply Layout 8, there will be two improvements to the histogram:
- The gaps between the bars will disappear.
- The frequency legend will disappear.

2. You may also wish to format the bars in the histogram so that they have borders. You do this by right-clicking on the bars. Click on **Format Data Series**, select **Border Color**, select **Solid Line**, and use the drop-down menu on **Color** to select a contrasting border colour. You can also use **Border Styles** options to change the thickness of the border.

3. Horizontal grid lines make it easier to interpret the heights of the bars on the histogram. Click on the graph, and then **Chart Tools** become available. Click on **Layout**, then select the drop-down menu under **Gridlines**, click on **Primary Horizontal Gridlines**, and then click on **Major Gridlines**.

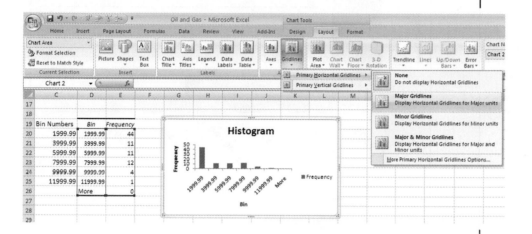

4. Convention is that the tick marks on the *x*-axis should indicate the *lower* limit of the class, but Excel's bin numbers are the *upper* limit of each class. There is a trick (in two steps) to give the appearance of lower class limits. If you round the bin numbers on the worksheet, they will look like the lower limits of the next class. Highlight the bin number cells on the worksheet (frequency distribution output). Under the **Home** tab, in the **Number** area, click on the icon to **Decrease Decimal**. Note that for this trick to work, you must always include the appropriate number of decimal places in your bin numbers (e.g., a bin number of "199.9," not "199").[2] This way, a bin number of 199.999 rounds to 200, which is the lower limit of the next class to the right. See Exhibits 2.31a and b on the next page, which illustrate the histograms before and after the bin numbers are rounded.

5. Excel generally places the bin numbers on the chart under the middle of each associated bar. Following on from step 4 above, you want to shift these labels to the right, so they are under the left edge of the bar for next class to the right.

---

[2] Probably because of the way Excel works, the traditional labelling convention (lower class limits on the *x*-axis of the histogram) is not always followed. You should communicate clearly that your histogram shows lower class limits (this will be obvious if your histogram is accompanied by a frequency distribution with clear class limits). You should also carefully examine any histogram you see, in case the standard convention is not followed.

EXHIBIT 2.31

Histograms with Unaltered and Rounded Bin Numbers

a) Histogram with Unaltered Bin Numbers

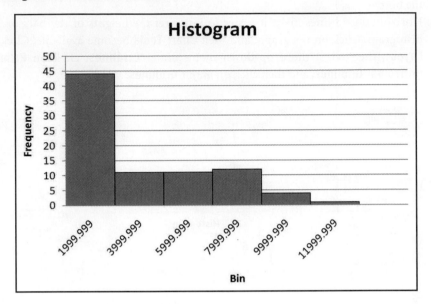

b) Histogram with Rounded Bin Numbers

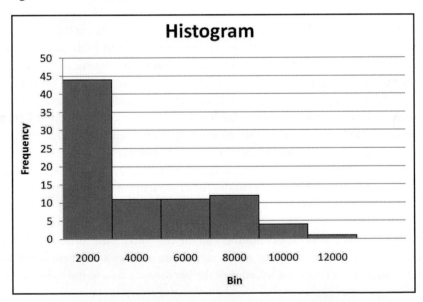

You can adjust the labels on the *x*-axis as follows: right-click on the *x*-axis labels, then click on **Format Axis…**. Under **Axis Options** click on **Alignment**, then set the **Custom angle** as 1°. The dialogue box is shown opposite.

This (perhaps surprisingly) will have the effect of shifting the *x*-axis labels to the right, closer to the appropriate tick mark on the chart. You may have to adjust the

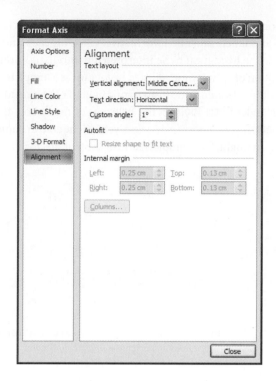

width of the chart to achieve the desired effect. It also helps to right-click on the axis labels, and right-justify them (using the justification available in the **Paragraph** area of the **Home** tab). This aligns the labels more closely with the tick marks.

See Exhibit 2.32 below, which illustrates.

EXHIBIT 2.32

Histogram with Bin Numbers Shifted Right

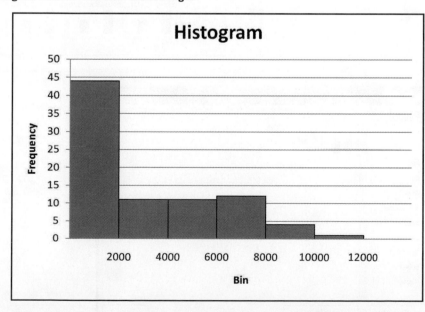

6. Delete the "More" label in the frequency distribution output.
7. The titles and axis labels must be informative. Click on each and type in titles and labels that allow the histogram to be interpreted without additional information.
8. You have the option of saving your adjusted histogram as a template that you can use to quickly reformat Excel's automatic histogram. Highlight the amended histogram, then click on **Design** under **Chart Tools**. In the **Type** area of the ribbon, there is an option to **Save As Template**. If you choose this option, you will be able to name the template and call on it later (you might, for example, name it "Histogram" for future reference).

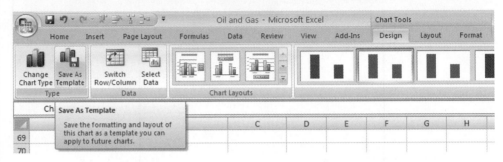

In future, if you want to apply the template to Excel's automatic histogram, do the following:

- Click on the graph.
- Under **Chart Tools**, click on **Design**.
- Under **Type**, click on **Change Chart Type**.
- Click on **Templates**, which is the top option in the **Change Chart Type** dialogue box, and select the template you created. Click on **OK**. Your automatic Excel histogram will now be much closer to what you want.

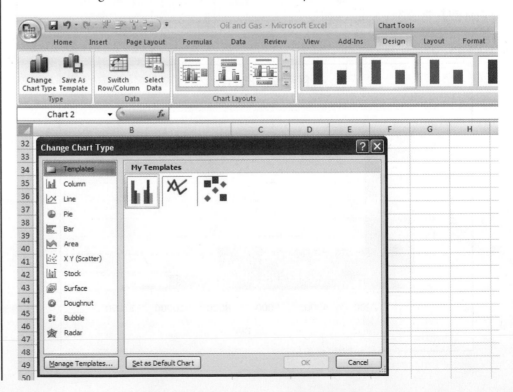

While making all of these adjustments may seem tedious at first, you will soon become accustomed to them. Using a chart template will speed things up (only adjustments 4, 6, and 7 will be required). The result will be a histogram that is much more useful, as illustrated in Exhibit 2.33 below.

EXHIBIT **2.33**

Before and After Histograms of Oil and Gas Quarterly Operating Profits

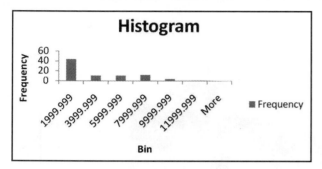

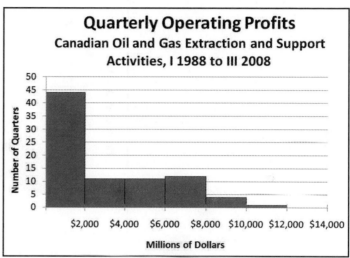

EXAMPLE **2.2B**

Modifying Excel's automatic histogram

The automatic histogram produced for the quarterly operating profits of the manufacturing sector (corresponding to the frequency distribution for Example 2.2A, Exhibit 2.27, page 44) looks as shown below in Exhibit 2.34. This must be adjusted.

EXHIBIT **2.34**

Automatic Histogram for Quarterly Operating Profits of Manufacturing Sector

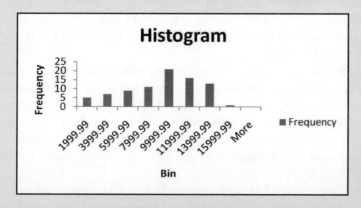

The adjusted histogram is shown below in Exhibit 2.35.

EXHIBIT 2.35

Adjusted Histogram for Quarterly Operating Profits of Manufacturing Sector

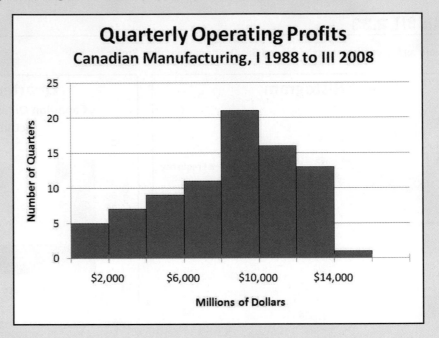

From this histogram we can see that the quarterly operating profits of the Canadian manufacturing sector have been at or above $14 billion only once in the last couple of decades. Also, we can see that for the majority of the quarters, the operating profits were between $8 billion and $14 billion. For a significant number of quarters, operating profits were less than $8 billion.

Symmetry and Skewness

Histograms are very useful graphs for summarizing quantitative data, and they are widely used. Histograms can also be used to decide if a sample data set has a desired or required distribution. You will often have to make this kind of decision as you learn the techniques covered in this text.

One characteristic of a data set that is usually of interest is whether it is *symmetric* or *skewed*. In a **symmetric distribution**, the right half of the distribution is a mirror image of the left half. A symmetric distribution is illustrated in the histogram shown in Exhibit 2.36, opposite. If this distribution were folded over along the dotted line, the left and right sides would match exactly. This kind of symmetry (and a shape like Exhibit 2.36) can be very desirable, although exact symmetry is rarely observed in real data.

In contrast, a non-symmetric distribution is described as being skewed. A distribution is **skewed to the right** (or **positively skewed**) when there are some unusually high

Symmetric distribution The right half of the distribution is a mirror image of the left half.

Skewed to the right (or positively skewed) distribution A distribution in which some unusually high values in the data set destroy the symmetry.

EXHIBIT 2.36

Symmetric Distribution

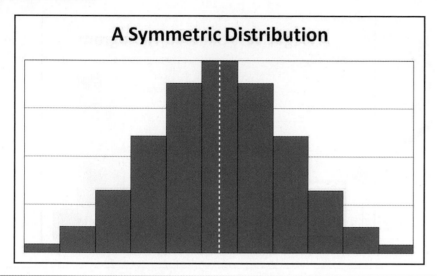

A Symmetric Distribution

values in the data set that destroy the symmetry. An example of a positively skewed distribution is shown in Exhibit 2.37 below.

EXHIBIT 2.37

Positively Skewed Distribution

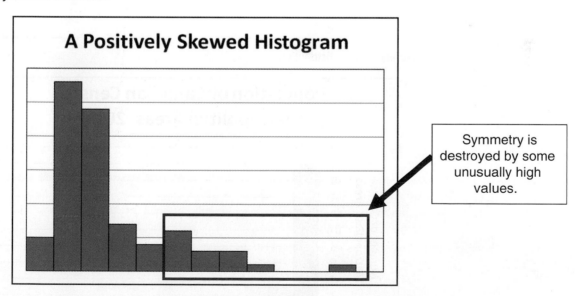

A Positively Skewed Histogram

Symmetry is destroyed by some unusually high values.

As you might guess, a distribution is described as **negatively skewed** (or **skewed to the left**) when some unusually small values destroy the symmetry. An example of a negatively skewed distribution is shown in Exhibit 2.38 on the next page.

Skewed to the left (or negatively skewed) distribution A distribution in which some unusually small values in the data set destroy the symmetry.

EXHIBIT **2.38**

Negatively Skewed Distribution

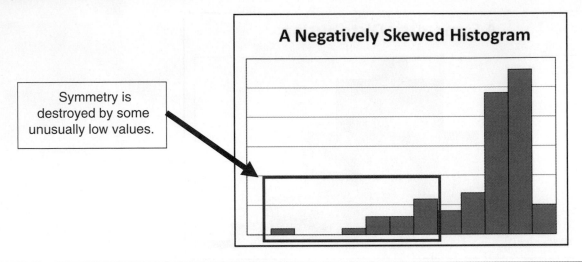

For an example of a data set that is severely skewed, see Exhibit 2.39 below. It shows the distribution of populations of metropolitan areas in Canada. You can see that most of these metropolitan areas have populations of less than 500,000. Canada's three largest cities (Vancouver, Montreal, and Toronto) are clearly seen in the histogram. In this data set, the populations of the three largest cities are unusually large, compared with the rest of the data.

EXHIBIT **2.39**

Severely Skewed Distribution

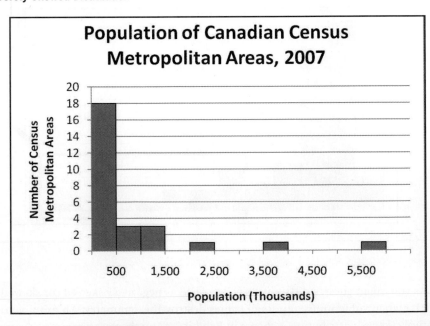

Source: "Population of Census Metropolitan areas," **www40.statcan. gc.ca/l01/cst01/demo05a-eng.htm,** accessed March 14, 2009.

These three data points could be referred to as *outliers*. An **outlier** is a data point that is unusually far from the rest of the data.

Outlier A data point that is unusually far from the rest of the data.

The presence of outliers in a data set usually raises questions. For example, it is often a requirement that a data set have a symmetric, bell-shaped distribution, and the existence of an outlier (or outliers) can destroy that required symmetry. Outliers are usually investigated carefully. Generally, outliers can exist for one of three reasons:

1. The outlier is a correct data point, and it exists because of the variability in the population data being sampled or studied. In this case, the observation is legitimately part of the data set.
2. The outlier is an error that was made when the data were being collected or recorded. If this is the case, the error should be corrected.
3. The outlier comes from a population that is distinctly different from the one being studied or sampled. In this case, it *may* be legitimate to eliminate the outlier from the data set, but you should never do this without explaining and justifying your action.

Comparing Histograms

Anne set out to compare the quarterly operating profits of the manufacturing and oil and gas sectors. She has chosen the same class width for both data sets, to make them easier to compare. This is not always possible. If the data sets are quite different, it may not be possible to find a class width that is reasonable for all.

Anne also realizes that anyone looking at the blue-shaded bars of the histograms will automatically compare the total area of the bars. The human eye responds to the visual "weight" of the coloured areas. This means that care should be taken to scale the two histograms in similar ways.

Exhibits 2.40 and 2.41 on the following pages illustrate.

When we look at the two histograms at once, it is clear that the quarterly operating profits of the manufacturing sectors were generally higher than for the oil and gas sector. However, this difference is emphasized because the vertical (*y*-) axes scales are different for the two histograms. As well, because the horizontal (*x*-) axes do not line up correctly, it is difficult to make a comparison between the two histograms. Exhibit 2.41 shows the two histograms with matching scales and sizes.

There is a further step you can take to make comparisons of histograms or frequency distributions easier to understand: you can convert the frequencies into relative frequencies. Relative frequencies are particularly useful when the data sets being compared have different numbers of data points. The **relative frequency** of a class is the percentage of total observations falling into that class.

Relative frequency The percentage of total observations that fall into a particular class.

For example, consider the frequency distribution for the quarterly operating profits of the oil and gas sector, in Exhibit 2.42 on page 58.

There are 83 data points in total. Therefore, the relative frequency for the $0 to < $2000 class is $44/83 = 0.53$. All of the relative frequencies are shown in Exhibit 2.43 on page 58.

Exhibit 2.44 on page 59 shows the two relative frequency histograms produced by Anne Morgan for the quarterly operating profits of the manufacturing and the oil and gas sectors. Note that the shapes of the histograms are unchanged when frequencies are converted to relative frequencies. The scale and the title on the vertical axes are the only things that change.

EXHIBIT 2.40

Histograms for Quarterly Operating Profits for the Manufacturing and Oil and Gas Sectors, Not Appropriate for Comparison

a) Quarterly Operating Profits, Oil and Gas Sector

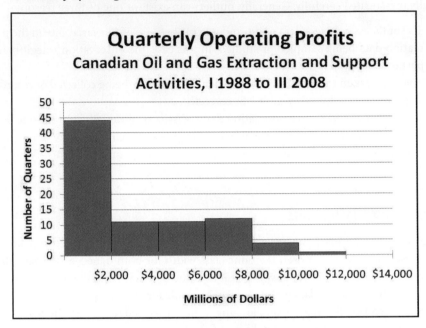

b) Quarterly Operating Profits, Manufacturing Sector

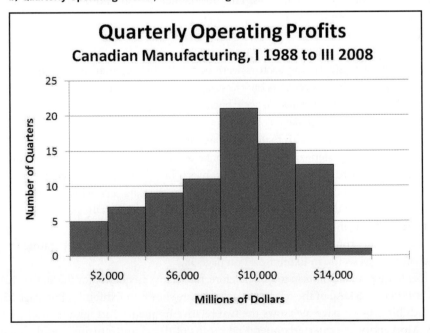

EXHIBIT **2.41**

Histograms for Quarterly Operating Profits for the Manufacturing and Oil and Gas Sectors,
Appropriate for Comparison

a) Quarterly Operating Profits, Oil and Gas Sector

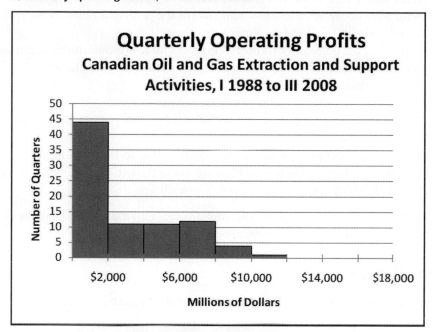

b) Quarterly Operating Profits, Manufacturing Sector

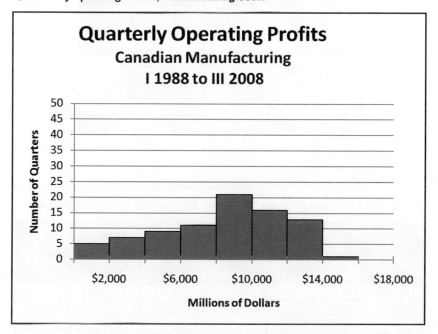

With the graphs set up for easy comparison, we can see a number of things:

- Generally, quarterly operating profits for the manufacturing sector were higher than for the oil and gas sector, from the first quarter of 1988 to the third quarter of 2008.
- For over half of the quarters under study, the operating profits of the oil and gas sector were under $2 billion. Quarterly operating profits for the manufacturing sector were under $2 billion less than 10% of the time, and generally were more variable than in the oil and gas sector.
- Over half of the time, quarterly operating profits for the manufacturing sector were above $8 billion. Quarterly operating profits for the oil and gas sector were above $8 billion less than 10% of the time.
- The quarterly operating profits of the oil and gas sector are skewed to the right. That is, most of the time the profits are below $2 billion, but in a few quarters the profits are unusually high.
- The quarterly operating profits of the manufacturing sector are more symmetric, although this distribution is somewhat skewed to the left. That is, there are a few quarters in which operating profits were unusually low.

The Guide to Technique on page 60 will remind you of important considerations when you are setting up histograms for comparison.

EXHIBIT 2.42

Frequency Distribution for Quarterly Operating Profits of the Oil and Gas Sector

Canadian Oil and Gas Extraction and Support Activities Quarterly Operating Profits, I 1988 to III 2008	
Quarterly Operating Profits (Millions of Dollars)	Number of Quarters
$0 to < $2,000	44
$2,000 to < $4,000	11
$4,000 to < $6,000	11
$6,000 to < $8,000	12
$8,000 to < $10,000	4
$10,000 to < $12,000	1

EXHIBIT 2.43

Relative Frequency Distribution for Quarterly Operating Profits of the Oil and Gas Sector

Canadian Oil and Gas Extraction and Support Activities Quarterly Operating Profits, I 1988 to III 2008		
Quarterly Operating Profits (Millions of Dollars)	Number of Quarters	Percentage of Quarters
$0 to < $2,000	44	44/83 = 0.53
$2,000 to < $4,000	11	11/83 = 0.13
$4,000 to < $6,000	11	0.13
$6,000 to < $8,000	12	0.14
$8,000 to < $10,000	4	0.05
$10,000 to < $12,000	1	0.01

EXHIBIT 2.44

Relative Frequency Histograms for Quarterly Operating Profits for the Manufacturing
and Oil and Gas Sectors

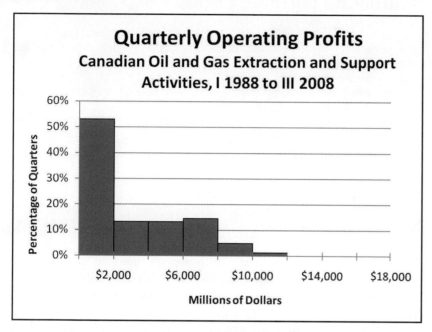

GUIDE TO TECHNIQUE

Comparing Histograms

1. Use the same class width for all the data sets being compared, if possible.
2. Use the same *x*-axis and *y*-axis scales for the data sets being compared, if possible. If the data sets are so different that using similar scales is not reasonable, signal the difference in scales to the reader.
3. Present the histograms one above the other on the same page, with the *x*-axis values lined up.
4. If the histograms being compared are based on data sets of different sizes, report relative frequencies on the *y*-axis, on the same scale.

DEVELOP YOUR SKILLS 2.2

6. Create a histogram for the ages of customers in the survey of drugstore customers. Do this three times, with three different class widths: 5, 10, and 15 years. Describe the histograms and comment on the differences among them. Which histogram do you think best summarizes the data?

DYS02-6

7. Create an appropriate frequency distribution and histogram for the incomes of customers in the survey of drugstore customers. Write a sentence or two to describe the data.

DYS02-7

8. Doug Brackett runs Downtown Automotive in Nelson, BC. The business is always under pressure to complete repairs quickly, correctly, and at a fair price. Doug is trying to understand how many different customers visit the shop per day, and he has collected customer counts for a random sample of days. Use a stem-and-leaf display to organize the resulting data set, shown in Exhibit 2.45 below. Comment on the data.

9. Consider the histogram shown in Exhibit 2.46 on the next page. There are several problems with this histogram. Describe the problems, and how you would fix them.

10. Patty Plainte wants to compare the final grades of the students in Mr. Mean's class with those in Ms. Nice's class. (Patty is a student in Mr. Mean's class, and thinks that her teacher's nasty personality is the reason she did so poorly in the course.) Patty has managed to collect a random sample of final grades from the students in the two classes. She has created the two histograms shown in Exhibit 2.47 on the next page so that she can make her comparison.

DYS02-10

Do you think that Patty deserved her low mark in statistics, based on these graphs? What would you do to improve the graphs?

EXHIBIT 2.45

Data Set for Downtown Automotive

Daily Customer Counts, Downtown Automotive				
24	19	27	41	17
26	34	17	25	31
23	29	26	18	24
31	24	14	29	36
31	29	40	12	26

EXHIBIT 2.46

Problematic Histogram

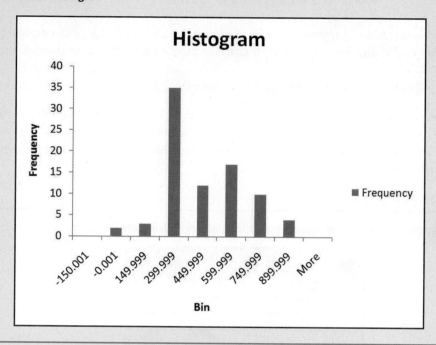

EXHIBIT 2.47

Histograms of Classes' Final Grades

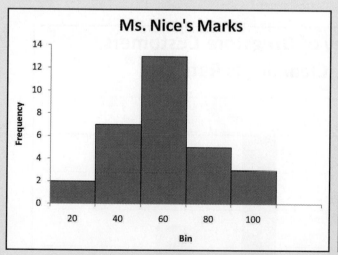

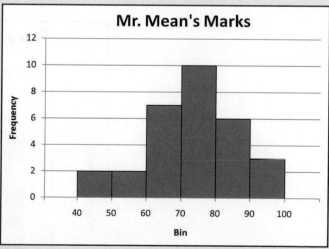

2.3 TABLES, BAR GRAPHS, AND PIE CHARTS FOR QUALITATIVE DATA

Setting up correct histograms with Excel involves a number of steps, and a number of decisions. Creating bar graphs and pie charts in Excel is relatively easy by comparison.

Bar Graphs and Pie Charts for a Simple Table

Lynda Parks, manager of the drugstore discussed in Section 2.1, wants to understand the perceptions of cleanliness from the survey of her customers. She reviews the data and produces a table summarizing the results. The table, which is another form of frequency distribution, is shown in Exhibit 2.48 below.

EXHIBIT 2.48

Frequency Distribution for Cleanliness Ratings, Survey of Drugstore Customers

Survey of Drugstore Customers, Cleanliness Ratings	
Rating	Number of Ratings
Excellent	20
Good	20
Fair	8
Poor	2

A bar graph that represents these data is shown in Exhibit 2.49.

EXHIBIT 2.49

Bar Graph of Drugstore Cleanliness Ratings

Notice the spaces between the bars. The heights of the bars in this graph represent counts (or frequencies) for distinct qualitative categories, so the bars must be separated by a space. This is in contrast to a histogram, where the classes have no gaps between them (and so there is no space between the bars). Also notice that the bars could have been presented in any order (again, in contrast to a histogram, where the bars correspond to quantitative data ranges on the *x*-axis).

This bar graph is created in Excel as follows:

1. Highlight the cells in the worksheet containing the number of items and the labels (the frequency distribution).
2. Click on **Insert** and then, in the **Charts** area, click on **Column**, and select the first **2-D Column** chart option available.

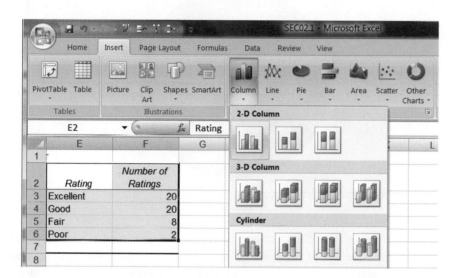

3. Click on the chart, and under **Chart Tools**, click on **Layout**. In the **Labels** area, you have available the tools necessary to adjust the labels and title of the chart (and you will probably want to clear the automatically created legend). For example, if you click on **Axis Titles**, and then on **Primary <u>V</u>ertical Axis Title**, then on **Rotated Title**, you will be able to enter a title for the *y*-axis of the graph. As usual, if you right-click on the axis labels or the title, you will be able to edit them as desired.

Bar graphs emphasize the relative sizes of the categories in qualitative data. Pie charts can also be used to display the data. Pie charts emphasize the share of the total represented by each category. A pie chart for the drugstore cleanliness survey data is shown below in Exhibit 2.50.

EXHIBIT 2.50

Pie Chart of Drugstore Cleanliness Survey Ratings

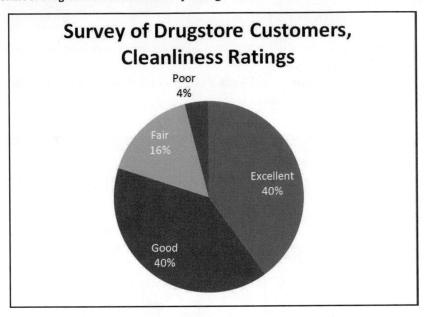

A pie chart can be created in Excel using essentially the same steps as for the bar graph, but selecting **Pie** as the type of chart to be inserted. Select the first **2-D Pie** option available.

With the chart highlighted, with **Chart Tools** available, you will see a number of options for **Chart Layouts**. **Chart Layout 1** shows the label and percentage accounted for by each slice of the pie, which is a common way to represent pie chart data. Exhibit 2.50 above shows how this looks.

It is usually best to have the category names right next to or on the pie slices in the graph, as shown in Exhibit 2.50, rather than in a separate legend. This is particularly true if the chart is going to be reproduced in black and white. If you plan to print the chart in black and white, highlight the chart so that **Chart Tools** are available. Click on the **Design** tab, and you will see a number of **Chart Styles** available. Choose one of the styles that shows in greyscale to ensure that your printed chart will be readable if you are printing in black and white. You can also right-click on the pie sections and use the **F̲ormat Data Point...** options to adjust the look of the chart.

EXAMPLE 2.3

Using Excel to create a bar graph with coded data

Create an appropriate graph to display the customer ratings of staff friendliness from the drugstore survey.

EXA02-3

The first task is to arrive at counts for each category of staff friendliness. Since the ratings are recorded as numbers, it is just a matter of using Excel's **Histogram** tool to create a frequency distribution, using bin numbers of 1, 2, 3, and 4 (the ratings). The result produced by Excel is shown below in Exhibit 2.51.

EXHIBIT 2.51

Excel Frequency Distribution for Staff Friendliness Ratings

Bin	Frequency
1	15
2	23
3	10
4	2
More	0

First, we can improve this table by adding a title and replacing the codes with their meanings. See the table shown in Exhibit 2.52 below.

EXHIBIT 2.52

Improved Frequency Distribution for Staff Friendliness Ratings

Survey of Drugstore Customers, Staff Friendliness Ratings	
Rating	Number of Ratings
Excellent	15
Good	23
Fair	10
Poor	2

If similar changes are made on the Excel spreadsheet, creating the bar graph is fairly straightforward. See Exhibit 2.53 below.

EXHIBIT 2.53

Bar Graph for Staff Friendliness Ratings

It is easy to see that most customers rate staff friendliness as either "excellent" or "good." We can also see that 10 customers rated the staff friendliness as "fair," and a few customers rated staff friendliness as "poor." If you were the owner of this drugstore, would you be happy with these results?

Bar Graphs for Contingency Tables

The owner of the drugstore is interested in the ratings of staff friendliness by gender. It is fairly easy to use Excel to organize the data to reveal these patterns, first by using the **Sort** tool to organize the data according to gender (0 for male, 1 for female). Once the data are sorted into male and female, the **Histogram** tool can be used to count the ratings for each gender.

The resulting contingency table (also called a cross-classification table) is shown below in Exhibit 2.54.

EXHIBIT 2.54

Contingency Table for Staff Friendliness Ratings, Survey of Drugstore Customers

	Staff Friendliness Ratings, Survey of Drugstore Customers				
	Excellent	Good	Fair	Poor	Total
Males	10	8	3	0	21
Females	5	15	7	2	29

Because there are 21 males and 29 females in the data set, it makes sense to calculate relative frequencies for each of the categories. The resulting contingency table is shown below in Exhibit 2.55.

EXHIBIT 2.55

Relative Frequency Contingency Table for Staff Friendliness Ratings, Survey of Drugstore Customers

	Staff Friendliness Ratings, Survey of Drugstore Customers			
	Excellent	Good	Fair	Poor
Percentage of Males	47.6%	38.1%	14.3%	0.0%
Percentage of Females	17.2%	51.7%	24.1%	6.9%

It is also possible to summarize this data set with a bar graph, as shown in Exhibit 2.56 on the next page. A pie chart would not be useful for cross-classified data of this type.

With this graph, a number of things are illustrated. For example:

1. A much higher percentage of males than females rated the staff friendliness as excellent. Just under 48% of males rated staff friendliness as excellent, compared with about 17% for female customers.

EXHIBIT 2.56

Bar Graph, Staff Friendliness Ratings, Survey of Drugstore Customers

2. A higher percentage of female customers rated staff friendliness as good, compared with male customers. Over 50% of female customers rated staff friendliness as good, while under 40% of male customers chose the "good" rating.
3. While no male customers rated staff friendliness as poor, some female customers did, although this accounted for less than 7% of female customers.

In general, there seems to be a relationship between gender and staff friendliness ratings. Male and female customers award the ratings differently.

It is also possible to create a bar graph that is organized according to the rows of the table, rather than the columns, as Exhibit 2.57 on the next page illustrates.

This presentation of the data allows us to make some other observations:

1. The majority of males rated staff friendliness as excellent or good, and none of them rated it as poor.
2. The majority of females rated staff friendliness as good, about 17% rated it as excellent, and some (fewer than 7%) rated it as poor.

Lynda Parks will decide which version of the bar graph to use, depending on what factors she wants to emphasize.

The more complicated bar graph based on table rows can be created in Excel by selecting the table in the worksheet (labels and numbers), as follows. Click on **Insert** and, in the **Chart** area, click on **Column** and then on the first **2-D Column** option. The default is to present the data with the categories defined (along the horizontal axis) by the columns in the table (as in Exhibit 2.56). You can change the graph to present the data with the column headings defining the categories (as in Exhibit 2.57) by using **Chart Tools**. Highlight the chart, and click on **Design** under **Chart Tools**. In the **Data** area, click on **Switch Row/Column**, and the chart will instantly adjust.

EXHIBIT 2.57

Alternative Bar Graph, Staff Friendliness Ratings, Survey of Drugstore Customers

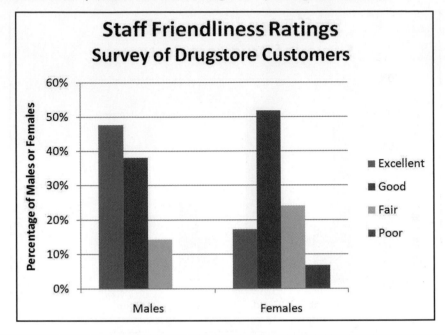

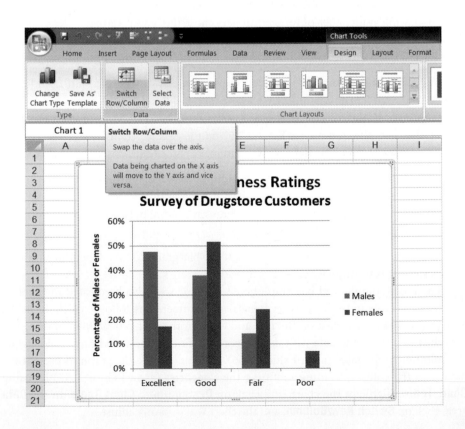

If you are going to present the chart in black and white, you should take care to ensure that it will be possible to tell the bars apart. With the chart highlighted, under the **Design** tab you will see a number of **Chart Styles** available. Choose one of the styles that shows in greyscale. You can also right-click on the bars and use the **Format Data Series...** options to adjust the look of the graph.

DEVELOP YOUR SKILLS 2.3   *MyStatLab*

11. Create an appropriate graph to summarize the "speed of service" rating data for the survey of drugstore customers. Comment on the data.
DYS02-11

12. A candy manufacturer has definite rules about the colour mixture of its candy-coated peanuts. Currently, the manufacturing process is set up to produce candies according to the distribution shown in Exhibit 2.58.

EXHIBIT 2.58

Candy Colour Desired Distribution

Candy Colours			
Red	Green	Blue	Yellow
40%	30%	20%	10%

The company wants to be sure it is still achieving this colour balance after a recent reorganization of the production process at one of its plants. A random sample of candies is selected. The breakdown of colours is shown in Exhibit 2.59.

EXHIBIT 2.59

Candy Colour Sample Distribution

Candy Colours			
Red	Green	Blue	Yellow
305	265	201	96

Create an appropriate graph to assess whether the company is still achieving the desired colour balance at the plant after reorganizing the production process.

13. Exhibit 2.60 shows some data on the number of defects observed during different shifts at a manufacturing plant. Create an appropriate graph to summarize these data, and comment.

EXHIBIT 2.60

Defects Observed at a Manufacturing Plant

Shift Items	Items with No Apparent Defects	Items with One Minor Defect	Items with More Than One Minor Defect
8:00 A.M.–4:00 P.M.	342	34	15
4:00 P.M.–Midnight	336	26	7
Midnight–8:00 A.M.	344	40	16

14. A financial services company conducted a survey of a random sample of its customers. One of the items on the survey was as follows: "The staff at my local branch can provide me with good advice on my financial affairs." Customers were asked to respond on the following scale: (1) strongly agree; (2) agree; (3) neither agree nor disagree; (4) disagree; (5) strongly disagree. The customer responses are summarized in Exhibit 2.61 on the next page.

EXHIBIT 2.61

Financial Services Company Customer Survey

Financial Services Company Customer Survey	
"The staff at my local branch can provide me with good advice on my financial affairs."	Number of Customers
Strongly agree	10
Agree	57
Neither agree nor disagree	32
Disagree	15
Strongly disagree	9

Create an appropriate graph to summarize the results, and comment. Do the results suggest any further investigation that might be worthwhile?

15. In MyStatLab there is a file containing data on favourite flavours of ice cream for a random sample of people DYS02-15 walking around Kempenfelt Bay one summer evening. The data are coded as follows: (1) vanilla, (2) chocolate, (3) strawberry, (4) maple walnut, (5) chocolate chip, (6) pralines, (7) other. Create an appropriate graph for the data set and comment.

2.4   TIME-SERIES GRAPHS

Time-series data are a sequence of observations made over time. These observations are plotted in the order in which they occurred, with time along the *x*-axis. Anne Morgan's boss is interested in the trends in quarterly operating profits over time for the oil and gas industry. A time-series graph of the operating profits is shown below in Exhibit 2.62.

Note that the original data points are shown in red on this graph (the colour has been changed from the default blue value, to emphasize the points for this discussion).

EXHIBIT 2.62

Time-Series Graph of Quarterly Operating Profits for Oil and Gas Sector

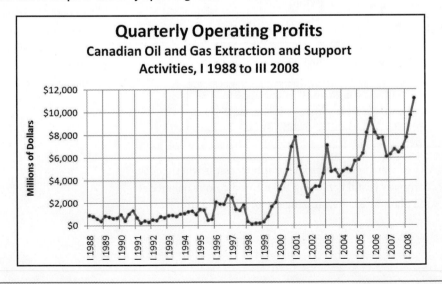

The lines joining the points do *not* represent data: the lines are added to make it easier to see any patterns or trends. When there are many data points (as in this case), the individual data points are sometimes not indicated in the graph, so that it is less cluttered.

There do appear to be some time-related trends in the quarterly operating profits of the oil and gas sector. Until the beginning of 1996, quarterly operating profits were below $2 billion. After somewhat higher levels in 1996 and 1997, quarterly operating profits dropped to quite low values for 1998. At the beginning of 1999, quarterly operating profits increased quite significantly from $333 million in the first quarter of 1999 to $7.8 billion in the first quarter of 2001. Quarterly operating profits then dropped significantly in 2001, to $2.4 billion. Since that time, quarterly operating profits have been on a general upward trend, with noticeable peaks in the first quarter of 2003 (at $7.1 billion), the last quarter of 2005 ($9.4 billion), and the third quarter of 2008 ($11.2 billion).

Notice that the discussion of trends above is descriptive. You may have some ideas about *why* the operating profits in the oil and gas sector have changed. The price of oil is certainly a contributing factor, but without any data on the price of oil, it is not legitimate to make any comment about this connection. Be sure to limit your descriptions of trends to the data you actually have. Also, notice that some particular values are cited in the description above. Clearly, these cannot be read directly from the graph. However, if you created the graph, you also have the original data points, and you should not ignore these. When the graph indicates that a particular value is of interest, you should quote it exactly from the original data.

It is also possible to present time-series data with a bar graph, but this is appropriate only if there are just a few time periods. For example, if you converted the time-series graph for the quarterly operating profits of the oil and gas sector to a bar graph, it would be more difficult to read (try it!). Bar graphs can be effective when time-series data are for only a limited number of observations, particularly if you want to clearly emphasize the differences from period to period.

The line graph is also useful if you want to compare time-series data. Exhibit 2.63 on the next page shows a time-series graph of quarterly operating profits for the oil and gas sector and the manufacturing sector.

This graph permits several observations about trends over time in the two sectors. For example:

1. Over the period from 1988 to 2008, the quarterly operating profits of the manufacturing sector were generally higher than for the oil and gas sector. However, in the period from the first quarter of 1988 to the fourth quarter of 1991, the quarterly operating profits of the manufacturing sector dropped from $5.9 billion to $475 million, which was similar to the level of quarterly operating profits for the oil and gas sector.
2. The quarterly operating profits in manufacturing showed significant growth over the period from 1992 to 1995. The quarterly operating profits of the oil and gas sector showed only a slight upward trend during this period.
3. Both sectors showed significant increases in quarterly operating profits in 1999, followed by significant decreases from 2000 to 2001.
4. Since 2001, quarterly operating profits in both sectors have generally been increasing.

EXHIBIT 2.63

Line Graph of Quarterly Operating Profits for Manufacturing and Oil and Gas Sectors

To create a line graph in Excel, first highlight the associated data table on the worksheet. Include the numbers and any column headings. Do not include the labels for the *x*-axis (dates in this case). Then click on **Insert** and, in the **Chart** area, click on **Line** and then on the first **2-D Line** option.

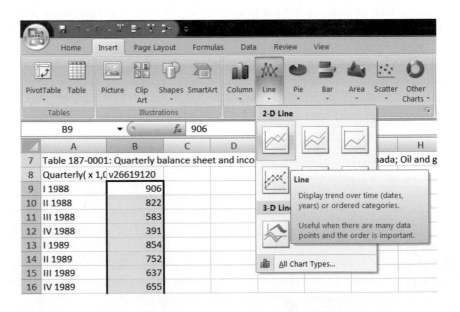

To add the data labels on the horizontal axis, highlight the chart, and under **Chart Tools**, click on **Design**. Then, in the **Data** area, click on **Select Data**. This will activate a window like the one shown opposite.

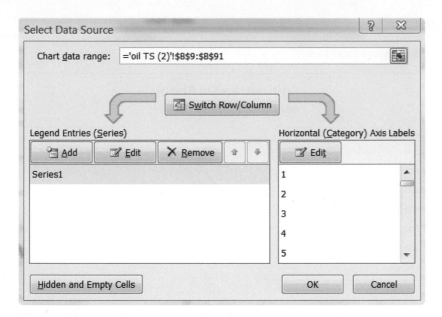

In the **Horizontal (Category) Axis Labels** window on the right-hand side, click on **Edit**, and then select the horizontal axis labels you want (the dates). Once the date labels are on the graph, you can right-click on the *x*-axis to modify them as you wish, with the **Format Axis** tools. For example, you might want to specify an interval between the labels, or change the alignment. You can also edit the data series itself with the **Select Data Source** dialogue box. If you choose **Edit** for the **Legend Entries (Series)** on the left side of the box, you will be able to type in (or select) a meaningful label for the data series.

Of course, the graph must have a meaningful title and *y*-axis label (generally the date labels are sufficient for the *x*-axis), and these elements can be accessed through the **Layout** tab of **Chart Tools**, as before (**Chart Tools** become available when you click on the graph). It is also often useful to have vertical gridlines on a time-series graph, and these can also be set up in the **Layout** tab of **Chart Tools**.

Under the **Design** tab of **Chart Tools** you will see a number of **Chart Styles** available. Choose one of the styles that shows in greyscale to ensure that your printed graph will be readable if you are printing in black and white. You can also right-click on the time-series lines and use the **Format Data Series...** options to adjust the look of the chart.

EXAMPLE 2.4

Graphing time-series data

The Collingtree Ski Shop has enjoyed a steadily growing business for about a decade. The company's owner believes that the increases in sales justify hiring another full-time sales associate. The company accountant wants to take a more cautious approach, hiring extra part-time sales staff as needed.

The owner is looking at annual sales data for the last 10 years. The accountant is looking at monthly sales data for the same period. Which data set should be the basis for analysis, and what hiring decision should be made?

 EXA02-4

Use Excel to create two time-series graphs—one for the monthly sales data, and one for the annual sales data. The Excel graphs are shown on the next page.

EXHIBIT 2.64

Collingtree Annual Sales Data

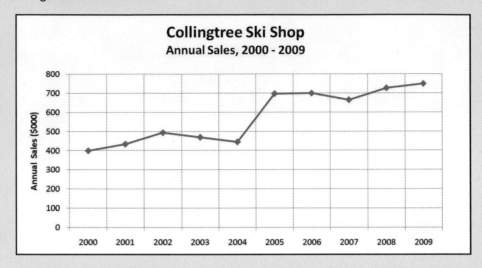

EXHIBIT 2.65

Collingtree Monthly Sales Data

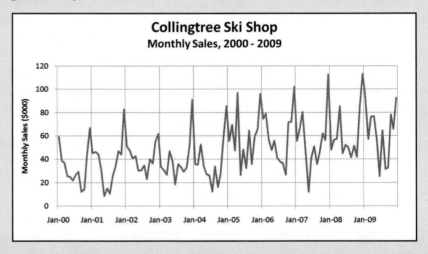

Note that it is difficult to see the increasing trend in sales in Exhibit 2.65, which shows the monthly sales. There is clearly a wide variation in sales, based on the season. It is easier to see the increasing trend in sales over the 10-year period in Exhibit 2.64, which shows annual sales.

Both graphs have their uses. For staffing purposes, the monthly sales data are more useful. While the monthly sales highs for each year have increased over the period, there are still many months with lower sales. This indicates that hiring another full-time sales associate may not be justified, because this staff member is likely not needed during the months with low sales. The accountant's recommendation to hire more part-time staff in the months with higher sales seems a more reasonable approach.

DEVELOP YOUR SKILLS 2.4

16. Suppose you are the sales manager at a car dealership. You want to examine data on past sales, with an eye to planning sales activities for the next year. Should you look at annual or monthly sales? Why?

17. Find some data on the Canada–U.S. exchange rate for the period from January 2000 to December 2008 (there are many reliable sources of such data available on the web, including the Bank of Canada website). Create a line graph, and comment on the pattern apparent in the graph.

18. Exhibit 2.66 below shows the Bank of Canada Bank Rate, on a monthly basis, from January 2007 to December 2008.
    a. Comment on what you observe in this graph.
    b. The other option for presenting these data would be a line graph. What is the advantage of using a bar graph in this case?

19. Many companies now provide information from their annual reports on their company websites. Find a company of your choice, and collect sales data for at least 10 periods. Create a graph of the data, and comment on what the graph tells you.

20. Statistics Canada collects data and computes a monthly index for computer prices. There is an index for computers sold to consumers, and one for business or government.

     A data set of this price index is available in MyStatLab. Create an appropriate graph for this data set, and comment on it. (*Source:* Adapted from Statistics Canada CANSIM in E-STAT, "Computer Prices Indexes, by Type of Purchaser, Monthly (index 2002=100), Jan 2002 to May 2008," CANSIM Table 331-0004, **http://estat.statcan.gc.ca**, accessed February 25, 2009.

EXHIBIT 2.66

Bank of Canada Bank Rate, Monthly, January 2007–December 2008

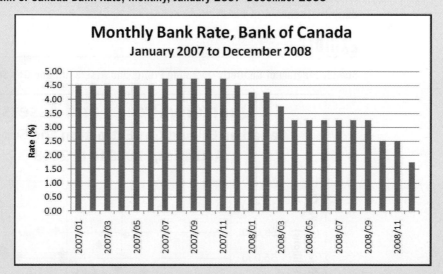

Source: Data from Rates and Statistics, Bank of Canada, **www.bankofcanada.ca/en/rates/interest-look.html** (accessed March 15, 2009). Used with permission.

2.5 SCATTER DIAGRAMS FOR PAIRED QUANTITATIVE DATA

When Lynda Parks examined the data from the drugstore survey on gender and staff friendliness ratings, she was investigating the relationship between these two *qualitative* variables. It is also possible to examine the relationship between two *quantitative* variables. Chapter 13 provides a more detailed discussion of the techniques involved, but it is possible to get a preliminary assessment of such a relationship by creating a graph called a scatter diagram. A **scatter diagram** displays paired *x-y* data points of the form (*x, y*).

For example, Mr. Big is interested in the relationship between total assets and quarterly operating profits for the oil and gas sector. With a large data set, it would be hard to tell anything about this relationship simply by looking at the numbers. It is much easier to see the relationship when the data are graphed in a scatter diagram.

It is customary to graph the explanatory variable on the *x*-axis, and the response variable on the *y*-axis, so before you create a scatter diagram, you must decide which is which. When the explanatory variable changes, it appears to (or is hypothesized to) cause a change in the response variable. The **explanatory variable** is observed (and sometimes controlled) by the researcher, and is the apparent cause of the change in the response variable. The **response variable** changes when the explanatory variable changes. Note that sometimes the explanatory variable is referred to as the "independent" variable, and the response variable is referred to as the "dependent" variable.

For the oil and gas sector data, it seems reasonable to expect that when total assets are higher, profits will be as well. Since we would expect assets to generate profits, the assets will be the explanatory variable, and the profits the response variable. The scatter diagram is shown in Exhibit 2.67 below.

Scatter diagram Displays paired *x-y* data points of the form (*x, y*).

Explanatory variable Variable observed (and sometimes controlled) by the researcher, which is the apparent cause of the change in the response variable.

Response variable Variable that changes when the explanatory variable changes.

EXHIBIT 2.67

Scatter Diagram of Quarterly Operating Profits and Assets, Oil and Gas Sector

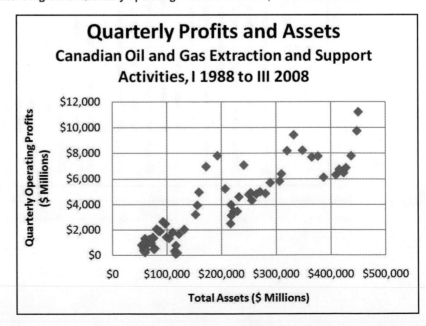

The scatter diagram shows us, more or less, the pattern we expected. When total assets are higher, quarterly operating profits are higher as well. The general shape of the pattern of data points is positive, indicating a positive relationship. In a **positive (direct) relationship**, increases in the explanatory variable correspond to increases in the response variable. In a **negative (inverse) relationship**, increases in the explanatory variable correspond to decreases in the response variable.

While there appears to be a positive relationship between total assets and quarterly profits, the profits are quite variable. It is likely that total assets is only one of the factors affecting profits.

You will learn more about investigating and modelling relationships in Chapters 13 and 14 of this text. One of the first steps in the more advanced techniques is creating a scatter diagram to picture the relationship, as we have done here.

The scatter diagram is created in Excel as follows:

1. Highlight the cells in the worksheet containing the *x*- and *y*-data. Note: Excel automatically interprets the left-most column as *x*-data. While this can be edited later, it is simplest to ensure that the *x*-data are in the left-most column.
2. Click on **Insert** and, in the **Charts** area, click on **Scatter**, and click on the first **Scatter** option.

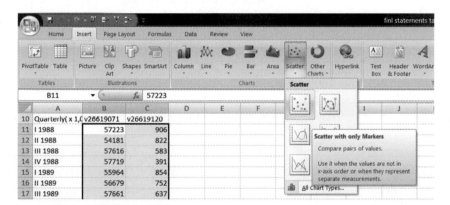

3. You will have to edit the chart that is produced to achieve the desired result. For example, delete the legend, and under **Chart Tools**, in the **Layout** area, use the **Chart Title** and **Axis Titles** buttons to enter an appropriate title and axis labels.

Positive (direct) relationship
Increases in the explanatory variable correspond to increases in the response variable.

Negative (inverse) relationship
Increases in the explanatory variable correspond to decreases in the response variable.

EXAMPLE 2.5

Graphing paired quantitative data

The marketing department at Smith & Klein Manufacturing is interested in the relationship between sales and promotional spending. Accountants have provided the annual figures in each category since 1980.

The first decision is which is the explanatory (*x*-axis) variable, and which is the response (*y*-axis) variable. In this case, spending is made on promotions with the goal of increasing sales, so amount of sales is the response variable.

Excel is used to create the scatter diagram shown in Exhibit 2.68 on the next page. It appears, from the scatter diagram, that there is a positive relationship between annual promotional spending and sales.

 EXA02-5

EXHIBIT 2.68

Scatter Diagram of Sales and Promotional Spending for Smith & Klein Manufacturing

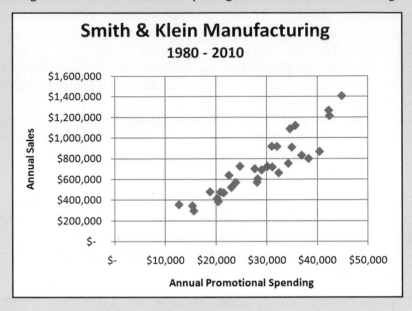

DEVELOP YOUR SKILLS 2.5

21. An economist wants to study the relationship between household income and monthly spending on restaurant meals. Data are collected from a random sample of households. Create an appropriate graph of the data, and comment.

DYS02-21

22. Jack runs a small convenience store, which sells freshly baked cookies (they are displayed near the cash register, to tempt buyers as they pay for their other purchases). Jack has been uncertain about how to price the cookies he sells (he vaguely remembers a concept called "price-elasticity of demand" from his class in economics at business school). Jack has experimented by charging a different price on a randomly selected number of days. The data he has collected are shown in Exhibit 2.69, opposite. Create an appropriate graph for these data, and comment on the relationship.

DYS02-22

23. Lynda Parks is wondering whether the size of a customer's most recent purchase at her drugstore is related to the customer's income. Create an appropriate graph for the data from the survey, and comment.

DYS02-23

24. A college professor is very concerned that her students' academic success is affected by the number of hours the students spend working at their jobs. She selects a random sample of 45 students and asks them to keep track of their total hours of paid employment for the semester (they all do, because she has promised them a bonus mark as a reward). The professor also records each student's average mark for the semester. Create an appropriate graph for the data, and comment.

DYS02-24

25. Which of the three scatter diagrams in Exhibit 2.70 opposite is the most likely representation of data on years of service and annual salary for a random selection of employees in an international organization? Why?

EXHIBIT 2.69

Sales Data for Jack's Cookies

Jack's Cookies	
Price ($)	Quantity Sold
1.00	50
0.90	51
0.80	58
0.75	59
0.70	58
0.65	55
0.60	63
0.55	60
0.50	65

EXHIBIT 2.70

Scatter Diagram Possibilities: Years of Service vs. Annual Salary

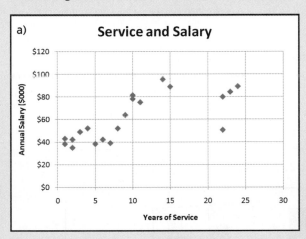

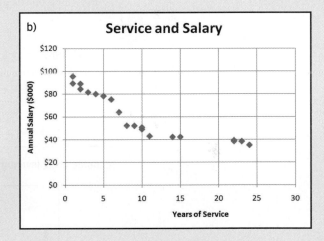

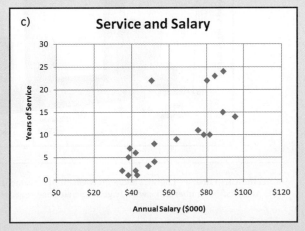

2.6 MISLEADING AND UNINTERESTING GRAPHS

Not all graphs are faithful and compelling visual representations of data sets. For various reasons, graphs can be either misleading or uninteresting, or both.

Misleading Graphs

Graphs and charts can provide useful summaries of data, but they can also mislead. As both a consumer and a producer of graphs, you should avoid misinterpreting others' graphs or misleading others with your own graphs. Some common problems with graphs are outlined below.

Non-Zero Origins

Good Graph Technique #1

By convention, the starting point (the origin) for the x- and y-axes of any graph is the point $(0, 0)$. Any departure from this convention must be clearly and visibly indicated on the graph.

Exhibit 2.71, below and on the next page, shows two graphs of the same data.

The graph in red and green was taken from a report produced by Industry Canada, on logistics and supply chain management. The report makes the point

EXHIBIT 2.71a

Manufacturing Inventory Turns, Non-Zero Origin

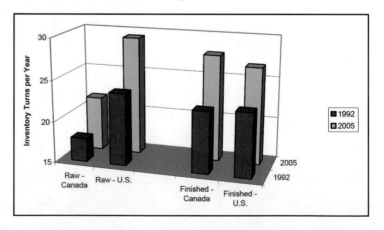

Source: Industry Canada, "Logistics and Supply Chain Management (SCM) Key Performance Indicators (KPI) Analysis," November 2006, **www.ic.gc.ca/eic/site/dsib-logi.nsf/eng/h_pj00220.html.**

that Canada lags behind the United States in inventory turns of raw materials. However, because the graph's vertical axis starts at 15, and not zero, the difference between the two is exaggerated. A more correct graph, with a zero origin, puts the difference between the raw materials inventory turnover in better context. See Exhibit 2.71b below.

With the corrected graph, it is easier to see the relative difference in manufacturing inventory turns for raw materials in Canada and the United States. In the first graph (Exhibit 2.71a), it appears that the inventory turns in raw materials in Canada are less than half those in the U.S. The second graph (Exhibit 2.71b) gives a clearer picture. The raw materials inventory turns are lower in Canada, both in 1992 and 2005, but they are only about 25% lower than the U.S. numbers in 1992, and about 26% lower in 2005.

There are cases when the (0, 0) origin cannot be reasonably used on a graph. For example, suppose you were investigating the scatter diagram shown in Exhibit 2.72 on the next page.

In this case, much of the area on the graph is unoccupied, and the data set is represented by a small cluster of points that cannot be seen very clearly. In a case like this, it is preferable to scale the axes of the graph (right-click on the axis in Excel, click on **Format Axis...**, and then click on **Axis options** and make the necessary adjustments).

EXHIBIT 2.71b

Manufacturing Inventory Turns, Zero Origin

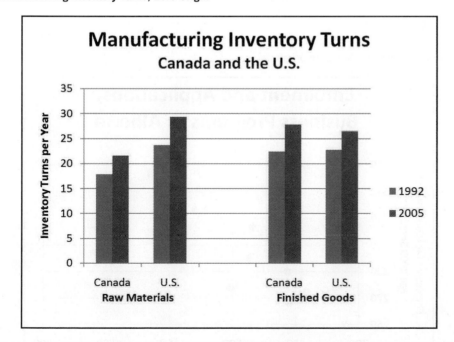

EXHIBIT 2.72

Scatter Diagram with (0, 0) Origin

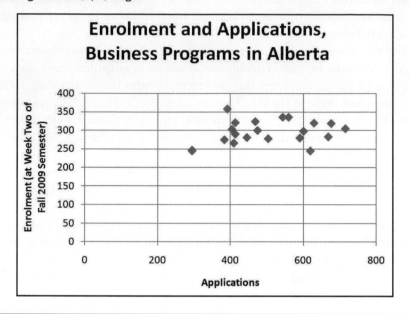

However, when you make an adjustment like this, it is crucial that you warn the reader that you have done so. Sometimes this is done by showing breaks in the axes or the plot area, as Exhibit 2.73 below illustrates.

EXHIBIT 2.73

Scatter Diagram with Non-Zero Origin

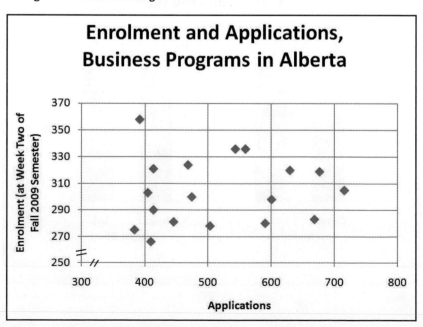

Distorted Images   The other difficulty with the graph shown in Exhibit 2.71a (page 80) is that it is distorted by the 3-D aspect. This makes it very hard to read the relative heights of the bars in the graph. Exhibit 2.71b (page 81) makes it much easier to do a direct comparison of the inventory turns for raw materials and finished goods, because it is set up in only two dimensions.

The wide availability of software such as Excel means that it is relatively easy to produce graphs to describe data. Unfortunately, if such software is not used judiciously, the graphs can be misleading or difficult to interpret. One of the most common errors is to add 3-D effects to a graph.

> **Good Graph Technique #2**
> It is *never* a good idea to add 3-D effects to a graph.

To see why, consider the pie charts shown below in Exhibit 2.74 below.

EXHIBIT 2.74

Pie Charts Based on Same Data, One with 3-D Effects

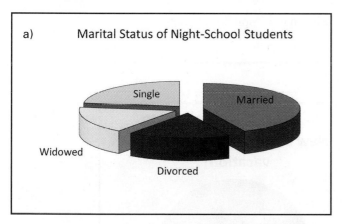
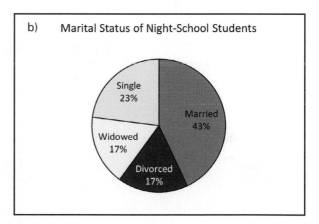

In Exhibit 2.74a, the pie chart is tilted and exploded, and has 3-D slices. Because of this, it is very difficult to judge the relative sizes of the slices of the pie. In Exhibit 2.74a, the "single" slice, at 23%, looks significantly larger than the "widowed" slice, at 17%, and it is not obvious that the "widowed" slice and the "divorced" slice are equal in size. It is far easier to judge the relative sizes of the slices in Exhibit 2.74b, where the graph is no longer tilted or exploded, and the 3-D aspect is removed. Exhibit 2.74a is not an acceptable graph, because it does not communicate clearly. Exhibit 2.74b is far better.

Sometimes graphs are cluttered with images. Often this is because the graphs themselves are not very interesting (see the section on "Uninteresting Graphs," which starts on page 88). Consider the graph shown in Exhibit 2.75a on the next page.

EXHIBIT 2.75a

Graph Cluttered with Images

An improved version is shown in Exhibit 2.75b, below.

EXHIBIT 2.75b

Improved, Uncluttered Graph

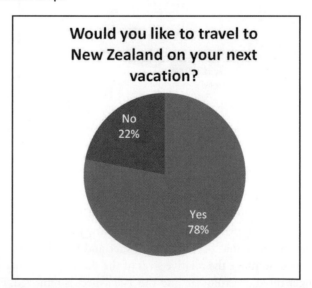

Exhibit 2.75b is easier to read, but it leaves a number of questions unanswered. Who was surveyed? When were the data collected? Even if we had answers to these questions, it is not clear that these data would be worth having. A more useful question might have been, "Are you actively considering travelling to New Zealand for your next vacation?" This might capture data about intentions (the original question is too vague, as it refers to wishes only).

The graph shown in Exhibit 2.75a does not really contain any useful data. The graph is superficially interesting only because of its vibrant colours and images. Beware of graphs that are cluttered with extraneous images. The clutter is often an indication that the creator of the graph cared less about communicating than about how fancy the graph looked.

> **Good Graph Technique #3**
> The primary goal of a graph is to summarize data in a way that communicates clearly.

Misleading or Missing Titles and Axis Labels   It is not unusual, particularly in the popular press, to see titles or captions on graphs that encourage the reader to draw conclusions about the data. This can be misleading. For example, an article in *The Globe and Mail* called "The Christmas that didn't register with retailers," published on February 24, 2009, it was suggested that Canada's retail sales had fallen "precipitously" since 2007. However, with the data available at that time (some of the data were preliminary), the graph shown in Exhibit 2.76 could have been created.

EXHIBIT **2.76**

Canadian Retail Sales, December 2007 and 2008

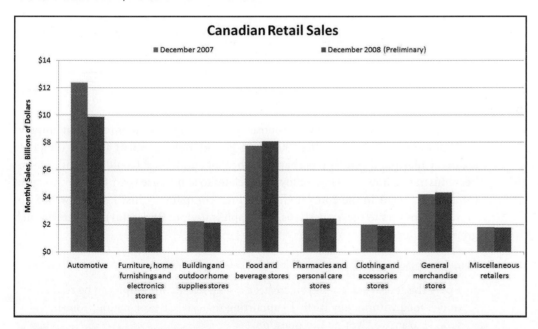

Source: Statistics Canada, "Retail Sales, by Industry (monthly)," CANSIM Tables 080-0014 and 080-0017, **www40.statcan.gc.ca/l01/ cst01/trad42a-eng.htm,** accessed February 25, 2009.

While the data (and the graph) certainly indicate some significant drops in retail sales in December 2008 compared with December 2007, it is also clear that the drop in sales in the automotive category is the most significant. Note that there were increases in retail sales for food and beverage stores and general merchandise stores, the two largest categories of retail sales after automotive. As well, changes in retail sales in the other categories are not relatively large. Whenever you are reading articles in the popular press, try to examine the data yourself, as the real story may be somewhat different from the reported story.

> **Good Graph Technique #4**
> Beware of titles on graphs that ask you to draw conclusions. Avoid using such titles. Titles and labels should objectively describe the associated data.

Another misleading feature of some graphs is missing or vague labels on the axes. See, for example, Exhibit 2.77 below.

EXHIBIT 2.77

Graph with Missing Labels on the Axes

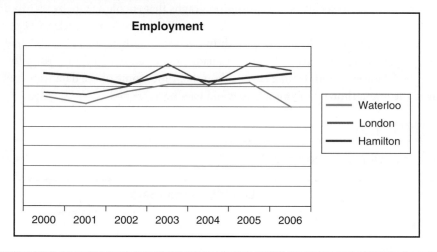

We can see that this graph is supposed to be telling us something about employment at three locations, over the 2000–2006 period. But it is not at all clear what data are being illustrated here. Is it perhaps numbers of employees? Could it be index numbers illustrating how current employment relates to some base year? Is it percentage of total employment in the company? And which company is this? Because we do not know the answers to these questions, the graph is useless. Be careful not to create such graphs.

> **Good Graph Technique #5**
> Apply this test to any graph you create: ask yourself if your graph can be read and understood without any further supporting material or explanation. You should be able to answer "yes" to this question.

Missing Data   Sometimes graphs are misleading because important data points are missing. Consider, for example, the time-series graph shown in Exhibit 2.78a opposite. The graph shows the quarterly operating profits in the Canadian oil and gas sector for the period from the fourth quarter of 2006 to the third quarter of 2008. Over this time period, the operating profits (especially in 2008) are on an upward trend. This graph gives no hint of the volatility in quarterly operating profits in the sector, as a more complete graph shows (see Exhibit 2.78b).

EXHIBIT 2.78a

Recent Quarterly Operating Profits for the Oil and Gas Sector

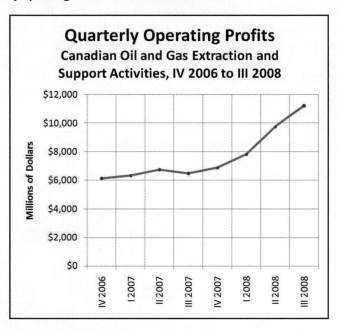

EXHIBIT 2.78b

More Complete Time Series of Operating Profits for the Oil and Gas Sector

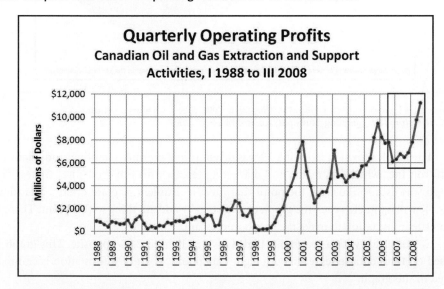

Good Graph Technique #6

Always check data sources to make sure that important data have not been omitted from a graph.

Uninteresting Graphs

As mentioned above, sometimes graphs are inherently uninteresting, and this can lead to a temptation to use colours, images, or 3-D aspects to try to make them look more interesting. However, trying to add interest to a graph with visual gimmicks will not work if the underlying data are not interesting. Consider the pie chart below in Exhibit 2.79.

EXHIBIT 2.79

Uninteresting Pie Chart

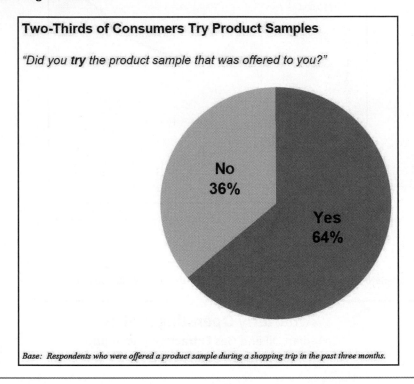

Two-Thirds of Consumers Try Product Samples

*"Did you **try** the product sample that was offered to you?"*

No 36%

Yes 64%

Base: Respondents who were offered a product sample during a shopping trip in the past three months.

Source: Olga Jourova, *Arbitron Product Sampling Study,* 2008, page 3. **www.arbitron.com/ downloads/product_sampling_study.pdf**, accessed March 27, 2009.

The graph shown in Exhibit 2.79 was taken from a product sampling study done by Arbitron Inc., which is a media and marketing research firm in the United States. The graph was used to illustrate the point that most consumers who are offered a product sample will try it. However, the graph does not really add anything to this point. There is too little information to make the graph interesting.

Contrast this with a graph like that shown in Exhibit 2.80 opposite. This graph is based on three data series, each with eight data points. A lot of information is summarized in this graph.

The graph provides the basis for a number of observations.

1. In 2006, more than 60% of the employed labour force drove to work by car, truck, or van in Canada's three largest cities. Employed workers in Vancouver were the most likely to drive to work, while employed workers in Toronto were least likely to drive to work.

EXHIBIT **2.80**

Modes of Transportation to Work for Employed Labour Force

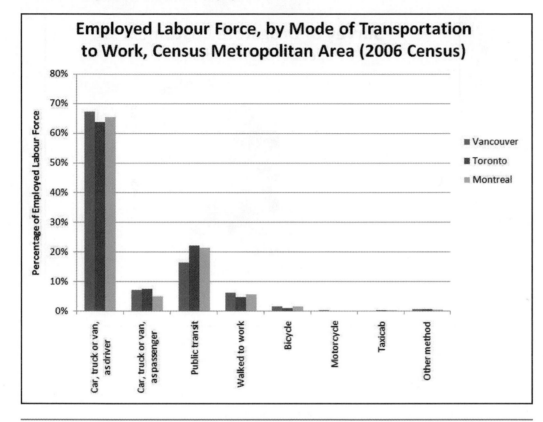

Sources: Statistics Canada, "Employed Labour Force by Mode of Transportation to Work, by Census Metropolitan Area (2006 Census)", Saguenay, Québec, Sherbrooke, Trois-Rivières, Montréal, Ottawa-Gatineau, Kingston, Peterborough, Oshawa, Toronto, Kelowna, Abbotsford, Vancouver, Victoria, **www40. statcan.gc.ca/l01/cst01/ labor42k-eng.htm;** all accessed March 26, 2009.

2. In 2006, the second most likely method for workers to travel to work in the three largest cities was public transit. In Toronto and Montreal, over 20% of the employed labour force used public transit to commute to work. Only 16% of Vancouver's employed labour force used public transit to commute to work.

3. In 2006, the percentages of the employed labour force who commuted to work as passengers were similar to the percentages who walked to work. In Montreal (in contrast to Toronto and Vancouver), a greater percentage of workers walked to work than commuted as passengers in a car, truck, or van.

DEVELOP YOUR SKILLS **2.6**

26. Exhibit 2.81 on the next page shows a graph of the speed-of-service ratings for the survey of drugstore customers. Comment on how you would improve the graph (if at all).

27. Pictographs are sometimes misleading. Visit a Statistics Canada website about pictographs: **www.statcan.gc.ca/** **edu/power-pouvoir/ch9/picto-figuratifs/5214825-eng .htm**. What is the problem with the pictograph for the purchasing power of the Canadian dollar?

28. Is Exhibit 2.82 on the next page an example of a good graph? Why or why not?

EXHIBIT 2.81

Survey of Drugstore Customers' Speed of Service Ratings

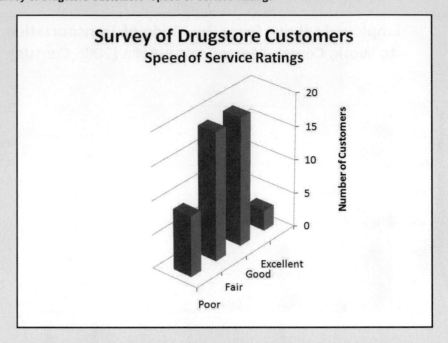

EXHIBIT 2.82

Scatter Graph of Sales Contacts and Sales, Hendrick Software

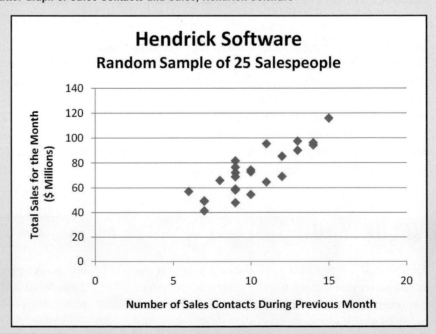

29. Is the graph shown in Exhibit 2.83 an interesting one? Explain why or why not.

30. Exhibit 2.84 below is one method of displaying the data on ice cream flavour preferences, first described in Develop Your Skills 2.3, Exercise 15 on page 70. Comment on this graph as a way of displaying the data.

EXHIBIT **2.83**

Histogram

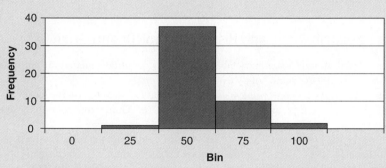

EXHIBIT **2.84**

Graph of Ice Cream Flavour Preferences

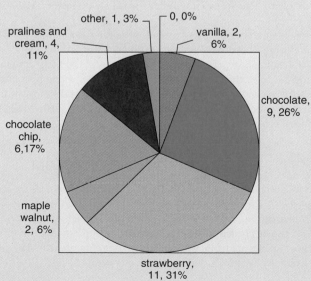

Chapter Summary

Types of Data

The methods used to analyze data and make decisions differ according to the type of data involved. Quantitative data contain numerical information, for which arithmetical operations such as averaging are meaningful. Qualitative data contain descriptive information, which may be recorded in words or numbers.

A continuous variable can take on *any* possible value on a number line (possibly within upper and lower limits). A discrete variable can take on only certain identifiable values on a number line (possibly within upper and lower limits). Ranked data are qualitative data that can be ordered according to size or quality.

Cross-sectional data are all collected in the same time period. Time-series data are collected over successive points in time.

Frequency Distributions and Histograms for Quantitative Data

A frequency distribution is a summary table that divides quantitative data into ranges (classes), and records the count (frequency) of data points in each range.

The number of classes appropriate for a particular data set depends on the number of observations, and the variability in the observations. See the Guide to Technique: Setting Up Appropriate Classes for a Frequency Distribution, page 38.

Excel can be used to count the frequencies for each class, using the **Data Analysis** tool called **Histogram** (see page 39). Classes are controlled using Excel's bin numbers, which are the upper limits of each class. Bin numbers must be typed into an Excel worksheet when the **Histogram** tool is used.

A histogram is a graph of a frequency distribution, with lower class limits shown along the *x*-axis, and frequencies shown along the *y*-axis. Histograms can also be created with Excel's **Histogram** tool (see page 45). Unfortunately, Excel's histograms require several adjustments. See the instructions for adjusting Excel's histograms on page 46 for details.

A distribution is symmetric if the right half of the distribution is a mirror image of the left half. A distribution is skewed to the right (or positively skewed) when there are some unusually large values in the data set that destroy the symmetry. A distribution is skewed to the left (or negatively skewed) when there are some unusually small values in the data set that destroy the symmetry.

Sometimes histograms illustrate the existence of outliers. An outlier is a data point that is unusually far from the rest of the data. Outliers are usually investigated carefully.

When you are creating histograms for comparison, you should take care to set them up so that comparison is easy. See the Guide to Technique for comparing histograms on page 60. Sometimes it is useful to create relative frequency distributions and histograms, particularly for comparison when the data sets have quite different frequencies. The relative frequency of a class is the percentage of total observations falling into that class.

Tables, Bar Graphs, and Pie Charts for Qualitative Data

Excel can be used to create bar graphs and pie charts for simple tables (see the Excel instructions on page 63 and page 64). Bar graphs emphasize the relative sizes of the categories in qualitative data. Pie charts emphasize the share of the total represented by each category.

Bar graphs can also be created to illustrate the relationship between two or more qualitative variables. Contingency tables are tables with more than one column, with data cross-classified by row and column headings. See the Excel instructions on page 67.

Time-Series Graphs

Time-series graphs are usually line graphs, with observations plotted against time on the *x*-axis. See the Excel instructions on page 72.

Graphs of Paired Quantitative Data

A scatter diagram displays paired x–y data points of the form (x, y). The response variable is plotted on the y-axis, and the explanatory variable on the x-axis. The explanatory variable is observed (and sometimes controlled) by the researcher.

In a positive (direct) relationship, increases in the explanatory variable correspond to increases in the response variable. In a negative (inverse) relationship, increases in the explanatory variable correspond to decreases in the response variable.

A scatter diagram is created in Excel using the XY (Scatter) type of chart. See the Excel instructions on page 77.

Misleading and Uninteresting Graphs

Graphs and charts can provide useful summaries of data, but they can also mislead. The primary goal of a graph is to summarize data, in a way that communicates clearly.

By convention, the starting point (the origin) for the x- and y-axes of any graph is $(0, 0)$. Any departure from this convention must be clearly and visibly indicated on the graph. Always check data sources to make sure that important data have not been omitted from a graph.

Beware of titles on graphs that ask you to draw conclusions. Avoid using such titles. Titles and labels should objectively describe the associated data.

Apply this test to any graph you create: ask yourself if the graph can be read and understood without any further supporting material or explanation. You should be able to answer "yes" to this question.

Graphs are interesting only if the underlying data are interesting. Trying to add interest with visual gimmicks will not improve a graph that is based on uninteresting data. It is never a good idea to add 3-D effects to a graph.

Go to MyStatLab at **www.mathxl.com**. You can practise the exercises indicated with red in the Develop Your Skills and Chapter Review Exercises as often as you want, and guided solutions will help you find answers step by step. You'll find a personalized study plan available to you too!

CHAPTER REVIEW EXERCISES

WARM-UP EXERCISES

1. What type of data are these? Which of these apply: quantitative (discrete or continuous?), qualitative (ranked or unranked?), cross-sectional, or time-series?
   a. A random sample of adult Moncton residents is surveyed, and data recorded about whether they are male or female, and whether they have fitness club memberships.
   b. The type of payment method used was recorded for a random sample of 100 customers from four different store locations.
   c. The number of pedestrians passing two prospective store locations in a given week was recorded.
   d. A restaurant owner who is trying to decide which of two chefs to promote asks a sample of diners to rate the food made by each of the chefs, on a scale of 1 to 4, where 1 corresponds to "barely edible" and 4 corresponds to "absolutely delicious."
   e. A company collects data for the past 10 years on sales and advertising.

2. What type of graph would be appropriate to display each of the data sets described in Exercise 1?

3. *USA Today* is an American newspaper that has an accompanying website. One of the features of the website is something called "Snapshots." These are graphical displays of data on a wide

range of topics. Go to the Snapshots section of the site, at **www.usatoday.com/news/ snapshot.htm**. View the graphical displays. What is the purpose of these graphs?

4. Pam Liddell collects data on the ages of a random sample of the people attending a local fall fair. The data are shown below in Exhibit 2.85. Use a stem-and-leaf display to organize the data. Describe the shape of the distribution.

EXHIBIT 2.85

Ages of a Random Sample of Attendees, Local Fall Fair

Ages of a Random Sample of Attendees, Local Fall Fair				
58	12	8	20	13
19	43	40	64	32
9	22	8	20	30
50	21	31	12	9

5. A human resources consultant produced the following graph, after selecting a random sample of employees and recording their salaries and months of experience with the company. Comment on the graph, shown below in Exhibit 2.86.

EXHIBIT 2.86

Employees' Salaries and Months of Experience

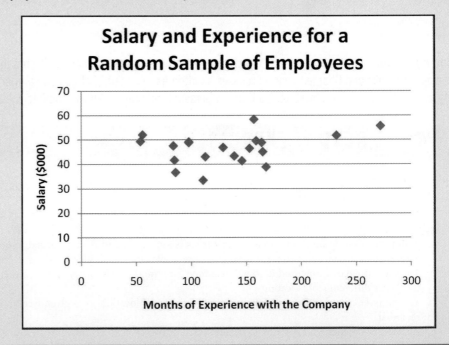

THINK AND DECIDE

(Note: The data sets are provided for these questions so you can sketch the appropriate graphs by hand. However, any graph that you use for presentation should be made with Excel.)

6. The owner of a music store is wondering if he should target female customers in particular, because he believes they tend to spend more than male customers. However, he wants to check

this belief. He asks the cashiers to keep track of the spending by a random sample of female customers and a random sample of male customers, over several days. The purchases are shown in Exhibit 2.87 below.

EXHIBIT 2.87

Music Store Purchases by a Random Sample of Customers

Music Store Purchases by a Random Sample of Customers	
Purchases by Females	**Purchases by Males**
$29.50	$32.49
$17.83	$29.88
$40.66	$32.77
$45.15	$25.95
$43.98	$22.26
$41.56	$28.66
$21.25	$26.77
$33.49	$35.32
$50.43	$19.29
$19.70	$40.25
$23.65	$28.09
$30.64	$31.51
$19.30	$25.96
$21.34	$25.34
$24.40	

Create appropriate graphical displays to summarize and compare these data. Comment.

7. A bank with a management training program has asked for 360° feedback for one of its trainees (that is, feedback from managers and peers). The ratings range from 1 to 6, where 1 corresponds to the worst performance, and 6 to the best. The results for one of the trainees are shown below in Exhibit 2.88. Create an appropriate graphical display and comment.

EXHIBIT 2.88

Results of a Trainee's 360° Feedback

Trainee Ratings
4
4
2
2
3
5
2
3
5
6
4
4
1
5
2

8. A random sample of employees is asked to rate the performance of a president. This president is fired and a new president is hired. After six months, another random sample of employees is asked to rate the performance of the new president. A rating of 1 corresponds to the worst performance, and 10 to the best possible performance. The ratings are shown below in Exhibit 2.89.

EXHIBIT 2.89

Employees' Ratings of Presidents' Performance

Rating of the Old President's Performance	Rating of the New President's Performance
10	9
7	6
2	2
8	1
8	2
6	4
4	5
6	7
8	8
9	7

Create an appropriate graphical display for these data. Comment on similarities or differences in the ratings of the two presidents.

9. A random sample of students was selected in Ontario and another in BC. The students were asked to rate a particular Canadian university, with a "1" if they considered it excellent, down to "4" if they considered it poor. The ratings of the students are shown below in Exhibit 2.90.

EXHIBIT 2.90

University Ratings

Ontario Student Rating	BC Student Rating
2	1
3	4
4	4
1	2
4	1
2	1
1	1
2	1
2	1
3	2
2	2
4	2
2	2
4	3
4	2
4	1
3	3
4	2
2	3
2	3

Create an appropriate graphical display and compare the ratings of this university by the Ontario students and the BC students.

10. The type of payment method used was recorded for a random sample of 100 customers from four different store locations. The data are shown below in Exhibit 2.91.

EXHIBIT 2.91

Customer Payment Method

Customer Payment Method					
	Store A	Store B	Store C	Store D	Total
Cash/Debit Card	40	65	20	25	150
Credit Card	30	80	30	40	180
Cheque	30	55	50	35	170
Total	100	200	100	100	500

Create an appropriate graphical display to summarize the data, and comment.

11. The marketing department of a college wanted to know if it there was a difference in the proportions of students drawn from inside or outside the college catchment area by program. A random sample of students from Business, Technology, and Hospitality and Tourism programs revealed the results shown in Exhibit 2.92.

EXHIBIT 2.92

Origin of Students in College Programs

Origin of Students in College Programs			
	Business	Technology	Hospitality and Tourism
From Local Area	65	45	68
Not from Local Area	85	55	72

Create an appropriate graphical display for these data. Does it appear there is a relationship between the program and whether or not students come from the local catchment area?

12. A new analyst at a soft drinks company was preparing a graph to illustrate the company's net operating revenues over the last five years. He decides the graph is boring so he adjusts it. The resulting graph is shown in Exhibit 2.93 on the next page. Comment on this graph.

THINK AND DECIDE USING EXCEL

13. For the data set of student marks from Ms. Nice's class and Mr. Mean's class (first discussed in the Develop Your Skills 2.2, Exercise 10), create appropriate graphs for comparison. Comment on the differences and similarities you see in the two data sets.

 CRE02-13

14. A survey of pedestrian traffic is conducted over 45 days for two areas where a manager is thinking of opening a new location. Create appropriate frequency distributions and histograms for these data sets, and comment on similarities and differences in the data.

 CRE02-14

15. Downtown Automotive in Nelson, BC, selects a random sample of daily sales. Create an appropriate graphical display for these data, and comment.

CRE02-15

EXHIBIT 2.93

Graph of Soft Drink Company's Net Operating Revenues

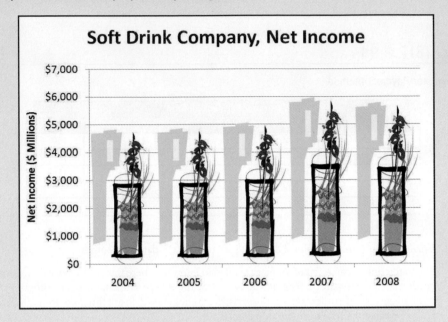

CRE02-16

16. Statistics Canada tracks prices on a number of products. Data about average retail prices of regular unleaded gasoline at self-service filling stations in Montreal are available in MyStatLab. Create an appropriate graph for the last 10 years of data available, and comment. (*Source:* Statistics Canada, "Average Retail Prices for Gasoline and Fuel Oil, by Urban Centre, Monthly (cents per litre)," CANSIM Table 326-0009, **http://cansim2.statcan.gc.ca/**.

CRE02-17

17. A Statistics teacher is wondering if there is a relationship between the marks of students in their first-year Business Math course, and their marks in the second-year Statistics course. She collects data from a random sample of students, and begins her analysis by creating an appropriate graph. Which is the explanatory variable? Which is the response variable? Would it be correct to say a high mark in Business Math *caused* a high mark in Statistics?

CRE02-18

18. Woodbon, a company that produces a limited line of high-quality wooden furniture, has enjoyed remarkable sales growth since its inception in 1980. Woodbon's owner Kate Cameron is looking back over the company's years of operation, and is trying to plan for the future. Kate collects the annual advertising and sales figures for the last several years. Create an appropriate graph to summarize the relationship between advertising and sales for Woodbon.

CRE02-19

19. Recall the drugstore survey mentioned at the beginning of the chapter. Sort the data on incomes into two groups, male and female customers. Use appropriate graphs to compare the incomes, and comment.

CRE02-20

20. Create an appropriate graph to compare speed of service ratings for male and female customers in the drugstore survey data. Does it appear that males and females rate speed of service differently?

CRE02-21

21. A major airport has been redesigned, with the goal of reducing flight delays. The delays (in minutes) for random samples of flights before and after the upgrade are available in

MyStatLab. Create appropriate graphs to summarize and compare the data sets, and comment.

22. Students in Business Studies, Computer Studies, and Engineering Technology Studies were asked to rate their college experience as excellent, good, fair, or poor. Create two graphs to compare the ratings, by program. In the first graph, use the frequencies in the table. In the second graph, use relative frequencies. Comment on how the use of frequencies distorts the analysis for this data set.

CRE02-22

23. Revisit the data on quarterly profits for the oil and gas sector. Create three histograms, one with a class width of $1 billion, one with a class width of $1.5 billion, and one with a class width of $2 billion. Compare the three histograms, and comment on which one does the best job of summarizing the data.

SEC02-2

TEST YOUR KNOWLEDGE

24. Textbooks are written at least a year in advance of their publication date. The data for operating profits in the Canadian oil and gas sector and the manufacturing sector that are referred to in this chapter were the most recent available in February 2009. If you have this textbook in your hands (or you are reading it in MyStatLab), more recent data will have become available. Go to the Statistics Canada website, access the most recent data available for the quarterly operating profits of the two sectors, and create revised histograms and time-series graphs. Be careful to note any revisions to earlier data when you do this. Write commentaries to compare the amounts of the quarterly operating profits, and the patterns over time.

CHAPTER **3**

Using Numbers to Describe Data

LEARNING OBJECTIVES

After mastering the material in this chapter, you will be able to:

1 Use conventions about the order of operations and summation notation to correctly evaluate common statistical formulas.

2 Choose and calculate the appropriate measure of central tendency for a data set.

3 Choose and calculate the appropriate measure of variability for a data set.

4 Choose, calculate, and interpret the appropriate measure of association for a paired data set.

INTRODUCTION

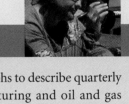

Anne Morgan has created some interesting graphs to describe quarterly operating profits for the Canadian manufacturing and oil and gas sectors (see Chapter 2 for details). Anne has noticed that profits are different for the two sectors, both in amount and variability. Anne now wants to prepare some numerical summary measures to describe the data.

Anne has also used a graph to illustrate the relationship between assets and profits in the oil and gas sector. She now wants to measure how strongly the two variables are related.

In this chapter, you will be introduced to some of the numerical measures Anne could use to describe the data sets of interest to her. In particular, you will be introduced to measures of central tendency (Section 3.2), measures of variability (Section 3.3), and measures of association (Section 3.4).

Construction of these measures involves some arithmetic, which will be summarized by standard mathematical notation. This notation is described in Section 3.1, so if you are already familiar with it, you should proceed directly to Section 3.2.

3.1   SOME USEFUL NOTATION

Statistics involves some arithmetic, much of it repetitive. While computers permit fast and easy calculation, you will probably have to do some of the arithmetic by hand (with the use of a calculator) as you learn new techniques or write tests for your Statistics course.

Doing the arithmetic by hand may help you develop an intuitive understanding of what the calculations mean, so it is important that you master the manual techniques. A basic calculator with at least one memory will come in handy (be sure you learn how to use your calculator's memory, because without it, the arithmetic can be *very* time-consuming).

Mathematical notation will also come in handy. Sometimes the arithmetic you must do will have a number of steps, and mathematical notation can help you remember the steps, *but only if you know how to read it!*

Fortunately, the notation is not that difficult to read. In this section, you will be introduced to some standard mathematical notation, and you will be shown how to read it and use it. The examples used are bits and pieces of formulas you will encounter as you go through this text, so you will be able to use this section as a reference when you encounter a formula in some other part of the book.

Order of Operations

There are some conventions in mathematics that help keep things organized, just as the convention of driving on the right-hand side of the road in Canada helps keep vehicle traffic from becoming dangerous and chaotic. One set of conventions is that some mathematical operations are always done first, before others, when an algebraic expression is being evaluated.

> **The Order of Operations**
> 1. First evaluate anything in *brackets*.
> 2. Then evaluate anything with an *exponent*.
> 3. Working from left to right, do any *division or multiplication*.
> 4. Working from left to right, do any *addition or subtraction*.

It is important to remember that the conventions about the order of operations always apply, and if you have trouble remembering what a mathematical formula means, it may help you to go back to these conventions.

Summation Notation

Suppose we have a data set for the variable called x (this is an example of a mathematical convention—x is a commonly assigned variable name, although we could have used any other letter, such as y or z). Suppose x is the name we give to the variable that is the ages of the five students sitting in the front row of Statistics class. If we collect the data from the five students, then the data set consists of

$$(17, 21, 20, 18, 20)$$

By convention, we refer to the first number in the data set (17) as x_1, that is, "x-one." This value is called x_1 simply because it is the *first* number in the list. Similarly, we would call the *fourth* number (which is 18) x_4, and so on.

Suppose we wanted to write an expression to indicate that all of the numbers in the data set should be added up, and we know that there will be five students in the front row of class, but we have not yet collected the data. We could write

$$x_1 + x_2 + x_3 + x_4 + x_5$$

as an indication of our plans. However, this is tedious to write out and, of course, writing it out could be time-consuming if there were many values.

Adding up all the numbers in a data set is one of the arithmetic tasks you will have to do repeatedly in Statistics. The commonly accepted notation for this task is Σ, which is a capital Greek letter called *sigma*. Greek letters are commonly used in statistics notation, and you will learn several more as you work through the material in this text.

The expression $\sum_{i=1}^{5} = x_i$ is mathematical notation that means "add up the first five values in your data set called *x*." This notation uses the subscript i as an index number. You can expand the notation by writing out the expression nestled beside the sigma operator, moving the index number from its lower limit (1 in this example) one by one to its upper limit (5 in this example), and then adding all the values.

$$\sum_{i=1}^{5} x_i$$

Write out the expression with each successive index number

$$x_1 \quad x_2 \quad x_3 \quad x_4 \quad x_5$$

and then add the terms (this is what the Σ operator is telling you to do):

$$x_1 + x_2 + x_3 + x_4 + x_5$$

So we see that

$$\sum_{i=1}^{5} x_i = x_1 + x_2 + x_3 + x_4 + x_5$$

But what if we do not know how many observations there are in the data set? There is a convention for this too. When we do not know, we refer to the total number of observations as n. If we wanted to indicate that all of the (unknown number of) observations in the data set should be added up, we would simply write

$$\sum_{i=1}^{n} x_i$$

This expression is used so often that there is an even shorter version, which is

$$\sum x$$

By convention, whenever the sigma sign does not have upper and lower limits, it means "add them all up." This more streamlined notation is the kind that will be used throughout this text.

Some Examples

Suppose we have two data sets. One is a set of observations for a variable x, as follows:

$$(1, 3, 5, 7)$$

Another is a set of observations for a variable y, as follows:

$$(2, 4, 6, 8)$$

EXAMPLE 3.1A

Evaluating Σx

What is Σx?

$$\Sigma x = x_1 + x_2 + x_3 + x_4 = 1 + 3 + 5 + 7 = 16$$

EXAMPLE 3.1B

Evaluating Σx^2

How would you evaluate the following expression? Σx^2

In this case, the x-values must be squared. Since exponents must be evaluated before addition (based on the order of operations), this means that each x-value is first squared, and then the resulting terms are added.

$$\Sigma x^2 = x_1^2 + x_2^2 + x_3^2 + x_4^2 = 1^2 + 3^2 + 5^2 + 7^2 = 1 + 9 + 25 + 49 = 84$$

EXAMPLE 3.1C

Evaluating $(\Sigma x)^2$

How would you evaluate the following expression? $(\Sigma x)^2$

In this case, the expression in the brackets must be evaluated *before* any squaring is done (based on the order of operations). Therefore, all of the x-values must first be added up, and then the resulting sum should be squared, as follows:

$$(\Sigma x)^2 = (x_1 + x_2 + x_3 + x_4)^2 = (1 + 3 + 5 + 7)^2 = 16^2 = 256$$

Notice that the result in Example 3.1C is quite different from the result in Example 3.1B. Be sure you understand and remember the difference between these two expressions.

EXAMPLE 3.1D

Evaluating Σxy

How would you evaluate the following expression? Σxy

If you know that both x and y are variables, this expression would be evaluated as follows:

$$\Sigma xy = x_1 y_1 + x_2 y_2 + x_3 y_3 + x_4 y_4 = 1(2) + 3(4) + 5(6) + 7(8)$$
$$= 2 + 12 + 30 + 56 = 100$$

Multiplication comes before addition in the conventions for order of operations. The first x-variable will be multiplied by the first y-variable, the second x-variable will be multiplied by the second y-variable, and so on, and the resulting terms will be added.

EXAMPLE 3.1E

Evaluating $\sum(x-6)$

How would you evaluate this expression? $\sum(x-6)$

What is in the brackets must be evaluated first for each value of x, and the resulting terms then added.

$$
\begin{aligned}
\sum(x-6) &= (x_1-6) + (x_2-6) + (x_3-6) + (x_4-6) \\
&= (1-6) + (3-6) + (5-6) + (7-6) \\
&= (-5) + (-3) + (-1) + 1 \\
&= -8
\end{aligned}
$$

EXAMPLE 3.1F

Evaluating $\sum(x-6)^2$

How would you evaluate this expression? $\sum(x-6)^2$

In this case, each of the terms in the brackets must be evaluated first, and then these results must be squared, and the resulting squares must be added up.

$$
\begin{aligned}
\sum(x-6)^2 &= (x_1-6)^2 + (x_2-6)^2 + (x_3-6)^2 + (x_4-6)^2 \\
&= (1-6)^2 + (3-6)^2 + (5-6)^2 + (7-6)^2 \\
&= (-5)^2 + (-3)^2 + (-1)^2 + 1^2 \\
&= 25 + 9 + 1 + 1 \\
&= 36
\end{aligned}
$$

EXAMPLE 3.1G

Evaluating $\sum \dfrac{(x-6)^2}{n-1}$

How would you evaluate this expression? $\sum \dfrac{(x-6)^2}{n-1}$

In this case, we can use the result from Example 3.1F to get the answer. Remember that n does not vary; it is a number. Although the number will be unknown until we determine how many observations there are in the data set, it is still just a number (not a variable). Therefore, the $\sum$ operator has no effect on it, and this expression can be rewritten and evaluated for the data set as follows:

$$
\sum \frac{(x-6)^2}{n-1} = \frac{1}{n-1} \sum(x-6)^2 = \frac{1}{4-1}(36) = \frac{1}{3}(36) = 12
$$

EXAMPLE 3.1H

Evaluating $\sum(x-6)(y-3)$

How would you evaluate this expression? $\sum(x-6)(y-3)$

First the terms in the brackets must be evaluated for all of the first, second, third, . . . sets of observations in the two data sets. The resulting pairs must be multiplied, and then all of those products must be added.

$$\sum (x - 6)(y - 3)$$

$$= (x_1 - 6)(y_1 - 3) + (x_2 - 6)(y_2 - 3) + (x_3 - 6)(y_3 - 3) + (x_4 - 6)(y_4 - 3)$$

$$= (1 - 6)(2 - 3) + (3 - 6)(4 - 3) + (5 - 6)(6 - 3) + (7 - 6)(8 - 3)$$

$$= (-5)(-1) + (-3)(1) + (-1)(3) + (1)(5)$$

$$= 5 + (-3) + (-3) + 5$$

$$= 4$$

DEVELOP YOUR SKILLS 3.1

1. Using the y data set $(2, 4, 6, 8)$, evaluate $\sum y$.
2. Using the y data set $(2, 4, 6, 8)$, evaluate $\sum y^2$. Also evaluate $(\sum y)^2$. Why are the answers different?
3. Using the y data set $(2, 4, 6, 8)$, calculate $\dfrac{\sum y}{n}$. Calculate $\dfrac{\sum x}{n}$ for the x data set $(1, 3, 5, 7)$.
4. Calculate $\sum(y - 4)$. Calculate $\sum(x - 5)$.

5. Consider the data set 34, 67, 2, 31, 89, 35. For this data set, calculate:
   a. $\sum x$
   b. $\sum x^2$
   c. $\dfrac{\sum x}{n}$
   d. $\sqrt{\dfrac{\sum x^2 - \dfrac{(\sum x)^2}{n}}{n - 1}}$

3.2   MEASURES OF CENTRAL TENDENCY

As we have already seen in Chapter 2, the quarterly operating profits of the Canadian manufacturing and oil and gas sectors are different. One of the ways to capture this difference is with a measure of central tendency. Some measure of central tendency is generally of interest when we examine a data set, and the *mean* is often used to represent a typical— or middle—value of a group of numbers. Another useful measure of central tendency is the *median*. A third, sometimes useful indication of central tendency is the *mode*.

The Mean

The mean is the most widely used measure of central tendency. You already know how to calculate a mean, although you may have referred to it as the *average*. We will capture the arithmetic in a formula, and introduce the usual notation for the mean of a data set.

Normally we are working with sample data. If this is the case, we use the notation $\bar{x}$ (x-bar) to denote the sample mean. We can then write the following formula to summarize the arithmetic involved in calculating the mean: the **mean** is calculated by adding up all the numbers in the data set, and then dividing by the number of numbers.

$$\bar{x} = \frac{\sum x}{n}$$

Mean A measure of central tendency calculated by adding up all the numbers in the data set, and then dividing by the number of numbers.

There is another symbol that we use to represent the mean (usually unknown) of a population of data. It is the Greek letter μ (called *mu* and pronounced "mew"). It is calculated the same way, that is:

$$\mu = \frac{\sum x}{N}$$

but the difference in notation is very important. We often say, for instance, that we are using $\bar{x}$ to estimate μ. In other words, we calculate $\bar{x}$ from the sample data, to get an estimate of the true population mean μ. (It is quite usual to use Greek letters to represent unknown population parameters.) The sample mean $\bar{x}$ is a sample statistic, and the population mean μ is the corresponding population parameter. The upper-case N in the formula for μ also reminds us that this calculation is based on population data.

Consider a sample data set of the days absent for a random sample of a company's workers.

$$(2, 2, 4, 4, 5, 5, 5, 6, 7, 7, 8)$$

In this case, the mean of the sample of days absent is

$$\bar{x} = \frac{\sum x}{n} = \frac{2 + 2 + 4 + 4 + 5 + 5 + 5 + 6 + 7 + 7 + 8}{11} = 5$$

The mean can be an important reference point for a data set. We often consider the location of each data point relative to the mean, with a concept called the deviation from the mean. This concept is illustrated in Exhibit 3.1, which shows a dot plot of the employee absence data. A dot plot is sometimes used to examine the distribution of values in a data set, particularly when there are too few values to create a meaningful histogram.

EXHIBIT 3.1

Deviations from the Mean

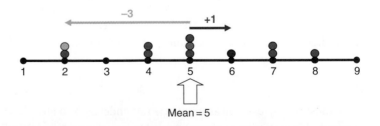

Mean = 5

Deviation from the mean The distance of the point from the mean value for each data point.

The **deviation from the mean** for each data point is the distance of the point from the mean. The deviation is positive for data points above the mean, and negative for data points below the mean. For example, for the data point represented by the red dot at 6, the deviation from the mean would be $(6 - 5) = +1$. For the data point represented by the green dot at 2, the deviation from the mean would be $(2 - 5) = -3$. For the data point represented by the blue dot at 5, the deviation from the mean would be $(5 - 5) = 0$.

We can use mathematical notation to indicate how to calculate a deviation from the mean, as follows.

$$\text{deviation from the mean} = (x - \bar{x})$$

The sum of the deviations from the mean for all the data points is always equal to zero. That is, the positive deviations from the mean always exactly cancel out the negative deviations from the mean, because of the way the mean is calculated.

The table shown in Exhibit 3.2 summarizes the calculation of the deviation from the mean for every data point in the sample data set.

EXHIBIT 3.2

Table of Deviations from the Mean

Deviations from the Mean for Employee Absences (Mean is 5)	
x	$x - \bar{x}$
2	$2 - 5 = -3$
2	$2 - 5 = -3$
4	$4 - 5 = -1$
4	$4 - 5 = -1$
5	$5 - 5 = 0$
5	$5 - 5 = 0$
5	$5 - 5 = 0$
6	$6 - 5 = +1$
7	$7 - 5 = +2$
7	$7 - 5 = +2$
8	$8 - 5 = +3$

$$\text{sum of deviations from the mean} \sum (x - \bar{x}) = 0$$

Of course, we could also use mathematical notation to summarize what we have observed, that is, that $\sum (x - \bar{x}) = 0$. We will use this mathematical relationship again, when we discuss measures of variability.

EXAMPLE 3.2A

Using Excel to calculate the mean

Anne Morgan decides to calculate the mean quarterly operating profits for the manufacturing and oil and gas sectors.

Anne uses Excel to calculate the mean quarterly operating profits. She types in = **AVERAGE( )**, with the location of the data indicated in the brackets. Note that Excel will calculate and return the average, with no label. It is good practice to type a label beside the cell containing the mean, so it will be easy to read the worksheet. The average quarterly profits for the manufacturing and oil and gas sectors over the 1988–2008 period are shown in Exhibit 3.3 on the next page.

 EXA03-2a

EXHIBIT 3.3

Mean Quarterly Operating Profits for Canadian Manufacturing and Oil and Gas Sectors

Mean Quarterly Operating Profits for Selected Canadian Sectors	
Sector	Mean Quarterly Operating Profits, I 1988–III 2008
Manufacturing	$8,330.2 Million
Oil and Gas	$3,090.5 Million

As we would have suspected from the histograms we saw in Chapter 2 (see page 57), mean quarterly operating profits are higher for the manufacturing sector. Notice also that the mean quarterly operating profit for the oil and gas sector is $3.1 billion dollars, yet we see from Exhibit 2.44 (see page 59) that over 50% of the time, quarterly operating profits were below $2 billion. Is the mean of $3.1 billion a good indication of a typical value or central tendency for the oil and gas sector? The answer is: probably not!

While the mean is the most widely used measure of central tendency, it has some limitations. It can be used only for quantitative data. It is also affected by extreme values (outliers), and this makes it a less satisfying indication of central tendency for skewed data sets, as Example 3.2B below illustrates.

EXAMPLE 3.2B

The mean is greatly affected by extreme values

Suppose that just one of the numbers in the sample data set of employee days absent illustrated in Exhibit 3.1 is changed. We will replace the 8 with a value of 58 (this might happen, for example, if one employee had a serious illness and missed a long period of work).

Data set 1: 2, 2, 4, 4, 5, 5, 5, 6, 7, 7, 8

Data set 2: 2, 2, 4, 4, 5, 5, 5, 6, 7, 7, **58**

What is the new mean?

$$\bar{x} = \frac{\sum x}{n} = \frac{2 + 2 + 4 + 4 + 5 + 5 + 5 + 6 + 7 + 7 + 58}{11} = 9.55$$

The new mean is now greater than 10 out of 11 points in the data set, and it no longer seems to be a very good measure of central tendency. Notice that the data point of 58 would be an outlier in the new data set. Because it is so different from the other data points, it should be investigated for accuracy.

The Median

Median The middle value (if there is a unique middle value), or the average of the two middle values (when there is not a unique middle value), in an ordered data set.

As we have seen in Example 3.2B, the mean is sometimes not the best measure of central tendency. When a data set is significantly skewed, or consists of ranked data, the median is a better measure of the middle of the data set. The **median** is the middle value (if there is a unique middle value), or the average of the two middle values (when there is not a unique middle value), in an ordered data set.

So, for example, for the original data set of days absent, the median would be 5. When the data are ordered, 5 (the sixth data point) is the unique middle value. There are five values in the data set that are higher than 5, and another five values that are lower than 5.

> Data set 1: 2, 2, 4, 4, 5, 5, 5, 6, 7, 7, 8

Notice that 5 is still the median when the data set is altered, with the 8 replaced by 58.

> Data set 2: 2, 2, 4, 4, 5, ⑤, 5, 6, 7, 7, **58**

In this case, when the data are highly skewed, the median is a more typical value than the mean, and a better measure of central tendency. For example, the median quarterly operating profit for the Canadian oil and gas sector (from the first quarter of 1988 to the third quarter of 2008) is $1.8 billion, compared with the mean of $3.1 billion. The median is a much better measure of central tendency and "typical" value than the mean in this case. See Exhibit 3.4 below.

EXHIBIT 3.4

Mean and Median for Quarterly Operating Profits of the Oil and Gas Sector

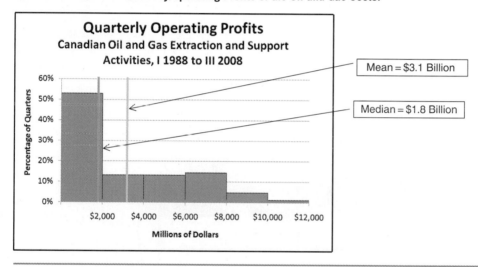

There is (strangely enough) no generally accepted notation for the median. As well, there can be no formula for the median, but there is a formula for the *location* of the median. In a data set of n ordered numbers, the median will be located at the $0.5(n + 1)^{th}$ place (this holds true whether we are dealing with sample or population data). So, for example, in the data set of 11 numbers, the median is located at the $0.5(n + 1) = 0.5(11 + 1) = 0.5(12) = 6^{th}$ place, as we found above.

Excel will calculate the median for a data set. The **MEDIAN** function is used. In a spreadsheet, type in =**MEDIAN()** with the location of the data typed into the brackets. Note that Excel will return the median, with no label. It is good practice to type a label beside the cell containing the median, so it will be easy to read the worksheet.

EXAMPLE 3.2C

Finding the median in a data set

The ages of a randomly selected group of applicants for a sales job at a small software firm are as shown in Exhibit 3.5 on the next page.

EXHIBIT 3.5

Ages of a Sample of Applicants for a Sales Job at a Software Firm

43	40
44	38
48	39
43	31
22	35
36	23
41	40
35	40
36	34
47	42

What is the median age of the applicants? What is the mean age? Which would be the better measure of central tendency, the mean or the median—and why?

The first step in finding the median age is to order the data. Note: One of the most common mistakes made by students in locating the median (with manual calculations) is forgetting this important step. Don't forget to order the data before you locate the median! Exhibit 3.6 below shows the ordered data set.

EXHIBIT 3.6

Sample of Software Firm Applicants' Ages, Ordered

Ages of a Sample of Applicants for a Sales Job at a Software Firm		
Ages	**Ordered Ages**	
43	22	
44	23	
48	31	
43	34	
22	35	Nine data points below the middle values
36	35	
41	36	
35	36	
36	38	
47	10th place: 39	Middle values
40	11th place: 40	
38	40	
39	40	
31	41	
35	42	Nine data points above the middle values
23	43	
40	43	
40	44	
34	47	
42	48	

In this sample, there is no unique middle value. There are two middle values, so we average them to get the median.

$$\text{median} = \frac{39 + 40}{2} = 39.5$$

This is straightforward, because the data set is small. We can also use the location formula to identify the median. In this sample, $n = 20$, so the median will be located at the $0.50(n + 1) = 0.50(20 + 1) = 0.50(21) = 10.5^{\text{th}}$ place. The meaning of "10.5" in this context is illustrated in Exhibit 3.7 below. The median is equal to:

10th place value $+ 0.5$(distance between 10th and 11th place value)

The 10th data point is 39, and the 11th is 40, so the median can be calculated as:

$39 + 0.5(40 - 39) = 39 + 0.5 = 39.5$

EXHIBIT 3.7

Meaning of a 10.5th Location

39	39.5	40
10th place	10.5^{th} place	11th place

The median age of the job applicants is 39.5.

The average age is 37.85 (you should verify this). This data set is somewhat skewed, because there are a couple of unusually young job applicants (one is 22 and one is 23). In this case, the median is a somewhat better measure of central tendency, because it is less affected by the unusually low values.

We can check our manual calculation of the median by using Excel. The data set for this problem is available in MyStatLab. Excel also calculates the median as 39.5.

 EXA03-2c

The Mode

Another measure of central tendency that is sometimes useful is the **mode**, the most frequently occurring value in the data set. In the data set of employee absences (from Exhibit 3.2), the mode is 5. It is the most frequently occurring value in the data set, and it is also a good indication of central tendency.

Mode The most frequently occurring value in the data set.

Orginal data set: $= (2, 2, 4, 4, \underbrace{5, 5, 5}_{\text{mode}}, 6, 7, 7, 8)$

However, if a data set contains only unique values, there will be no mode. As well, there may be more than one mode and, in such a case, the multiple modes may not be good measures of central tendency. Consider the following slightly amended data set, which is the employee absences data with one value removed.

Data set with one value removed: $(2, 2, 4, 4, 5, 5, 6, 7, 7, 8)$

This amended data set has four modes: 2, 4, 5, and 7. It would be hard to justify that all four are good measures of central tendency, or a good reflection of a typical value.

For this reason, the mode is most often used in reference to the shape of a histogram. For example, a histogram with the shape shown in Exhibit 3.8 would be described as *unimodal*, as there is a unique modal class.

EXHIBIT 3.8

Histogram of a Unimodal Distribution

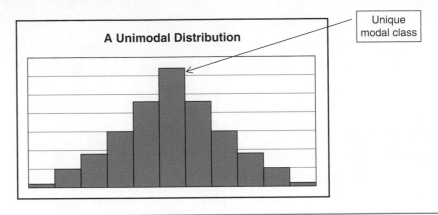

In contrast, the distribution shown in Exhibit 3.9 would be described as *bimodal*, because there are two distinct modal classes.

EXHIBIT 3.9

Histogram of a Bimodal Distribution

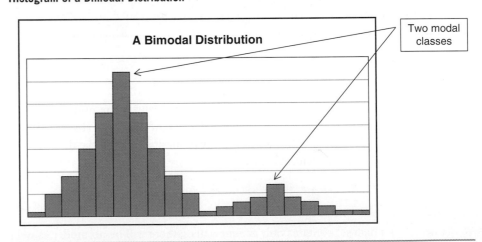

Excel will calculate the mode for a data set (if one exists) using the **MODE** function. In a spreadsheet, type in =**MODE()** with the location of the data typed into the brackets. If there is more than one mode, Excel will not identify this, and it will return only the first mode in the data set. As usual, you should type a label beside the cell containing the mode.

Which Measure of Central Tendency Is Best?

You will usually have to choose between the mean and the median as a measure of central tendency for quantitative data. In general, the mean is preferred, because its calculation is based on all of the information in the data set (each value is used in the calculation). However, the mean is not a good measure of central tendency when the data set is significantly skewed. But how do you determine whether the data set is too skewed to rely on the mean as the measure of central tendency? As your experience in analyzing data increases, your judgment about the best measure of central tendency will likely improve.

Sometimes we can easily tell which measure to use by inspection of a histogram, such as in the case of the quarterly operating profits for the Canadian oil and gas sector. Another helpful thing to do is calculate both the mean and the median. If they are not significantly different (a judgment that you will have to make, based on the particular data set), use the mean. If the two measures are significantly different, use the median.

Exhibits 3.10a and b provide some examples.

The histogram depicted in Exhibit 3.10a is somewhat skewed to the right. The mean is 133.7, and the median is 122.2. When considered relative to the range of values

EXHIBIT 3.10a

Histogram Is Not Significantly Skewed

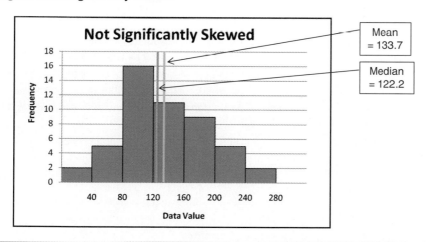

in the data set, the difference between the two is not that large. In this case, the mean would probably be the best choice for the measure of central tendency.

The histogram depicted in Exhibit 3.10b is significantly skewed to the right. The mean is 129.0, and the median is 105.7. When considered relative to the range of values in the data set, the difference between the two is large. In this case, the mean would probably not be the best choice for the measure of central tendency. The median would be a better choice.

EXHIBIT 3.10b

Histogram Is Significantly Skewed

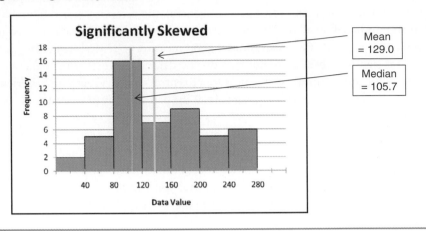

GUIDE TO DECISION MAKING

Choosing a Measure of Central Tendency

1. The mean is the preferred measure of central tendency for quantitative data. However, it is significantly affected by outliers, and should not be used for significantly skewed data.

2. The median can be used as a measure of central tendency for quantitative or ranked data. It is preferred for quantitative data when the data are significantly skewed.

3. The mode can give an indication of central tendency for quantitative or ranked data, but there may be no mode, or there may not be a unique mode.

4. When comparing distributions, use the same measure of central tendency for all. If one distribution's central tendency is better represented by the median, calculate the median for all distributions.

DEVELOP YOUR SKILLS 3.2

6. Calculate the mean, median, and mode for the ages of customers in the survey of drugstore customers. Which is the best measure of central tendency in this data set? Why?

DYS03-6

7. Calculate the mean and the median for the incomes of customers in the survey of drugstore customers.

DYS03-7 Comment on the difference between the two measures of central tendency. Which one is best, and why?

8. Doug Brackett runs Downtown Automotive in Nelson, BC. He has collected customer counts for a random sample of days. The data set is shown below in Exhibit 3.11. Calculate an appropriate measure of central tendency for this data set.

9. The mean amount of the most recent purchase made by customers in the survey of drugstore customers is

$26.19. The median amount is $26.44. What does this tell you about the distribution of customer purchases?

10. Calculate an appropriate measure of central tendency for the quarterly operating profits of the

DYS03-10

Canadian manufacturing sector. Compare the oil and gas and manufacturing sectors, in terms of central tendency.

EXHIBIT 3.11

Downtown Automotive, Daily Customer Counts

24	19	27	41	17
26	34	17	25	31
23	29	26	18	24
31	24	14	29	36
31	29	40	12	26

3.3   MEASURES OF VARIABILITY

We are usually also interested in the variability in a data set. When Anne Morgan created histograms for the manufacturing and oil and gas sectors, she noticed several differences in the quarterly operating profits of the manufacturing sector and the oil and gas sector. One thing Anne noticed was that the quarterly operating profits for the oil and gas sector were concentrated in the first class, below $2 billion, while the quarterly operating profits for the manufacturing sector were more widely scattered across the classes. Anne is now wondering if there is some numerical measure she can use to capture the differences in variability between the data sets.

The Range

The **range** of the data set is a number that is calculated as the difference between the maximum and minimum values in the data set.

Notice that the range is a *single* number. For the oil and gas sector, the minimum quarterly operating profit is $105.0 million, and the maximum quarterly operating profit is $11,228.0 million.

range = $11,228.0 million − $105.0 million = $11,123.0 million

Notice that the range is *not* "$105 million to $11,228 million," which is how you might have described it in everyday English. This does not correspond to the precise meaning of the term in statistical language. Remember the range is one number, calculated as the difference between the maximum and minimum values in the data set.

The range for the quarterly operating profits of the manufacturing sector is $13,803 million. The higher range for the manufacturing sector corresponds to Anne's observation that the quarterly profits for manufacturing are more widely scattered than for the oil and gas sector.

Range A number that is calculated as the difference between the maximum and minimum values in the data set.

The Standard Deviation

While the range can give an indication of the variability in the data, it does not distinguish between data sets with the same maximum and minimum values but very different variability. Consider the histograms in Exhibit 3.12, which summarize the purchase amounts made by random samples of customers at two gas bars (each with a convenience store attached).

EXHIBIT 3.12

Histograms of Gas Bar Purchases with the Same Range but Different Variability

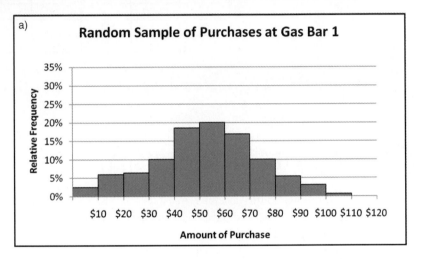

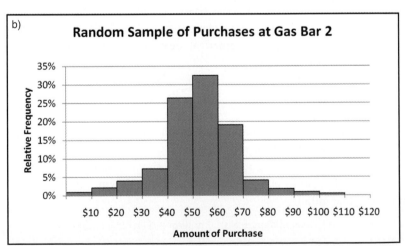

The data sets for both samples have exactly the same range of $104.70. However, we can see that the purchases for Gas Bar 1 have more widely scattered amounts than the purchases for Gas Bar 2. About 78% of the purchases at Gas Bar 2 are in the two central classes ($40 to < $60), but only about 56% of the purchases at Gas Bar 1 are accounted for in these two classes.

A better measure of variability would focus not only on the maximum and minimum values in the data set, but on every value. The most-used measure of variability does this. It is called the **standard deviation**, and is a measure of variability in a data set that is based on deviations from the mean.

Standard deviation A measure of variability in a data set that is based on deviations from the mean.

You have already been introduced to the idea of a deviation from the mean. The deviations from the mean for the purchases at Gas Bar 1 will, overall, be larger than the deviations from the mean for the purchases at Gas Bar 2. If we want a single number to represent the variability in the two data sets, we could consider calculating the average deviation from the mean for each. Unfortunately, if we did this, we would realize that the average deviation from the mean was zero for both distributions. This is because (as was pointed out earlier), for all data sets, the deviations from the mean will *total* to zero. The positive and negative deviations from the mean always exactly cancel each other out, for every data set, so the average deviation will always be zero.

In order to prevent this cancelling out, calculation of the standard deviation involves *squaring* the deviations from the mean. An average of the squared deviations is then calculated. Finally, the square root of this value is taken, to "undo" the squaring and return the measure to units like the units in the original data set.

When we refer to the standard deviation of the population, the notation is σ, which is the Greek letter *sigma* (this is the lower-case version of the upper-case Σ that is used to denote summation). The formula capturing the arithmetic for calculation of the population standard deviation is as follows.

$$\sigma = \sqrt{\frac{\Sigma(x - \mu)^2}{N}}$$

Some statistical formulas require the use of the squared version of this measure, which is called the variance,[1] with the notation (reasonably enough) σ^2.

The notation for a sample standard deviation is different, and in this case, the formula is also slightly different. We denote the sample standard deviation with s. The formula differs in that the divisor is $(n - 1)$, not n, as follows:[2]

$$s = \sqrt{\frac{\Sigma(x - \bar{x})^2}{n - 1}}$$

The sample mean is referred to as $\bar{x}$ in this formula for the sample standard deviation, as it should be.

We use s to estimate the (usually unknown) value of σ. The formula shown above for s (with the $n - 1$ divisor) provides a reliable and unbiased estimate of σ. It can be

---

[1] Of course, the formula for the population variance is $\sigma^2 = \dfrac{\Sigma(x - \mu)^2}{N}$

[2] Similarly, the formula for the sample variance is $s^2 = \dfrac{\Sigma(x - \bar{x})^2}{n - 1}$

shown that if the sample standard deviation was calculated with just n in the divisor, it would tend to underestimate the true population value, which is of course undesirable. Dividing by $n - 1$ removes this bias.

Let's return to the employee absence data set from the beginning of the chapter to demonstrate calculation of the standard deviation. Since we have already calculated deviations from the mean for this data set, we will build on this base, as shown below in Exhibit 3.13.

EXHIBIT 3.13

Employee Absences Data: Deviations

Employee Absences		
x	$(x - \bar{x})$	$(x - \bar{x})^2$
2	$2 - 5 = -3$	$(-3)^2 = 9$
2	$2 - 5 = -3$	$(-3)^2 = 9$
4	$4 - 5 = -1$	$(-1)^2 = 1$
4	$4 - 5 = -1$	$(-1)^2 = 1$
5	$5 - 5 = 0$	$0^2 = 0$
5	$5 - 5 = 0$	$0^2 = 0$
5	$5 - 5 = 0$	$0^2 = 0$
6	$6 - 5 = +1$	$1^2 = 1$
7	$7 - 5 = +2$	$2^2 = 4$
7	$7 - 5 = +2$	$2^2 = 4$
8	$8 - 5 = +3$	$3^2 = 9$
sum	0	38 ← $\boxed{\sum(x - \bar{x})^2}$

There are 11 data points in this sample data set, so $n = 11$. We can now use the formula, as follows.

$$s = \sqrt{\frac{\sum(x - \bar{x})^2}{n - 1}} = \sqrt{\frac{38}{11 - 1}} = \sqrt{\frac{38}{10}} = \sqrt{3.8} = 1.949$$

The standard deviation for this sample data set is 1.949. What does this mean? Think of it, for now, simply as a measure, or a score, of variability. The larger the standard deviation is, the more variable the data are.

EXAMPLE **3.3A**

Calculating standard deviation with Excel

Calculate the standard deviations of the purchases at the two Gas Bars mentioned above.

EXA03-3a

You can use the **STDEV** function in Excel to find the sample standard deviation. Type in =**STDEV( )**, with the location of the data typed into the brackets. As usual, you should type a label beside the cell containing the standard deviation.

A summary table of the standard deviations is shown in Exhibit 3.14.

EXHIBIT 3.14

Standard Deviations of Purchases at Two Gas Bars

	Gas Bar 1 Purchases	Gas Bar 2 Purchases
Standard Deviation	$20.73	$15.21

The standard deviation of the purchases at Gas Bar 1 is higher than at Gas Bar 2. This is what we would expect, given our observation that the purchases at Gas Bar 1 are more variable than at Gas Bar 2.

The formula for standard deviation introduced above can help you understand how deviations from the mean are used to calculate this measure of variability. However, if you want to calculate the sample standard deviation by hand with a calculator, you should use another version of the formula, as follows.

$$s = \sqrt{\frac{\Sigma x^2 - \frac{(\Sigma x)^2}{n}}{n-1}}$$

We will refer to this as the "computational formula" for the standard deviation. This formula will result in the same value for the standard deviation, and although it looks more complicated, you will find it quicker to use, so be sure that you master it. Example 3.3B illustrates the use of the computational formula.

EXAMPLE 3.3B

Calculating the standard deviation with the computational formula

We will use the computational formula to calculate the standard deviation for the employee absences data set. This will show you how to use the formula, and should reassure you that it gives the same end result. Exhibit 3.15 shows the employee absences data, and some other calculations.

$$s = \sqrt{\frac{\Sigma x^2 - \frac{(\Sigma x)^2}{n}}{n-1}}$$

First, break the formula into pieces.

$$s = \sqrt{\frac{\Sigma x^2 - \frac{(\Sigma x)^2}{\textcircled{n}}}{n-1}}$$

As usual, n is the number of observations, and $n = 11$ in this case.

EXHIBIT 3.15

Employee Absences

x	x^2
2	$2^2 = 4$
2	$2^2 = 4$
4	$4^2 = 16$
4	$4^2 = 16$
5	$5^2 = 25$
5	$5^2 = 25$
5	$5^2 = 25$
6	$6^2 = 36$
7	$7^2 = 49$
7	$7^2 = 49$
8	$8^2 = 64$
$\Sigma x = 55$	$\Sigma x^2 = 313$

$$s = \sqrt{\frac{\Sigma x^2 - \frac{(\Sigma x)^2}{n}}{n-1}}$$

Σx^2 requires squaring each data point, and then adding the results (see the second column of Exhibit 3.15). In this case, $\Sigma x^2 = 2^2 + 2^2 + 4^2 + 4^2 + 5^2 + 5^2 + 5^2 + 6^2 + 7^2 + 7^2 + 8^2 = 313$.

$$s = \sqrt{\frac{\Sigma x^2 - \frac{(\Sigma x)^2}{n}}{n-1}}$$

$(\Sigma x)^2$ requires adding up all the data points (see the first column of Exhibit 3.15 above), and then squaring the sum.

$$(\Sigma x)^2 = (2 + 2 + 4 + 4 + 5 + 5 + 5 + 6 + 7 + 7 + 8)^2 = 55^2 = 3025$$

Now we have all the pieces necessary for the calculation, as follows.

$$s = \sqrt{\frac{\Sigma x^2 - \frac{(\Sigma x)^2}{n}}{n-1}} = \sqrt{\frac{313 - \frac{3025}{11}}{11-1}} = \sqrt{\frac{313 - 275}{10}} = \sqrt{\frac{38}{10}} = \sqrt{3.8}$$
$$= 1.949$$

This matches our earlier calculation of the standard deviation.

With some practice, you should be able to do this calculation, using the memory of your calculator, without stopping to write down any intermediate answers. Since you will probably be required to do this calculation on tests or exams, you should learn to do it efficiently.

The Empirical Rule   So far, we have used the standard deviation as a measure of variability, with a larger standard deviation indicating greater variability. However, for certain types of data sets, the standard deviation has some very useful additional properties.

We can regard the standard deviation as a typical deviation from the mean in a data set. We can also use the standard deviation as a unit of measurement, something that is very common and very useful in statistical decision-making techniques. The Empirical Rule is an introduction to this use of the standard deviation.

Consider the following data set, which represents the number of diners at a small Winnipeg restaurant, for a random sample of 30 different evenings. The sample data are shown below in Exhibit 3.16.

EXHIBIT 3.16

Number of Diners at a Winnipeg Restaurant, Random Sample of 30 Evenings

104	112	94
100	109	93
115	100	104
107	106	97
88	113	118
107	94	111
121	103	97
80	96	97
111	88	108
125	101	109

For the Empirical Rule to apply, the data set must be symmetric and bell-shaped. The desired shape is shown in Exhibit 3.17 below.

EXHIBIT 3.17

Distribution Shape Required for Application of the Empirical Rule

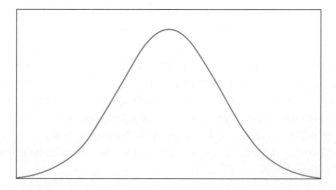

One way to check on the symmetry and shape of the data is to create a histogram for the data set. If the histogram is approximately the correct shape, it is appropriate to apply the Empirical Rule. A histogram of the data set of diners (see the table in Exhibit 3.16) is shown below in Exhibit 3.18. Since this histogram has the required shape, we can proceed with the Empirical Rule.

EXHIBIT 3.18

Histogram of Data on Diners at a Winnipeg Restaurant

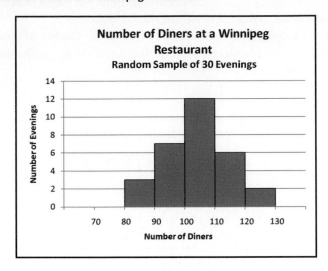

The Empirical Rule

The Empirical Rule applies *only* to a symmetric bell-shaped distribution:

1. About 68% of the data points will lie within one standard deviation of the mean.
2. About 95% of the data points will lie within two standard deviations of the mean.
3. Almost all of the data points will lie within three standard deviations of the mean.

The Empirical Rule is illustrated in Exhibit 3.19 opposite. Strictly speaking, the Empirical Rule applies to *population* data that have a symmetric bell-shaped distribution. However, if we have a representative sample data set, we can use $\bar{x}$ as an estimate of μ, and s as an estimate of σ, and apply the rule to make some inferences about the population.

The sample data set of the number of diners at the Winnipeg restaurant has a mean of 103.6 and a standard deviation of 10.23. First, we will directly apply the Empirical Rule (we have already established that the sample data have a symmetric, bell-shaped distribution). This will illustrate the use of the standard deviation as a unit of measurement. Then we will explore the implications of the Empirical Rule.

For the Winnipeg diners data set, $s = 10.23$. This distance will be the unit of measurement in the discussion.

$$\underset{10.23}{\overset{1s}{\vdash\!\!\!-\!\!\!\dashv}}$$

1. About 68% of the numbers of diners visiting the Winnipeg restaurant in the evening are within one standard deviation of the mean. We will explore the data set

EXHIBIT **3.19**

The Empirical Rule for Symmetric Bell-Shaped Distributions

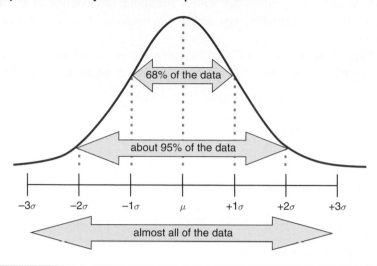

by first locating the points that are one standard deviation away from the mean (that is, 10.23 units away from the mean of 103.6). We have to calculate

$$\bar{x} + 1s = 103.6 + (1)10.23 = 113.83$$

We also have to calculate

$$\bar{x} - 1s = 103.6 - (1)10.23 = 93.37$$

Exhibit 3.20 below illustrates this calculation.

EXHIBIT **3.20**

One Standard Deviation from the Mean

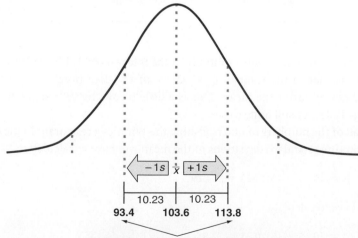

How many of the sample data points are in the interval (93.4, 113.8)? Refer to Exhibit 3.16. You should be able to count 22. This means that in the sample, $\frac{22}{30} = 73.3\%$ of the data points are within one standard deviation of the mean. This is a little above the 68% suggested by the Empirical Rule, but still reasonably close.

2. About 95% of the numbers of diners visiting the Winnipeg restaurant in the evening are within two standard deviations of the mean. We have to calculate

$$\bar{x} + 2s = 103.6 + (2)10.23 = 124.06$$

We also have to calculate

$$\bar{x} - 2s = 103.6 - (2)10.23 = 83.14$$

Exhibit 3.21 below illustrates this calculation.

EXHIBIT 3.21

Two Standard Deviations from the Mean

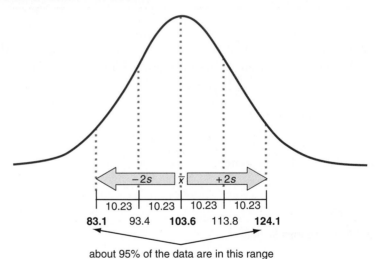

about 95% of the data are in this range

How many of the sample data points are in the interval (83.1, 124.1)? We count 28. This means that in the sample, $\frac{28}{30} = 93.3\%$ of the data points are within two standard deviations of the mean. This is a little below the 95% suggested by the Empirical Rule, but still quite close.

3. Almost all of the numbers of diners visiting the Winnipeg restaurant in the evening are within three standard deviations of the mean. We have to calculate

$$\bar{x} + 3s = 103.6 + (3)10.23 = 134.29$$

We also have to calculate

$$\bar{x} - 3s = 103.6 - (3)10.23 = 72.91$$

Exhibit 3.22 below illustrates this calculation.

EXHIBIT 3.22

Three Standard Deviations from the Mean

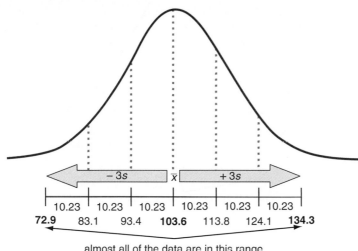

almost all of the data are in this range

How many of the sample data points are in the interval (72.9, 134.3)? All of them are, so in the sample 100% of the data points are within three standard deviations of the mean. This is what the Empirical Rule suggests (almost all).

So what? This is a case where we can infer characteristics of the population data on the basis of the sample data, presuming that we have a representative sample. While the Empirical Rule holds (approximately) for the sample data, what is more interesting is that it also probably holds for the population data.

This means, for example (using the third part of the Empirical Rule), that this restaurant would almost never have fewer than about 73 diners in the evening, or more than about 134 diners. This could have implications for ordering supplies and setting staff schedules.

Because wasted food is expensive, the restaurant might decide to plan for a maximum of 124 diners in the evening. The second part of the Empirical Rule says that about 95% of the numbers of diners at this Winnipeg restaurant, in the evening, will be between 83.1 and 124.1. If 95% of the numbers of diners are within this range, then only 5% are outside this range, in what are referred to as the "tails" of the distribution. Since the distribution appears to be symmetric, this would indicate that about 2.5% of the time, there would be fewer than 83 diners, and about 2.5% of the time, there would be more than 124 diners. Planning for a maximum of 124 diners, then, would leave the restaurant short of supplies only about 2.5% of the time—a risk the owner might take, to save on costs. Exhibit 3.23 on the next page illustrates this calculation.

EXHIBIT 3.23

The Tails of the Distribution

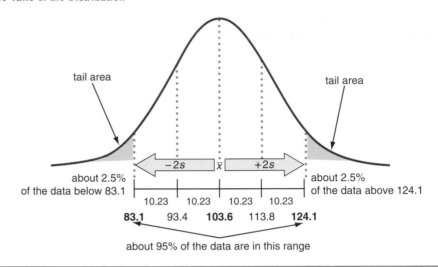

In Chapter 8, we will explore these estimation procedures in more detail. For now, the Empirical Rule provides a way to make some educated guesses about population data, *if the sample data set is symmetric and bell-shaped.* Example 3.3C shows another application of the Empirical Rule.

EXAMPLE 3.3C

Applying the Empirical Rule

Holly Sarton has just received the mark on her first Statistics test. She would like to have some idea of how her mark compares to the marks of other students on the test, but her professor will not tell her what her relative standing is. However, Holly's professor did give Holly a random sample of 50 of the marks of the other students who took the test. When Holly created a histogram of the sample data set, it was fairly bell-shaped and symmetric. The sample mean mark was 58.3, and the sample standard deviation was 13.7. Holly's mark was 75.

The sample size, at 50, is fairly large. Because a histogram of the sample data is bell-shaped and symmetric, Holly feels comfortable applying the Empirical Rule. Holly starts by calculating the points that are one standard deviation from the mean.

$$\bar{x} + 1s = 58.3 + 13.7 = 72$$
$$\bar{x} - 1s = 58.3 - 13.7 = 44.6$$

The Empirical Rule suggests that about 68% of the marks on the Statistics test are between 44.6 and 72. This means that about 32% of the marks are outside this range. Because the distribution is symmetric, Holly expects that about 16% (half of 32%) of the marks are above 72, and about 16% are below 44.6. Since Holly's mark is 75, she estimates that just fewer than 16% of her fellow students got a better mark than she did. Although Holly was hoping to achieve a higher mark on the test, she feels better knowing that she is likely in the top 16% of the class. However, she makes a commitment to spend more time doing statistics exercises so that she can do better on the next test.

Example 3.3C illustrated the usefulness and also the limitations of the Empirical Rule. For example, Holly's estimate of the percentage of students with a higher mark than she received is approximate, because her mark is not exactly one or two standard deviations from the mean. In fact, Holly's mark is $75 - 58.3 = 16.7$ marks away from the mean, and this is a distance of $\frac{16.7}{13.7} = 1.22$ standard deviations. Similarly, it is difficult to estimate what percentage of students passed the test, as the mark of 50 is not exactly one or two standard deviations from the mean, but $\frac{50 - 58.3}{13.7} = -0.6$ standard deviations from the mean. In Chapter 5, you will be introduced to the normal distribution, and you will learn how to go beyond the limitations of the Empirical Rule to deal with cases like these.

The Interquartile Range

While the standard deviation is the preferred measure of variability for quantitative data, it can be significantly affected by outliers (which is reasonable, since it is based on deviations from the mean, a measure also affected by outliers).

Let us return to the data sets of employee days absent that we used to explore the mean.

Data set 1 (Original data): (2, 2, 4, 4, 5, 5, 5, 6, 7, 7, 8)

Data set 2 (New data): (2, 2, 4, 4, 5, 5, 5, 6, 7, 7, **58**)

Calculate the standard deviation for data set 1 (we will refer to this as s_1).

$$s_1 = \sqrt{\frac{\sum x^2 - \frac{(\sum x)^2}{n}}{n-1}} = \sqrt{\frac{313 - \frac{(55)^2}{11}}{10}} = 1.949$$

The standard deviation for data set 2 will be:

$$s_2 = \sqrt{\frac{\sum x^2 - \frac{(\sum x)^2}{n}}{n-1}} = \sqrt{\frac{3{,}613 - \frac{(105)^2}{11}}{10}} = 16.158$$

Now, there is no doubt that data set 2 is more variable than data set 1. However, the standard deviation was significantly affected by the change in only one data point. In this case, where data set 2 is significantly skewed by the outlier of 58, the standard deviation gives a somewhat misleading impression of variability. As a contrast, consider data set 3 shown below, which has a mean of 9.5 (almost the same mean as data set 2) and a standard deviation of 16.0 (very close to that of data set 2). Data set 2 is repeated, for ease of comparison.

Data set 2: 2, 2, 4, 4, 5, 5, 5, 6, 7, 7, 58

Data set 3: $-12, -10, -9, 0, 2, 12, 16, 22, 27, 27, 30$

Most people would agree that there is more variability in data set 3 than in data set 2. It seems that the standard deviation gives a somewhat misleading measure of variability for the skewed data set.

So, what could we use instead? The answer is the interquartile range. But before we discuss its calculation, we must first discuss quartiles and percentiles.

If 75% of the other marks on a test were lower than yours, then your test mark is the 75th percentile. If 38% of the other marks were lower than yours, then your test mark is the 38th percentile. In general, if $P\%$ of the data points are lower than x_p, then x_p is the **P^{th} percentile**.

P^{th} percentile x_p, the data point that is above $P\%$ of the data points.

Notice that the median is the 50th percentile, as 50% of the data points are below the median. To locate a particular percentile, we use a formula that is a generalization of the location formula for the median. In a data set of n ordered numbers, the Pth percentile will be located at the $\frac{P}{100}(n + 1)^{\text{th}}$ place.

EXAMPLE **3.3D**

Finding the 75th percentile

Find the 75th percentile for the following data set:
3, 6, 8, 8, 12, 34, 56, 79

In this case, there are eight data points, so $n = 8$. The 75th percentile will be located at the $\dfrac{P}{100}(n + 1) = \dfrac{75}{100}(8 + 1) = 6.75^{\text{th}}$ place.

Since the data are already ordered, we can proceed directly to the calculation of the 75th percentile. The 6th data point is 34, and the 7th data point is 56. The value of the 6.75th location is equal to:

6th place value + 0.75(distance between 6th and 7th place values)

The 75th percentile will be:

$$34 + 0.75(56 - 34) = 34 + 0.75(22) = 34 + 16.5 = 50.5$$

Exhibit 3.24 illustrates the 6.75th location.

EXHIBIT **3.24**

Meaning of a 6.75 Location

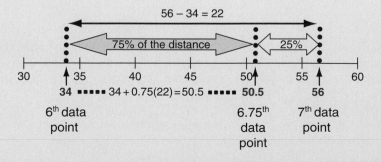

1st quartile Quartile usually denoted Q_1; is the 25th percentile.

3rd quartile Quartile usually denoted Q_3; is the 75th percentile.

Interquartile range (IQR) $Q_3 - Q_1$; it measures the range of the middle 50% of the data values.

Quartiles are particular percentiles, which divide the data set into quarters. The **1st quartile**, usually denoted Q_1, is the 25th percentile. The **3rd quartile**, usually denoted Q_3, is the 75th percentile. Of course, the median is also the 2nd quartile.

The **interquartile range (IQR)** is $Q_3 - Q_1$. It measures the range of the middle 50% of the data values. Because the IQR is calculated on the basis of the middle 50% of the data values, it is not affected by outliers, so it is a better measure of variability for skewed data sets.

EXAMPLE 3.3E

Calculate the interquartile range for data set 2 and data set 3, first discussed above.

Calculate the interquartile range

Data set 2: 2, 2, 4, 4, 5, 5, 5, 6, 7, 7, 58

Data set 3: −12, −10, −9, 0, 2, 12, 16, 22, 27, 27, 30

For data set 2:

Q_1's location is $0.25(n + 1) = 0.25(11 + 1) = 0.25(12) = 3$

So Q_1 is the 3rd data point (the data are already ordered).

$Q_1 = 4$

Similarly, Q_3's location is $0.75(n + 1) = 0.75(11 + 1) = 0.75(12) = 9$

Q_3 is the 9th data point, so $Q_3 = 7$

$IQR_2 = Q_3 - Q_1 = 7 - 4 = 3$

Repeat for data set 3, which also has 11 data points.

Q_1 is the 3rd data point (the data are already ordered).

$Q_1 = -9$

Q_3 is the 9th data point.

$Q_3 = 27$

$IQR_3 = 27 - (-9) = 36$

Notice that IQRs are quite different for these two data sets, which share an almost equal standard deviation. In this case, the interquartile range is a better measure of variability, because it more appropriately distinguishes between these two data sets.

Notice that the interquartile range can also be used as a measure of variability for ranked data, although there are not many instances where this would be useful.

Excel does not have a built-in tool to calculate the interquartile range. However, Excel does have a function to calculate Q_1 and Q_3. Exhibit 3.25 on the next page shows the function arguments dialogue box for the **QUARTILE** function.

EXHIBIT 3.25

Function Arguments Dialogue Box for the QUARTILE Function

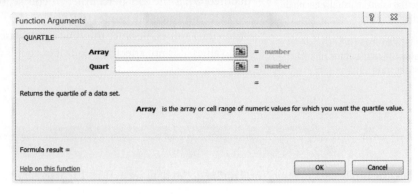

The dialogue box is filled in as follows:

1. **Array** is the location of the data to be analyzed.
2. **Quart** is where you indicate which quartile you want to calculate. As the dialogue box indicates when you activate this input area, you must enter **1** for the 1st quartile, and **3** for the 3rd quartile.

The Excel function will output the quartile value, with no label. You should type a label into an adjacent cell, so that your spreadsheet is easy to read.

Once you have calculated the 1st and 3rd quartiles, you have to enter a formula into Excel to calculate the difference. Exhibit 3.26 below shows an excerpt from an Excel spreadsheet in

EXHIBIT 3.26

IQR Calculation in Spreadsheet

	A	B
1	Data Set 2	
2	2	
3	2	
4	4	
5	4	
6	5	
7	5	
8	5	
9	6	
10	7	
11	7	
12	58	
13		
14	Q1	=QUARTILE(A2:A12,1)
15	Q3	=QUARTILE(A2:A12,3)
16	IQR	=B15-B14
17		

which the IQR is calculated. The formulas are revealed for your reference. Notice that the labels in cells A14, A15, and A16 have been typed in so that the spreadsheet is easy to read.

You may be surprised to find that the values calculated by Excel for the quartiles (and thus the interquartile range) do not exactly match the manual calculations above. Exhibit 3.27 summarizes the differences.

EXHIBIT 3.27

Differences between Manual Calculations and Spreadsheet

	Data Set 2 Calculations	
	As Calculated by Hand	As Calculated by Excel
Q_1	4	4
Q_3	7	6.5
IQR	3	2.5

As you can see from the table above, Excel's calculations of the quartiles differ from the calculations shown in the manual method above. It is interesting that there is not widespread agreement about how to calculate percentiles and quartiles. The manual method shown above is widely accepted (and somewhat easier), and you should continue to use it with confidence. Because the methods differ somewhat in their results, you should always compare IQRs calculated using the same method so that your comparisons will be valid.

GUIDE TO DECISION MAKING

Choosing a Measure of Variability

1. The standard deviation is the preferred measure of variability for quantitative data. However, it can be significantly affected by outliers, and should not be used for badly skewed data.

2. The interquartile range can be used as a measure of variability for quantitative or ranked data. It is preferred for quantitative data when the data are skewed. When comparing data sets, never compare an IQR calculated by hand with an IQR calculated with Excel, as the methods are not directly comparable.

3. If the mean is an appropriate measure of central tendency for a data set, use the standard deviation as a measure of variability. If the median is the best measure of central tendency for a data set, use the interquartile range as a measure of variability.

DEVELOP YOUR SKILLS 3.3

11. Calculate an appropriate measure of variability for the ages of customers in the survey of drugstore customers. Would it be appropriate to use the Empirical Rule with this data set?

DYS03-11

12. Calculate an appropriate measure of variability for the incomes of customers in the survey of drugstore customers.

DYS03-12

13. Doug Brackett runs Downtown Automotive in Nelson, BC. He has collected customer counts for a random sample of days. The data set is shown below in Exhibit 3.28. Calculate an appropriate measure of variability for this data set.

EXHIBIT 3.28

Downtown Automotive, Daily Customer Counts

24	19	27	41	17
26	34	17	25	31
23	29	26	18	24
31	24	14	29	36
31	29	40	12	26

14. Would it be appropriate to apply the Empirical Rule to the data set of customer counts for Downtown Automotive, shown in Exhibit 3.28? Why or why not?

15. Doug Brackett wants to have enough mechanics on hand to take care of his customer requests, but he does not want to be paying mechanics to sit around doing nothing. Doug needs to know a reasonable upper limit on the number of customers so he can plan his staff schedule. About 97.5% of the time, what is the maximum number of customers should Doug plan for?

3.4 MEASURES OF ASSOCIATION

Correlation analysis can be used to measure the degree (and direction) of association between two variables.

The Pearson Correlation Coefficient for Quantitative Variables

In Chapter 2, Anne Morgan created a scatter diagram to investigate the relationship between assets and quarterly operating profits of the oil and gas sector. This scatter diagram is reproduced below, in Exhibit 3.29.

EXHIBIT 3.29

Scatter Diagram for Oil and Gas Sector Profits and Assets

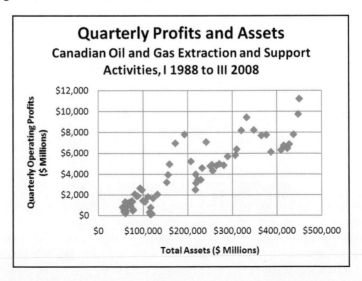

There appears to be a positive relationship between the two variables; that is, when total assets are higher, quarterly operating profits are higher. The relationship is not perfect, because for a given level of assets, there is a range of observed profit levels.

If profits were perfectly predicted by assets, the relationship would appear as depicted in Exhibit 3.30.

EXHIBIT 3.30

Perfect Positive Linear Relationship

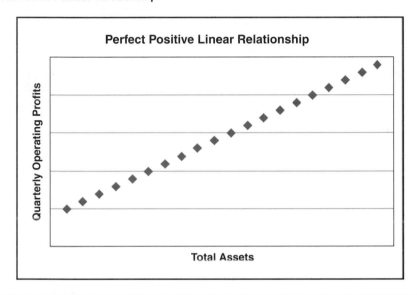

The stronger linear correlation is between two variables, the closer the *x*–*y* data points are to lining up in a straight line.

The **Pearson correlation coefficient** is a numerical measure that indicates the strength and direction of the linear relationship between two quantitative variables. The notation for the Pearson correlation coefficient is *r* (or sometimes the "Pearson *r*"), and the coefficient can take on values between −1 and +1. An *r* of −1 signifies a perfect negative linear relationship. An *r* of +1 signifies a perfect positive relationship. An *r* of 0 indicates no apparent linear relationship. The stronger the relationship, the further the *r*-value is from zero in either direction. Exhibit 3.31 on the next page illustrates this.

While interpretation of the *r*-value cannot follow any fixed rules, it is generally considered that an *r* in the range from −0.5 to +0.5 indicates that there is no strong linear relationship between the *x*- and *y*-values. Note that an *r*-value close to +1 or −1 does not *prove* that there is a cause-and-effect relationship between the *x*- and *y*-variables involved—all we can say is that the variables are highly correlated, and any conclusions about causality must be made on the basis of an understanding of the context of the data being analyzed.

Pearson correlation coefficient A numerical measure that indicates the strength and direction of the linear relationship between two quantitative variables.

EXHIBIT 3.31

Values of the Pearson Correlation Coefficient

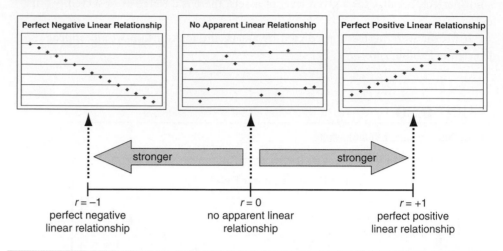

A high value of the Pearson correlation coefficient, r, (close to $+1$ or close to -1) indicates a strong linear correlation between the x- and y-variables, but it does not prove that changes in the x-variable caused changes in the y-variable.

There are many famous examples of so-called spurious (false or misleading) correlations. For example, the "Halloween effect" refers to the fact that the US stock market has typically performed better in the winter months than in the summer.[3] You may have heard this effect referred to as "Go away in May." However, it seems unreasonable to believe that stock market performance changes because a calendar page turns over.

We will use Excel to calculate the correlation coefficient. To calculate r for a sample data set (the most usual case), use the **PEARSON** function in Excel. Type =**PEARSON()** into a cell on the worksheet, with the locations of the x- and y-values input into the brackets. As usual, you should create a label beside the cell where the function result is located.

Excel calculates the correlation coefficient for the assets and profit data of the oil and gas sector to be $+0.91$. This is an indication of a strong positive relationship between assets and quarterly operating profits.

Calculation of r Is Based on Deviations from the Mean   While the correlation coefficient is not normally calculated by hand, the formula on which it is based is of interest. This formula illustrates that r is based on deviations from the mean, for both x- and y-values.

One formula for r is as follows.

$$r = \frac{\sum (x - \bar{x})(y - \bar{y})}{(n - 1)s_x s_y}$$

---

[3] Ben Jacobsen and Nuttawat Visaltanachoti, "The Halloween Effect in US Sectors," *The Financial Review* 44(3) (August, 2009), **www.thefinancialreview.org/abstracts/Financial-Review-Abstracts-August-2009.html**, accessed August 26, 2009.

where s_x is the standard deviation of the x-values in the sample, and s_y is the standard deviation of the y-values in the sample. The sign of r is determined by the numerator, $\sum(x - \bar{x})(y - \bar{y})$, because all of the terms in the denominator will always be positive.

The numerator of this formula for r is the sum of the products of the deviations from the mean for each pair of (x, y) variables. An example will help you understand how this formula works. Exhibit 3.32 below shows a scatter diagram of results from a study of a weight-loss program run by a fitness club that wants to advertise its success.

EXHIBIT 3.32

Scatter Diagram of Weight-Loss Results

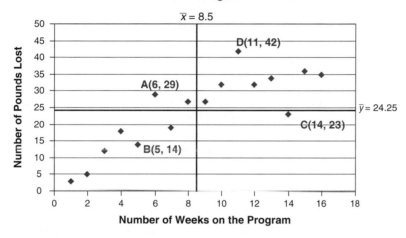

A random sample of participants reported how many weeks they had been on the program, and the number of pounds lost.

$$r = \frac{\sum(x - \bar{x})(y - \bar{y})}{(n - 1)s_x s_y}$$

We will focus on the numerator of this calculation, since it governs the sign of the r-value. While we will not evaluate every term in $\sum(x - \bar{x})(y - \bar{y})$, it is instructive to look at some examples. For this data set, $\bar{x} = 8.5$ and $\bar{y} = 24.25$, and these means are shown on the graph in Exhibit 3.32, dividing the graph into four areas.

Now consider the point labelled A on the graph, at $(6, 29)$. For this point,

$$(x_A - \bar{x})(y_A - \bar{y}) = (6 - 8.5)(29 - 24.25) = (-2.5)(4.75) = -11.875$$

which is, of course, a negative number. Notice that the term for the other point in this area of the graph will also produce a negative number. This is because in this area of the graph, all of the *x*-values are *below* $\bar{x}$, so $(x - \bar{x}) < 0$. However, all of the *y*-values are *above* $\bar{y}$, so $(y - \bar{y}) > 0$. Multiplying a negative number by a positive number yields a negative result.

With similar reasoning, we can see that all of the points in the area of the graph where B is located will contribute a *positive* term to the calculation of *r*. All of the *x*-values in this area are *below* $\bar{x}$, so $(x - \bar{x}) < 0$. All of the *y*-values are *below* $\bar{y}$, so $(y - \bar{y}) < 0$. Multiplying two negative terms yields a positive result. For the point labelled B, the term is

$$(x_B - \bar{x})(y_B - \bar{y}) = (5 - 8.5)(14 - 24.25) = (-3.5)(-10.25) = +35.875$$

Following on, you should be able to see that all of the points in the area of point C on the graph will contribute a negative term to the calculation of *r*. All of the points in the area of point D will contribute a positive term to the calculation of *r*. These conclusions are summarized in Exhibit 3.33 below.

EXHIBIT 3.33

Scatter Diagram of Weight-Loss Results

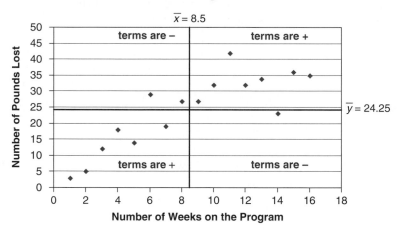

Finally, you should be able to see that the number and the value of positive terms (there are 13 positive terms) in the calculation of *r* far outweigh the number of negative terms (there are only 3 negative terms) for this data set. As a result, $\sum(x - \bar{x})(y - \bar{y})$ will be a positive number, leading to a positive correlation coefficient. In fact, in this case, $r = 0.84$, indicating a strong positive correlation between the number of weeks on the program and the number of pounds lost.

Now, apply the same reasoning about positive and negative terms in the $\sum(x - \bar{x})(y - \bar{y})$ calculation for the scatter diagram shown in Exhibit 3.34 opposite.

In this case, the negative terms far outweigh the positive terms, and so the correlation coefficient will be negative. In fact, for the data set shown above, $r = -0.87$.

EXHIBIT **3.34**

r < 0 for a Negative Relationship

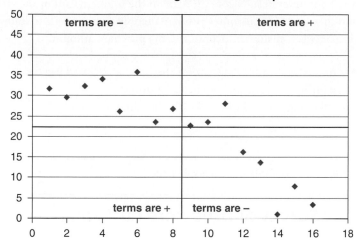

EXHIBIT **3.35**

Now consider the case illustrated by Exhibit 3.35 below. In this case, the numbers and values of the positive and negative terms in the $\sum(x - \bar{x})(y - \bar{y})$ calculation will approximately offset each other, leading to a correlation coefficient near zero. In fact, for this data set, $r = 0.08$.

EXHIBIT **3.35**

r Is Close to Zero

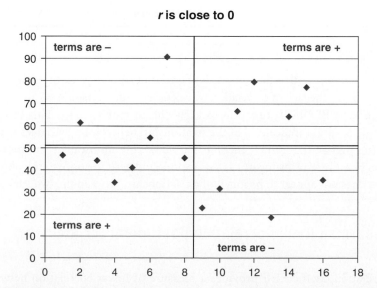

EXAMPLE 3.4A

Calculating the Pearson correlation coefficient

EXA03-4a

Lynda Parks has surveyed a random sample of the customers who shop at the drugstore she owns. The survey results contain data on the total amount of the customer's most recent purchase, and the customer's annual income. Lynda wants to know if there is a relationship between customer income and the purchase amount.

The first step is to create a scatter diagram for the data set. We will use this to see if the data appear to be linearly related, and to check for outliers.

An Excel scatter diagram is shown below in Exhibit 3.36.

EXHIBIT 3.36

Scatter Diagram of Drugstore Customer Survey Results

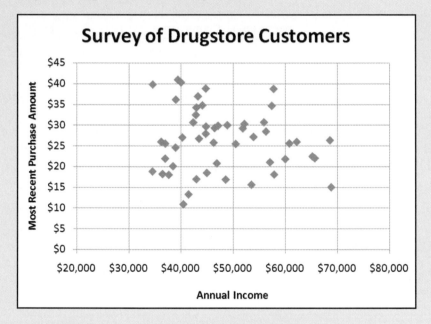

It does not appear that there is much of a relationship between these two variables, but we'll confirm the lack of correlation by calculating the Pearson *r*.

Use Excel's **PEARSON** function to arrive at an *r* of −0.119. This might seem surprising, because it indicates that the relationship between the variables is negative, that is, the higher the annual income, the *lower* the amount of the most recent purchase. However, this value of *r* is close enough to zero to confirm the observation that there does not appear to be much of a relationship between the two variables.

The Spearman Rank Correlation Coefficient for Ranked Variables

The correlation coefficient *r* provides a measure of linear correlation between two quantitative variables. However, it has some weaknesses:

1. The correlation coefficient r does not identify non-linear correlations.
2. The correlation coefficient r can be greatly affected by outliers, to the extent that it may give a misleading indication of correlation.

There is an alternative measure of correlation that identifies both linear and non-linear correlations, and is not so affected by outliers. It is called the Spearman rank correlation coefficient, and is usually denoted r_S. The Spearman rank correlation coefficient has another advantage: it can be used to calculate a measure of association between two variables when one or both of them are ranked data. The **Spearman rank correlation coefficient** is a numerical measure that indicates the strength and direction of the relationship (linear or non-linear) for two variables, one or both of which may be ranked.

The Spearman rank correlation coefficient is calculated in the same way as the Pearson correlation coefficient, but is based on the ranks of the x- and y-variables, not the actual values of the data. The ranking process is fairly straightforward. All of the x-values are ranked from smallest to largest, with ranks from 1 to n. Similarly, all y-values are ranked from smallest to largest, with ranks from 1 to n. The only complication arises when a value occurs more than once. When this occurs, the ranks of the tied values are averaged. Example 3.4B below illustrates the ranking process, and calculation of the Spearman rank correlation coefficient.

Spearman rank correlation coefficient A numerical measure that indicates the strength and direction of the relationship (linear or non-linear) for two variables, one or both of which may be ranked.

EXAMPLE 3.4B

Calculating the Spearman rank correlation coefficient

A head office manager is concerned about the employee turnover rate at some of the local branches. On the basis of an employee survey, the manager ranks the branches according to how satisfied the employees are with the working conditions at the branch (the branch rated 1 is the branch where employees are most satisfied). The manager then collects some data on employee turnover, calculated as the number of employee terminations (because of firing or someone quitting) as a percentage of the total number of employees. Since a high turnover rate may suggest retention issues, the manager wants to see if there is an association between the branch ranking by the employees and the turnover rate. The data for the 10 branches is shown in Exhibit 3.37 below.

EXHIBIT 3.37

Employee Ranking and Turnover Rate

Branch Location	Rank of Branch by Local Employees	Employee Turnover Rate
Whitby	1	4.50
Ajax	2	4.00
Pickering	3	4.50
Oshawa	4	5.70
Scarborough	5	15.20
Oakville	6	14.70
Woodbridge	7	10.30
Mississauga	8	13.40
Hamilton	9	9.60
Waterloo	10	17.00

Since the rankings of each branch by the local employees are ranked data, the manager must use the Spearman rank correlation coefficient to measure the association between the two variables. In this case, the ranking of the branches is already done. The ranking process is illustrated in Exhibit 3.38 below.

EXHIBIT 3.38

Ranking Process

Branch Location	Rank of Branch by Local Employees	Employee Turnover Ratio	Ranks to Be Assigned	Assigned Ranks
Whitby	1	4.50	3	2.5
Ajax	2	4.00	1	1
Pickering	3	4.50	2	2.5
Oshawa	4	5.70	4	4
Scarborough	5	15.20	9	9
Oakville	6	14.70	8	8
Woodbridge	7	10.30	6	6
Mississauga	8	13.40	7	7
Hamilton	9	9.60	5	5
Waterloo	10	17.00	10	10

The employee turnover ratios must be ranked, from smallest to largest, with ranks from 1 to 10. There are two locations with the same employee turnover ratio (Whitby and Pickering). The ranks that must be assigned to the two locations are 2 and 3. Since the employee turnover ratios are the same, the associated ranks should also be the same. This is achieved by averaging the two ranks involved, and assigning the averaged rank to each location. We assign a rank of $\frac{2 + 3}{2} = 2.5$ to each location.

Now that the ranks are calculated, the Spearman rank correlation coefficient can be calculated. This can be done with Excel, as usual, using the **PEARSON** function on the ranks of the data. The result for this data set is $r_S = 0.75$ (you should check this in Excel). This indicates that the ranking of the branch by local employees is fairly strongly associated with the employee turnover ratio. The higher the turnover ratio, the lower the ranking by employees.

Notice that in Example 3.4B, the employee rating of 1 corresponds to "best," and so the lowest assigned rank corresponds to the best employee rating. If we thought that low employee turnover ratios (low assigned ranks) were associated with good ratings by employees (low assigned ranks), we would expect a positive correlation between the assigned ranks.

However, suppose that instead of employee turnover ratios, we had data about the number of employees with at least three years of service. The lowest assigned rank of 1 would then be assigned to the lowest number of employees with at least three years of experience, the worst case. In this case, if we thought that good employee ratings (low ranks) were associated with a greater number of employees with at least three years of service (high ranks), we would expect a negative correlation between the assigned ranks. Always take a minute to think about the rankings before you assign them, and you will avoid confusion about the meaning of the Spearman *r*. Otherwise, you might confuse the meaning of negative and positive correlations.

While ranking the data was straightforward in this example, it can be quite tedious for larger data sets. Unfortunately, Excel does not provide for this ranking process. There is an Excel add-in that comes with the text, which ranks the data correctly and calculates the Spearman rank correlation coefficient.

Once the add-ins are installed (see instructions on page xxx), click on **Add-Ins**, then **Non-parametric Tools**, and then select **Spearman Rank Correlation Coefficient Calculations** as illustrated in Exhibit 3.39 below.

EXHIBIT 3.39

Non-parametric Tools Dialogue Box

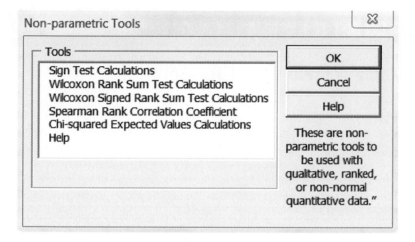

Exhibit 3.40 shows the next dialogue box, which is self-explanatory.

EXHIBIT 3.40

Spearman Rank Correlation Coefficient Calculation

You must indicate where the sample data are located, and where you want the output to go. The output will be as shown below in Exhibit 3.41.

EXHIBIT 3.41

Spearman Rank Correlation Coefficient Calculation

Spearman Rank Correlation Coefficient Calculation	
Spearman r	0.747724

GUIDE TO DECISION MAKING

Choosing a Measure of Association

1. The Pearson correlation coefficient (r) is the preferred measure of association for quantitative data. However, it can be affected by outliers, and is less reliable when these are present in the data. As well, it is a measure of linear association only.

2. The Spearman rank correlation coefficient (r_S) can be used as a measure of both linear and non-linear association between two variables. It may provide a better indication of the correlation between two quantitative variables when there are outliers in the data. The Spearman rank correlation coefficient can also be used as a measure of association when one or both of the variables are ranked.

DEVELOP YOUR SKILLS 3.4

16. In Develop Your Skills 2.5, Exercise 21, you were asked to produce a scatter diagram for data on household income and monthly spending on restaurant meals. Calculate an appropriate measure of association for these two variables.

DYS03-16

17. Jack runs a small convenience store, where he sells freshly baked cookies. Jack has experimented by charging different prices for the cookies on randomly selected days, and recording the quantity sold. A scatter diagram for the data is shown opposite in Exhibit 3.42.

Which of the following r-values best matches this scatter diagram? Why?
a. $+0.75$
b. -0.88
c. $+0.22$
d. -0.11

18. The human resources department is interested in whether there is a relationship between the rankings of new hires by their recruiter and by their supervisor. A random sample of 10 employees is selected from a large group of employees hired by a single

DYS03-18

EXHIBIT 3.42

Scatter Diagram of Cookie Prices and Quantities Sold

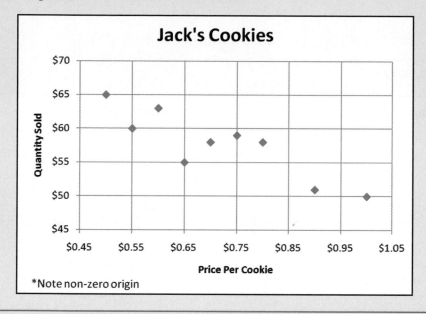

recruiter, to be assigned to a single supervisor. The recruiter is asked to rank the 10 employees at the time of hiring. The supervisor is then asked to rank them a year later.

Does it appear that there is a correlation between the recruiter's rankings and the supervisor's rankings? Explain.

19. A college professor has collected data for a random sample of 45 students. She has asked them to keep track of their total hours of paid employment for the semester, and she has also recorded each student's semester average mark. Does it appear that there is a linear correlation between the hours of work and the average mark? Explain.

DYS03-19

20. Two of the data sets depicted in Exhibit 3.43 below have an *r*-value of 0.73, and one has an *r*-value of −0.90. Indicate which *r*-value belongs to each graph. How can the *r*-values be the same for the two graphs you have picked?

EXHIBIT **3.43**

Three Graphs of Service and Salary

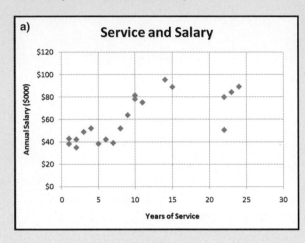

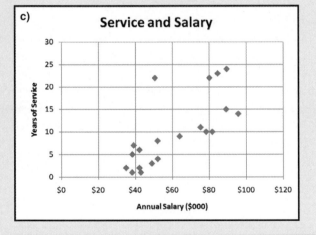

Some Useful Notation

Summation notation is frequently used in statistical formulas. For example:

$$\sum_{i=1}^{n} x_1 = \sum x = x_1 + x_2 + x_3 + \cdots + x_n$$

Examples 3.1A to 3.1H on pages 103 to 105 illustrate how to evaluate some terms you will encounter in statistical formulas.

Measures of Central Tendency

Some measure of central tendency is generally of interest when we examine a data set.

The mean is calculated by adding up all the numbers in the data set, and then dividing by the number of numbers. The sample mean is given the notation $\bar{x}$, and the population mean is given the notation μ. Formulas for their calculation are:

$$\bar{x} = \frac{\sum x}{n} \quad \text{and} \quad \mu = \frac{\sum x}{N}$$

The deviation from the mean for each data point is the distance of the point from the mean value. The sum of all the deviations from the mean is always zero; that is, $\sum (x - \bar{x}) = 0$.

While the mean is the most widely used measure of central location, it has some limitations. It can be used only for quantitative data. It is also affected by extreme values, and this makes it a less satisfying indication of central tendency for skewed data sets. Calculation of the mean is done with the **AVERAGE** function in Excel.

The median is the middle value (if there is a unique middle value), or the average of the two middle values (when there is not a unique middle value) in an ordered data set. There is no commonly accepted notation for the median. In a data set of n numbers, the median will be located at the $0.50(n + 1)^{\text{th}}$ place (this holds true for both sample and population data). Calculation of the median is done with the **MEDIAN** function in Excel.

The mode is another measure of central tendency that is sometimes useful. The mode is the most frequently occurring value in the data set. The mode is most often used in reference to the shape of a histogram. Calculation of the mode can be done with the **MODE** function in Excel, although this function will identify only one mode (the first in the list), and is therefore not reliable for multi-modal data.

A Guide to Decision Making for choosing a measure of central tendency is shown on page 114.

Measures of Variability

Some measure of variability is generally of interest when we examine a data set. One measure of variability is the range. The range of the data set is a number that is calculated as the difference between the maximum and minimum values in the data set.

The standard deviation is a measure of variability in a data set that is based on deviations from the mean. The sample standard deviation is given the notation s, and the population standard deviation is given the notation σ. The formulas are as follows:

$$s = \sqrt{\frac{\sum (x - \bar{x})^2}{n - 1}} \quad \text{and} \quad \sigma = \sqrt{\frac{\sum (x - \mu)^2}{N}}$$

The computational formula for the sample standard deviation is

$$s = \sqrt{\frac{\sum x^2 - \frac{(\sum x)^2}{n}}{n - 1}}$$

The standard deviation is a measure of variability, with a larger standard deviation indicating greater variability. For data sets with a symmetric bell-shaped distribution, the standard deviation has some very useful additional properties. In such cases, the Empirical Rule applies.

1. About 68% of the data points will lie within one standard deviation of the mean.
2. About 95% of the data points will lie within two standard deviations of the mean.
3. Almost all of the data points will lie within three standard deviations of the mean.

You can check to see if the distribution has the appropriate shape by creating a histogram for the data.

The sample standard deviation is calculated with the **STDEV** function in Excel. The standard deviation is affected by outliers, and so is not an appropriate measure of variability for badly skewed data. In this case, the interquartile range (IQR) should be used. $IQR = Q_3 - Q_1$, where Q_3 is the 75th percentile of the data set, and Q_1 is the 25th percentile. Q_1 is located at the $0.25(n + 1)$th place in an ordered data set. Q_3 is located at the $0.75(n + 1)$th place in an ordered data set.

Excel does not have a built-in tool to calculate the interquartile range. However, Excel does have a function to calculate Q_1 and Q_3. Once you have calculated the 1st and 3rd quartiles, you have to enter a formula into Excel to calculate the difference. Exhibit 3.26 on page 130 shows an excerpt from an Excel spreadsheet where the IQR is calculated. The formulas are revealed for your reference. Excel produces slightly different values for Q_1 and Q_3 than those produced by the formulas given above.

A Guide to Decision Making for choosing the best measure of variability for a data set is shown on page 131.

Measures of Association

The Pearson correlation coefficient is a numerical measure that indicates the strength and direction of the linear relationship between two quantitative variables. The notation for the correlation coefficient is r (or sometimes the "Pearson r"). The Pearson correlation coefficient can take on values between -1 and $+1$. An r of -1 signifies a perfect negative linear relationship. An r of $+1$ signifies a perfect positive relationship. An r of 0 indicates no apparent linear relationship. The relationship is stronger the further the r-value is from zero in either direction.

A value of r that is close to $+1$ or -1 does not *prove* that there is a cause-and-effect relationship between the x- and y-variables involved. All we can say is that the variables are highly correlated, and any conclusions about causality must be made on the basis of an understanding of the context of the data being analyzed. Calculation of the Pearson r is done in Excel with the **PEARSON** function.

The correlation coefficient r provides a measure of linear correlation between two quantitative variables. However, it has some weaknesses:

1. The correlation coefficient r does not identify non-linear correlations.
2. The correlation coefficient r can be greatly affected by outliers, to the extent that it may give a misleading indication of correlation.

The Spearman rank correlation coefficient (usually denoted r_S) is an alternative measure of correlation that identifies both linear and non-linear correlations, and is not so affected by outliers. It can also be used to calculate a measure of association between two variables when one or both of them are ranked data.

The Spearman rank correlation coefficient is calculated in the same way as the Pearson correlation coefficient, but is based on the ranks of the x- and y-variables, not the actual values of the data. All of the x-values are ranked from smallest to largest, with ranks from 1 to n. Similarly, all y-values are ranked from smallest to largest, with ranks from 1 to n. When a value appears more than once in the x- or y-values, the ranks for the tied values are averaged.

An Excel add-in that comes with the text ranks the data and calculates the Spearman rank correlation coefficient. Instructions for its use are given on page 141.

A Guide to Decision Making for choosing the best measure of association is shown on page 142.

CHAPTER REVIEW EXERCISES

It is usual, when investigating a data set, to examine it both graphically and with numerical summary measures. Often, it is necessary to create a graph for the data to assess the shape of the distribution before deciding on the appropriate measures of central tendency and variability. Some of these exercises refer to data sets you have already examined graphically in Chapter 2.

WARM-UP EXERCISES

1. The mean mark on Test 1 in a Microeconomics course was 62%, while the median mark was 54%. What do these two measures tell us about the distribution of marks on this Microeconomics test?

2. Suppose you are planning to buy a personal service business, and you are trying to decide between a haircutting salon and a day spa offering manicures, pedicures, and massages. Some summary data for the two businesses are shown below in Exhibit 3.44.

EXHIBIT 3.44

Summary Data for Two Potential Businesses

Historical Weekly Sales for Two Businesses		
	Haircutting Salon	Day Spa
Mean	$4,720	$4,850
Standard Deviation	$226	$1,215

What do these measures tell you about the businesses? Other things being equal, which one would you be likely to purchase, and why?

3. Calculate the mean, median, mode, standard deviation, and interquartile range for this data set of ages of a random sample of people attending a local fall fair.

EXHIBIT 3.45

Ages of People Attending a Fall Fair

Ages of a Random Sample of Attendees at a Local Fall Fair				
58	12	8	20	13
19	43	40	64	32
9	22	8	20	30
50	21	31	12	9

4. For the first three semesters at college, Jane has been keeping track of the amount of time she spends studying for each test, and her mark on the test. For a similar time period, Don has been keeping track of the number of calories he consumes the day before he writes each test, and his mark on the test. Jane has calculated a Pearson r of $+0.71$, and Don has calculated a Pearson r of $+0.88$. Indicate what these values tell us about the correlations in

Jane's and Don's data sets. In which case is the cause-and-effect relationship likely to be stronger, and why?

5. In Example 3.4A, no linear relationship was found between the amount of the most recent purchase and income in the survey of drugstore customers. Does this result from the survey prove that there is no relationship? Explain.

THINK AND DECIDE

6. The owner of a music store asks the cashiers to keep track of the spending by a random sample of female customers, and a random sample of male customers, over several days. The purchases are shown in Exhibit 3.46 below.

EXHIBIT 3.46

Music Store Purchases by a Random Sample of Customers

Purchases by Females	Purchases by Males
$29.50	$32.49
$17.83	$29.88
$40.66	$32.77
$45.15	$25.95
$43.98	$22.26
$41.56	$28.66
$21.25	$26.77
$33.49	$35.32
$50.43	$19.29
$19.70	$40.25
$23.65	$28.09
$30.64	$31.51
$19.30	$25.96
$21.34	$25.34
$24.40	

Calculate appropriate measures of central tendency and variability, and comment. (Refer to graphs you created for Chapter Review Exercise 6 in Chapter 2.)

7. A clothing manufacturer is concerned that the heights of young men aged 18 to 24 might have changed since the patterns in use were first designed. A random sample of young men aged 18 to 24 was selected. The average height in the sample data was 177.2 cm, with a standard deviation of 7.2 cm. A histogram of the sample data was symmetric and bell-shaped. Assuming this sample is representative of the population, what proportion of young men aged 18 to 24 are shorter than 170 cm? What proportion of young men aged 18 to 24 are taller than 199 cm?

8. Annual sales for two printing shop franchises are shown opposite in Exhibit 3.47. Calculate an appropriate measure of variability. Which enterprise had more variable sales over the period?

EXHIBIT 3.47

Printing Shop Annual Sales ($000)

	Annual Sales ($000)	
	Red Deer	**Vernon**
2004	109.55	122.01
2005	102.52	118.14
2006	114.91	107.85
2007	122.48	121.34
2008	122.12	112.30
2009	123.96	117.29
2010	122.36	122.27

9. Hannah Milne is investigating the cost of cartridges for her inkjet printer. She decides to call several local suppliers of cartridges to collect data on prices. The results are shown in Exhibit 3.48 below.

EXHIBIT 3.48

Prices of Inkjet Printer Cartridge

$19.99	$24.97	$33.13	$26.92	$34.50	$29.99	$23.95	$21.97

What is the mean price? What is the median price?

10. A manufacturer sells plastic jars of alfalfa honey, in 500 g containers. The actual (carefully measured) weights of 10 jars of honey are recorded (the weights are adjusted for the weight of the jar itself). What is the mean weight of honey in the jars? Do you think this result means that the company is systematically under-filling the honey jars? The weights are shown in Exhibit 3.49 below.

EXHIBIT 3.49

Precise Weights (g) of 500 g Jars of Honey

510	491	489	504	490	513	502	480	488	506

11. A company is trying a new product line in a random sample of stores. Previously, the average of sales at all stores was $5,000 a week. Weekly sales at the stores trying out the new product line were recorded, with the results shown in Exhibit 3.50 below.

EXHIBIT 3.50

Weekly Sales at Random Sample of Stores Trying the New Product Line

$5,117	$5,167	$5,267	$5,451	$5,430
$5,577	$4,900	$5,036	$5,601	$4,801
$5,224	$4,635	$4,592	$4,831	$4,887

Calculate appropriate measures of central tendency and variability for this data set. Would it be appropriate to apply the Empirical Rule to this data set? If so, almost all of the sales would be in what range?

12. An automotive parts manufacturing plant has been working hard to reduce employee absences. In the past, the average number of days off work (other than vacation) per year has been 6.6. The company has introduced a wellness program to encourage workers to eat well, exercise regularly, and lead healthier lifestyles. The absences of a random sample of 25 employees were examined for the current year, and are shown in Exhibit 3.51 below.

EXHIBIT 3.51

Annual Days Off Work (Other than Vacation) for a Random Sample of Employees

4	4.5	5.5	5	5.5	9	7.5	4	7.5	6.5
6	5.5	6.5	6.5	6	5	6	4.5	7	7
8	7	4.5	5.5	7					

Calculate appropriate measures of central tendency and variability for this data set. Do you think the annual days off work have decreased because of the wellness program?

13. Some management trainees across several branches of an electronics store were rated by their customers, and by their bosses. Comment on the correlation between the two sets of ratings. The data are shown in Exhibit 3.52 below. A rating of "1" is excellent, and a rating of "5" is poor. Do the ranking by hand, and then use Excel to calculate the Spearman rank correlation coefficient, using the **PEARSON** function on your assigned ranks. Also, use the add-in for Spearman Rank Correlation Coefficient on the data. (You should get the same answer.)

EXHIBIT 3.52

Management Trainees' Ratings

Ratings by Customers	Ratings by Bosses
2	3
2	4
3	2
4	1
3	2
3	2
2	4
2	1
1	3
2	2

THINK AND DECIDE USING EXCEL

CRE03-14

14. A survey of pedestrian traffic is conducted over 45 days for two locations where a manager is thinking of opening a new location. Calculate appropriate measures of central tendency and variability for these data, and comment. (Refer to graphs you created for Chapter Review Exercise 14 in Chapter 2.)

15. A Statistics teacher is wondering whether there is a relationship between the marks of students in their first-year Business Math course, and their marks in the second-year Statistics course. Calculate the appropriate measure of association for these data, and comment. (Refer to a graph you created for Review Exercise 17 in Chapter 2.)

CRE03-15

16. Woodbon produces high-quality wooden furniture. Woodbon's owner, Kate Cameron, collects the annual advertising and sales figures for the last several years. Calculate an appropriate measure of association for these data, and comment. (Refer to a graph you created for Review Exercise 18 in Chapter 2.)

CRE03-16

17. Calculate appropriate measures of central tendency and variability for the incomes of customers in the survey of drugstore customers, first discussed in Chapter 2, and comment. (Refer to the graph you created for Develop Your Skills 2.2, Exercise 7.)

CRE03-17

18. Two financial advisors who have been working at the same company for about five years have decided to compare their customer characteristics. Wally Johnson has 167 clients with Registered Retirement Savings Plans (RRSPs). Kate Moore has 202 clients with RRSPs. The amounts in the RRSPs for both sets of customers are available in MyStatLab. Use appropriate numerical measures to compare the amounts of client RRSPs for Kate and Wally.

CRE03-18

19. Cans of soup are supposed to contain 540 mL. A random sample of 35 cans of soup is selected from the production line, and their contents measured carefully. Assume this sample is representative of the population. The company wants to be sure that the soup cans contain no more than 556 mL. Based on this sample, is there any cause for concern that the cans being produced contain more than 556 mL? The company is also concerned about customer complaints. About what percentage of the soup cans being produced will have less than 530 mL?

CRE03-19

20. Repeat Exercise 19 above, but with the new data set for this exercise.

CRE03-20

TEST YOUR KNOWLEDGE

21. Access Statistics Canada Table 187-0001, "Quarterly Balance Sheet and Income Statement," by North American Industry Classification System (NAICS) (you can access these data through E-STAT). From this table, retrieve data about quarterly operating profits for the retail trade sector, from the first quarter of 1988 to the most recent data available. Use appropriate graphical and numerical measures to summarize these data, commenting on the amounts of quarterly profits, and patterns over time. Compare the operating profits of the retail sector with those of the manufacturing sector, and analyze the nature and strength of any relationship between the quarterly profits of the two sectors.

CHAPTER 4

Calculating Probabilities

LEARNING OBJECTIVES

After mastering the material in this chapter, you will be able to:

1 Understand what probability is, and use both the classical and relative frequency probability approaches.

2 Calculate conditional probabilities and use them to test for independence.

3 Use basic probability rules to calculate "and," "or," and "not" probabilities.

INTRODUCTION

Most business decisions must be made with incomplete information, and there is usually some uncertainty about the impacts of particular decisions. Probability analysis allows us to make the best use of the (usually limited) information that is available to us, and to measure or estimate uncertainty. More importantly, probability analysis allows us to draw generally reliable inferences from sample data. In this chapter, we will cover some basic probability concepts, and start to build the probability skills needed for statistical inference.

Probability analysis involves experiments, events, and sample spaces. An **experiment** is any activity with an uncertain outcome. An **event** is one or more outcomes of an experiment. A **sample space** is a complete list or representation of all of the possible outcomes of an experiment. **Probability** is a measure of the likelihood of an event. It indicates the percentage of times the event is likely to occur when the experiment is repeated a large number of times.

Let's put this language in a particular context. Suppose George Wilson is running an Internet service provider called GeorgeConn, and he has an accurate database of customer information, including whether each customer has an urban or a rural address.

Here is an *experiment:* George randomly selects one customer from his database. Suppose George is interested in whether the customer lives in an urban or rural area, and whether the customer is satisfied with the service or not. Then George can create the *sample space* of his experiment, that is, a list of all possible outcomes: {urban and satisfied, urban and dissatisfied, rural and satisfied, rural and dissatisfied}. Here is an *event* George might be interested in: whether the customer has an urban address or not.

The **classical definition of probability** is based on counting. If there are n equally likely possible outcomes of an experiment, and m of them correspond to the event you are interested in, then the probability of the event is $\frac{m}{n}$. Suppose George has 800 customers in total, and 480 of them are urban. Then the probability of randomly selecting an urban customer is $\frac{480}{800} = 0.60$.

The standard notation for probability is P(event). The P here stands for *probability* and P followed by brackets means *the probability of.* Notice that the P and the brackets () cannot be separated (and do not, in this case, indicate multiplication). The uppercase P is a mathematical operator that is standard mathematical shorthand for *the probability of.* So, P(urban customer) = 0.60.

The **relative frequency approach to probability** is based on a large number of repeated trials of an experiment. Probability is the relative frequency of an event over this large number of trials.

Suppose George conducts his experiment just once, and he selects an urban customer. Based on only one trial, his estimate of the probability of selecting an urban customer would be 100%, which we know is not accurate. If George repeats his experiment 10 times, it is more likely that he will select some urban and some rural customers, and his estimate of the probability of selecting an urban customer will improve. If George repeats his experiment 10,000 times, it is quite likely that he will have randomly selected close to 6,000 urban customers, and his estimate of P(urban customer) will be very close to 0.60.

George may not have a customer database, or have time to conduct 10,000 experiments. It is still possible for George to obtain some probability information about his customers by taking a random sample of them. Suppose George does this, and records two types of data:

• whether they are satisfied or dissatisfied with the service
• whether they are urban customers or rural customers

For the sake of the discussion that follows, we will assume that although George surveyed only 10 customers, this sample is representative of *all* of his customers. The customer data can be represented as shown in Exhibit 4.1.

Experiment Any activity with an uncertain outcome.

Event One or more outcomes of an experiment.

Sample space A complete list or representation of all of the possible outcomes of an experiment.

Probability A measure of the likelihood of an event.

Classical definition of probability If there are n equally likely possible outcomes of an experiment, and m of them correspond to the event you are interested in, then the probability of the event is $\frac{m}{n}$.

Relative frequency approach to probability Probability is the relative frequency of an event over a large number of repeated trials of an experiment.

EXHIBIT 4.1

A Random Sample of GeorgeConn's Customers

Customer	Urban or Rural? R: Customer is rural U: Customer is urban	Satisfied or Not? S: Customer is satisfied N: Customer is not satisfied
1	U	N
2	R	S
3	U	S
4	R	N
5	U	S
6	U	S
7	R	S
8	R	S
9	U	N
10	U	S

4.1   SAMPLE SPACES AND BASIC PROBABILITIES

One of the keys to successful probability analysis is a good understanding of the sample space, that is, all the possible outcomes of an experiment. Usually, you will have partial information about the probabilities of the outcomes in the sample space, and you will have to use this information and the structure of the sample space to calculate the missing probabilities.

There is more than one way to represent a sample space, and we will examine three of them for the GeorgeConn sample. We often streamline our references to particular events with letters, so that our probability arithmetic is easier to do. The sample spaces shown below rely on the following notation:

- *S*: customer is satisfied
- *N*: customer is not satisfied
- *U*: customer is urban
- *R*: customer is rural

List of All Possible Outcomes   A sample space can be represented with a list of all possibilities. One way to list the sample space for selection of one of GeorgeConn's customers is {*R* and *S*, *R* and *N*, *U* and *S*, *U* and *N*}. If we were interested only in whether customers were urban or rural, we could list the sample space as {*U*, *R*}. If we were interested only in whether the customers were satisfied or not, we could list the sample space as {*S*, *N*}. The particular representation we choose depends on the characteristics and events we are investigating.

If we refer to Exhibit 4.1, we can count the number of customers in the sample who are urban or rural, and satisfied or not. The counts are shown in Exhibit 4.2 below.

EXHIBIT 4.2

Sample Space and Customer Counts for a Random Sample of GeorgeConn's Customers

Sample Space Listing	Count from Random Sample
R and S	3
R and N	1
U and S	4
U and N	2
Total	10

With this information, it is easy to estimate some probabilities. For example, what is the probability that a randomly selected customer is satisfied with GeorgeConn's service? From the list, we can see that there are 3 rural customers who are satisfied and 4 urban customers who are satisfied, out of a total of 10 customers. This yields a relative frequency of $\frac{3+4}{10} = \frac{7}{10} = 0.70$. This relative frequency gives us an estimate of the probability of selecting a satisfied customer. It may be difficult or expensive to get information about the satisfaction levels of all GeorgeConn's customers, so we will use relative frequencies from sample data as probability estimates. The larger the sample size, the better the probability estimate will be.

We can write P(satisfied customer) = P(S) = 0.70.

While it is appropriate to talk about probabilities as percentages, we will use the decimal equivalents (0.70 instead of 70%) because it makes the arithmetic easier.

Tables of Counts or Joint Probabilities   It is also possible (sometimes) to describe the sample space as a table, and this can be useful for organizing information we may have about counts or probabilities. The data collected in the GeorgeConn customer survey could be summarized as a table, as in Exhibit 4.3.

EXHIBIT 4.3

Contingency Table for GeorgeConn's Customers

	Satisfied	Not Satisfied	Total
Rural	3	1	4
Urban	4	2	6
Total	7	3	10

This is an example of a cross-classification table, or contingency table. Such a table is a very useful way of organizing the data. When row and column totals are computed, the table gives us a quick and easy way to calculate probabilities. For example, we can easily see from the table that $P(S) = P(\text{satisfied customer}) = \frac{7}{10} = 0.70$. We can also easily see that $P(U) = P(\text{urban customer}) = \frac{6}{10} = 0.60$.

One further variation is to convert the counts in the table cells to relative frequencies, which can be interpreted as probabilities. Exhibit 4.4 illustrates this for GeorgeConn's customers. Now we can read some probabilities directly from the table. For example, $P(R) = P(\text{rural customer}) = 0.4$. We will discuss *joint* probabilities in this table in more detail later in this chapter.

EXHIBIT 4.4

Joint Probability Table for GeorgeConn's Customers

	Satisfied	Not Satisfied	Total
Rural	$\frac{3}{10} = 0.3$	0.1	0.4
Urban	$\frac{4}{10} = 0.4$	0.2	0.6
Total	$\frac{7}{10} = 0.7$	0.3	1.0

Tree Diagrams   Sometimes diagrams or pictures can be helpful to represent a sample space. We will examine a particular kind of diagram, called a tree diagram. Such diagrams are particularly helpful when there are stages to a probability experiment (for example, select the first customer, then select the second customer) or when there are cross-classifications. Building a tree diagram can be a good way to keep track of all the possible outcomes of an experiment in complicated situations. A tree diagram for GeorgeConn's customer data would look like Exhibit 4.5.

EXHIBIT 4.5

Tree Diagram for GeorgeConn's Customers

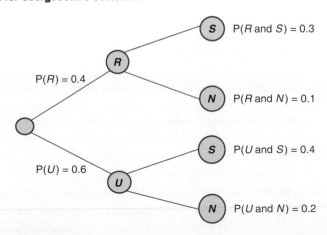

The first stage of the tree splits the data into rural and urban categories. The second stage then splits the data into satisfied and not satisfied customers. Note the probabilities along the first branches. In a tree diagram, the sum of the probabilities over the branches from one node (one of the circles in the diagram) has to equal 1 or 100% (if it does not, you have missed some part of the sample space). All of the branches have probabilities associated with them. At present, this tree diagram is incomplete because some of the probabilities are missing. We will complete it when we have covered conditional probabilities.

Notice that at the end stage of the tree diagram are the four events that correspond to the cells of the tables we already created. The probabilities of these events also sum to 1 or 100%.

Of course, only one representation of the sample space is necessary, and the one you choose will depend on the information available and your personal preferences. It is always a good idea to start your probability calculations with some careful thinking about the sample space.

EXAMPLE 4.1

Representing a sample space with a contingency table, a joint probability table, and a tree diagram

A company has made a health and fitness centre available to its employees. Records show that over the last year, 210 of the 350 employees used the facilities at some time. Of the 170 males who worked for the company, 65 used the facilities.

Create a listing of the sample space for randomly selecting one employee and determining whether the person is male or female, and has or has not used the facilities. Then set up a contingency table to represent the sample space. Finally, use relative frequencies to create a joint probability table, and set up a tree diagram.

Workers can be classified into male and female categories, and then further classified by whether or not they used the health and fitness centre in the last year. One representation of the sample space is shown below in Exhibit 4.6.

EXHIBIT 4.6

Representation of a Sample Space

Sample Space for Employee Use of a Company Health and Fitness Centre
Male and used health and fitness centre
Male and did not use health and fitness centre
Female and used health and fitness centre
Female and did not use health and fitness centre

In order to use the sample space to calculate probabilities, we will have to know the counts for each of the items in the sample space. There are 350 employees altogether, and 170 of these are male. This means there must be $350 - 170 = 180$ females. We are told that 210 workers used the facilities at some time, and that 65 males used the facilities. This means that $210 - 65 = 145$ females used the facilities. If 65 males out of

170 used the facilities, this means that 105 male employees did not use the facilities. If 145 out of 180 females used the facilities, then 35 female employees did not use the facilities. Exhibit 4.7 below shows the sample space with the associated counts.

EXHIBIT 4.7

Sample Space with Associated Counts

Sample Space for Employee Use of a Company Health and Fitness Centre	
Male and used health and fitness centre	65
Male and did not use health and fitness centre	105
Female and used health and fitness centre	145
Female and did not use health and fitness centre	35

The contingency table to summarize the information could look as shown in Exhibit 4.8. The numbers that were given originally are shown in black. The numbers we calculated above are shown in red. Totals calculated from these are shown in blue.

EXHIBIT 4.8

Contingency Table

Employee Use of a Company Health and Fitness Centre			
	Males	Females	Total
Used the facilities	65	145	210
Did not use the facilities	105	35	140
Total	170	180	350

It is straightforward to convert the frequencies into probabilities. The probability of a randomly selected person from the sample being a male who used the facilities is $\frac{65}{350} = 0.1857$. The probability that a randomly selected person from the sample is a female who used the facilities is $\frac{145}{350} = 0.4143$. The probability that a randomly selected person from the sample used the facilities is $\frac{210}{350} = 0.6$, and so on. A completed table of probabilities is shown below in Exhibit 4.9.

EXHIBIT 4.9

Joint Probability Table

Probabilities of Employee Use of a Company Health and Fitness Centre			
	Males	Females	Total
Used the facilities	$\frac{65}{350} = 0.1857$	0.4143	0.6
Did not use the facilities	0.3000	0.1000	0.4
Total	0.4857	0.5143	1.0

Finally, a tree diagram to represent the sample space might look as shown in Exhibit 4.10 (notice that the tree diagram might just as well have started with the split between those who used the facilities and those who did not). We will use the letters
- *M* to represent the event that an employee is male
- *F* to represent the event that an employee is female
- *U* for the event that the employee used the health and fitness facilities
- *D* for the event that the employee did not use the health and fitness facilities

EXHIBIT **4.10**

Employee Use of a Company Health and Fitness Centre

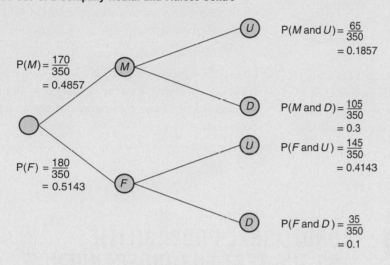

$P(M) = \frac{170}{350}$
$= 0.4857$

$P(F) = \frac{180}{350}$
$= 0.5143$

$P(M \text{ and } U) = \frac{65}{350}$
$= 0.1857$

$P(M \text{ and } D) = \frac{105}{350}$
$= 0.3$

$P(F \text{ and } U) = \frac{145}{350}$
$= 0.4143$

$P(F \text{ and } D) = \frac{35}{350}$
$= 0.1$

Notice that we have still not filled in the probabilities along some of the branches. We will learn how to do this in the next section, where we explore conditional probabilities.

DEVELOP YOUR SKILLS **4.1**

For each of the exercises below, start by creating a representation of the sample space (your choice). Then use it to calculate the probabilities.

1. A random sample of 350 workers at a car parts manufacturing plant are surveyed. Of the 350, all come to work by car. 246 commute more than 40 kilometres to work. 150 of the employees arrange rides with other workers. 135 of those who commute more than 40 kilometres to work drive alone.

a. What is the probability that a randomly selected employee from the sample commutes more than 40 kilometres to work?

b. What is the probability that a randomly selected employee from the sample arranges rides with other workers?

2. The human resources department has classified all company employees according to highest level of education attained, and job classification. Education

levels are high school, up to four years of post-secondary education, graduate degree, and post-graduate studies. Job classifications are clerical, professional, and managerial. The company has 37 managers, 10 of whom have either a graduate degree or post-graduate studies. None of these has only high school education. What is the probability that a randomly selected manager has up to four years of post-secondary education?

3. Refer back to the information contained in Exercise 2 above. The company has 520 employees, of whom 372 are professionals. What is the probability that a randomly selected employee is in the professional classification? What is the probability that a randomly selected employee is in the clerical classification?

4. A random sample of 100 customers at a grocery store were asked to classify themselves as making a quick trip, doing a major stock-up, or doing a fill-in shop. 62 of the customers said they were making quick trips, and 13 were doing major stock-ups. What is the probability that a grocery store customer is doing a fill-in shop? Assume the relative frequencies from the sample are good estimates of the probabilities.

5. On the first day of class, a statistics teacher asked the class to choose one of the following items as the best description of their previous experience in math courses.

- loved previous math courses
- worked very hard in previous math courses, but did not enjoy them
- thought previous math courses were far too difficult
- equated previous math courses with sticking needles in the eyes

Of the 225 students surveyed, 56 said they loved previous math courses. What is the probability that a randomly selected student from the survey did not love his/her previous math courses?

4.2 CONDITIONAL PROBABILITIES AND THE TEST FOR INDEPENDENCE

Conditional Probabilities

While it might be interesting to George Wilson that 60% of his customers are urban, there are other, perhaps more interesting questions that he might want to ask. For example, does the level of satisfaction with his service differ between the rural customers and the urban customers? If it does, he might want to figure out why, and change his approach accordingly.

In order to judge whether location (urban vs. rural) is related to customer satisfaction, you have to understand something about conditional probabilities. A **conditional probability** is the probability of an event (call it A), *given that* another event (call it B) has already occurred. The usual notation is $P(A|B)$, read *the probability* of A, *given* B.

What is the probability that a randomly selected urban customer is satisfied with GeorgeConn's service? This is a conditional probability, because George is no longer interested in *all* of his customers. He is interested only in urban customers. A more formal way to put this would be, what is the probability that a customer is satisfied with GeorgeConn's service, *given that* the customer is urban? The standard notation for this is P(satisfied *given* urban) = $P(S|U)$. The vertical line in the notation corresponds to the words *given that,* which will rarely appear in probability discussions. It will be up to you to recognize conditional probabilities without these words as a guide. Another word that might give you a clue that a conditional probability is required is *if* (e.g., "If the customer is urban, what is the probability that she is satisfied with GeorgeConn's service?"). Often, however, there is no explicit word clue. Remember that the probability is conditional

Conditional probability The probability of an event *A* given that another event *B* has already occurred; the usual notation is P(*A*|*B*), read *the probability of* A, *given* B.

whenever we are examining only a subset (that is, a limited part) of the entire sample space. This will be your only reliable indication that a conditional probability is required. Consider the list of GeorgeConn's customers shown in Exhibit 4.11 below.

The customer list has been rearranged so that all the satisfied urban customers are listed first.

EXHIBIT 4.11

A Random Sample of GeorgeConn's Customers

Customer	Urban or Rural? R: Customer is rural U: Customer is urban	Satisfied or Not? S: Customer is satisfied N: Customer is not satisfied
3	U	S
5	U	S
6	U	S
10	U	S
1	U	N
9	U	N
2	R	S
4	R	N
7	R	S
8	R	S

From this list, we can see that there are six urban customers, of whom four are satisfied with GeorgeConn's service.

Therefore, P(satisfied *given* urban) = $P(S|U) = \frac{4}{6} = 0.6667$.

We can also use the contingency table of customer counts to calculate the probability that a customer is satisfied with GeorgeConn's service, given that he or she is urban. See Exhibit 4.12 below.

EXHIBIT 4.12

Contingency Table

	GeorgeConn's Customers		
	Satisfied	Not Satisfied	Total
Rural	3	1	4
Urban	4	2	6
Total	7	3	10

We focus only on the subset of GeorgeConn's customers who are urban, which is the row that is shaded in the table. There are six urban customers, and of these, four are satisfied with GeorgeConn's service. We calculate that P(satisfied *given* urban) = $P(S|U) = \frac{4}{6} = 0.6667$. We can also do a parallel calculation on the contingency table of probabilities: $P(S|U) = \frac{0.4}{0.6} = 0.6667$.

EXAMPLE 4.2A

Calculating conditional probabilities

Suppose you are wondering whether your TV advertising actually affects a consumer's decision about buying your product. You conduct a random sample of 300 people in your market area, and ask them if they saw your TV ad and whether they purchased your product within the last six months. The results are summarized in Exhibit 4.13.

What is the probability that one of the people in the sample purchased the product? What is the probability that one of the people who saw the TV ad purchased the product?

EXHIBIT 4.13

Results of Advertising Survey

In the Last Six Months	Random Sample of Customers	
	Purchased Product	Did Not Purchase Product
Saw the TV ad	152	36
Did not see the TV ad	76	36

Out of the 300 people surveyed, 228 purchased the product (152 + 76). So $P(\text{purchased product}) = \frac{228}{300} = 0.76$.

There were 188 people in the sample who saw the TV ad (152 + 36). Of those, 152 purchased the product. So $P(\text{purchased the product}|\text{saw the TV ad}) = \frac{152}{188} = 0.8085$.

There is some evidence the ad is working. Those who saw the ad were more likely to have purchased the product.

The Test for Independence

George Wilson wants to figure out whether customer location is related to customer satisfaction. One way to do this is to compare the probability of satisfaction for an urban customer with the probability of satisfaction for all of his customers. We already know that in the entire sample, 7 out of the 10 customers were satisfied, so $P(S) = 0.7$. Above, we calculated $P(S|U) = 0.6667$. These probabilities allow us to see that the customer location *is* related to customer satisfaction, as urban customers are less satisfied with GeorgeConn's service than customers overall.

There is something important that you should note at this stage: we can say only that customer location and level of satisfaction are related *in the sample*. In order to draw such a conclusion for the entire population of customers on the basis of the sample, we need some statistical tools that will be covered in Chapter 12.

The probability comparison that we have just completed is a test for independence. Two events are **independent** if the probability of one of the events is unaffected by whether the other event has occurred. If two events A and B are independent, then $P(A|B) = P(A)$ and $P(B|A) = P(B)$. The general approach to checking for independence is described opposite.

Independent events Two events A and B are independent if the probability of one of the events is unaffected by whether the other event has occurred; $P(A|B) = P(A)$ and $P(B|A) = P(B)$.

The Test for Independence

To check whether two events A and B are independent:

- compare P($A|B$) with P(A), or
- compare P($B|A$) with P(B)

It is necessary to do only one of these comparisons. If the compared probabilities are equal, then events A and B are independent. If the compared probabilities are not equal, then events A and B are not independent (that is, they are related).

Note that you have different options for checking for independence. In the GeorgeConn example, we compared P(satisfied customer) = P(S) with P(satisfied given urban) = P($S|U$) to test for independence. However, we could also have compared P(S) with P($S|R$). Either of these comparisons is sufficient to establish independence (or lack of it).

EXAMPLE 4.2B

Testing for independence

Suppose an industry association conducted a survey of companies in the industry to collect information about the educational background of different types of employees. The data are summarized in Exhibit 4.14.

In this sample, is being a supervisor independent of whether or not the employee completed graduate studies?

EXHIBIT 4.14

Industry Association Survey of Employees

	Highest Level of Education Attained		
	High School	College/University	Graduate Studies
Hourly worker	790	265	2
Supervisor	7	145	12
Manager	1	75	23
Senior executive	0	15	10

We calculate that the total number of employees in the sample is 1,345. Of these, 164 are supervisors. We calculate

$$P(\text{supervisor}) = \frac{164}{1,345} = 0.1219$$

We the compare this to P(supervisor|graduate studies). In the sample, there are 47 employees who completed graduate studies and, of these, 12 are supervisors.

$$P(\text{supervisor|graduate studies}) = \frac{12}{47} = 0.2553$$

The two probabilities are not equal, so being a supervisor is not independent of whether an employee completed graduate studies. In this sample, employees who completed graduate studies are about twice as likely to be supervisors compared to employees as a whole.

DEVELOP YOUR SKILLS 4.2

6. Out of 100 gas station customers, 80 customers pay with a credit card. Twenty-five gas station customers buy something other than gas (e.g., chips or pop) and 20 customers pay with a credit card and buy something other than gas. If a station customer buys something other than gas, what is the probability that he/she pays with a credit card? If the customer pays with a credit card, what is the probability that he/she buys something other than gas? Are paying with a credit card and buying something other than gas related?

7. A breakfast cereal comes in several versions. It can be purchased in a regular size or a larger family size. As well, it can be purchased in regular flavour or in a honey-nut version. Sales data are shown in Exhibit 4.15 below.

If a customer buys a family size box of cereal, what is the probability that it is the honey-nut flavour? Are the size of the box and the flavour related?

8. Exhibit 4.16 below shows employment in Canada, by industry and sex, for 2008 (numbers are in thousands).

What is the probability that someone employed in the agriculture industry in Canada in 2008 was female? What is the probability that a male worker was employed in public administration? What is the probability that a randomly selected employee worked in public administration? Were sex of employee and industry of employment independent in Canada in 2008?

9. A roofing company has analyzed its accounts receivable, and produced the cross-classification table shown in

EXHIBIT 4.15

Probabilities of Sales of Breakfast Cereal

	Regular Size	Family Size
Regular flavour	270	135
Honey-nut flavour	315	180

EXHIBIT 4.16

Employment in Canada by Industry and Sex, 2008

Canada, Employment by Industry And Sex (Numbers in Thousands)		
	2008	
	Number Employed	
	Men	Women
Goods-producing sector	3,123.20	898.1
Agriculture	230.5	96.5
Forestry, fishing, mining, oil and gas	279.4	60.7
Utilities	115.6	36.1
Construction	1,087.30	144.8
Manufacturing	1,410.40	559.9
Services-producing sector	5,898.10	7,206.40
Trade	1,353.30	1,325.40
Transportation and warehousing	647.5	210.2
Finance, insurance, real estate and leasing	465	610.4
Professional, scientific, and technical services	693.7	506.3
Business, building, and other support services	366.7	319.8
Educational services	405.9	787
Health care and social assistance	342.4	1,561.00
Information, culture, and recreation	400.3	359.4
Accommodation and food services	433	640.4
Other services	336.3	414.8
Public administration	454	471.7
All industries	9,021.30	8,104.50

Source: Statistics Canada, "Labour Force Survey Estimates (LFS), by North American Industry Classification System (NAICS), Sex and Age Group, Annual," CANSIM Table 282-0008, **http://cansim2 .statcan.gc.ca**, accessed May 25, 2009.

Exhibit 4.17. What is the probability that one of the company's accounts receivable is < 30 days? What is the probability that an account of ≤ $5,000 is < 30 days? Are the age of the account and its amount independent?

EXHIBIT 4.17

Accounts Receivable for a Roofing Company

Age	Amount		
	≤ $5,000	$5,000–< $10,000	≥ $10,000
< 30 days	12	15	10
30–< 60 days	7	11	2
60 days and over	3	4	1

10. A dry cleaning company has done some research into how customers rate its services, and whether the customer will use its services again. The data are summarized in Exhibit 4.18.

EXHIBIT 4.18

Customer Survey for a Dry Cleaning Company

Service Rating	Will Use Services Again	Will Not Use Services Again
Poor	174	986
Fair	232	928
Good	2,436	174
Excellent	754	116

What is the probability that a customer will use the dry cleaning company's services again? What is the probability that a customer who rates the services as "good" or "excellent" will not use the services again? What does this indicate? Are the service rating and the tendency to use the services again independent?

4.3   "AND," "OR," AND "NOT" PROBABILITIES

"And" Probabilities

There are other straightforward probabilities that we can calculate from the GeorgeConn customer survey. For example, what is the probability that a randomly selected customer from GeorgeConn's sample of customers is urban *and* satisfied with the service? Look at Exhibit 4.19 below.

Note that the customers who are urban and satisfied with the service are highlighted in the table.

EXHIBIT 4.19

A Random Sample of GeorgeConn's Customers

Customer	Urban or Rural? R: Customer is rural U: Customer is urban	Satisfied or Not? S: Customer is satisfied N: Customer is not satisfied
3	U	S
5	U	S
6	U	S
10	U	S
1	U	N
9	U	N
2	R	S
4	R	N
7	R	S
8	R	S

$P(\text{urban } and \text{ satisfied}) = \frac{4}{10} = 0.4$. We can also see this in the contingency table shown in Exhibit 4.20 below. We can see that of the 10 customers surveyed, 4 were *both* urban and satisfied, so $P(\text{urban } and \text{ satisfied}) = P(U \text{ and } S) = \frac{4}{10} = 0.4$.

EXHIBIT 4.20

GeorgeConn's Customers

	Satisfied	Not Satisfied	Total
Rural	3	1	4
Urban	④	2	6
Total	7	3	10

This is an example of a *joint* probability. Notice the *and* in the description. The customer had to be *both* urban *and* satisfied with the service to be counted in the probability calculation. This is illustrated with Exhibit 4.21. The probability we want is at the intersection of the second column and the third row of the table.

EXHIBIT 4.21

GeorgeConn's Customers

	Satisfied	Not Satisfied	Total
Rural	3	1	4
Urban	④	2	6
Total	7	3	10

Make sure you understand the difference between a joint probability and a conditional probability. For a joint probability, we are considering the entire sample space. We want to know how many customers, out of *all* customers, are both urban and satisfied. This is different from a conditional probability, where we consider only a subset of the sample space. If we were trying to calculate the conditional probability of an urban customer being satisfied, we would be focusing on only the urban customers, a subset of the sample space.

- $P(\text{satisfied } given \text{ urban}) = P(S|U) = \frac{4}{6} = 0.6667 \, (\text{a conditional probability})$
- $P(\text{satisfied } and \text{ urban}) = P(S \text{ and } U) = \frac{4}{10} = 0.4 \, (\text{a joint probability})$

Now that we have introduced the idea of a joint probability, we can point out a relationship between joint and conditional probabilities.

Conditional Probability Calculation

For two events A and B, the conditional probability can be calculated as follows:

$$P(A|B) = \frac{P(A \text{ and } B)}{P(B)}$$

This formula corresponds exactly to the method we used to calculate the probability of a GeorgeConn customer being satisfied, given that he or she is urban. Translating from the general statement above, we see that

$$P(\text{satisfied}|\text{urban}) = \frac{P(\text{satisifed } and \text{ urban})}{P(\text{urban})}$$

$$P(S|U) = \frac{P(S \text{ and } U)}{P(U)}$$

$$P(S|U) = \frac{0.4}{0.6}$$

$$= 0.6667$$

as we calculated before.

You should realize that it is not required that you use the approach shown above every time you calculate a conditional probability. The approach shown above can be useful, if you have the necessary pieces of information. However, sometimes you can do the calculation by inspection, as we first did for the GeorgeConn problem. As long as the end result is correct, use whatever approach works!

Suppose that we have 10 female job applicants and 12 male job applicants waiting for an interview. If the company doing the hiring randomly selects two applicants to interview, what is the probability that both of them are male? We might be interested in this, if there was concern about gender bias in the interviewing process.

If you think about it, you will see that P(both applicants are male) is a joint probability. For both applicants to be male, the first one has to be male *and* the second one has to be male. But how do we figure out the probability?

Break this down into two parts. First, what is the probability that the first applicant is male? There are 22 applicants altogether (10 female + 12 male), and of these, 12 are male. $P(1^{st}\text{applicant selected is male}) = \frac{12}{22} = 0.5455$. Now, what is the probability that the second applicant selected is male as well? There are 21 applicants left, 11 of whom are male, so $P(2^{nd}\text{applicant selected is male}|1^{st}\text{applicant selected was male}) = \frac{11}{21} = 0.5238$.

Now, how do we put these calculations together to arrive at the joint probability? For this, we need the rule of multiplication.

The Multiplication Rule

For two events *A* and *B*, the probability of *A* and *B* occurring can be calculated using the rule of multiplication (the dot is a symbol for multiplication):

$$P(A \text{ and } B) = P(A) \cdot P(B|A).$$

You should be able to see that this rule is just a rearrangement of the rule for calculating conditional probability. If $P(A|B) = \frac{P(A \text{ and } B)}{P(B)}$, then it follows that $P(A \text{ and } B) = P(B) \cdot P(A|B)$ (just cross-multiply to get this). Of course, we can also say that $P(B \text{ and } A) = P(A \text{ and } B) = P(A) \cdot P(B|A)$.

Now apply the multiplication rule directly to the job applicant problem.

P(both applicants are male)

= P(1st applicant is male *and* 2nd applicant is male)

= P(1st applicant is male) • P(2nd applicant is male|1st applicant was male)

$$= \frac{12}{22} \cdot \frac{11}{21}$$

$$= \frac{132}{462}$$

$$= 0.2857$$

For this kind of calculation, it may be easier to leave the intermediate probabilities in fraction form, rather than converting them to decimals (that is, use $\frac{12}{22}$ in the calculation, rather than 0.5455, which is a rounded value). This is a good way to preserve accuracy.

Now that we have covered conditional and joint probabilities, we can use them to complete a tree diagram corresponding to the job interview example.

EXHIBIT 4.22

Tree Diagram for Job Applicants

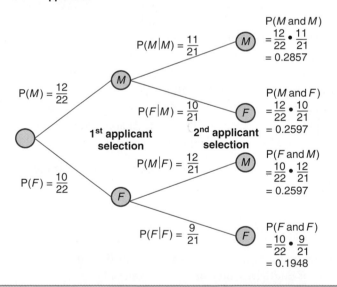

Notice that the second stage probabilities in the tree diagram are conditional. When we assess the probabilities of the second applicant being male or female, we have to take into account what the gender of the first applicant is. The result is that you can multiply the probabilities along a set of branches to get the joint probability at the end, using the multiplication rule. For example, P(F) = $\frac{10}{22}$ for the first applicant, and this is the probability shown along that branch. Then P(F|F) = $\frac{9}{21}$ for the second applicant.

When we get to the end of the two branches, we arrive at $P(F \text{ and } F) = P(F) \cdot P(F|F) = \frac{10}{22} \cdot \frac{9}{21} = 0.1948$.

The rule of multiplication has a special form when the two events involved are independent. Remember, when two events A and B are independent, the probability of one happening is unaffected by whether the other event has occurred, and $P(B) = P(B|A)$, for example. This means that for the special case of independent events, we can simplify the rule of multiplication as follows:

$P(A \text{ and } B)$

$= P(A) \cdot P(B|A)$

$= P(A) \cdot P(B)$

Here is an example. Suppose an international music production company is launching new CDs for two artists. One of the artists is a country singer, and one is an opera singer. The probability that the country singer's CD will be a big hit is estimated to be 0.07. The probability that the opera singer's CD will be a hit is estimated to be 0.03. What is the probability that both CDs will be a hit for the company? Market research has indicated that country music fans generally do not listen to opera, and vice versa.

In this case, although we are not directly told that the two events are independent, we are told that customers who buy country music are different from customers who buy operatic music, so it is probably safe to conclude that the two CD launches are independent. Therefore

$P(\text{country CD is a hit } and \text{ opera CD is a hit})$

$= 0.07 \cdot 0.03$

$= 0.0021$

There is only a very small probability that both new CDs will be hits.

EXAMPLE 4.3A

The rule of multiplication: calculating "and" probability

The probability of your company winning a large government contract to supply computers is considered to be 0.3. Budget projections indicate that the probability of earning a profit this quarter if the company wins the government contract is 0.75. The probability of earning a profit this quarter if the company does not win the government contract is 0.4. What is the probability of earning a profit and winning the government contract?

$P(\text{winning the government contract and earning a profit})$

$= P(\text{winning the government contract}) \cdot P(\text{earning a profit } given \text{ government contract won})$

$= 0.3 \cdot 0.75$

$= 0.225$

Finally, you should realize that it is not required that you use the multiplication rule every time you want to calculate an "and" probability. Sometimes these probabilities are already present in the information provided in the problem. As we saw at the beginning of this section, we could simply count the number of customers who were both urban and satisfied to arrive at $P(U \text{ and } S) = \frac{4}{10} = 0.4$. No fancy multiplication was required!

"Or" Probabilities

George Wilson is thinking of placing an advertisement for GeorgeConn in the local newspapers. He is not sure which newspaper(s) would be best for the ad, but the newspapers give him some information about their readership that will help him with his decision. Suppose George is told that 60% of local residents read the morning paper, 40% read the evening paper, and 20% read both. What percentage of residents read at least one of the two papers?

Your first reaction might be to think that almost everybody reads at least one of the papers. After all, P(morning paper read) = 0.6, and P(evening paper read) = 0.4, and the sum of those two probabilities is 100%. However, simply adding the two probabilities is not correct, because it will result in double-counting the 20% of residents who read both papers. They are counted in the probability for the morning paper, and they are counted again in the probability for the evening paper. So, we have to subtract the 20% who are double-counted to get the final probability, as follows:

P(at least one of the two papers read)

= P(morning paper read *or* evening paper read *or* both read)

= P(morning paper read) + P(evening paper read) − P(both papers read)

= 0.6 + 0.4 − 0.2

= 0.8

This is an example of an "*or*" probability. Note that there was no *or* in the original question ("at least one"). As usual, it will be up to you to recognize when an "or" probability is required. Usually this is a matter of checking to see if the event can be described correctly using the word "or." The event "*A* or *B*" means that *A* occurs, or *B* occurs, or they both occur. The rule for calculating these probabilities is the rule of addition.

The Addition Rule

For two events *A* and *B,* the probability of *A* or *B* occurring can be calculated using the rule of addition:

$$P(A \text{ or } B) = P(A) + P(B) - P(A \text{ and } B)$$

Once again, you should realize that it is not required that you use the addition rule as shown above every time you have an "or" probability. Sometimes you can do the calculation another way, and you should use whatever approach yields the correct answer.

We can examine how the addition rule operates with the GeorgeConn customer data.

P(satisfied or urban)

= P(S or U)

= P(S) + P(U) − P(S and U)

= 0.7 + 0.6 − 0.4

= 0.9

Exhibit 4.23 illustrates the double-counting that must be corrected. P(urban) = 0.6, and P(satisfied) = 0.7, but this double-counts P(urban and satisfied) = 0.4.

EXHIBIT **4.23**

GeorgeConn's Customers

	Satisfied	Not Satisfied	Total
Rural	0.3	0.1	0.4
Urban	(0.4)	0.2	0.6
Total	0.7	0.3	1.0

The rule of addition has a special case for **mutually exclusive events**, events that cannot happen simultaneously. If two events A and B are mutually exclusive, then P(A and B) = 0.

For example, suppose you have some information about your customers, according to level of income. The information is summarized in Exhibit 4.24.

Mutually exclusive events Events that cannot happen simultaneously; if two events A and B are mutually exclusive, then P(A and B) = 0.

EXHIBIT **4.24**

Customer Income Analysis

Annual Income Level	Number of Customers
$0–<$25,000	29
$25,000–<$50,000	152
$50,000–<$75,000	353
$75,000–<$100,000	12
Total	546

What is the probability that a randomly selected customer has an income below $25,000, or $75,000–<$100,000?

$$P(\text{income}<\$25,000) = \frac{29}{546} = 0.0531$$

$$P(\text{income } \$75,000-<\$100,000) = \frac{12}{546} = 0.0220$$

$$P(\text{income}<\$25,000 \;\; or \;\; \$75,000-<\$100,000) = \frac{29}{546} + \frac{12}{546} = \frac{41}{546} = 0.0751$$

Notice that since the income categories are mutually exclusive (a customer cannot have an income <$25,000 and at the same time have an income $75,000–<$100,000), the probabilities can simply be added.

EXAMPLE **4.3B**

The rule of addition: calculating "or" probabilities

Your large company has suppliers all across Canada. The joint probability table shown in Exhibit 4.25 on the next page summarizes the location and size (by annual sales) of these suppliers. What is the probability that a supplier has sales < $1 million or is located in BC?

EXHIBIT 4.25

Joint Probability Table for Company Suppliers

Location	Annual Sales		
	<$1 million	$1 million–<$5 million	≥$5 million
BC	0.02	0.06	0.15
AB, SK, MB	0.01	0.07	0.01
ON	0.03	0.10	0.40
QC	0.02	0.01	0.07
PE, NB, NS, and NL	0.01	0.02	0.02

First we calculate the probability of a supplier having sales of <$1 million. We get this by adding the probabilities in the second column of Exhibit 4.25 (these are all mutually exclusive outcomes, so we can just add the probabilities).

P(supplier has sales <$1 million) = 0.02 + 0.01 + 0.03 + 0.02 + 0.01 = 0.09

Similarly, we calculate the probability of a supplier being located in BC by adding the probabilities along the first row of the table.

P(supplier located in BC) = 0.02 + 0.06 + 0.15 = 0.23

For one of the company's suppliers

P(sales < $1 million *or* located in BC)

= P(sales <$1 million) + P(located in BC) − P(sales <$1 million *and* located in BC)

= 0.09 + 0.23 − 0.02 (the joint probability is simply read from the table)

= 0.30

"Not" Probabilities

Complement of an event *A* Everything in the sample space that is not *A*.

If the probability that one of GeorgeConn's customers is urban is 0.6, what is the probability that a customer is *not* urban? One way to calculate this is P(not urban) = 1 − P(urban) = 1 − 0.6 = 0.4. We can do this because all of GeorgeConn's customers are either urban or not (rural). Generally, the sum of probabilities for all the non-overlapping events in a sample space has to add up to 1 or 100%. If they do not, something must be missing from the list of all possible events. *Not urban* is called the complement of *urban*. The **complement of an event *A*** is everything in the sample space that is not *A*. Various notations are used to describe complements. The complement of *A* might be noted as $\overline{A}$ or ~*A* or A^C or A'. In this text, we will use the notation A^C for the complement of *A*. The complement rule summarizes the relationship between P(*A*) and P(A^C).

> **The Complement Rule**
>
> The probability of an event *A* can be calculated using the complement rule:
>
> P(*A*) = 1 − P(A^C)

The complement rule can be a very powerful tool for probability calculation. Let's look at an example. A company is submitting tenders for two road construction jobs in Calgary. The smaller of the two jobs is a contract to repair a major city street. The larger job is new street construction in a new residential development. The company's president estimates that the probability of winning the smaller job (which comes up first) is 0.70. She also believes that the probability of winning the larger job, if the company wins the smaller job, is 0.50. On the other hand, if the company does not win the smaller job, she believes the probability of winning the larger job to be only 0.20. According to the president's probability estimates, what is the probability that the company will win both jobs?

There is no probability rule for "both," but we recognize that "winning both jobs" is logically equivalent to "winning the smaller job *and* winning the larger job." We will denote "winning the smaller job" with the letter S, and winning the larger job with the letter L. We can now summarize the information we have been given:

- P(winning smaller job) = $P(S)$ = 0.70
- P(winning larger job, given that the smaller job is won) = $P(L|S)$ = 0.50
- P(winning larger job, given that the smaller job is not won) = $P(L|S^C)$ = 0.20

To calculate the probability of winning both jobs, proceed as follows.

$P(S \text{ and } L)$

$= P(S) \cdot P(L|S)$

$= 0.70 \cdot 0.50$

$= 0.35$

So, the probability of winning both jobs is 0.35.

What is the probability of losing both jobs?

$P(\text{losing both jobs})$

$= P(S^C \text{ and } L^C)$

$= P(S^C) \cdot P(L^C|S^C)$

$= (1 - 0.70) \cdot (1 - 0.20)$

$= 0.30 \cdot 0.80$

$= 0.24$

What is the probability of winning just one of the two jobs? This could be a lengthy probability calculation. We could calculate the probability of winning the smaller job and losing the larger job, and then add that to the probability of losing the smaller job and winning the larger job. However, there is an easier way, which involves the complement rule. This is a case where a tree diagram can be helpful to keep track of the sample space. Exhibit 4.26 on the next page illustrates the sample space for this example.

The probabilities in black in Exhibit 4.26 correspond to the probabilities given in the problem description. The probabilities in red are calculated using the complement rule. For example, if $P(L|S)$ = 0.5, then $P(L^C|S)$ = 1 − 0.5 = 0.5. The end-stage probabilities, in blue, are calculated using the multiplication rule. For example, $P(S \text{ and } L)$ = $P(S) \cdot P(L|S)$ = $0.7 \cdot 0.5$ = 0.35.

EXHIBIT 4.26

Tree Diagram for Road Construction Jobs

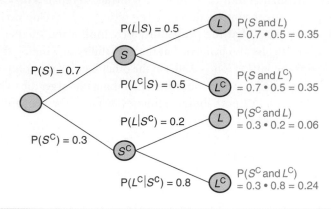

This tree diagram now gives quite a full picture of the sample space, and a number of related probabilities. It also allows us to see clearly how to calculate the probability of winning exactly one of the contracts. Using the information in the tree diagram, we can now go through the long probability calculation for winning exactly one contract.

P(winning exactly one contract)

$= $ P[(winning the smaller job *and* not winning the larger job)
$\quad$ *or* (not winning the smaller job *and* winning the larger job)]

$= $ P[(S and L^C) or (S^C and L)]

$= $ P(S and L^C) $+$ P(S^C and L) (mutually exclusive events)

$= $ [P(S) • P($L^C|S$)] $+$ [P(S^C) • P($L|S^C$)] (multiplication rule)

$= $ (0.7 • 0.5) $+$ (0.3 • 0.2)

$= $ 0.35 $+$ 0.06

$= $ 0.41

However, the tree diagram also gives us a clear picture of an easier way to calculate this probability. We have already calculated P(winning both contracts) and P(losing both contracts). So, using the complement rule, we can calculate

P(winning exactly one contract)

$= $ 1 $-$ P(winning both contracts *or* losing both contracts)

$= $ 1 $-$ (0.35 $+$ 0.24)

$= $ 1 $-$ 0.59

$= $ 0.41

This approach takes advantage of the calculations we have already done. The complement rule leads to a much easier calculation in this case. A tree diagram can often be useful to determine when the complement rule would be helpful.

Return to the situation described in Example 4.3A, in which your company was bidding on a large government contract to supply computers. The information provided was:

- P(winning government contract) = 0.3
- P(earning a quarterly profit, given that government contract won) = 0.75
- P(earning a quarterly profit, given that government contract not won) = 0.4

What is the probability that the company will earn a profit in the next quarter?

Recognize that there are two (mutually exclusive) ways for the company to earn a profit in the next quarter: when it wins the government contract, and when it does not. It might be helpful to draw a tree diagram for this situation, to illustrate the sample space. To simplify the notation, we will use the following letters:

- W for winning the government contract
- P for earning a profit in the next quarter

The appropriate tree diagram is shown in Exhibit 4.27 below.

EXHIBIT **4.27**

Tree Diagram for Company Bidding on Government Contracts

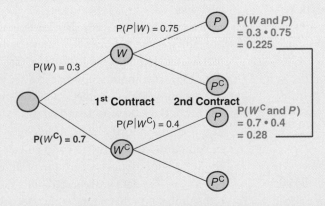

$P(P)$

$= P[(W \text{ and } P) \text{ or } (W^C \text{ and } P)]$

$= P(W \text{ and } P) + P(W^C \text{ and } P)]$ (mutually exclusive events)

$= P(W) \cdot P(P|W) + P(W^C) \cdot P(P|W^C)$

$= (0.3 \cdot 0.75) + (0.7 \cdot 0.4)$ (using the complement rule)

$= 0.225 + 0.28$

$= 0.505$

While the notation looks a little complicated, the calculations are fairly straightforward when the tree diagram is used.

Mutually Exclusive vs. Independent Events If you are going to be successful with probability calculations, it is important that you understand the difference between mutually exclusive and independent events. These conditions are not the same. As a reminder, here are the definitions of both.

- Events A and B are *mutually exclusive* if $P(A \text{ and } B) = 0$. This means that A and B cannot both happen.
- Events A and B are *independent* if $P(A) = P(A|B)$; that is, the fact that B happened does not affect the chances of A happening (or vice versa).

DEVELOP YOUR SKILLS 4.3

11. Your company has two employees, Jane Morton and Oscar Wildman, who are experts at rescuing computers from viruses. One morning, you arrive at work to find that a virus has totally incapacitated the computers on the company network. The probability that Jane Morton will be late for work in the morning is 0.02. The probability that Oscar Wildman will be late for work in the morning is 0.04. If the employees live in different parts of the city, what is the probability that both will be late for work this morning when you really need their help?

12. Three women who have been friends since childhood have just graduated from college. The friends are very different, and have different abilities and skills. All three of them are trying to get jobs in the financial services industry. Their probabilities of succeeding are 0.4, 0.5, and 0.35. Find the probability that

a. all of them succeed
b. none of them succeeds
c. at least one of them succeeds

13. A software company is about to release three new software programs, one from each of three very distinct business divisions. The first program is a new game aimed at 15- to 25-year-olds. Its probability of succeeding is estimated to be 0.34. The second program is an accounting application for small business. Its probability of succeeding is estimated to be 0.12. The third program is a payroll system designed for government organizations. Its probability of succeeding is 0.10. ("Success" is defined as earning enough profits to fully recover development, production, and marketing costs within one year.) What is the probability that all three software programs will succeed? What is the probability that at least two out of three of them will succeed? You may assume that the success of each product is independent of the success of the others.

14. Draw a fully labelled tree diagram for the GeorgeConn customer data at the beginning of the chapter (see Exhibit 4.5 on page 156). Notice that the end-stage probabilities are the ones that show up in the cells of the related joint probability table (see Exhibit 4.3, page 155). Use another approach to set up a different tree diagram for the GeorgeConn problem.

15. Return to the situation described in Example 4.2B on page 163. An industry association conducted a survey of companies in the industry to collect information about the educational background of different types of employees. The data are repeated in Exhibit 4.28. What is the probability that a randomly selected employee in this industry is an hourly worker or someone with only a high school education?

EXHIBIT 4.28

Industry Association Survey of Employees

	Highest Level of Education Attained		
	High School	College/University	Graduate Studies
Hourly worker	790	265	2
Supervisor	7	145	12
Manager	1	75	23
Senior executive	0	15	10

Sample Spaces and Basic Probabilities

An experiment is any activity with an uncertain outcome. An event is one or more outcomes of an experiment. A sample space is a complete list or representation of all of the possible outcomes of an experiment. Sample spaces can be represented with a list, a contingency table, a joint probability table, or a tree diagram.

Probability is a measure of the likelihood of an event. The classical definition of probability is based on counting. If there are n equally likely possible outcomes of an experiment, and m of them correspond to the event you are interested in, then the probability of the event is $\frac{m}{n}$.

The relative frequency approach to probability is based on a large number of repeated trials of an experiment. Probability is the relative frequency of an event over this large number of trials. Often relative frequencies from samples are used to estimate the probabilities of populations.

Conditional Probabilities and the Test for Independence

A conditional probability is the probability of an event (call it A), *given that* another event (call it B) has already occurred. The usual notation is P($A|B$), read *the probability of* A, *given* B. For two events A and B, the conditional probability can be calculated as follows:

$$P(A|B) = \frac{P(A \text{ and } B)}{P(B)}$$

Two events are independent if the probability of one of the events is unaffected by whether the other event has occurred. To see whether two events A and B are independent, do *one of* the following comparisons:

- compare P($A|B$) with P(A), or
- compare P($B|A$) with P(B)

If the compared probabilities are equal, then events A and B are independent. If the compared probabilities are not equal, then events A and B are not independent (that is, they are related).

"And," "Or," and "Not" Probabilities

For two events A and B, the probability of A and B occurring can be calculated using the rule of multiplication:

$$P(A \text{ and } B) = P(A) \cdot P(B|A)$$

For the special case of independent events, we can simplify the rule of multiplication as follows:

$$P(A \text{ and } B) = P(A) \cdot P(B)$$

For two events A and B, the probability of A or B occurring can be calculated using the rule of addition:

$$P(A \text{ or } B) = P(A) + P(B) - P(A \text{ and } B)$$

Mutually exclusive events are events that cannot happen simultaneously. If two events A and B are mutually exclusive, then

$$P(A \text{ and } B) = 0$$

For the special case of mutually exclusive events, we can simplify the rule of addition as follows:

$$P(A \text{ or } B) = P(A) + P(B)$$

The complement of an event A is everything in the sample space that is not A. The complement of event A is denoted A^C. The probability of an event A can be calculated using the complement rule:

$$P(A) = 1 - P(A^C)$$

Chapter Summary

4

Go to MyStatLab at www.mathxl.com. You can practise the exercises indicated with red in the Develop Your Skills and Chapter Review Exercises as often as you want, and guided solutions will help you find answers step by step. You'll find a personalized study plan available to you too!

CHAPTER REVIEW EXERCISES

WARM-UP EXERCISES

1. A company accountant did a study of 750 accounts receivable. She found that 119 accounts were paid early, 320 were paid on time, 200 were paid late, and 111 were considered uncollectable. Assume the past experience with accounts receivable is a good indication of the future. Estimate the probabilities for each category of accounts receivable for the future.

2. GeorgeConn has 100 employees. There are 60 men and 40 women. Of these, 25 of the women and 30 of the men have a Business diploma. One employee is randomly selected. What is the probability of the following outcomes?
   a. man
   b. man with a Business diploma
   c. woman
   d. woman with a Business diploma
   e. employee with a Business diploma
   f. man without a Business diploma
   g. employee without a Business diploma
   h. woman without a Business diploma
   i. woman or employee with a Business diploma
   j. man or employee with a Business diploma
   k. woman or employee without a Business diploma
   l. man or employee without a Business diploma

3. Refer to the information about GeorgeConn employees, in Exercise 2 above. If the selected employee is a woman, what is the probability she has a Business diploma? Are gender and possession of a Business diploma related for GeorgeConn employees?

4. Suppose that there is an 80% probability that a caller will be directly connected when he or she calls a computer help line, and a 20% probability the caller will be forced to wait while listening to a recorded message. Assume that the caller experience with each call is independent if the calls are placed on different days. What is the probability that a caller making three calls (on different days) will be directly connected each time? What is the probability that a caller making three calls (on different days) will have to wait each time?

5. An employment agency has analyzed the skills and experience of its employees, with the results shown in Exhibit 4.29.

EXHIBIT 4.29

Skills and Experience of Employment Agency Employees

Experience	Primary Skill		
	Bookkeeping	Reception	Document Management
Less Than One Year	5	15	30
One to Two Years	10	6	7
More Than Two Years	15	4	8

One person's file is selected at random. What is the probability that the selected person will have the following characteristics?
a. Primary skill is bookkeeping.
b. Employee has less than one year of experience.
c. Primary skill is reception.

    d. Employee has one to two years of experience.

    e. Primary skill is document management.

    f. Employee has more than two years of experience.

THINK AND DECIDE

6. A restaurant chain regularly surveys its customers about the quality of the food and the quality of the service. The survey responses are summarized in the Exhibit 4.30 below. The relative frequencies are considered good estimates of the associated probabilities.

EXHIBIT 4.30

Survey of Restaurant Customers

Opinion about Food	Satisfied with Service	Not Satisfied with Service
Excellent	0.36	0.06
Good	0.18	0.07
Fair	0.10	0.08
Poor	0.05	0.10

    a. What is the probability that a randomly selected customer is satisfied with the service and rates the restaurant's food as poor?

    b. What is the probability that a randomly selected customer is not satisfied with the service?

    c. What is the probability that a customer who rated the food as poor was not satisfied with the service?

    d. Are the service rating and the food rating related? You must use probabilities to prove your answer to this question.

7. Past experience shows that the probability that a salespeople will exceed their sales targets in a given year is 15%, provided that they exceeded their targets in the previous year. If the probability of a salesperson exceeding his/her target in any given year is 78%, what is the probability the salesperson will exceed target two years in a row?

8. In a follow-up survey of people who purchased netbook computers, the buyers were asked if they were satisfied with their purchase. The answers were classified according to whether or not the netbook had more than 1 GB of RAM. The probability table shown in Exhibit 4.31 was created.

EXHIBIT 4.31

Follow-Up Survey of Customers Who Bought Netbook Computers

	Satisfied	Not Satisfied
1 GB of RAM or Less	0.30	0.05
More than 1 GB of RAM	0.50	0.15

    a. What is the probability that a customer who bought a netbook computer was satisfied with his/her purchase?

    b. What is the probability that a customer who bought a netbook with more than 1 GB of RAM was satisfied with his/her purchase?

    c. Does the amount of RAM affect whether the purchaser was satisfied with his/her purchase? You must use probabilities to answer this question.

9. Students who wish to become chartered accountants (C.A.s) must pass a set of exams to qualify. Suppose that in Ontario, the pass rate is 75%. Candidates who fail the exams the first time may take them again later. Of those who fail the first time, 90% pass the second time. What is the probability that a randomly selected student qualifies to become a C.A. with no more than two attempts at passing the exams? (Hint: Use a tree diagram. Be sure to consider all the ways that a candidate can pass the exam.)

10. An insurance company has collected data on the gender and marital status of 300 customers, shown in Exhibit 4.32 below.

EXHIBIT 4.32

Customers of an Insurance Company

	Single	Married	Divorced
Male	25	125	30
Female	50	50	20

Suppose a customer is selected at random from this sample.
a. What is the probability that the customer is female or married?
b. What is the probability that the customer is married if the customer is male?
c. Are gender and marital status independent? Prove your answer.

11. At the beginning of each year, an investment newsletter predicts whether or not the stock market will rise over the following year. Historical evidence reveals that there is a 60% chance of the market rising, in any given year. The newsletter has predicted a rise for 70% of the years when the market actually rose, and has predicted a rise for 30% of the years when the market actually fell. Find the probability that the newsletter's prediction for next year will be correct. (Hint: Use a tree diagram. Be sure to consider all the ways in which the prediction can be correct.)

12. A company has decided to hire some summer students. A local high school has provided the names of 10 students who have been academically successful, and who have good work habits. The company decides to pick three students from this group at random, rather than taking the time to interview the students. If six of the students are female, what is the probability that all of the students selected by the company are female? What is the probability that all of the students selected by the company are male?

13. Refer back to Example 4.1, about the employee health and fitness facilities (page 157). Are gender and tendency to use the health and fitness facilities related in this sample? You must use probabilities to support your answer.

14. Refer back to Example 4.1 on page 157, and particularly to the tree diagram in Exhibit 4.10 on page 159. Construct another tree diagram for the data, using the first node to distinguish those who did or did not use the facilities. Are the joint probabilities at the end of the branches the same? Did you expect them to be?

15. Refer back to Example 4.2A, about a survey to determine whether people saw a TV ad or purchased a product. In the sample, is purchasing behaviour related to seeing the TV ad? You must use probabilities to support your answer.

16. Brenda Miner has just graduated with a Business diploma. She has applied for a job at the largest Canadian bank. The probability that she will get the job is 0.25. The probability that she will move to Alberta if she is offered this job is 0.70. The probability that she will move to Alberta if she does not get this job is 0.35. Create a tree diagram, complete with probabilities, to describe all of the possible outcomes for Brenda. What is the probability that she will be offered the job and not move to Alberta?

17. The probability that a Canadian adult has taken some instruction in canoeing is 0.03. The probability that a Canadian adult who has taken some instruction in canoeing will go on a canoe trip this summer is 0.46. The probability that a Canadian adult who has taken no instruction in canoeing is going on a canoe trip this summer is 0.20. Create a tree diagram to represent all the possibilities for Canadian adults taking instruction in canoeing, and going on a canoe trip this summer.

18. Using the tree diagram you created in Exercise 17 above, calculate the probability that a randomly selected Canadian adult is going on a canoe trip this summer, and has taken some canoeing instruction. What is the probability that a randomly selected Canadian adult is going on a canoe trip this summer, and has not taken any canoeing instruction?

19. Suppose a survey of customers from stores A, B, C, and D recorded the method of payment by customers. The data are shown below in Exhibit 4.33.

EXHIBIT 4.33

Customer Payment Method

	Store A	Store B	Store C	Store D	Total
Cash or debit card	40	65	20	25	150
Credit card	30	80	30	40	180
Cheque	30	55	50	35	170
Total	100	200	100	100	500

Based on the survey, what is the probability that a randomly selected customer from one of these stores uses a cash/debit card or a credit card for payment?

20. Refer to Exhibit 4.33 in Exercise 19. Is the payment method independent of the store in this sample?

21. You are thinking about investing in a fitness facility. The current owner tells you that, based on past experience, the following probabilities apply to someone who visits the facility. The probability that a visitor will buy a membership is 40%. The probability that a visitor will buy a membership and sign up for fitness classes is 30%. What is the probability that a visitor will sign up for fitness classes, if he or she buys a membership?

22. Refer back to Exercise 21 above. Are buying a membership and signing up for fitness classes mutually exclusive? Are buying a membership and signing up for fitness classes independent?

23. A restaurant is interested in whether there is a difference in the tendency to drink beer, wine, and other alcoholic drinks, by gender. If there appears to be a difference, the servers will be trained to promote the most preferred types of drinks to male and female customers. A survey of a random sample of customers who bought alcoholic beverages revealed the data shown in Exhibit 4.34, below.

EXHIBIT 4.34

Sample of Restaurant Customers Ordering Alcoholic Drinks

	Beer	Wine	Other Alcoholic Drinks
Male	42	36	22
Female	63	54	33

Is the tendency to order beer related to the gender of the customer? Is the tendency to order wine related to the gender of the customer?

24. A shipment contains 500 circuit boards. Suppose that 30 of them are defective. What is the probability that if you randomly selected three circuit boards, all three of them would be defective? How does this compare to the probability you would obtain if you considered that the selection of each circuit board was independent of selection of the others, using the initial probability of selecting a defective circuit board?

25. Polls show that 25% of Canadians plan to make a contribution to their RRSPs over the next year. What is the probability that four randomly selected Canadians are all planning to make a contribution to their RRSPs over the next year?

TEST YOUR KNOWLEDGE

26. A small company that provides customer assistance with computer software has the following group of employees.

EXHIBIT 4.35

Employees of Software Help Company

Name	Specialty	Experience
Amy Jacobs	Presentation Software	Low
Christopher Johnson	Spreadsheet Software	High
Jacqueline Brown	Word Processing Software	High
Amanda Brandon	Spreadsheet Software	High
Ainslie Burgess	Spreadsheet Software	Low
Tim Dayman	Spreadsheet Software	Low
Norma Chambers	Presentation Software	Low
Shannon Greig	Spreadsheet Software	Low
Lisa Breau	Presentation Software	Low
Amy Ross	Word Processing Software	High
Paul Gurr	Word Processing Software	High
Adam King	Word Processing Software	Low
Samuel Babcock	Presentation Software	Low
Joshua Quesnelle	Database Software	High
Jeffery McGuire	Spreadsheet Software	Low
Shelley Saad	Word Processing Software	High
Martha Vassair	Word Processing Software	Low
Curtis Dingle	Spreadsheet Software	High
Jennifer Arsenault	Spreadsheet Software	Low
Graham Anderson	Spreadsheet Software	High
Thomas Monaghan	Word Processing Software	High
Kenneth Day	Spreadsheet Software	Low
Jason Truax	Word Processing Software	High
Crystal Beaumont	Spreadsheet Software	Low

Using the information in this table, calculate the following probabilities.
a. One employee will be selected at random to plan the company picnic. What is the probability that he or she will be:
   • someone with low experience
   • someone with high experience
   • someone whose specialty is spreadsheet software
   • someone whose specialty is presentation software

b. Suppose the first two client requests are for someone who specializes in spreadsheet software. How many employees could meet this request? What is the probability that the first employee selected has high experience? What is the probability that both employees have high experience? What is the probability that at least one of the employees has high experience?

c. Create a joint probability table for specialty and experience for the employees. What is the probability that an employee has high experience, if his/her specialty is word processing? What is the probability that an employee has low experience, if his/her specialty is spreadsheet software?

d. Create a joint probability table for gender and specialty for the employees. What is the probability that an employee specializes in word processing software if she is female? What is the probability that an employee is male if he specializes in spreadsheet software?

e. Create a tree diagram that illustrates the possibilities for randomly selecting an employee. In the first stage, show the probabilities of selecting a male or female employee. In the second stage, show the probabilities for each type of software specialty. In the third stage, show the probabilities for high or low experience. Leave the probabilities in fractional form. Calculate the end-stage probabilities.

f. Create a tree diagram that illustrates the possibilities for randomly selecting an employee. In the first stage, show the probabilities of selecting an employee with high or low experience. In the second stage, show the probabilities of selecting a male or female employee. In the third stage, show the probabilities for each type of software specialty. Leave the probabilities in fractional form. Calculate the end-stage probabilities. Do they match the corresponding end-stage probabilities you calculated in part e above?

Probability Distributions

LEARNING OBJECTIVES

After mastering the material in this chapter, you will be able to:

1 Understand the concepts of discrete and continuous random variables and their associated probability distributions.

2 Recognize situations when the binomial probability distribution applies, and use a formula, Excel, or tables to calculate binomial probabilities.

3 Recognize the normal probability distribution, and use Excel or tables to calculate normal probabilities.

INTRODUCTION

Chapter 4 introduced basic probability concepts and rules. Many of the problems considered in Chapter 4 involved counts of outcomes with particular characteristics. For example, how many of GeorgeConn's customers are urban? How many are satisfied? It is possible to associate a random variable with these counts. For example, we could define a random variable x as the number of rural customers GeorgeConn would find, if two customers were randomly selected. The value of x will be determined only when GeorgeConn randomly selects two customers and determines if they have rural addresses. A **random variable** is a variable whose value is determined by the outcome of a random experiment.

In Chapter 2, the distinction between discrete and continuous variables was made. Random variables can also be discrete or continuous. The number of rural customers out of two randomly selected GeorgeConn customers is a discrete random variable. The possible values that this random variable x can take are 0, 1, and 2. Because we can list all the possible values of x, it is a discrete random variable. A **discrete random variable** can take any value from a list of distinct possible values.

Discrete random variables are often counts, and we looked at several examples of these kinds of experiments in Chapter 4. A probability distribution is associated with a discrete random variable. The **probability distribution for a discrete random variable** is often illustrated with a list of all the possible values of the random variable, and their associated probabilities. We will see, in Section 5.1, that these probability distributions can be constructed with the probability rules of Chapter 4. We will also see that once these distributions are known, they can be used to calculate probabilities in a wide range of situations. In Chapter 5 we will look at one particular discrete probability distribution, the binomial distribution, in Section 5.2.

A **continuous random variable** can take on any value from a continuous range. Continuous random variables are often measurements of some kind. For example, a random variable y could be defined as the height of a student in your statistics class. Because y could take on any of the values in some range[1] (from the shortest possible height to the tallest), it is a continuous random variable. In Chapter 5 we will look at one particular continuous probability distribution, the normal distribution, in Section 5.3. Of course, it is not possible to list the infinite number of possible values for a continuous random variable, so the associated probability distribution cannot take the form of a list. The **probability distribution of a continuous random variable** is described graphically, or with a mathematical formula.

Chapter 5 examines two important probability distributions (one discrete, one continuous) that have many applications for statistical inference. Later in the text, we will encounter other important probability distributions, such as the t-distribution and the Chi-square distribution.

Random variable A variable whose value is determined by the outcome of a random experiment.

Discrete random variable A random variable that can take on any value from a list of distinct possible values.

Probability distribution for a discrete random variable A list of all the possible values of the random variable, and their associated probabilities.

Continuous random variable A random variable that can take on any value from a continuous range.

Probability distribution of a continuous random variable A graph or a mathematical formula describing the probabilities in a continuous range.

5.1   PROBABILITY DISTRIBUTIONS

Building a Discrete Probability Distribution

Define a random variable x as "the number of rural customers, out of two randomly selected GeorgeConn customers." We know that the random variable x has three possible values: 0, 1, or 2 (that is, none or one or both of the customers may be rural). There are probabilities associated with each of these possible values of x, and we can use the probability rules from Chapter 4 to calculate them.

In Chapter 4, we learned that P(rural customer) = 0.4 among GeorgeConn's customers. Assume for now that GeorgeConn's customer base is so large that this probability does not change when two customers are selected from the customer base (we will discuss this idea more fully later in the chapter). Exhibit 5.1 on the next page shows a tree diagram to illustrate the possible values for x and the associated probabilities.

We see that $P(x = 2) = 0.16$, and $P(x = 0) = 0.36$. We see that there are two ways for x to equal 1, and since these are mutually exclusive, we can simply add the related probabilities to get $P(x = 1) = 0.24 + 0.24 = 0.48$. This information can be summarized in a table such as the one shown in Exhibit 5.2 on the next page.

Note that the possible values of the random variable x represent mutually exclusive outcomes (having exactly one rural customer is mutually exclusive with having exactly two rural customers). This means that if we want to calculate $P(x = 1 \text{ or } 2)$, we can simply add the related probabilities.

$$P(x = 1 \text{ or } 2) = 0.48 + 0.16 = 0.64$$

---

[1] Subject to the limitations of the measuring device, as noted in Chapter 2.

EXHIBIT 5.1

Tree Diagram for Characteristics of Two Randomly Selected GeorgeConn Customers

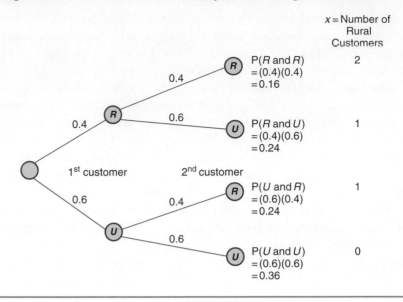

EXHIBIT 5.2

Number of Rural Customers Out of Two Randomly Selected GeorgeConn Customers

x	0	1	2
P(x)	0.36	0.48	0.16

We could also have used the complement rule to get this probability.

P(x = 1 or 2) = 1 − P(x = 0) = 1 − 0.36 = 0.64

The probability rules from Chapter 4 will still come in handy when you are working with discrete probability distributions.

The table shown in Exhibit 5.2 is one way to represent the probability distribution of the random variable x. It is also possible to represent this information graphically, with the random variable x on the x-axis and P(x) on the y-axis, as shown opposite in Exhibit 5.3.

Of course, the sum of the probabilities in any probability distribution has to be 100% (or 1, in decimal form), because the probability distribution lists *all* of the possible values of the random variable, and these in turn must account for all of the possible outcomes of the experiment.

Mean and Standard Deviation of a Probability Distribution

Most probability distributions can be summarized with:

- expected values (or means), which are (not surprisingly) measures of the centre of the probability distribution, and
- standard deviations, which are measures of the variability of the probability distribution

EXHIBIT 5.3

Graph of a Probability Distribution

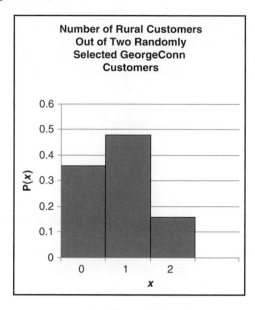

The calculations depend on the particular probability distribution.

The mean, μ, of a discrete probability distribution can be calculated as follows:

$$\mu = \sum(x \cdot P(x))$$

That is, the mean is a weighted average of the possible values of the random variable x, where the weights are the associated probabilities. The mean of a probability distribution is also referred to as the *expected value* of the random variable.

The standard deviation, σ, of a probability distribution can be calculated as follows:

$$\sigma = \sqrt{\sum(x - \mu)^2 \, P(x)}$$

This formula shows that calculation of the standard deviation is based on deviations from the mean, as we would expect from our work on standard deviations in Chapter 3. While this formula is correct, if you want to calculate the standard deviation by hand, there is another version of the formula that you will find easier to use:

$$\sigma = \sqrt{\sum x^2 P(x) - \mu^2}$$

We can apply these formulas to calculate the mean and standard deviation for the probability distribution for the GeorgeConn example. Exhibit 5.4 on the next page shows the probability distribution again.

$$\begin{aligned}
\mu &= \sum(x \cdot P(x)) \\
&= 0 \cdot 0.36 + 1 \cdot 0.48 + 2 \cdot 0.16 \\
&= 0.8
\end{aligned}$$

The expected number of rural customers, out of a random sample of two, is 0.8.

EXHIBIT 5.4

Probability Distribution for Number of Rural Customers Out of Two Randomly Selected GeorgeConn Customers

x	0	1	2
P(x)	0.36	0.48	0.16

$$\sigma = \sqrt{\Sigma x^2 P(x) - \mu^2}$$

$$= \sqrt{(0^2 \cdot 0.36 + 1^2 \cdot 0.48 + 2^2 \cdot 0.16) - 0.8^2}$$

$$= \sqrt{1.12 - 0.64}$$

$$= \sqrt{0.48}$$

$$= 0.6928$$

The standard deviation of this probability distribution is 0.6928.

EXAMPLE 5.1

Calculating the mean and standard deviation of a discrete probability distribution

Suppose every year you bid for the $5,000 contract to cut the lawns at a townhouse condominium in your town. Suppose also that each year there is a 50% chance you will get the contract, because the condominium board makes the decision by flipping a coin to choose between you and your arch-rival. Prepare a probability distribution table for x, the amount of money you will make from this lawn-cutting contract in a particular year. Calculate the mean and standard deviation of this probability distribution.

The associated probability distribution for this contract is illustrated in Exhibit 5.5.

EXHIBIT 5.5

Probability Distribution for Lawn-Cutting Contract

Contract value, x	$0	$5,000
Probability, P(x)	0.50	0.50

Imagine bidding on this contract year after year for many, many years. About half the time you will earn $5,000, and about half the time you will earn $0. So, your expected earnings over many years will be about $2,500; that is, $0.50(\$0) + 0.50(\$5,000) = \$2,500$. This is of course the expected value of the probability distribution.

$$\sigma = \sqrt{\Sigma x^2 P(x) - \mu^2}$$

$$= \sqrt{(0^2 \cdot 0.50 + 5,000^2 \cdot 0.50) - 2,500^2}$$

$$= \sqrt{12,500,000 - 6,250,000}$$

$$= \sqrt{6,250,000}$$

$$= 2,500$$

The standard deviation for the contract value is $2,500.

DEVELOP YOUR SKILLS 5.1

1. Which of the following random variables are discrete, and which are continuous?

   a. The number of passengers on a flight from Toronto to Paris
   b. The time it takes you to drive to work in the morning
   c. The number of cars that arrive at the local car dealership for an express oil-change service on Wednesday
   d. The time it takes to cut a customer's lawn
   e. The number of soft drinks a student buys during one week
   f. The kilometres driven on one tank of gas

2. Revisit the situation first described in Develop Your Skills 4.3, Exercise 12 (page 176). Three women who have been friends since childhood have just graduated from college. The friends are very different, and have different abilities and skills. All three of them are trying to get jobs in the financial services industry. Their probabilities of succeeding are 0.4, 0.5, and 0.35. Define x as the number of these three friends who get a job in the financial services industry. Build the probability distribution for x. If you did the earlier Develop Your Skills exercise, you have already calculated some of the probabilities.

3. Revisit the situation first described in Develop Your Skills 4.3, Exercise 13 (page 176). A software company is about to release three new software programs, one from each of three very distinct business divisions. The first program is a new game aimed at 15- to 25-year-olds. Its probability of succeeding is estimated to be 0.34. The second program is an accounting application for small business. Its probability of succeeding is estimated to be 0.12. The third program is a payroll system designed for government organizations. Its probability of succeeding is 0.10. Define x as the number of the three new software programs that are a success for this company. Build the associated probability distribution (you should have already calculated some of the probabilities). What is the expected number of successes?

4. A shipment contains 5,000 circuit boards, and 30 of them are defective. Define x as the number of defective boards in two selections from the shipment. Build the probability distribution for x. (You may find it easiest to use a computer to do these calculations.)

5. Exhibit 5.6 below shows a probability distribution for the number of restaurant customers who will order the daily special, out of the next six customers who come through the door. Fill in the missing probability, and calculate the mean and standard deviation of this probability distribution.

EXHIBIT 5.6

Number of Customers Who Will Order the Daily Special at a Restaurant, Out of the Next Six Customers

x	0	1	2	3	4	5	6
P(x)	0.03	0.05	0.28	0.45	0.12	0.04	?

5.2   THE BINOMIAL PROBABILITY DISTRIBUTION

Conditions for a Binomial Experiment

The binomial probability distribution often applies when we are interested in the number of times a particular characteristic turns up. For example, in a paint factory, we might be interested in the number of dented paint cans we find in the next 500 cans. Or, we might want to know how many of the next 50 customers who come into the store will opt for the bonus offer. Notice that what is of interest here is a count (how many out of a particular number), which can also be expressed as a percentage or proportion (that is, 32 customers out of the next 50 corresponds to 64%).

This count that we are interested in is a random variable, because its outcome is determined by chance. A binomial random variable counts the number of times one of only two possible outcomes takes place (thus the *bi-* part of the binomial's name). Because the binomial distribution can apply in a wide range of circumstances, we use some general language to cover all of these cases. When we find what we are looking for, this is called a *success*, and the other outcome (the complement of success) is a *failure*. So, if a customer comes into the store and opts for the bonus offer, this is a success. When a customer does not opt for the bonus offer, this is a failure. Similarly, if we find a dented paint can (this is what we are looking for), this is a success. This may seem a bit odd (surely we are hoping that the paint cans will *not* be dented), but if you think of a success as *finding what you are looking for*, the language will be more comfortable. In a binomial experiment, we are doing something repeatedly, such as examining a paint can to see if it is dented. These repeated actions are referred to as *trials*.

Requirements for a Binomial Experiment

The requirements for a random variable to be binomial are as follows:

1. There are only two possible outcomes to each trial of the experiment: success and failure. The probability of success in a given trial is denoted p. The probability of failure is $1 - p$ (often denoted as q).
2. The binomial random variable is the number of successes in a fixed number of trials (n).
3. Each trial is independent of every other trial. The probability of success, p, stays constant from trial to trial, as does the probability of failure, q.

Mean and Standard Deviation of a Binomial Distribution

A binomial probability distribution has a mean (expected value) and a standard deviation, as most probability distributions do. For a binomial random variable, the general formula for the mean simplifies to $\mu = np$. For example, when there are 10 trials (so $n = 10$), and the probability of success on each trial is 0.60, the expected value (or mean) of the binomial random variable would be $10(0.6) = 6$. This seems reasonable: if we repeated this experiment many times, we could expect the average outcome to be 6.

The general formula for the standard deviation of the binomial random variable simplifies to $\sigma = \sqrt{npq}$. Following on with the example above, the standard deviation would be $\sqrt{10(0.6)(0.4)} = 1.5492$.

Checking the Conditions for a Binomial Experiment

There are many situations where the binomial distribution applies. If you can recognize these situations, then you will be able to rely on a theoretical mathematical model to calculate probabilities (which is easier than it sounds!). The key to recognizing an application of the binomial probability distribution is to check against the requirements outlined above. For example, suppose we want to know the probability that a student can pass a 25-question multiple choice exam, if each question has five choices, and the student guesses. Is this a case where the binomial probability distribution applies?

First, there are 25 trials in this experiment. In each trial, the student guesses the answer to a multiple choice question. Although the student is picking from among five choices, there are in fact only two outcomes of interest: either the student guesses correctly (which has a probability of $\frac{1}{5} = 0.20$), or the student guesses incorrectly (which has a probability of $\frac{4}{5} = 0.80$). If a student is to pass the exam, then he or she must get at least 13 of the 25 questions correct. Therefore, we want to know $P(x \geq 13, n = 25, p = 0.20)$. So far, this situation seems to fit the binomial model.

The last requirement is that each trial is independent of every other trial, and that the probability of success, p, stays constant from trial to trial. If the student is truly guessing at each question, then this would be the case. We can use the binomial model to calculate the probability of passing the multiple choice test (you should do so, once you learn how to do the calculations, in case you are harbouring any misconceptions that multiple choice tests are easy to pass!).

Here is another example. What is the probability that in a sample of 20 tires in a tire factory, one will be defective, if 3% of all such tires produced at a particular plant are defective?

There are 20 trials in this experiment. Each trial consists of checking a tire to see if it is defective or not. Success in this case is defined as finding a defective tire, and we are told that $P(\text{success}) = p = 0.03$. The only other outcome is that a tire is not defective. So, we want to know $P(x = 1, n = 20, p = 0.03)$.

The last requirement is that each trial is independent of every other trial, and that the probability of success stays constant from trial to trial. When we sample a tire to see if it is defective, we would not return the sampled tire back into the population of tires. Therefore, each time we check a tire and set it aside, we are changing the probability that the next tire we sample will be defective. In terms of the binomial distribution, this means that the probability of success is changing from trial to trial, and the trials are not independent. This would seem to indicate that the binomial distribution does *not* apply in this case. But there is more to this.

Sampling Without Replacement   In the tire example, sampling is being done *without replacement*. This means that the trials are *not* independent, and so the experiment is not truly binomial. However, the binomial distribution can still be used in *certain* situations where the trials are not truly independent.

A numerical example will help you understand why. For example, suppose a tire factory produces 100,000 tires in a production run. If 3% of the tires are defective, then there are 3,000 defective tires in the population. The first time a tire is selected, the probability of finding a defective tire will be $\frac{3,000}{100,000} = 0.03$. The probability that the second tire will be defective will depend on whether the first tire was defective:

- it will be $\frac{2,999}{99,999} = 0.0299903$ (if the first tire was defective), or
- it will be $\frac{3,000}{99,999} = 0.0300003$ (if the first tire was not defective)

Notice that although the second-round selection probability is changing, it is not changing by much, and this is what is important here.

By the time the 20th tire is selected, the number of defective tires left in the population can be as low as 2,981 (if all of the previous 19 tires were defective) or as high as 3,000 (if none of the previous 19 tires was defective). This means that on the 20th trial, the probability of finding a defective tire can range from

- $\frac{2,981}{99,981} = 0.0298157$ to
- $\frac{3,000}{99,981} = 0.0300057$

While these probabilities are different from 3%, they are not much different. Because of this, we can still use the binomial distribution in this situation, because the probabilities will be close enough to the exact calculations.

This is appropriate only when the sample size is small relative to the population (otherwise, the binomial probabilities would be too far off the correct ones). How small should the sample be, relative to the population, for the binomial distribution to be used when we are sampling without replacement? Generally, if the sample is no more than 5% of the population, the binomial distribution can still be used. Another way to state this condition is: The population should be at least 20 times larger than the sample.

> **Using the Binomial Distribution when Sampling Without Replacement**
>
> When the other conditions for a binomial experiment apply but sampling is done without replacement, the binomial distribution can be used to approximate probabilities as long as the sample is no more than 5% of the population (that is, the population should be at least 20 times larger than the sample).

In fact, most of the useful applications of the binomial distribution rely on this result, because it is rare to encounter a real-life situation where sampling is done with replacement. Opinion polls are one of the most widely known applications of the binomial distribution. Obviously, the interviews are conducted without replacement. Once a pollster has talked with a respondent, that respondent is *not* added back into the population so that he or she might be called again.

Calculating Binomial Probabilities

Now that we know how to recognize when the binomial distribution applies, the next step is to calculate binomial probabilities. We will begin by calculating a binomial probability using the probability rules from Chapter 4, and then introduce a general formula. We will also use Excel to calculate binomial probabilities, and, finally, we will use tables in the back of this textbook.

Suppose a polling company has sent you to a large shopping mall to do some research into buying habits. Past polls done by the company in this mall have indicated that 60% of the shoppers are female, and there is no reason to believe that the customer base has changed significantly. You are standing by one of many entrances to the mall and approaching every customer who comes through the door to complete your survey, in the belief that this will give you a random sample of customers (suppose it does). What is the probability that two of the next three customers are female?

First we have to decide if this situation fits the binomial probability distribution. There will be three trials, as you ascertain whether each of the next three customers is female (success, in this case). The probability of a customer being female is 0.6, based on past research. Are the trials independent? No, because you are sampling without replacement.

However, it is likely that your sample of three customers is much less than 5% of the population of mall customers, so we can still use the binomial distribution to figure out probabilities. Although the probability of a customer being female will change *slightly* from trial to trial, it will still be approximately 0.6, and that is the value we will use.

The tree diagram shown in Exhibit 5.7 outlines the situation. There are eight possible outcomes, of which three correspond to the desired result (two out of the next three customers are female). These are highlighted in blue on the tree diagram.

EXHIBIT 5.7

Tree Diagram for Customers Entering a Mall

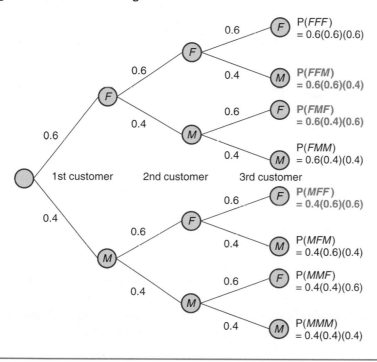

To calculate the probability we want, we can simply add the probabilities of the three appropriate end outcomes (they are mutually exclusive). We calculate:

P(next 2 out of 3 customers female)

$$= (0.6)(0.6)(0.4) + (0.6)(0.4)(0.6) + (0.4)(0.6)(0.6)$$

$$= 0.144 + 0.144 + 0.144$$

$$= 0.432$$

Obviously, we could repeat this sort of probability calculation until we had the complete probability distribution for the random variable x, which is the number of females among the next three customers you encounter. This random variable can take four possible values (0, 1, 2, or 3). A complete probability distribution for this random variable is summarized in the table shown in Exhibit 5.8 on the next page.

Particularly if you take the time to verify the other probability entries in this table, you will notice that there is a pattern to the probability calculation. This pattern applies

EXHIBIT 5.8

Probability Distribution for the Number of Female Customers Out of the Next Three Entering a Mall

x	0	1	2	3
P(x)	0.064	0.288	0.432	0.216

whether we are analyzing customers at a mall or faulty tires on an assembly line. The pattern of calculations can be captured mathematically in a formula, which underlies the probability calculations in Excel and the tables in the back of the book.

Calculating Binomial Probabilities with a Formula   The formula is as follows. For a binomial experiment with n trials, probability of success p, and probability of failure $q = 1 - p$:

$$P(x \text{ successes}) = \binom{n}{x} p^x q^{n-x}$$

where $\binom{n}{x}$ is the number of combinations of x items you can choose from n items, and is evaluated as follows:

$$\binom{n}{x} = \frac{n!}{x!(n-x)!} = \frac{n(n-1)(n-2)\cdots(1)}{x(x-1)(x-2)\cdots 1(n-x)(n-x-1)\cdots(1)}$$

This formula looks more complicated than it is. When you see the actual calculations, you will realize that they are fairly straightforward. $n!$ is read as n *factorial*. An example of a factorial calculation is $5! = 5 \times 4 \times 3 \times 2 \times 1$.

In these calculations, you will see that there is always a fair amount of cancelling out in the factorial portion of the formula. Another fact you will need to know is that $0! = 1$, by definition.

For the example above, where we wanted to know how many female customers there would be out of the next three customers entering the mall,

- $n = 3$
- $p = 0.60$ (and $q = 1 - 0.60 = 0.40$)

Suppose we want to calculate P($x = 2$).

$$P(x = 2) = \binom{n}{x} p^x q^{n-x}$$

$$= \binom{3}{2} 0.06^2 \, 0.40^{3-2}$$

$$= \frac{3!}{2!(3-2)!} 0.60^2 \, 0.40^1$$

$$= \frac{3 \cdot 2 \cdot 1}{(2 \cdot 1)(1 \cdot 1)} 0.36 \cdot 0.40$$

$$= 3(0.36)(0.40)$$

$$= 0.432$$

This agrees exactly with the value we calculated before (see Exhibit 5.8).

EXAMPLE 5.2A

Calculating binomial probabilities
with a formula

The probability that an adult resident of Hamilton is going to purchase a new vehicle in the next six months is 0.12. If six adult residents of Hamilton are randomly selected and asked whether they intend to buy a new vehicle in the next six months, what is the probability that two will indicate they plan to do so?

In this case, sampling is done without replacement, but the population of Hamilton is over 500,000. The sample size of six is much less than 5% of the population, so the binomial distribution can still be used to approximate the probability.

For this experiment, $n = 6$, $p = 0.12$, and we want to calculate $P(x = 2)$.

$$
\begin{aligned}
P(x = 2) &= \binom{n}{x} p^x q^{n-x} \\
&= \binom{6}{2} 0.12^2 \, 0.88^{6-2} \\
&= \frac{6!}{2!(6-2)!} 0.12^2 \, 0.88^4 \\
&= \frac{6 \cdot 5 \cdot 4 \cdot 3 \cdot 2 \cdot 1}{(2 \cdot 1)(4 \cdot 3 \cdot 2 \cdot 1)} 0.12^2 \, 0.88^4 \\
&= \frac{6 \cdot 5}{(2 \cdot 1)} 0.12^2 \, 0.88^4 \\
&= (3 \cdot 5)(0.0144)(0.59969536) \\
&= 0.1295
\end{aligned}
$$

When using your calculator, do not round the probabilities until you get to the end of the calculation.

The probability that two out of six randomly selected adult Hamilton residents plan to buy a new vehicle in the next six months is 0.1295.

It is easier to use a computer (or the tables, if a computer is not at hand) to do binomial probability calculations than to do them with a calculator.

Calculating Binomial Probabilities with Excel   As with the formula, in order to use Excel, we need to identify the particular binomial distribution of interest. We need to know:

- n, the number of trials
- p, the probability of success
- x, the number of successes for which we want the probability.

In the example about the mall customers, $n = 3$, $p = 0.6$, and $x = 2$. The Excel function we need is called **BINOMDIST**, and has the dialogue box shown on the next page in Exhibit 5.9.

The function arguments in Excel are:

- **Number_s** is x, the number of successes we are interested in
- **Trials** is n, the number of trials
- **Probability_s** is the probability of success, p
- **Cumulative** requires either *false* or *true* depending on whether you want a probability of a single number of successes (as in $P(x = 2)$, enter *false* in this case) or a cumulative probability of the form $P(x \leq 2)$ (enter *true* in this case).

EXHIBIT 5.9

BINOMDIST Dialogue Box

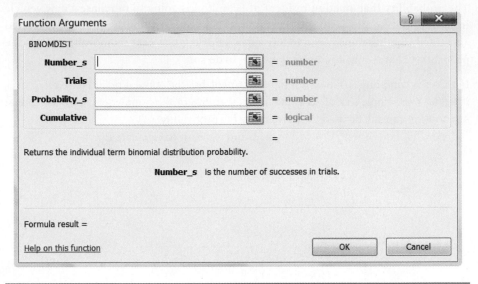

Notice that as you place your cursor in each of the individual slots on the dialogue box, Excel provides a description of what is needed in the bottom part of the box. When you click **OK**, Excel returns the value into the cell in the spreadsheet where your cursor is located. You should type some text into an adjoining cell, to describe what the calculation is about.

Excel produces the same result we arrived at through calculation, $P(x = 2) = 0.432$, as illustrated in Exhibit 5.10.

EXHIBIT 5.10

BINOMDIST Excel Function Result

Function Arguments

BINOMDIST

Number_s	2	= 2
Trials	3	= 3
Probability_s	.6	= 0.6
Cumulative	False	= FALSE

= 0.432

Returns the individual term binomial distribution probability.

Cumulative is a logical value: for the cumulative distribution function, use TRUE; for the probability mass function, use FALSE.

Formula result = 0.432

Help on this function   OK   Cancel

Excel's **BINOMDIST** provides not only probabilities for a single number of successes, but also *cumulative* probabilities. These are of the form $P(x \leq x^*)$, where x^* is a particular number of successes. For example, $P(x \leq 2)$ in the mall survey example would be the answer to the question, What is the probability that two or fewer of the next three customers are female?

$P(x \leq 2) = P(x = 0 \text{ or } 1 \text{ or } 2)$. The values of x in a binomial experiment represent mutually exclusive outcomes. Cumulative probabilities are calculated by adding the associated probabilities. This is effectively what Excel does when you enter **TRUE** in the **Cumulative** slot of the **BINOMDIST** dialogue box.

The probability function of Excel and the complement rule enable us to calculate *any* binomial probability we need.

EXAMPLE 5.2B

Using Excel to calculate the binomial probabilities

Use Excel to calculate the following probabilities.

   1. $P(x = 13, n = 50, p = 0.12)$
   2. $P(x \leq 13, n = 50, p = 0.12)$
   3. $P(x > 13, n = 50, p = 0.12)$
   4. $P(x < 13, n = 50, p = 0.12)$
   5. $P(8 \leq x \leq 15)$
   6. $P(8 < x < 15)$

Solutions

   1. $P(x = 13, n = 50, p = 0.12) = 0.0034$. This is a straightforward, non-cumulative binomial probability. See the Excel result in Exhibit 5.11.

EXHIBIT 5.11

BINOMDIST Result for $P(x = 13, n = 50, p = 0.12)$

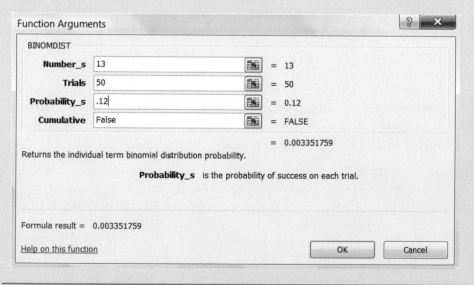

2. $P(x \le 13, n = 50, p = 0.12) = 0.9982$. This is a straightforward cumulative binomial probability. See the Excel result in Exhibit 5.12, below.

EXHIBIT 5.12

BINOMDIST Result for $P(x \le 13, n = 50, p = 0.12)$

Function Arguments				?	x

BINOMDIST

Number_s	13	📷	=	13
Trials	50	📷	=	50
Probability_s	.12	📷	=	0.12
Cumulative	True	📷	=	TRUE

= 0.998236281

Returns the individual term binomial distribution probability.

Cumulative is a logical value: for the cumulative distribution function, use TRUE; for the probability mass function, use FALSE.

Formula result = 0.998236281

Help on this function   OK   Cancel

3. $P(x > 13, n = 50, p = 0.12)$. This poses a problem, since it does not correspond exactly to either of the two probabilities that Excel calculates. However, we can use the complement rule to calculate this answer. This allows us to work with probabilities that **BINOMDIST** does calculate.

$P(x > 13)$
$= 1 - P(x \le 13)$
$= 1 - 0.998236281$ (shown above)
$= 0.001763719$

Be sure to use Excel to do the subtraction shown above. Exhibit 5.13 oppposite gives an example of how to set up a spreadsheet correctly. The calculations done by Excel are contained in cells B4 and B7. All of the other text has been typed into Excel. This allows you (or anyone else) to read the spreadsheet.

4. $P(x < 13, n = 50, p = 0.12)$. This probability also does not correspond directly to one that Excel calculates. Here we have to realize that for the binomial, $P(x < 13) = P(x \le 12)$. $(x = 13)$ is *not* included in this calculation, while it *is* included in $P(x \le 13)$.

$P(x < 13) = P(x \le 12) = 0.9949$

EXHIBIT 5.13

Correct Spreadsheet Setup

	A	B
1	n	50
2	p	0.12
3		
4	P(x<=13)	0.998236281
5		
6	P(x>13)	=1 - P(x<=13)
7		0.001763719

5. $P(8 \leq x \leq 15)$. Again, we have to do some thinking before we turn to Excel.

$$P(8 \leq x \leq 15) = P(x = 8 \text{ or } 9 \text{ or } 10 \text{ or } 11 \text{ or } 12 \text{ or } 13 \text{ or } 14 \text{ or } 15)$$

One way we could do this would be to figure out all of these individual probabilities and simply add them together (the outcomes are mutually exclusive). However, this is a lot of work and there is an easier way.

We can use Excel to calculate $P(x \leq 15)$ directly. This is almost the probability we want, except that it includes $P(x \leq 7)$, which we do not want. We can use Excel to calculate $P(x \leq 7)$ directly, and then subtract to get what we want.

$$P(8 \leq x \leq 15)$$
$$= P(x \leq 15) - P(x \leq 7)$$
$$= 0.99984 - 0.75325$$
$$= 0.2466$$

6. $P(8 < x < 15)$. Use similar reasoning to get this probability.

$$P(8 < x < 15)$$
$$= P(9 \leq x \leq 14)$$
$$= P(x \leq 14) - P(x \leq 8)$$
$$= 0.999444 - 0.860799$$
$$= 0.1386$$

Now that you have seen these examples, that's it! You should be able to use Excel to calculate *any* binomial probability you encounter.

Calculating Binomial Probabilities with Tables   For some situations, binomial tables are available (see Appendix 1 at the back of this textbook). As with Excel, you need to know n (the number of trials), p (the probability of success on any trial), and x (the number of successes you are interested in), to use the tables. Binomial tables are available in two forms:

- tables showing $P(x = \text{a particular value})$
- tables showing $P(x \leq \text{a particular value})$

The tables in the back of this textbook are of the second form, that is, they show $P(x \leq$ a particular value). To get $P(x =$ a particular value) from these tables, perform a subtraction as follows:

$$P(x = \text{a particular value}) = P(x \leq \text{the particular value}) - P(x \leq (\text{the particular value} - 1))$$

For example,

$$P(x = 4, n = 8, p = 0.3)$$
$$= P(x \leq 4) - P(x \leq 3) \text{ (both of these values are in the table; see the excerpt in Exhibit 5.14)}$$
$$= 0.942 - 0.806$$
$$= 0.136$$

EXHIBIT 5.14

Table Value = P ($x \leq$ number of successes)
Cumulative Binomial Probabilities for $n = 8$

no. of successes \ P	0.01	0.05	0.10	0.20	0.25	0.30	0.40
0	0.923	0.663	0.430	0.168	0.100	0.058	0.017
1	0.997	0.943	0.813	0.503	0.367	0.255	0.106
2	1.000	0.994	0.962	0.797	0.679	0.552	0.135
3	1.000	1.000	0.995	0.944	0.886	0.806	0.594
4	1.000	1.000	1.000	0.990	0.973	0.942	0.826
5	1.000	1.000	1.000	0.999	0.996	0.989	0.950
6	1.000	1.000	1.000	1.000	1.000	0.999	0.991
7	1.000	1.000	1.000	1.000	1.000	1.000	0.999

Generally, binomial probability tables do not include the last row, $P(x \leq n)$, which is $P(x \leq 8)$ in the example above. This is because $P(x \leq 8) = 1$ when $n = 8$. The sum of the probabilities for all possible outcomes *must* add up to 100%. Of course, the tables work for only the probabilities shown across the top row. In cases where the tables do not provide the answer, you can always turn to Excel for the answer.

EXAMPLE 5.2C

Calculating binomial probabilities with tables

The probability that a paint can will be dented during the production process in a factory is 0.01. If 25 paint cans are randomly selected from production, what is the probability that three or more of them will be dented?

In this case, sampling is done without replacement, but we assume the factory produces many thousands of cans of paint. The sample size is probably much less than 5% of the population, so the binomial distribution can still be used to approximate the probabilities.

$$n = 25, p = 0.01$$

$$P(x \geq 3) = 1 - P(x \leq 2) = 1 - 0.998 = 0.002$$

The probability of getting three or more dented cans out of 25 when they are randomly selected from the paint production process is 0.002.

Graphical Representation of Binomial Probability Distributions   It is possible to present the binomial distribution graphically, by plotting probabilities on the y-axis and values of x on the x-axis. Exhibit 5.15 below shows $P(x =$ number of successes) for $n = 8$ and $p = 0.3$. The probabilities were calculated using Excel.

EXHIBIT 5.15

Table of Binomial Probabilities (Non-Cumulative) for $n = 8$

no. of successes \ P	0.3
0	0.05765
1	0.19765
2	0.29648
3	0.25412
4	0.13614
5	0.04668
6	0.01000
7	0.00122
8	0.00007

$P(x = 4)$, for example, is represented by the shaded area in the graph in Exhibit 5.16, where $n = 8$ and $p = 0.3$. Because this is a probability distribution, the sum of all the probabilities and the total area of the bars has to add up to 1 (or 100%).

EXHIBIT 5.16

Graph of Probability Distribution

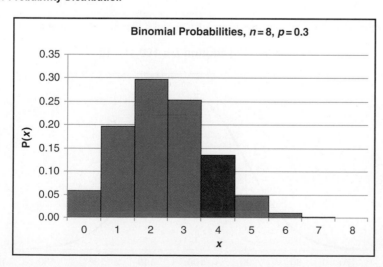

DEVELOP YOUR SKILLS 5.2

Do these calculations both with Excel and with tables (and with the binomial formula, if this is straightforward). You should get the same answers! Think about how you would recognize these as binomial probability calculations if you did not have the clues here (the title of this section, for example) to let you know.

6. A campus newspaper claims that 80% of students on campus support the newspaper's position on various issues affecting the college. A random sample of 10 students is taken, and in the sample, only four students say they support the newspaper's position. What is the probability of four or fewer students agreeing with the newspaper's position, if the newspaper's claim about 80% support is correct? Do you believe the newspaper's claim?

7. What is the probability that a student can pass a 25-question multiple choice exam, if each question has five choices and the student guesses?

8. What is the probability that in a sample of 20 tires, one will be defective, if 5% of all such tires produced at a particular plant are defective?

9. A poll on a website asked respondents what they thought was the best method of losing weight. 65% picked *exercise* as the answer. If five randomly selected visitors to the website were asked this question, what is the probability that three of them would pick *exercise?* Are you sure? Think carefully.

10. According to a recent survey conducted by a management recruiting firm, more than one third (34.2%) of executives polled thought that business casual dress has gone too casual. Suppose you randomly selected 30 executives, and asked them if they thought that business casual dress had gone too casual. What is the probability that 10 or fewer would agree?

5.3 THE NORMAL PROBABILITY DISTRIBUTION

The normal distribution is the most important probability distribution in the world! It applies to many natural and physical situations, it is absolutely essential for many types of statistical inference, and it can also be used to approximate other distributions (even the binomial, as we will see in Chapter 6).

Even if you have never studied statistics before, you have probably seen or heard about the normal curve. It is sometimes referred to as the *bell curve*, because it is shaped like a bell. Exhibit 5.17 shows an example of a normal probability distribution

EXHIBIT 5.17

Normal Probability Distribution with a Mean of 100 and a Standard Deviation of 10

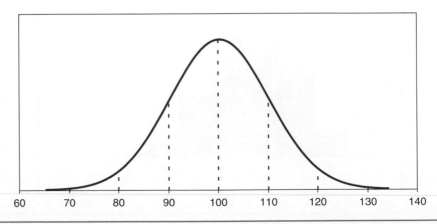

Normal Distribution $\mu = 100$, $\sigma = 10$

centred on 100, with a standard deviation of 10. Notice that the normal distribution is symmetric.

Many continuous random variables have normal distributions. Many normal random variables are related to a measurement of some kind. For example, if you made a histogram of the heights of all the students in your Statistics class (assuming the class is fairly large), it is likely that this histogram would look fairly *normal*. As well, measurements such as the exact weight of cereal in cereal boxes tend to fit the normal distribution.

You may recall from Chapter 2 that in theory, a continuous random variable can take any value in a continuous range or interval. In practice, our measuring devices are limited (you probably cannot measure the height of your classmates more accurately than to the centimetre, unless you have some unusual measuring tools). Nevertheless, a normal random variable is theoretically continuous, and so the graph is a smooth line. As with the binomial distribution, the total area under the curve has to equal 1 (this is a probability distribution).

Because a normal random variable can take an uncountable number of possible values, it is not possible to list all values in a table with the associated probability, as we could for the binomial distribution. In this case another approach is needed, but it is very similar to the graphical approach we used for the binomial distribution.

Exhibit 5.18 on the next page shows a probability graph for a binomial distribution with $n = 100, p = 0.5$. $P(40 \leq x \leq 45)$ here is equivalent to the red-shaded area in the graph in Exhibit 5.18.

Exhibit 5.19 is a normal distribution that is quite similar to the binomial distribution shown in Exhibit 5.18. The shaded area in this graph corresponds to $P(40 \leq x \leq 45)$.

Using the Normal Distribution to Approximate a Discrete Distribution   The normal distribution is continuous, but it can sometimes be used to approximate the distribution of a discrete random variable. In Chapter 6 we will see how to create normal distributions that approximate the distributions of certain binomial random variables. Normal distributions can also be used to approximate the distributions of other discrete random variables. For example, x might be the number of packages dropped off for next-day delivery at a courier service. Obviously, x is not a continuous random variable, because it is impossible to drop off $1\frac{1}{2}$ packages. However, the probability graph for the number of packages dropped off might be very close to a normal distribution (see Exhibit 5.20 on page 205).

Therefore, you should not be surprised to see the normal distribution being used to calculate probabilities for some discrete random variables.

Calculating Normal Probabilities with Excel   But how do we figure out how much this area is? As with the binomial, this can be done with a formula (and in this case, some calculus). However, we will rely on Excel and a table to do normal probability calculations.

Before we turn to Excel, there is one more important point. When we are using the binomial probability distribution, there can be a big difference between, for

EXHIBIT 5.18

Probability Graph for a Binomial Distribution with $n = 100$, $p = 0.5$

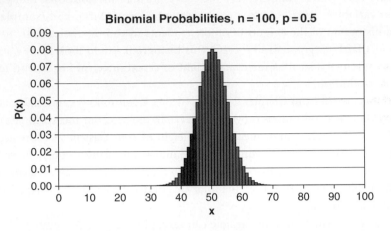

EXHIBIT 5.19

Normal Distribution Corresponding to Binomial Distribution with $n = 100$, $p = 0.5$

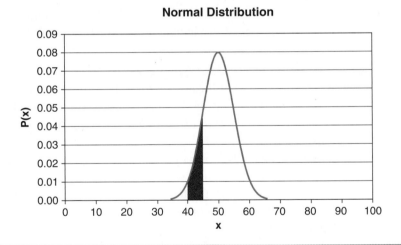

example, $P(x \leq 4)$ and $P(x < 4)$, because $P(x < 4) = P(x \leq 3)$. When we are calculating normal probabilities, however, $P(x \leq 4)$ is approximately equal to $P(x < 4)$, because $P(x < 4) = P(x \leq 3.9999999999999\ldots)$. The difference between the normal probabilities $P(x \leq 4)$ and $P(x < 4)$ is so small that it is approximately zero.

EXHIBIT 5.20

The Normal Curve Can Be Used to Approximate the Probability Distribution of a Discrete Random Variable

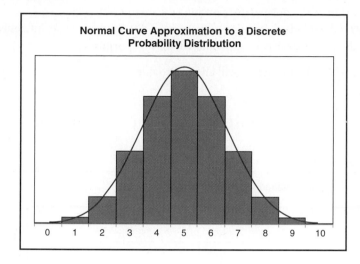

Excel has a number of functions associated with the normal distribution. The one we will use most often is **NORMDIST**. In order to use this Excel function, we need to identify the particular normal distribution we are interested in. There are an infinite number of different normal distributions, but each one is uniquely determined by its mean and standard deviation. The dialogue box for **NORMDIST** is shown below in Exhibit 5.21.

EXHIBIT 5.21

Dialogue Box for NORMDIST

Function Arguments	?	X

NORMDIST		
X		= number
Mean		= number
Standard_dev		= number
Cumulative		= logical
		=

Returns the normal cumulative distribution for the specified mean and standard deviation.

X   is the value for which you want the distribution.

Formula result =

Help on this function   OK   Cancel

The function arguments in Excel are:

- **x** is the upper limit of the probability you are interested in. For example if you wanted to know $P(x \leq 4)$, you would enter 4 here.
- **Mean** is the mean of the normal distribution you are interested in
- **Standard_dev** is the standard deviation of the normal distribution you are interested in
- **Cumulative** should *always* have "true" entered, for our purposes

Used this way, the **NORMDIST** function will always provide

$$P(x \leq \text{the particular value of } x \text{ you provide})$$

Graphically, it looks like the example in Exhibit 5.22, where $P(x \leq 4)$ is illustrated.

EXHIBIT 5.22

$P(x \leq 4)$, NORMDIST Reports Shaded Area Under Curve

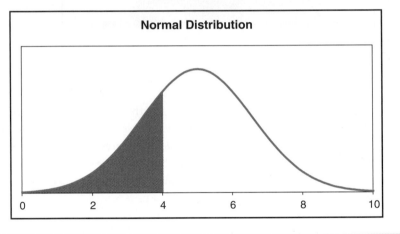

Normal Distribution

EXAMPLE 5.3A

Calculating normal probabilities with NORMDIST

For a normal distribution with a mean of 10 and a standard deviation of 2, calculate the following probabilities.

1. $P(x \leq 8)$
2. $P(8 \leq x \leq 13)$
3. $P(x \geq 12)$

Solutions

1. Probability calculations such as $P(x \leq 8)$ are quite straightforward with **NORMDIST**. Simply enter the mean, the standard deviation, and the value 8 into the appropriate areas, and the probability will be calculated for you. See Exhibit 5.23 opposite.

   $$P(x \leq 8) = 0.1587$$

   This probability is the shaded area under the curve shown in Exhibit 5.24.

EXHIBIT 5.23

P($x \leq 8$)

Function Arguments		?	✕

NORMDIST

X	8	▦	= 8
Mean	10	▦	= 10
Standard_dev	2	▦	= 2
Cumulative	true	▦	= TRUE

= 0.158655254

Returns the normal cumulative distribution for the specified mean and standard deviation.

Cumulative   is a logical value: for the cumulative distribution function, use TRUE; for the probability mass function, use FALSE.

Formula result =   0.158655254

Help on this function   OK   Cancel

EXHIBIT 5.24

P($x \leq 8$) = 0.1587, Shaded Area Under Curve

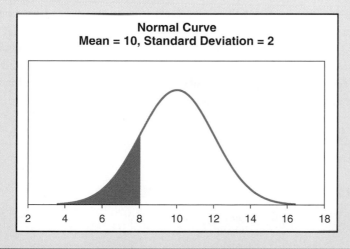

2. What if we want P($8 \leq x \leq 13$)? It should be easy to see that we can arrive at this answer by first calculating P($x \leq 13$), and then subtracting off the area where P($x \leq 8$) (the cross-hatched area in Exhibit 5.25, on the next page).

$$P(8 \leq x \leq 13) = P(x \leq 13) - P(x \leq 8) = 0.933193 - 0.158655 = 0.774538$$

EXHIBIT 5.25

P(8 ≤ x ≤ 13)

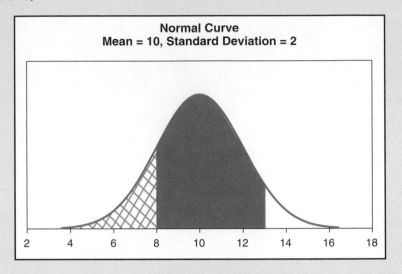

3. What if we wanted P($x \geq 12$)? For this case, we can use the complement rule. P($x \geq 12$) = 1 − P($x \leq 12$) = 1 − 0.8413455 = 0.158655 (notice this is the same value as P($x \leq 8$), which we would expect, since the distribution is symmetric).

Once you have mastered the three variations in the preceding example, you should be able to use **NORMDIST** to calculate any normal probability that you need. You should type some descriptive text into your spreadsheet so that you can identify the mean and standard deviation of the normal distribution you worked with, and you have a description of what the calculated probabilities refer to. Exhibit 5.26 below shows an example of how you could set up your spreadsheet.

EXHIBIT 5.26

Example of Spreadsheet Setup

	A	B	C
1	normal distribution		
2	mean	10	
3	standard deviation	2	
4			
5	P(x<=8)	0.158655	
6			
7	P(x<=13)	0.933193	
8	P(8<=x<=13)	0.774538	
9			
10	P(x<=12)	0.841345	
11	P(x>=12)	0.158655	

NORMDIST function results show in cells B5, B7, B8, B10, and B11. Everything else in the spreadsheet is typed in, so that the spreadsheet is easy to read and understand.

Another Excel function that we will use when calculating normal probabilities is **NORMINV**. We will use this function when we want the *x*-value that corresponds to a particular probability (this is the reverse of what we have done so far, where we started with an *x*-value and ended up with a probability).

EXAMPLE 5.3B

Using **NORMINV** to calculate *x*-values for normal probabilities

Suppose that past research has shown that the amount of paint in paint cans is normally distributed, with a mean of 3 litres and a standard deviation of 0.01 litres. The company controller is concerned that the company is giving away a lot of free paint in cans that are overfull. You want to reassure her by telling her that 98% of the cans have no more than *x* amount of paint in them. What is *x*? Exhibit 5.27 illustrates this problem.

EXHIBIT 5.27

Normal Distribution of Paint Volume in Cans

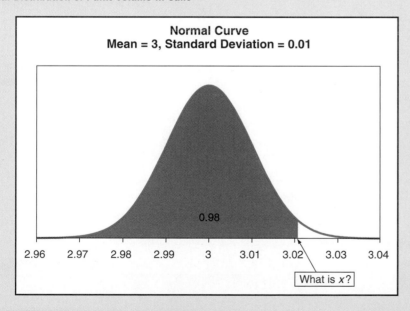

You can find the required *x* with **NORMINV**. The dialogue box for the function is shown on the next page in Exhibit 5.28.

The function arguments in Excel are as follows.

- **Probability** is the (left-side) probability you are starting with (98%, in this case)
- **Mean** is the mean of the normal distribution (3, in this case)
- **Standard_dev** is the standard deviation of the normal distribution (0.01, in this case)

EXHIBIT 5.28

Dialogue Box for NORMINV

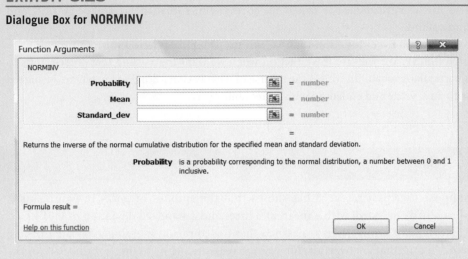

Since the probability problem is set up in a way that corresponds exactly to the Excel function, we can get the answer directly from Excel. The completed dialogue box is shown below in Exhibit 5.29.

EXHIBIT 5.29

Completed Dialogue Box for NORMINV

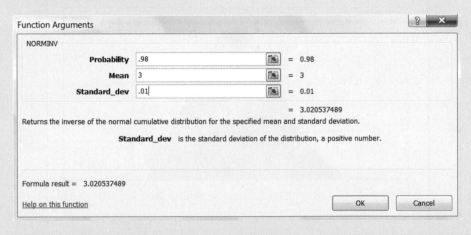

So, we can assure the controller that 98% of the paint cans have less than 3.020537 litres in them.

Calculating Normal Probabilities with a Table   If you do not have access to Excel to calculate normal probabilities, there is a table in Appendix 2, at the back of this textbook, that you can use. It might seem surprising or mysterious that there is only *one* table, when there are an infinite number of normal distributions. The solution to the mystery lies in the fact that all normal distributions are symmetric probability distributions. The total area under each curve is equal to 1. As a result, corresponding probabilities from all of the normal distributions are equal.

This might be more obvious if we look at a couple of normal distributions. We will compare two normal distributions: one with a mean of 15 and a standard deviation of 2, and another with a mean of 16 and a standard deviation of 3. If we put both curves on the same graph (which ensures that the axis scales for the two curves are identical), the normal curves look different. This is illustrated in Exhibit 5.30.

EXHIBIT 5.30

Two Normal Distributions, Same Axis

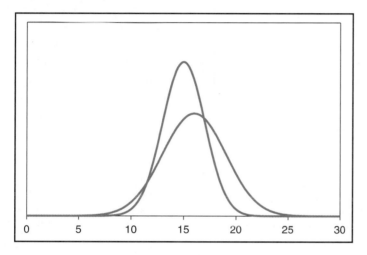

However, if we put the curves on two different graphs, and change the scales on the axes, the curves look the same, as illustrated in Exhibit 5.31 below.

EXHIBIT 5.31

Two Normal Distributions, Different Axis Scales

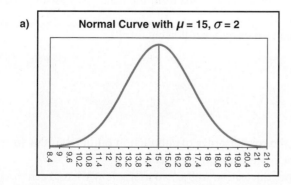
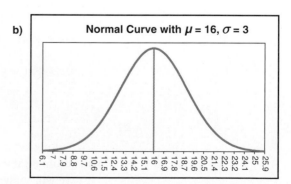

Some of the similarities are obvious. $P(x \leq 15)$ for the normal curve in Exhibit 5.31a will be equal to $P(x \leq 16)$ for the normal curve in Exhibit 5.31b. In both cases, of course, this probability will be equal to 50%, since the curves are symmetric, and half of the total 100% probability lies to the left of the mean and half to the right.

We can also see that P($x ≤ 12$) for the normal curve centred on 15 will be equivalent to P($x ≤ 11.5$) for the normal curve centred on 16, as illustrated in Exhibit 5.32.

EXHIBIT 5.32

Two Normal Distributions

a)
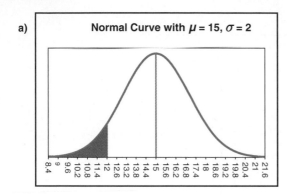

b)
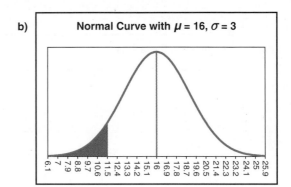

But how do we work with the normal distribution so that we can identify similar areas and probabilities? We do this by *standardizing* every normal probability calculation, that is, relating it back to a normal distribution with a mean of 0 and a standard deviation of 1 (this is the distribution that matches the table in the back of this book). We do this by calculating a *z-score*. The z-score translates the *x*-value of any normal distribution into a measure of how far that *x*-value is from the mean, in numbers of standard deviations. When an *x*-value is to the left of the mean (below the mean), the z-score has a negative value. When an *x*-value is to the right of the mean (above the mean), the z-score has a positive value.

We first used the standard deviation as a unit of measurement when we discussed the Empirical Rule, in Chapter 3. Then, we worked with *x*-values located at distances of exactly one, two, and three standard deviations from the mean. Now, with z-scores, we will be able to work with any *x*-value.

The z-score can be calculated using the following formula.

Calculating a z-score

$$z = \frac{x - \mu}{\sigma}$$

As long as you follow the correct order of subtraction outlined in this formula, it will automatically assign the correct sign to the z-score.

We will apply the z-score calculation to the two examples we have been discussing. For the first distribution ($\mu = 15, \sigma = 2$), the z-score for an *x*-value of 12 is calculated as

$$z = \frac{x - \mu}{\sigma} = \frac{12 - 15}{2} = -1.5$$

For the second distribution ($\mu = 16$, $\sigma = 3$), the z-score for an x-value of 11.5 is calculated as

$$z = \frac{x - \mu}{\sigma} = \frac{11.5 - 16}{3} = -1.5$$

The z-scores are the same, so these x-values are an equivalent distance from the mean in their respective distributions. Therefore, the area (and probability) to the left of the x-values will be the same.

The table in the back of the textbook works with these z-scores, so once you have translated any x-value into a z-score, you can use the table for *any* normal distribution. You may have to rely on the complement rule to complete your calculations. The illustration at the top of the table shows what the table tells you. For a given z-score (call it z_0), the table gives $P(z \leq z_0)$, that is, the area under the normal curve to the left of the z-score. The table reports z-scores to two decimal places. Find the first decimal place by looking down the first column. Locate the second decimal place by looking across the top row of the table. The intersection of the column and row you selected gives you the associated probability for the z-score. Exhibit 5.33 below provides an excerpt from the normal table, and illustrates how to use it.

EXHIBIT 5.33

Excerpt of Standard Normal Table

z	0.00	0.01	0.02	0.03	0.04
−0.1	0.4602	0.4562	0.4522	0.4483	0.4443
−0.0	0.5000	0.4960	0.4920	0.4880	0.4840
0.0	0.5000	0.5040	0.5080	0.5120	0.5160
0.1	0.5398	0.5438	0.5478	0.5517	0.5557
0.2	0.5793	0.5832	0.5871	0.5910	0.5948
0.3	0.6179	0.6217	0.6255	0.6293	0.6331
0.4	0.6554	0.6591	0.6628	0.6664	0.6700
0.5	0.6915	0.6950	0.6985	0.7019	0.7054
0.6	0.7257	0.7291	0.7324	0.7357	0.7389
0.7	0.7580	0.7611	0.7642	0.7673	0.7704
0.8	0.7881	0.7910	0.7939	0.7967	0.7995
0.9	0.8159	0.8186	0.8212	0.8238	0.8264
1.0	0.8413	0.8438	0.8461	0.8485	0.8508

Suppose you calculated a z-score of 0.43. This table says that $P(z \leq 0.43) = 0.6664$. This is illustrated in Exhibit 5.34 on the next page.

There is one more point about the normal tables. What if your calculations lead to a z-score that is not included in the tables? For example, what if you calculated a z-score of 4? And why do the tables go only as high as 3.99? If you look at the table, you will see that $P(z \leq 3.99) = 1.0000$. This probability is equal to 100%, to four decimal places of accuracy, although a more exact value is 0.999967. Although theoretically a normal random variable can be infinitely large or small, almost 100% of the probability is accounted for with a z-score of 3.99, and so the table stops there. If you have a z-score any larger than 3.99, and you are using the tables, keep in mind that there is only negligible area under the normal curve beyond a z-score of 3.99 (or −3.99).

EXHIBIT 5.34

$P(z \leq 0.43) = 0.6664$

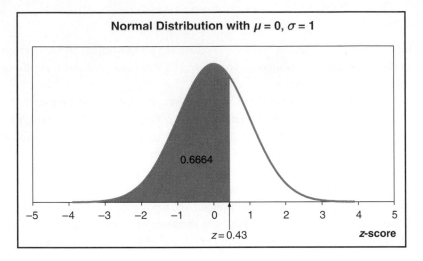

How do we solve the problems that start with a probability and require us to find a corresponding x-value, using the normal tables? For example, how do we solve the problem from Example 5.3B (page 209)? In this example, the amount of paint in paint cans is normally distributed, with a mean of 3 litres and a standard deviation of 0.01 litres. The company controller is concerned that the cans are overfull, and you want to reassure her that 98% of the cans have no more than x amount of paint in them. What is x?

In this case, the fact we are given is that $P(x \leq$ unknown x-value$) = 0.98$. We have to scan the *body* of the normal table for an entry that is as close as possible to 0.98. The closest entry is 0.9798 (and here is one of the problems associated with using tables—often, you have to approximate the answer). This is the left-side probability for a z-score of 2.05. The z-score tells us that the correct x-value is 2.05 standard deviations above the mean. Therefore, the required x-value $= 3 + 2.05\,(0.01) = 3.0205$. Because of the approximation, the x-value calculated with the table does not exactly match the value we calculated with **NORMINV** (3.020537), but it is fairly close.

Notice that this calculation is just a rearrangement of the formula for a z-score, as follows:

$$z = \frac{x - \mu}{\sigma} \text{ (cross-multiply)}$$
$$x - \mu = z \cdot \sigma \text{ (add } \mu \text{ to both sides)}$$
$$x = \mu + z \cdot \sigma$$

Whenever you do normal probability calculations, it is a good idea to draw a normal curve and sketch the area you are trying to find. This will allow you to relate the Excel output or the entry in the normal table to the probability you are trying to calculate. Example 5.3C opposite illustrates.

EXAMPLE **5.3C**

Calculating normal probabilities
with a table

Suppose the listing prices for all three-bedroom, two-bathroom bungalows for sale in Barrie in May of 2009 are normally distributed, with a mean of $265,800 and a standard deviation of $28,600.

1. What is the probability that such a bungalow will list for less than $240,000?
2. What is the probability that such a bungalow will list for more than $300,000?
3. What is the probability that such a bungalow will list for between $225,000 and $300,000?
4. 75% of such bungalows list for more than what price?

1. What is the probability that such a bungalow will list for less than $240,000? First, sketch a graph that illustrates the probability we are trying to find.

EXHIBIT **5.35**

Distribution of Bungalow Prices P(x < $240,000)

The required probability is on the left side of the distribution, which matches the way the tables are set up.

$$P(x < \$240{,}000)$$
$$= P\left[z < \left(\frac{240{,}000 - 265{,}800}{28{,}600}\right)\right]$$
$$= P(z < -0.90)$$
$$= 0.1841$$

2. What is the probability that such a bungalow will list for more than $300,000? First, sketch the appropriate diagram.

EXHIBIT 5.36

Distribution of Bungalow Prices P(x > $300,000)

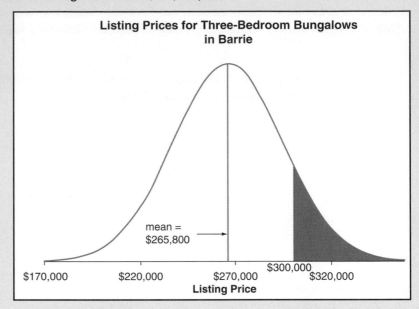

In this case, the required probability is on the right side of the distribution. We can use the table to look up the complementary probability on the left side, and subtract that probability from 1.

$P(x > \$300,000)$

$$= 1 - P\left[z < \left(\frac{300,000 - 265,800}{28,600}\right)\right]$$
$$= 1 - P(z < 1.20)$$
$$= 1 - 0.8849$$
$$= 0.1151$$

Notice that it is very important to round the z-score correctly to two decimal places when working with the table.

3. What is the probability that such a bungalow will list for between $225,000 and $300,000? First, sketch the appropriate diagram (see Exhibit 5.37 opposite).

In this case, we will have to subtract the probability to the left of $225,000 from the probability to the left of $300,000 to get the desired probability.

$P(\$225,000 < x < \$300,000)$

$$= P\left[z < \left(\frac{300,000 - 265,800}{28,600}\right)\right] - P\left[z < \left(\frac{225,000 - 265,800}{28,600}\right)\right]$$
$$= P(z < 1.20) - P(z < -1.43)$$
$$= 0.8849 - 0.0764$$
$$= 0.8085$$

4. 75% of such bungalows list for more than what price? Again, begin with a sketch of the distribution (see Exhibit 5.38 opposite).

To work with the tables, we must work with a left-side probability. If 75% of such bungalows list for more than the price we want to find, then 25% must list for less. We must search the body of the normal table for a probability as close as possible

EXHIBIT **5.37**

Distribution of Bungalow Prices   P($225,000 < x < $300,000)

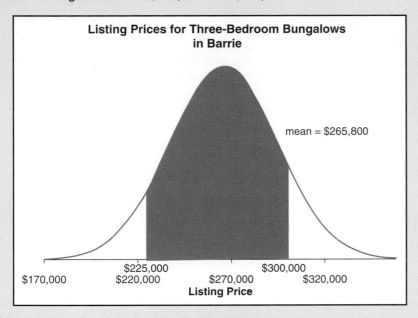

EXHIBIT **5.38**

Distribution of Bungalow Prices, 75% of Prices Are Above x

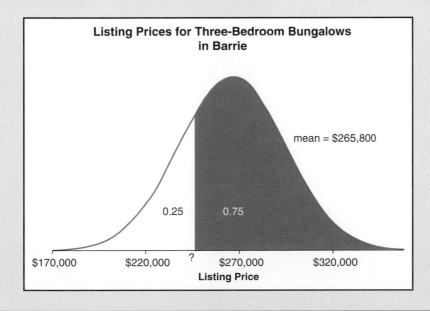

to 0.2500. The closest value is 0.2514, which corresponds to a *z*-score of −0.67. This means that the *x*-value we seek is 0.67($28,600) below the mean price of $265,800.

$$x = \mu + z \cdot \sigma$$
$$x = \$265,800 - 0.67(\$28,600)$$
$$= \$246,638$$

DEVELOP YOUR SKILLS 5.3

Do the following probability calculations with Excel first, and then with the tables in Appendix 2. You should get the same answers no matter how you do the calculations, although the tables will sometimes force you to approximate.

11. Your company manufactures light bulbs. You know from past experience that the number of hours the bulbs will last is a normally distributed random variable, with a mean of 5,000 hours and a standard deviation of 367 hours. What percentage of the bulbs will last at least 6,000 hours?

12. Using the light bulb distribution in Exercise 11 above, calculate what length-of-life guarantee your company should issue so that no more than 2.5% of light bulbs will fail to meet the guarantee.

13. Rocky Hill Bikes (RHB) manufactures high-end bicycles. Rocky Hill's vice-president of finance asked you to investigate the warranty expense for RHB's dual-suspension hybrid bike. You sampled 600 warranty claims and found that the average warranty expense per bike appeared to be normally distributed with an average of $53 (to your surprise, every bike in your sample had a warranty expense). You may assume that the standard deviation is $9. Assuming the normal distribution is an accurate probability model, answer the following questions.

   a. What is the probability that a randomly selected warranty expense for these dual suspension hybrid bikes would be less than $38?

   b. What is the probability that a randomly selected warranty expense for these bikes would be between $38 and $62?

   c. Your boss has reminded you that RHB loses money on these bikes when the warranty expense exceeds $68. What is the probability that a randomly selected warranty expense for these bikes would be above $68?

14. Trading volume on a major stock exchange is approximately normally distributed with a mean of 232 million shares and a standard deviation of about 44 million shares.

   a. What is the probability that the trading volume will be less than 200 million shares?

   b. If the exchange wants to issue a press release when trading volume is in the top 2% of trading days, what trading volume would trigger a press release?

   c. What percentage of the time does the trading volume exceed 300 million shares?

15. The time that it takes a worker to finish a particular assembly line task is normally distributed, with a mean of 32 seconds and a standard deviation of 10 seconds. The slowest 10% of workers (those with the slowest 10% of times) will be required to spend the weekend training, to try to improve their times. What is the minimum speed a worker must achieve to escape the weekend training?

A random variable is a variable whose value is determined by the outcome of a random experiment. A discrete random variable can take on any value from a list of distinct possible values. The probability distribution for a discrete random variable is often illustrated with a list of all the possible values of the random variable and their associated probabilities. A continuous random variable can take on any value from a continuous range. The probability distribution of a continuous random variable is described graphically, or with a mathematical formula.

Probability Distributions

It is possible to build a discrete probability distribution with probability rules. Discrete probability distributions can be represented with a table listing all possible values of the random variable and their associated probabilities. The distribution can also be represented graphically, with the possible values of the random variable along the x-axis, and the associated probabilities shown on the y-axis.

Most probability distributions can be summarized with

- expected values (or means), which are measures of the centre of the probability distribution, and
- standard deviations, which are measures of the variability of the probability distribution

The mean of a discrete probability distribution, μ, can be calculated as follows.

$$\mu = \Sigma(x \cdot P(x))$$

The standard deviation of a probability distribution, σ, can be calculated as follows.

$$\sigma = \sqrt{\Sigma(x - \mu)^2 P(x)}$$

There is another version of the formula that you will find easier to use when doing calculations by hand, as follows.

$$\sigma = \sqrt{\Sigma(x^2 P(x) - \mu^2)}$$

The mean and standard deviation of a continuous probability distribution depend on the particular mathematical model.

The Binomial Probability Distribution

A binomial random variable counts the number of times one of only two possible outcomes takes place. In a binomial experiment, something is done repeatedly, for example, examining a paint can to see if it is dented. These repeated actions are referred to as trials.

There are a number of requirements for a random variable to be binomial, as follows:

1. There are only two possible outcomes to each trial of the experiment: success and failure. The probability of success in a given trial is denoted p. The probability of failure is $1 - p$ (often denoted as q).
2. The binomial random variable is the number of successes in a fixed number of trials (n).
3. Each trial is independent of every other trial. The probability of success, p, stays constant from trial to trial, as does the probability of failure, q.

The mean of a binomial random variable is $\mu = np$. The standard deviation of the binomial random variable is $\sigma = \sqrt{npq}$.

Most of the useful applications of the binomial distribution are not truly binomial, because sampling is done without replacement. When the other conditions for a binomial experiment apply, but sampling is done without replacement, the binomial distribution can be used to approximate probabilities, as long as the sample is no more than 5% of the population (that is, the population is at least 20 times as large as the sample).

For a binomial experiment with *n* trials, probability of success *p*, and probability of failure $q = 1 - p$,

$$P(x \text{ successes}) = \binom{n}{x} p^x q^{n-x}$$

Example 5.2A on page 195 illustrates the use of the formula.

The Excel function used to calculate binomial probabilities is called **BINOMDIST**.

Example 5.2B on page 197 illustrates the use of Excel to calculate binomial probabilities. It is also possible to calculate a limited number of binomial probabilities using the tables in the back of the book (see Appendix 1). Example 5.2C on page 200 illustrates how to use the tables to calculate binomial probabilities.

The Normal Probability Distribution

The normal distribution applies to many natural and physical situations, it is absolutely essential for many types of statistical inference, and it can even be used to approximate other distributions. Many continuous random variables have normal distributions. Many normal random variables are related to a measurement of some kind.

For a normal random variable, $P(x = \text{a particular value}) \simeq 0$. This means that for a normal random variable, say, 4, for example, $P(x < 4) = P(x \le 4)$.

Excel has a number of functions associated with the normal distribution. Two that are described in this chapter are **NORMDIST** and **NORMINV**. Example 5.3A on page 206 illustrates the use of **NORMDIST**. Example 5.3B on page 209 illustrates the use of **NORMINV**.

It is also possible to use the standard normal distribution and a table (see Appendix 2 at the back of the book) to calculate normal probabilities. It is necessary to standardize the probability calculation using a *z*-score, which translates the location of a particular *x* in a normal probability distribution into a number of standard deviations from the mean. The calculation of the *z*-score is as follows:

$$z = \frac{x - \mu}{\sigma}$$

See page 213 for instructions on how to read the normal table. Example 5.3C on page 215 illustrates the use of the normal tables to calculate probabilities.

You can also use the tables to locate an *x*-value that corresponds to a particular probability. Once you locate the desired probability in the body of the normal table and the associated *z*-score, you can calculate the desired *x*-value with the following formula.

$$x = \mu + z \cdot \sigma$$

If any of your normal probability calculations lead to a *z*-score that is not included in the tables, remember that although theoretically a normal random variable can be infinitely large or small, almost 100% of the probability is accounted for with a *z*-score of 3.99, and so the table stops there. Therefore, if you have a *z*-score any larger than 3.99, and you are using the tables, keep in mind that there is only negligible area under the normal curve beyond a *z*-score of 3.99 (or −3.99).

Go to MyStatLab at www.mathxl.com. You can practise the exercises indicated with red in the Develop Your Skills and Chapter Review Exercises as often as you want, and guided solutions will help you find answers step by step. You'll find a personalized study plan available to you too!

CHAPTER REVIEW EXERCISES

WARM-UP EXERCISES

1. Which of the following is a binomial random variable? Which one(s) could possibly have a normal distribution? Explain your answers.
   a. The number of magazines subscribed to by a Canadian household.
   b. An opinion poll of 1,235 Canadians, asking if they subscribe to at least one magazine.
   c. The annual expenditure by Canadian households on magazine subscriptions.

2. Suppose the random variable x is the number of magazines subscribed to by a Canadian household. The probability distribution for x is shown in Exhibit 5.39 below.

EXHIBIT 5.39

Probability Distribution for the Number of Magazine Subscriptions in a Canadian Household

x	0	1	2	3	4	5
P(x)	0.15	0.38	0.27	0.11	0.06	0.03

   a. What is the probability that a Canadian household subscribes to three or more magazines?
   b. What is the probability that a Canadian household subscribes to two or three magazines?
   c. What is the expected number of magazine subscriptions in a Canadian household?
   d. What is the standard deviation of the number of magazine subscriptions in a Canadian household?

3. Suppose that 20% of students in the Business program read the financial section of the daily newspaper. Develop the probability distribution for x, the number out of three randomly selected students from the Business program who read the financial section of the daily newspaper.

4. Calculate the mean and standard deviation for the probability distribution you created in Exercise 3 above. Represent the probability distribution graphically.

5. Create the probability distribution for a binomial random variable with $n = 2, p = 0.4$, using basic probability rules. Verify that the expected value is equal to np, using the general formula for the mean of a probability distribution.

THINK AND DECIDE

6. A construction company is bidding on a contract. The company believes that it has a 25% chance of winning the contract. If the company wins, it will earn a profit of $50,000. If the company does not win the contract, it will lose the $1,845 it spent preparing the bid. What is the company's expected value of this contract?

7. The marks in an Economics class are normally distributed, with a mean of 65% and a standard deviation of 12%.
   a. What percentage of the class passed (that is, received a mark of 50% or higher)?
   b. What percentage of the class received a mark of 45% or lower?
   c. What percentage of the class received a mark between 50% and 75%?
   d. What percentage of the class received a mark of 90% or higher?

8. The leading brand of toothpaste has a 5% market share.
   a. A sample of 15 customers is taken. What is the probability that three or fewer of them use the leading brand of toothpaste?
   b. A sample of four customers is selected. What is the probability that two of them use the leading brand of toothpaste?

9. The number of pages printed before the ink cartridge has to be replaced on an inkjet printer is normally distributed, with a mean of 840 pages and a standard deviation of 224 pages. A new print cartridge has just been installed.
   a. What is the probability that the printer produces more than 1,000 pages before this cartridge needs to be replaced?
   b. What is the probability that the printer produces fewer than 600 pages before this cartridge needs to be replaced?
   c. 95% of the time, a cartridge will produce at least how many pages?

10. Warranty records show that the probability that a new computer will need warranty service in the first 90 days is 0.01.
    a. If a sample of five computers is selected, what is the probability that one of them will require service in the first 90 days?
    b. If a sample of four computers is selected, what is the probability that one of them will require service in the first 90 days?

11. An official from the securities commission estimates that 25% of all investment bankers have profited from the use of insider information. If 15 investment bankers are selected at random, find the probability that:
    a. All 15 have profited from insider information.
    b. At least six have profited from insider information.
    c. Suppose the experiment was repeated, and three investment bankers were selected. What is the probability that one of them profited from insider information?

12. Companies that sell mutual funds charge their investors expense fees to offset the costs of research and administration. The distribution of expense fees is normal, with a mean of 2.5% and a standard deviation of 1.0%.
    a. Find the probability that a mutual fund has an expense fee of between 2.5% and 3.5%.
    b. What is the probability that a mutual fund has expense fees greater than 3%?
    c. 90% of mutual funds have expense fees below what percentage?

13. The recent average starting salary for new college graduates employed as business systems analysts is $49,879. Assume salaries are normally distributed with a standard deviation of $7,088.
    a. What is the probability of a new graduate receiving a salary between $45,000 and $50,000?
    b. What is the probably of a new graduate getting a starting salary more than $55,000?
    c. If you wanted to be earning more than 90% of new college graduates in computer information systems, what salary would you have to earn?

THINK AND DECIDE USING EXCEL

(Note that the normal probability problems in this section could also be done with tables.)

14. The probability that a college student will cheat on his or her Statistics assignment by copying the work of other students is 0.043. If a professor has 175 Statistics students, what is the probability that at least one of them will cheat?

15. A long-life flood lamp has a lifetime that is normally distributed with a mean of 10,000 hours and a standard deviation of 2,525 hours.
    a. What percentage of the flood lamps would last for more than 12,000 hours?
    b. What lifetime should the manufacturer advertise for these lamps so that only 2% will burn out before the advertised lifetime?

16. A study was made of frequent fliers, and it was found that 53% had an income over $65,000 a year.
    a. Fifteen frequent fliers were selected at random, and their incomes recorded. What is the probability that at least 10 had an income over $65,000 a year?
    b. A further group of 12 fliers was selected at random. What is the probability that exactly eight had an income over $65,000 a year?

17. Suppose the average credit card debt of Canadian households is normally distributed, with a mean of $2,400 and a standard deviation of $756.
    a. What proportion of credit card debt is less than $1,000?
    b. What proportion of credit card debt is more than $1,500?
    c. 75% of credit card debt is more than what amount?

18. 42% of Lindsay's population is opposed to the proposed widening of Highway 35 to four lanes. If 10 Lindsay residents are selected at random,
    a. What is the probability that all 10 of them are opposed to the proposed highway widening?
    b. What is the probability that none of them is opposed to the proposed highway widening?
    c. What is the probability that five or fewer of them are opposed to the proposed highway widening?

19. Over time, the owner of a bicycle store has come to the conclusion that about 3.2% of the customers who enter her store are prepared to purchase a new bicycle. What is the probability that one out of the 25 customers who enter the store today will purchase new bicycles (you may assume these 25 customers are randomly selected).

20. The time that it takes an emergency car repair service to arrive at the car that has broken down is a normally distributed random variable, with a mean of 42 minutes and a standard deviation of 12 minutes. What is the probability that the customer will have to wait more than 45 minutes for help to arrive?

TEST YOUR KNOWLEDGE

21. In Chapter 6, you will see that the normal distribution can sometimes be used to approximate the binomial distribution. This exercise is designed to illustrate how good the normal approximation to the binomial can be.
    a. Consider a binomial distribution with $n = 200$ and $p = 0.5$. Calculate $P(x \leq 100)$. (Use Excel to do this).
    b. What is the mean and standard deviation for the distribution you used in part a?
    c. Using a normal distribution with the same mean and standard deviation you calculated in part b, calculate $P(x \leq 100)$.
    d. The probabilities you calculated in parts a and c should be similar. Why do you think this is so?
    e. Now calculate $P(x \leq 100.5)$ for the normal distribution. The extra 0.5 is added to provide a "continuity correction factor." It compensates for the fact that the normal distribution is continuous (so $P(x \leq 100) = P(x < 100)$, for example), and the binomial distribution is not ($P(x \leq 100) \neq P(x < 100)$). How close are the binomial and normal probabilities now?

CHAPTER **6**

Using Sampling Distributions to Make Decisions

LEARNING OBJECTIVES

After mastering the material in the chapter, you will be able to:

1. Understand how probability calculations and sampling distributions can be used to make conclusions about populations on the basis of sample results.

2. Infer whether a population mean is as claimed or desired, on the basis of a particular sample mean, using the appropriate sampling distribution and probability calculations, when σ is known.

3. Infer whether a population proportion is as claimed or desired, on the basis of a particular sample proportion, using the appropriate sampling distribution and probability calculations.

INTRODUCTION

Eleanor Bennett is a quality control inspector in a paint factory, and she knows that machines suffer wear and tear and operators fall asleep or go for coffee breaks, so there is no guarantee that the right amount of paint is always going into the paint cans. If there is too little paint in each can, there will be customer complaints and perhaps a loss of business. If there is too much paint in each can, the company is giving away free paint, which is not good for profits.

Suppose the paint cans are designed to hold 3 litres of paint. Eleanor wants to be sure that, on average, there are 3 litres of paint in every can, with limited variability. But how will Eleanor determine if this is the case?

It is not practical to measure the amount of paint in every can. Fortunately, Eleanor can make a reliable conclusion about the average amount of paint in all the paint cans, on the basis of a random sample of paint cans, using inferential statistics. In Section 6.1, you will be introduced to the general decision-making process for statistical inference. You will see how probability calculations and sampling distributions are used to make decisions about population parameters, on the basis of sample results. You will be given all the necessary details about the sampling distribution so you can concentrate on learning how to use a sample result and a probability calculation to make a statistical inference. In Sections 6.2 and 6.3, you will learn how to determine the necessary details of two important sampling distributions yourself. In Section 6.2, you will be introduced to the sampling distribution of the sample mean, which can be used to make decisions about a population mean. In Section 6.3, you will be introduced to the sampling distribution of the sample proportion, which can be used to make decisions about population proportions.

6.1 THE DECISION-MAKING PROCESS FOR STATISTICAL INFERENCE

Suppose Eleanor Bennett takes the following approach to deciding whether the paint-filling line is putting the correct amount of paint in the paint cans.

1. She randomly selects 25 cans of paint from the paint-filling line.
2. She carefully measures the amount of paint in each can, and computes a sample mean amount of paint ($\bar{x}$).

Eleanor will not expect to get an $\bar{x}$ of exactly 3 litres. Even when the paint-filling line is working perfectly, there will not be *exactly* 3 litres of paint in each can. Normal mechanical variability in the filling process results in some cans having a little less than 3 litres, and some having a little more.

Eleanor wants to be sure to adjust the paint-filling line when there is sample evidence that it needs adjusting. But she does not want to adjust the line when it is in fact working well. But how does Eleanor decide which values of $\bar{x}$ should trigger adjustment of the line, and which values should not?

The decision about what values of $\bar{x}$ should trigger adjustment of the paint-filling line is straightforward if we know the sampling distribution of the sample mean. A **sampling distribution** is the probability distribution of all possible sample results for a given sample size.

Suppose Eleanor knows that when the paint-filling line is adjusted properly (with a mean of 3 litres in all cans of paint), the sampling distribution of the $\bar{x}$-values for a sample of size 25 will be normally distributed, with a mean of 3 litres and a standard deviation of 0.01 litres. Now Eleanor knows something about the $\bar{x}$-values she can expect to get from her sample of 25 paint cans when the paint-filling line is working as it should. Eleanor would not be surprised to get an $\bar{x}$-value of 3.01 litres if the paint-filling line were set up properly; she would expect to get a sample mean as high as 3.01 litres almost 16% of the time if the line were set up properly. So an $\bar{x}$-value of 3.01 litres would not trigger adjustment of the paint-filling line. However, Eleanor would not expect to get an $\bar{x}$-value of 3.05 litres if the paint-filling line were set up properly; she would expect to get a sample mean as high as 3.05 litres with a probability of 0.00000029—almost impossible! So if Eleanor did actually get an $\bar{x}$-value of 3.05 litres, this would be a clear signal that the paint-filling line needed to be adjusted.

Sampling distribution The probability distribution of all possible sample results for a given sample size.

The sampling distribution is key to being able to distinguish unusual sample results from usual sample results. The sampling distribution is closely related to the distribution of the population from which the sample is drawn. The details of how to arrive at a sampling distribution will be covered in later sections of this chapter. In this section, we will instead focus on how to use the sampling distribution to decide if a sample result is unusual. Your general understanding of this decision-making approach will allow you to use statistical inference in a variety of situations.

Depending on the situation, the sample result could be a mean, a proportion, a standard deviation, or any one of many other possible sample statistics. Whatever population parameter we are interested in, no matter what corresponding sample statistic is calculated, the decision-making process is the same. In the following discussion of the decision-making process, we will simply refer to the sample statistic as the sample result (SR). The sampling distribution used in this discussion will be normal, as many sampling distributions are (although certainly not all are).

We will examine a situation in which it is claimed or desired that the population has a parameter of 100. Suppose we know that when the population has a parameter of 100, the sample results for a sample of size 25 will be normally distributed, with a mean of 100 and a standard deviation of 20. (Note the more general language here. We are not necessarily talking about paint now.) The sample results would have the sampling distribution that is shown in Exhibit 6.1.

EXHIBIT 6.1

Expected Distribution of Sample Results, Mean of 100 and Standard Deviation of 20

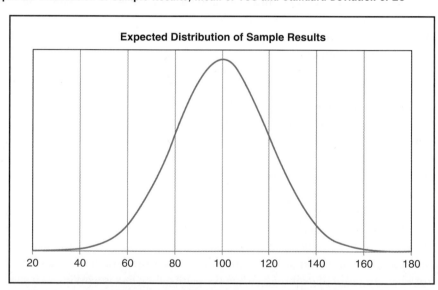

Expected Distribution of Sample Results

20   40   60   80   100   120   140   160   180

Suppose we collect a sample of 25, and calculate a sample result. Now we have to make one of two decisions:

1. The sample result *is NOT unusual*, and there is insufficient evidence that the population parameter is not as desired.
2. The sample result *is unusual*, and there is sufficient evidence that the population parameter is not as desired.

Which of the two possible decisions should we make if:

a. the sample result is 100?
b. the sample result is 180 (or 20)?
c. the sample result is 120 (or 80)?
d. the sample result is 140 (or 60)?
e. the sample result is 160 (or 40)?

a. If the sample result is 100 (as in Exhibit 6.2), no one would conclude that the sample result was unusual, or that there was any evidence that the population parameter was not 100.

EXHIBIT 6.2

Sample Result Is 100

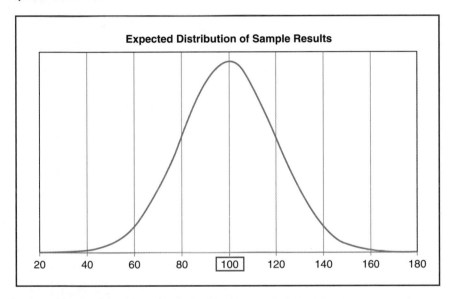

b. If the sample result is 180 (as in Exhibit 6.3), we would conclude that the sample result is unusual, and there is evidence that the population parameter is not 100.

The probability of getting a sample result as high as 180 is:

$$P(SR \geq 180)$$

$$= P\left(z \geq \frac{180 - 100}{20}\right)$$

$$= P(z \geq 4)$$

$$\approx 0$$

(Excel provides a more exact calculation of 0.0000316860. Throughout this chapter, the normal probabilities will be calculated using z-scores and tables, so you can follow along even if you do not have a computer at hand.)

This sample result 180 is four standard deviations away from the mean of the sampling distribution. This is highly unlikely in a normal distribution. Such a sample result is unlikely to occur if the population mean is actually 100. Because it *did* occur, we have evidence that the population parameter is not 100.

EXHIBIT 6.3

Sample Result is 180

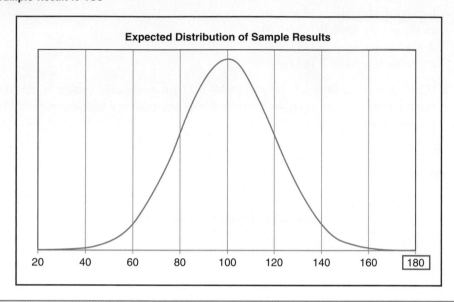

c. The decisions get a little harder once we move to a sample result such as 120 (Exhibit 6.4).

EXHIBIT 6.4

Sample Result Is 120

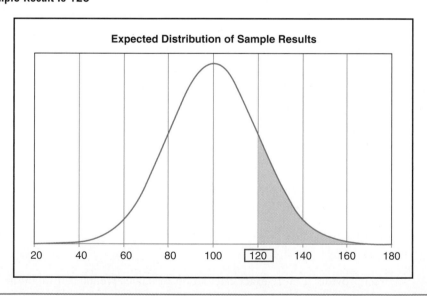

This result is higher than the mean of all the expected sample results, but is it *unusually* high? We have to have some consistent way of deciding this. Since we are trying to decide if a result is unusual or unlikely, it seems logical to do a probability calculation. This sample result is "high," so what is the probability of getting a sample result this high or higher?

$$P(SR \geq 120)$$

$$= P\left(z \geq \frac{120 - 100}{20}\right)$$

$$= P(z \geq 1)$$

$$= 1 - 0.8413$$

$$= 0.1587$$

There is an almost 16% probability of getting a sample result this high or higher. For the purposes of statistical inference, such a result would not be considered unusual. In this case, we would conclude that the sample result is *not unusual* if the population parameter is 100. The sample does not provide enough evidence to conclude that the population parameter is greater than 100.

We need a precise guide to our decision making, based on the probability of the sample result. In Chapter 7, we will discuss how such decision-making rules are set, and we will use different variations of such rules. For now, we use one simple rule. We will conclude that the population is not as claimed or desired if the probability of the sample result is 5% or less.

When Is a Sample Result Unusual?

We calculate the probability of the sample result as follows:
- if the sample result is higher than expected, calculate $P(SR \geq$ observed value)
- if the sample result is lower than expected, calculate $P(SR \leq$ observed value)

We conclude that the population parameter is not as claimed or desired only if the probability of such an extreme sample result is 5% or less.

Notice that the decision about the population can be made only when we know the probability of the observed sample result. Without probability analysis, there is no way to know if a sample result of 120 is usual or unusual. Be very careful as you proceed with this analysis. Sometimes your intuition may suggest that a sample result is highly unusual, but you can never decide this without doing a probability calculation based on the sampling distribution.

Using the decision-making rule above as a guide, with a sample result of 120 or 80, the inspector should not adjust the paint-filling line, since the sample result would occur with a probability of just under 16% if the population mean were actually 100. This is not that unusual.

d. What is the probability of getting a result as high as 140, or as low as 60? $P(SR \geq 140) = P(SR \leq 60) = P(z \leq -2)$ is a little more than 2% (you should check this calculation). This is an unusual sample result. Such a sample result is unlikely to occur if the population parameter is actually 100. Because it *did* occur, we have evidence that the population parameter is not 100.

e. Similarly, a sample result of 100 or 40 would be highly unusual if the population parameter were actually 100. Because it did occur, we have evidence that the population parameter is not 100. Try the probability calculation yourself.

The decisions are easy with results such as in part a or b above. In those cases, we can be fairly certain of making the right decision. With results such as in parts c to e, the decisions seem less certain. We can't be absolutely sure that the population parameter is not as claimed. There is a very small chance that we actually got a highly unusual sample. With any of the sample results, though, there is always the chance that this one sample is a fluke, and that the wrong decision is being made. Taking another sample might be tempting, but in practice, this may not be possible—the decision has to be made. We find it acceptable to live with this uncertainty (and in practice, we reduce it by using sample sizes as large as are affordable). It is worth the price of occasionally being wrong, because measuring or testing the entire population is impossible or expensive, and *most* of the time, statistical inference will lead to the correct decision.

EXAMPLE 6.1A

Using a sampling distribution to decide if a sample mean is unusual

Suppose an inspector is concerned that too much cereal is going into the cereal boxes in a factory. The boxes are supposed to contain 645 grams of cereal. The inspector takes a random sample of 30 boxes of cereal, and calculates the sample mean ($\bar{x}$), which turns out to be 648 grams. Assume that if the cereal-filling line is properly adjusted, the $\bar{x}$-values will be normally distributed, with a mean of 645 grams and a standard deviation of 5 grams. Should the line be adjusted?

In this case, the sample result is $\bar{x}$, so we will refer to $\bar{x}$ specifically, and not the general "SR" for sample result.

EXHIBIT 6.5

Expected Distribution of Sample Means for Example 6.1A

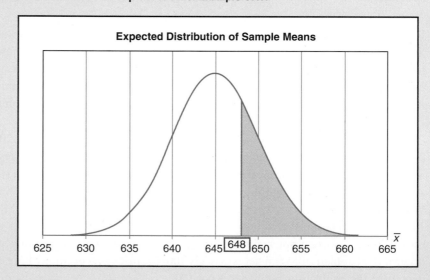

$P(\bar{x} \geq 648)$

$= P\left(z \geq \dfrac{648 - 645}{5}\right)$

$= P(z \geq 0.6)$

$= 1 - 0.7257$

$= 0.2743$

No, the cereal-filling line should not be adjusted, because the sample result is not unusual. If the average amount of cereal in the boxes is 645 grams, we would get a sample mean at least as high as 648 grams with a probability of 0.2742. There is not enough evidence to suggest that the cereal boxes contain more than 645 grams of cereal, on average.

EXAMPLE 6.1B

Using a sampling distribution to decide whether a sample proportion is unusual

A computer manufacturing company regularly monitors the percentage of customers who require technical assistance within 30 days of the purchase of a new computer. In the past, 17% of new computer owners accessed technical assistance within 30 days of purchase. A random sample of 250 recent purchasers reveals that 14% of new computer owners accessed technical assistance within 30 days of purchase. Assume that if the percentage of new computer owners needing technical assistance in the first 30 days of ownership is 17%, the sample proportions (for which we use the notation $\hat{p}$) will be normally distributed, with a mean of 0.17 and a standard deviation of 0.023757. Is there evidence that the proportion of new computer owners who require technical assistance in the first 30 days has decreased?

EXHIBIT 6.6

Expected Distribution of Sample Proportions for Example 6.1B

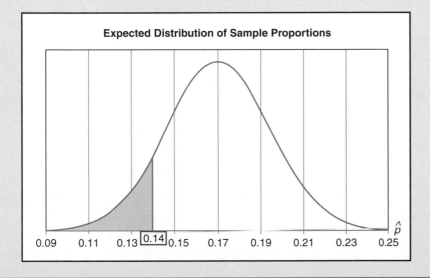

$P(\hat{p} \leq 0.14)$

$= P\left(z \leq \dfrac{0.14 - 0.17}{0.023757} \right)$

$= P(z \leq -1.26)$

$= 0.1038$

The sample result is not unusual. If the percentage of new computer owners needing technical assistance in the first 30 days of ownership is actually 17%, we would expect to get a sample proportion as low as 14% more than 10% of the time. The sample proportion is not unusual enough to allow us to conclude that the proportion of new computer owners who need technical assistance in the first 30 days has declined.

DEVELOP YOUR SKILLS 6.1

1. Suppose a college claims that its graduates from the business programs earn $40,000 a year, on average, after graduation. You are making only $38,000, so you have reason to doubt the college's claim. You take a random sample of 35 graduates, and calculate an average salary of $39,368. Assume that if the college's claim is true, sample means of one-year-after-graduation salaries would be normally distributed, with a mean of $40,000 and a standard deviation of $554. Does your sample result suggest that the college's claim overstates salaries?

2. Suppose an ad for an automotive service centre claims that at least 90% of its customers would gladly recommend the centre to friends. Since you have heard nothing but complaints about this service centre, you doubt that the claim is true. Your friend who works at the service centre helps you to conduct a survey of 300 customers, and you discover that only 87% of them would recommend the centre to friends. Assume that if the centre's claim were true, sample proportions would be normally distributed, with a mean of 0.90 and a standard deviation of 0.01732. Does your sample result indicate that the centre's ad overstates the percentage of customers who would provide a positive recommendation?

3. A company is wondering if it should subsidize the tuition costs of employees who are furthering their education. The company feels that it could afford a subsidy program if 25% or fewer of its employees enrolled in programs that would be eligible for subsidies. The chief accountant conducted a random sample of 400 employees and calculated that 26% would enroll in eligible programs if the subsidy were available.

   Suppose that if only 25% of employees actually enrolled in eligible programs, the sample proportions would be normally distributed, with a mean of 0.25 and a standard deviation of 0.021651. Does the sample result indicate that more than 25% of employees would enroll in eligible programs?

4. Your statistics teacher claims that the average mark on the mid-term statistics exam for students in the business program is 67%. You survey a random sample of 30 of the business students taking statistics, and you calculate an average mark of 62%. The statistics teacher tells you that if her claim is true, the sample means will be normally distributed, with a mean of 67%, and a standard deviation of 3.2%. Does your sample evidence indicate that the teacher's claim overestimates the true average mark for the mid-term stats exam?

5. According to the personnel department, the average commuting time for workers within a 50-kilometre radius of your company's head office is 32 minutes. You suspect that, because of development in the area and increased traffic, the average commuting time has increased. Suppose you know that if the personnel department's estimate was correct, sample means would be normally distributed, with a mean of 32 minutes and a standard deviation of 5 minutes. You take a random sample of 20 employees, and calculate a sample mean of 40 minutes. Does this provide evidence that commuting times have increased?

6.2   THE SAMPLING DISTRIBUTION OF THE SAMPLE MEAN

In Section 6.1, you were given the details about the distribution of sample results. Now the question is: how do you figure out what the sampling distribution should look like? To start with, we will cover two sampling distributions: the sampling distribution of the sample mean, $\bar{x}$, which is discussed in Section 6.2, and the sampling distribution of the sample proportion, $\hat{p}$ (pronounced "p-hat"), which is presented in Section 6.3.

The probability distribution of the sample means (the $\bar{x}$-values) is related to the distribution of the original population (the x-values). For example, the distribution of the average content for 25-can samples of paint (the $\bar{x}$-values) is related to the distribution of fill volumes for individual cans of paint (the x-values). The details are outlined below.

The Sampling Distribution of $\bar{x}$ (The Sample Mean)

For a sample of size n, and a population with a claimed or desired mean of μ,

1. The standard deviation of the sample means (the $\bar{x}$-values) is equal to the population standard deviation, divided by the square root of the sample size. In other words:

$$\sigma_{\bar{x}} = \frac{\sigma}{\sqrt{n}}$$

We will refer to the standard deviation of the sample means ($\sigma_{\bar{x}}$) as the *standard error*.

2. The mean of the sample means (the $\bar{x}$-values) is equal to the mean of the original population. To put this into mathematical shorthand, we would say:

$$\mu_{\bar{x}} = \mu$$

3. The sampling distribution of the sample means ($\bar{x}$'s) will be normally distributed if the original population of x's is normally distributed, or the sample size is large enough.

Now we can apply this information about the sampling distribution and its relationship to the population distribution, using the paint-filling line as an example.

Suppose the average amount of paint in the population is supposed to be 3 litres. Suppose we know that the population of paint can volumes (the x's) is normally distributed, and that the population standard deviation is 0.05 litres (of course, it is unlikely that we would know the population standard deviation, but we will deal with this difficulty in Chapter 7).

For samples of size 25, we can calculate that:

1. the standard error of the sampling distribution of the $\bar{x}$-values is

$$\sigma_{\bar{x}} = \frac{\sigma}{\sqrt{n}} = \frac{0.05}{\sqrt{25}} = \frac{0.05}{5} = 0.01$$

2. the mean of the $\bar{x}$-values is 3 litres (the same as the population mean)
3. because the population is normally distributed, the sampling distribution will be normally distributed

So, by using the information about the population and the sample size, we have come up with the sampling distribution that was first discussed on page 225, as shown in Exhibit 6.7.

EXHIBIT 6.7

Distribution of Sample Means, Sample Size of 25

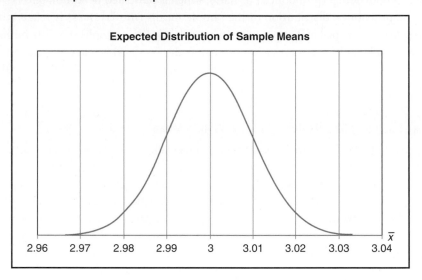

2.96 2.97 2.98 2.99 3 3.01 3.02 3.03 3.04

Suppose Eleanor randomly samples 25 cans of paint, and calculates a sample mean of 3.016 litres. Are the paint cans being overfilled?

EXHIBIT 6.8

Distribution of Sample Means, Sample Result is 3.016 litres

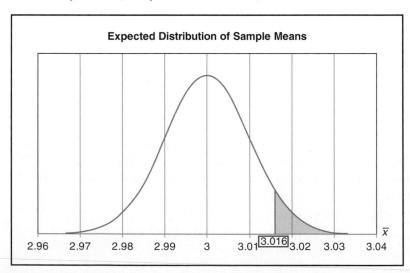

2.96 2.97 2.98 2.99 3 3.01 3.016 3.02 3.03 3.04

Since 3.016 litres is more than the desired volume of 3 litres, we calculate the probability of the sample result as follows:

$$= P(\bar{x} \geq 3.016)$$

$$= P\left(z \geq \frac{3.016 - 3}{0.01}\right)$$

$$= P(z \geq 1.6)$$

$$= 1 - 0.9452$$

$$= 0.0548$$

The probability of getting a sample mean as high as 3.016 is 0.0548, if the population mean is 3. Since the probability of such a sample mean is greater than 5%, the sample mean is not unusual, according to our decision rule. Therefore, although the sample mean is on the high side, no adjustment is made to the paint-filling line. There is not enough evidence to conclude that the mean volume of paint in all the cans is more than the desired 3 litres.

You might be slightly uncomfortable about this decision. The probability of such a high sample mean is more than 5%, but not by much! Shouldn't Eleanor adjust the paint-filling line anyway? The answer is no. While this sample mean might make us uncomfortable, the paint-filling line should not be adjusted unless it truly needs adjustment.

Close decisions such as the one above may not be entirely comfortable, but over the long run decisions made this way will generally be correct. We are willing to live with a little discomfort in decision making, since this method is far superior to guessing. The only way to be absolutely certain about the paint cans is to exactly measure the quantity of paint going into each and every can, and this is likely impossible or prohibitively expensive.

EXAMPLE 6.2A

Constructing a sampling distribution and using it to decide about a population mean

Suppose a random sample of 35 cans of paint yields a sample mean of 2.984 litres. Are the paint cans being underfilled? Assume, as before, that the population of individual fill volumes is normally distributed, with a desired mean of 3 litres and a standard deviation of 0.05 litres.

First, what will the sampling distribution look like? It will be normally distributed, because the population is normally distributed. It will have a mean of 3 litres (the population mean). It will have a standard error of $\sigma_{\bar{x}} = \dfrac{\sigma}{\sqrt{n}} = \dfrac{0.05}{\sqrt{35}} = 0.0084515$. The sampling distribution will look like Exhibit 6.9 on the next page.

Notice that this sampling distribution is different from the one we used for the previous problem, when only 25 cans of paint were sampled. With a larger sample, the standard error will be smaller, and so the distribution is narrower and taller. This sample result is exactly the same distance from the mean as the measurement in the previous example (3.016 is 0.016 above the mean, and 2.984 is 0.016 below the mean). However, because the sample size is different, the sampling distribution has changed. The same distance from the mean now represents a more extreme result.

EXHIBIT 6.9

Distribution of Sample Means, Sample Size Is 35, Sample Result Is 2.984 Litres

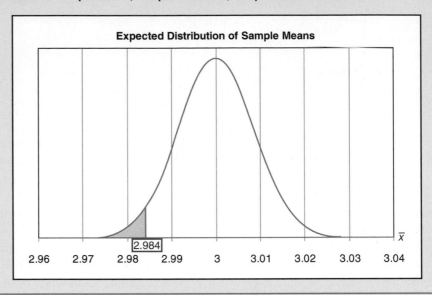

We have to do the probability calculation to see if the paint-filling line should be adjusted.

$$= P(\bar{x} \leq 2.984)$$

$$= P\left(z \leq \frac{2.984 - 3}{0.0084515}\right)$$

$$= P(z \leq -1.89)$$

$$= 0.0294$$

When the paint-filling line is properly adjusted, the probability of getting a 35-can sample mean as low as 2.984 litres is a little less than 3%. In other words, it would be unusual to get such a sample result, were the paint-filling line properly set up. Since we actually did get such a result, this is an indication that the paint-filling line needs adjustment.

Notice that although this sample mean is the same distance from the mean as in the previous example, we made a different decision, because the sample sizes and the sampling distributions were different. We cannot simply say, "Oh, 3.016 litres isn't *that* far from 3 litres, so everything is okay." We must do a probability-based calculation to decide.

The decision-making procedure here is the same as in Section 6.1. The only difference is that now we are figuring out what the details of the sampling distribution are, rather than being told what they are. This simply means some extra work before we can do the probability calculation and make the decision.

An Empirical Exploration of the Sampling Distribution of $\bar{x}$

The relationship between the population distribution of x's and the sampling distribution $\bar{x}$'s can be proven mathematically, although the mathematics is beyond the level of this text. However, you can also think of the sampling distribution as something that could be derived empirically. That is, for a given population, you could imagine taking random samples of 25 and calculating $\bar{x}$ over and over again, a very large number of times. If you could somehow do this a very large number of times, you could create the probability distribution of the $\bar{x}$-values for samples of size 25. You could list all the possible values of $\bar{x}$, with the relative frequencies as the probabilities. This is just the sampling distribution of $\bar{x}$.

If we explore this empirical approach, you may be able to develop some intuition about the differences between the population distribution and the sampling distributions, and how the two types of distributions are related.

We will do this by looking at Exhibit 6.10, on page 238. That page lists (in order) the exact volumes for 500 cans of paint with a normal distribution with a mean of 3 litres and a standard deviation of 0.05 litres. You can think of that page full of numbers as a *population* of paint can volumes (x-values). The values have been rounded to numbers with four decimal places. In practical terms, it is unlikely that fill volumes would be measured to the nearest ten-thousandth of a litre, and so the level of precision should help us think of these as population values.

$\sigma_{\bar{x}} = \dfrac{\sigma}{\sqrt{n}}$**—An Exploration**   Suppose you began by taking samples of size 9 from this population. What is the largest possible $\bar{x}$ you could get, with a sample of 9? The highest possible $\bar{x}$ would come from averaging the 9 fullest paint cans. In that case would be $\dfrac{3.1090 + 3.1093 + \cdots + 3.1585}{9} = 3.1211$ litres. Similarly, the smallest possible $\bar{x}$ would come from averaging the 9 least full cans, and this results in an $\bar{x}$ value of 2.8832 litres.

What if we increased the sample size to 25? With similar calculations, we find that the largest possible $\bar{x}$ from a sample of 25 cans is 3.1056 litres. The smallest possible $\bar{x}$ from a sample of 25 cans is 2.9037 litres.

These results are summarized in the table shown in Exhibit 6.11 on page 239. The smallest and largest $\bar{x}$-values for both sample sizes are shown, as well as the smallest and largest x-values from this population.

This information is also captured on the number line shown in Exhibit 6.12.

Clearly the $\bar{x}$-values cannot vary as much as the original x-values in the population. Additionally, the variability in the $\bar{x}$-values has to decrease when the sample size increases. Note that this is just what the formula for the standard error is telling us. For a sample size of 9, the standard error of the $\bar{x}$-values would be only $\frac{1}{3}$ of the standard deviation of the x-values. You can see this with the following arithmetic:

$$\text{If } n = 9, \sigma_{\bar{x}} = \frac{\sigma}{\sqrt{n}} = \frac{\sigma}{\sqrt{9}} = \frac{\sigma}{3} = \frac{1}{3}\sigma$$

Similarly, if the sample size is increased to 25, the standard error of the $\bar{x}$-values will be only $\frac{1}{5}$ of the standard deviation of the x-values.

$$\text{If } n = 25, \sigma_{\bar{x}} = \frac{\sigma}{\sqrt{n}} = \frac{\sigma}{\sqrt{25}} = \frac{\sigma}{5} = \frac{1}{5}\sigma$$

As the sample size (n) gets larger, the standard error gets smaller (you can see the actual values in Exhibit 6.11). The ends of the sampling distribution get pulled in toward the mean as the sample size increases. Exhibit 6.13 on page 239 illustrates this.

EXHIBIT 6.10

Population of Paint Can Volumes (Litres)

2.8679	2.9430	2.9622	2.9773	2.9906	3.0050	3.0129	3.0262	3.0426	3.0656
2.8714	2.9433	2.9626	2.9779	2.9907	3.0050	3.0134	3.0264	3.0427	3.0667
2.8718	2.9436	2.9631	2.9782	2.9908	3.0054	3.0134	3.0266	3.0442	3.0703
2.8756	2.9438	2.9635	2.9784	2.9914	3.0054	3.0134	3.0272	3.0446	3.0704
2.8817	2.9441	2.9635	2.9786	2.9918	3.0056	3.0134	3.0274	3.0446	3.0712
2.8859	2.9442	2.9636	2.9788	2.9919	3.0057	3.0136	3.0275	3.0448	3.0731
2.8936	2.9466	2.9640	2.9789	2.9920	3.0059	3.0137	3.0276	3.0457	3.0731
2.8989	2.9469	2.9640	2.9791	2.9921	3.0059	3.0143	3.0280	3.0459	3.0740
2.9022	2.9486	2.9642	2.9793	2.9923	3.0060	3.0146	3.0283	3.0474	3.0741
2.9027	2.9486	2.9645	2.9795	2.9930	3.0060	3.0147	3.0284	3.0475	3.0743
2.9058	2.9487	2.9647	2.9796	2.9934	3.0063	3.0153	3.0292	3.0476	3.0744
2.9069	2.9497	2.9651	2.9798	2.9935	3.0063	3.0161	3.0300	3.0478	3.0757
2.9099	2.9502	2.9655	2.9800	2.9935	3.0067	3.0163	3.0303	3.0479	3.0773
2.9103	2.9508	2.9657	2.9808	2.9936	3.0068	3.0171	3.0313	3.0481	3.0774
2.9121	2.9513	2.9660	2.9808	2.9937	3.0069	3.0172	3.0317	3.0492	3.0779
2.9162	2.9513	2.9666	2.9811	2.9943	3.0070	3.0174	3.0321	3.0500	3.0787
2.9163	2.9516	2.9681	2.9811	2.9945	3.0071	3.0178	3.0325	3.0503	3.0788
2.9174	2.9525	2.9681	2.9817	2.9949	3.0073	3.0179	3.0335	3.0504	3.0789
2.9184	2.9528	2.9682	2.9818	2.9951	3.0073	3.0182	3.0336	3.0508	3.0790
2.9186	2.9529	2.9686	2.9818	2.9952	3.0074	3.0187	3.0340	3.0510	3.0808
2.9196	2.9529	2.9687	2.9823	2.9955	3.0077	3.0189	3.0343	3.0513	3.0810
2.9212	2.9530	2.9691	2.9824	2.9958	3.0078	3.0195	3.0345	3.0523	3.0815
2.9221	2.9532	2.9694	2.9828	2.9962	3.0078	3.0196	3.0347	3.0525	3.0862
2.9225	2.9533	2.9696	2.9829	2.9965	3.0079	3.0200	3.0349	3.0535	3.0865
2.9236	2.9536	2.9705	2.9833	2.9965	3.0084	3.0207	3.0351	3.0543	3.0867
2.9237	2.9538	2.9708	2.9835	2.9966	3.0088	3.0208	3.0356	3.0551	3.0872
2.9243	2.9541	2.9710	2.9842	2.9967	3.0090	3.0210	3.0356	3.0556	3.0878
2.9249	2.9544	2.9716	2.9843	2.9969	3.0092	3.0215	3.0360	3.0556	3.0883
2.9254	2.9547	2.9716	2.9843	2.9969	3.0093	3.0217	3.0365	3.0557	3.0899
2.9265	2.9549	2.9724	2.9847	2.9970	3.0097	3.0218	3.0366	3.0561	3.0906
2.9266	2.9551	2.9724	2.9849	2.9975	3.0098	3.0222	3.0371	3.0564	3.0936
2.9283	2.9552	2.9725	2.9856	2.9976	3.0098	3.0223	3.0372	3.0565	3.0952
2.9283	2.9552	2.9725	2.9856	2.9981	3.0098	3.0224	3.0376	3.0570	3.0983
2.9317	2.9556	2.9726	2.9860	2.9987	3.0099	3.0227	3.0377	3.0578	3.0984
2.9324	2.9565	2.9733	2.9861	2.9988	3.0100	3.0229	3.0377	3.0583	3.0994
2.9328	2.9568	2.9739	2.9865	2.9989	3.0100	3.0229	3.0379	3.0586	3.1009
2.9333	2.9568	2.9742	2.9868	2.9990	3.0103	3.0230	3.0382	3.0605	3.1025
2.9339	2.9573	2.9742	2.9870	2.9993	3.0106	3.0232	3.0387	3.0609	3.1038
2.9345	2.9576	2.9743	2.9870	3.0000	3.0107	3.0233	3.0387	3.0609	3.1039
2.9350	2.9581	2.9747	2.9871	3.0001	3.0107	3.0235	3.0388	3.0619	3.1050
2.9351	2.9584	2.9748	2.9874	3.0003	3.0107	3.0235	3.0390	3.0626	3.1062
2.9373	2.9590	2.9748	2.9876	3.0006	3.0111	3.0236	3.0395	3.0626	3.1090
2.9386	2.9592	2.9750	2.9880	3.0010	3.0115	3.0238	3.0397	3.0629	3.1093
2.9392	2.9593	2.9752	2.9890	3.0014	3.0117	3.0247	3.0398	3.0634	3.1096
2.9410	2.9593	2.9753	2.9898	3.0019	3.0118	3.0251	3.0406	3.0637	3.1162
2.9414	2.9594	2.9758	2.9899	3.0019	3.0119	3.0254	3.0407	3.0640	3.1188
2.9414	2.9601	2.9760	2.9900	3.0031	3.0120	3.0256	3.0408	3.0642	3.1200
2.9415	2.9601	2.9761	2.9902	3.0035	3.0123	3.0258	3.0410	3.0644	3.1227
2.9418	2.9606	2.9762	2.9904	3.0036	3.0125	3.0260	3.0412	3.0652	3.1255
2.9421	2.9610	2.9766	2.9904	3.0040	3.0128	3.0262	3.0413	3.0655	3.1585

EXHIBIT 6.11

x-Values and $\bar{x}$-Values, Paint Can Volumes

	Smallest Possible Value	Largest Possible Value	Standard Deviation or Standard Error			
x from Population	2.8679	3.1585				$\sigma = 0.05$
$\bar{x}$ from Samples of Size 9	2.8832	3.1211	$\sigma_{\bar{x}} = \dfrac{\sigma}{\sqrt{n}} = \dfrac{0.05}{\sqrt{9}} = \dfrac{1}{3}(0.05) = 0.01667$			
$\bar{x}$ from Samples of Size 25	2.9037	3.1056	$\sigma_{\bar{x}} = \dfrac{\sigma}{\sqrt{n}} = \dfrac{0.05}{\sqrt{25}} = \dfrac{1}{5}(0.05) = 0.01$			

EXHIBIT 6.12

Extreme x-Values and $\bar{x}$-Values, Paint Can Volumes

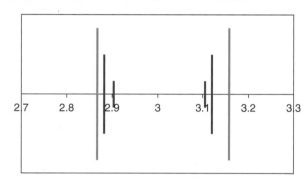

	x's Population
	$\bar{x}$'s for Sample Size 9
	$\bar{x}$'s for Sample Size 25

EXHIBIT 6.13

Population and Sampling Distributions

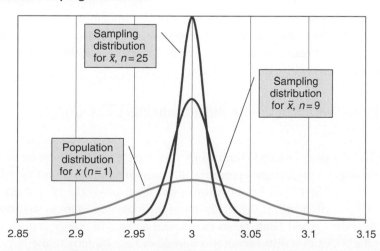

$\mu_{\bar{x}} = \mu$ **—An Exploration**   Something else that you will notice from Exhibit 6.13 is that the centres (the means) of the population and both sampling distributions are the same. This is what is meant by $\mu_{\bar{x}} = \mu$. The mean of the $\bar{x}$-values is the same as the mean of the x-values.

If you think about it, this should seem sensible to you. Think of selecting sample after sample after sample of size 9 from the population in Exhibit 6.10. Some of the x-values selected for the samples will be below 3 litres (about half the time), and some will be above (about half the time). Similarly, some of the $\bar{x}$-values will be below 3 litres and some will be above. Over a very large number of samples, these differences would tend to average out, and the mean of the $\bar{x}$-values would be 3 litres.

PAINT

You might want to experiment with this yourself. The data from Exhibit 6.10 are available in a spreadsheet called PAINT. You can use Excel to take a number of random samples from this data set (as described in Chapter 1) and calculate sample means. Of course, none of us has time to take an infinite number of samples. Exhibit 6.14 shows 20 sample means, based on 20 random samples from the population shown in Exhibit 6.10 (the sample size was 25).

EXHIBIT 6.14

Sample Means of 20 Random Samples from the Population in Exhibit 6.10 (Litres)

2.9874	3.0053
2.9902	3.0068
2.9917	3.0069
2.9950	3.0070
2.9956	3.0073
2.9960	3.0104
2.9961	3.0117
2.9964	3.0122
2.9997	3.0190
3.0035	3.0200

Of course, 20 samples is nowhere near a "very large" number of samples, which we would have to take to build the sampling distribution empirically. However, even these 20 sample means show the kinds of results we would expect. Some of the sample means are below 3 litres; some are above 3 litres. The average of these sample means is 3.0029 litres, which is quite close to 3 litres.

When Is the Sampling Distribution Normal? The Central Limit Theorem

So far, all of the sampling distributions of $\bar{x}$ we have examined have been normal, because the original population was normal. But sampling distributions of $\bar{x}$ will also be normal—even if the original population is not normal—*if the sample size is large enough*. This somewhat surprising fact is one of the most important in statistics, and is referred to as the Central Limit Theorem. There is a practical matter first. How would we know if a population distribution was normal or not? We have to use the information we have about the population—the sample data—to make this decision.

Generally, we will create a histogram of the sample data and try to decide if it looks normal. There are formal techniques to help with this decision, but although they can be helpful, none of them works well with small sample sizes. Often, with small sample sizes the decision about normality of the population is a judgment call.

As sample sizes get larger, the decision about normality becomes less crucial, because of the Central Limit Theorem. But how large a sample size is *large enough*? The answer is: it depends. The less normal the population is (or appears to be, based on the sample data), the larger the sample size that is necessary for the sampling distribution of $\bar{x}$ to be normal.

Assessing the Normality of the Sampling Distribution of $\bar{x}$

The normality of the sampling distribution of $\bar{x}$ is affected by sample size and the normality of the population. To assess population normality, create a histogram of sample data (unless there are too few data points). Here are some guidelines to help you decide whether a sampling distribution of $\bar{x}$ is likely to be normal.

1. If there are outliers in the sample data, you should proceed with caution, no matter what the sample size.
2. If there is more than one mode in the sample data, you should proceed thoughtfully. While large enough sample sizes could result in a normal sampling distribution of $\bar{x}$, you should investigate whether your data might be coming from more than one population.
3. With small sample sizes, less than about 15 or 20, the population data must be normal for the sampling distribution to be normal. The histogram of sample data should have a normal shape, with one central mode and no skewness.
4. With sample sizes in the range of about 15 or 20 to 40, the histogram of sample data should have a normal shape, with one central mode and not much skewness. If these conditions are met, the sampling distribution will likely be normal.
5. With sample sizes above 40 or so, the sampling distribution will probably still be normal, even if the sample histogram is somewhat skewed.

EXAMPLE 6.2B

Assessing population normality, constructing a sampling distribution, and using it to decide about a population mean

It has been suggested that the average price of a three-bedroom brick bungalow in Peterborough is $239,000. You collect a random sample of 30 sales of this type of house, and calculate a sample mean of $236,767. You may assume that the standard deviation for house selling prices is $33,500. A histogram of the sample data are shown on the next page in Exhibit 6.15. Does the sample result suggest that the average price of a three-bedroom brick bungalow in Peterborough is less than $239,000?

The histogram of the sample data looks fairly normal, and with a sample size of 30, it is reasonable to assume that the sampling distribution is normal. The mean of the sampling distribution of sample average house prices will be $239,000, if the claim is true. The standard error of the sampling distribution will be

$$\sigma_{\bar{x}} = \frac{\sigma}{\sqrt{n}} = \frac{33,500}{\sqrt{30}} = 6,116.23523$$

EXHIBIT 6.15

Prices of Three-Bedroom Brick Bungalows in Peterborough

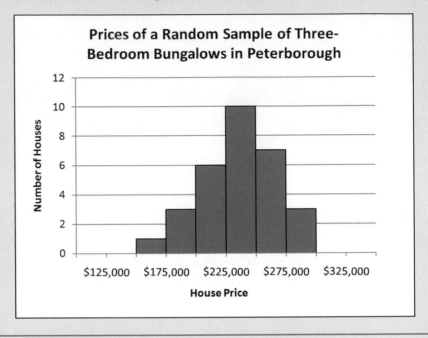

The sample mean is lower than expected. We calculate

$$P(\bar{x} \le \$236{,}767) = P\left(z \le \frac{\$236{,}767 - \$239{,}000}{6{,}116.23523}\right) = P(z \le -0.37) = 0.3557$$

If the claim about the average house price being \$239,000 is true, it would not be unusual to get a sample mean from 30 randomly selected houses that was as low as \$236,767. In fact, we would get a sample mean that low with a probability of 0.3557 (about 36% of the time). This suggests that although the sample mean is below the claimed average house price, it is not far enough below to provide convincing evidence that the average price of a three-bedroom brick bungalow in Peterborough is below \$239,000.

Notice that the decision-making procedure depends on knowing σ. If you think about it, you will realize that if we do not know μ, it would be impossible to know σ. If σ is given, then either the people collecting the data have superhuman powers or the data are fake. In Chapter 7, you will learn what to do when you do not know σ (which will be all the time!). The decision-making process will be very similar, but it requires a new probability distribution (the t-distribution, rather than the normal distribution). At this stage, the focus is on learning how the decision-making process works. Once you have mastered this, in the "pretend" world where we know σ, you should find it straightforward to transfer your knowledge to the real world, where σ is not known. It is important to remember that the decision-making process outlined above is temporary. After you cover the material in Chapter 7, you should not use the normal distribution to make a decision about μ.

GUIDE TO DECISION MAKING

Using the Sampling Distribution of $\bar{x}$ to Decide About μ When σ Is Known

When:

- quantitative data, one sample, one population
- trying to make a decision about μ on the basis of $\bar{x}$
- σ given

Steps:

1. Identify or calculate

- $\bar{x}$, the sample mean
- σ, the population standard deviation
- μ, the desired or claimed population mean
- n, the sample size

2. Check for normality of the sampling distribution by assessing the normality of the population (usually with a histogram of the sample values).

3. If the sampling distribution is likely to be normal, proceed by identifying or calculating the mean and standard deviation of the sampling distribution, using the following formulas:

- $\mu_{\bar{x}} = \mu$

- $\sigma_{\bar{x}} = \dfrac{\sigma}{\sqrt{n}}$

4. Use this sampling distribution to calculate the probability of a sample result as extreme as the $\bar{x}$ from the sample.

- If $\bar{x}$ is above μ, calculate $P(\bar{x} \geq$ observed sample mean)
- If $\bar{x}$ is below μ, calculate $P(\bar{x} \leq$ observed sample mean)

5. If the calculated probability is 5% or less, there is convincing evidence that the population mean is not as claimed or desired.

See Example 6.2B on page 241.

DEVELOP YOUR SKILLS 6.2

6. Suppose the cereal boxes in a factory are supposed to contain 645 grams of cereal. Assume that when the filling line is properly adjusted, the weights of the cereal boxes are normally distributed, with a standard deviation of 5 grams. The inspector selects 10 boxes from the line, and determines that their average weight is 648 grams. What would the sampling distribution of the $\bar{x}$-values look like? What is the probability of getting an

$\bar{x}$-value as high as 648 grams? Should the cereal-filling line be adjusted?

7. Suppose a college claims that its graduates from the business program earn at least $40,000 a year, on average, in the first year after graduation. Assume that the year-after-graduation salaries are normally distributed, with a standard deviation of $3,300. You survey a random sample of 20 graduates of the program, and find

that, one year after graduation, the average salary is $38,000. What would the sampling distribution of the $\bar{x}$-values look like? What is the probability of getting an $\bar{x}$-value as low as $38,000? Does this mean that the average salary of graduates from the business program is less than $40,000 in the first year after graduation?

8. The new tire you bought for your car is guaranteed to last an average of 25,000 kilometres. Your new tire wears prematurely, so you talk the tire store owner into surveying a random sample of 19 other tire buyers. When you survey them to see how long their tires lasted, and add your own disappointing result, you find an average of 24,000 kilometres. Assume that the tire life is a variable with a standard deviation of 500 kilometres. Do you think you could successfully sue the company for false advertising? (Be careful!)

9. A local bank claims that it takes no more than 1.5 working days on average to approve loan requests. Examination of the bank's records for 64 randomly selected loan requests produced a sample mean of 1.8 working days. Assume that the standard deviation for the number of days to approve loan requests is 2.0 days, and that the population data are approximately normally distributed. On the basis of the sample result, does it appear that the bank's claim understates the average amount of time to approve loan requests?

10. The manager at Big Package Express knows that in the past, the packages the company handled had a mean weight of 36.7 kg. A random sample of last month's shipping records yielded a mean weight of 32.1 kg for 64 packages. Assume that the standard deviation of package weights is 14.2 kg, and that the package weights are approximately normally distributed. Does the sample result tell us that the average weight of the packages has decreased?

THE SAMPLING DISTRIBUTION OF THE SAMPLE PROPORTION

Eleanor Bennett, the quality control inspector at the paint factory, is probably interested in quality measures other than the amount of paint going into the cans. Some of these other measures may be qualitative characteristics, such as whether the cans coming off of the paint-filling line are dented. In Section 6.3, you will see how to make decisions about the proportion of dented cans in the population of all paint cans, on the basis of a sample of paint cans.

Making Decisions About Population Proportions with the Binomial Distribution

Suppose the paint factory has decided that no more than 4% of the paint cans should be dented. Eleanor examines a random sample of 30 cans of paint. She notes that two of them are dented. If the dent rate is actually 4%, she would expect $0.04 \cdot 30 = 1.2$ dented cans, so two cans is a higher number than expected (of course, it is not actually possible to have 1.2 dented cans, but this is still the expected number). The question is whether this sample has an *unusually* high number of dented cans.

The decision-making process is the same as the one we have used before. We need to calculate the probability of getting two or more dented cans in a sample of 30, if the population proportion of dented cans is 4%. If it is unusual to get this number of dented cans, we will have evidence that something is wrong and too many cans are being dented. However, we cannot use the sampling distribution of $\bar{x}$ to calculate this probability, because the underlying data are qualitative, not quantitative. What probability distribution should we use?

The appropriate probability distribution is the binomial. Although we are sampling without replacement, it is likely that the population is large enough that we can treat this as an approximately binomial problem, with $n = 30$ and $p = 0.04$ (the paint line probably produces thousands of cans). There are 30 trials; on each trial there is a success (in this case, success would be defined as getting a dented can) or a failure; the probability of getting a dented can is the same (approximately) from trial to trial; and the trials are (approximately) independent. Using Excel, for example, we discover that this probability is $P(x \geq 2, n = 30, p = 0.04) = 0.3388$. Therefore, this is not an unusual sample result. It would not be unusual to get two or more dented cans in a sample of 30, if the actual dent rate is 4%.

So far, there is nothing new here. We are calculating binomial probabilities, as we have before, and we are applying the decision-making criteria from Section 6.2.

EXAMPLE 6.3A

Using the binomial distribution to make a decision about a population proportion

A large manufacturing firm has analyzed its records and discovered that, in the past, 32% of all materials shipments were received late. The company receives many thousands of shipments, so this is a significant number of late arrivals. However, the company has recently installed a just-in-time system, which links suppliers more closely to the manufacturing process. A random sample of 400 deliveries since the new system was installed revealed 89 late deliveries. What is the probability of getting 89 or fewer late deliveries if the percentage of late shipments is still 32%? What does this tell you about the effectiveness of the new just-in-time system in reducing late deliveries?

Although the trials are not truly independent, we can still model this as a binomial problem, since the company receives many thousands of shipments. We can use Excel to calculate:

$$P(x \leq 89, n = 400, p = 0.32) = 0.000010481$$

This means that a sample result of only 89 late deliveries out of 400 would be *very* unlikely if the proportion of late shipments was still 32%. We have evidence that the proportion of late shipments is lower than it was. It seems reasonable to conclude that the new just-in-time system is responsible, but we cannot draw this conclusion from the sample data alone. Other factors may have contributed to the reduction in late deliveries.

The Sampling Distribution of $\hat{p}$ While it is possible to make inferences with the binomial distribution, as in the examples above, this is not the usual approach. Instead, such inferences are made by focusing not on the *number* of successes, but on the *proportion* of successes. For example, in Example 6.3A, above, there were 89 late shipments out of 400. This is equivalent to $\frac{89}{400} = 0.2225$ as a proportion of late shipments. These are two methods of representing the same information. When you are asked about a sample proportion, you can always turn it into an equivalent binomial problem, with the appropriate number of successes. As long as you have access to a computer to provide the probabilities, these problems are straightforward. However, traditionally, inferences about qualitative data have focused on the proportion of successes, and we will also cover this approach. It is possible to make such statistical inferences without the aid of a computer, in certain cases.

If we focus on the proportion of successes rather than the count of successes, we can make decisions about a population proportion using the sampling distribution of $\hat{p}$, the sample proportion. If you are not given the sample proportion, then it should be possible to calculate it by expressing the number of successes as a percentage of the total sample, that is, $\hat{p} = \dfrac{x}{n}$. For example, if you are told that there are three dented paint cans in a sample of 30, then $\hat{p} = \dfrac{x}{n} = \dfrac{3}{30} = 0.10$.

The sampling distribution of $\hat{p}$ is normal, under the right conditions. This is because the binomial distribution can sometimes be approximated by the normal distribution. This may be somewhat surprising, since binomial random variables are discrete, while normal random variables are continuous. However, if we look at some graphs and do some calculations, you may become convinced of this fact (which is a special case of the Central Limit Theorem).

The graph of the binomial distribution has a shape similar to the normal distribution whenever the probability of success (p) is close to 0.5, or whenever the number of trials is *large*. Generally, the binomial distribution can be approximated by a normal distribution whenever the following two conditions hold:

- $np \geq 10$ and
- $nq \geq 10$ (where $q = 1 - p$ is the probability of failure)

Exhibits 6.16, 6.17, and 6.18 illustrate this.

EXHIBIT 6.16

Binomial Distribution, $n = 10$, $p = 0.1$

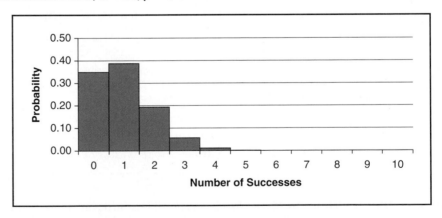

Exhibit 6.16 is a graph of a binomial distribution with $n = 10$ and $p = 0.1$. It does not look normal, because it is skewed to the right. Notice that it does not meet the required conditions ($np = 10(0.1) = 1 < 10$). In this case, we could *not* approximate the binomial distribution with the normal distribution.

Exhibit 6.17 opposite is a graph of a binomial distribution with $n = 20$ and $p = 0.5$. It looks like a normal distribution. Notice that it does meet the required conditions ($np = 20(0.5) = 10$, $nq = 20(0.5) = 10$). In this case, we could use the normal distribution to approximate the binomial distribution.

EXHIBIT **6.17**

Binomial Distribution, *n* = 20, *p* = 0.5

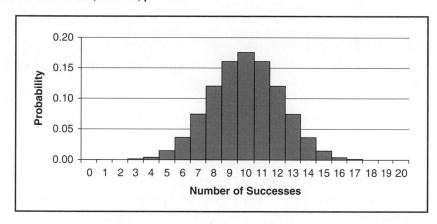

Exhibit 6.18 is a graph of a binomial distribution with $n = 100$ and $p = 0.1$. In this case, the conditions for normal approximation are just met ($np = 100(0.1) = 10$, $nq = 90$). Even though the probability of success is far from 0.5, the graph still looks fairly normal, because of the high number of trials. In this case, we could use the normal distribution to approximate the binomial distribution.

EXHIBIT **6.18**

Binomial Distribution, *n* = 100, *p* = 0.1

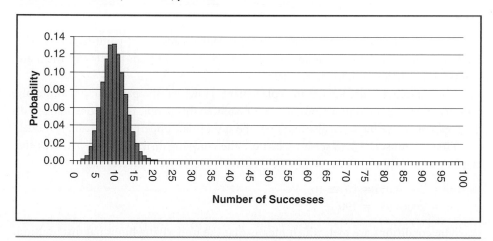

Once we have established that the binomial distribution we are interested in is *normal* enough, the next question is: which normal distribution should we use to approximate it? Remember that:

• the mean of a binomial distribution is np
• the standard deviation of a binomial distribution is $\sqrt{npq}$

So, the normal distribution with a mean of np and a standard deviation of $\sqrt{npq}$ can be used to approximate a binomial distribution, under the right conditions (np and nq both ≥ 10).

If the binomial distribution can be approximated by the normal distribution, then it is also true that the sampling distribution of proportions is also normally distributed. The sampling distribution of $\hat{p}$ is as follows.

The Sampling Distribution of $\hat{p}$ (The Sample Proportion)

For a sample of size n and a binomial distribution with a claimed or desired proportion p:

1. The standard deviation of the sample proportions (the $\hat{p}$-values) is

$$\sigma_{\hat{p}} = \sqrt{\frac{pq}{n}}$$

We will refer to $\sigma_{\hat{p}}$ as the *standard error* of the sample proportion.

2. The mean of the sample proportions is equal to the population proportion. In other words:

$$\mu_{\hat{p}} = p$$

3. The sampling distribution will be approximately normal as long as both of the required conditions are met:

- $np \geq 10$ and
- $nq \geq 10$

Note: This last result means that you must check these conditions before you use the sampling distribution of $\hat{p}$. If these conditions are not both met, you will have to use the binomial distribution to make your decision.

Suppose that the acceptable proportion of dented cans in the paint factory is 5%. Eleanor Bennett examines a random sample of 200 cans and finds that 6% of them are dented. What action should Eleanor take?

The sampling is done without replacement. However, the paint factory probably produces thousands and thousands of cans of paint, so this sample is not more than 5% of the population. The binomial distribution is the appropriate underlying probability model.

First, we must check to see if we can use the sampling distribution of $\hat{p}$. Check the conditions:

- $np = 200(0.05) = 10 \geq 10$
- $nq = 200(0.95) = 190 \geq 10$

The conditions are met, which means that the underlying binomial distribution can be approximated with the normal distribution, and that we can use the sampling distribution of $\hat{p}$. The sampling distribution of $\hat{p}$ will be approximately normal, with

$$\sigma_{\hat{p}} = \sqrt{\frac{pq}{n}} = \sqrt{\frac{(0.05)(0.95)}{200}} = 0.015411035$$

and

$$\mu_{\hat{p}} = p = 0.05$$

The observed sample proportion is higher than we expected, so we want to calculate $P(\hat{p} \geq 0.06)$. The tail area corresponding to the probability we need to calculate is shaded in Exhibit 6.19.

EXHIBIT 6.19

Sampling Distribution of Sample Proportion, $n = 200$, $p = 0.05$

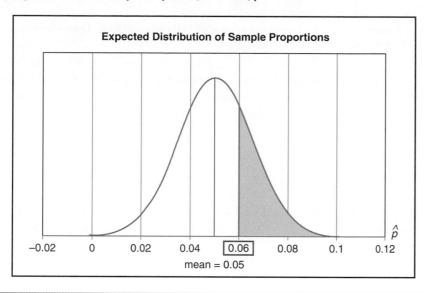

The probability calculation is once again a straightforward normal probability calculation.

$$P(\hat{p} \geq 0.06)$$

$$= P\left(z \geq \frac{0.06 - 0.05}{0.015411035} \right)$$

$$= P(z \geq 0.65)$$

$$= 1 - 0.7422$$

$$= 0.2578$$

The probability of getting a sample proportion of 6% dented cans is 0.2578, if the population proportion of dented cans is 5%. This sample result would not be unusual. We do not have evidence that the true proportion of dented cans is higher than the acceptable level. So, no action is required.

For comparison's sake, we can also calculate this probability directly, using the binomial distribution and a computer. If 6% of 200 paint cans had dents, that would correspond to $(0.06 \cdot 200) = 12$ dented cans. $P(x \geq 12, n = 200, p = 0.05) = 0.3002$. You might think that this is not that close to the approximated value of about 26% that we calculated above.

There is a reason for the discrepancy. Because we are approximating a discrete probability distribution with a continuous one, the straightforward calculation that we did using $\hat{p}$ will tend to underestimate the true probability. This bias can be corrected through the use of something called the *continuity correction factor*, which is beyond the scope of this text. The good news is that the continuity correction factor is not so important for larger values of n, and that is the situation we will assume throughout the rest of the exercises. If you think about it, you will realize that it is easier to get large sample sizes when we are collecting qualitative data. A quick inspection is enough to determine whether a can is dented or not. This is much less time-consuming than exactly measuring the amount of paint in the can.

To demonstrate that the accuracy of the approximation is better for large sample sizes, we will redo the dented paint can example with a sample size of 500.

EXAMPLE 6.3B

Using the sampling distribution of $\hat{p}$ to make a decision about a population proportion

Suppose that the acceptable proportion of dented cans in the paint factory is 5%. Eleanor Bennett examines a random sample of 500 cans and finds that 6% of them are dented. What action should Eleanor take?

It is likely that the sample of 500 cans is not more than 5% of the total population of paint cans. Therefore, even though the sampling is done without replacement, it is still appropriate to use the binomial distribution as the underlying probability model. Check the conditions:

- $np = 500(0.05) = 25 \geq 10$
- $nq = 500(0.95) = 475 \geq 10$

A normal distribution could be used to approximate the underlying binomial distribution. It is appropriate to use the sampling distribution of $\hat{p}$, which will be approximately normal, with:

$$\sigma_{\hat{p}} = \sqrt{\frac{pq}{n}} = \sqrt{\frac{(0.05)(0.95)}{500}} = 0.009746794$$

and

$$\mu_{\hat{p}} = p = 0.05$$

The observed sample proportion is higher than the desired level, so we want to calculate $P(\hat{p} \geq 0.06)$. The area corresponding to the probability we need to calculate is shaded in Exhibit 6.20.

EXHIBIT 6.20

Sampling Distribution of Sample Proportion, $n = 500$, $p = 0.05$

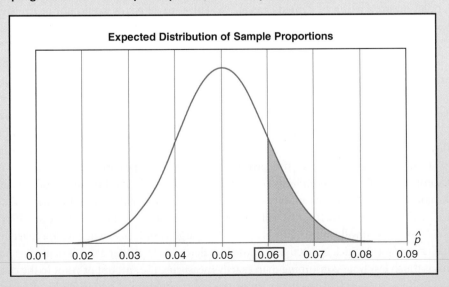

$$P(\hat{p} \geq 0.06)$$

$$= P\left(z \geq \frac{0.06 - 0.05}{0.009746794}\right)$$

$$= P(z \geq 1.03)$$

$$= 1 - 0.8485$$

$$= 0.1515$$

If we do the corresponding binomial probability calculation (with the aid of a computer), we find that $P(x \geq 30, n = 500, p = 0.05) = 0.1765$. This time, the approximation (0.1515) is closer to the actual value (0.1765). Note that because the underlying binomial distribution is skewed (the probability of success is only 5%, which is quite far from 50%), the approximation will not be perfect.

Whether we calculate the probability of the sample result with the binomial distribution or approximate it with the sampling distribution of $\hat{p}$, we will reach the same decision. Because a sample proportion as high as 6% would occur more than 15% of time, if the actual proportion of dented cans were actually 5%, the sample result is not unusual. We do not have evidence that there are more dented cans than there should be. No action should be taken.

EXAMPLE 6.3C

Using the sampling distribution of $\hat{p}$ to make a decision about a population proportion

In a recent survey about the acceptability of a new breakfast cereal, the respondents were asked to indicate whether they would use the cereal regularly after trying it. The cereal's manufacturer thought that the new cereal would be worthwhile to launch if the probability of an individual saying yes was more than 20%.

Suppose the research company surveyed 200 people and found 46 who said they would use the cereal regularly after trying it. What is the probability of this happening, assuming that the actual probability of using the cereal after trying it is only 20%? Does the sample result provide evidence that the proportion of all people who would use the cereal regularly after trying it is more than 20%?

First, we have to recognize that this is a situation in which the binomial distribution applies. As with other opinion surveys, sampling is done without replacement. The population of breakfast cereal eaters is probably quite large, so the sample size of 200 is probably much less than 5% of the population. The binomial distribution is an appropriate underlying model here, with $n = 200$ and $p = 0.20$.

Next, we have to see if this binomial distribution can be approximated by a normal distribution. We check np and nq.

- $np = 200(0.20) = 40$
- $nq = 200(0.80) = 160$

Both are ≥ 10, so we can use the sampling distribution of $\hat{p}$.

The sample proportion is $\frac{46}{200} = 0.23$. We now have to calculate the probability of a sample proportion as high as the observed sample result, if the population proportion is 0.20.

$$P(\hat{p} \geq 0.23) = P\left(z \geq \frac{0.23 - 0.20}{\sqrt{\dfrac{0.20(0.80)}{200}}}\right) = P(z \geq 1.06) = (1 - 0.8554) = 0.1446$$

The probability of getting a sample proportion as high as 23% is 0.1446, if 20% of all customers would use the cereal after trying it. This sample result is not unusual. While the sample results looked promising ($\hat{p}$ was greater than 20%), the sample result was not enough greater than 20% to be convincing. Therefore, we do not have enough evidence from the sample to conclude that more than 20% of people would use the cereal regularly after trying it. This means it would not be worthwhile to launch this breakfast cereal (if this criterion is the only one determining the launch, which is unlikely).

GUIDE TO DECISION MAKING

Using the Sampling Distribution of $\hat{p}$ to Decide About p

When:

- qualitative data, one sample, one population
- trying to make a decision about p on the basis of $\hat{p}$
- sample size (n) large
- computer not available, so using a binomial probability calculation is not practical

Steps:

1. Identify or calculate

   - p, the desired or claimed population proportion
   - $\hat{p}$, the sample proportion
   - n, the sample size

2. If sampling is being done without replacement, check that the sample is not more than 5% of the total population, so the binomial distribution is an appropriate underlying model.

3. Check that the underlying binomial distribution can be approximated by a normal distribution, which requires *both*

   - $np \geq 10$ and
   - $nq \geq 10$

   If these conditions are met, the sampling distribution of $\hat{p}$ will be approximately normal.

4. *If* the sampling distribution is approximately normal, proceed by identifying or calculating the mean and standard deviation of the sampling distributions, using the following formulas:

   - $\mu_{\hat{p}} = p$
   - $\sigma_{\hat{p}} = \sqrt{\dfrac{pq}{n}}$

5. Use this sampling distribution to calculate the probability of a sample result as extreme as the $\hat{p}$ from the sample.

- If $\hat{p}$ is above p, calculate P($\hat{p} \geq$ observed sample proportion).

- If $\hat{p}$ is below p, calculate P($\hat{p} \leq$ observed sample proportion).

If the calculated probability is 5% or less, there is convincing evidence that the population proportion is not as claimed.

See Example 6.3B on page 250, or Example 6.3C on page 251.

DEVELOP YOUR SKILLS 6.3

11. A cereal manufacturer claims that 10% of its cereal boxes contain a free ticket to the movies. Because you have eaten several boxes of cereal without finding a movie ticket, you are suspicious of this claim. You set up a website to ask people about their experience with the cereal boxes. Once you have 250 responses, you shut the website down, and do some calculations. You discover that 20 of your 250 respondents have found free movie tickets. Do you have a case against the manufacturer's claim? (Is this really a random sample? Why or why not? What do you have to think about in order to answer this question?)

12. A college claims that 97% of its graduates find jobs in their field within a year of graduation. Since you graduated from the program a year ago and have not been able to find a job, you think that the college has overestimated the job placement rate of its graduates. The alumni office contacts a random sample of 200 students from your college who graduated when you did, and discovers that 5% of the group do not have a job in their field. Does this mean that the college has overstated the proportion of graduates who find jobs in their field within a year of graduation?

13. A tire company claims that no more than 1% of its tires are defective. A national survey shows that 8 out of 500 tires purchased in the last year from this company were defective. Does the sample provide evidence that the

percentage of defective tires is more than 1%? (What bias might you be concerned about, with the national survey?)

14. An advertisement for Cold-Over claims an 80% success rate in preventing a cold from developing, if the patient starts the treatment immediately upon getting a sore throat or a runny nose. A random sample of 300 patients who are just developing symptoms are given Cold-Over, and are later checked to see if the treatment was successful. It is found that 235 of them found the treatment successful. Does the sample provide evidence that fewer than 80% of patients taking Cold-Over prevent a cold from developing, if they take it as directed?

15. A survey by a research company reported that 40% of retired people eat out at least once a week. You run a restaurant, and you are wondering if you should focus more of your advertising on retired people. However, you are concerned that the research might not apply to your city. You decide to check on the research results. You hire a statistics student to conduct a random sample of 150 retired people in your city. The student reports that 44 of them eat out at least once a week. Do these sample results suggest that the percentage of retired people who eat out at least once a week in your city is less than in the research study? Is there anything else you should consider?

6.4 HYPOTHESIS TESTING

In Chapter 6, we have explored the use of sampling distributions and probability calculations to make decisions about population parameters, based on sample results. The formal method of doing this is called a hypothesis test, and you will be introduced to it in Chapter 7. The methods applied in this chapter, while fundamentally correct, have been somewhat informal and streamlined. The goal was to help you develop an intuitive understanding of the decision-making process, without being distracted by too many details.

We have glossed over some important issues. For example, we assumed that σ was known when we were making decisions about population means. This is clearly unrealistic, as was pointed out. However, this unrealistic approach allowed us (temporarily) to work with the familiar normal distribution. In Chapter 7, you will learn how to deal with the more realistic situation where σ is unknown, and you need to make decisions about means.

In Chapter 6 we used a general rule of declaring a sample result *unusual* if the associated tail probability was 5% or less. This is a streamlined approach. In formal hypothesis tests, the probability level that is used to distinguish an unusual sample result can be different from 5%, depending on the situation (although generally it will not be more than 5%). In Chapter 7, you will learn how to deal with these different situations.

There is more to learn about the topics covered in Chapter 6, and you should realize that Chapter 6 represents an interim step in your learning. However, if you have understood what a sampling distribution is, and how it can be used to make a decision about a population distribution, this is a major accomplishment. This decision-making process is the cornerstone of inferential statistics. If you have understood it, the rest is just details. You should find that you can easily build on this understanding to conduct the formal hypothesis tests discussed in Chapter 7 and beyond.

The Decision-Making Process for Statistical Inference

Statistical inference is a set of techniques to allow reliable conclusions to be drawn about population data on the basis of sample data. A random sample is drawn from the population, and a sample statistic is calculated. While the sample statistic is unlikely to be exactly equal to the claimed or desired value of the population parameter, some sample results are very unlikely to occur. If such a sample result is observed, there is evidence to conclude that the population parameter is not as claimed or desired.

The sampling distribution is key to the ability to distinguish whether sample results are consistent with the claimed or desired value of the population parameter. A sampling distribution is the probability distribution of all possible sample results for a given sample size. We use the sampling distribution to calculate the probability of getting a sample result as extreme as the one we observed from the sample, assuming the claim about the population is true. For the purposes of this chapter, we used a general rule of declaring a sample result unusual if the associated tail probability was 5% or less.

The sampling distribution is closely related to the distribution of the population from which the sample is drawn. Once we know what the population characteristics are supposed to be, we can calculate the characteristics of the sampling distribution. Two particular sampling distributions are described in this chapter.

The Sampling Distribution of the Sample Mean

Sometimes we want to make a decision about a population mean, μ, on the basis of a sample mean, $\bar{x}$. For this we need the sampling distribution of the sample mean.

For a sample of size n, and a population with a claimed or desired mean of μ:

1. The standard deviation of the sample means (the $\bar{x}$-values) is equal to the population standard deviation, divided by the square root of the sample size. In other words:

$$\sigma_{\bar{x}} = \frac{\sigma}{\sqrt{n}}$$

   We refer to the standard deviation of the sample means ($\sigma_{\bar{x}}$) as the *standard error*.

2. The mean of the sample means (the $\bar{x}$-values) is equal to the mean of the original population. That is,

$$\mu_{\bar{x}} = \mu$$

3. The sampling distribution of the sample means is normal if the original population is normally distributed, or the sample size is large enough.

The Central Limit Theorem tells us that sampling distributions of $\bar{x}$ will be normal—even if the original population is not normal—if the sample size is large enough. How large is "large enough" depends on how far from normal the population is.

To assess population normality, create a histogram of sample data (unless there are too few data points). Some guidelines to help you decide whether a sampling distribution of $\bar{x}$ is normal are outlined on page 241. Also, there is a Guide to Decision Making using sampling distributions of $\bar{x}$ when σ is known, on page 243. Example 6.2B on page 241 illustrates.

The Sampling Distribution of the Sample Proportion

Sometimes we want to make decisions about a population proportion, p, on the basis of the sample proportion, $\hat{p}$. We can do this by two different methods, depending on whether we focus on the counts (the number of successes) or the proportion of successes. For example, in Example 6.3A on page 245, the problem focused on 89 late shipments out of 400. This could also be expressed as $\frac{89}{400} = 0.2225$, a proportion of late shipments. These are just two ways of representing the same information.

No matter which method is used, if sampling is done without replacement, ensure that the sample is no more than 5% of the total population, so that the binomial distribution is the appropriate underlying probability model.

If we focus on the counts (the number of successes) rather than the proportion of successes, we can calculate the probability of a sample result as extreme as the one we observed using the binomial probability distribution. Generally this will require the use of a computer. The approach is the same as before: if the probability of getting a sample result as extreme as the one we observed is 5% or less, we consider that to be evidence that the population proportion is not as claimed. Example 6.3A on page 245 illustrates.

If we focus on the proportion of successes, we can (in some cases) use the sampling distribution of $\hat{p}$ to assess the probability of a sample result as extreme as the one we observed.

For a sample of size n and a binomial distribution with a claimed or desired proportion p:

1. The standard deviation of the sample proportions (the $\hat{p}$-values) is as follows:

$$\sigma_{\hat{p}} = \sqrt{\frac{pq}{n}}$$

We refer to $\sigma_{\hat{p}}$ as the *standard error* of the sample proportion.

2. The mean of the sample proportions is equal to the population proportion. In other words:

$$\mu_{\hat{p}} = p$$

The sampling distribution will be approximately normal as long as both of the required conditions are met:

- $np \geq 10$ and
- $nq \geq 10$

Note: This last result means that you must check these conditions before you use the sampling distribution of $\hat{p}$. If these conditions are not both met, you will have to use the binomial distribution to make your decision.

There is a Guide to Decision Making using the sampling distribution of $\hat{p}$ on page 252. Example 6.3B on page 250 illustrates.

 Go to MyStatLab at www.mathxl.com. You can practise the exercises indicated with red in the Develop Your Skills and Chapter Review Exercises as often as you want, and guided solutions will help you find answers step by step. You'll find a personalized study plan available to you too!

CHAPTER REVIEW EXERCISES

When you do these exercises, you will have to decide whether to use the sampling distribution of $\bar{x}$, or the sampling distribution of $\hat{p}$ (or the binomial distribution). It should not be difficult to distinguish between the two situations, if you keep the following in mind.

- If the data are quantitative, and there is reference to averages or means, you will need to use the sampling distribution of $\bar{x}$. Remember to check for normality of the sample data set.
- If the data are qualitative, and there is reference to percentages or proportions or counts, you will need to use the sampling distribution of $\hat{p}$ (or the binomial distribution). Remember to check the conditions for normality of the sampling distribution.

These Chapter Review Exercises will give you practice in handling sampling distributions. Remember that the informal, streamlined approach you are using for these questions is temporary, and that Chapter 7 will introduce you to formal hypothesis tests.

WARM-UP EXERCISES

1. Suppose the population data of heights of students at your college (the *x*-values) is normally distributed, with a mean of 167.5 centimetres and a standard deviation of 12 centimetres.
   a. Sketch the normal distribution of heights (*x*-values) in the population.
   b. Describe the sampling distribution of sample means (the $\bar{x}$-values) for samples of size 25 drawn from this population. Sketch this distribution, using the same horizontal axis scale as you used in part a.
   c. Describe the sampling distribution of sample means for samples of size 40 drawn from this population. Sketch this distribution, using the same horizontal axis scale as you used in part a.
   d. Comment on the similarities and differences in the distributions from parts a, b, and c.

2. Use the distributions from Exercise 1 to answer the following questions.
   a. What is the probability that an individual student will be taller than 180 centimetres?
   b. Suppose a random sample of 25 students is selected from the population. What is the probability that the mean height of these 25 students will be more than 180 centimetres?
   c. Suppose a random sample of 40 students is selected from the population. What is the probability that the mean height of these 40 students will be more than 180 centimetres?
   d. Why are your answers to parts a, b, and c of this question different?

THINK AND DECIDE

3. The manufacturer of a pill for back pain claims that 86% of those who take the pill get relief within one hour. You work for a consumer organization and you want to check the claim. You take a random sample of 350 people with back pain who took the pill and find that 287 of them got relief within one hour. Is there evidence that the proportion of back pain sufferers who get relief within one hour is lower than the manufacturer claims?

4. The college cafeteria manager claims that 90% of cafeteria customers are satisfied with the range of food served and prices. Suppose that in a random sample of 500 cafeteria customers, 438 say they are satisfied with the cafeteria. Does the sample result suggest that fewer than 90% of the cafeteria's customers are satisfied with the range of food served and prices?

5. A survey of the morning beverage market shows that the primary breakfast beverage of 17% of Americans is milk. A Canadian dairy company believes the figure is higher in Canada. The company contacts a random sample of 500 Canadians and asks what primary beverage they consumed for breakfast that day. Suppose 102 replied that milk was their primary beverage. Does this sample result provide evidence that a greater proportion of Canadians drink milk as the primary breakfast beverage, as compared to Americans?

6. A tourist attraction gets over 50,000 visitors a year, but traffic has declined over the last few years. The manager has recently refurbished the buildings, added new activities, and generally spruced up the facility. A survey of customers done two years ago revealed that only 65% of them felt they had had an enjoyable experience. A survey of 400 visitors, done after the upgrades, indicated that 282 of them felt they had had an enjoyable experience. Does this provide any evidence that the upgrades improved visitor enjoyment?

7. An analyst in a government ministry is interested in the average cost of textbooks per semester for a college student. A previous estimate suggests that the average cost of textbooks per semester is $700. The analyst wants to check this and conducts a random sample of 75 college students, asking them what their textbook costs were for the last semester. The sample results show an average cost of $756, with a standard deviation of $132. Is there evidence that average textbook costs per semester have increased for college students? You may assume that the standard deviation of all textbook costs is actually $132, and that the population data are normally distributed.

8. Automated teller machines must be stocked with enough cash to satisfy customers making withdrawals over an entire weekend. At one branch, a random sample of the total withdrawals

on 36 weekends showed a sample mean of $8,400. Suppose that the branch manager has always claimed the average total withdrawal over the weekend is $7,500. On the basis of the sample taken, is there evidence to suggest that the bank manager's claim about the true average total withdrawal per weekend is too low? You may assume the population data are normally distributed, and that the standard deviation is $3,700.

THINK AND DECIDE WITH EXCEL

CRE06-9

9. The operations manager at a factory is interested in the lifespan of an electronic component used in one of the factory's machines. The producer of the electronic component claims that it has an average life of 6,200 hours. A random sample of 40 components is studied, and their lifespans recorded.

   What is the probability of getting a sample result as low as this if the average life of the component is actually 6,200 hours, as the component's producer claims? Does this sample provide evidence that component lifespan is less than the producer claims? You may assume the population standard deviation is equal to the sample standard deviation.

CRE06-10

10. A small college in southern Ontario advertises that its business graduates earn an average annual income of $37,323 the first year after graduation. A researcher has been given the task of checking the claim for the 2010 year.

    A random survey of 45 of the college's business graduates produces a data set that is available in MyStatLab. Does this sample provide evidence that the average annual income of Business graduates in the first year after graduation is less than $37,323? You may assume that the standard deviation of all graduates' salaries is equal to the sample standard deviation.

CRE06-11

11. When Doug Brackett bought Downtown Automotive, the previous owner suggested to him that average daily sales at the shop were $2,000. A random sample of daily sales is available in MyStatLab.

    Do the sample data suggest that the average daily sales at the shop are less than the previous owner claimed? You may assume the population standard deviation is equal to the sample standard deviation.

12. In the past, 25% of a college's students lived in the immediate area. In recent years, the college has been trying to attract students from farther afield. A random sample of 400 students revealed that 82 lived in the immediate area. The college has over 10,000 students.
    a. Use Excel to calculate the probability of 82 or fewer students out of 400 coming from the immediate area, assuming the percentage of such students is still 25%.
    b. What is $\hat{p}$ for this random sample?
    c. What is the probability of getting a sample proportion as low as the $\hat{p}$ you calculated in part b if the percentage of students from the immediate area is still 25%? Use the sampling distribution of $\hat{p}$ to answer this question.
    d. Why are the probabilities calculated in parts a and c different?
    e. Is there evidence that the percentage of college students from the immediate catchment area is lower than in the past?

13. A college is considering making the purchase of a laptop computer a requirement for some of its programs. In the past, only 20% of students owned laptop computers. A random sample of 300 students revealed that 77 of them had laptop computers. Is there evidence that the percentage of students with laptop computers is now more than 20%?

CRE06-14

14. A winery owner believes that 60% of the customers visiting her retail wine shop are women. To check this belief, a random sample of visitors is taken. The results are in the file called CRE06-14, where "0" corresponds to male and "1" corresponds to female. Do these data provide evidence that the proportion of female customers is lower than the owner believes?

CHAPTER 7

Making Decisions with a Single Sample

INTRODUCTION

Chapter 6 illustrated how to use a sampling distribution and a probability calculation to make a decision about a population parameter on the basis of a sample result. In this chapter, we will use this decision-making approach in a more formal way, that is, a test of hypothesis. This chapter introduces some commonly used language for this type of decision making. Once the formal hypothesis-testing framework is set up (Section 7.1), you will see how to apply it to make decisions about proportions (Section 7.2) and means (Section 7.3), on the basis of single samples.

In Chapter 6, as an interim step, you learned how to make decisions about population means when the population standard deviation was known. This was clearly unrealistic, and so in Chapter 7 you will learn how to make decisions about a population mean when the population standard deviation is not known (which will be always).

In Chapter 6, the problems we looked at (paint in cans, cereal in boxes, etc.) started out with a goal. For example, the paint cans were supposed to hold 3 litres of paint. We recognized that not every paint

LEARNING OBJECTIVES

After mastering the material in this chapter, you will be able to:

1 Set up appropriate null and alternative hypotheses, and make appropriate conclusions by comparing *p*-values with significance levels.

2 Use a formal hypothesis test to make appropriate conclusions about a population proportion, on the basis of a single sample.

3 Use a formal hypothesis test to make appropriate conclusions about a population mean, on the basis of a single sample.

can would hold *exactly* 3 litres of paint, but we wanted to recognize any case when there was a significantly different amount of paint going into the cans.

If the paint-filling line is set up properly, then the population mean will be 3 litres. In this example, it is our hypothesis (that is, idea or theory or goal) that the population mean is 3 litres, because the paint-filling line is designed to put 3 litres of paint into every can.

7.1 FORMAL HYPOTHESIS TESTING

The Null and the Alternative Hypotheses

Null hypothesis What you are going to believe about the population unless the sample gives you strongly contradictory evidence.

Alternative hypothesis What you are going to believe about the population when there is strong evidence against the null hypothesis.

In a formal hypothesis test, there are always two hypotheses. The **null hypothesis** is what you are going to believe about the population, unless the sample gives you strongly contradictory evidence. The **alternative hypothesis** (sometimes called the *research hypothesis*) is what you are going to believe about the population when there is strong evidence against the null hypothesis.

For example, in the paint-filling line example, the null hypothesis is that in the population, the mean amount of paint in the cans is 3 litres. We could use some mathematical shorthand, and say the following:

$$H_0: \mu = 3 \text{ litres}$$

H_0, read *H-nought*, is standard notation to depict the null hypothesis.

The alternative hypothesis, denoted H_1 (or sometimes H_A), could then take one of three forms:

- $H_1: \mu > 3$ litres (if we were concerned about the cans having too much paint in them) or
- $H_1: \mu < 3$ litres (if we were concerned about the cans having too little paint in them) or
- $H_1: \mu \neq 3$ litres (if we were concerned about the cans having either too little or too much paint in them)

Notice some important things about the null and alternative hypotheses.

1. The hypotheses are statements about a population parameter. They will never be about sample statistics. If we have sample data, we can calculate the sample statistic—no hypothesis is required.
2. The hypotheses *match*, in the sense that if the null hypothesis (H_0) is that $\mu = 3$ litres, the alternative hypothesis (H_1) will be some statement about μ and 3 litres.
3. The null hypothesis (H_0) always contains an equality. The alternative hypothesis never contains an equality (or $\leq$ or $\geq$).

EXAMPLE 7.1A

Setting up correct null and alternative hypotheses

Which of the following are legitimate hypothesis-testing pairs? If a pair is not a legitimate hypothesis-testing pair, explain why.

a. $H_0: \mu = 15$; $H_1: \mu = 14$
b. $H_0: \sigma = 0.4$; $H_1: \sigma > 0.6$

c. $H_0: \mu = 123; H_1: \mu \neq 123$

d. $H_0 = 150; H_1 > 150$

e. $H_0: p = 0.15; H_1: p \geq 0.15$

f. $H_0: \bar{x} = 15; H_1: \bar{x} > 15$

Solutions:

a. $H_0: \mu = 15; H_1: \mu = 14$

No, this is not a legitimate hypothesis-testing pair. Both the null and alternative hypotheses contain equalities. As well, the hypotheses refer to two different numbers. If there was evidence against the null hypothesis that $\mu = 15$, it would not be logical to conclude $\mu = 14$ instead.

b. $H_0: \sigma = 0.4; H_1: \sigma > 0.6$

No, this is not a legitimate hypothesis-testing pair. The hypotheses refer to two different numbers. The numbers must match. If there was evidence against the null hypothesis that $\sigma = 0.4$, it would not be sensible to conclude instead that $\sigma > 0.6$!

c. $H_0: \mu = 123; H_1: \mu \neq 123$

Yes, this is a legitimate hypothesis-testing pair.

d. $H_0 = 150; H_1 > 150$

No, this is not a legitimate hypothesis-testing pair. No population parameter is mentioned. H_0 and H_1 cannot equal anything, or be greater than anything. H_0 simply means *the null hypothesis* and H_1 means *the alternative hypothesis*. If this pair were rewritten with reference to a population parameter, the pair would be legitimate. For example:

$$H_0: \mu = 150; H_1: \mu > 150$$

e. $H_0: p = 0.15; H_1: p \geq 0.15$

No, this is not a legitimate hypothesis-testing pair. Both hypotheses contain an equality. If we reject the idea that $p = 0.15$, it would not be reasonable to conclude p might be equal to (or greater than) 0.15. If H_1 were rewritten to read "$p > 0.15$," the pair would be legitimate.

f. $H_0: \bar{x} = 15; H_1: \bar{x} > 15$

No, this is not a legitimate hypothesis-testing pair. Both hypotheses refer to $\bar{x}$, which is a sample statistic, not a population parameter. We have no doubt about what $\bar{x}$ is, because we can calculate it from the sample. The mystery is about μ, not $\bar{x}$!

Setting up the correct null and alternative hypotheses is important because they guide your analysis. There are many things to think about.

One-Tailed and Two-Tailed Hypothesis Tests

In general, the alternative hypothesis can take one of three forms:

1. H_1: population parameter > some particular value
2. H_1: population parameter < some particular value
3. H_1: population parameter ≠ some particular value

The first two forms are referred to as *one-tailed tests* because sample results in only one tail of the sampling distribution provide evidence against the null hypothesis, in favour of the alternative hypothesis.

Suppose you have been working to reduce the time it takes for loan requests to be approved (or denied) at your financial institution. You know the average time was 2 working days in the past, and this sets up the null hypothesis, H_0: $\mu = 2$ working days. You take a random sample of loan requests, and track how long it takes until a decision is made. In this case, you are looking for evidence that the average time has been reduced. The alternative hypothesis is H_1: $\mu < 2$ working days. This is a one-tailed (also called a left-tailed) test: only unusually low values of $\bar{x}$ from the sample (in the left tail of the sampling distribution) will convince you that average time to process the loan requests has been reduced.

As another example, suppose you have developed a new marketing plan, and now you want to see if average weekly sales have increased. In the past, average weekly sales were $5,000, so the null hypothesis will be H_0: $\mu = \$5,000$. Since you are wondering if sales have increased, this will also be a one-tailed test (in this case, a right-tailed test), with H_1: $\mu > \$5,000$: only unusually high values of $\bar{x}$ from the sample (in the right tail of the sampling distribution) will convince you that sales have improved.

In the streamlined approach we used in Chapter 6, all of our informal tests were one-tailed. This was a simplification. Now we are also going to deal with two-tailed tests. In Chapter 6, we also looked at sample evidence about the amount of paint in paint cans. The goal was to have an average of 3 litres of paint in every can. So the null hypothesis is H_0: $\mu = 3$ litres. The quality control procedures should identify cases in which there is either significantly too little or significantly too much paint in the cans, so the alternative hypothesis will be H_1: $\mu \neq 3$ litres. This is described as a *two-tailed* test of hypothesis, because both sample results that are significantly too low (from the left tail of the sampling distribution) and significantly too high (from the right tail of the sampling distribution) would provide evidence against the null hypothesis. Many quality control hypothesis tests are two-tailed.

Making a Decision: Rejecting or Failing to Reject the Null Hypothesis

In a hypothesis test, we are using sample data to decide between two conflicting ideas, expressed as H_0 and H_1. If we get significant evidence from the sample data against the null hypothesis, then we are going to change our minds about something, and probably take some action. In the paint-filling line example, if the sample data provide convincing evidence that the mean amount of paint going into the paint cans is *not* 3 litres, then some action will be taken to adjust the machines, and there will be good reason for doing so. Also notice this: if the sample does not provide convincing evidence against the null hypothesis, no action will be taken. This makes sense: the company does not want to adjust machines when they don't really need it. But this is a weaker result, in the sense that it does not *guarantee* that the average amount of paint going into the cans is actually 3 litres.

In the first case (convincing evidence against the null hypothesis), the usual language is to say that we *rejected* the null hypothesis, and that there is sufficient evidence to support the alternative hypothesis. This is a fairly strong conclusion. In the second case, we say that we *failed to reject* the null hypothesis, and that there is insufficient evidence to support the alternative hypothesis. This is a weaker conclusion. Above all, it does *not* imply that the null hypothesis is *true*. We can never be that definitive unless we have examined the entire population of data. Therefore, if you fail to reject the null hypothesis, you should *not* say "the null hypothesis is true," or even that you "accept" the null hypothesis. All you can say is that you do not have strong evidence against it.

Significance Level and Type I and Type II Errors

Once the null and alternative hypotheses are set up, the next step is to establish the significance level of the test. The usual notation for the significance level is α, that is, the Greek letter alpha. For example, you might see $\alpha = 0.05$, which means that the significance level is set at 5%.

But what does *significance level* mean? To understand this, you must understand that you can make two types of errors when you are doing a test of hypothesis. Both of these potential errors arise because we are using sample data to make a conclusion about a population. The best we can do is control the possibility of these kinds of errors. We cannot eliminate them completely, as long as we are using sample data (and not population data) to make decisions.

A **Type I error** arises when we mistakenly reject the null hypothesis when it is in fact true. In the paint-filling line example, this would correspond to deciding to adjust the machines on the line when they were in fact working correctly. This could happen if we observed a very unusual sample result. The **significance level** is the maximum allowable probability of a Type I error. It is something that you will control in the hypothesis test.

Your first instinct would probably be to set the significance level quite low, although of course, we would never set $\alpha = 0$ (We would never be able to reject H_0 if we did this). Suppose the quality control inspector at the paint factory set the significance level at a low value, for example, $\alpha = 0.01$. Then there would be only a small chance of adjusting the machines on the paint-filling line when they did not actually need adjusting. With α set so low, the inspector would have to get very strong evidence from the sample data to be convinced to adjust the paint-filling line. The only difficulty with this approach is that it has the effect of increasing the chance that machines would *not* be adjusted when they did need to be adjusted, with the result being either angry customers or lower profits because the company was giving away free paint. This is called a Type II error. A **Type II error** arises when we mistakenly fail to reject the null hypothesis when it is in fact false. Exhibit 7.1 on the next page illustrates the trade-off.

So, how do you set α? First, realize that if you set α at 5%, this means that if you repeat the hypothesis test over and over a large number of times, then you will end up incorrectly rejecting a true null hypothesis about 5% of the time. So, over many, many quality control tests in the paint factory, the machines on the paint-filling line would be adjusted when they did not actually need it about 5% of the time. If you set α lower, at 2%, for example, the machines would be incorrectly adjusted only about 2% of the time, in the long run. However, lowering α would have the result that the machines would more often not be adjusted when they should be (Type II error). It is important to recognize that there is always a trade-off between Type I and Type II errors—reducing the chances of one type of error will always increase the chances of the other.

Type I error Error that arises when we mistakenly reject the null hypothesis when it is in fact true.

Significance level The maximum allowable probability of a Type I error in a hypothesis test.

Type II error Error that arises when we mistakenly fail to reject the null hypothesis when it is in fact false.

EXHIBIT 7.1

Trade-Off in Type I and Type II Error

High Significance Level Increases the Chance of Rejecting H_0 (Possibly When It Is True)

Low Significance Level Decreases the Chance of Rejecting H_0 (Possibly When It Is False)

a)

Sampling Distribution

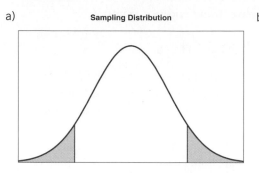

b)

Sampling Distribution

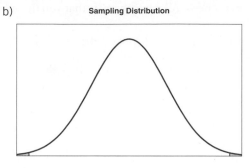

Both kinds of errors have cost and other consequences. The way to set α is to think about the costs and consequences of both types of errors, and then set α at the maximum tolerable level (which keeps the probability of Type II error as low as possible). It is possible to calculate the probability of a Type II error in a particular hypothesis test, but this is beyond the scope of this text.

In practice, the most commonly used levels of significance are 5% and 1%, and these are the levels you will most often see in problems and examples in this text. In the informal hypothesis tests in Chapter 6, we used just one significance level (5%). Now we will introduce other possibilities.

Notice that the lower the significance level is, the harder it is to reject the null hypothesis. This also means that the lower the significance level, the stronger and more persuasive your result will be if you do in fact reject the null hypothesis. If you set α fairly low, say at 1%, then you have to get a sample result that would be highly unusual (that is, it should happen only 1% of the time or less) in order to reject the null hypothesis and decide in favour of the alternative hypothesis. If we set α at 1%, and the sample evidence convinced us to adjust the machines on the paint-filling line, we would be fairly confident that the machines did in fact need adjustment. There is one more point about the significance level of the hypothesis test. The significance level should be set *before* any data are collected, on the basis of the considerations outlined above. It can be tempting to collect some sample data and then set the significance level so that you get the result you want, but this is not the correct way to proceed.

EXAMPLE 7.1B

Type I and Type II errors

The college information technology (IT) department is interested in computer usage among students, because it has to plan to provide adequate service. The former standard for planning purposes was that students spent an average of 10 hours per week using college computers, but the director of IT thinks that students are now making greater use of computers than in the past.

   a. What are the null and alternative hypotheses for this situation?

   b. Explain the Type I and Type II errors in the context of computer use.

   c. From the IT director's point of view, which type of error would be the most important? Why?

   d. From the students' point of view, which type of error would be the most important? Why?

Solutions:

   a. H_0: $\mu = 10$ hours per week
      H_1: $\mu > 10$ hours per week

   b. A Type I error occurs when we reject the null hypothesis when it is actually true. In this context, that would mean mistakenly believing that computer use had increased, when in fact it had not.

      A Type II error occurs when we fail to reject the null hypothesis when it is in fact false. In this context, that would mean concluding that computer use had not increased, when in fact it had.

   c. A Type I error would mean that extra resources would be put into computing when they were not needed. This would mean incurring unnecessary extra costs.

      A Type II error would mean not recognizing the case when extra resources were in fact needed. This would mean that inadequate service would be provided to students, leading to complaints and more computer down-time.

      With the extreme resource limitations in the post-secondary sector in Canada, the Type I error would probably be more important to the IT director, in the short run. However, a Type II error might lead to decreased enrollment in the long run, as word got out about poor computer resources at the college.

   d. A Type II error would be more important to students, as it would mean their being without crucial computing services.

Deciding on the Basis of *p*-Values

Although most of the problems in this text assume that data have already been collected, when you apply the hypothesis testing approach in your work, you will have to collect the sample data, as discussed in Chapter 1. Once you have the sample data, you will use it and the sampling distribution to determine whether the sample result gives you convincing evidence against the null hypothesis. This requires doing a probability calculation, based on the sampling distribution, as we did in Chapter 6.

This probability calculation results in what is called the **_p_-value** of a hypothesis test—the probability of getting a sample result at least as extreme as the observed sample result. The probability calculation is based on the sampling distribution that would exist if the null hypothesis were true. We have already calculated *p*-values, in Chapter 6, although we did not call them *p*-values. Most statistical computer software reports the *p*-value of any hypothesis test, so it is crucial that you understand what the *p*-value

_p_-value In a hypothesis test, the probability of getting a sample result at least as extreme as the observed sample result; the probability calculation is based on the sampling distribution that would exist if the null hypothesis were true.

means. Notice that a low p-value means that the sample result would be highly unlikely if the null hypothesis were true. Put more casually, we could say: we shouldn't be getting this sample result, if the null hypothesis were true. But we did! This gives us evidence against the null hypothesis. On the other hand, if the p-value is high, then the sample result is not unusual, and we do not have enough evidence to reject the null hypothesis. What do *high* and *low* mean? In fact, the significance level of the hypothesis test is what decides this.

> ### Using p-Values in Hypothesis Tests
>
> We reject the null hypothesis whenever the p-value $\leq \alpha$. The lower the p-value is, the stronger is the evidence against H_0.

Comparison of the p-value with the significance level allows us to make the decision that is supported by the data. However, the p-value also gives us something more: an indication of the strength of the evidence. Suppose α is set at 5%. Both a p-value of 4% and a p-value of 1% would lead to a rejection of the null hypothesis, because both p-values are less than 5%. However, we would have stronger evidence against the null hypothesis when the p-value was 1%. A p-value of 1% tells us that we would get sample results like the ones we have observed only 1% of the time, if the null hypothesis were true. This is highly improbable (yet it happened), and so we can be quite confident in our decision in favour of the alternative hypothesis. A p-value of 4% gives us somewhat less confidence, even though the decision is the same.

There is one more point worth making about the p-value. It is unfortunate that the standard notation is so close to the notation we use for the population proportion. This can get confusing, particularly when we are doing hypothesis tests about population proportions. Keep in mind that "p," by itself, is the notation for a population proportion (or the probability of success in a binomial experiment). The term "p-value" refers to the probability calculation done for a hypothesis test.

GUIDE TO TECHNIQUE

Calculating p-Values

The p-value is the probability of getting a sample result at least as extreme as the observed sample result. The probability is calculated from the appropriate sampling distribution, which is always based on the assumption that the null hypothesis is true. The p-value probability calculation must match the alternative hypothesis used in the test. For tests of means and proportions, p-values are calculated as follows:

- P(sample statistic $\geq$ observed sample result) when H_1 contains "$>$"
- P(sample statistic $\leq$ observed sample result) when H_1 contains "$<$"
- $2 \times$ P(tail area beyond the observed sample result) when H_1 contains "$\neq$"

EXAMPLE **7.1C**

Calculating *p*-values

A Nanos national poll conducted between April 25th and April 30th in 2009 surveyed 1,001 Canadians about the harmonization of the GST with the provincial sales tax in Ontario.[1] The poll reported that 28% of those surveyed thought that the impact on the Ontario economy would be "positive" or "somewhat positive." Is there enough evidence to conclude that more than a quarter of all Canadians think the effect of harmonization of the GST with the provincial sales tax in Ontario would have a positive or somewhat positive impact on the Ontario economy? Set up the null and alternative hypotheses, check conditions, and calculate the *p*-value. If $\alpha = 0.05$, what conclusion should be made?

$$H_0: p = 0.25$$
$$H_1: p > 0.25$$

Sampling is done without replacement, but there are millions of Canadians 18 years and older, so the sample is not more than 5% of the population. Now, check that the sampling distribution of $\hat{p}$ will be approximately normal.

$$np = 1,001(0.25) = 250.25 \geq 10$$
$$nq = 1,001(1 - 0.75) = 750.75 \geq 10$$

The necessary conditions are met for us to use the sampling distribution of $\hat{p}$ to make the decision.

$$P(\hat{p} \geq \text{observed sample statistic})$$
$$= P(\hat{p} \geq 0.28)$$

$$= P\left(z \geq \frac{0.28 - 0.25}{\sqrt{\dfrac{0.25(0.75)}{1,001}}} \right)$$

$$= P(z \geq 2.19)$$
$$= 1 - 0.9857$$
$$= 0.0143$$

The probability of observing a sample proportion as high as 28%, if the true proportion is 25%, is only 0.0143. It is highly unlikely that we would observe such a sample result if the true proportion is 25%. Because we did observe this sample result, we have fairly convincing evidence against the idea that the true proportion is 25%. The *p*-value is less than $\alpha = 0.05$. Our sample result is as unlikely as it needs to be, to convince us to reject the idea that the true proportion is 25%. There is enough evidence to suggest that more than a quarter of Canadians think the effect of harmonization of the GST with the provincial sales tax in Ontario would have a positive or somewhat positive impact on the Ontario economy.

---

[1] *Source:* Nanos National Poll, "Canadians Divided on Impact of GST Harmonization," **www.nanosresearch.com/library/polls/POLNAT-S09-T374E.pdf**, accessed May 29, 2009.

Steps in a Formal Hypothesis Test

1. Specify H_0, the null hypothesis.
2. Specify H_1, the alternative hypothesis.
3. Determine or identify α, the significance level.
4. Collect or identify the sample data. Calculate the p-value of the sample result.
5. If p-value $\leq \alpha$, reject H_0 and conclude that there is sufficient evidence to decide in favour of H_1. If p-value $> \alpha$, fail to reject H_0 and conclude that there is insufficient evidence to decide in favour of H_1. Always state your conclusions in units of measurement and language appropriate to the problem.

DEVELOP YOUR SKILLS 7.1

MyStatLab

1. A manufacturer receives large shipments of keyboards that will be sold with its computers. The computer manufacturer does not accept any shipments unless there is evidence that fewer than 5% of the keyboards are defective.

   a. What are the null and alternative hypotheses for this situation?

   b. Explain the Type I and Type II errors in the context of the keyboard shipments.

   c. From the computer manufacturer's point of view, which type of error would be the most important? Why?

   d. From the keyboard supplier's point of view, which type of error would be the most important? Why?

2. A drug company has developed a new formulation of a popular pain reliever. It appears that the new formula provides quicker pain relief than the old formula, which provided relief in 15 minutes, on average. The company wants to gather evidence to see if the new drug provides relief faster than the old one.

   a. What should the null and alternative hypotheses be for this situation?

   b. Explain the Type I and Type II errors in the context of the pain reliever.

   c. If the company reported that it had rejected the null hypothesis at a 10% significance level, would you be inclined to switch to the new drug for faster pain relief? Why or why not?

   d. If the company reported that it had rejected the null hypothesis, and that the test had a p-value of 1%, would you be inclined to switch to the new drug? Why or why not?

3. The quality control manager at a plant that produces canned peaches is setting up a hypothesis test about the amount of peaches in the can. The cans are supposed to contain 142 mL of peaches.

   a. What should the null and alternative hypotheses be for this situation?

   b. Explain the Type I and Type II errors in the context of the canned peaches.

   c. If you were a consumer buying the peaches, which type of error would be most important to you? Why?

4. Suppose you have null and alternative hypotheses as follows.

   $H_0: p = 0.35$

   $H_1: p > 0.35$

   The sample size is 500, sampling is done without replacement, and the sample is less than 5% of the population. The sample proportion is 0.36. What is the p-value?

5. Alter the information in Exercise 4 above by replacing the alternative hypothesis with:

   $H_1: p \neq 0.35.$

   Now what is the p-value?

7.2   DECIDING ABOUT A POPULATION PROPORTION—THE z-TEST OF p

Now we can apply the formal hypothesis-testing procedure to a situation in which we are trying to make a decision about a population proportion. As we did in Example 7.1C, we can use the sampling distribution of $\hat{p}$ when np and nq are both ≥ 10. Remember also that if these conditions hold, the sampling distribution of $\hat{p}$ will be approximately normal, with the mean and standard deviation as follows:

- $\mu_{\hat{p}} = p$

- $\sigma_{\hat{p}} = \sqrt{\dfrac{pq}{n}}$

We will start with a problem that we already did in Chapter 6. This will allow you to see the hypothesis-testing language being used in a situation that is already familiar to you.

EXAMPLE 7.2A

Hypothesis test about a population proportion, summary data

Let's revisit Example 6.3C on page 251. In a recent survey about the acceptability of a new breakfast cereal, 200 respondents were asked to indicate whether they would use the cereal regularly after trying it, and 46 said they would. The cereal's manufacturer thought that the new cereal would be worthwhile to launch only if the probability that someone would regularly use the cereal after trying it was more than 20%. Does the sample provide evidence that this is the case?

What should the null and alternative hypotheses be in this case? The cereal will be worthwhile only if $p > 0.20$. In other words, the company needs to find convincing evidence that the proportion of people who would regularly use the cereal after trying it is more than 20%. This is the alternative hypothesis:

$H_1: p > 0.20$

This leads directly to a null hypothesis of $p = 0.20$. We could also say that $p \leq 0.20$, and sometimes you will see a null hypothesis specified in this way. However, we have to pick a particular value for p in order to proceed with the hypothesis test, and the value chosen must match the alternative hypothesis, so we work with $p = 0.20$. So, at this point, the null and alternative hypotheses are as follows:

$H_0: p = 0.20$

$H_1: p > 0.20$

The next step is to set the significance level for the test. To do this, we must think about the possible errors. A Type I error occurs when we reject the null hypothesis and it is actually true. Here, this would correspond to deciding that more than 20% of people who tried the cereal would actually use it, when in fact they would not. The consequences of this error would be that the company would launch the new cereal, and it would not be as successful as required.

A Type II error occurs when we fail to reject the null hypothesis and it is in fact false. Here, this would correspond to deciding that not enough people who tried the cereal would actually use it, when in fact they would. The consequences of this error would be that the company would not launch the new cereal when it would have been successful.

Without more detail about the potential costs of the two kinds of errors, it is difficult to decide what the significance level of the test should be. However, it is likely that the launch of a new cereal is fairly costly, and so we would want to be fairly sure that people who tried the cereal would actually use it. In this case, we will set $\alpha = 0.01$.

The survey of 200 people found 46 who said they would use the cereal regularly after trying it. This gives us $\hat{p} = \frac{46}{200} = 0.23$, which looks promising, as $\hat{p} > 0.20$.

The next step is to calculate the appropriate p-value. This means that we must check conditions and set up the appropriate sampling distribution, as was done in Chapter 6. Since we already did this in Example 6.3C, we will not repeat the details here. We concluded that although sampling was done without replacement, the sample size was probably not more than 5% of the population, so the binomial distribution was the appropriate underlying model. We calculated:

$$np = 200(0.20) = 40$$

$$nq = 200(0.80) = 160$$

Since both np and nq are ≥ 10, the sampling distribution of $\hat{p}$ will be approximately normal. Recall that the alternative hypothesis is $p > 0.20$. The p-value calculation is therefore:

$$P(\hat{p} \geq 0.23) = P\left(z \geq \frac{0.23 - 0.20}{\sqrt{\frac{0.20(0.80)}{200}}} \right) = P(z \geq 1.06) = 1 - 0.8554 = 0.1446$$

The p-value is more than 14%. It would not be that unusual to get $\hat{p} = 23\%$, even if only 20% of customers would actually use the cereal after trying it. The p-value, at more than 14%, is quite a lot higher than the significance level of 1%. Therefore, we fail to reject H_0, as we do not have enough evidence from the sample to conclude that more than 20% of people would use the cereal regularly after trying it. This means that on the basis of this criterion alone, it would not be worthwhile to launch this breakfast cereal.

The launch of a new breakfast cereal is a big undertaking, and it is unlikely that the decision would be made on the basis of this analysis alone. However, you should notice something important about this example. Before you learned about hypothesis testing, what would you have concluded about the proportion of people who would use the cereal after trying it? Since $\hat{p} = 0.23$ in this sample, you probably would have concluded that p was greater than 20%, but this conclusion is not supported by the data. It would be useful to get a more comprehensive estimate of the true value of p based on sample data, and this will be discussed in Chapter 8.

Particularly when samples are large, the data may be collected with the help of computers. Codes are often used to collect qualitative data, for example, 1 = excellent service, 2 = good service, etc. Such data have to be organized before any hypothesis test can be done. Fortunately, we have already encountered such data sets. In Chapter 2, we learned how to use Excel's **Histogram** tool to organize this kind of qualitative data. The next example illustrates what to do in a case such as this, and also introduces an Excel template to help with the analysis.

EXAMPLE 7.2B

Hypothesis test about a population proportion with coded data

During the fall of 2008, newspapers were filled with gloomy headlines about the global financial crisis. A poll of Canadians was taken in December of 2008, asking them if they expected Canada's employment conditions to improve, not change, or worsen over the next year (respondents were also given the option of saying they didn't know). The data are available in MyStatLab, with the following codes:

 EXA07-2b

1: **Employment conditions will improve over the next year.**
2: **Employment conditions will not change over the next year.**
3: **Employment conditions will worsen over the next year.**
4: **Don't know.**

At a 5% level of significance, is there enough evidence to suggest that fewer than 20% of Canadians expected employment conditions to improve in 2009?

It is always a good idea to think about the problem before you look at the sample data. First, set up the null and alternative hypotheses, and set the significance level.

$$H_0: p = 0.20$$
$$H_1: p < 0.20$$
$$\alpha = 0.05$$

The next step is to organize the coded data so we know the sample size, and what proportion of respondents expected employment conditions to improve. Using bin numbers 1 to 4 and Excel's **Histogram** tool, we find the results shown in Exhibit 7.2.

EXHIBIT 7.2

Excel Histogram Output for Employment Conditions Survey

Bin	Frequency
1	30
2	26
3	130
4	14
More	0

We can use Excel formulas to calculate the sum of the frequencies, and then calculate the proportion of responses for each code. The results of these calculations are shown on the next page in Exhibit 7.3. The "Bin" heading has been altered and the bin numbers have been replaced with appropriate labels to make the spreadsheet more readable (something you should always do).

EXHIBIT 7.3

Excel Calculations for Employment Conditions Survey

Opinion About Canada's Employment Conditions Over the Next Year	Frequency	Proportion
Improve	30	0.15
Not Change	26	0.13
Worsen	130	0.65
Don't Know	14	0.07
Total	200	

From the Excel calculations we can see that the proportion of those surveyed who thought that employment conditions were going to improve over the next year was 0.15. So, for this problem, $\hat{p} = 0.15$. We can also see that $n = 200$. We know that there are millions of Canadians, so we can be sure that the sample is $\leq 5\%$ of the population of those who might have been surveyed about this issue. This allows us to use the binomial distribution, despite sampling without replacement.

We must also check to see that the sampling distribution of $\hat{p}$ will be approximately normal.

$$np = 200(0.20) = 40 \geq 10$$
$$nq = 200(1 - 0.20) = 160 \geq 10$$

Because the necessary conditions are met, we can use the sampling distribution of $\hat{p}$ to calculate the p-value.

$$P(\hat{p} \leq \text{observed sample statistic})$$
$$= P(\hat{p} \leq 0.15)$$
$$= P\left(z \leq \frac{0.15 - 0.20}{\sqrt{\frac{0.20(0.80)}{200}}} \right)$$
$$= P(z \leq -1.77)$$
$$= 0.0384$$

The sample result is fairly unlikely. There is less than a 4% chance of getting a sample proportion as low as 15%, if in fact 20% of Canadians expect employment conditions to improve. Since we got this fairly unlikely sample result, we have enough evidence to reject H_0 and suggest that fewer than 20% of Canadians expected employment conditions to improve in 2009.

Using the Excel Template for Making Decisions About a Population Proportion with a Single Sample   In the example above, we used Excel to organize the sample data, and we finished the calculations manually. However, it makes more sense to get Excel to do the p-value calculations.

A worksheet template is available to help you with these calculations. Several templates are available, in the workbook called "Templates." The worksheet used here is labelled "z-Test of Proportion" (check the labels at the bottom of the Excel screen).

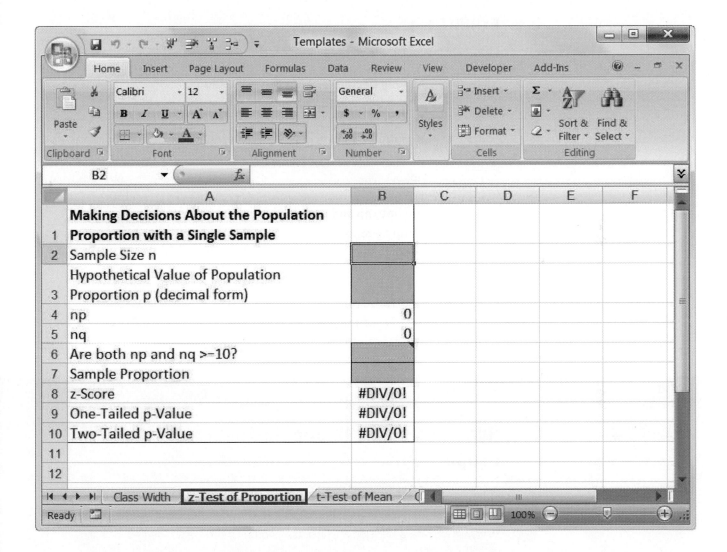

The template automates the calculations you would do by hand for a hypothesis test about a population proportion. You have to input values into the blue-shaded cells. When you do this, the built-in formulas will fill in the other required values. This template has a built-in formula for checking for normality (calculating np and nq), for calculating the z-score, and for both the one-tailed and two-tailed p-values of the hypothesis test (you will have to decide which you need, depending on H_1). You can copy and paste this template onto the worksheet containing your data and initial analysis. Then you can simply link most of the values you need for the blue-shaded cells to calculated values on your spreadsheet.

The completed template for Example 7.2B is shown in Exhibit 7.4 below.

Since the hypothesis test in Example 7.2B was one-tailed, the appropriate p-value from the template is 0.03855. Remember that we previously calculated a p-value of 0.0384. The Excel template gives a slightly more accurate answer (when we use the normal table, we round the z-score to only two decimal places).

EXHIBIT 7.4

Completed Excel Template for Example 7.2B

Making Decisions About the Population Proportion with a Single Sample	
Sample Size n	200
Hypothetical Value of Population Proportion p (decimal form)	0.2
np	40
nq	160
Are both np and nq >=10?	yes
Sample Proportion	0.15
z-Score	-1.7678
One-Tailed p-Value	0.03855
Two-Tailed p-Value	0.0771

GUIDE TO DECISION MAKING

Hypothesis Test to Decide About a Population Proportion

When:

- qualitative data, one sample, one population
- trying to make a decision about p, the population proportion, on the basis of $\hat{p}$, the sample proportion
- sample size (n) large

Steps:

1. Specify H_0, the null hypothesis.
2. Specify H_1, the alternative hypothesis.
3. Determine or identify α, the significance level.
4. Collect or identify the sample data. Identify or calculate:
   - $\hat{p}$, the sample proportion
   - n, the sample size
5. If sampling is done without replacement, make sure that the sample size is not more than 5% of the population, so that the binomial distribution is the appropriate underlying model.

6. Check for (approximate) normality of the sampling distribution, which requires BOTH:
   - $np \geq 10$ and
   - $nq \geq 10$

7. *If* the sampling distribution is approximately normal, proceed by identifying or calculating the mean and standard deviation of the sampling distribution, with:

   - $\mu_{\hat{p}} = p$

   - $\sigma_{\hat{p}} = \sqrt{\dfrac{pq}{n}}$

8. Use the approximately normal sampling distribution of $\hat{p}$ to calculate the appropriate *p*-value for the hypothesis test. When done by hand, the calculation will involve the *z*-score:

$$z = \frac{\hat{p} - \mu_{\hat{p}}}{\sigma_{\hat{p}}} = \frac{\hat{p} - p}{\sqrt{\dfrac{pq}{n}}}$$

9. If *p*-value $\leq \alpha$, reject H_0 and conclude that there is sufficient evidence to decide in favour of H_1. If *p*-value $> \alpha$, fail to reject H_0 and conclude that there is insufficient evidence to decide in favour of H_1. State your conclusions in language appropriate to the problem.

See Example 7.2B on page 271.

DEVELOP YOUR SKILLS 7.2

6. A poll conducted by Decima Research in September 2005 said that 27% of Canadian homeowners spent more than they planned on home renovation projects. The results were based on a random sample of 1,006 homeowners.[2] At the 5% significance level, does the survey support the notion that more than a quarter of homeowners spent more than they planned on home renovation projects?

7. The same poll referred to above said that 34% of homeowners are borrowing to renovate. At the 2% significance level, does the survey support the claim that more than a third of homeowners borrow to renovate?

8. An online poll conducted by Ipsos Reid on behalf of Rogers Wireless in May 2009 concluded that "two in ten (17%) of cellphone and smartphone users typically access the Internet on a daily basis from their phone."[3] Although this online poll was not a probability sample, assume that it was. 1,403 Canadians were surveyed. Is there enough evidence, at the 4% level of significance, to conclude that more than 15% of all Canadian cellphone and smartphone users typically access the internet on a daily basis from their phone?

9. A retail electronics shop is thinking of mounting a sales push to get customers to buy the extended warranty available for their purchases. The sales manager believes that fewer than 10% of customers currently opt for the extra coverage. A random sample of 200 customers revealed that 18 opted for the extended warranty. Do the sample results confirm the sales manager's belief? Use $\alpha = 0.05$.

10. The owner of a diner wants to know if more than 25% of customers choose salad instead of fries with their main course. A random sample of 50 customers reveals that 14 chose salad instead of fries. What can you tell the diner's owner, on the basis of this sample? Use $\alpha = 4\%$.

[2] *Source:* "Design Shows Blamed for High Reno Spending," *The Globe and Mail,* October 21, 2005, Section G.

[3] *Source:* Ipsos North America, "Two in Ten (17%) Cellphone and Smartphone Users Typically Access The Internet on a Daily Basis From Their Phone," May 20, 2009, **www.ipsos-na.com/news/pressrelease.cfm?id=4398#**, accessed May 29, 2009.

<table>
<tr><td>**7.3**</td><td></td></tr>
</table>

7.3 DECIDING ABOUT THE POPULATION MEAN—THE *t*-TEST OF μ

In Chapter 6, we made some conclusions about population means on the basis of sample means, using the sampling distribution of $\bar{x}$. This was a useful introduction, but in Chapter 6, we assumed that we knew σ, the population standard deviation. Of course, if we do not even know μ, it is highly unlikely that we will know σ! In this section, we will learn how to deal with the more realistic case where we do not know σ.

Remember that the sampling distribution of $\bar{x}$ will be normal if the population is normal, something that you can check by examining a histogram of the sample data. The mean and standard deviation of the $\bar{x}$-values will be:

- $\mu_{\bar{x}} = \mu$
- $\sigma_x = \dfrac{\sigma}{\sqrt{n}}$

The difficulty is that we do not know σ, so we cannot calculate $\sigma_{\bar{x}}$.

Although we do not know σ, we can use s, the sample standard deviation, as an estimate. The bigger the sample size, the better s will be as an estimate of σ. However, s is not σ (although it may be close) and we have to take this into consideration.

The sampling distribution of $\bar{x}$ has a mean of μ, and a standard error of $\sigma_{\bar{x}} = \dfrac{\sigma}{\sqrt{n}}$.

The closest we can come to this is an approximation of the sampling distribution, with a mean of μ and an approximate standard error of $s_{\bar{x}} = \dfrac{s}{\sqrt{n}}$. While there is only one true sampling distribution, there will be a number of these approximate sampling distributions, because each one depends on the value of s taken from a particular sample. This adds some extra uncertainty into our calculations.

The *t*-Distribution

Fortunately, in 1908, a man named William S. Gosset, who worked for the Guinness brewing company in Dublin, Ireland, discovered how to handle this extra uncertainty. He developed something that is now called the *t*-distribution, which allows us to conduct reliable hypothesis tests about μ when σ is unknown.

The *t*-distributions are symmetric probability distributions, which look similar to the normal distribution, but with more area under the tails. There is a different *t*-distribution for each sample size, and each *t*-distribution is distinguished by its degrees of freedom. For single sample tests about μ, the degrees of freedom are calculated as $n - 1$.

Probability calculations for the *t*-distribution are based on the standardized *t*-score (even those in Excel), which is calculated for tests about μ as follows:

$$t = \frac{\bar{x} - \mu}{s \big/ \sqrt{n}}$$

The *t*-score calculation is parallel to the calculation of the *z*-score in the probability calculations in Section 6.2, with *s* replacing the unknown *σ*.

Exhibit 7.5 shows a *t*-distribution with three degrees of freedom (the red curve on the graph), one with six degrees of freedom (the blue curve on the graph), and a normal distribution (the green curve on the graph).

EXHIBIT 7.5

Two *t*-Distribution Curves and a Normal Curve

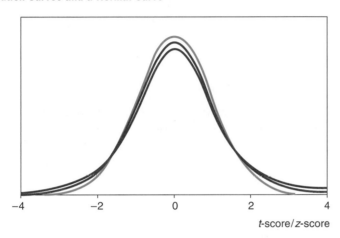

t-score/*z*-score

You can see that as the degrees of freedom (and sample size) increase, the *t*-distribution has less area under the tails. This is reasonable. As the sample size increases, *s* will be a better estimate of *σ*, and so there will be less variability in the *t*-score. In fact, when the degrees of freedom reach 30 or so, the *t*-distribution is very close to the normal distribution.

The *t*-distribution can be used for inferences about *μ* if it appears that the population data are normally distributed. We checked for normality of the population data in Chapter 6 by examining histograms of the sample data, and we must continue to do so here.

We can use Excel or *t*-tables for the probability calculations we need in order to do hypothesis tests about *μ*, *σ* unknown. Examples 7.3A, 7.3B, and 7.3C illustrate the use of Excel. Examples 7.3D and 7.3E illustrate the use of the *t*-tables.

EXAMPLE 7.3A

Right-tailed hypothesis test about a population mean

Suppose a company is trying a new marketing approach in a random sample of its stores. The average of sales at all stores was $5,000 a week before the new marketing plan was introduced. Weekly sales at the stores trying out the new marketing approach are shown in Exhibit 7.6 on the next page. Do the sample data indicate that the new marketing approach has increased weekly sales? Use a 5% significance level.

EXHIBIT 7.6

Weekly Sales at a Random Sample of Stores Trying Out a New Marketing Approach

Weekly Sales ($)				
5,117	5,167	5,267	5,451	5,430
5,577	4,900	5,036	5,601	4,801
5,224	4,635	4,592	4,831	4,887

In this case, we are looking for evidence that μ has increased. The null and alternative hypotheses will be as follows:

H_0: μ = $5,000 in sales per week

H_1: μ > $5,000 in sales per week

The significance level was given as 5%. Now we must determine what the sampling distribution of the $\bar{x}$-values will look like, and use it (if appropriate) to determine the p-value.

The first step is to try to assess whether weekly sales at all the locations are normally distributed. To do this, we will create a histogram of the sample data. One possible histogram is shown below in Exhibit 7.7.

EXHIBIT 7.7

Histogram of the Sample Data

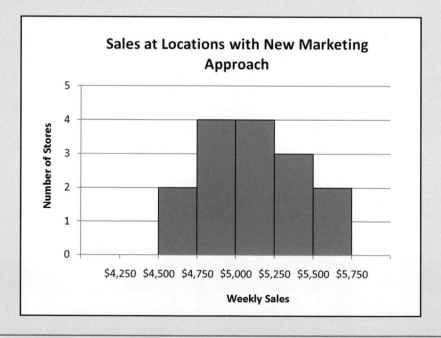

This data set looks approximately normal, so we can proceed. The next step is to calculate the appropriate t-score, so that we can assess the p-value associated with the observed sample mean.

$$t = \frac{\bar{x} - \mu}{s / \sqrt{n}}$$

Before we can calculate the t-score, we must first calculate its components. We can do this most easily with Excel, but we can also calculate the components by hand. The manual calculations are shown below. You should refer to Chapter 3 for a reminder about the use of Excel functions such as **AVERAGE** and **STDEV**.

$$\bar{x} = \frac{\Sigma x}{n} = \frac{\$76,516}{15} = \$5,101.06667$$

$$s = \sqrt{\frac{\Sigma x^2 - \frac{(\Sigma x)^2}{n}}{n - 1}} = \sqrt{\frac{391,797,390.00 - \frac{(76,516)^2}{15}}{14}} = \$325.59538$$

The t-score can be calculated as follows.

$$t = \frac{\bar{x} - \mu}{s / \sqrt{n}} = \frac{\$5,101.06667 - \$5,000}{\$325.59538 / \sqrt{15}} = 1.20220$$

Since this is a right-tailed hypothesis test, we calculate the p-value as $P(t \geq 1.20220)$, for a t-distribution with 14 degrees of freedom (remember, degrees of freedom = $n - 1$). We can use the **TDIST** function in Excel to calculate this probability. The dialogue box is shown below, in Exhibit 7.8

EXHIBIT 7.8

Dialogue Box for TDIST Function in Excel

Function Arguments		?	X
TDIST			
X		= number	
Deg_freedom		= number	
Tails		= number	
		=	
Returns the Student's t-distribution.			
	X is the numeric value at which to evaluate the distribution.		
Formula result =			
Help on this function		OK	Cancel

The function arguments in Excel are as follows.

- **x** is the t-score you calculated. Note that **TDIST** works only with positive numbers.
- **Deg_freedom** is the degrees of freedom for the t-distribution you are working with. It is equal to $n - 1$ for single-sample tests about μ.

- **Tails** requires you to specify 1 or 2, depending on whether you want the probability in one or both tails of the distribution.

The completed dialogue box, with the result, is shown in Exhibit 7.9.

EXHIBIT 7.9

Completed Dialogue Box for TDIST Function in Excel

Function Arguments			
TDIST			
X	1.20220		= 1.2022
Deg_freedom	14		= 14
Tails	1		= 1
			= 0.124613207

Returns the Student's t-distribution.

Tails specifies the number of distribution tails to return: one-tailed distribution = 1; two-tailed distribution = 2.

Formula result = 0.124613207

Help on this function   [OK]   [Cancel]

TDIST tells us that $P(t \geq 1.2022) = 0.124613$. Since this is a fairly high probability, the observed sample result would not be unusual, if the average weekly sales were $5,000. We do not have convincing evidence that average weekly sales have increased. The p-value of $0.124613 > 0.05$, the significance level of this test.

We fail to reject H_0, and can also say that there is insufficient evidence to conclude that average weekly sales have increased for the stores using the new marketing approach.

Note that if you are using **TDIST** in Excel, you cannot enter a negative t-score (Excel will produce an error if you do). The **TDIST** function does not work with negative numbers, but this does not pose a problem for left-tailed tests, because the t-distribution is symmetric. Simply enter the absolute value of any t-score into the **TDIST** function, and it will calculate the tail area beyond that t-score. If you use the template described below, you will not have to worry about this technical detail.

Using the Excel Template for Making Decisions About the Population Mean with a Single Sample   An Excel template is available in the workbook called "Templates," in a worksheet called "t-Test of Mean." The template is shown in Exhibit 7.10 opposite.

The template has a built-in formula for the t-score, and for both the one-tailed and two-tailed p-values of the hypothesis test (you have to decide which you need, depending on H_1). As usual, you will have to input values into the blue-shaded cells in the template. This template will handle negative t-scores.

EXHIBIT **7.10**

Excel Template for t-Test of Mean

Making Decisions About the Population Mean with a Single Sample	
Do the sample data appear to be normally distributed?	
Sample Standard Deviation s	
Sample Mean	
Sample Size n	
Hypothetical Value of Population Mean	
t-Score	#DIV/0!
One-Tailed p-Value	#DIV/0!
Two-Tailed p-Value	#DIV/0!

The template explicitly reminds you that the data must be normal for this test to be used. You will usually have to create a histogram for the sample data to decide this. You can use the Excel functions **AVERAGE** and **STDEV** to calculate the sample mean and sample standard deviation. An Excel function called **COUNT** will count the number of values in the data set to get *n*, the sample size.

EXAMPLE **7.3B**

Right-tailed hypothesis test about a population mean

A human resources consulting firm has been hired to do some salary research. The company is trying to find out if its junior managers' salaries are competitive, and in particular, if the average salary of such managers in the region is more than $40,000.

The results collected from a random sample are available in MyStatLab. Is there evidence that the average salary of junior managers is more than $40,000? Use an $\alpha = 5\%$.

EXA07-3b

The first step is to specify the null and alternative hypotheses. The company wants to know if the average salary of junior managers is more than $40,000.

$H_0: \mu = \$40,000$

$H_1: \mu > \$40,000$

The level of significance is 5%. The sample mean, standard deviation, and sample size can be computed with Excel.

$\bar{x} = \$40,648$

$s = \$3,782.84$

$n = 50$

The next step is to check for normality of the sample data. One possible histogram for the data set is shown on the next page in Exhibit 7.11.

EXHIBIT 7.11

Histogram for Junior Managers' Salary Data

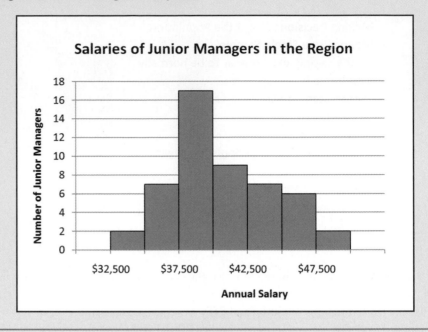

The histogram is somewhat skewed to the right, but it is unimodal and the sample size is fairly large (at 50), so using the *t*-distribution is acceptable.

An analyst at the consulting firm uses the Excel template for this problem. The result is shown below in Exhibit 7.12.

EXHIBIT 7.12

Excel Template for Junior Managers' Salary Data

Making Decisions About the Population Mean with a Single Sample	
Do the sample data appear to be normally distributed?	yes
Sample Standard Deviation s	3782.84
Sample Mean	40648
Sample Size n	50
Hypothetical Value of Population Mean	40000
t-Score	1.21127
One-Tailed p-Value	0.1158
Two-Tailed p-Value	0.2316

This is a one-tailed test, so the relevant *p*-value is 0.1158. Since this is > 0.05, we fail to reject the null hypothesis. The sample evidence is insufficient for us to infer that the average salary of junior managers in the region is more than $40,000.

Using the Table of Critical Values for the *t*-Distribution   It is also possible to estimate *p*-values with the help of the table of critical values for the *t*-distribution, at the back of this textbook in Appendix 3 (page 580). This table presents some limited information for a series of *t*-distributions (there are, of course, many of these), organized by degrees of freedom. In the current example, the sample size is $n = 50$, so the degrees of freedom value is 49. The first thing you will notice is that there is no entry in the table for 49 degrees of freedom. The closest you can come is 50, so that is the row we will use (tables often require this kind of approximation, which is why it is always preferable to use a computer). There are five entries in the table for 50 degrees of freedom, and they are shown in Exhibit 7.13.

EXHIBIT 7.13

Excerpt from Table of Critical Values for *t*-Distribution

Degrees of Freedom	$t_{.100}$	$t_{.050}$	$t_{.025}$	$t_{.010}$	$t_{.005}$
50	1.299	1.676	2.009	2.403	2.678
60	1.296	1.671	2.000	2.390	2.660
70	1.294	1.667	1.994	2.381	2.648
80	1.292	1.664	1.990	2.374	2.639
90	1.291	1.662	1.987	2.368	2.632
100	1.290	1.660	1.984	2.364	2.626

The notation t_x indicates that beyond this particular *t*-score, in the tail of the distribution, lies an area equal to *x*. So, for example, $P(t \geq t_{.100}) = 0.100$, and $P(t \geq t_{.005}) = 0.005$, and so on.

Exhibit 7.14 below illustrates $t_{.025}$.

EXHIBIT 7.14

Illustration of $t_{.025}$

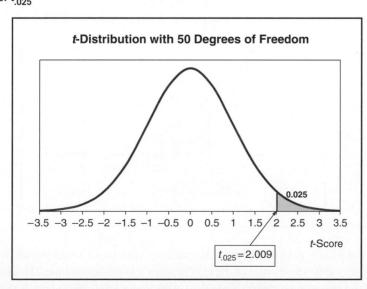

t-Distribution with 50 Degrees of Freedom

0.025

$t_{.025} = 2.009$

t-Score

To put this more mathematically, for a t-distribution with 50 degrees of freedom, $t_{.025} = 2.009$, so $P(t \geq 2.009) = 0.025$. In general:

$$P(t \geq t_x) = x$$

If we wanted to use the t-table to make the decision for Example 7.3B, how would we do this? The calculated t-score is equal to 1.21127 (see Exhibit 7.12 on page 282, and of course, we could have calculated this by hand). The p-value $= P(t \geq 1.21127)$. There is no t-score of 1.21127 for 50 degrees of freedom in the table, so we will not be able to get the p-value directly. However, if we were going to place the t-score of 1.21127 in the row for 50 degrees of freedom, it would be located to the left of 1.299, as shown in Exhibit 7.15 below.

EXHIBIT **7.15**

Excerpt from Table of Critical Values for t-Distribution

Degrees of Freedom	$t_{.100}$	$t_{.050}$	$t_{.025}$	$t_{.010}$	$t_{.005}$
50	1.299	1.676	2.009	2.403	2.678

$t = 1.21127$

From the table, we see that $P(t \geq 1.299) = 0.100$. Since the t-score of 1.21127 is less than 1.299, we know that $P(t \geq 1.21127)$ must be greater than 10%. Exhibit 7.16 below illustrates this.

EXHIBIT **7.16**

t-Distribution with 50 Degrees of Freedom

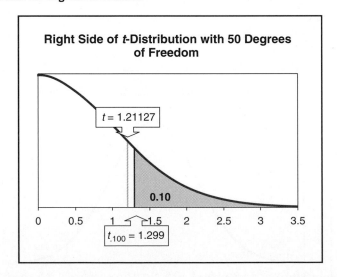

The shaded area in the right tail has an area equal to 0.10, and the left-hand edge of this area is 1.299. The t-score of 1.21127 is shown at the green line. The area in the tail beyond the green line is clearly more than 10%. So we know that $P(t \geq 1.21127) > 0.10$.

While we cannot be precise about the *p*-value when we are using the *t*-tables, we can still make a decision. Since the *p*-value is more than 10%, we fail to reject the null hypothesis. The sample evidence is insufficient for us to infer that the average salary of junior managers in the region is more than $40,000.

EXAMPLE 7.3C

Estimating p-values from the table of critical values for the t-distribution

For the following hypothesis tests and *t*-scores, estimate the *p*-value of the sample result.

a. $H_0: \mu = 56$

$H_1: \mu > 56$

The sample size is 30, and the calculated *t*-score is 1.74.

b. $H_0: \mu = 100$

$H_1: \mu < 100$

The sample size is 20, and the calculated *t*-score is −2.96.

c. $H_0: \mu = 300$

$H_1: \mu \neq 300$

The sample size is 25, and the calculated *t*-score is −2.36.

Solutions:

a. $H_0: \mu = 56$

$H_1: \mu > 56$

The sample size is 30, so degrees of freedom = 30 − 1 = 29. The appropriate row from the *t*-table is shown in Exhibit 7.17. The calculated *t*-score is 1.74, which is in between $t_{.050}$ and $t_{.025}$.

EXHIBIT 7.17

Excerpt from Table of Critical Values for *t*-Distribution

Degrees of Freedom	$t_{.100}$	$t_{.050}$	$t_{.025}$	$t_{.010}$	$t_{.005}$
29	1.311	1.699	2.045	2.462	2.756

$t = 1.74$

We see that $0.025 < P(t > 1.74) < 0.050$. This is a one-tailed test. We conclude that $0.025 < p\text{-value} < 0.050$.

b. $H_0: \mu = 100$

$H_1: \mu < 100$

The sample size is 20, so degrees of freedom = 20 − 1 = 19. The appropriate row from the *t*-table is shown on the next page in Exhibit 7.18. The calculated

EXHIBIT 7.18

Excerpt from Table of Critical Values for *t*-Distribution

Degrees of Freedom	$t_{.100}$	$t_{.050}$	$t_{.025}$	$t_{.010}$	$t_{.005}$
19	1.328	1.729	2.093	2.539	2.861

$t = 2.96$

t-score is -2.96. We know that $P(t < -2.96) = P(t > +2.96)$, so we locate 2.96 on the table, to the right of $t_{.005}$.

We see that $P(t > 2.96) < 0.005$. This is a one-tailed test. We conclude that *p*-value < 0.005.

c. $H_0: \mu = 300$

$H_1: \mu \neq 300$

The sample size is 25, so degrees of freedom $= 25 - 1 = 24$. The appropriate row from the *t*-table is shown below in Exhibit 7.19. The calculated *t*-score is -2.36. We know that $P(t < -2.36) = P(t > +2.36)$, so we locate 2.36 on the table between $t_{.025}$ and $t_{.010}$.

EXHIBIT 7.19

Excerpt from Table of Critical Values for *t*-Distribution

Degrees of Freedom	$t_{.100}$	$t_{.050}$	$t_{.025}$	$t_{.010}$	$t_{.005}$
24	1.318	1.711	2.064	2.492	2.797

$t = 2.36$

We see that $0.010 < P(t > 2.36) < 0.025$. This is a two-tailed test, so we have to double these probabilities to estimate the *p*-value.

$0.010 \cdot 2 < p\text{-value} < 0.025 \cdot 2$

$0.020 < p\text{-value} < 0.050$

The Decision Rule Approach   There is another way to make the decision for this hypothesis test. In Example 7.3B, the level of significance was 5%. From the table, we see that $t_{.050}$ for 50 degrees of freedom is 1.676. Therefore, we know that if the *t*-value we calculate for the sample result is ≥ 1.676, we should reject the null hypothesis. The area where $t \geq 1.676$ is called the rejection region for this test, and the *t*-score is called a critical value.

To recap, we could have conducted the hypothesis test for Example 7.3C as follows:

$H_0: \mu = \$40,000$

$H_1: \mu > \$40,000$

The level of significance is 5%.
Decision rule: Reject H_0 if $t \geq 1.676$.

$$t = \frac{\bar{x} - \mu}{s / \sqrt{n}} = \frac{\$40,648 - \$40,000}{\$3,782.84 / \sqrt{50}} = 1.21127\$$$

Since $t < 1.676$, we fail to reject H_0. There is insufficient evidence to conclude that the average salary of junior managers is more than \$40,000.

The decision rule approach does not require us to estimate the p-value, but of course, it provides us with less information. This approach is a holdover from the days before personal computers—the p-value approach is now the accepted method.

EXAMPLE 7.3D

Two-tailed hypothesis test about a population mean

For this example, we will revisit Chapter Review Exercise 8 in Chapter 6, about automated teller machines (ATMs), in a more realistic context. At one particular branch, a random sample of the total withdrawals on 36 weekends showed a sample mean of \$8,400, and a sample standard deviation of \$3,700. Suppose the branch manager has always claimed that the average total withdrawal over the weekend is \$7,500. On the basis of the sample, is there evidence to suggest that the true average total withdrawal per weekend is different from \$7,500? You may assume that the population data are normally distributed. Use a 5% significance level.

In this case, we should conduct a two-tailed hypothesis test, because we have been asked if there is evidence to suggest that the average total withdrawal per weekend is *different from* \$7,500. The question was phrased this way because either too little or too much cash in the ATM will cause problems.

H_0: $\mu = \$7,500$

H_1: $\mu \neq \$7,500$

$\alpha = 0.05$

We know from the problem description that:

$\bar{x} = \$8,400$

$s = \$3,700$

$n = 36$

We are told to assume that the data are normally distributed. We now go on to calculate the standardized t-score.

$$t = \frac{\bar{x} - \mu}{s / \sqrt{n}} = \frac{\$8,400 - \$7,500}{\$3,700 / \sqrt{36}} = 1.459$$

With 36 observations in the sample, the appropriate t-distribution will have 35 degrees of freedom. The appropriate row from the t-table is reproduced on the next page in Exhibit 7.20.

Our calculated t-score of 1.459 is between $t_{.100}$ and $t_{.050}$, so we know:

$0.050 < P(t \geq 1.459) < 0.100$

EXHIBIT 7.20

Excerpt from Table of Critical Values for *t*-Distribution

Degrees of Freedom	$t_{.100}$	$t_{.050}$	$t_{.025}$	$t_{.010}$	$t_{.005}$
35	1.306	1.690	2.030	2.438	2.724

$t = 1.459$

This is a two-tailed test, so we have to double these probabilities to estimate the *p*-value.

$$0.050 \cdot 2 < p\text{-value} < 0.100 \cdot 2$$

$$0.100 < p\text{-value} < 0.200$$

We fail to reject the null hypothesis, as the *p*-value is more than the significance level of 5%. There is insufficient evidence in the sample to infer that the average cash withdrawal from the ATM over the weekend is different from $7,500.

GUIDE TO DECISION MAKING

Hypothesis Test to Decide About a Population Mean

When:

- quantitative data, one sample, one population
- trying to make a decision about μ, the population mean, on the basis of $\bar{x}$, the sample mean

Steps:

1. Specify H_0, the null hypothesis.
2. Specify H_1, the alternative hypothesis.
3. Determine or identify α, the significance level.
4. Collect or identify the sample data. Identify or calculate:

- $\bar{x}$, the sample mean
- s, the sample standard deviation
- n, the sample size

5. Check for normality of the population (usually with a histogram of the sample values).
6. *If* the sampling distribution is normal, proceed by calculating the appropriate *t*-score for the sample mean, using the following formula:

$$t = \frac{\bar{x} - \mu}{s / \sqrt{n}}$$

7. Use the appropriate *t*-distribution, with $n - 1$ degrees of freedom, to calculate (or approximate, if using tables) the appropriate *p*-value for the hypothesis test.

8. If *p*-value $\leq \alpha$, reject H_0 and conclude that there is sufficient evidence to decide in favour of H_1. If *p*-value $> \alpha$, fail to reject H_0 and conclude that there is insufficient evidence to decide in favour of H_1. State your conclusions in language appropriate to the problem.

See Example 7.3D on page 287 (using the table) and Example 7.3B on page 281 (using Excel).

How Normal Is Normal Enough?

Step 5 above requires you to check for normality of the population. We have done this quite informally, with an eyeball test: a histogram of the sample data is created, and if it looks normal, we proceed. This is an inexact approach, and certainly it is not always clear how normal the sample data are. We already discussed this problem in Chapter 6.

The larger the sample is, the more reliable the results of any hypothesis test about the population mean will be. There are two reasons that larger samples are better:

1. With larger sample sizes, the *s* calculated from the sample will be closer to the true value of σ, even if the population is not normal.
2. The sampling distribution of $\bar{x}$ becomes more normal as the sample size increases, no matter what the shape of the population distribution, because of the Central Limit Theorem.

The good news is that the *t*-distribution approach for deciding about μ is what statisticians call *robust*, that is, it is not strongly affected by non normality of the data. However, this *t*-distribution–based approach should not be relied on if there are outliers in the data, or strong skewness.

Here are some general rules to guide you, until you develop enough experience and judgment to decide for yourself. You should not make important decisions about means with a sample size of less than 15 or 20, unless you have very good reason to believe that the population is normally distributed. Once sample sizes become as large as 40 or more, reliable decisions can be made even if the data are somewhat skewed. But there is no magic about these numbers, and the general rule will always be that decisions will be more reliable with larger sample sizes.

DEVELOP YOUR SKILLS 7.3

11. A marketing research organization wanted to see if the average household incomes in a particular suburb of Halifax were more than $50,000 a year.

DYS07-11

A random sample of 40 households revealed the household income data available in a MyStatLab. At the 3% level of significance, what can you conclude, on the basis of the sample data?

12. The 2008 MasterIndex™ Report produced for MasterCard indicated that women spend an average of $34.21 on quick trips to the grocery store.[4] This estimate is based on a survey of 1,000 Canadians, and you may assume that half of them were women. Assume the standard deviation is $10 and the sample data are normally distributed. Is there evidence, at the 3% level of

[4] *Source:* MasterCard Canada, "2008 MasterIndex™ Report: Checking Out the Canadian Grocery Experience," May 2008, **www.mastercard.com/ca/wce/PDF/TRANSACTOR_REPORT_E.pdf**, accessed June 2, 2009.

significance, that all Canadian women spend more than $33, on average, when they make quick trips to the grocery store?

13. The human resources department wants to be sure that the average salary of entry-level clerks in the company (which is $37,876) is higher than the average in the surrounding area.

    DYS07-13   A random sample of salaries of clerks in the surrounding area reveals the data available in the file called DYS07-13. At the 2% significance level, can you conclude that these salaries are lower than $37,876, on average?

14. A company that produces stereo equipment for home listening is interested in the average age of the equipment in the homes of so-called baby boomers. A random sample of 60 baby boomer households was surveyed. The average age of their stereo equipment was 8.9 years, with a standard deviation of 5.5 years. The data appear to be normally distributed. Do the data contradict the company's idea that most baby boomer households have stereo equipment that is at least 10 years old? Use $\alpha = 4\%$.

15. A carpet cleaning company is doing some research to determine if its rates are lower than those of its competitors. A researcher posed as a householder to get prices for cleaning a bedroom carpet. The average of 15 such prices was $87.43, with a standard deviation of $16.23. Is this average significantly higher than the company's own price of $85 for such a job? You may assume that the population data are normally distributed. What should the company do? Use $\alpha = 0.05$.

Formal Hypothesis Testing

In a hypothesis test, we use sample data to decide between two conflicting ideas, expressed as H_0 and H_1. The null hypothesis (denoted H_0) is what you are going to believe about the population, unless the sample gives you strongly contradictory evidence. The alternative hypothesis (denoted H_1) is what you are going to believe about the population when there is strong evidence against the null hypothesis.

The null hypothesis is of the form: population parameter = some particular value.

In general, the alternative hypothesis can take one of three forms:

1. H_1: population parameter > some particular value
2. H_1: population parameter < some particular value
3. H_1: population parameter ≠ some particular value

The first two forms are referred to as one-tailed tests because sample results in only one tail of the sampling distribution provide evidence against the null hypothesis, in favour of the alternative hypothesis. The third form is a two-tailed test, because sample results in either tail of the sampling distribution provide evidence against the null hypothesis, in favour of the alternative hypothesis.

If there is convincing evidence against the null hypothesis, we say that we *rejected* the null hypothesis and there is sufficient evidence to support the alternative hypothesis. This is a fairly strong conclusion. If there is not convincing evidence against the null hypothesis, we say that we *failed to reject* the null hypothesis and there is insufficient evidence to support the alternative hypothesis. This is a weaker conclusion. Above all, it does *not* imply that the null hypothesis is true. If you fail to reject the null hypothesis, you should *not* say "the null hypothesis is true," or even that you "accept" the null hypothesis. All you can say is that you do not have strong evidence against it.

There are two types of possible error in a test of hypothesis, and we cannot completely eliminate them. A Type I error arises when we mistakenly reject the null hypothesis when it is in fact true. A Type II error arises when we mistakenly fail to reject the null hypothesis when it is in fact false. Both kinds of errors have costs and consequences. The significance level of a test of hypothesis is the maximum allowable probability of a Type I error. It is denoted α and is set by the researcher. The *p*-value is the probability of getting a sample result at least as extreme as the observed sample result. The probability is calculated from the appropriate sampling distribution, which is always based on the assumption that the null hypothesis is true.

The *p*-value probability calculation must match the alternative hypothesis used in the test. For tests of means and proportions, the *p*-value is calculated as follows:

- P(sample statistic ≥ observed sample result) when H_1 contains ">"
- P(sample statistic ≤ observed sample result) when H_1 contains "<"
- $2 \times$ P(tail area beyond the observed sample result) when H_1 contains "≠"

A low *p*-value means that the sample result would be highly unlikely (if the null hypothesis were true). This gives us strong evidence against the null hypothesis. If the *p*-value is high, then the sample result is not unusual, and we do not have enough evidence to reject the null hypothesis. We reject the null hypothesis whenever the *p*-value is less than or equal to α, the significance level of the test. The lower the *p*-value, the stronger is the evidence against H_0.

A Guide to Technique on page 268 outlines the general steps in a formal hypothesis test.

Deciding About a Population Proportion

Hypothesis tests about *p* are illustrated in Examples 7.2A and 7.2B. Example 7.2A applies the formal hypothesis testing format to a Chapter Review Exercise from Chapter 6. Example 7.2B illustrates how to handle coded data with Excel, and illustrates the use of an Excel template for making decisions about the population proportion with a single sample (see page 271).

A Guide to Decision Making for hypothesis tests about a population proportion is on page 274.

Deciding About the Population Mean

We generally do not know σ, the population standard deviation, and have to estimate it with s, the sample standard deviation. To take care of the resulting extra variability in the sampling distribution, we must use the t-distribution for hypothesis tests about the population mean. The t-distribution is actually a family of distributions, distinguished by their degrees of freedom, which are equal to $n - 1$ for tests about the mean.

Examples 7.3A (page 277) and 7.3B (page 281) illustrate the use of Excel to conduct hypothesis tests about μ. Example 7.3B also illustrates the use of an Excel template for making decisions about the population mean with a single sample.

It is also possible to estimate p-values from a t-table of critical values. Example 7.3D (page 287) illustrates.

A Guide to Decision Making for hypothesis tests about a population mean is on page 288.

Use of the t-distribution is dependent on the population being normal. We check this by creating a histogram of the sample data, and assessing whether it appears normally distributed. The t-distribution is robust, that is, it is not strongly affected by non-normality of the data. However, the t-distribution should not be relied on if there are outliers in the data, or strong skewness.

You should not make important decisions about means with sample sizes of less than 15 or 20, unless you have very good reason to believe that the population is normally distributed. Once sample sizes become as large as 40 or more, reliable decisions can be made even if the data are somewhat skewed. But there is no magic about these numbers, and the general rule will always be that decisions will be more reliable with larger sample sizes.

Go to MyStatLab at www.mathxl.com. You can practise the exercises indicated with red in the Develop Your Skills and Chapter Review Exercises as often as you want, and guided solutions will help you find answers step by step. You'll find a personalized study plan available to you too!

CHAPTER REVIEW EXERCISES

WARM-UP EXERCISES

1. A toy manufacturer receives large shipments of electronic components that will be used in the dolls that it makes. It is too expensive to test every component to see whether it functions properly, so the manufacturer inspects a random sample of components from every shipment. The toy manufacturer does not accept any shipments unless there is evidence that fewer than 3% of the components are defective.
   a. What are the null and alternative hypotheses for this situation?
   b. Explain the Type I and Type II errors in the context of the component shipments.
   c. From the toy manufacturer's point of view, which type of error would be the most important? Why?

2. A gasoline refinery has developed a new gasoline that theoretically reduces gas consumption per 100 kilometres driven (or, to use a non-metric phrase, provides improved gas mileage). The company wants to gather evidence to see whether the new gasoline actually does provide better gas mileage. Suppose the refinery knows that for a wide range of four-passenger compact cars, the average gas consumption per 100 kilometres was 10.6 litres for the old gasoline formulation.
   a. What are the null and alternative hypotheses for this situation?
   b. Explain the Type I and Type II errors in the context of testing the new gasoline.

3. The quality control manager at a plant that produces bottled water is setting up a hypothesis test for the amount of water in the bottle, which is supposed to be 750 millilitres.
   a. What should the null and alternative hypotheses be for this situation?
   b. Explain the Type I and Type II errors in the context of the bottled water.
   c. If you were a consumer buying the bottled water, which type of error would be most important to you? Why?

4. Suppose you have null and alternative hypotheses as follows:

   H_0: $\mu = 300$

   H_1: $\mu < 300$

   A histogram of the sample data appears normal. The sample mean is 296.5 and the sample size is 40. The sample standard deviation is 35.6. Estimate the p-value for this test.

5. Suppose you have null and alternative hypotheses as follows:

   H_0: $p = 0.26$

   H_1: $p \neq 0.26$

   Assume that the sample size, at 200, is less than 5% of the population. The sample proportion is 0.30. Estimate the p-value for this test.

THINK AND DECIDE

6. Your radio station, which has generally targeted the so-called baby-boomers, is starting to reorient its programming to a younger audience. Formats have been changed, some new on-air personalities have been hired, and generally efforts have been made to come up with a fresh approach. Now the radio station wants to see whether these efforts have been successful in reaching a younger audience. In the past, the average listener age was 48.2.
   a. What null and alternative hypotheses would be appropriate here?
   b. Explain the Type I and Type II errors in the context of the radio audience.
   c. Suppose you rejected the null hypothesis with a p-value of 1%. What does this tell you? Does it mean the radio station has accomplished its goal?
   d. Suppose the situation described in part c occurs, and the sample mean is 46. Does this mean the radio station has accomplished its goal?

7. An online retailer believes that Canadian Internet users spent an average of $725 shopping online annually. A survey of 2,711 Canadian Internet users reports average spending of $641, with a standard deviation of $234. You may assume that the sample data are normally distributed. At the 5% level of significance, is there evidence that annual Internet spending by Canadians is lower than the online retailer believes? How sure of your answer are you?

8. The college cafeteria manager claims that 90% of cafeteria customers are satisfied with the range of food served and prices. Suppose that in a random sample of 500 cafeteria customers, 438 say they are satisfied with the cafeteria. Does the sample result suggest that fewer than 90% of the cafeteria's customers are satisfied with the range of food served and prices? You have already examined this problem, in Chapter 6 Review Exercise 4. Complete a formal hypothesis test. Use $\alpha = 4\%$.

9. A survey of the morning beverage market shows that the primary breakfast beverage of 17% of Americans is milk. A Canadian dairy company believes the figure is higher in Canada. The company contacts a random sample of 500 Canadians and asks what primary beverage they consumed for breakfast that day. Suppose 102 replied that milk was their primary beverage. Does this sample result provide evidence that a greater proportion of Canadians drink milk as the primary breakfast beverage, as compared to Americans? You have already examined this problem, in Chapter 6 Review Exercise 5. Complete a formal hypothesis test. Use $\alpha = 0.01$.

10. A tourist attraction gets over 50,000 visitors a year, but traffic has declined over the last few years. The manager has recently refurbished the buildings, added new activities, and generally spruced up the facility. A survey of customers done two years ago revealed that only 65% of them felt they had had an enjoyable experience. A survey of 400 visitors, done after the upgrades, indicated that 282 of them felt they had had an enjoyable experience. Does this provide any evidence that the upgrades improved visitor enjoyment? You have already examined this problem, in Chapter 6 Review Exercise 6. Complete a formal hypothesis test. Use $\alpha = 0.03$.

11. A human resources manager claims that tuition subsidies for employees are not an important benefit, as only 5% of employees would use such a program. The union president thinks this estimate is too low. A survey of 500 revealed that 38 of them would use the tuition subsidy program. Does the sample provide evidence that the HR manager's estimate of the percentage of employees who would use the program is too low? Use a 2% level of significance.

12. An analyst in a government ministry is interested in the average cost of textbooks per semester for a college student. A previous estimate suggests that the average cost of textbooks per semester is $700. The analyst conducts a random sample of 75 college students, with a sample average cost of $756 and a standard deviation of $132. Is there evidence that average textbook costs per semester have increased for college students? You have already examined this problem, in Chapter 6 Review Exercise 7. Complete a formal hypothesis test, with a 5% level of significance.

13. A financial services company conducted a survey of a random sample of its customers. One of the items on the survey was as follows:
    "The staff at my local branch can provide me with good advice on my financial affairs."
    Customers were asked to respond on the following scale:
    1 – strongly agree
    2 – agree
    3 – neither agree nor disagree
    4 – disagree
    5 – strongly disagree
    The customer responses are summarized in Exhibit 7.21 below.

EXHIBIT 7.21

Financial Services Customer Survey

"The staff at my local branch can provide me with good advice on my financial affairs."	Number of Customers
Strongly agree	20
Agree	47
Neither agree nor disagree	32
Disagree	15
Strongly disagree	9

Based on the sample results, can you infer that more than half of customers agree or strongly agree that the staff at the local branch can provide good advice on their financial affairs? Use $\alpha = 0.05$.

14. As a student, you are suspicious that some teachers give easier tests than others. You have heard that Mr. Wilson is one such teacher, and you are thinking of switching to his class. However, you want to be sure that Mr. Wilson's tests are easier. Ms. Hardy has told you that the class average on the first test of the semester was 58.2%. Mr. Wilson did not give out the class average, so you conduct a random sample of 20 students from his class, and get an

average mark of 65.4%, with a standard deviation of 18.6. At the 5% level of significance, does this provide evidence that the average mark was higher in Mr. Wilson's class? If so, does this mean that Mr. Wilson's test was easier than Ms. Hardy's? What other explanations should you consider? You may assume the test marks are normally distributed.

THINK AND DECIDE USING EXCEL

15. The operations manager at the factory is interested in the lifespan of an electronic component used in one of the factory's machines. The producer of the electronic component claims that it has an average life of 6,200 hours. A random sample of 40 components is studied, and their lifespans are recorded. You have already examined this data set, in Chapter 6 Review Exercise 9.

    Is there evidence that the average lifespan of the electronic components is less than the manufacturer claims? Complete a formal hypothesis test, using $\alpha = 0.05$.

    CRE07-15

16. When Doug Brackett bought Downtown Automotive, the previous owner suggested to him that average daily sales at the shop were $2,000. You have already examined this data set, in Chapter 6 Review Exercise 11.

    Is there evidence that average daily sales at the shop are less than the previous owner claimed? Complete a formal hypothesis test, using a 4% level of significance.

    CRE07-16

17. A smart meter tracks household electricity use and the time of use. With smart meters, consumers have a price incentive to use electricity at off-peak hours, when rates are cheaper. After having smart meters described to them, a survey asked 2,400 Canadians about their interest level in having a smart meter installed. At the 5% level of significance, is there evidence that fewer than one quarter of all Canadians are extremely interested or very interested in having smart meters installed in their homes?

    CRE07-17

18. Lynda Parks has surveyed a random sample of the customers who shop at the drugstore she owns. Is there evidence that the average purchase amount is more than $25? Use a 5% level of significance.

    CRE07-18

19. The survey of drugstore customers mentioned in Exercise 18 also includes data about staff friendliness. Based on the survey, can Lynda Parks conclude that fewer than 5% of customers rate staff friendliness as "poor"? Use a 4% significance level.

    CRE07-19

20. The survey of drugstore customers also collected data on incomes. At the 4% level of significance, can Lynda Parks conclude that the average income of her drugstore customers is more than $45,000?

    CRE07-20

21. The survey of drugstore customers also collected data on ages. Lynda Parks has always thought that the average age of her customers is around 40. At the 5% level of significance, what can you conclude, based on the sample data?

    CRE07-21

22. The survey of drugstore customers also collected data on speed of service. At the 3% level of significance, is there evidence that more than 40% of customers rate the service as good or excellent?

    CRE07-22

23. The Office of Economic Development in your city has conducted a survey of a random sample of city households, and has collected data on reported after-tax income for families with two or more people. Is there enough evidence to suggest that the average after-tax income for such families is more than $60,000 in your city? Use $\alpha = 0.05$.

    CRE07-23

TEST YOUR KNOWLEDGE

24. A college surveys incoming students every year. An excerpt of one such survey, for Business students only, is available in MyStatLab. For this question, consider these particular incoming students as a random sample of all students entering Business programs in

    CRE07-24

Canadian colleges for this year (for convenience, we will refer to these students simply as "incoming students"). Complete a formal hypothesis test to answer the following questions, if necessary conditions exist.

a. Is there sufficient evidence to conclude that over 25% of incoming students have laptops? Use $\alpha = 0.04$.

b. Is there sufficient evidence to conclude that 10% of incoming students rent rooms? Use a 4% level of significance.

c. Is there sufficient evidence to conclude that the average mark of incoming students is over 80%? Use $\alpha = 0.04$.

d. Is there sufficient evidence to conclude that the amount of savings available for education is less than $6,500? Use $\alpha = 0.04$.

CHAPTER 8

Estimating Population Values

INTRODUCTION

In Chapter 7, we learned how to make conclusions about population means and proportions with hypothesis tests. In Example 7.2B, we saw enough evidence in the sample to conclude that fewer than 20% of Canadians expected employment conditions to improve. The next logical question is, what *was* the percentage of Canadians who expected employment conditions to improve? The hypothesis test told us that it was less than 20%, but was it 18% or 10%? Of course, we cannot know for sure (unless we can somehow ask all Canadians), but we can use the sample data to come up with a useful estimate.

Estimation begins with a sample statistic that corresponds to the population parameter of interest. For example, it makes sense to use the sample proportion ($\hat{p}$) from Example 7.2B, which was 15%, to estimate the proportion (p) of all Canadians who expected employment conditions to improve. Similarly, it makes sense to use the average amount of cash withdrawals over a sample of weekends (the sample mean $\bar{x}$) to estimate the average amount of cash withdrawals at an automated teller machine (ATM) over all weekends

LEARNING OBJECTIVES

After mastering the material in this chapter, you will be able to:

1 Estimate a population proportion.

2 Estimate a population mean.

3 Decide on the appropriate sample size to estimate a population mean or proportion, given a desired level of accuracy for the estimate.

4 Use confidence intervals to draw appropriate hypothesis-testing conclusions.

Point estimate A single-number estimate of a population parameter that is based on sample data.

Confidence interval estimate A range of numbers of the form (*a, b*) that is thought to enclose the parameter of interest, with a given level of probability.

(the population mean μ). Such sample statistics are called point estimates. A single-number estimate of a population parameter that is based on sample data is called a **point estimate**.

We know that there is variability in sampling distributions, and so, for example, the $\bar{x}$ we calculate from the sample may or may not be close to μ. Instead of relying on a point estimate such as $\bar{x}$ or $\hat{p}$, we construct something called a confidence interval estimate. A **confidence interval estimate** of the form (*a, b*) is a range of numbers that is thought to enclose the parameter of interest, with a given level of probability. For example, we might estimate that the interval ($520, $600) contains the average amount of cash withdrawn from the ATM at night, with 95% confidence. It might help you to visualize this by thinking of the confidence interval as a horseshoe we are trying to throw at the (always unknown) population parameter. Properly constructed, a 95% confidence interval is a horseshoe that will land on the unknown population parameter 95 times out of 100, if we repeated the sampling process and constructed the interval many, many times.

> **The General Form of a Confidence Interval**
>
> Confidence interval estimates have a general form as follows:
>
> (point estimate) ± (critical value) • (estimated standard error of the sample statistic)

Exhibit 8.1 illustrates the general form of a confidence interval estimate.

EXHIBIT 8.1

The General Form of a Confidence Interval Estimate

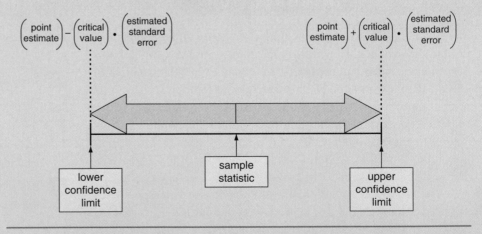

In Chapter 8, we will use sampling distributions (and probability concepts) to create confidence intervals for population proportions (Section 8.1) and means (Section 8.2). As well, we will introduce some methods to help us decide how large a sample size we should take to make reliable estimates (Section 8.3). Finally, we will demonstrate the link between estimation techniques (in particular, confidence intervals) and hypothesis tests (Section 8.4).

8.1   ESTIMATING THE POPULATION PROPORTION

Suppose we wanted to estimate the proportion of bank customers who come to the branch to access their safety deposit boxes. A random sample of 200 customers revealed 43 who had come to the branch primarily to access their safety deposit boxes. We now want to estimate p, the proportion of *all* customers who come to the branch primarily to access their safety deposit boxes, with 95% confidence.

We can use the sampling distribution of $\hat{p}$ for this estimation, as long as the (probably now familiar) required conditions hold:

- The sample size must be $\leq$ 5% of the population if sampling is done without replacement (as it is in this case).
- np and nq must be $\geq$ 10, for normality of the sampling distribution of $\hat{p}$.

In the hypothesis tests we did in Chapter 7, we used the hypothesized values for p and q to check that np and nq were $\geq$ 10. In estimation, we have no hypothesized value for p (or q). Therefore, to check for normality, we use $\hat{p}$ and $\hat{q}$, calculated from the sample data.

If the required conditions are met, we construct a confidence interval estimate as follows. First, record the relevant information from the problem.

- $n = 200$
- $\hat{p} = \dfrac{43}{200} = 0.215$
- so $\hat{q} = 1 - 0.215 = 0.785$

A bank branch probably has thousands of customers, so it is reasonable to conclude that the sample of 200 is not more than 5% of the population of customers.

We check the conditions for normality.

- $n\hat{p} = 200\left(\dfrac{43}{200}\right) = 43 \geq 10$
- $n\hat{q} = 200(0.785) = 157 \geq 10$

The critical value for a 95% confidence interval estimate is 1.96 (we will illustrate why a little later on). The confidence interval estimate for the proportion of all customers who come to the branch primarily to access their safety deposit boxes will be as follows.

(point estimate) $\pm$ (critical value) $\cdot$ (estimated standard error of the sample statistic)

$$= \hat{p} \pm 1.96\sqrt{\frac{\hat{p}\hat{q}}{n}}$$

$$= 0.215 \pm 1.96\sqrt{\frac{0.215(0.785)}{200}}$$

$$= 0.215 \pm 1.96(0.029049527)$$

$$= 0.215 \pm 0.0569371$$

The value on the right-hand side of the confidence interval calculation above is the *half-width* of the interval. This is the amount we add to—and subtract from—the point estimate to arrive at the upper and lower confidence limits. We will use the notation HW to refer to the half-width, as Exhibit 8.2 below illustrates.

EXHIBIT 8.2

95% Confidence Interval for *p*

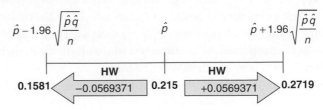

To finish the calculation:

$$0.215 \pm 0.0569371$$
$$(0.1581, 0.2719)$$

We estimate that the interval $(0.1581, 0.2719)$ encloses the true proportion of all customers who come to the branch primarily to access their safety deposit boxes, with 95% confidence. Notice the wording that is used here. The 95% confidence is associated with the interval. Remember that we are saying we have 95% confidence that the horseshoe we constructed landed around the true population proportion. It is *not* correct to say we have 95% confidence that the population proportion is between 0.1581 and 0.2719. The population proportion is *not* a random variable, and so there is no probability associated with its location, except for 100% probability that it is exactly what it is. Be careful not to make this common mistake when you are interpreting a confidence interval.

The question we have not yet answered is this: why is 1.96 the critical value in this case?

Remember that when the required conditions are met, the sampling distribution of $\hat{p}$ is approximately normal, with a mean and standard deviation as follows:

- $\mu_{\hat{p}} = p$

- $\sigma_{\hat{p}} = \sqrt{\dfrac{pq}{n}}$

The sampling distribution of $\hat{p}$ would as illustrated in Exhibit 8.3 opposite.

Marked on the sampling distribution are arrows corresponding to the confidence interval half-width of $1.96\sigma_{\hat{p}}$. Of course, we do not know exactly what this sampling distribution looks like, because we do not know what p or $\sigma_{\hat{p}}$ are, exactly. However, we can estimate the standard error based on sample information. In the bank example, we estimated the standard error as follows:

$$\sigma_{\hat{p}} \cong \sqrt{\frac{\hat{p}(\hat{q})}{n}} = \sqrt{\frac{0.215(0.785)}{200}} = 0.02905$$

and so the distance that corresponds to the arrow in Exhibit 8.3 is $1.96\sigma_{\hat{p}} \cong 1.96(0.02905) = 0.0569$. The length of the arrow (the confidence interval half-width) will of course depend on the particular sampling distribution you are working with.

We can use the normal table in the back of the textbook to confirm that a *z*-score of -1.96 leaves an area of 0.025 in the left-hand tail of this normal distribution. Because the

EXHIBIT 8.3

Sampling Distribution of the Sample Proportion

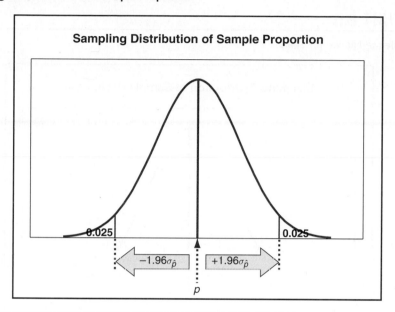

Sampling Distribution of Sample Proportion

distribution is symmetric, we know that there is also 0.025 in the right-hand tail of the distribution.

Now, let's simulate sampling and constructing a confidence interval, over and over. Suppose the first $\hat{p}$ we get (we'll call it $\hat{p}_1$) is somewhat to the right of the mean, as shown in Exhibit 8.4 below. When we construct the confidence interval, does it enclose the true population proportion, p? The answer is yes.

EXHIBIT 8.4

Confidence Interval for Sample 1

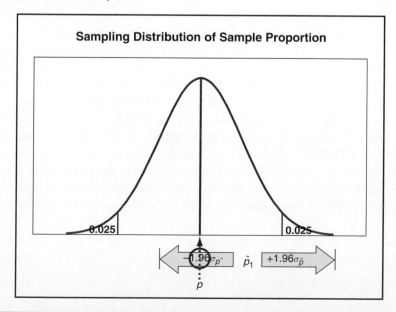

Sampling Distribution of Sample Proportion

Suppose we take another sample, and this time the $\hat{p}$-value is to the left of the mean, as shown in Exhibit 8.5. Does the confidence interval enclose p? Again, the answer is yes.

EXHIBIT 8.5

Confidence Interval for Sample 2

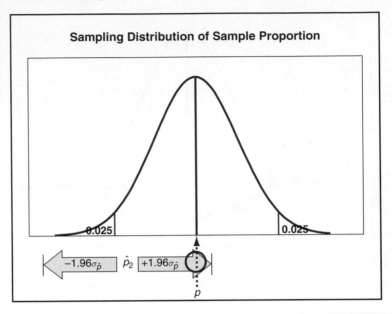

If we imagine sampling over and over again, when will the confidence intervals *not* enclose p? The answer is whenever the sample proportion $\hat{p}$ is in one of the tail areas of the sampling distribution. And this will happen, in the long run, just 5% of the time $(0.025 + 0.025 = 0.05)$. This means that 95% of the time, the confidence interval *will* enclose p, and this is what gives us the 95% confidence level.

Now you should be able to figure out the critical value for a 99% confidence level. This will be the z-score that leaves 99% in the middle of the distribution, with the remaining 1% split between the two tails of the distribution, leaving 0.005 in each tail. We can use notation similar to the notation for critical t-scores here. We need to identify $z_{.005}$.

If we use the normal table in the back of the book to identify $z_{.005}$, we are faced with a problem: a z-score of -2.57 leaves 0.0051 in the tail of the distribution, and a z-score of -2.58 leaves 0.0049 in the tail. Neither of these is exactly what we want, and they are tied in terms of closeness to the desired probability. However, if we go to Excel and use **NORMINV** (or **NORMSINV**, which is the inverse for the standard normal distribution), we see that a z-score of -2.57583 will leave 0.005 in the tail of the distribution. The minus sign on the z-score is not relevant (it is already built into the formula), so the z-score we will use for a 99% confidence interval is 2.57583 (round this to 2.576 for manual calculations).

You should know how to identify the correct z-score for any confidence level, although there are just a few common ones. For a confidence level of x (the percentage in decimal form) the critical z-score will leave $\dfrac{(1 - x)}{2}$ in each tail of the distribution. For example, for a confidence level of 94%, the z-score will leave $\dfrac{(1 - 0.94)}{2} = 0.03$ in each

tail. The correct z-score is located by looking at the body of the normal table for an entry as close as possible to 0.03. In this case, $z_{0.03}$ is –1.88. We ignore the minus sign, as it is already accounted for in the formula.

A table showing the z-scores used for calculating some common confidence interval estimates for p is provided below in Exhibit 8.6.

EXHIBIT 8.6

Critical *z*-Scores for Calculating Confidence Interval Estimates for *p*

Confidence level	99%	98%	95%	90%
z-score	2.576	2.326	1.96	1.645

A higher level of confidence requires a wider interval. Let's return to the initial example, of estimating the proportion of bank customers who come to the branch to access their safety deposit boxes. If we wanted a 99% confidence interval, the calculations would be as follows:

(point estimate) $\pm$ (critical value) $\cdot$ (estimated standard error of the sample statistic)

$$= \hat{p} \pm 2.576\sqrt{\frac{\hat{p}\hat{q}}{n}}$$

$$= 0.215 \pm 2.576\sqrt{\frac{0.215(0.785)}{200}}$$

$$= 0.215 \pm 2.576(0.029049527)$$

$$= 0.215 \pm 0.0748316$$

$$= (0.1402, 0.2898)$$

Exhibit 8.7 illustrates the 99% and 95% confidence interval estimates for p. The 99% confidence interval is (0.1402, 0.2898), wider than the 95% interval we first calculated at (0.1581, 0.2719).

EXHIBIT 8.7

99% and 95% Confidence Interval Estimates for *p*

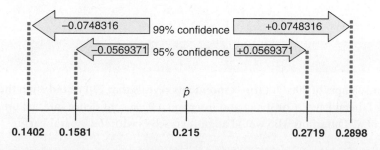

GUIDE TO TECHNIQUE

Creating a Confidence Interval Estimate for *p*

When:

- qualitative data, one sample
- trying to estimate *p*, the population proportion, on the basis of $\hat{p}$, the sample proportion
- sample size (*n*) large

Steps:

1. Collect or identify the sample data. Identify or calculate:

   - $\hat{p}$, the sample proportion,
   - $\hat{q} = 1 - \hat{p}$
   - *n,* the sample size.

2. If sampling is done without replacement, make sure that the sample size is not more than 5% of the population, so that the binomial distribution is the appropriate underlying model.

3. Check for (approximate) normality of the sampling distribution of $\hat{p}$, which requires BOTH:

   - $n\hat{p} \geq 10$
   - $n\hat{q} \geq 10$

4. If the sampling distribution is approximately normal, proceed by calculating the confidence interval estimate with the following formula:

$$\hat{p} \pm (\text{critical } z\text{-score})\sqrt{\frac{\hat{p}\hat{q}}{n}}$$

The critical *z*-score corresponds to the level of confidence required. First, check the table of critical *z*-scores in Exhibit 8.6 on page 303. If the required *z*-score is not there, identify the required critical *z*-score as follows:

- Calculate $\dfrac{(1 - x)}{2}$, where *x* is the desired level of confidence (percentage in decimal form).
- Look in the body of the normal table (Appendix 2) for the entry that is as close as possible to the value calculated above, and identify the corresponding *z*-score. Ignore the minus sign, and use it as the critical *z*-score in the formula.

See Example 8.1, below.

EXAMPLE 8.1

Constructing a confidence interval estimate for *p*

A random sample of 500 Ontario respondents reveals that 230 would align themselves with the Liberal Party. Construct and interpret a 97% confidence interval for the percentage of all Ontarians who would align themselves with the Liberal Party.

First, summarize the information provided.

- $n = 500$
- $\hat{p} = \dfrac{230}{500} = 0.46$
- $\hat{q} = 1 - 0.46 = 0.54$

Sampling is done without replacement, but the sample of 500 is much less than 5% of all Ontario voters, so we can proceed.

Next, check conditions for normality of the sampling distribution of $\hat{p}$.

- $n\hat{p} = 500\left(\dfrac{230}{500}\right) = 230 \geq 10$
- $n\hat{q} = 500(0.54) = 270 \geq 10$

Conditions for normality are met.

We need the critical z-score for a 97% confidence interval estimate. First, check Exhibit 8.6 on page 303. The required z-score is not there. Next, calculate $\dfrac{(1 - x)}{2} = \dfrac{(1 - 0.97)}{2} = 0.015$. Look in the body of the normal table for an entry as close as possible to 0.015. In this case, we can identify an entry exactly equal to this value, with a corresponding z-score of -2.17. We ignore the minus sign and plug the z-score into the formula.

$$\hat{p} \pm (z\text{-score})\sqrt{\dfrac{\hat{p}\hat{q}}{n}}$$

$$0.46 \pm (2.17)\sqrt{\dfrac{0.46(0.54)}{500}}$$

$$0.46 \pm (2.17)(0.022289011)$$

$$0.46 \pm 0.048367153$$

We have 97% confidence that the interval (0.411, 0.508) contains the true proportion of Ontarians who would align themselves with the Liberal Party.

Using the Excel Template for a Confidence Interval Estimate of the Population Proportion   While it is fairly straightforward to construct confidence intervals for a population proportion by hand with a calculator and a normal table, this approach will often be slightly less accurate than with a computer.

A worksheet template for the confidence interval for a proportion is available in the workbook called "Templates." It is called "CI for Proportion." The template is shown on the next page in Exhibit 8.8, with the values from Example 8.1 filled in. Note that you should always use Excel to do any calculations when you are using this template. For Example 8.1, you should enter the formula "=230/500" into the slot for $\hat{p}$, not "0.46." You should *never* use your calculator to calculate a value that you then input into an Excel spreadsheet (employers cite this behaviour as a prime indicator of lack of skill with Excel).

Notice that the Excel template arrived at the same answers we got when we did this by hand. As usual, some input is required for all the blue-shaded areas in the template.

EXHIBIT 8.8

Excel Template for the Confidence Interval Estimate for the Population Proportion

Confidence Interval Estimate for the Population Proportion	
Confidence Level (decimal form)	0.97
Sample Proportion	0.46
Sample Size n	500
np-hat	230
nq-hat	270
Are np-hat and nq-hat >=10?	yes
Upper Confidence Limit	0.50837
Lower Confidence Limit	0.41163

DEVELOP YOUR SKILLS 8.1

MyStatLab

Try doing these by hand, and then use the Excel template to verify your answers.

1. A company is trying to decide whether to provide an outdoor gazebo for the smokers on its staff. Before any money is spent on construction costs, the company would like to estimate the percentage of its workers who smoke. A random sample of 300 employees reveals 56 smokers. Construct a 99% confidence interval for the proportion of smokers in this company.

2. A company wants to design a daycare program for its staff. A random sample of 200 employees reveals that 142 have children of daycare age. Construct a 95% confidence interval for the proportion of all employees who have children of daycare age.

3. A manufacturer of high-definition, flat-panel LCD (liquid crystal display) televisions surveyed 1,000 Canadians about their knowledge of such features as 1080p resolution and pixel response times. Forty-eight percent of those surveyed confessed they were not at all knowledgeable about such features. Construct a 90% confidence interval estimate for the proportion of all Canadians who do not feel knowledgeable about such television features.

4. You are trying to estimate the percentage of households who have high-speed Internet access in the east end of St. John's, Newfoundland. A random sample of 50 households reveals 37 with high-speed Internet access. Estimate the percentage of all the households in the east end who have high-speed Internet access, with 98% confidence.

5. A random sample of 1,202 British Columbia residents was given a list of several approaches for retailers to deal with plastic bags. Of those surveyed, 469 said that retailers should provide biodegradable plastic bags to consumers, at no charge. The survey was reported as accurate to within 2.9%, 19 times out of 20. What confidence interval can you construct from these results?

8.2 ESTIMATING THE POPULATION MEAN

Suppose we want to estimate the average number of customers who come into the bank branch over the noon hour, with 90% confidence. A random sample of 50 noon hours yields a sample mean of 30.98, with a sample standard deviation of 10.686. We can use the sampling distribution of $\bar{x}$ to construct the confidence interval. Because we do not know the population standard deviation σ, we will use the t-distribution, as we did for hypothesis tests about μ in Chapter 7. Of course, we cannot proceed unless we have some reason to believe that the population data are normally distributed. A histogram of the sample data is shown in Exhibit 8.9.

EXHIBIT 8.9

Histogram of Noon Hour Traffic at a Bank Branch

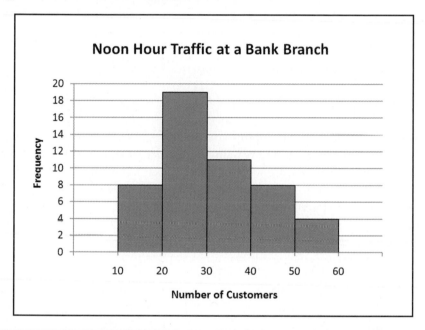

Although this histogram is somewhat skewed to the right, the sample size is fairly large at 50, and so we will proceed with the use of the t-distribution.

As usual, we first summarize the relevant details from the sample.

- $\bar{x} = 30.98$
- $s = 10.686$
- $n = 50$

As before, the confidence or interval will take the general form of

(point estimate) $\pm$ (critical value) · (estimated standard error of the sample statistic)

This translates to:

$$\bar{x} \pm (\text{critical } t\text{-score})\left(\frac{s}{\sqrt{n}}\right)$$

Exhibit 8.10 below illustrates the confidence interval estimate for μ.

EXHIBIT 8.10

Confidence Interval Estimate for μ

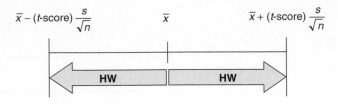

Filling in the information from the sample, this leads to:

$$30.98 \pm (t\text{-score}) \frac{10.686}{\sqrt{50}}$$

Now we must identify the appropriate t-score. Since $n = 50$ in the sample, the degrees of freedom $= n - 1 = 49$. We want to construct a 90% confidence level, meaning that the appropriate t-score will leave 5% in each tail of the distribution. This means we want to identify $t_{.050}$. Since the t-table has no row for 49 degrees of freedom, we must use the row for 50 degrees of freedom. In that row, $t_{.050} = 1.676$. The final result is as follows.

$$\bar{x} \pm (t\text{-score}) \frac{s}{\sqrt{n}}$$

$$= 30.98 \pm (1.676) \frac{10.686}{\sqrt{50}}$$

$$= 30.98 \pm 2.5328192$$

$$= (28.447, 33.513)$$

Exhibit 8.11 illustrates the final result.

EXHIBIT 8.11

90% Confidence Interval for μ (Sample Size of 50)

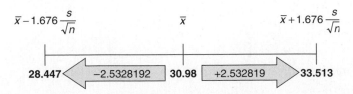

The 90% confidence interval for the average number of customers in the bank branch over the noon hour is (28.447, 33.513). This information will help branch management decide how many counter officers should be scheduled to work over the noon hour.

GUIDE TO TECHNIQUE

Creating a Confidence Interval Estimate for μ

When:

- quantitative data, one sample, one population
- trying to estimate μ, the population mean, on the basis of $\bar{x}$, the sample mean

Steps:

1. Collect or identify the sample data. Identify or calculate:

    - $\bar{x}$, the sample mean
    - s, the sample standard deviation
    - n, the sample size

2. Check for normality of the population, with a histogram of sample values.
3. *If* the sample data appear normal, proceed by calculating the confidence interval estimate with the following formula:

$$\bar{x} \pm (\text{critical } t\text{-score})\left(\frac{s}{\sqrt{n}}\right)$$

The critical t-score corresponds to the level of confidence required. Use the t-table in Appendix 3 on page 580.

- Degrees of freedom $= n - 1$
- Calculate $\dfrac{(1 - x)}{2}$, where x is the desired level of confidence (percentage in decimal form). The resulting value will be the subscript of the correct t-score. For example, for a 95% confidence interval estimate, $\dfrac{(1 - x)}{2} = \dfrac{(1 - 0.95)}{2} = 0.025$, and the correct t-score will be $t_{0.025}$.

See Example 8.2, below.

EXAMPLE 8.2

Constructing a confidence interval estimate for μ

A manager in the shipping and receiving area of a large company has noticed an increase in her department's number of employee absences due to work-related injuries, and she has started to wonder if the average weight of the packages handled by workers has increased. She wants to calculate a 95% confidence interval for the average package weight. A random sample of package weights (in kilograms) is shown in Exhibit 8.12 below.

EXHIBIT 8.12

Random Sample of Package Weights (in kilograms)

11.2	9.3	13.1	9.3	13	14.8	9.9	9	8.5	9.8
12.4	8.6	7.4	9.6	5	16.7	11.5	4.2	6.4	11.5

The first step is to check for normality. One possible histogram of the data, shown below in Exhibit 8.13, seems approximately normal.

EXHIBIT 8.13

Histogram of Package Weight Data

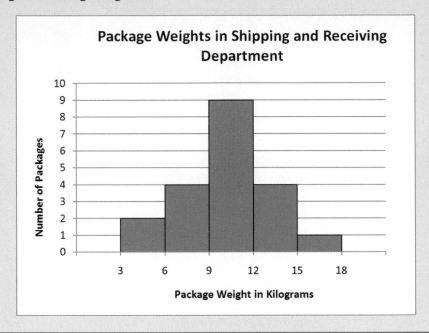

The next step is to calculate the sample mean and standard deviation.

$$\bar{x} = \frac{\Sigma x}{n} = \frac{201.2}{20} = 10.06$$

$$s = \sqrt{\frac{\Sigma x^2 - \frac{(\Sigma x)^2}{n}}{n-1}} = \sqrt{\frac{2207 - \frac{(201.2)^2}{20}}{19}} = 3.103$$

There are 20 observations in the sample, yielding 19 degrees of freedom. For a 95% confidence interval estimate, $\frac{(1-x)}{2} = \frac{(1-0.95)}{2} = 0.025$, and the correct t-score will be $t_{0.025}$ with 19 degrees of freedom. The t-table tells us that this value is 2.093. The confidence interval is constructed as follows.

$$\bar{x} \pm (t\text{-score})\frac{s}{\sqrt{n}}$$

$$= 10.06 \pm (2.093)\frac{3.103}{\sqrt{20}}$$

$$= 10.06 \pm 1.452$$

We have 95% confidence that the interval (8.61 kg, 11.51 kg) contains the true average package weight handled in shipping and receiving.

Using the Excel Template for a Confidence Interval Estimate of the Population Mean   A worksheet template for the confidence interval for a mean is available in the workbook called "Templates." The worksheet is called "CI for Mean." The template is shown below in Exhibit 8.14, with the values from Example 8.2 filled in. As usual, you will have to use this template in conjunction with the **Histogram** tool of Excel, so you can check for normality.

EXHIBIT 8.14

Excel Template for the Confidence Interval Estimate for the Population Mean

Confidence Interval Estimate for the Population Mean	
Do the sample data appear to be normally distributed?	yes
Confidence Level (decimal form)	0.95
Sample Mean	10.06000
Sample Standard Deviation s	3.10287
Sample Size n	20
Upper Confidence Limit	11.5122
Lower Confidence Limit	8.60781

Note that the values for the sample mean, standard deviation, and sample size can be calculated with Excel functions (**AVERAGE**, **STDEV**, and **COUNT**).

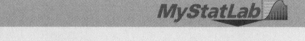

DEVELOP YOUR SKILLS 8.2

MyStatLab

Do these exercises by hand, and with the Excel template.

6. A random sample of 25 families leaving a supermarket yields an average grocery bill of $112.36, with a standard deviation of $32.45. A histogram of the data is approximately normal. Construct a 95% confidence interval for the average grocery bill of all households whose members shop at this store.

7. A random sample of 100 Canadians revealed that they spent an average of $22.58 eating dinner out (at a restaurant) on a weekly basis, with a standard deviation of $26.90. A histogram of the sample data is shown on the next page in Exhibit 8.15. If appropriate, construct a 98% confidence interval estimate for the average amount spent weekly by all Canadians eating dinner out.

8. A random sample of monthly daycare costs for 50 households in Halifax, Nova Scotia, yields an average of $460, with a standard deviation of $65. Estimate the average monthly daycare costs for all Halifax households, with 98% confidence. You may assume that the daycare costs are normally distributed.

9. You want to know the average grade on a Statistics test, but the teacher will not provide the information. You take a random sample of the marks of 20 students who wrote the test.

DYS08-9
    The results are available in MyStatLab. Construct a 95% confidence interval estimate for the average grade on the statistics test.

10. A human resources consulting firm wants to estimate the average salary of university graduates with a bachelor's degree in science, and 10 years of working experience, in the Toronto area. A sample of 50 such employees reveals an average of $56,387 and a standard deviation of $5,435. Assuming the salary data are approximately normally distributed, construct a 90% confidence interval for the salaries.

EXHIBIT 8.15

Histogram of Weekly Amount Spent Eating Dinner Out

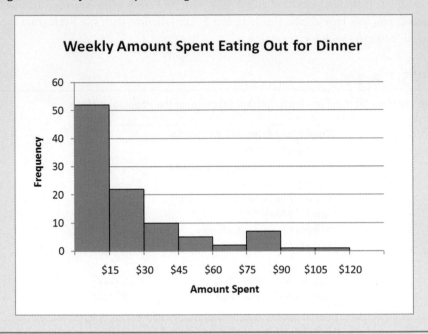

8.3 SELECTING THE SAMPLE SIZE

Sample Size to Estimate a Mean

Deciding on the size of the sample you plan to take is important. If you take a sample that is larger than necessary, you will be wasting money. If your sample is too small, the results may not achieve the desired level of accuracy. Deciding on the sample size is a challenge, not because it is technically difficult but because you need information you do not normally have until *after* you have taken a sample.

Suppose you wanted to take a sample to estimate the average number of customers in the bank branch over the noon hour to within 3 customers, with a 95% level of confidence. Think again of the confidence interval being a horseshoe we are trying to throw around μ. Suppose we just barely catch μ inside the horseshoe (with the true μ being at either the upper or the lower limit of the interval). Even in this worst case, the farthest $\bar{x}$ can be from μ is equal to the half-width of the interval, since $\bar{x}$ is in the centre of the confidence interval (as shown in Exhibit 8.16). For this reason, the half-width of a confidence interval is sometimes referred to as the *margin of error* or *allowable error*. Since there is actually no *error* involved, we have referred to it as the half-width (or HW).

If we want the estimate to be within 3 units of the true value of μ, we simply set the half-width of the interval equal to 3.

EXHIBIT 8.16

$\bar{x}$ Will Be Within a Half-Width of μ

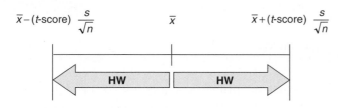

$$\bar{x}-(t\text{-score})\,\frac{s}{\sqrt{n}} \qquad\qquad \bar{x} \qquad\qquad \bar{x}+(t\text{-score})\,\frac{s}{\sqrt{n}}$$

$$\text{HW} = (t\text{-score})\,\frac{s}{\sqrt{n}} = 3$$

We cannot solve for the sample size *n* until we fill in the other unknowns in this equation. The first problem is that we need an estimate for *s,* the standard deviation. Since we have not yet done any sampling, this may pose a problem! However, there are several possible approaches.

1. Past or similar studies may provide a useful estimate of the standard deviation. For example, the bank may have done customer traffic studies in this or similar branches.

2. It may be possible to estimate the standard deviation from the range of the data. For example, counter staff may be quite sure that there are never fewer than 10 customers in the branch over the noon hour, and never more than 50. This yields a range of 40. Remember that in a normal data set, almost all of the observations will lie within three standard deviations of the mean. This means that the range of the data would occupy six standard deviations (three to the right of the mean plus three to the left of the mean). If you have reason to believe that customer traffic numbers are normally distributed (something else you are guessing about), you could estimate the standard deviation by dividing the range by 6. However, a more conservative (and the recommended) approach would be to divide the range by 4. This is less likely to give you a sample size too small for your purposes.

3. If all else fails, you may have to do a small preliminary sample to estimate the standard deviation before you proceed with your real sample.

The other value that we have to fill into the equation is the *t*-score. Once again we have a difficulty: the appropriate *t*-score depends on the degrees of freedom, which depends on *n,* the sample size, which is exactly what we are trying to figure out! We solve this problem by turning to the normal distribution (which is the *t*-distribution with infinite degrees of freedom).

Going back to the example, we can complete the calculations as follows. For a 95% confidence interval, the *z*-score would be 1.96. We will use the range-based estimate of the standard deviation mentioned above; that is, we will set $s = \frac{\text{range}}{4} = \frac{40}{4} = 10$.

$$(z\text{-score})\,\frac{s}{\sqrt{n}} = 3$$

$$(1.96)\,\frac{10}{\sqrt{n}} = 3$$

cross-multiply to get

$$3\sqrt{n} = (1.96)(10)$$

$$\sqrt{n} = \frac{(1.96)(10)}{3}$$

$$n = \left(\frac{1.96(10)}{3}\right)^2 = 42.684$$

This calculation indicates that we need a sample size of 43 days to get an estimate with the desired level of accuracy. Notice an important point: even if the calculation had yielded a number such as 42.01, we would *still* take a sample of 43 days. We do not *round* the results of the sample size calculation. Instead we always use the whole number next-highest to the result of the calculation.

It makes sense to come up with a general formula for *n* to summarize the algebraic manipulations required.

GUIDE TO TECHNIQUE

Choosing the Sample Size to Estimate μ

Steps:

1. Identify the *z*-score corresponding to the desired level of confidence. Start with the table of critical *z*-scores in Exhibit 8.6 on page 303. If the required *z*-score is not there, identify the required critical *z*-score as follows:

   - Calculate $\frac{(1 - x)}{2}$, where *x* is the desired level of confidence (percentage in decimal form).
   - Look in the body of the normal table for the entry that is as close as possible to the value calculated above, and identify the corresponding *z*-score. Ignore the minus sign, and use it as the *z*-score in the formula.

2. Identify the best estimate available for *s*.

   - Use *s* from past or similar studies.
   - Approximate with $\frac{range}{4}$, if information about the range is available.
   - Do a small preliminary sample to estimate the standard deviation.

3. Identify the half-width (HW) of the interval. The goal is a sample estimate that is *within* this distance of the population value.

4. Use this formula:

$$n = \left(\frac{(z\text{-score})(s)}{HW}\right)^2$$

Recommended sample size *n* should be set at the whole number next highest to the result of the calculation.

See Example 8.3A on page 315.

One of the most common mistakes students make when using the formula for sample size is forgetting to square the right-hand side—so don't forget! Of course, this formula is appropriate only if the data turn out to be normally distributed, but we cannot assess that until a sample is taken.

EXAMPLE 8.3A

Deciding on sample size to estimate μ

Recall Example 8.2, about the average weight of packages in shipping and receiving. Suppose the manager is not satisfied with the accuracy of the estimate obtained. She wants to estimate the average weight of the packages to within half a kilogram. How large a sample must she take?

From earlier calculations, we know that the data are approximately normally distributed. The manager wants the estimate to be within half a kilogram of the true value, so HW = 0.5. For a 95% confidence level, we use a z-score of 1.96. From earlier calculations, $s = 3.103$.

$$n = \left(\frac{(z\text{-score})(s)}{HW} \right)^2$$

$$n = \left(\frac{(1.96)(3.103)}{0.5} \right)^2$$

$$n = 147.96$$

The manager will have to take a random sample of 148 packages to get an estimate with the desired accuracy.

Sample Size to Estimate a Proportion

Similar reasoning leads us to a formula for sample size for estimating p, the population proportion. The confidence interval is set up as shown in Exhibit 8.17 below.

EXHIBIT 8.17

Confidence Interval Estimate for p

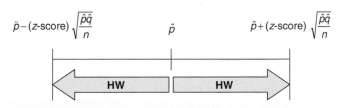

We can solve for the appropriate sample size by solving for n in the formula for the half-width.

$$HW = (z\text{-score})\sqrt{\frac{\hat{p}\hat{q}}{n}}$$

We are temporarily stopped by the need for $\hat{p}$ (and $\hat{q}$). As before, if some appropriate estimate of $\hat{p}$ exists from previous or similar studies, we would use that value. If no estimate of $\hat{p}$ exists, then we set $\hat{p} = 0.5$. This is because whatever $\hat{p}$ turns out to be, the sample size required will never be larger than the one required when $\hat{p} = 0.5$ (try using various levels of $\hat{p}$ in your calculations to see for yourself that this is true).

The algebraic manipulations to isolate n, the sample size, result in the formula shown in the following Guide to Technique.

GUIDE TO TECHNIQUE

Choosing the Sample Size to Estimate *p*

Steps:

1. Identify the *z*-score corresponding to the desired level of confidence. Start with the table of critical *z*-scores in Exhibit 8.6 on page 303. If the required *z*-score is not there, identify the required critical *z*-score as follows:

   - Calculate $\dfrac{(1 - x)}{2}$, where *x* is the desired level of confidence (percentage in decimal form).

   - Look in the body of the normal table for the entry that is as close as possible to the value calculated above, and identify the corresponding *z*-score. Ignore the minus sign, and use it as the *z*-score in the formula.

2. Use any available estimate for $\hat{p}$. If no estimate is available, use $\hat{p} = 0.5$.
3. Identify the half-width (HW) of the interval. The goal is a sample estimate that is *within* this distance of the population value.
4. Use this formula:

$$n = \hat{p}\hat{q}\left(\frac{z\text{-score}}{\text{HW}}\right)^2$$

Recommended sample size *n* should be set at the whole number next highest to the result of the calculation.

See Example 8.3B, below.

Again, be sure you remember to square the term on the right-hand side when you use this formula. Of course, this formula is only appropriate if the conditions for normality of the sampling distribution of $\hat{p}$ are met, but we cannot assess this until we have an estimate for *p* (that is, until a sample is taken).

EXAMPLE 8.3B

Deciding on sample size to estimate *p*

Recall Example 8.1, about the proportion of Ontarians who would align themselves with the Liberal Party. Suppose the party wanted to be able to estimate this proportion to within 2% of the true value, with 97% confidence. How big a sample size would be necessary?

From the first sample, $\hat{p} = 0.46$. As before, the appropriate z-score for a 97% confidence interval will be 2.17. Using the formula for sample size, we get the following result.

$$n = \hat{p}\hat{q}\left(\frac{z\text{-score}}{HW}\right)^2$$

$$= (0.46)(0.54)\left(\frac{2.17}{0.02}\right)^2$$

$$= 2{,}924.2$$

For the desired level of accuracy, a random sample of 2,925 Ontarians is required.

DEVELOP YOUR SKILLS 8.3

MyStatLab

11. A company wants to estimate the proportion of smokers on staff to within 5%, with 99% confidence. A preliminary estimate of the proportion of smokers is 0.1867. How big a sample size is necessary?

12. A company wants to estimate the proportion of employees who have children of daycare age to within 5%, with 95% confidence. No estimate is available. How big a sample size is necessary? How big a sample size would be required if the confidence level increased to 98%?

13. A researcher wants to estimate the average grocery bill of households whose members shop at a particular supermarket to within $10, with 95% confidence. How big a sample size is necessary? A preliminary sample revealed a standard deviation of $32.45.

14. A student wants to estimate the average mark on a statistics test to within 5 marks (out of 100), with 95% confidence. A preliminary sample yielded a standard deviation of 15.54. How big a sample size is necessary?

15. How large a sample should be taken to estimate the percentage of Canadian Internet users who visit social networking sites, to within 4%, with 96% confidence?

8.4 CONFIDENCE INTERVALS AND HYPOTHESIS TESTS

There is a direct correspondence between a two-tailed hypothesis test and the corresponding confidence interval. *If the confidence interval contains the hypothesized value of the population parameter, there is insufficient evidence to reject the null hypothesis.* And of course, the reverse is also true: *If the confidence interval does not contain the hypothesized value of the population parameter, there is sufficient evidence to reject the null hypothesis.*

Exhibit 8.18 on the next page illustrates why this is so. The exhibit shows the sampling distribution of $\hat{p}$, based on the hypothesized value of p, and sets up the 95% confidence interval half-width. Exhibit 8.18 shows the results of four separate sample results.

The confidence interval constructed for sample 1 contains the hypothesized value of p. As well, since the sample proportion is not extreme (not in the tail area of the

EXHIBIT 8.18

Correspondence Between Confidence Intervals and Two-Tailed Hypothesis Tests

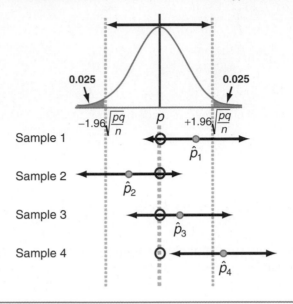

distribution), we would fail to reject the null hypothesis. The same can be said for the results of samples 2 and 3. Only in sample 4 do we get a sample mean so extreme that we would reject the null hypothesis. Notice that the confidence interval constructed in this case does *not* include p.

Of course, this correspondence holds only if the tail areas from the confidence interval match the level of significance in the two-tailed hypothesis test. For example, a 95% confidence interval corresponds to a two-tailed hypothesis test with $\alpha = 0.05$. A 99% confidence interval corresponds to a two-tailed hypothesis test with $\alpha = 0.01$.

A confidence interval cannot be directly used to draw a hypothesis testing conclusion when the hypothesis test is one-tailed. With some thought, you could work out the relationship between a particular confidence interval and a one-tailed hypothesis test.

Finally, notice that while it is possible to draw a hypothesis testing conclusion from a confidence interval estimate in some situations, this approach does not provide a p-value for the hypothesis test, so the results are somewhat limited.

EXAMPLE 8.4

Using a confidence interval for a hypothesis test

Refer to Example 8.2 on page 309, about the weights of packages handled at shipping and receiving. A 95% confidence interval for the average package weight was (8.61 kg, 11.51 kg). The manager thought that the average package weight was 12 kg. Based on this confidence interval, does the sample evidence support the manager's claim? What level of significance applies?

Since the 95% confidence interval does *not* include a weight of 12 kg, there is sufficient evidence to reject the hypothesis that $\mu = 12$ kg. There is sufficient evidence from the sample to infer that $\mu \neq 12$ kg, with a 5% significance level.

DEVELOP YOUR SKILLS 8.4

Answer the following questions without doing any additional calculations beyond the confidence intervals you have already constructed.

16. Return to the confidence interval you constructed for Develop Your Skills 8.2, Exercise 6. The owner of the supermarket claims that the average household grocery bill is $95. Does the sample evidence support the owner's claim? What level of significance applies to your conclusion?

17. Return to the confidence interval you constructed for Develop Your Skills 8.1, Exercise 1. The company nurse claims that the percentage of smokers on staff is 20%. Does the sample evidence support the nurse's claim? What level of significance applies to your conclusion?

18. The manager of a college coffee shop believes that members of the college community spend an average of about $6 a week on morning coffees. You conduct a random sample of the college community, and find that the data on weekly spending for morning coffees are approximately normally distributed. You construct a 99% confidence interval estimate of ($3.24, $5.76). What does this tell you about the manager's claim?

19. Return to the confidence interval you constructed for Develop Your Skills 8.2, Exercise 9. You believe that the average mark on the statistics test was 50%. Does the sample evidence support your belief? What level of significance applies to your conclusion?

Chapter Summary

Estimation procedures rely on sampling (as usual), and we will continue to assume simple random sampling. Estimation begins with a sample statistic that corresponds to the population parameter of interest. For example, it makes sense to estimate the population mean, μ, with the sample mean, $\bar{x}$. A single-number estimate of a population parameter that is based on sample data is called a point estimate. A confidence interval estimate of the form (a, b) is a range of numbers that is thought to enclose the parameter of interest, with a given level of probability.

Confidence intervals have a general form as follows:

(point estimate) $\pm$ (critical value) $\cdot$ (estimated standard error of the sample statistic)

Estimating the Population Proportion

A confidence interval for a population proportion has the following general form:

$$\hat{p} \pm (\text{critical } z\text{-score})\sqrt{\frac{\hat{p}\hat{q}}{n}}$$

See the Guide to Technique: Creating a Confidence Interval Estimate for p, on page 304.

An Excel template for constructing a confidence interval for the population proportion is available in MyStatLab. It is described on page 306.

Estimating the Population Mean

A confidence interval for a population mean has the following general form:

$$\bar{x} \pm (\text{critical } t\text{-score})\left(\frac{s}{\sqrt{n}}\right)$$

See the Guide to Technique: Creating a Confidence Interval Estimate for μ, on page 309. An Excel template for constructing a confidence interval for the population mean is available in MyStatLab. It is described on page 311.

Selecting the Sample Size

Deciding on the sample size is a challenge because you need information that you do not normally have until *after* you have taken your sample.

The formula to select the appropriate sample size to estimate the mean is as follows:

$$n = \left(\frac{(z\text{-score})(s)}{\text{HW}}\right)^2$$

See Guide to Technique: Choosing the Sample Size to Estimate μ, on page 314.

The formula to select the appropriate sample size to estimate the proportion is as follows:

$$n = \hat{p}\hat{q}\left(\frac{z\text{-score}}{\text{HW}}\right)^2$$

See Guide to Technique: Choosing the Sample Size to Estimate p, on page 316.

Confidence Intervals and Hypothesis Tests

There is a direct correspondence between a two-tailed test of hypothesis with a significance level of α and an interval estimate with a confidence level of $(1 - \alpha)$. If the confidence interval contains the hypothesized value of the population parameter, there is insufficient evidence to reject the null hypothesis. If the confidence interval does not contain the hypothesized value of the population parameter, there is sufficient evidence to reject the null hypothesis.

Go to MyStatLab at www.mathxl.com. You can practise the exercises indicated with red in the Develop Your Skills and Chapter Review Exercises as often as you want, and guided solutions will help you find answers step by step. You'll find a personalized study plan available to you too!

CHAPTER REVIEW EXERCISES

WARM-UP EXERCISES

1. A random sample of 400 Canadian grocery shoppers reveals that 26% of them are trying to make healthier food choices.
    a. Construct a 90% confidence interval estimate of the proportion of all Canadian grocery shoppers who are trying to make healthier food choices.
    b. Construct a 96% confidence interval estimate of the proportion of all Canadian grocery shoppers who are trying to make healthier food choices.
    c. Construct a 99% confidence interval estimate of the proportion of all Canadian grocery shoppers who are trying to make healthier food choices.
    d. Compare the three intervals you created for parts a, b, and c of this question. What happens to the width of the confidence interval as the desired level of confidence increases?

2. Using the information provided in Exercise 1 above, how large a sample size should be taken to estimate the proportion of all Canadian grocery shoppers who are trying to make healthier food choices to within 3%, with 95% confidence? How large a sample would you choose if there was no sample information available about the proportion of Canadian grocery shoppers who are trying to make healthier food choices? Why is it better to have an estimate of the proportion?

3. A random sample of 212 Canadian Internet users reveals that they visited an average of 1,576 web pages per month.
    a. Assume the standard deviation from the sample was 521. Construct a 95% confidence interval estimate of the average number of web pages visited per month by Canadian Internet users.
    b. Assume the standard deviation from the sample was 321. Construct a 95% confidence interval estimate of the average number of web pages visited per month by Canadian Internet users.
    c. Assume the standard deviation from the sample was 201. Construct a 95% confidence interval estimate of the average number of web pages visited per month by Canadian Internet users.
    d. Compare the three intervals you created for parts a, b, and c of this question. What happens to the width of the confidence interval as the variability in the data decreases?

4. Refer to the information in Exercise 3a above.
    a. How large a sample would be required to estimate the average number of web pages visited per month by Canadian Internet users to within 100 pages, with 95% confidence?
    b. How large a sample would be required to estimate the average number of web pages visited per month by Canadian Internet users to within 50 pages, with 95% confidence?
    c. How large a sample would be required to estimate the average number of web pages visited per month by Canadian Internet users to within 10 pages, with 95% confidence?
    d. Compare your answers to parts a, b, and c of this question. What happens to the sample size required as the desired level of accuracy increases?

5. How big a sample is necessary to estimate, to within 2 percentage points, the proportion of new graduates of a Business program who are willing to relocate to find a job, with 90% confidence? If your college graduates only 350 students from the Business program, what does this tell you?

THINK AND DECIDE

6. A poll taken for *Toronto Life* magazine in the fall of 2005 surveyed 316 adults in the greater Toronto area. Four in 10 said they would keep their jobs even if they won $10 million in the lottery. Provide a 90% confidence interval for the proportion of people in the greater Toronto area who would keep their jobs after winning $10 million in the lottery.[1]

7. A survey of 30 employees living in a large metropolitan area yielded an average of 54.2 hours of work per week, with a standard deviation of 3.2 hours. Provide a 99% confidence interval for average hours of work per week for employees in this metropolitan area. The data appear to be normally distributed.

8. A statistics professor wants to estimate the average number of hours per week that students in statistics classes spend (outside class) working on statistics. The professor wants to estimate the number of hours to within one hour, with 95% confidence. The professor thinks that the range of hours is probably from 1 to 10. How large a sample should she take? The professor knows she should be cautious about interpreting the results of any such survey. Why?

9. A car manufacturer, worried about how increasing gasoline prices are going to affect sales, wants to estimate the percentage of the adult population in Canada who would consider buying a hybrid vehicle for their next purchase. How big a sample size should the manufacturer take if the company wants to estimate the proportion to within 2% and the manufacturer is fairly certain that the proportion is in the neighbourhood of 10%? The desired confidence level is 95%.

10. The City of Moose Jaw wants to estimate the percentage of households that make consistent efforts to separate recyclable materials from their garbage. How many households should be included in the random sample if the city wants its estimate to be within 3 percentage points, with 95% confidence?

11. In a survey, 43% of the 2,450 respondents said they had phoned in sick when they were not ill. Construct a 99% confidence interval estimate for the proportion of workers who phone in sick when they are not ill. Do you think the results of such a survey would be reliable?

12. A restaurant is trying to decide how to target its marketing. The owner thinks that diners on business expense accounts typically spend more on food and wine than other diners. The restaurant takes a random sample of 40 diners who pay with corporate credit cards. The average bill (per person) is $68.52, with a standard deviation of $14.89. Construct a 98% confidence interval estimate of the average amount spent (per person) in this restaurant by diners with business expense accounts. You may assume that the spending is normally distributed.

13. A college is concerned that the scarcity of housing in the immediate area has made it difficult for students to find affordable accommodation. It is claimed that the average monthly rent paid by a student at the college is $500. A random sample of 40 students is surveyed, and their monthly rent costs are recorded. The sample mean was $543.21, with a sample standard deviation of $47.89. The sample data appear normally distributed. Construct a 95% confidence interval estimate for the average monthly rent paid by students at this college. What does this allow you to conclude about the claim that the average monthly rent is $500?

14. A college wants to estimate the proportion of its students who live at home with their parents. How large a sample size should be taken if the desire is to estimate the proportion to within 3%, with 98% confidence? Past research indicated that the proportion was in the neighbourhood of 35%.

---

[1] *Source:* "Would You Keep Job If You Won $10 Million?" **www.theglobeandmail.com**, accessed October 26, 2005.

THINK AND DECIDE USING EXCEL

15. An ice cream store wants to expand its range of flavours, and has decided to do some research to select which flavours to add. Customers were presented with a range of new flavours, and asked which one they would like to try, if any.

CRE08-15

   The codes are as follows:
   1 – pecan and fudge
   2 – apple pie
   3 – banana caramel ripple
   4 – ginger and honey
   5 – would not try any of these flavours
   Create a 95% confidence interval estimate for the percentage of customers who would try the banana caramel ripple flavour.

16. A maker of toothpaste is doing quality control tests on the amount of toothpaste in the tubes. Thirty tubes of toothpaste are randomly selected, and the quantity of toothpaste in each tube is precisely measured, in millilitres.

CRE08-16

   Construct a 95% confidence interval for the average amount of toothpaste in the tubes.

17. A car rental agency is trying to make staffing plans. The early morning is always a busy time for rentals. The agency keeps track of the number of customers who pick up rental cars in the 8 A.M. to 10 A.M. period for a random sample of days.

CRE08-17

   Construct a 99% confidence interval for the average number of customers picking up rental cars in the 8 A.M. to 10 A.M. period.

18. A manufacturer of cars that have had a poor quality rating in the past wants to estimate the average annual maintenance expenditure for its entry-level compact in the third year of its life. A random sample of 60 customers with such cars is selected, and annual maintenance costs are tracked.

CRE08-18

   Create a 98% confidence interval estimate for the annual maintenance spending on this car in the third year of its life.

19. How large a sample size should the manufacturer described in Exercise 18 take if it wants to estimate annual maintenance costs for this entry-level compact in the 3rd year of its life to within $10, with 98% confidence?

CRE08-19

20. A large company is trying to manage its accounts receivable more efficiently than in the past. It selects a random sample of 100 these accounts, and tracks how old they are. (The company's accounting system does not track account age, although there are plans for an upgrade soon.) The codes associated with the account ages are shown below:

CRE08-20

   1 – 0 to 30 days old
   2 – 31 to 60 days old
   3 – more than 60 days old.
   Create a 95% confidence interval estimate for the proportion of the company's accounts that are 0 to 30 days old.

21. The confidence interval created in Exercise 20 is quite wide. How large a sample would be necessary if the company wanted to estimate the percentage of its accounts receivable that were 0 to 30 days old to within 5%, with 95% confidence?

TEST YOUR KNOWLEDGE

22. A college surveys incoming students every year. An excerpt of one such survey, for Business students only, is available in MyStatLab (you may have looked at this data set for the Test Your Knowledge exercise at the end of Chapter 7). For this question, consider these particular incoming students as a random sample of all students entering Business programs in Canadian colleges for this year (for convenience, we will refer to these students simply as "incoming students").

CRE08-22

a. Construct a 96% confidence interval estimate of the proportion of incoming students who have laptops.

b. How large a sample size would be required to estimate the proportion of incoming students with laptops to within 2%, with 96% confidence?

c. Construct a 96% confidence interval estimate of the proportion of incoming students who rent rooms.

d. Construct a 96% confidence interval estimate of the average mark of incoming students.

e. Construct a 96% confidence interval estimate of the amount of savings available for education.

f. How large a sample would be required to estimate the amount of savings available for education to within $200, with 96% confidence?

CHAPTER 9

Making Decisions with Matched-Pairs Samples, Quantitative or Ranked Data

INTRODUCTION

So far, we have been investigating only one population at a time. We have covered techniques to examine quantitative data (confidence intervals and hypothesis tests of the mean) and qualitative data (confidence intervals and hypothesis tests of the proportion).

In Chapters 9, 10, 11, and 12, we will cover techniques to compare two or more populations. Chapter 9 investigates matched-pairs samples for normal and non-normal quantitative data, and also for ranked data. Chapter 10 looks at comparisons of two independent samples, again for normal and non-normal quantitative data, and ranked data. Chapter 11 provides a technique to compare three or more samples of quantitative data. Chapter 12 presents methods to compare two or more samples of qualitative data.

Matched-pairs analysis is a special case of comparing two populations, but we will start here because the methods for matched pairs of normal quantitative data and ranked data are simply new applications of techniques that you have already seen. Matched-pairs experiments are also a powerful technique, because they often allow us to draw stronger conclusions about cause and effect. For example,

LEARNING OBJECTIVES

After mastering the material in this chapter, you will be able to:

1 Choose and conduct the appropriate hypothesis test to make conclusions about the mean difference in matched populations, on the basis of matched-pairs samples, for normally distributed quantitative data.

2 Choose and conduct the appropriate hypothesis test to make conclusions about the difference in matched populations, on the basis of matched-pairs samples, for non-normally distributed quantitative data.

3 Choose and conduct the appropriate hypothesis test to make conclusions about the difference in matched populations, on the basis of matched-pairs samples, for ranked data.

in Chapter 1 we discussed the difficulties in deciding whether training methods were effective in reducing the number of worker errors. We discussed comparing workers at two plants—one where the workers had not gone through the training program, and one where they had been trained. We realized that although the data could tell us if there was a difference in error rates at the two plants, we could not come to a strong conclusion that the training programs were the cause of any difference, because too many other factors could have played a part.

A better method of comparison is a matched-pairs experiment, where worker errors are recorded both before and after training. If the number of errors fell in this case, we would be able to make a stronger conclusion that the training was the cause of the improvement.

When applying the techniques covered in Chapter 9, it will be extremely important to assess the situation before proceeding. The first step will be to decide whether you have matched-pairs data or independent samples. With matched-pairs samples, there is some kind of relationship between an observation in the first sample and the corresponding observation in the second sample. With independent samples, there is no such relationship.

There are two situations in which sample data are matched pairs:

1. *Observational studies with matched pairs*—Suppose you wanted to compare starting salaries of graduates of the Business program with salaries of graduates of the Computer Studies program. Obviously, there are many factors that could affect salary, such as work experience, intelligence, location of job, and so on. If you wanted to make a valid comparison by program, you would match each graduate of the Business program in your sample to a graduate of the Computer Studies program. If the graduates were matched as closely as possible according to these other factors, you could more safely suggest that any observed difference was caused by program of study. In this case, you would want to directly compare the salary of the Business graduate with the salary of the corresponding graduate of the Computer Studies program.

2. *Experimental studies with matched pairs*—Suppose a company wants to test the effects of a training program on worker errors (this situation was first discussed in Example 1.4A on page 16). A group of workers is randomly selected at a particular plant, and the number of errors made by each worker is recorded over a period of time. The workers are then put through a training program, and the numbers of errors are recorded again after the training. It makes sense to compare the errors of each worker before the training to the same worker's errors after the training.

In either situation, it is crucial that you recognize that you have matched-pairs data. If you miss this, you might draw the wrong conclusion!

If the data were produced from a matched-pairs experiment, then the techniques of Chapter 9 apply, and the other decisions you will have to make are whether the data are normal or non-normal quantitative data, or ranked data. The headings in the chapter will guide you to the appropriate techniques: Section 9.1 for matched pairs with normally distributed differences, Section 9.2 for matched pairs with non-normally distributed differences, and Section 9.3 for matched pairs of ranked data. If the samples are independent, you will need techniques from Chapter 10, 11, or 12 to complete your analysis.

9.1

MATCHED PAIRS, QUANTITATIVE DATA, NORMALLY DISTRIBUTED DIFFERENCES—THE t-TEST AND CONFIDENCE INTERVAL OF μ_D

The foreman in a small assembly plant wants to see if a training program results in a reduced number of worker errors. The foreman records the weekly number of errors for a random sample of workers before the training, and again after the training. In some cases, the number of worker errors decreased, in other cases, the number of errors stayed about the same, and in still other cases, the number of errors actually increased after the training. The foreman now has to decide whether to continue the training. The foreman is in a situation that is by now familiar to us: he has to decide whether the training would reduce the number of errors if it were applied to the population of *all* workers, on the basis of these data about a sample of workers.

This is a matched-pairs experiment. The foreman should compare the errors before and after the training for each particular worker. In a situation like this (a matched-pairs experiment and quantitative data), we focus on the differences in the matching observations in the samples.

If the positive and negative differences are offsetting, this results in an average difference of zero, indicating that there is no significant difference in the before and after measurements. However, even if the average difference in the population is actually zero, we would not expect the average difference in the sample to be *exactly* zero, because of sampling variability. Therefore, we have to do a test of hypothesis to determine if the average difference is significantly different from zero.

We will use the subscript D to remind us that we are dealing with the differences between corresponding observations. Generally, then, we will be comparing a null hypothesis H_0: $\mu_D = 0$ (that is, no significant difference) with one of three possible alternative hypotheses:

- $\mu_D > 0$
- $\mu_D < 0$
- $\mu_D \neq 0$

A decision about which of the three possible alternative hypotheses to use will depend on the context of the analysis, *and the order of subtraction.*

The first step in the analysis is to calculate the differences between the corresponding observations to produce the single data set that we will focus on. The order of subtraction does not matter, *as long as the subtraction is done consistently.* If you are calculating the difference as [(sample 1 observation) − (sample 2 observation)], all the differences must be calculated in the same way. The foreman might calculate the differences in the number of worker errors as [(number of errors before training) − (number of errors after training)], or the other way around. The order does not matter, as long as it is consistent. Once the data set of differences is created, you proceed with a hypothesis test of the mean, as in Chapter 7. There is really nothing new here, because we are focusing on a single data set of differences. The technique you have already learned is simply being applied to a new situation, as Example 9.1A illustrates.

EXAMPLE 9.1A

The *t*-test for matched pairs

Suppose you wanted to study the effect of receiving a promotion on how often people visit the gym, because you believe that promotions lead to increased work and reduced visits to the gym. You examine a random sample of people who have received a promotion, and you gather data on their monthly gym visits before and after their promotions. The data are provided in the table shown in Exhibit 9.1.

EXHIBIT 9.1

Sample Data: Monthly Gym Visits Before and After a Promotion, Section 9.1

	Monthly Gym Visits	
Person	Before Promotion	After Promotion
Joe	10	7
Sally	13	11
Hugo	14	10
Meriel	15	15
Juanita	15	14
Tadashi	15	14
Noel	18	19
Joanne	22	21
Heather	23	25
Barb	25	20

This is certainly a matched-pairs sample. It would not make sense to compare the gym visits of Joe after promotion with the gym visits of Heather before promotion!

The first step is to calculate the differences in the number of visits. The order of subtraction does not matter, so we will simply subtract as [(visits before promotion) – (visits after promotion)]. This leads to the data set of differences shown in Exhibit 9.2.

EXHIBIT 9.2

Differences in Monthly Gym Visits Before and After Promotion, Section 9.1

	Monthly Gym Visits
Person	Visits Before Promotion – Visits After Promotion
Joe	3
Sally	2
Hugo	4
Meriel	0
Juanita	1
Tadashi	1
Noel	−1
Joanne	1
Heather	−2
Barb	5

Now we will follow the steps for a hypothesis test of the mean, as outlined in Chapter 7.

First we have to specify H_0 and H_1, the null and alternative hypotheses. As noted above, the null hypothesis is that the average difference is zero, so we have $H_0: \mu_D = 0$. Now we have to determine the alternative hypothesis. In this case, it is believed that promotions lead to fewer gym visits.

This is where you have to think about the order of subtraction. If promotions reduced the number of gym visits (this is the alternative hypothesis), then the number of visits to the gym *before* the promotion should be higher than the number of gym visits *after* the promotion. We will be examining the data to see if there is evidence that the average difference is positive, given the [(before) − (after)] order of subtraction we chose. This leads to $H_1: \mu_D > 0$, for the order of subtraction used here.

What if we had used the [(after) − (before)] order of subtraction? Then the null hypothesis would be $H_1: \mu_D < 0$. This is a completely equivalent way of approaching the analysis. You should always think carefully about the order of subtraction before you specify the alternative hypothesis in a matched-pairs analysis.

Suppose we use $\alpha = 0.05$. The data have already been collected, and the differences have been calculated. We must now identify or calculate the average difference in the sample, the standard deviation of the differences in the sample, and the sample size (as in Chapter 7).

Continuing on with the subscripts to remind ourselves that we are working with differences, and using the standard formulas, we find the following values.

- There are 10 observations, so $n_D = 10$.

$$\bar{x}_D = \frac{\sum x_D}{n_D} = \frac{14}{10} = 1.4$$

$$s_D = \sqrt{\frac{\sum x_D^2 - \frac{(\sum x_D)^2}{n_D}}{n_D - 1}} = \sqrt{\frac{62 - \frac{(14)^2}{10}}{10 - 1}} = 2.17051$$

As in Chapter 7, we must check for normality of the sample data, by creating a histogram of the differences. One possible histogram is shown on the next page in Exhibit 9.3.

As usual, it is difficult to assess normality with a small sample. Since the histogram appears to be somewhat normal, we will assume that the population of differences is also normally distributed. We now calculate the appropriate t-score, again using the familiar formula.

$$t = \frac{\bar{x}_D - \mu_D}{s_D / \sqrt{n_D}} = \frac{1.4 - 0}{2.17051 / \sqrt{10}} = 2.0397$$

With 10 matched pairs, there are 10 differences and $n_D - 1 = 10 - 1 = 9$ degrees of freedom. Exhibit 9.4 shows the appropriate row from the t-table.

This is a one-tailed test, so the p-value is somewhere between 2.5% and 5%. Since this is less than the α of 5%, we reject the null hypothesis. There is sufficient evidence to suggest that gym visits decline after a promotion.

Notice that we have put the conclusion in terms of the original question. If we had said instead that there was sufficient evidence to suggest that $\mu_D > 0$, very few people would understand the result. Your analysis will be useful only if it is clearly communicated.

EXHIBIT 9.3

Histogram of the Differences in Monthly Gym Visits Before and After Promotion, Section 9.1

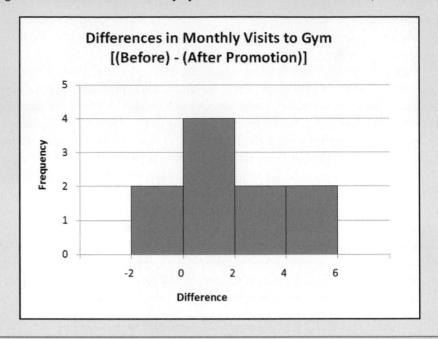

EXHIBIT 9.4

t-Distribution Critical Values

Degrees of Freedom	$t_{.100}$	$t_{.050}$	$t_{.025}$	$t_{.010}$	$t_{.005}$
9	1.383	1.833	2.262	2.821	3.250

2.0397

Using the Excel Template for Making Decisions About the Population Mean with a Single Sample Of course, we could have done this analysis using an Excel formula to calculate the differences in the matched pairs of observations. Then we could have used the template introduced in Chapter 7 for hypothesis tests about the mean, with a single sample. Remember that, effectively, we are dealing with only one sample here—the sample of differences. A completed template is shown in Exhibit 9.5.

As usual, the values of the standard deviation, the mean, and the sample size are calculated using the **STDEV**, **AVERAGE**, and **COUNT** functions of Excel. Be sure that you use Excel to calculate the differences in the before and after data values. Note that you can also use this template whenever you have only summary data from the samples.

Using the Data Analysis *t*-Test: Paired Two Sample for Means Excel has a built-in Data Analysis tool that allows you to do matched-pairs data comparisons when you have normally distributed data. Exhibit 9.6 opposite shows the **Data Analysis** menu (under the **Data** tab). The correct choice is highlighted: ***t*-Test: Paired Two Sample for Means**.

EXHIBIT 9.5

Excel Template for Making Decisions About the Population Mean with a Single Sample

Making Decisions About the Population Mean with a Single Sample	
Do the sample data appear to be normally distributed?	yes
Sample Standard Deviation s	2.17051
Sample Mean	1.4
Sample Size n	10.00
Hypothetical Value of Population Mean	0
t-Score	2.0397
One-Tailed p-Value	0.0359
Two-Tailed p-Value	0.0718

EXHIBIT 9.6

Excel Data Analysis Menu

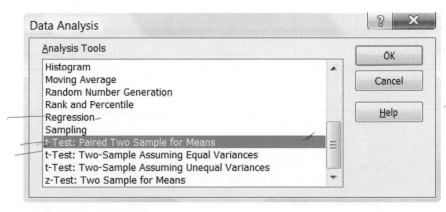

You should do some thinking about your hypothesis test before you activate the Excel tool. As well, you must check for normality of the differences. Excel does not do this; it will conduct the *t*-test whether the data are normal or not! Exhibit 9.7 on the next page shows the *t*-test dialogue box.

The dialogue box requires you to indicate to Excel where the sample data are stored (**Variable 1 Range:** and **Variable 2 Range:**). As indicated in Exhibit 9.7, the **Hypothesized Mean Difference** is zero (and usually will be). The Excel output for Example 9.1A is shown in Exhibit 9.8.

We can see from the output that the one-tailed *p*-value is 0.0359 (see the highlighted row in the table—note that it will *not* be highlighted in the Excel output). This of course agrees with our previous calculations. The **Data Analysis** tool in Excel can be used whenever you have data sets for matched-pairs data comparisons, and you have established that the data are normally distributed. *Be sure to check for normality of differences first.*

EXHIBIT 9.7

Dialogue Box for *t*-Test: Paired Two Sample for Means

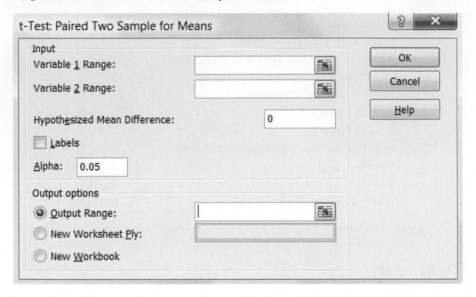

EXHIBIT 9.8

Excel Output for Example 9.1A

t-Test: Paired Two Sample for Means

	Before	After
Mean	17	15.6
Variance	23.55556	31.15556
Observations	10	10
Pearson Correlation	0.922838	
Hypothesized Mean Difference	0	
df	9	
t Stat	2.0397	
P(T<=t) one-tail	0.0359	
t Critical one-tail	1.833113	
P(T<=t) two-tail	0.0718	
t Critical two-tail	2.262157	

EXAMPLE 9.1B

The *t*-test for matched pairs

A random sample of three-bedroom bungalows in one particular Edmonton suburb was selected. In the month of July, two real estate agents were asked to look at the properties and suggest listing prices.

The data are shown in Exhibit 9.9 below. At the 3% level of significance, is there evidence that Amanda Hargreave suggests listing prices that are different from those suggested by Nick O'Brien?

EXA09-1b

EXHIBIT 9.9

Two Agents' Suggested Listing Prices, Edmonton Bungalows

	Random Sample of Three-Bedroom Bungalows in an Edmonton Suburb, July	
House	Amanda Hargreave's Suggested Listing Price	Nick O'Brien's Suggested Listing Price
1	250,900	249,600
2	242,700	242,200
3	256,600	255,200
4	263,600	263,200
5	263,600	262,800
6	264,600	264,800
7	239,050	239,900
8	251,100	250,300
9	263,900	262,300
10	244,200	243,200
11	246,000	246,000
12	239,800	240,700
13	210,500	210,100
14	245,100	243,800
15	245,700	245,300
16	241,000	240,000
17	247,300	247,000
18	249,300	248,600
19	254,600	254,100
20	249,800	248,900

Since this data set is available in an Excel worksheet, we will use Excel for the analysis. The first step is to calculate the differences in the prices recommended by the two agents, and then check to see if the differences are normally distributed. We will subtract as follows: [(Amanda Hargreave's suggested listing price) − (Nick O'Brien's suggested listing price)]. A histogram of the differences is shown in Exhibit 9.10 on the following page.

The histogram is somewhat negatively skewed, but fairly normal, so we will proceed.

- H_0: $\mu_D = 0$
- H_1: $\mu_D \neq 0$
- $\alpha = 0.03$

A completed template for the differences is shown in Exhibit 9.11 on the next page.

This is a two-tailed test, so the appropriate p-value from the template is 0.00184. The p-value is $< \alpha$, so we reject H_0. There is sufficient evidence to suggest that the recommended listing prices of the two agents are different.

EXHIBIT **9.10**

Histogram of Differences in Agents' Listing Prices

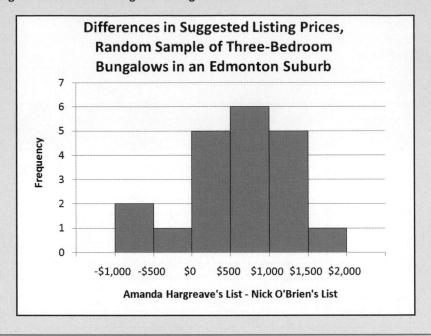

EXHIBIT **9.11**

Completed Excel Template for Making Decisions About the Population Mean with a Single Sample

Making Decisions About the Population Mean with a Single Sample	
Do the sample data appear to be normally distributed?	yes
Sample Standard Deviation s	683.157
Sample Mean	552.5
Sample Size n	20
Hypothetical Value of Population Mean	0
t-Score	3.61682
One-Tailed p-Value	0.00092
Two-Tailed p-Value	0.00184

GUIDE TO DECISION MAKING

Matched Pairs, Quantitative Data, Normal Differences—The t-Test to Decide About the Average Population Difference (μ_D)

When:

- matched pairs of quantitative data with normally distributed differences
- trying to make a decision about the average difference, μ_D, on the basis of $\bar{x}_D$, the average of the sample differences

Steps:

1. Specify H_0, the null hypothesis, which will be $\mu_D = 0$. Specify your hypotheses in words that reflect the context of the problem.
2. Specify H_1, the alternative hypothesis.
3. Determine or identify α, the significance level.
4. Collect or identify the sample data. Identify or calculate the differences between the matching observations in the samples (keeping the order of subtraction consistent).
5. Check for normality of sample differences with a histogram. If the histogram is non-normal, particularly with small sample sizes, do not proceed with the t-test (use the Wilcoxon Signed Rank Sum Test instead, described on page 339).
6. *If* the sample differences appear to be normally distributed, identify or calculate:

   - $\bar{x}_D$, the average of the differences (*including* zero differences)
   - s_D, the standard deviation of the differences
   - n_D, the number of differences (*including* zero differences)

7. Calculate the appropriate t-score, using the following formula:

$$t = \frac{\bar{x}_D - \mu_D}{s_D/\sqrt{n_D}}$$

8. Use the t-distribution with $n_D - 1$ degrees of freedom to calculate (or approximate, if using tables) the appropriate p-value for the hypothesis test, keeping in mind the order of subtraction used when calculating the differences.
9. If p-value $\leq \alpha$, reject H_0 and conclude that there is sufficient evidence to decide in favour of H_1. If p-value $> \alpha$, fail to reject H_0 and conclude that there is insufficient evidence to decide in favour of H_1. State your conclusions in language appropriate to the problem.

See Example 9.1A on page 328 (using the t-tables), and Example 9.1B on page 332 (using Excel).

Confidence Interval Estimate of μ_D

Following directly from the sampling distribution and the discussion of the hypothesis test, a confidence interval estimate can be constructed for the average difference in population means, as follows:

(point estimate) $\pm$ (critical value) • (estimate standard error of the sample statistic)

$$\bar{x}_D \pm \text{critical } t\text{-score}\left(\frac{s_D}{\sqrt{n_D}}\right)$$

where the critical t-score corresponds to the desired level of confidence, and has $n_D - 1$ degrees of freedom. Of course, the histogram of differences must be normal for this formula to be appropriate. Example 9.1C below illustrates the construction of the confidence interval.

EXAMPLE 9.1C

Confidence interval for μ_D

Financial planners collect data about their clients' circumstances, and then use a number of assumptions about the future to recommend savings plans. A researcher wanted to determine if a financial planner at a local bank branch was consistently using pessimistic assumptions about the future, resulting in recommendations for higher-than-necessary savings for clients. A random sample of 15 clients was sent to the bank's financial planner, and to a highly respected fee-for-service financial advisor. The differences in recommended monthly savings, calculated as [(bank planner's recommended savings) – (fee-for-service advisor's recommended savings)] appeared to be normally distributed. The mean difference in monthly savings recommended was $45.21, with a standard deviation of $12.35. Construct a 95% confidence interval estimate for the mean difference in recommended monthly savings.

We have been told that the sample differences are normally distributed, and we will assume that the population of differences is also. We proceed by substituting the sample statistics into the confidence interval estimate formula.

$$\bar{x}_D \pm \text{critical } t\text{-score}\left(\frac{s_D}{\sqrt{n_D}}\right)$$

$$= 45.21 \pm t\text{-score}\left(\frac{12.35}{\sqrt{15}}\right)$$

The t-score for a 95% confidence interval with $15 - 1 = 14$ degrees of freedom is 2.145, as illustrated in the excerpt from the t-table shown in Exhibit 9.12.

EXHIBIT 9.12

t-Distribution Critical Values

Degrees of Freedom	$t_{.100}$	$t_{.050}$	$t_{.025}$	$t_{.010}$	$t_{.005}$
14	1.345	1.761	2.145	2.624	2.977

for 95% CI

The remaining calculations are as follows.

$$45.21 \pm 2.145\left(\frac{12.35}{\sqrt{15}}\right)$$

$$= 45.21 \pm 6.8399$$

$$= (38.37, 52.05)$$

A 95% confidence interval for the mean difference in recommended monthly savings is ($38.37, $52.05). In other words, we have 95% confidence that the interval ($38.37, $52.05) contains the average amount that the bank's financial planner is recommending in monthly savings above the savings recommended by the fee-for-service financial planner.

Notice that since this confidence interval does not contain zero, we know that a hypothesis test would conclude that there is sufficient evidence to reject the null hypothesis of no difference in recommended monthly savings between the two financial advisors (two-tailed test, with $\alpha = 0.05$).

Using the Excel Template for a Confidence Interval Estimate of μ_D You can use the template for the confidence interval of a population mean (first discussed in Chapter 8 on page 311) to construct this confidence interval. A completed template for the example above is shown in Exhibit 9.13.

EXHIBIT 9.13

Completed Excel Template for the Confidence Interval Estimate for the Population Mean

Confidence Interval Estimate for the Population Mean	
Do the sample data appear to be normally distributed?	yes
Confidence Level (decimal form)	0.95
Sample Mean	45.21
Sample Standard Deviation s	12.35
Sample Size n	15
Upper Confidence Limit	52.0492
Lower Confidence Limit	38.3708

As usual, Excel yields a slightly more accurate confidence interval estimate than our manual calculations.

DEVELOP YOUR SKILLS 9.1

1. The foreman in a small assembly plant believes that playing classical music in the plant will improve worker productivity. To try to prove his point, the foreman conducts an experiment. He records the average daily production levels for a random sample of workers over a four-week period. He then plays music in the plant, and records the average daily production levels for the same workers over another four-week period (some time after the music was started). The results of the study are shown on the next page in Exhibit 9.14.

DYS09-1

EXHIBIT 9.14

Worker Production

Worker	Average Daily Production Before Music	Average Daily Production After Music
1	18	18
2	14	15
3	10	12
4	11	15
5	9	7
6	10	11
7	9	6
8	11	14
9	10	11
10	12	12

EXHIBIT 9.15

Cookie Sales Data, Develop Your Skills 9.1

Weekly Sales Before and After Product Redesign		
Store	Sales After	Sales Before
51 Bayfield	842.42	813.67
109 Mapleview Drive	831.54	698.71
137 Wellington	822.86	734.48
6 Collier	876.97	832.46
421 Essa Road	776.44	791.22
19 Queen	793.19	766.73
345 Cundles	730.17	668.66
D-564 Byrne Drive	576.95	631.05
24 Archer	758.87	724.39
15 Short St.	736.04	766.76

Is there sufficient evidence, at the 4% significance level, to suggest that playing classical music led to increased worker productivity?

2. A small company that specializes in gourmet cookies decides to redesign its packaging. The company owner is certain that the new package will lead to increased sales. Weekly sales at a random sample of stores in the Barrie area are recorded before and after the change in package design. Using the 5% level of significance, analyze the data to see if the owner's idea is correct. Also, construct a 90% confidence interval estimate of the differences in sales after the product redesign.

DYS09-2

The data set is available in MyStatLab and is reproduced in Exhibit 9.15.

3. Telemarketers generally read from a prepared script when they make their sales calls. A firm decides to change this prepared script, making it both friendlier and shorter. Daily sales are recorded for a random sample of telemarketers, before and after the script change. The average difference—using a [(before the change) − (after the change)] order of subtraction—is +4.2, with a sample size of 56. The differences have a standard deviation of 23.4. Do the data suggest that there is a difference in daily sales before and after the script change? Use $\alpha = 0.05$. What assumption do you have to make in order to answer this question?

4. The Student Services Department at a Prince Edward Island college wants to see whether there are differences in the study habits of male and female students. A

DYS09-4

random sample of female students is selected, and then a corresponding sample of male students is designed—same programs, ages, previous educational experience, and living arrangements (that is, all of the students are living away from their parents). The students are asked to keep track of the number of hours they study over a four-week period.

Does it appear, based on these data, that male students study less than female students? Use a 2% significance level. Construct a 96% confidence interval estimate of the average amount of time that male students study less than their female counterparts.

5. An automobile association wants to demonstrate that maintaining tire pressure results in better fuel economy. The association selected a random sample of its members, and asked them to record their fuel consumption in litres per 100 km for all of their driving for one month. It then asked the members to check and adjust tire pressures every 3 to 4 days, for another month, and record their fuel consumption again. The average difference in number of litres per 100 km was 0.4, with the standard deviation of the differences being 1.4. The order of subtraction was [(fuel consumption without checking tires) − (fuel consumption with checking tires)]. The sample size was 20. The histogram of differences appears to be normally distributed. Do these data support the association's claim that maintaining tire pressure improves fuel economy? Use a 4% significance level. What else might explain the results in this case?

9.2   MATCHED PAIRS, QUANTITATIVE DATA, NON-NORMAL DIFFERENCES—THE WILCOXON SIGNED RANK SUM TEST

What if you have a matched-pairs sample with quantitative data, but the histogram of differences reveals significant non-normality (particularly with small sample sizes)? Fortunately, you can still proceed with the analysis, using a technique called the Wilcoxon Signed Rank Sum Test (WSRST). This is an example of a distribution-free statistical method, which does not require that the populations conform to any particular distribution (such as the normal).

The WSRST can be used whenever the differences in matched data points are symmetric about their median. This will be the case whenever the matched populations have similar shape and spread. As usual, we check for required symmetry in the population differences by constructing a histogram of the sample differences.

For the WSRST, the analysis begins in exactly the same way as with normal quantitative data. Differences between corresponding observations in each sample are computed. One change with WSRST is that we will disregard any differences that are zero (these differences are included in the t-test of μ_D, but are not included in the WSRST—make sure you remember this distinction). We will refer to the number of non-zero differences as n_W.

As before, if the positive and negative differences are offsetting, we would have evidence of *no difference* in the before and after measurements. We assess the positive and negative differences by looking not at the values of the differences but at the *ranks* of the differences.[1] We begin by assigning ranks (1, 2, 3, 4, . . . , n, from smallest to largest) to the absolute values of the differences (that is, we ignore the minus signs on the negative differences when the ranks are assigned). We then compare the sum of the ranks for the negative differences and the positive differences. If the positive and negative differences are approximately offsetting, then the ranks would be fairly evenly distributed between the positive and negative differences, and the sums of the ranks would be about the same. Only if the sums of the ranks are significantly different do we have evidence that there is a difference in population locations.

First we will look at a small numerical example to illustrate how to assign the ranks properly. Then we will go back to the gym visits example, with a larger data set having non-normal differences, to show the complete hypothesis testing procedure.

A small numerical example of before and after matched-pairs data is shown in Exhibit 9.16 on the next page, with the differences calculated as [(before event) − (after event)].

We will go through the ranking process step by step. Since we ignore the signs on the differences when we assign ranks, the next step is to record the absolute value of the differences. Ultimately, though, we will want to be able to tell which ranks were assigned to positive differences, and which were assigned to negative differences. To make this easy, we will record negative differences and their assigned ranks in red. This is shown in Exhibit 9.17.

---

[1] You have seen the ranking process before, when the Spearman Rank Correlation Coefficient was discussed, in Chapter 3.

EXHIBIT 9.16

Data Set for Rank Assignment Demonstration

	Sample Data	
Before	**After**	**Differences**
119	133	−14
105	127	−22
130	130	0
145	119	26
144	133	11
148	154	−6
101	107	−6
120	114	6
143	134	9
107	121	−14

EXHIBIT 9.17

Data Set for Rank Assignment Demonstration, Absolute Value of Difference

	Sample Data		
Before	**After**	**Differences**	**Absolute Value of Differences**
119	133	−14	14
105	127	−22	22
130	130	0	0
145	119	26	26
144	133	11	11
148	154	−6	6
101	107	−6	6
120	114	6	6
143	134	9	9
107	121	−14	14

Next, we put the differences in order, from smallest to largest (in absolute value). For the WSRST, we eliminate any differences of zero. The ordered differences are shown opposite in Exhibit 9.18. Also shown is a column of the ranks that must be assigned to the non-zero differences.

We cannot assign the ranks exactly as shown here, because we have to deal with tied differences carefully. The example contains a couple of cases in which the differences are of the same size, but the ranks initially assigned to them are different. For example, there are three differences of 6 (in absolute value) and, in Exhibit 9.18, one has a rank of 1, one has a rank of 2, and one has a rank of 3. It does not seem sensible to assign unequal rankings to equal differences of 6, simply as a result of the order in which the differences were recorded. So that each difference of the same absolute value is treated equally, we average the ranks of tied differences, and assign the averaged rank to each of the tied values. The ranks of 1, 2, and 3 have to be equally allocated to the three differences of 6. We assign each difference a rank of $\dfrac{1 + 2 + 3}{3} = \dfrac{6}{3} = 2$. Similarly, there are two

EXHIBIT 9.18

Demonstration Data with Ordered Differences and Ranks to Be Assigned

Absolute Value of Differences	Ordered Differences	Ranks to be Assigned
14	0	ignore
22	6	1
0	6	2
26	6	3
11	9	4
6	11	5
6	14	6
6	14	7
9	22	8
14	26	9

EXHIBIT 9.19

Demonstration Data, Ranked

Absolute Value of Differences	Ordered Differences	Ranks to Be Assigned	Assigned Ranks
14	0		
22	6	1	2
0	6	2	2
26	6	3	2
11	9	4	4
6	11	5	5
6	14	6	6.5
6	14	7	6.5
9	22	8	8
14	26	9	9

differences of 14, with associated ranks of 6 and 7. We assign a rank of $\dfrac{6 + 7}{2} = 6.5$ to each difference of 14. Once the tied values are accounted for, the final assigned ranks are as shown in Exhibit 9.19 above.

Next, we sum the ranks of the positive differences to get what we will refer to as W^+, and we sum the ranks of the negative differences to get what we will refer to as W^-. This is shown in Exhibit 9.20, on the next page.

We see that $W^+ = 20$ and $W^- = 25$. One way to check that you have assigned the ranks correctly is to total W^+ and W^-: the sum should be equal to the sum of the column of ranks to be assigned. This is a quick way to pick up any errors you might have made in averaging the tied ranks—in this case, $20 + 25 = 45$.

In general, when we rank n numbers, the sum of the ranks will be equal to $\dfrac{n(n + 1)}{2}$. This means that $W^- + W^+ - \dfrac{n(n + 1)}{2}$. Notice that if the positive and

EXHIBIT 9.20

Demonstration Data with Rank Sums

Sample Data					
Absolute Value of Differences	Ordered Differences	Ranks to Be Assigned	Assigned Ranks	Positive Ranks	Negative Ranks
14	0				
22	6	1	2		2
0	6	2	2		2
26	6	3	2	2	
11	9	4	4	4	
6	11	5	5	5	
6	14	6	6.5		6.5
6	14	7	6.5		6.5
9	22	8	8		8
14	26	9	9	9	
Sum of the Ranks		45	45	$W^+ = 20$	$W^- = 25$

negative differences are approximately offsetting, the ranks will be fairly evenly distributed between the positive and negative differences, and the sums of the positive and negative ranks would be about the same. With 9 data points, the sum of all the ranks would be $\frac{9(9+1)}{2} = 45$, and W^- and W^+ would both be close to $\frac{45}{2} = 22.5$.

To develop your intuition about possible values of the sums of the ranks, we will consider some specific cases. First, suppose there were only negative differences. This would provide strong evidence that the first measurements were smaller than the second. In this extreme case, $W^- = 1 + 2 + \cdots + 9 = 45$, and $W^+ = 0$. Exhibit 9.21 below illustrates.

EXHIBIT 9.21

Possible Values of W^- and W^+, Negative Difference

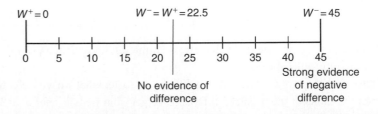

Another extreme case would be only positive differences. This would provide strong evidence that the first measurements were larger than the second. In this extreme case, $W^+ = 1 + 2 + \cdots + 9 = 45$, and $W^- = 0$. Exhibit 9.22 opposite illustrates this.

Now, suppose there are only two negative differences, and they are the smallest (in absolute value). In this case, the positive differences would overwhelm the negative differences, providing strong evidence of a positive difference. In this case, $W^- = 1 + 2 = 3$, and $W^+ = 3 + 4 + \cdots + 9 = 42$. Exhibit 9.23 illustrates this.

EXHIBIT **9.22**

Possible Values of W^- and W^+, Positive Difference

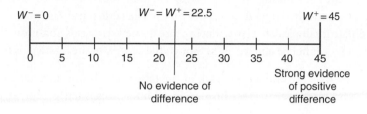

EXHIBIT **9.23**

Possible Values of W^- and W^+, Positive Difference

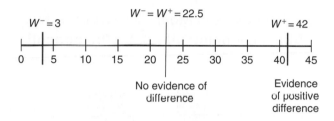

The further apart W^- and W^+ are, the greater the evidence of difference. The tail probabilities are equal; that is, $P(W^+ \geq 42) = P(W^- \leq 3) = 0.010$. But how do we calculate the tail probabilities? As usual, we need a sampling distribution of the rank sums so that we can decide whether the sample results are sufficiently unusual to allow us to reject the null hypothesis of no difference. When sample sizes are large, the sampling distribution of W is approximately normal, and when sample sizes are small, we use the tables in Appendix 4.

Sampling Distribution of W (Wilcoxon Signed Rank Sum Test)

For $n_W \geq 25$, the sampling distribution of either W is approximately normally distributed.

1. The standard error of the sampling distribution is calculated with the following formula, where n_W is the number of non-zero differences:

$$\sigma_W = \sqrt{\frac{n_W(n_W + 1)(2n_W + 1)}{24}}$$

2. The mean of the sampling distribution is as follows:

$$\mu_W = \frac{n_W(n_W + 1)}{4}$$

This information about the sampling distribution allows us to calculate p-values for the hypothesis tests (whenever sample sizes are 25 or more). As usual, when you are doing the exercises by hand and using the normal table, you would calculate a z-score of the usual form:

$$z = \frac{W - \mu_W}{\sigma_W} = \frac{W - \dfrac{n_W(n_W + 1)}{4}}{\sqrt{\dfrac{n_W(n_W + 1)(2n_W + 1)}{24}}}$$

EXAMPLE 9.2A

Wilcoxon Signed Rank Sum Test, sample size ≥25

 EXA09-2a

Now that we have gone through the process for assigning ranks, we will go back to the gym visits example, but with a larger data set with non-normal differences (in other words, same problem, different sample data). Note that because the new data set is non-normal, the *t*-test from Section 9.1 cannot be applied, even though the context of the problem is the same.

We have a new data set, and a histogram of the differences is non-normal, as shown in Exhibit 9.24 below. Notice that the histogram of differences is fairly symmetric.

EXHIBIT 9.24

Histogram of Differences in Gym Visits, Section 9.2

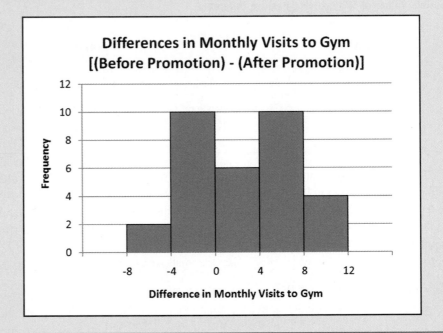

The data set is shown opposite in Exhibit 9.25, as are all the steps to order the data and assign ranks. As before, the negative differences are recorded in red for easy tracking. There are many tied differences in this data set, and so many of the ranks have to be averaged.

Exhibit 9.25 looks a bit daunting, but if you follow it step by step, you will see that the process of assigning ranks is not that difficult. As well, an Excel add-in is available to help you assign ranks and calculate rank sums for larger data sets such as the one in Exhibit 9.25.

We can focus on either W^+ or W^- to make a decision. You may find one of the values more logical for your focus, in the context of the order of subtraction you chose and the alternative hypothesis.

As before, the null hypothesis is that there is no difference in the visits to the gym before promotion and after promotion. We will use a significance level of 5% for this example.

- H_0: There is no difference in monthly gym visits before and after promotion.
- H_1: Monthly gym visits decreased after promotion.

EXHIBIT 9.25

Gym Visits, Section 9.2 With Ordering and Ranking

Monthly Gym Visits								
Before Promotion	After Promotion	Differences [(Before Promotion) − (After Promotion)]	Absolute Value of Differences	Ordered Differences	Ranks to Be Assigned	Assigned Ranks	+Ranks	−Ranks
10	2	8	8	0	Ignore			
13	6	7	7	1	1	4.5		4.5
14	8	6	6	1	2	4.5		4.5
15	15	0	0	1	3	4.5		4.5
15	5	10	10	1	4	4.5		4.5
15	18	−3	3	1	5	4.5	4.5	
18	25	−7	7	1	6	4.5	4.5	
22	25	−3	3	1	7	4.5	4.5	
23	25	−2	2	1	8	4.5		4.5
25	17	8	8	2	9	10		10
11	12	−1	1	2	10	10		10
14	15	−1	1	2	11	10		10
15	10	5	5	3	12	13.5		13.5
16	11	5	5	3	13	13.5		13.5
16	9	7	7	3	14	13.5	13.5	
17	12	5	5	3	15	13.5	13.5	
19	21	−2	2	4	16	16	16	
23	28	−5	5	5	17	19.5	19.5	
21	22	−1	1	5	18	19.5	19.5	
15	12	3	3	5	19	19.5	19.5	
21	17	4	4	5	20	19.5		19.5
8	9	−1	1	5	21	19.5	19.5	
5	4	1	1	5	22	19.5	19.5	
13	12	1	1	6	23	23	23	
12	7	5	5	7	24	25.5	25.5	
11	13	−2	2	7	25	25.5		25.5
23	20	3	3	7	26	25.5	25.5	
18	17	1	1	7	27	25.5	25.5	
19	20	−1	1	8	28	29	29	
19	12	7	7	8	29	29	29	
10	2	8	8	8	30	29	29	
15	10	5	5	10	31	31	31	
			Sum of the Ranks		496	496	$W^+ =$ 371.5	$W^- =$ 124.5

- $\alpha = 0.05$, as given above
- $W^+ = 371.5$ and $W^- = 124.5$, as calculated above
- $n_W = 31$ (there are 31 non-zero differences)

Since $n_W \geq 25$, we can use the sampling distribution of W described on page 343.

We can focus on either W^+ or W^-. Because the sampling distribution of W is symmetric, P($W \geq$ largest rank sum) = P($W \leq$ smallest rank sum). This is a one-tailed test, so the p-value will be P($W^+ \geq 371.5$) = P($W^- \leq 124.5$). To see why this is so, remember that the alternative hypothesis is that monthly gym visits decreased after the person received a promotion. If this were true, then the number of before promotion monthly gym visits would generally be higher than the after promotion gym visits. Because the order of subtraction was [(before promotion) − (after promotion)], the alternative hypothesis implies more positive differences than negative ones. This also means that the sum of the ranks of the positive differences should be large, and the sum of the ranks of the negative differences should be small. A large W^+ *or* a small W^- would provide evidence in favour of the alternative hypothesis, contrary to the null hypothesis.

This does not mean that you can ignore the order of subtraction. In this problem, if the largest rank sum was W^-, this would seem to indicate that gym visits *increased* after promotion! So that you do not miss this situation (somewhat unlikely, given H_1), you should always think about the order of subtraction in these problems when you are doing a one-tailed test.

Suppose we focus on W^+.

$$\mu_W = \frac{n_W(n_W + 1)}{4} = \frac{31(31 + 1)}{4} = 248$$

$$\sigma_W = \sqrt{\frac{n_W(n_W + 1)(2n_W + 1)}{24}} = \sqrt{\frac{31(31 + 1)(2(31) + 1)}{24}} = 51.0294$$

$$z = \frac{W^+ - u_W}{\sigma_W} = \frac{371.5 - 248}{51.0294} = 2.42$$

The p-value = P($W^+ \geq 371.5$) = P($z \geq 2.42$) = $1 - 0.9922 = 0.0078$. The p-value is very small. If the null hypothesis were true, it would be highly unlikely that we could get a sample result like the one we got. The sample evidence gives us reason to reject the null hypothesis. There is sufficient evidence to suggest that individuals who received a promotion reduced their monthly visits to the gym.

You should notice two things about Example 9.2A. First, the conclusion is stated in language that relates to the original example, and is understandable, even by someone who did not fully understand the details of the analysis. Second, this is just a hypothesis test like any of the others we have already done. Once the initial conditions are examined and the correct sampling distribution is identified, the process is the same as usual.

As well, you should now be able to see why the Wilcoxon Signed Rank Sum Test is called a *distribution-free* technique: the decision is made based on the *ranks* of the differences; there is no longer a requirement that the actual differences be normally distributed. This technique is also sometimes referred to as a *non-parametric* technique, because the null and alternative hypotheses do not refer to a population parameter such as μ.

Using the Excel Add-in and Template for Sample Sizes ≥25 There is no built-in data analysis tool in Excel to allow you to conduct a Wilcoxon Signed Rank Sum Test. Some Excel add-ins are available in MyStatLab, however, and once these add-ins are installed (see the instructions on p. xxx), you will be able to use Excel to calculate the sums of the ranks for the Wilcoxon Signed Rank Sum Test. Click on the **Add-Ins** tab, then click on **Non-Parametric Tools**, then choose **Wilcoxon Signed Rank Sum Test Calculations**, as illustrated in Exhibit 9.26 below.

EXHIBIT 9.26

Excel Dialogue Box for Non-Parametric Tools

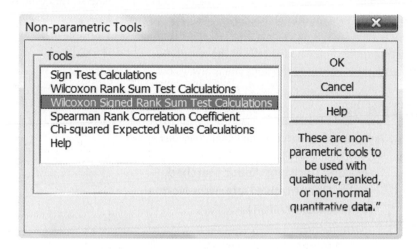

The next dialogue box is shown in Exhibit 9.27.

You must indicate where the sample data are located, and where you want the output to go. The output is shown on the next page in Exhibit 9.28.

Note that the order of subtraction for the Excel add-in is always (sample one observation − sample two observation).

EXHIBIT 9.27

Excel Dialogue Box for Wilcoxon Signed Rank Sum Test Calculations

EXHIBIT 9.28

Wilcoxon Signed Rank Sum Test Calculations Output

Wilcoxon Signed Rank Sum Test Calculations	
sample size	31
W+	371.5
W-	124.5

You can then use the worksheet template called "WSRST Matched Pairs" (available in MyStatLab in the workbook called "Templates"). This template should only be used if the number of non-zero differences is at least 25.

Shown below in Exhibit 9.29 is the worksheet template for Example 9.2A. As always, you must fill in the blue-shaded cells in the template.

Note that the z-score in the template is always based on the largest of W^- and W^+.

EXHIBIT 9.29

Worksheet Template for Wilcoxon Signed Rank Sum Test

Making Decisions About Matched Pairs, Quantitative Data, Non-Normal Differences (WSRST)	
Sample Size	31
Is the sample size at least 25?	yes
Is the histogram of differences symmetric?	yes
W+	371.5
W-	124.5
z-Score	2.42017331
One-Tailed p-Value	0.00775656
Two-Tailed p-Value	0.01551311

Using the Wilcoxon Signed Rank Sum Test Table for Sample Sizes < 25

There is only one more variation when you are dealing with matched pairs of quantitative data with non-normal differences. The sampling distribution outlined on page 343 is approximately normal only for fairly large sample sizes, that is, $n \geq 25$. What if we have a smaller sample? The process is the same. Differences are ranked, and the sums of the ranks are computed. However, we must turn to tables to estimate p-values in these cases, because the sampling distribution is not normally distributed.

As discussed above, when there is no difference in the populations, the sums of the ranks for the positive differences and the negative differences would be about the same. The more different the rank sums are, the more evidence there is of a difference in the populations. The Wilcoxon Signed Rank Sum Test table in Appendix 4 shows rank sums (for a given sample size) that are so different that they provide evidence of a difference in the populations. The tables show these selected rank sums for each sample size (n_W) from 4 to 25.

Some of the rank sums are at the lower end of possible rank sums (referred to as W_L), and some of them are at the upper end of possible rank sums (referred to as W_U). The table lists just the rank sums with p-values that are either equal to or closest to the common p-values of 0.010, 0.025, and 0.050. An excerpt of the table is shown below in Exhibit 9.30, with $n_W = 10$.

EXHIBIT 9.30

Wilcoxon Signed Rank Sum Test, Critical Values and p-Values

	W_L	W_U	$P(W \leq W_L) = P(W \geq W_U)$
$n_W = 10$	5	50	0.010
	8	47	0.024
	9	46	0.032
	10	45	0.042
	11	44	0.053

For example, in the table above, there is no simple rank sum that has a p-value of 0.025, so the rank sums with p values just above and below 0.025 are shown.

Suppose you calculated a rank sum of 5.5 with 10 matched pairs. No rank sum of 5.5 is shown in the table above. We can proceed as usual by identifying where in the table the rank sum of 5.5 would belong, and estimating the p-value accordingly, as Exhibit 9.31 below illustrates.

The rank sum of 5.5 is between 5 and 8 in the table, so its p-value is between 0.010 and 0.024.

EXHIBIT 9.31

Wilcoxon Signed Rank Sum Test, Critical Values and p-Values, Estimating p

	W_L	W_U	$P(W \leq W_L) = P(W \geq W_U)$
5.5	5	50	0.010
	8	47	0.024
	9	46	0.032
	10	45	0.042
	11	44	0.053

Now that we have seen how the table is set up, we will once again return to the gym visits example, with yet another data set. In the new data set, the differences are non-normal, so we cannot use the t-test from Section 9.1. The sample size is small, so we cannot use the approximately normal sampling distribution of W, as in Example 9.2A. We will conduct a Wilcoxon Signed Rank Sum Test, but use the table to estimate the p-value. The Wilcoxon Signed Rank Sum Test table is in Appendix 4 on page 581 at the back of the text.

EXAMPLE 9.2B

Wilcoxon Signed Rank Sum Test, small sample

Suppose we return to the gym visits analysis discussed in Example 9.1A, but with different data. The differences are non-normal, and the sample size is < 25. The third data set is shown in **Exhibit 9.32**.

EXHIBIT 9.32

Gym Visits, Example 9.2B

Person	Monthly Gym Visits		Differences [(Before) − (After)]
	Before Promotion	After Promotion	
#1	10	17	−7
#2	13	15	−2
#3	14	14	0
#4	15	14	1
#5	15	11	4
#6	15	10	5
#7	18	25	−7
#8	22	13	9
#9	23	26	−3
#10	25	15	10

A histogram of the differences is shown in Exhibit 9.33. It is non-normal but perfectly symmetric. This is evidence that the populations are similar in shape and variability.

The ranking process is illustrated in Exhibit 9.34 opposite.

EXHIBIT 9.33

Histogram of Differences in Gym Visits, Example 9.2B

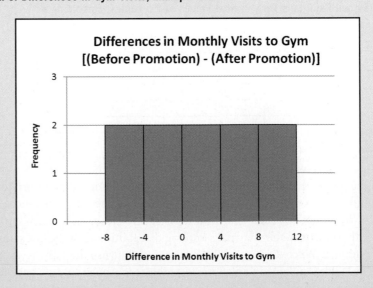

EXHIBIT 9.34

Ranking Process Illustration for Gym Visits, Example 9.2B

Monthly Gym Visits					
Differences in Monthly Gym Visits [(Before Promotion) – (After Promotion)]	Absolute Value of Differences (Negative Differences Recorded in Red)	Differences Reordered from Smallest to Largest (Absolute Value)	Ranks to Be Assigned	Ranks for Positive Differences	Ranks for Negative Differences
−7	7	0	ignore	ignore	ignore
−2	2	1	1	1	
0	0	2	2		2
1	1	3	3		3
4	4	4	4	4	
5	5	5	5	5	
−7	7	7	6		$(6 + 7)/2 = 6.5$
9	9	7	7		$(6 + 7)/2 = 6.5$
−3	3	9	8	8	
10	10	10	9	9	
Sum of the Ranks			45	$W^+ = 27$	$W^- = 18$

First, set up the hypothesis test. Use $\alpha = 0.025$ in this case.

- H_0: The populations of monthly gym visits are the same for individuals before and after promotion.
- H_1: The population of monthly gym visits before an individual received a promotion is to the right of the population of monthly gym visits after the promotion.
- $\alpha = 0.025$, as given above
- $W^+ = 27$ and $W^- = 18$, as calculated above
- $n_W = 9$ (there are 9 non-zero differences)

Let's focus on W^+ (we could also have chosen to focus on W^-). The question is whether a W of 27 gives us sufficient evidence to reject the null hypothesis. We have to refer to the Wilcoxon Signed Rank Sum Test table in Appendix 4 to find out. We want

EXHIBIT 9.35

Wilcoxon Signed Rank Sum Test, Critical Values and *p*-Values

n	W_L	W_U	$P(W \leq W_L) = P(W \geq W_U)$
9	3	42	0.010
	5	40	0.020
	6	39	0.027
	8	37	0.049
	9	36	0.064

27 ⟩

to know P($W^+ \geq 27$) for this sample, when $n_W = 9$. An excerpt from the table is shown on the previous page in Exhibit 9.35, for $n_W = 9$.

There is no rank sum of 27 in the table, so we can proceed as usual. We can identify where in the table the rank sum would belong, and estimate the *p*-value accordingly.

In Example 9.2B, $W^+ = 27$. This value is not on the table, but we can see that P($W \geq 36$) = 0.064. We know that P($W \geq 27$) > 0.064, which is also greater than our level of significance, at 0.025. Exhibit 9.36 below illustrates.

We fail to reject the null hypothesis. In this case, there is insufficient evidence to suggest that visits to the gym decreased after promotion.

EXHIBIT 9.36

p-Values for Example 9.2B

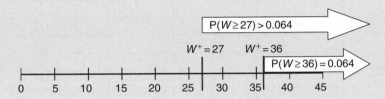

GUIDE TO DECISION MAKING

Matched Pairs, Quantitative Data, Non-Normal Differences—The Wilcoxon Signed Rank Sum Test to Decide About the Difference in Matched Populations

When:

- matched pairs of quantitative data, non-normally distributed differences
- trying to make a decision about the difference in the matched observations

Steps:

1. Specify H_0, the null hypothesis, which is that the population locations are the same.
2. Specify H_1, the alternative hypothesis.
3. Determine or identify α, the significance level.
4. Collect or identify the sample data. Identify or calculate the differences between the matching observations in the samples (keeping the order of subtraction consistent).
5. Check for normality of sample differences with a histogram. If the histogram of differences appears normal, use the *t*-test (described on page 335). If the histogram of differences is non-normal, check that it is fairly symmetric.

6. *If* the histogram of differences is non-normal and fairly symmetric, identify or calculate n_W, the number of non-zero differences between the matching observations in the samples.
7. Rank the absolute values of the non-zero differences, from 1 to n_W, averaging the ranks for tied differences.
8. Calculate

   - W^+, the sum of the ranks of the positive differences.
   - W^-, the sum of the ranks of the negative differences

9. *If* $n_W \geq 25$, the sampling distribution of W is approximately normal, with

   $$\sigma_W = \sqrt{\frac{n_W(n_W + 1)(2n_W + 1)}{24}}$$

   $$\mu_W = \frac{n_W(n_W + 1)}{4}$$

   Using either W^+ or W^- (choose by thinking about H_1 and the order of subtraction), use the normal sampling distribution to calculate the *p*-value of the result. When doing this by hand, the calculation will involve the *z*-score:

   $$z = \frac{W - \mu_W}{\sigma_W}$$

10. If $n_W < 25$, use Appendix 4 on page 581 to approximate the *p*-value of the chosen *W*.
11. If *p*-value $\leq \alpha$, reject H_0 and conclude that there is sufficient evidence to decide in favour of H_1. If *p*-value $> \alpha$, fail to reject H_0 and conclude that there is insufficient evidence to decide in favour of H_1. State your conclusions in language appropriate to the problem.

See Example 9.2A on page 344 ($n \geq 25$), and Example 9.2B on page 350 ($n < 25$, using tables).

Quantitative Matched-Pairs Data: Which Test?

We have now looked at matched pairs of quantitative data, and we have presented decision-making techniques to use when the differences are normally distributed and when they are not.

When the differences are normally distributed, the *t*-test about the mean difference applies (you first learned about the *t*-test in Chapter 7). When the differences are not normally distributed but symmetric, the Wilcoxon Signed Rank Sum Test can be used.

When deciding whether to use the *t*-test or the WSRST, we are faced once again with the question: how normal is normal enough? The *t*-test is robust but, as before, it performs better with larger sample sizes. If there are outliers, do not use the *t*-test. If the sample size is small (less than about 15 or 20), and the differences are clearly non-normal, do not use the *t*-test. If the sample size is more than 15 or 20, you can use the *t*-test, even with some skewness in the histogram of differences. Once samples are as large as 40 or so, the *t*-test can be used even if there is significant skewness in the differences. The *t*-test is preferred to the Wilcoxon Signed Rank Sum Test, if the necessary conditions are met. The *t*-test is based on the actual data values, while the WSRST is based only on the ranks of the values. Using the WSRST means giving up some information, and this should be done only if necessary.

DEVELOP YOUR SKILLS 9.2

6. The foreman in a small assembly plant wants to see whether a training program has reduced the number of worker errors. The foreman records the weekly number of errors for a random sample of workers before the training, and again after the training. Is there sufficient evidence, at the 4% significance level, to suggest that the training led to a reduced number of worker errors?

DYS09-6

7. A small company that specializes in gourmet cookies decides to redesign its packaging. The company owner is certain that the new package will lead to increased sales. Weekly sales at a random sample of stores in the Barrie area are recorded before and after the change in package design. Using the 5% level of significance, analyze the data to see if the owner's idea is correct. The data set is shown in Exhibit 9.37.

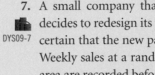

DYS09-7

EXHIBIT 9.37

Cookie Sales Data, Develop Your Skills 9.2

Weekly Sales Before and After Product Redesign		
Store	Sales After	Sales Before
51 Bayfield	942.00	813.67
109 Mapleview Drive	698.71	831.54
137 Wellington	646.10	734.48
6 Collier	976.97	832.46
421 Essa Road	676.44	791.22
19 Queen	793.19	766.73
345 Cundles	607.15	668.66
D–564 Byrne Drive	785.15	631.05
24 Archer	858.87	724.39
15 Short St.	636.04	766.76

8. Telemarketers generally read from a prepared script when they make their sales calls. A firm decides to change this prepared script, making it both friendlier and shorter. The numbers of daily sales are recorded for a random sample of telemarketers, before and after the script change. The data are shown in Exhibit 9.38. Do the data suggest that there is a difference in the numbers of daily sales before and after the script change? Use $\alpha = 0.05$.

9. The Student Services Department at a Prince Edward Island college wants to see whether there are differences in the study habits of male and female students. A random sample of female students is selected, and then a corresponding sample of male students is designed—same programs, ages, previous educational experience, and living arrangements (that is, all of the students are living away from their parents). The students are asked to keep track of the number of hours they study over a four-week period. Does it

DYS09-9

EXHIBIT 9.38

Telemarketers' Numbers of Sales

Sales Before Script Change	Sales After Script Change
52	63
35	45
47	57
69	78
54	55
63	62
47	45
36	29
51	49

appear, based on these data, that male students study less than female students? Use $\alpha = 0.04$.

10. An automobile association wants to demonstrate that maintaining tire pressure results in better fuel economy.

DYS09-10

The association selected a random sample of its members, and asked them to record their fuel consumption in litres per 100 km for all of their driving for one month. It then selected another sample of members whose driving habits and car models were the same as the original sample, and asked these drivers to check and adjust tire pressures every 3 to 4 days, for another month, and record their fuel consumption again. Do the data support the association's claim that maintaining tire pressure improves fuel economy? Use $\alpha = 0.04$.

9.3   MATCHED PAIRS, RANKED DATA— THE SIGN TEST

What if we want to examine matched pairs of ranked data? This section describes the appropriate decision-making technique, which is called the Sign Test.

Suppose an advertising agency wants to analyze the impact of a new advertisement about HDTVs (high definition televisions). The agency selects a random sample of potential consumers of the televisions, and asks them to rate their readiness to buy an HDTV before and after seeing the ad. The ratings are on a scale of 1 to 4, where 1 corresponds to *unwilling to buy*, and 4 corresponds to *ready to buy*. When the data are ranked, as they are here, we cannot calculate the difference in the corresponding sample values (how do you subtract [(ready to buy) − (unwilling to buy)], for example?). However, we can keep track of whether the difference is positive or negative (whether the ad increased or decreased the consumer's willingness to buy). We record positive differences with a plus sign, and negative differences with a minus sign, and then we examine the numbers of each in the Sign Test.

If there was no difference in the ratings in the two samples, then the number of positive differences should be about the same as the number of negative differences. About the same number of people would have increased their readiness to buy HDTVs as decreased their readiness to buy, after seeing the ad. We can use a binomial distribution with $p = 0.5$ to test whether the observed number of positive (or negative) differences is significantly different from a half-and-half split. If sample sizes are sufficiently large, we can also do a population proportion hypothesis test of $p = 0.5$ (generally we would do this only if the test must be done without a computer). Examples 9.3A and 9.3B illustrate the two approaches to this test. In both cases, the test uses techniques you have already learned, and applies the techniques to new situations.

EXAMPLE 9.3A

Sign Test, using the binomial distribution

Suppose a polling company found a random sample of Canadian students who were considering going to university. The polling company then asked the students to rate two Canadian universities—one in Ontario and one in British Columbia—using the following rating system: (1) excellent; (2) good; (3) fair; and (4) poor.

The company wants to test the hypothesis that students rate the Ontario university less favourably than the BC university, with a 5% level of significance.

The results for the university ratings are shown in Exhibit 9.39.

EXHIBIT 9.39

University Ratings

Student	Ontario University Rating	BC University Rating
1	2	1
2	3	4
3	4	4
4	1	2
5	4	1
6	2	1
7	1	1
8	2	1
9	2	1
10	3	2
11	2	2
12	4	2
13	2	2
14	4	3
15	4	2
16	4	1
17	3	3
18	4	2
19	2	3
20	2	3

Once again, it is clear that we have a matched-pairs experiment. It makes sense to compare the rating of the Ontario university with the rating of the BC university by the same student. The data are ranked. Again, we will examine the data set of differences, but we cannot simply calculate the differences in the numerical ratings because the results would not be meaningful. Instead, we keep track only of whether the Ontario university's numerical rating was higher or lower than that of the BC university by the same student.

Exhibit 9.40 opposite shows the data again, with an extra column. The column records a + whenever the numerical value of the Ontario university rating is higher than the numerical value of the BC university rating, a 0 when the student gave the universities the same numerical rating, and a – when the numerical value of the Ontario university rating is lower than the numerical value of the BC university rating.

It is simplest, and most computer-friendly, simply to subtract the numerical values of the ratings to determine the pluses and minuses. You can ignore the value of the difference, and just focus on the sign. As usual, you will have to think carefully about what a plus or a minus means when you are conducting this test. (As always, the order of subtraction must be consistent.)

In this example, a higher *numerical* rating means a less favourable *actual* opinion—since the highest rating is 1. This is often the case ("We're number one!" is usually a good thing), but it is not always the case. We subtracted as follows: [(Ontario university rating) − (BC university rating)]. This results in a plus sign whenever the numerical value of the Ontario university rating is higher. The more plus signs there are, the greater the evidence that students rate the Ontario university less favourably than the BC university.

In this data set, we have observed 11 plus signs (so $n^+ = 11$), 4 minus signs (so $n^- = 4$), and 5 cases of no difference. The polling company wants to test the hypothesis H_1: students rate the Ontario university less favourably than the BC university. Now we have to decide whether this sample evidence supports this idea.

EXHIBIT 9.40

Positive or Negative Differences in University Ratings

Student	Ontario University Rating	BC University Rating	Ontario Rating Versus BC Rating
1	2	1	+
2	3	4	−
3	4	4	0
4	1	2	−
5	4	1	+
6	2	1	+
7	1	1	0
8	2	1	+
9	2	1	+
10	3	2	+
11	2	2	0
12	4	2	+
13	2	2	0
14	4	3	+
15	4	2	+
16	4	1	+
17	3	3	0
18	4	2	+
19	2	3	−
20	2	3	−

With the Sign Test, we ignore cases where there is no difference in the rating, so the sample size (adjusted for the Sign Test) is $n_{ST} = 15$. With 15 non-zero differences, we would expect about 7.5 (that is, 7 or 8) to be positive and 7.5 to be negative.

We can focus on either the number of pluses or the number of minuses because we are testing to see if there is about a half-and-half split in plus signs and minus signs. The binomial distribution will be symmetric, because $p = 0.5$: $P(n^+ \geq 11) = P(n^- \leq 4)$.

This does not mean that you can ignore the order of subtraction. In this problem, if the results were reversed ($n^+ = 4$, $n^- = 11$), this would seem to indicate that students rated the Ontario university more highly than the BC university! So that you do not miss this situation (somewhat unlikely, given H_1), you should always think about the order of subtraction in these problems when you are doing a one-tailed test.

In this case, we have been focusing on whether the student ratings of the Ontario university are less favourable than the BC student ratings, so we will focus on the plus signs. We observed 11 plus signs. We will use the notation n^+ to refer to the number of plus signs.

The question we have to ask is this: does the result of 11 out of 15 give us convincing evidence that all students rate the Ontario university less favourably than the BC university?

- H_0: Students rate the Ontario and BC universities about the same.
- H_1: Students rate the Ontario university less favourably than the BC university.
- The polling company wants to use $\alpha = 0.05$.
- The p-value will be $P(n^+ \geq 11, n_{ST} = 15, p = 0.5)$.

This is a binomial probability calculation. As we discussed in Chapter 5, we can use the binomial distribution here, even though we do not have a *true* binomial experiment (we are sampling without replacement). As long as the sample size is not more than 5% of the population, the binomial distribution will still give us a good estimate of the probability. It is clear that the sample size of 15 is not more than 5% of the total population of Canadian students considering going to university.

Of course, we can use Excel to calculate the p-value. In this case, we can also use the tables in the textbook. Locate the binomial table where $n = 9$, and find the column in which $p = 0.50$. The calculation (similar to the ones we did in Chapter 5) is as follows.

$$p\text{-value} = P(n^+ \geq 11) = 1 - P(n^+ \leq 10) = 1 - 0.941 = 0.059$$

Since p-value $> \alpha$, we fail to reject H_0. There is insufficient evidence to suggest that students rate the Ontario university less favourably than the BC university.

Using the Excel Add-in and Template There is an Excel add-in that will calculate the number of positive and negative differences for matched-pairs ranked data. Once the add-in is installed, click on the the **Add-Ins** tab, click on **Non-Parametric Tools**, and choose **Sign Test Calculations**. The next dialogue box is self-explanatory, as shown in Exhibit 9.41 opposite.

You must indicate where the sample data are located, and where you want the output to go. The output is shown opposite in Exhibit 9.42.

There is a worksheet template called "Sign Test," in the Templates workbook in MyStatLab. You can use this template to complete the hypothesis test for matched pairs of ranked data. A completed template for the university rating problem is shown in Exhibit 9.43. As usual, you must fill in the blue-shaded cells in the template.

The template is also useful if you have only summary data from the samples.

EXHIBIT 9.41

Excel Dialogue Box for Sign Test Calculations

Sign Test Calculations

Sample One

Sample Two

Help

Cancel

OK

Output Options

○ Output Range

● New Worksheet

Use:
The Sign Test is used for matched pairs of ranked data.

EXHIBIT 9.42

Excel Output for Sign Test Calculations

Sign Test Calculations	
# of non-zero differences	15
# of positive differences	11
# of negative differences	4

EXHIBIT 9.43

Completed Excel Template for Making Decisions About Matched Pairs, Ranked Data (Sign Test)

Making Decisions About Matched Pairs, Ranked Data (Sign Test)	
Number of Non-Zero Differences	15
Number of Positive Differences	11
Number of Negative Differences	4
One-Tailed p-Value	0.05923
Two-Tailed p-Value	0.11847

Using the Sampling Distribution of $\hat{p}$ for Large Sample Sizes   If the sample size is fairly large, it is possible to do the Sign Test as a hypothesis test of $p = 0.50$. Because $p = 0.50$, we know that the underlying binomial distribution will be symmetric. However, with smaller sample sizes, the normal approximation is not very accurate (a continuity correction factor is required, as discussed in Chapter 6), and your approach should be to use the template shown above. If the sample size is fairly large, however, and you have to do the problem by hand, you can use the approach illustrated in Example 9.3B on the next page.

When we want to work with the sampling distribution of $\hat{p}$, we have to check for normality, which requires np and $nq \geq 10$. In every case of the Sign Test, because we are checking for *no difference in the ratings,* we use a null hypothesis of $p = 0.50$. This means that $q = 0.50$ as well. So, whenever $n \geq 20$, both np and nq will be ≥ 10.

EXAMPLE 9.3B

Sign Test, large sample, using the sampling distribution of $\hat{p}$

A fine-living magazine asked its subscribers to rate two local restaurants—Jane's Fish and Chips and Archie's Tea Room. Response rates were high, because the magazine was going to randomly select one respondent to receive a free meal for two at one of the two restaurants being rated. (Are the target and sampled populations actually the same here? Should this be a concern?)

There were 280 responses. Of those, 26 rated the two restaurants the same. Of the 254 remaining respondents, 145 rated Jane's Fish and Chips higher than Archie's Tea Room. From this sample, is there evidence that this magazine's subscribers rate Jane's Fish and Chips higher than Archie's Tea Room (the magazine has more than 7,000 subscribers)? Use $\alpha = 0.025$.

Since we are interested in cases where Jane's Fish and Chips gets higher ratings than Archie's Tea Room, we will calculate this proportion as $\hat{p} = \dfrac{145}{254} = 0.570866$.

Take a minute to think about the focus of the analysis. It is important to realize that if Jane's restaurant is rated higher, this is the same as Archie's restaurant being rated lower. These are just two different ways of describing the same condition.

Let's proceed with a hypothesis test like the ones we did in Chapter 7. The underlying distribution is the binomial. Although we are sampling without replacement, we are told that the magazine has more than 7,000 subscribers. A sample of 280 represents only 4% of the population, and so the binomial distribution will be a reasonable model.

- $H_0: p = 0.50$, that is, Archie's restaurant and Jane's restaurant are rated about the same
- $H_1: p > 0.50$ (with p defined as the proportion of times that Jane's restaurant is rated higher than Archie's restaurant)
- $\alpha = 0.025$

We check for normality of the sampling distribution of $\hat{p}$, and note that $n_{ST} = 254 > 20$, so the conditions are met.

We are using the normal approximation to the binomial in this case so that we can complete the test by hand (if a computer is available, there is no reason to use the approximation). We know from Chapter 7 that the standard error of the sample proportion is

$$\sigma_{\hat{p}} = \sqrt{\frac{pq}{n_{ST}}} = \sqrt{\frac{(0.5)(0.5)}{254}} = 0.03137279$$

so the z-score will be

$$z = \frac{\hat{p} - p}{\sigma_{\hat{p}}} = \frac{\hat{p} - p}{\sqrt{\dfrac{pq}{n_{ST}}}} = \frac{0.570866 - 0.5}{0.03137279} = 2.26$$

Using the normal tables, we find the p-value as $P(\hat{p} \geq 0.570866) \doteq$ $P(z \geq 2.26) = (1 - 0.9881) = 0.0119$. Since this is less than 0.025, the significance level of the hypothesis test, we will reject the null hypothesis. There is sufficient evidence to suggest that the magazine's subscribers rate Jane's Fish and Chips higher than Archie's Tea Room. Remember to state the conclusion in terms of the original problem. Concluding that there is evidence that $p > 0.50$ here would be technically correct, but not helpful!

As well, in this case, the sample is self-selected, so we have to be careful about interpreting results. Respondents might have been motivated by the promise of winning a free meal, and their opinions might differ from the population of magazine subscribers.

GUIDE TO DECISION MAKING

Matched Pairs, Ranked Data—The Sign Test to Decide About the Difference in Matched Populations

When:

- matched pairs of ranked data
- trying to make a decision about the difference in the matched observations

Steps:
1. Specify H_0, the null hypothesis.
2. Specify H_1, the alternative hypothesis.
3. Determine or identify α, the significance level.
4. Collect or identify the sample data. Identify or count:
   - the number of times sample 1 values are greater than sample 2 values (the $+$ signs), n^+
   - the number of times sample 1 values are less than sample 2 values (the $-$ signs), n^-
   - n_{ST}, the number of non-zero differences between the matching observations in the samples

5. Using the binomial distribution with n_{ST} trials, $p = 0.5$, calculate the p-value for either n^+ or n^- (depending on H_1 and the way the comparison was made). When doing the problem by hand, with a sufficiently large sample size, conduct this as a test of $p = 0.50$, with the p-value based on $z = \dfrac{\hat{p} - p}{\sigma_{\hat{p}}} = \dfrac{\hat{p} - p}{\sqrt{\dfrac{pq}{n_{ST}}}}$.

6. If p-value $\leq \alpha$, reject H_0 and conclude that there is sufficient evidence to decide in favour of H_1. If p-value $> \alpha$, fail to reject H_0 and conclude that there is insufficient evidence to decide in favour of H_1. State your conclusions in language appropriate to the problem.

See Example 9.3A on page 355 (using the binomial distribution) and Example 9.3B on p 360 (using the sampling distribution of $\hat{p}$)

DEVELOP YOUR SKILLS 9.3

11. A marketing team wanted to run a taste test between a particular brand of cola and its major competitor. A random sample of 16 cola drinkers was selected. Each was asked to taste a sample of the two colas and say which one they preferred, if any. The order in which the colas were tasted was randomly assigned. Of the 16 testers, 1 preferred the colas equally and 9 preferred cola A. Is there evidence, at the 5% level of significance, that cola A is preferred by cola drinkers?

12. A Honda automobile dealer was interested in how his sales staff compared with the salespeople at the Ford dealership across the road. The Honda dealer hired a research organization to investigate. The company selected a group of adults and asked them to shop for (but not to buy) a particular make and model of car— one at the Honda dealer and one at the Ford dealer— and then rate their experiences on the following scale: (1) the best car-shopping experience I have ever had; (2) a very positive experience; (3) some positive and some negative aspects; (4) a very negative experience; and (5) the worst car-shopping experience I have ever had. The results are shown in Exhibit 9.44. At the 4% significance level, is there any evidence of a difference in the ratings for the two auto dealerships?

EXHIBIT 9.44

Car Shopping Experience

Shopper	Rating for Ford Dealer	Rating for Honda Dealer
1	5	1
2	2	3
3	3	4
4	4	2
5	2	3
6	2	2
7	5	1
8	3	2
9	3	3

13. A number of economic analysts were asked to rate their expectations for the economies of North America and Europe over the coming year, according to the following scale: (4) prospects are very promising; (3) prospects are promising in terms of growth, but with some potential for slowdown; (2) the economy is expected to slow down from the previous year; and (1) a serious downturn is expected. The analysts' ratings are shown in Exhibit 9.45 below. At the 3% level of significance, is there evidence that all economic analysts rate prospects for the North American and European economies differently?

14. A random sample of 250 attendees of a wine and cheese festival were asked to rate Californian and French wines. Of the 250, 25 rated the wines about equal. Of the remainder, 150 rated Californian wines higher than French wines. At the 3% level of significance, is there evidence to suggest that all wine drinkers rate Californian wines higher than French wines?

15. An advertising agency wants to analyze the impact of a new advertisement about HDTVs (high definition televisions). The agency selects a random sample of potential consumers of the televisions, and asks them to rate their readiness to buy an HDTV before and after seeing the ad. The ratings are on a scale of 1 to 4, where 1 corresponds to *unwilling to buy*, and 4 corresponds to *ready to buy*. Is there evidence, at the 5% significance level, that consumers' willingness to buy would be higher after seeing the ad? Do this question with the Excel template, and compare your answer to the results you get when you do it by hand.

DYS09-15

EXHIBIT 9.45

Analysts' Ratings of Economic Prospects for North America and Europe

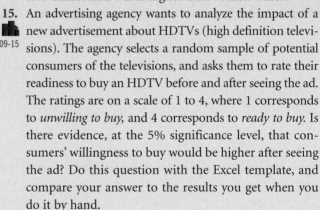

Analyst	Rating for North America	Rating for Europe
1	3	4
2	2	3
3	4	2
4	3	2
5	3	1
6	2	3
7	3	2
8	3	2
9	3	4
10	2	1
11	4	4

All of the techniques in this chapter apply to matched-pairs data. There are two situations when sample data are matched pairs:

1. *A matched-pairs experimental study*—There is a measurement or count, followed by an action of some kind, followed by a second measurement or count.
2. *A matched-pairs observational study*—There is a matching or pairing of observations, designed so that it is easier to decide what caused any observed change between the observations.

In all cases with matched pairs, it is essential that the order of subtraction (or comparison) be consistent. As well, you will have to think about what the order of subtraction tells you about the alternative hypothesis, so that you can do the correct *p*-value calculation (or estimation).

Matched Pairs, Quantitative Data, Normal Differences—The *t*-Test and Confidence Interval of μ_D

When the quantitative matched-pairs data have normally distributed differences, a *t*-test of the mean difference is used to make decisions. The null hypothesis is always that there is no difference, on average, between the two measurements for the matched pairs. A comparison is made of a null hypothesis H_0: $\mu_D = 0$ with one of three possible alternative hypotheses:

- $\mu_D > 0$
- $\mu_D < 0$
- $\mu_D \neq 0$

A decision about which of the three possible alternative hypotheses to use will depend on the context of the analysis, *and the order of subtraction* used to arrive at the differences.

The *t*-score is calculated as follows, with the subscript D reminding us that we are looking at a data set of differences:

$$t = \frac{\bar{x}_D - \mu_D}{s_D/\sqrt{n_D}}, \text{ with } n_D - 1 \text{ degrees of freedom}$$

If you have raw or summary data, you can use the template illustrated on page 330 to make your calculations in Excel (as Example 9.1B on page 332 illustrates). With raw sample data, you can also use the Excel data analysis tool **t-Test: Paired Two Sample for Means** (see page 330). Its use is demonstrated on pages 330–331, with data from Example 9.1A. A Guide to Decision Making for matched pairs, quantitative data, normal differences is shown on page 335.

A confidence interval estimate of μ_D can be calculated, as follows:

$\bar{x}_D \pm$ critical *t*-score $\left(\dfrac{s_D}{\sqrt{n_D}} \right)$. Example 9.1C on page 336 illustrates.

Matched Pairs, Quantitative Data, Non-Normal Differences— The Wilcoxon Signed Rank Sum Test

When the histogram of differences for quantitative data is not normally distributed (particularly with small sample sizes), the Wilcoxon Signed Rank Sum Test is used to make decisions. The requirement is that the histogram of differences be symmetric. The null hypothesis is that there is no difference in the population locations.

The absolute values of differences are ranked from smallest to largest. When differences are tied, the associated ranks are averaged. The sums of the ranks for the positive and negative differences are calculated. Differences of zero are ignored. The procedure for assigning ranks is described on page 339.

When n_W, the number of non-zero differences, is at least 25, an approximately normal sampling distribution can be used, with a *z*-score of

$$z = \frac{W - \mu_W}{\sigma_W} = \frac{W - \left(\dfrac{n_W(n_W + 1)}{4} \right)}{\sqrt{\dfrac{n_W(n_W + 1)(2n_W + 1)}{24}}}$$

The Excel add-in that comes with the textbook (**Non-Parametric Tools**) contains a tool called **Wilcoxon Signed Rank Sum Test Calculations** that will calculate the W^+ and W^- for the Wilcoxon Signed Rank Sum Test. You can then use the worksheet template titled "Making Decisions About Matched Pairs, Quantitative Data, Non-Normal Differences (WSRST)" for p-value calculations when the sample size is ≥ 25. See page 348.

When $n_W < 25$, the table in Appendix 4 should be used to estimate p-values to make decisions, as Example 9.2B on page 350 illustrates.

A Guide to Decision Making for matched pairs, quantitative data, non-normal differences is shown on page 352.

Matched Pairs, Ranked Data—The Sign Test

When the data are ranked, the corresponding sample data points cannot be subtracted (what does [(good) − (excellent)] mean?). However, we can keep track of whether differences are positive or negative. If there is no difference in the rankings of the matched pairs, on average, then the number of positive differences should be about equal to the number of negative differences (again, for this test, differences of zero are ignored).

This binomial probability distribution, with $p = 0.50$, can be used to calculate the p-value of the sample result, as Example 9.3A on page 355 illustrates. There is no built-in data analysis function in Excel to conduct a Sign Test. The Excel add-in that come with the text (**Non-Parametric Tools**) contains a tool called **Sign Test Calculations** that will calculate the numbers of positive and negative differences for a data set. You can then use the worksheet template titled "Making Decisions About Matched Pairs, Ranked Data (Sign Test)" for p-value calculations (see page 359). If you have to do this test by hand, and the sample size is large, you can make a decision using a hypothesis test of $p = 0.50$, as Example 9.3B on page 360 illustrates.

A Guide to Decision Making for matched pairs, ranked data, is shown on page 361.

 Go to MyStatLab at www.mathxl.com. You can practise the exercises indicated with red in the Develop Your Skills and Chapter Review Exercises as often as you want, and guided solutions will help you find answers step by step. You'll find a personalized study plan available to you too!

CHAPTER REVIEW EXERCISES

WARM-UP EXERCISES

1. Why are matched-pairs samples better than independent samples for exploring cause and effect?

2. Suppose you have a set of "before" and "after" sample measurements, and you do not know whether the data are matched pairs or independent samples. Suppose $n_1 = 25$ and $n_2 = 28$. Are these matched pairs? Why or why not?

3. Suppose you have a sample of 50 measurements of matched-pairs data, and the histogram of differences is fairly, but not perfectly, normal. The t-test of μ_D leads to a rejection of the null hypothesis, indicating that the average difference between the populations is not zero. You decide to conduct a Wilcoxon Signed Rank Sum Test, just to be sure, but you find that you fail to reject the null hypothesis of no difference. How could this happen? What does it mean?

4. Why is the computer-based version of the Sign Test preferred to the version using the sampling distribution of $\hat{p}$?

5. You use matched-pairs sample data concerning customer ratings of a new version of a company's website compared with the old version. Your conclusion is that customers rate the new version more highly than the old version. Your friend Tom examines the same data and concludes that customer ratings of the old version of the website are lower than customer ratings of the new version. Is Tom right or wrong?

THINK AND DECIDE

6. A new microbrewery has opened in southern Ontario. The aim is to produce an English-style ale adapted to Canadian tastes. While developing the beer recipe, the company periodically asked a panel of beer drinkers to rate the beer, on a scale of 1 to 5, where 1 is excellent and 5 is undrinkable. The ratings for one taste test are shown below in Exhibit 9.46.

EXHIBIT 9.46

Beer Taste Test

Tester	Beer Recipe #3	Beer Recipe #4
1	1	4
2	3	2
3	2	1
4	5	3
5	3	4
6	2	1
7	4	5
8	1	3
9	2	1
10	3	4

At the 5% level of significance, is there evidence of a difference in ratings for the two beer recipes?

7. A random sample of 400 college students was asked to rate two potential designs for the new Student Centre on campus. Of these, 27 rated the designs equally. Of the remainder, 207 gave a higher rating to the more modern design. At the 2.5% level of significance, is there evidence to suggest that students rate the two designs differently?

8. A new tool is supposed to reduce the time it takes to assemble a component in a factory. A random sample of workers is selected, and the assembly times are measured with and without the new tool. The average difference in assembly time is 3.4 minutes, with a standard deviation of 4.6 minutes. Sample size is 18. You may assume that the differences are normally distributed. Is there evidence, at the 5% level of significance, that the new tool speeds up assembly time? The order of subtraction is (time without tool – time with tool).

9. A random sample of 10 contractors was asked to quote a price for a bathroom renovation in two different houses. The bathroom renovation was technically the same in each house, with the same amount of labour and materials required. One house was in a very wealthy neighbourhood, and the other was in a more run-down neighbourhood. The average difference was $1,262, with a standard deviation of $478. At the 5% level of significance, is there evidence that contractors quote higher prices for jobs in houses in wealthier neighbourhoods? Differences were calculated as (price for job in wealthy neighbourhood – price for job in run-down neighbourhood). You may assume the differences were normally distributed.

10. Construct a 95% confidence interval for the average difference in prices quoted for the bathroom renovation, based on the data in Exercise 9 above.

11. A restaurant owner wanted to gather some data on customer taste preferences about two new salads on the menu, one a mixed-greens salad, and one a roasted vegetable salad. A random sample of diners was selected, and each diner was asked to taste both of the new salads and indicate which was preferred. There were 35 diners in the sample. Of these, three liked the salads equally. Of the remainder, 20 gave a higher rating to the mixed-greens salad. Is there evidence, at the 3% level of significance, that diners prefer the mixed-greens salad?

12. A researcher is interested in the price people would be willing to pay for a spa weekend in the country, compared with the price they would be willing to pay for a spa weekend in the city. The researcher collected data from a random sample of potential spa customers. When he created a histogram of the differences, he noted it was not normal, but was fairly symmetric. The researcher used the Wilcoxon Signed Rank Sum Test Calculations add-in, and produced the output shown in Exhibit 9.47 below.

EXHIBIT 9.47

Excel Output for Spa Research Data

Wilcoxon Signed Rank Sum Test Calculations	
sample size	75
W+	1751
W-	1099

Is there evidence, at the 5% level of significance, that people are willing to pay more for a spa weekend in the country? The order of subtraction was (price for country spa weekend – price for city spa weekend).

13. An accounting firm is testing a new software program. The company selects a random sample of workers and trains them on the new software until the employees are equally comfortable with the two programs. These workers are then asked to complete a set of tasks—with the old software and the new software (order of software randomly assigned)—and keep track of how long (in minutes) the work takes. A 95% confidence interval of the average difference in time is (3.9, 14.3). The order of subtraction was (time with old software – time with new software). Without doing any further calculations, what can you conclude about whether the tasks are completed in the same amount of time with the two software programs? What level of significance applies? Which software program would you recommend? Explain your reasoning.

14. A company decides to test two package designs for canned soup by placing cans with each design at opposite ends of the soup aisle in a random sample of 26 supermarkets. Data were collected on weekly sales for each soup. Differences in sales were symmetric, but not normally distributed. The rank sum of the positive differences was 300, and the rank sum of the negative differences was 51. Is there sufficient evidence to suggest that sales of the soup in the two different packages differ? Use $\alpha = 0.05$.

15. The manager of a financial planning firm is trying to train her staff to make greater use of their working time. To see whether this training is having any effect, she keeps track of monthly new business generated before and after the training, for all six staff members. The results are as shown in Exhibit 9.48 opposite.

Has the manager's training resulted in increased new business? Use $\alpha = 0.025$. The sample size is too small to judge normality, but you may assume that the differences are normally distributed.

EXHIBIT 9.48

New Business Before and After Training

Staff Member	Monthly New Business Before Training ($000s)	Monthly New Business After Training ($000s)
Shirley	230	240
Tom	150	165
Janice	100	90
Brian	75	100
Ed	340	330
Kim	500	525

16. Create a 95% confidence interval estimate for the average difference between monthly new business before training and after training. Based on your answer to Exercise 15, would you expect this interval to contain zero?

17. Repeat the analysis for Exercise 15 above, but this time assume the differences are not normally distributed.

18. A dairy products company is developing a new organic yogurt. The company assembles a panel of tasters to compare two possible formulations of the new product. The panellists are asked to rate the taste of each yogurt on a scale of 1 to 5, with 1 corresponding to "absolutely delicious," and 5 corresponding to "inedible." The results of the taste test are shown below in Exhibit 9.49.

EXHIBIT 9.49

Taste Test of Yogurt Formulations

Taster	Recipe #1	Recipe #2
1	1	2
2	4	1
3	2	3
4	5	4
5	3	2
6	2	1
7	3	2
8	2	5
9	5	2
10	4	3

Is there evidence, at the 2.5% level of significance, that the tasters prefer one yogurt recipe over the other?

19. A drill manufacturer wants to draw attention to a new design, which theoretically allows quicker changes between drill bits. The manufacturer gathers a random sample of 20 amateurs who have some experience using drills around the home. They are asked to complete a prescribed set of tasks with the new drill and with the old drill (which drill is used first is randomly assigned). The total time to complete the tasks (in minutes) is recorded for each drill. The order of subtraction is (time with the new-style drill – time with the old-style drill). The average difference is –5.2, with a standard deviation of 12.2. Is there sufficient evidence to

suggest that the tasks are completed more quickly with the new-style drill? Use $\alpha = 0.05$. You may assume the differences in completion times are normally distributed.

THINK AND DECIDE USING EXCEL

CRE09-20

20. A company hires a consulting firm to conduct a seminar to improve workers' sense of self-esteem. Employees are given a test to assess their self-esteem before the seminar, and again afterwards. The test scores are shown below in Exhibit 9.50. A higher score indicates higher self-esteem.

EXHIBIT 9.50

Results of Employees' Self-Esteem Test

Self-Esteem Test Score Before Seminar	Self-Esteem Test Score After Seminar
70	76
84	89
74	69
61	65
82	88
55	59
43	40
56	63
84	80
67	64
63	61
76	82
62	57
83	79
56	54
44	47
52	56
85	90

a. What kind of data are these?
b. Is there sufficient evidence, at a 5% significance level, to suggest that the seminar improved employees' self-esteem?

CRE09-21

21. A large college was interested in the salaries of graduates from its Business and Computer Studies programs. The college randomly selected a number of graduates from each program, and then matched the graduates as closely as possible in terms of age, experience, achievement at school, and location. The college collected data on the annual salaries of the graduates.

At the 2.5% significance level, is there evidence of a difference in salaries of Computer Studies and Business graduates from this college?

CRE09-22

22. A large number of workers commute to work at the Honda assembly plant in Alliston, Ontario, every day. The commute can be quite long, depending on traffic conditions. Suppose the company decided to experiment with flexible hours for office workers at the plant. A random sample of these workers was asked to precisely time (in minutes) how long their drive to work took, over a random sample of days. On half of those days, the workers were to leave home to arrive for an 8 A.M. start, on the other half, they were to arrive for a

9 A.M. start. The average commuting time for each worker was recorded for each start time, and the results are shown below in Exhibit 9.51. Is there evidence, at a 4% significance level, that the earlier arrival time reduces the time it takes for workers to commute to work?

EXHIBIT 9.51

Commuting Time for Workers to Honda Plant in Alliston (in minutes)

8:00 A.M. Start	9:00 A.M. Start
23	15
74	64
116	113
76	89
94	102
56	65
74	80
76	90
72	67
91	95
85	79
93	100
101	100
105	113
91	90
62	66
80	73
57	67
56	70
91	86
67	68
71	80
58	54
89	93
70	83
50	58
76	86
82	74
99	111
52	68

23. A golf course was concerned that many of its golfers were playing too slowly, thus reducing the number of players the course could host (and profits). The course marshal recorded the time (in minutes) for randomly selected foursomes in the ladies' league to play nine holes (walking). The marshal then implemented measures designed to encourage greater speed of play, and recorded the playing time for the same foursomes. Is there sufficient evidence, at the 5% level of significance, to conclude that the new approach increased the speed of play at the course?

 CRE09-23

24. Construct a 90% confidence interval estimate of the reduction in playing time at the golf course (see Exercise 23, above).

25. A random sample of employees is asked to rate the performance of a president. This president is fired, and a new president hired. After six months, the same employees are asked to

 CRE09-25

rate the performance of the new president. A rating of 1 corresponds to the best performance, and 10 the worst possible. Is there evidence, at the 4% level of significance, that employees rate the new president higher than the old president?

TEST YOUR KNOWLEDGE

CRE09-26

26. A software company has designed a new version of its search engine, and wants to investigate consumer response. A randomly selected group of users of the old search engine is selected, and given training with the new version of the search engine.
    a. The users are given a set of search tasks to complete. The total time required to locate the required information with the old search engine and the new version is recorded for each user (the order of use of the search engines is randomized). Is there evidence, at the 5% level of significance, that the new search engine is faster?
    b. Researchers realized that the data from part a would be affected by the knowledge gained during the first search. They design similar tasks, and then repeat the test. Under the new conditions, is there evidence, at the 5% level of significance, that the new search engine is faster?
    c. Users are also asked to rate their impressions of the old and new search engines. Twenty-one of the users preferred the new version, eight preferred the old version, and five found them about the same. Is there evidence, at the 5% level of significance, that users prefer the new search engine?

CHAPTER 10

Making Decisions with Two Independent Samples, Quantitative or Ranked Data

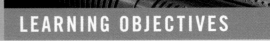

INTRODUCTION

Suppose that a doughnut shop is considering opening a new location in the downtown area. After considering many criteria, the manager has narrowed the choices down to two. All other things being about equal, she wants to choose the location with greater pedestrian traffic. The manager hires a student to count the number of pedestrians passing by each of the two locations, on a random sample of days.

The result of the survey will be two independent samples. When samples are independent, there is no relationship between, for example, observation 1 from sample 1 and observation 1 from sample 2. Conclusions about differences in populations based on independent samples are not as strong as those based on matched pairs (as was discussed in Chapter 9).

Despite the weaker conclusions, independent samples are often used because they are less costly to obtain. In some cases, matched-pairs experiments would not be appropriate or even possible. For example, it would be impossible to design a sensible matched-pairs experiment to

LEARNING OBJECTIVES

After mastering the material in this chapter, you will be able to:

1 Choose and conduct the appropriate hypothesis test to compare two populations, based on independent samples, for normal quantitative data.

2 Choose and conduct the appropriate hypothesis test to compare two populations, based on independent samples, for non-normal quantitative or ranked data.

compare amounts of pedestrian traffic at the two potential doughnut shop locations; there are too many factors that might contribute to different traffic levels, and they cannot all be controlled.

Making a decision about which store location actually has more pedestrian traffic (if there is a difference) requires a hypothesis test of the difference between two means, which is covered in Section 10.1. As you might expect, the kind of test required depends on the normality of the populations.

In Section 10.2, we will examine comparisons of two independent samples when the populations do not appear to be normal. The hypothesis test that we'll use is another non-parametric test, the Wilcoxon Rank Sum Test (WRST). The WRST has some similarities to the Wilcoxon Signed Rank Sum Test covered in Chapter 9, and so you should find it fairly easy to understand. The WRST can also be used to compare independent samples of ranked data, and this is also discussed in Section 10.2.

10.1 INDEPENDENT SAMPLES, NORMAL QUANTITATIVE DATA—THE *t*-TEST AND CONFIDENCE INTERVAL ESTIMATE OF $\mu_1 - \mu_2$

Let's return to the doughnut shop location decision described in the introduction. After considering many criteria for the location decision, the manager wants to focus on pedestrian traffic at the two locations. The manager believes the traffic at location 2 to be higher, but she decides to gather some data to check her belief. A survey over 45 days reveals that location 1 has an average of 108.4 pedestrians per day, and location 2 has an average of 124.4 pedestrians per day. But there is considerable variability in the daily traffic patterns, so is this really evidence that location 2 actually gets more pedestrian traffic, on average? Or is the difference in the two sample means only due to sampling variability?

The manager wants to know if μ_1 (the average daily pedestrian traffic at location 1) is smaller than μ_2 (the average daily pedestrian traffic at location 2). As in the matched-pairs analysis, the focus is the differences, this time between μ_1 and μ_2. Usually (although not always), the null hypothesis is that there is no difference between the two averages—that is, $\mu_1 - \mu_2 = 0$. This leaves three possibilities for the alternative hypothesis:

- If the population 1 mean is greater than the population 2 mean, then H_1 is $\mu_1 - \mu_2 > 0$.
- If the population 1 mean is less than the population 2 mean, then H_1 is $\mu_1 - \mu_2 < 0$.
- If the population 1 mean is different from the population 2 mean, then H_1 is $\mu_1 - \mu_2 \neq 0$.

Of course, we will examine the difference between the two sample means (that is, $\bar{x}_1 - \bar{x}_2$) in order to decide. We need to know what the sampling distribution of $\bar{x}_1 - \bar{x}_2$ looks like in order to make a decision.

Sampling Distribution of $\bar{x}_1 - \bar{x}_2$ with Two Independent Samples

The sampling distribution of $\bar{x}_1 - \bar{x}_2$ is normally distributed if the populations are normal.

1. The standard error of the sampling distribution is

$$\sigma_{\bar{x}_1 - \bar{x}_2} = \sqrt{\frac{\sigma_1^2}{n_1} + \frac{\sigma_2^2}{n_2}}$$

2. The mean of the sampling distribution is

$$\mu_{\bar{x}_1 - \bar{x}_2} = \mu_1 - \mu_2$$

As discussed in Chapter 6, the sampling distributions of the sample means will be approximately normal as long as the populations are not extremely non-normal, or sample sizes are fairly large. The sampling distribution of the differences in the means will also be approximately normal under these conditions.

This information about the sampling distribution cannot be directly applied, as we do not know what σ_1 or σ_2 (the true population standard deviations) are. We have to approximate σ_1 and σ_2 with the sample estimates, that is, s_1 and s_2. We will proceed by using them in place of the unknown population parameters in the formula (as we have before). This means that the test statistic will become

$$t = \frac{(\bar{x}_1 - \bar{x}_2) - \mu_{\bar{x}_1 - \bar{x}_2}}{s_{\bar{x}_1 - \bar{x}_2}} = \frac{(\bar{x}_1 - \bar{x}_2) - (\mu_1 - \mu_2)}{\sqrt{\frac{s_1^2}{n_1} + \frac{s_2^2}{n_2}}}$$

When we estimate both standard deviations, the resulting sampling distribution is not actually a t-distribution, but fortunately it can be approximated with a t-distribution. Perhaps unfortunately, the approximate degrees of freedom for the relevant t-distribution are as follows:

$$df = \frac{\left(\frac{s_1^2}{n_1} + \frac{s_2^2}{n_2}\right)^2}{\frac{\left(\frac{s_1^2}{n_1}\right)^2}{(n_1 - 1)} + \frac{\left(\frac{s_2^2}{n_2}\right)^2}{(n_2 - 1)}}$$

Using Data Analysis t-Test: Two-Sample Assuming Unequal Variances

It should be obvious that such an expression is best evaluated by computer (although it is certainly possible to do it with a calculator). Excel has a built-in **Data Analysis** tool that supports hypothesis testing of the difference in means for normal data, with independent samples. It can be used when you have the raw data from the samples on which the analysis is based

Exhibit 10.1 below shows the **Data Analysis** menu. The correct choice is as highlighted: ***t*-Test: Two-Sample Assuming Unequal Variances**.

As always, you should set up the hypothesis test and do your thinking before you turn to the computer. Example 10.1A illustrates this.

EXHIBIT 10.1

Excel Data Analysis Dialogue Box

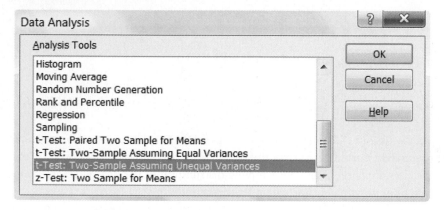

EXAMPLE 10.1A

t-Test for independent samples, using Excel

EXA10-1a

The manager of a doughnut shop is trying to decide between two potential locations for a new shop. The manager believes the traffic at location 2 to be higher, but she decides to gather some data to check her belief.

- $H_0: \mu_1 - \mu_2 = 0$ (that is, there is no difference in the means of the two populations; this is the null hypothesis in most cases)
- $H_1: \mu_1 - \mu_2 < 0$ (this is based on our question: does location 2 actually get more pedestrian traffic?)
- Use $\alpha = 0.04$

The first thing we must assess is the normality of the populations. As usual, we do that by creating histograms of the sample data. The histograms shown opposite in Exhibit 10.2 are reasonably normal. Both sample sizes are fairly large, at 45, and so we can proceed.

Exhibit 10.3 on page 376 shows the ***t*-Test** dialogue box.

The dialogue box requires you to indicate where the sample data are stored (**Variable 1 Range:** and **Variable 2 Range:**). As indicated in Exhibit 10.3, the **Hypothesized Mean Difference** is usually zero (although there are instances when it is another value). The Excel output is shown in Exhibit 10.4, on page 376.

EXHIBIT 10.2

Histograms of Daily Pedestrian Traffic at Two Potential Doughnut Shop Locations

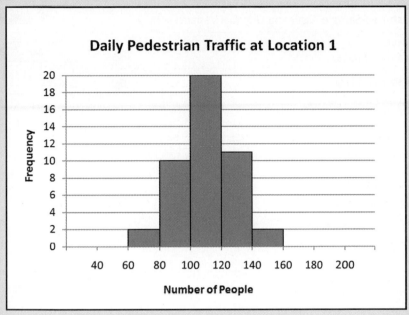

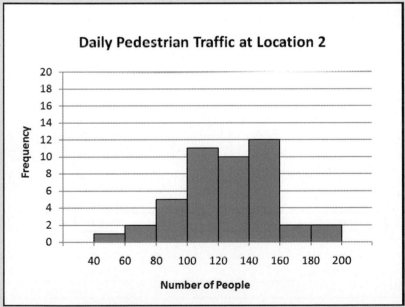

We can see from the output shown on page 376 that the p-value is 0.00104 (the row is highlighted in the table, although it will not be in the Excel output). Since this is less than the α of 0.04, we reject the null hypothesis. There is sufficient evidence to conclude that average daily pedestrian traffic at location 2 is higher than at location 1. (An equivalent way to say this is that average pedestrian traffic at location 1 is lower than at location 2.)

EXHIBIT 10.3

t-Test Dialogue Box

t-Test: Two-Sample Assuming Unequal Variances

Input
Variable 1 Range:
Variable 2 Range:

Hypothesized Mean Difference: 0

☐ Labels
Alpha: 0.05

Output options
◉ Output Range:
◯ New Worksheet Ply:
◯ New Workbook

OK
Cancel
Help

EXHIBIT 10.4

Excel Output for *t*-Test: Two-Sample Assuming Unequal Variances

t-Test: Two-Sample Assuming Unequal Variances

	Location 1	Location 2
Mean	108.378	124.622
Variance	298.649	863.786
Observations	45	45
Hypothesized Mean Difference	0	
df	71	
t Stat	-3.19615	
P(T<=t) one-tail	0.00104	
t Critical one-tail	1.6666	
P(T<=t) two-tail	0.00208	
t Critical two-tail	1.99394	

Now, what if you want to do a comparison of means with independent samples by hand? With courage and a good calculator, you can calculate the degrees of freedom with the formula shown on page 373, and use the *t*-table to estimate the *p*-value. However, if your courage fails, you can use a simpler approach to the degrees of freedom. Instead of the complicated formula for degrees of freedom shown on page 373, use the lesser of $(n_1 - 1)$ and $(n_2 - 1)$ as the degrees of freedom. The result will not be as accurate, but will provide a conservative answer, in that it will tend to overestimate the

p-value (and so you will be somewhat less likely to reject the null hypothesis with the manual method).

While the computer-based approach is preferred, you can do these problems by hand with tables. Example 10.1B below illustrates the approach, and compares the results with the computer-based analysis.

EXAMPLE 10.1B

t-Test for independent samples, using *t*-table

A toy company is trying to decide which brand of battery to install in its battery-operated toys. A random sample of 45 AA batteries from the Everlife battery company yields a mean life of 28.5 hours, with a standard deviation of 5.3 hours. A random sample of 42 AA batteries from the Durible battery company produces a mean life of 30.2 hours, with a standard deviation of 6.9 hours. At the 4% level of significance, is there evidence of a difference in mean battery life? You may assume that the battery life data are normally distributed, for both manufacturers.

Again, recognize that these are independent samples. There is no correspondence between battery 1 in the Everlife sample and battery 1 in the Durible sample. Also, the sample sizes are different, which guarantees that this cannot be a matched-pairs sample.

Let's designate the Everlife sample as sample 1 from population 1, and the Durible sample as sample 2 from population 2 (you should always state your designation explicitly when you do one of these problems, so that you don't get confused about which population is which).

- $H_0 : \mu_1 - \mu_2 = 0$ (mean battery life is the same for Everlife and Durible)
- $H_1 : \mu_1 - \mu_2 \neq 0$ (mean battery life is different for Everlife and Durible)
- $\alpha = 0.04$
- $t = \dfrac{(\bar{x}_1 - \bar{x}_2) - (\mu_1 - \mu_2)}{\sqrt{\dfrac{s_1^2}{n_1} + \dfrac{s_2^2}{n_2}}} = \dfrac{(28.5 - 30.2) - (0)}{\sqrt{\dfrac{5.3^2}{45} + \dfrac{6.9^2}{42}}} = -1.282$

We will have to use the t-table to approximate the p-value. We approximate the degrees of freedom as the minimum of $(n_1 - 1)$ and $(n_2 - 1)$.

$$n_1 - 1 = 45 - 1 = 44$$

$$n_2 - 1 = 42 - 1 = 41$$

The minimum is 41. We have no row in the t-table for 41 degrees. The closest is the row with 40 degrees of freedom, which is illustrated in Exhibit 10.5 below.

EXHIBIT 10.5

t-Distribution Critical Values

Degrees of Freedom	$t_{.100}$	$t_{.050}$	$t_{.025}$	$t_{.010}$	$t_{.005}$
40	1.303	1.684	2.021	2.423	2.704

1.282

We can see that the one-tailed *p*-value is >10%, which means that the two-tailed *p*-value (appropriate for this test) is >20%. We fail to reject the null hypothesis. There is insufficient evidence to conclude that there is a difference in AA battery life between the Everlife and Durible brands.

Using the Excel Template for *t*-Test of Means   Now we can turn to Excel for a more accurate result. In this example, we do not have the data on which the summary statistics are based. There is a worksheet template called "*t*-Test of Means, Independent" in the workbook called "Templates." You can use this template if you have only the summary statistics available (sample mean, etc.). You could also use the template if you have calculated the summary statistics from the raw data (preferably using a computer!). The completed template for Example 10.1B is shown below in Exhibit 10.6.

EXHIBIT 10.6

Completed Excel Template for Example 10.1B

Making Decisions About the Difference in Population Means with Two Independent Samples	
Do the sample data appear to be normally distributed?	yes
Sample 1 Standard Deviation	5.3
Sample 2 Standard Deviation	6.9
Sample 1 Mean	28.5
Sample 2 Mean	30.2
Sample 1 Size	45
Sample 2 Size	42
Hypothetical Difference in Population Means	0
t-Score	-1.28223
One-Tailed p-Value	0.10183
Two-Tailed p-Value	0.20366

When we used the simplified approach for degrees of freedom and estimated the *p*-value, we concluded that it was > 20%. The two-tailed *p*-value shown in the template is 20.4%, so our manual method was pretty close. This will not always be the case. You should always use the computer to do these tests if possible.

Equal or Unequal Variances?

In Example 10.1A, the sample variance for the location 1 data was 298.649 (see the Excel output in Exhibit 10.4 on p. 376), and the sample variance for the location 2 data was 863.786. In Example 10.1B, sample 1's standard deviation was 5.3 (making the variance = $5.3^2 = 28.09$), and sample 2's standard deviation was 6.9 (making the variance = $6.9^2 = 47.61$). Since the variances were fairly far apart in both cases, it seems reasonable that we chose the *t*-test with unequal variances.

In some cases, we might suspect that population variances are equal, which would allow us to use another version of the *t*-test that is available in Excel—namely, ***t*-Test: Two-Sample Assuming Equal Variances**. There are some advantages to the equal-variances version of this hypothesis test. Since the variances are assumed to be equal, the sample data can be pooled, which should lead to a better estimate of the variance (and the standard deviation). As well, the sampling distribution is exactly a *t*-distribution when the variances are equal.

However, there is an important difficulty in using the equal-variances version of the test: how do we know if the population variances are equal? Several statistical tests are available to help with this decision, but they are sensitive to non-normality (some of them quite highly so). This makes it difficult to decide whether the variances are equal, especially when sample sizes are small.

As well, any test of variances should be independent of the test of means. Remember, for a hypothesis test, the significance level is the cut-off for deciding whether a sample result is so unusual that we have convincing evidence against the null hypothesis. However, there is always the chance that the null hypothesis is true, and we have actually observed a highly unusual sample. If we reject the null hypothesis in such a case, we are committing a Type I error. The significance level is the upper limit on Type I error. But it's only the upper limit if we conduct just one test. If we conduct another test with the same data, we are increasing the possibility of Type I error. Think of it this way: suppose you are skating across a frozen lake, and there is a 5% chance that you will fall through the ice (an unusual event). If you skate across the lake only once, then it is unlikely that you will fall through the ice. But if you keep skating back and forth across the lake, your chances of falling in (the unusual event) will increase. Doing repeated hypothesis tests on the same data set is like skating across the lake more than once. There is an increased chance of actually observing an unusual sample, and rejecting the null hypothesis when we shouldn't. So, we cannot safely use the same data set to test for equality of variances and also equality of means. Testing the variances thus requires additional sampling, *before* you sample to make a decision about the means.

Finally, if you mistakenly assume that the variances are equal when they are not, your results will be unreliable, particularly when sample sizes differ (and especially when the smaller sample has the larger variance).

> **Equal-Variances and Unequal-Variances Versions of the *t*-Test of $\mu_1 - \mu_2$**
>
> It is recommended that you always use the unequal variances version of the *t*-test to compare population means with independent normally distributed samples, unless you have strong independent evidence that the variances are the same.

Using the unequal variances version of the *t*-test will lead to the right decision, even if the variances are in fact equal (with very few exceptions). One reason for this is that if the variances *are* equal, then s_1^2 and s_2^2 will be fairly close, so that the *pooled* version of the variance will be close to the *unpooled* version. Also, when sample sizes are close to the same, the results of the *t*-test assuming equal variances will be very close to the results for the *t*-test assuming unequal variances.

To illustrate, we will redo the calculations of Example 10.1B, but this time we will assume *equal* population variances. The pooled variance is a weighted average of the sample variances.

$$s_p^2 = \frac{(n_1 - 1)s_1^2 + (n_2 - 1)s_2^2}{(n_1 + n_2 - 2)} = \frac{(45 - 1)5.3^2 + (42 - 1)6.9^2}{(45 + 42 - 2)} = 37.50553$$

The t-score then becomes

$$t = \frac{(\bar{x}_1 - \bar{x}_2) - (\mu_1 - \mu_2)}{\sqrt{s_p^2\left(\frac{1}{n_1} + \frac{1}{n_2}\right)}} = \frac{(28.5 - 30.2) - (0)}{\sqrt{37.50553\left(\frac{1}{45} + \frac{1}{42}\right)}} = -1.2938$$

Using Excel, we calculate the p-value as 0.1992. This is very close to the p-value we calculated for the unequal-variances version of the test, which was 0.2037 (see Exhibit 10.6 on p. 378). Certainly, the conclusion is not affected by the choice of the equal or unequal variances version of the t-test for Example 10.1B.

GUIDE TO DECISION MAKING

Independent Samples, Normal Quantitative Data—The t-Test of $\mu_1 - \mu_2$ to Decide About the Difference in Two Population Means

When:

- normal quantitative data, independent samples
- trying to make a decision about $\mu_1 - \mu_2$ (the difference in population means) on the basis of $\bar{x}_1 - \bar{x}_2$ (the difference in the sample means)
- variances are unequal (this version of the test is recommended, unless you have strong independent evidence that variances are equal)

Steps:
1. Specify H_0, the null hypothesis, which will usually be H_0: $\mu_1 - \mu_2 = 0$.
2. Specify H_1, the alternative hypothesis.
3. Determine or identify α, the significance level.
4. Collect or identify the sample data. Identify or calculate:

   - the sample means, $\bar{x}_1$ and $\bar{x}_2$
   - the sample standard deviations, s_1 and s_2
   - the sample sizes, n_1 and n_2

5. Check for normality of populations with histograms of the sample data. If even one of the histograms is non-normal, particularly with small sample sizes, do not proceed with the t-test (use the Wilcoxon Rank Sum Test instead, described on page 384).
6. *If* the samples appear to be normally distributed, calculate the appropriate t-score, using the following formula:

$$t = \frac{(\bar{x}_1 - \bar{x}_2) - (\mu_1 - \mu_2)}{\sqrt{\frac{s_1^2}{n_1} + \frac{s_2^2}{n_2}}}$$

7. Calculate or estimate the degrees of freedom for the appropriate t-distribution. If you are using a computer, the degrees of freedom will be calculated for you. If you are doing the problem by hand, approximate the degrees of freedom by choosing the minimum of $(n_1 - 1)$ and $(n_2 - 1)$.

8. Use the *t*-distribution to calculate (or approximate, if using tables) the appropriate *p*-value for the hypothesis test, keeping in mind the order of subtraction used when calculating the differences.

9. If *p*-value $\leq \alpha$, reject H_0 and conclude that there is sufficient evidence to decide in favour of H_1. If *p*-value $> \alpha$, fail to reject H_0 and conclude that there is insufficient evidence to decide in favour of H_1. State your conclusions in language appropriate to the problem.

See Example 10.1A on page 374 (using Excel), and Example 10.1B on page 377 (using the *t*-table).

Confidence Interval for $\mu_1 - \mu_2$

Following directly from the sampling distribution and the discussion of the hypothesis test, a confidence interval estimate can be constructed for the difference in population means, as follows:

$$\text{(point estimate)} \pm \text{(critical value)} \cdot \text{(estimated standard error of the sample statistic)}$$

$$(\bar{x}_1 - \bar{x}_2) \pm t\text{-score}\sqrt{\frac{s_1^2}{n_1} + \frac{s_2^2}{n_2}}$$

where the *t*-score corresponds to the desired level of confidence, and has approximately

$$\frac{\left(\dfrac{s_1^2}{n_1} + \dfrac{s_2^2}{n_2} \right)^2}{\dfrac{\left(\dfrac{s_1^2}{n_1} \right)^2}{(n_1 - 1)} + \dfrac{\left(\dfrac{s_2^2}{n_2} \right)^2}{(n_2 - 1)}}$$

degrees of freedom. As above, when you are creating a confidence interval estimate by hand, you may use minimum $(n_1 - 1, n_2 - 1)$ as the degrees of freedom. Of course, normality of the populations is required for this formula to be appropriate.

Example 10.1C below illustrates construction of a confidence interval for the life of the batteries described in Example 10.1B.

EXAMPLE **10.1C**

Confidence interval for difference in means

The toy company wants to estimate the difference in average battery life between AA batteries from the Everlife battery company and those from the Durible battery company. A random sample of 45 AA batteries from the Everlife battery company yields a mean life of 28.5 hours, with a standard deviation of 5.3 hours. A random sample of 42 AA batteries from the Durible battery company produces a mean life of 30.2 hours, with a standard deviation of 6.9 hours. Construct a 99% confidence interval estimate for the difference in average battery life between the two kinds of batteries. You may assume that the battery life data are normally distributed.

We use the formula for the confidence interval:

$$(\bar{x}_1 - \bar{x}_2) \pm t\text{-score}\sqrt{\frac{s_1^2}{n_1} + \frac{s_2^2}{n_2}}$$

$$(28.5 - 30.2) \pm t\text{-score}\sqrt{\frac{5.3^2}{45} + \frac{6.9^2}{42}}$$

When doing this by hand, we will use the t-score with degrees of freedom = minimum$(n_1 - 1, n_2 - 1)$. The minimum of $(45 - 1, 42 - 1)$ is 41. We find no row in the table for 41 degrees of freedom, so we will use the row for 40. It is illustrated in Exhibit 10.7 below.

EXHIBIT 10.7

t-Distribution Critical Values

Degrees of Freedom	$t_{.100}$	$t_{.050}$	$t_{.025}$	$t_{.010}$	$t_{.005}$
40	1.303	1.684	2.021	2.423	2.704

for 99% CI

We will now complete the calculations.

$$(28.5 - 30.2) \pm (2.704)\sqrt{\frac{5.3^2}{45} + \frac{6.9^2}{42}}$$

$$= -1.7 \pm (2.704)(1.3258)$$

$$= -1.7 \pm 3.5850$$

$$= (-5.29, 1.89)$$

With a confidence level of 99%, we believe that the interval $(-5.29, 1.89)$ contains the true difference in average battery life between the Everlife and Durible batteries. Notice that this interval contains zero, which we would expect, since the hypothesis test concluded that there was no evidence of a significant difference in battery life. (We have to be careful in establishing this correspondence between the hypothesis test and the confidence interval. They do not correspond exactly, because the significance level of 4% does not match with a confidence level of 99%.)

Using the Excel Template for Confidence Interval Estimate for the Difference in Population Means   There is a template on the worksheet called "CI for Diff in Means" in the workbook called "Templates." This template allows you to calculate confidence interval estimates more accurately. As always, you are required to fill in the blue-shaded cells in the template. A completed template for Example 10.1C is shown opposite in Exhibit 10.8.

The approximation done by hand produced an interval of $(-5.29, 1.89)$. This is fairly close to the more accurate interval shown in the template of $(-5.20, 1.80)$.

EXHIBIT 10.8

Completed Excel Template for Confidence Interval Estimate for the Difference in Population Means, Example 10.1C

Confidence Interval Estimate for the Difference in Population Means	
Do the sample data appear to be normally distributed?	yes
Sample 1 Standard Deviation	5.3
Sample 2 Standard Deviation	6.9
Sample 1 Mean	28.5
Sample 2 Mean	30.2
Sample 1 Size	45
Sample 2 Size	42
Confidence Level (decimal form)	0.99
Upper Confidence Limit	1.80292
Lower Confidence Limit	-5.20292

DEVELOP YOUR SKILLS 10.1

1. The foreman at an assembly plant is concerned that the number of defective items produced on the night shift seems to be higher than during the day shift. A random sample of 45 night shifts had an average of 35.4 defects, with a standard deviation of 15.3. A random sample of 50 day shifts had an average of 27.8 defects, with a standard deviation of 7.9. Is there sufficient evidence, at the 5% significance level, to indicate that the number of defects is higher on the night shift than on the day shift? You may assume that the population distributions of errors are normally distributed.

2. The owner of a drugstore is wondering whether he should target female customers in particular, because he
DYS10-2 believes that they tend to spend more than male customers. He asks the cashiers to keep track of the spending by a random sample of female customers, and a random sample of male customers, over several days. The purchases are shown in Exhibit 10.9. At the 2.5% level of significance, do the data provide evidence to support the drugstore owner's idea that female customers spend more than male customers?

EXHIBIT 10.9

Drugstore Purchases by a Random Sample of Customers

Purchases by Females ($)	Purchases by Males ($)
30.5	31.49
28.73	28.88
38.66	30.77
44.15	24.95
42.98	23.26
39.56	27.66
36.25	25.77
31.49	33.32
49.43	18.29
29.36	38.25
24.65	25.09
29.64	30.51
17.30	24.96
20.34	26.34
23.40	

3. Construct a 95% confidence interval estimate for the average difference in purchases made by female customers compared to male customers, based on the data in Exercise 2 above. Do you expect this confidence interval to contain zero? Why or why not?

4. A hotgog vendor who operates just outside the front door of a major hardware store wants to know if his daily sales have increased this summer, compared with last summer. He does not have electronic records, so he selects a random sample of days from last summer, and calculates daily sales from his records. He does the same for a random sample of days from this summer.

 DYS10-4

Is there sufficient evidence for the owner to conclude that daily sales are higher than last year, on average? Use $\alpha = 0.03$.

5. A radio station is interested in whether listening habits differ by age. The station identified a random sample of 30 listeners aged 25 and younger, and asked them to keep track of the number of minutes they listened to the station in a week. The station also identified a random sample of 35 listeners who were over 25 years of age, and asked them to record their listening times. The data from the younger listeners yielded an average of 256.8 minutes, with a standard deviation of 50.3 minutes. The data from the older listeners yielded an average of 218.3 minutes, with a standard deviation of 92.4 minutes. At the 5% significance level, is there evidence of a difference in listening times between the two age groups?

10.2 INDEPENDENT SAMPLES, NON-NORMAL QUANTITATIVE DATA OR RANKED DATA—THE WILCOXON RANK SUM TEST

There are two remaining situations in which you might want to compare two independent samples. The first follows from the previous section—what if the quantitative data do not appear to be normally distributed? The second arises when the data points themselves are ranked data. In both situations, it is possible to use the Wilcoxon Rank Sum Test (WRST) to make decisions. The WRST is quite similar to the WSRST, in that it involves ordering the data, assigning ranks, and calculating rank sums. Examples 10.2A and 10.2B illustrate the use of this test. As with the Wilcoxon Signed Rank Sum Test, we can make conclusions about population locations (and average values) only if the populations are similar in shape and spread. Therefore, we begin by creating histograms of sample data to check for similarity in shape and spread. As usual, this can be difficult to assess with small data sets.

The WRST requires you to calculate the sum of the ranks for each sample. All of the values in both samples are considered simultaneously when ranks are assigned, and so the ranks will go from 1 to $(n_1 + n_2)$. As with the Wilcoxon Signed Rank Sum Test, ranks are averaged for tied values. The ranks for each sample are summed, to arrive at W_1 for sample 1 and W_2 for sample 2. If the samples come from populations in the same location, we would expect the rank sums to be about equal, while allowing for different sample sizes (smaller samples will have smaller rank sums, because there are fewer terms to add up). If the samples come from populations in different locations, we would expect the rank sums to be very different. It is possible to draw conclusions by examining either W_1 or W_2. For consistency, we will focus on W_1. In particular, when we are working with tables, we will designate W_1 as the rank sum of the *smaller* sample (if the samples are of different sizes).

Of course, we need a sampling distribution to know when the rank sums are significantly different. When sample sizes are large, the sampling distribution of W_1 is approximately normal; when sample sizes are small, we use the tables in Appendix 5.

Sampling Distribution of W_1 with Two Independent Samples

When both sample sizes are at least 10, the sampling distribution of W_1 is approximately normally distributed.

1. The standard error of the sampling distribution is calculated with the following formula, where n_1 is the size of sample 1, and n_2 is the size of sample 2.

$$\sigma_{W_1} = \sqrt{\frac{n_1 n_2 (n_1 + n_2 + 1)}{12}}$$

2. The mean of the sampling distribution of W_1 is

$$\mu_{W_1} = \frac{n_1(n_1 + n_2 + 1)}{2}$$

If you are doing these problems by hand, you will use a *z*-score of the usual form, that is:

$$z = \frac{W_1 - \mu_{W_1}}{\sigma_{W_1}} = \frac{W_1 - \dfrac{n_1 n_2(n_1 + n_2 + 1)}{2}}{\sqrt{\dfrac{n_1 n_2(n_1 + n_2 + 1)}{12}}}$$

Independent Samples, Non-Normal Quantitative Data

The ranking process in the Wilcoxon Rank Sum Test is very similar to the ranking process for the Wilcoxon Signed Rank Sum Test from Chapter 9, as Example 10.2A illustrates.

EXAMPLE **10.2A**

Wilcoxon Rank Sum Test, sample sizes $\geq$ 10

A company that manages a number of golf course properties is trying to decide between two types of accounting software, CreditIt and DoubleEntry. One of the criteria the company is using to make its decision is the number of times per day that the system locks up, requiring a supervisor override to complete an entry. The company wants to determine whether there are fewer supervisor overrides with the CreditIt software. A random sample of days is chosen, and the number of supervisor overrides is recorded.

EXA10-2a

First, notice that these are independent samples, and not matched pairs. The software users are doing a variety of tasks (not matched) on different days (also not matched).

Histograms for this data set do show some similarity in shape and spread. The range is the same, and there is notable skewness to the right. The histograms are shown below in Exhibit 10.10.

EXHIBIT 10.10

Histograms of Overrides for Accounting Software

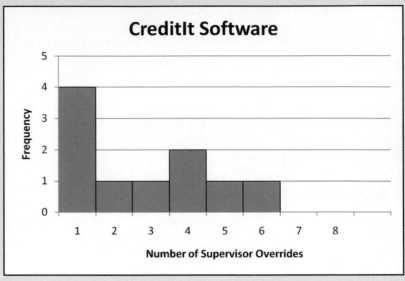

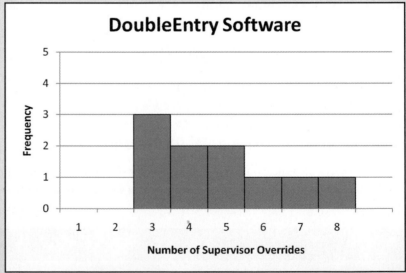

Because of the significant skewness and small sample size, it would not be appropriate to use a *t*-test to analyze this data set.

- H_0: The CreditIt and DoubleEntry software require the same number of daily supervisor overrides.
- H_1: The CreditIt software requires a lower number of daily supervisor overrides.
- Use $\alpha = 0.05$.

Exhibit 10.11 below shows the assigned ranks for the two samples.

EXHIBIT 10.11

Supervisor Overrides for Accounting Software

CreditIt Supervisor Overrides	DoubleEntry Supervisor Overrides	CreditIt Supervisor Overrides (Ordered Data)	Initial Ranks	Final Ranks (Adjusted for Tied Values)	DoubleEntry Supervisor Overrides (Ordered Data)	Initial Ranks	Final Ranks (Adjusted for Tied Values)
6	8	1	1	2.5	3	7	7.5
1	5	1	2	2.5	3	8	7.5
4	4	1	3	2.5	3	9	7.5
5	4	1	4	2.5	4	10	11.5
3	3	2	5	5	4	11	11.5
4	3	3	6	7.5	5	15	15
1	5	4	12	11.5	5	16	15
1	6	4	13	11.5	6	17	17.5
1	7	5	14	15	7	19	19
2	3	6	18	17.5	8	20	20
				$W_1 = 78$			$W_2 = 132$

When values are tied, the associated ranks are averaged. For example, there are four values of 1 in this sample data set. They are the four lowest values, and the ranks 1, 2, 3, and 4 have to be assigned to them. These ranks are averaged.

$$\frac{1 + 2 + 3 + 4}{4} = 2.5$$

This average rank of 2.5 is assigned to all four values of 1. This process is repeated any time the values are tied.

Because the samples are the same size, we can designate either sample as sample 1. We will designate the data set for the CreditIt data as sample 1, and the sum of the ranks for this sample W_1.

The sample sizes are just large enough for the normal approximation.

$$z = \frac{W_1 - \mu_{W_1}}{\sigma_{W_1}} - \frac{78 - \dfrac{10(10 + 10 + 1)}{2}}{\sqrt{\dfrac{10(10)(10 + 10 + 1)}{12}}} = -2.04$$

In order to get the p-value, we have to think about the alternative hypothesis and what W_1 tells us. We are wondering if the supervisor overrides with the CreditIt software are lower than with the DoubleEntry software. If this were the case, then the number of overrides in sample 1 (the CreditIt sample) would be lower than in sample 2. This would lead to a lower rank sum for sample 1. Therefore, the p-value will be $P(W_1 \leq 78)$.

$$P(W_1 \leq 78) = P(z \leq -2.04) = 0.0207$$

Since this p-value is less than the α of 5%, we reject the null hypothesis. There is sufficient evidence to infer that fewer supervisor overrides are required with the CreditIt software.

Using the Excel Add-in and Template for Sample Sizes ≥10   There is no built-in **Data Analysis** function in Excel to allow you to conduct a Wilcoxon Rank Sum Test. One of the Excel add-ins that comes with this textbook allows you to quickly and easily calculate W_1 and W_2 for any data set. Once the add-ins are installed, click on the **Add-Ins** tab, click on **Non-Parametric Tools**, and then choose **Wilcoxon Rank Sum Test Calculations**. As usual, you will have to fill in the dialogue box to indicate where sample 1 and sample 2 data are stored, and where you want the output placed. You should keep track of which sample you designated as sample 1, and which as sample 2, to help you understand the results. The output for the data in Example 10.2A is shown in Exhibit 10.12. Again, for consistency, you should designate the smaller sample as sample 1, if the samples are not the same size.

EXHIBIT **10.12**

Excel Output for Wilcoxon Rank Sum Test Calculations, Example 10.2A

Wilcoxon Rank Sum Test Calculations	
sample 1 size	10
sample 2 size	10
W1	78
W2	132

You can then use the worksheet template called "WRST Independent" (which is available in the workbook called "Templates") for *p*-value calculations. This template should only be used when sample sizes are at least 10. Exhibit 10.13 shows the worksheet template for Example 10.2A.

EXHIBIT **10.13**

Excel Template for Making Decisions About Two Population Locations, Non-Normal Quantitative Data or Ranked Data (WRST), Example 10.2A

Making Decisions About Two Population Locations, Two Independent Samples of Non-Normal Quantitative Data or Ranked Data (WRST)	
Sample 1 Size	10
Sample 2 Size	10
Are both sample sizes at least 10?	yes
Are the sample histograms similar in shape and spread?	yes
W1	78
W2	132
z-Score (based on W1)	-2.04100815
One-Tailed p-Value	0.02062501
Two-Tailed p-Value	0.04125002

As usual, you must fill in the blue-shaded cells in the template. The *p*-value is slightly more accurate than the one we calculated by hand.

Wilcoxon Rank Sum Test or *t*-Test of $\mu_1 - \mu_2$?

We have now looked at two ways to draw a conclusion about two populations of quantitative data: one for normal data, and one for non-normal data. You might be tempted to choose the WRST whether the data are normal are not, since normal data fit the requirements for the WRST (that is, that the distributions be similar in shape and spread). But you should *not* succumb to this temptation.

The *t*-test is preferred to the Wilcoxon Rank Sum Test, because the *t*-test is more powerful than the WRST when the data are normal, in the sense that it is better at detecting false hypotheses. You should always use the *t*-test if you can.

How normal is normal enough? As always, this depends on sample size. The *t*-test works well, particularly when sample sizes are equal and sample histograms are similar, even if they are somewhat non-normal and skewed. The larger the sample sizes are, the more reliable the *t*-test will be. As always, you should be cautious about using a *t*-test when there are outliers in the data.

Independent Samples, Ranked Data

As mentioned above, the WRST is also useful in comparing two populations of ranked data, as Example 10.2B below illustrates. This example also illustrates the use of the Wilcoxon Rank Sum tables for sample sizes < 10.

EXAMPLE **10.2B**

Wilcoxon Rank Sum Test, sample size < 10

A restaurant owner is trying to decide which of two chefs she should promote. Both of the chefs work at a small restaurant that is known for its interesting fusion of French and Asian cooking styles. The owner is currently leaning toward Chef Lee as worthy of promotion. Her accountant has accused her of personal bias, and she is determined to refute this accusation by using data in her decision-making process. The owner decides to do a hypothesis test with a 5% level of significance.

The owner selects a random sample of customers who are dining when Chef Lee is cooking, and asks them to rate the food. She does the same for a random sample of customers when Chef Girard is cooking. The rating scale is as follows: (1) barely edible; (2) passable; (3) good; and (4) absolutely delicious.

The survey results and assigned ranks are shown in Exhibit 10.14 on the next page. The data are similar in spread (ratings are from 1 to 4) and similar in shape, so we can use the Wilcoxon Rank Sum Test to draw a conclusion about population locations.

- H_0: the ratings for Chef Lee's food and Chef Girard's food are the same
- H_1: the ratings for Chef Lee's food are higher than for Chef Girard's food
- $\alpha = 5\%$

Since we have different sample sizes here, we designate the smallest sample (Chef Girard's ratings) as sample 1. Notice that we need calculate only W_1 to complete our analysis. We choose to calculate W_1 from the smallest sample because it's less work! As well, the Wilcoxon Rank Sum Table is based on the rank sum from the smallest sample.

EXHIBIT 10.14

Restaurant Food Ratings

Ratings Assigned to Chef Lee's Food	Ratings Assigned to Chef Girard's Food	Ratings Assigned to Chef Lee's Food (Ordered)	Ranks	Ratings Assigned to Chef Girard's Food (Ordered)	Ranks
2	2	1	2	1	2
4	3	2	5.5	1	2
3	3	2	5.5	2	5.5
4	2	3	11	2	5.5
2	1	3	11	3	11
1	4	3	11	3	11
3	3	3	11	3	11
3	1	4	16	4	16
3		4	16		
			$W_2 = 89$		$W_1 = 64$

Before we calculate the p-value, we have to think about W_1 and what it tells us. In this case, higher numerical rankings correspond to higher actual rankings (the highest rank is 4, which corresponds to *absolutely delicious*). If the ratings for Chef Lee's food are higher than for Chef Girard's food, then the rank sum for the Chef Lee ratings sample should be higher, and the rank sum for Chef Girard's food should be lower, although we have to take into consideration that Chef Girard's sample is smaller. Therefore, to get the p-value, we need to figure out $P(W_1 \leq 64)$ when $n_1 = 8$ and $n_2 = 9$.

Before we go to the table, notice something very important: because sample 1 is smaller, its rank sum will be smaller, even when there is no difference in the two population locations. The Wilcoxon Rank Sum Test table is based on the calculation of W_1 from the smaller sample. It is critical that you always calculate W_1 from the smaller of the two samples when you are using the tables. Otherwise, your conclusion may be incorrect.

The table for the Wilcoxon Rank Sum Test is at the back of the book, in Appendix 5 on page 582. The table lists the rank sums (for the smaller sample) with p-values that are either equal to or close to the common levels of significance of 0.010, 0.025, and 0.05. The sampling distribution of W_1 is symmetric, so $P(W_1 \geq W_U) = P(W_1 \leq W_L)$.

When you use the table, you first have to identify n_1 (the size of the smaller sample), n_2 (the size of the larger sample), and W_1 (the rank sum for the smaller sample). In Example 10.2B, $n_1 = 8$, $n_2 = 9$, and $W_1 = 64$. An excerpt from the table is shown opposite in Exhibit 10.15.

$W_1 = 64$. This value is not on the table, but we can proceed as usual. $P(W_1 \leq 55) = 0.057$, so we know $P(W_1 \leq 64) > 0.057$. Since the p-value is greater than α, we fail to reject H_0. There is insufficient evidence to conclude that Chef Lee's ratings are higher than Chef Girard's. The data do not support promotion of Chef Lee on the basis of this criterion. The owner is going to have to find some other way to justify her promotion of Chef Lee.

EXHIBIT 10.15

Wilcoxon Rank Sum Test Critical Values and p-Values

n_1	n_2	W_L	W_U	$P(W_1 \leq W_L) = P(W_2 \geq W_U)$
8	9	55	89	0.057
		54	90	0.046
		52	92	0.030
		51	93	0.023
		48	96	0.010

GUIDE TO DECISION MAKING

Independent Samples, Non-Normal Quantitative Data or Ranked Data—The Wilcoxon Rank Sum Test to Decide About the Difference in Two Population Locations

When:

- non-normal quantitative data or ranked data, independent samples
- trying to make a decision about the locations of two populations

Steps:

1. Specify H_0, the null hypothesis, which is normally that there is no difference in the population locations.
2. Specify H_1, the alternative hypothesis. Specify the hypothesis in words that reflect the context of the problem.
3. Determine or identify α, the significance level.
4. Collect or identify the sample data.
5. Create histograms of the data, and check for normality. If the histograms appear normal and the data are quantitative, use the t-test of $\mu_1 - \mu_2$ (described on page 380). If the histograms are non-normal, they should be similar in shape and spread for conclusions to be drawn about population locations.
6. Considering all of the data (from both samples) simultaneously, rank the data from 1 to $(n_1 + n_2)$. Average the ranks for tied data points. Calculate W_1, the sum of the ranks for sample 1, which is the *smallest* sample.
7. *If* both n_1 and n_2 are ≥ 10, the sampling distribution of W_1 is approximately normal, with

$$\sigma_{W_1} = \sqrt{\frac{n_1 n_2(n_1 + n_2 + 1)}{12}}$$

$$\mu_{W_1} = \frac{n_1(n_1 + n_2 + 1)}{2}$$

Use the normal sampling distribution to calculate the p-value of the result. When doing this by hand, the calculation will involve the z-score:

$$z = \frac{W_1 - \mu_{W_1}}{\sigma_{W_1}}$$

If either of n_1 or n_2 is < 10, use the table in Appendix 5 on page 582 to approximate the p-value. The table provides p-values for W_1, assuming it is calculated from the smallest sample.

8. If p-value $\leq \alpha$, reject H_0 and conclude that there is sufficient evidence to decide in favour of H_1. If p-value $> \alpha$, fail to reject H_0 and conclude that there is insufficient evidence to decide in favour of H_1. State your conclusions in language appropriate to the problem.

See Example 10.2A on page 385 (sample sizes $\geq$ 10), and Example 10.2B on page 389 (sample sizes < 10).

DEVELOP YOUR SKILLS 10.2

6. A bank with a management training program is considering promotion of one of two trainees in the Metro West division. The bank has asked for 360° feedback for each of the trainees (that is, feedback from managers and peers). The overall ratings for each trainee are shown in Exhibit 10.16 below. The ratings range from 1 to 6, where 1 corresponds to the best performance, and 6 corresponds to the worst performance. At the 2.5% level of significance, is there evidence of a difference in the performance ratings of the two trainees? Based on these performance ratings, which trainee should be promoted?

EXHIBIT 10.16

Performance Ratings

Trainee #1	Trainee #2
1	4
5	5
3	4
2	5
3	6
4	2
4	5
5	5
4	

The results are shown below in Exhibit 10.17. Is there evidence that the new golf ball travels longer distances? Use $\alpha = 0.05$.

EXHIBIT 10.17

Distances Travelled by Current Best-Selling and New Golf Balls

Distances Travelled (Metres) by Current Best-Selling Golf Ball	Distances Travelled (Metres) by New Golf Ball
260	310
266	286
254	292
302	276
241	269
249	293
262	346
255	279
252	262
244	321
286	336
276	341
308	
310	
309	

7. A company that produces golf balls is trying to develop a new ball that will travel farther than its current best-seller. A golf pro hits a number of balls of each type off a tee, and the distance travelled is measured exactly.

DYS10-7

8. A major airport has been redesigned, with the goal of reducing flight delays. The delays (in minutes) for random samples of flights before and after the upgrade are recorded. Is there evidence, at the 5% significance level, that the upgrades reduced flight delays?

DYS10-8

9. A pharmaceutical manufacturer undertakes a study to prove the effectiveness of its diet pill. The company selects a random sample of 50 young women aged 18 to 25, and puts them on a weight-loss program. Half of them (randomly selected) are given the diet pill, and half are given a placebo. Total weight loss, after 30 days, is recorded for all the participants in the study. The distributions of weight loss are non-normal, but both are skewed to the right, with some unusually high weight losses recorded. The rank sum of the weight losses with the diet pill is 700, and the rank sum of the weight losses with the placebo is 575. Do these data prove that the diet pill is effective? Use $\alpha = 4\%$.

10. A restaurant asked a random sample of its weeknight customers to rate their food on the following scale: 1—excellent, 2—good, 3—fair, 4—poor, 5—awful. Another random sample of weekend diners was asked to rate their food. The results are shown in Exhibit 10.18. At the 5% level of significance, is there evidence that weekend and weeknight diners rate the restaurant's food differently?

EXHIBIT 10.18

Ratings by Weeknight and Weekend Diners at a Restaurant

Ratings by Weeknight Diners	Ratings by Weekend Diners
4	1
5	3
1	2
2	1
1	1
2	1
2	3
1	2
1	3

Chapter Summary

10

This chapter presents hypothesis tests to make decisions when comparing two independent samples of normal or ranked data (if the data are unranked and qualitative, refer to Chapter 12). When samples are independent, there is no relationship between, for example, observation #1 from sample 1 and observation #1 from sample 2. Conclusions about differences in populations based on independent samples are not as strong as those based on matched pairs (which we covered in Chapter 9). Despite the weaker conclusions, independent samples are often used because matched-pairs data are more costly or even impossible to obtain.

Independent Samples, Normal Quantitative Data—The t-Test and Confidence Interval Estimate of $\mu_1 - \mu_2$

If the data are quantitative and the histograms of sample data appear normal, the hypothesis test is a t-test, assuming unequal variances, with $H_0: \mu_1 - \mu_2 = 0$. (There is an equal-variances version of this test, but since it can be difficult to establish whether variances are actually equal, it is not recommended.)

The sampling distribution is approximately a t-distribution, with degrees of freedom as follows:

$$df = \frac{\left(\dfrac{s_1^2}{n_1} + \dfrac{s_2^2}{n_2} \right)^2}{\dfrac{\left(\dfrac{s_1^2}{n_1} \right)^2}{(n_1 - 1)} + \dfrac{\left(\dfrac{s_2^2}{n_2} \right)^2}{(n_2 - 1)}}$$

The t-score used in calculating p-values is:

$$t = \frac{(\bar{x}_1 - \bar{x}_2) - \mu_{\bar{x}_1 - \bar{x}_2}}{s_{\bar{x}_1 - \bar{x}_2}} = \frac{(\bar{x}_1 - \bar{x}_2) - (\mu_1 - \mu_2)}{\sqrt{\dfrac{s_1^2}{n_1} + \dfrac{s_2^2}{n_2}}}$$

The Excel Data Analysis tool for raw sample data, **t-Test: Two-Sample Assuming Unequal Variances**, is illustrated in Example 10.1A on page 374. These problems can also be done by hand, using minimum $(n_1 - 1, n_2 - 1)$ as the degrees of freedom, as illustrated in Example 10.1B on page 377. There is an Excel template for problems with summary sample data; it is illustrated on page 378.

A confidence interval estimate for the difference in means is

$$(\bar{x}_1 - \bar{x}_2) \pm t\text{-score}\sqrt{\dfrac{s_1^2}{n_1} + \dfrac{s_2^2}{n_2}}$$

where the t-score corresponds to the desired level of confidence, and has approximately

$$\frac{\left(\dfrac{s_1^2}{n_1} + \dfrac{s_2^2}{n_2} \right)^2}{\dfrac{\left(\dfrac{s_1^2}{n_1} \right)^2}{(n_1 - 1)} + \dfrac{\left(\dfrac{s_2^2}{n_2} \right)^2}{(n_2 - 1)}}$$

degrees of freedom. An Excel template is available, and is illustrated on page 383. Again, if a confidence interval is created without a computer, use minimum $(n_1 - 1, n_2 - 1)$ as the approximate degrees of freedom.

The Guide to Decision Making for independent samples, normal quantitative data, is on page 380.

Independent Samples, Non-Normal Quantitative Data or Ranked Data—The Wilcoxon Rank Sum Test

If the data are quantitative, sample sizes are small, and histograms are non-normal, you should use the Wilcoxon Rank Sum Test. This requires that the histograms be similar in shape and spread (if not, the test may indicate only that the population distributions are different in some way: location, shape, or spread, and this may not be very helpful). The null hypothesis is that the population locations are the same. If the data are ranked, then the Wilcoxon Rank Sum Test is also appropriate, with the same requirements.

When sample sizes are at least 10, the sampling distribution is approximately normal, and the z-score used to calculate p-values is

$$z = \frac{W_1 - \mu_{W_1}}{\sigma_{W_1}} = \frac{W_1 - \dfrac{n_1(n_1 + n_2 + 1)}{2}}{\sqrt{\dfrac{n_1 n_2(n_1 + n_2 + 1)}{12}}}$$

There is an Excel add-in to allow you to calculate W_1 and W_2 from a data set, and there is an Excel template you can use to calculate p-values. These are both illustrated in Example 10.2A on page 385.

When the sample size is small, problems can be done by hand using the tables in Appendix 5 on page 582, as Example 10.2B on page 389 illustrates.

The Guide to Decision Making for independent samples, non-normal quantitative or ranked data, is on page 391.

Go to MyStatLab at www.mathxl.com. You can practise the exercises indicated with red in the Develop Your Skills and Chapter Review Exercises as often as you want, and guided solutions will help you find answers step by step. You'll find a personalized study plan available to you too!

CHAPTER REVIEW EXERCISES

WARM-UP EXERCISES

1. Why is it preferable to use the t-test of $\mu_1 - \mu_2$ instead of the Wilcoxon Rank Sum Test, if the necessary conditions are met?

2. Suppose you are conducting a Wilcoxon Rank Sum Test to determine if population 1 is to the right of population 2. You have two samples of size 10. $W_1 = 78$. What does this tell you?

3. Why is it important, when conducting a Wilcoxon Rank Sum Test using Appendix 5 on page 582, to calculate W from the smallest sample?

4. Why is the unequal-variances version of the t-test of μ_1 μ_2 generally preferred to the equal-variances version? Mention three reasons.

5. Why is the Excel template for the Confidence Interval Estimate for the Difference in Population Means preferred to the manual calculation?

THINK AND DECIDE

6. A large accounting firm is concerned about the amount of time its managers spend dealing with email. A random sample of 27 managers taken in the past revealed that they spent, on average, 49.2 minutes per day on email, with a standard deviation of 22.3 minutes. Since then, new procedures have been put in place. Another random sample of 25 managers reveals that they spent, on average, 39.6 minutes per day on email, with a standard deviation of 10.6 minutes. Is there evidence, at the 5% level of significance, that the new procedures have reduced the amount of time managers spend on email? You may assume that the sample data sets appear normally distributed.

7. Construct a 90% confidence interval estimate of the average amount of time that is saved for managers spending time on email, as a result of the new procedures described in Exercise 6.

8. A random sample of 55 Canadian men aged 25 to 54 were asked to keep a daily log of the hours spent doing unpaid work around the home. The time was averaged over the week. The survey was conducted in 2000 and 2009. In 2000, the average number of hours men spent doing unpaid work around the home was 2.2, with a standard deviation of 0.6. In 2009, the average number of hours men spent doing unpaid work around the home was 2.6, with a standard deviation of 1.3. Both sample data sets appear to be normally distributed. At the 2.5% level of significance, is there evidence that the average number of hours men spent doing unpaid work around the home was higher in 2009 than in 2000?

9. Construct a 95% confidence interval estimate of the increase in the amount of time that men spent doing unpaid work around the house in 2009, compared with 2000, based on the data in Exercise 8 above.

CRE10-10 10. The management of a grocery store chain knows that the appearance of its stores is very important to customers. Regular surveys of customers are conducted so that appearance can be rated. The results of two surveys done in a particular store are shown below in Exhibit 10.19. Is there evidence, at a 5% level of significance, of a change in the store's ratings? A rating of 5 is the best, and 1 is the worst.

EXHIBIT 10.19

Customers' Ratings of Store's Appearance

Random Sample of Grocery Store Customers	
Appearance Ratings Six Months Ago	Current Appearance Ratings
5	1
4	5
5	4
4	5
2	4
1	4
4	5
4	3
3	5
3	4
5	3
5	

CRE10-11 11. A consumer is interested in whether the price of books in Canada has declined as a result of the strengthening of the Canadian dollar. She records the prices of several books she bought last year, and uses her bookstore's website to discover current prices for these books. The prices are shown in Exhibit 10.20. At the 5% significance level, is there evidence of a decrease in book prices compared with last year? What cautions should you have about your conclusion?

12. One of the criteria Statistics professors use to select a textbook is the number of exercises provided. One particular topic in Statistics is selected: the t-test of the mean. A random sample of 15 professors is asked how many exercises students should do in order to master the topic. The sample average was 19.2, with a standard deviation of 5.2. A random sample of 20 students who demonstrated that they had mastered the topic by successfully completing

EXHIBIT 10.20

List Price of Books Last Year and This Year

Books Bought by a Consumer	
Last Year's Price	This Year's Price
$8.99	$4.90
$17.04	$17.37
$9.07	$10.06
$11.00	$9.95
$21.45	$21.87
$19.25	$16.72
$21.79	$15.35
$21.12	$16.97
$10.91	$10.82
$19.79	$12.72
$19.22	$16.23
$10.17	$8.87
$5.49	$2.82
$18.69	$20.31
$9.99	$6.92
$8.99	$7.91
$19.10	$21.47
$19.76	$15.98
$9.99	$7.11
$8.99	$8.17

some related questions was selected from these professors' classes. The students were asked how many exercises they actually completed for this topic. The sample average was 12.3, with a standard deviation of 3.6. Is there evidence, at the 1% level of significance, that the professors overestimate the number of exercises that students need to do to master this topic? You may assume the sample data for both professors and students appear normally distributed.

13. Construct a 99% confidence interval estimate for the difference in the number of exercises professors think are necessary, and the number the students deem necessary, for the situation described in Exercise 12. Do you expect the confidence interval estimate to include zero? Why or why not?

14. A consumer group tested two brands of inkjet printer cartridges for a particular printer, to see whether there was a difference in the number of pages produced before the cartridge ran out of ink. The printers were tested in a random sample of offices where they were used for printing invoices. Brand A cartridges produced an average of 862 pages, with a standard deviation of 362, for a sample size of 31. Brand B cartridges produced an average of 731 pages, with a standard deviation of 223, for a sample size of 25. Is there evidence of a difference in the number of pages produced by the two brands of cartridges? Use $\alpha = 5\%$. You may assume that the sample data appear normally distributed.

15. Construct a 90% confidence interval estimate for the difference in the number of pages produced by the two different cartridges described in Exercise 14 above.

16. A large college was considering switching brands of the laptop computers they lease for faculty. To test the quality of the support available, IT workers made a number of calls throughout one week to the support lines for each manufacturer. The workers recorded the number of minutes that they waited on the phone before a technician became available. The average wait time for the

ITM brand was 8.5 minutes, with a standard deviation of 2.6 minutes, with a sample size of 34. The average wait time for the Dull brand was 6.5 minutes, with a standard deviation of 1.9 minutes, for a sample size of 36. You may assume the wait times are normally distributed. Is there evidence of a difference in wait times between the two brands? Use $\alpha = 5\%$.

17. Construct a 95% confidence interval estimate for the difference in wait times for ITM and Dull computers, based on the data in Exercise 16 above. Do you expect this interval to contain zero? Why or why not?

THINK AND DECIDE WITH EXCEL

CRE10-18

18. A financial advisor is concerned that the time she has to spend with her clients has increased, because of the increasing complexity of the investment products available. The advisor asks her assistant to keep track of exactly how many minutes she spends with a random sample of her clients every January.

    At the 3% level of significance, is there evidence that the amount of time the advisor spends with her clients has increased from a year ago? Can she attribute this to the increasing complexity of the investment products available?

19. Create a 97% confidence interval estimate of the average increase in the amount of time the financial advisor described in Exercise 18 above is spending with each of her clients.

CRE10-20

20. A company with a large sales force has implemented a pilot project to test new sales management software, hoping it will reduce the amount of time sales representatives spend on the computer. A random sample of sales reps is selected, 30 of them with the old software and 35 with the new software. They are asked to keep track of the total amount of time they spend on the computer (in minutes) over a two-week period.

    Is there evidence, at the 4% significance level, that the new software has reduced the amount of time sales reps spend on the computer? Are you sure that the new software is the cause of any difference you see?

21. Construct a 96% confidence interval estimate for the average amount of time the new software has saved sales reps, based on the data in Exercise 20 above.

CRE10-22

22. Two random samples of home computer users in Vancouver are asked to test two different types of high-speed Internet access, one provided by a cable TV company and one provided by a telephone company. The computer users are asked to rate the service after three months on a five-point scale, where 1 corresponds to very satisfied and 5 corresponds to very dissatisfied. At a 2.5% level of significance, is there evidence that the consumers rate the two services differently?

TEST YOUR KNOWLEDGE

CRE10-23

23. A lawnmower manufacturer sells partially assembled lawnmowers through large hardware stores. The manufacturer typically receives a number of calls to its toll-free line from consumers who have questions about the assembly of the lawnmowers. The manufacturer wants to reduce the number of these calls, so it creates a new version of the written instructions that accompany the lawnmower. The manufacturer, working with retail outlets, randomly selects two groups of consumers: some who buy the lawnmower with the old assembly instructions, and some who buy the lawnmower with the new assembly instructions.
    a. The manufacturer contacts consumers and asks them to rate the written assembly instructions, on a scale of 1 to 5, with 1 corresponding to "very easy to read and follow," and 5 corresponding to "very difficult to read and follow."
        Is there evidence that consumers find the new instructions easier to read and follow? Use $\alpha = 0.05$.
    b. The lawnmower company also asks consumers to report how long it took them to assemble their new lawnmowers (in minutes).
        Is there evidence that assembly times for consumers using the new instructions are lower than for consumers using the old instructions? Use $\alpha = 4\%$. Is there any reason the company should be cautious in concluding the new instructions are better?

CHAPTER 11

Making Decisions with Three or More Samples, Quantitative Data—Analysis of Variance (ANOVA)

INTRODUCTION

In Chapters 9 and 10, we described techniques for making decisions when comparing two populations. In Chapter 11, we will describe hypothesis tests for comparing the means of three or more populations of quantitative data. There are many situations in which multiple comparisons of this type are made. Suppose, for example, that a college wants to compare the annual salaries of graduates of the four different streams of its Business diploma program, five years after graduation. The college could randomly select graduates from each of the streams (Marketing, Accounting, Human Resources, General Business) and, with appropriate reassurances about maintaining confidentiality, collect the data.

You might be tempted to apply the *t*-test technique (covered in Chapter 10) repeatedly to make these comparisons. You might think, for example, to make the following pair-wise comparisons of graduate salaries:

- Marketing with
  - Accounting
  - Human Resources
  - General

LEARNING OBJECTIVES

After mastering the material in this chapter, you will be able to:

1. Check the required conditions for the analysis of variance (ANOVA).

2. Choose and conduct the appropriate hypothesis test to compare the means of three or more populations, based on independent samples, for normally distributed quantitative data.

3. Make appropriate multiple comparisons to decide which means differ when a test of hypothesis indicates that at least one of the means of three or more populations is different from the others.

- Accounting with
  - Human Resources
  - General Business
- Human Resources with
  - General Business

Making six pair-wise comparisons is a lot of work, but just think: if there were five different streams in the Business program, you would need to do 10 pair-wise comparisons!

There are a couple of reasons why making repeated pair-wise comparisons is *not* the correct approach. The first reason is that doing so many *t*-tests increases the possibility of a calculation error.

More importantly, when repeated tests are done, there is an increased probability that a null hypothesis will be falsely rejected, purely by chance. That is, we may erroneously conclude that graduate salaries differ among the different streams of Business studied, when in fact they do not (a Type I error). Although we can control the possibility of this type of error for a single *t*-test through the level of significance (α), the possibility of this type of error becomes larger with repeated tests—the greater the number of tests, the larger the chance of at least one Type I error.[1]

The good news is that multiple comparisons can be made simultaneously with a set of techniques called "analysis of variance," and usually referred to as ANOVA (***AN**alysis **O**f **VA**riance*). In the most straightforward case (one-way ANOVA), we can compare the salaries of graduates from the four streams of the Business program. The null hypothesis is that all the mean salaries are equal, and the alternative hypothesis is that the mean salaries are not all equal (at least one mean salary differs from the others). If the null hypothesis is rejected, further analysis is required to find out which means differ, and how. One such technique is covered in Section 11.3.

Another way to describe the graduate salary question is this: does the type of Business education have an effect on graduate salaries? If the answer is no, then the mean graduate salaries will be the same. If the answer is yes, then at least one stream of the Business program will have graduates with a different mean salary. In general, ANOVA is used to determine whether different levels of a factor[2] have a significant effect on the response variable. A **factor** is a qualitative explanatory characteristic that might distinguish one group or population from another. In the Business example, the factor is the stream of the Business program. A **level** is a value or setting that the factor can take. In the example, the factor has four levels because the Business program has four different streams. A **response variable** is a quantitative variable that is being measured or observed. We are interested in how this variable responds to the different levels of the factor. In the Business program example, we want to know if graduate salaries vary according to the stream of the Business program.

Factor A qualitative explanatory characteristic that might distinguish one group or population from another.

Level A value or setting that the factor can take.

Response variable A quantitative variable that is being measured or observed. We are interested in how this variable responds to the different levels of the factor.

---

[1] This was first discussed in Chapter 10, on page 379. Remember: the more times you skate back and forth across a frozen lake, the greater the chance you will fall through the ice!

[2] "Factors" are sometimes referred to as "treatments."

Some other examples we will consider in this chapter are:

1. Does the brand of battery make a difference in battery life? The response variable being measured is battery life, in minutes. The factor is the brand, and there will be three different levels because three brands will be compared.
2. Does the setup of a voicemail system affect how long it takes a caller to connect to the right person? The factor is the voicemail system, and there will be four different levels because four systems are going to be compared.

Once we have formulated the research questions this way, it is easier to see why the appropriate technique is referred to as "analysis of variance." Let's go back to the Business program example. We would really like to know if different levels (streams) of the Business program (the factor) are causing variation in the graduate salaries (the response variable). In other words, does changing the Business stream result in differences in graduate salaries? If it does, then the mean salaries will be different.

There are potentially two sources of variability in the entire data set:

1. The salaries of the graduates in the sample will vary because of factors other than the stream of Business education, or because of random variation. We will estimate this with the "within-sample variability" in the sample data.
2. The salaries may actually differ because of the stream of Business program studied. We will estimate this with the "between-sample[3] variability" in the sample data.

The ANOVA hypothesis test compares the between-sample variation (associated with different levels of the factor) to the within-sample variation (random variation). We use within-sample variation as the standard against which the between-sample variation is measured. The F distribution (described in Section 11.2) is used to determine whether the variability in the sample means is significantly greater than the random variability in the data. If it is, then we can conclude that variations in graduate salaries in the population are associated with the different streams of Business studied. This implies that the mean salary of graduates of at least one of the program streams is different from the mean salaries of graduates of other program streams.

Of course, we have to be careful about drawing conclusions about whether differences in the stream of Business studied actually *caused* any observed differences in graduate salaries. We can think of a number of other explanatory factors that might affect graduate salaries: natural ability and work habits of the graduate, location of employment, type of employer, other experience or training, and so on. If we take large and truly random samples for each stream of Business education, we could hope that the influence of the other factors is randomized (that is, the effects cancel out across the samples). In any case, as usual, we must be cautious about cause-and-effect conclusions based on observational data.

---

[3] Because there are more than two samples, this should really be called the "among-sample variability." This slightly grammatically incorrect term is traditional, and it matches Excel terminology.

CHECKING CONDITIONS FOR ONE-WAY ANALYSIS OF VARIANCE (ANOVA)

Suppose we want to know if some brands of batteries last longer than others. We could investigate by buying 10 batteries from each of three major brands, and using them to power a flashlight (the same type of flashlight would be used for all of the experiments). The number of minutes before the flashlight went dark for the three battery types is shown below.

EXHIBIT 11.1

Data for the Battery Example

Battery Life in Minutes		
Onever	Durible	PlusEnergy
811	787	1,614
942	925	1,655
1,078	935	1,999
1,263	1,134	1,321
1,331	1,243	1,777
1,374	1,326	970
1,509	1,449	1,928
1,594	1,499	1,557
1,732	1,546	1,310
1,821	1,666	1,513

At first glance, it is hard to tell if there is any difference in the batteries. Of course, our initial examination of the data would include both graphical and numerical measures. The mean battery life for the three brands is shown in the table below.

EXHIBIT 11.2

Sample Means for the Battery Example

	Onever	Durible	PlusEnergy
Mean Battery Life in Minutes	$\bar{x}_1 = 1,345.5$	$\bar{x}_2 = 1,251$	$\bar{x}_3 = 1,564.4$

Note that we use subscripts to differentiate among the three sample means: 1 = Onever, 2 = Durible, 3 = PlusEnergy.

The PlusEnergy battery has the longest mean life in the sample data. But is this significantly longer, or simply the result of sampling variability? We need to do some further examination of the data before we can decide.

Required Conditions for ANOVA Analysis

As usual, before we proceed with our analysis, we have to check whether the data meet the conditions required for ANOVA techniques. These conditions are

1. The data points are independent and randomly selected from each population.
2. Each population is normally distributed.
3. The populations all have the same variability. In particular, the variances are equal.[4]

Independent Randomly Selected Data   As usual, it is important to select a random sample of independent observations. In the battery life example, it might be difficult to obtain a truly random sample. However, we would probably buy the batteries at different locations, to try to ensure that the ones we tested were not related, as they might be if they were all manufactured in the same lot and shipped to the same store.

Normal Populations   We are by now accustomed to checking for the normality of the populations by examining histograms of the sample data. As always, with a small sample size, it can be difficult to assess normality. Histograms of the three sample data sets are shown below in Exhibit 11.3.

EXHIBIT 11.3

Histograms of the Sample Data for the Battery Example

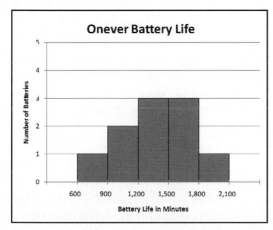

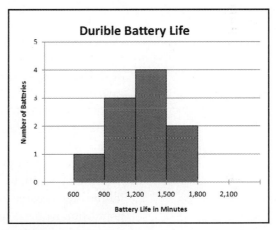

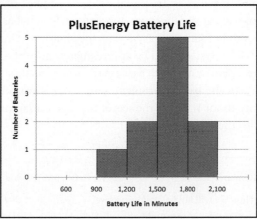

---

[4] We could equally require that the standard deviations be equal. Traditionally, ANOVA techniques focus on variance, not standard deviation. Remember the variance (σ^2 for the population and s^2 for the sample) is just the square of the standard deviation (σ or s).

The ANOVA technique is fairly robust, in that it can safely be used with populations that are somewhat skewed, particularly when sample sizes are large. It is best if sample sizes are equal, or nearly equal (often referred to as a "balanced" design).

For the battery life data, sample sizes are equal, and histograms of the sample data appear approximately normal. We will assume that the population data are normally distributed.

Equality of Variances   Finally, we must decide whether the population variances are equal. We start by calculating the sample variances,[5] which are as follows:

EXHIBIT 11.4

Variances for the Battery Example

	Onever	Durible	PlusEnergy
Variance	110,206.056	88,973.778	95,213.378

The sample variances for the batteries are not exactly equal, but we would not expect them to be, even if the population variances are actually equal, because of sampling variability. It is possible to do a formal hypothesis test to check for equality of variances in the population. However, as we discussed in Chapter 10, any test of variances should be independent of the test of means, because if it is not, the significance level will not be reliable. A reliable hypothesis test of the variances would require a different sample data set, something which may not be available or affordable. If we must rely on a single sample data set, we will use a general rule (and not a hypothesis test) to assess equality of variances.[6]

In Chapter 10, we recommended assuming that population variances are unequal for the t-test to compare two sample means. Fortunately, the ANOVA test for comparing population means is not greatly affected by inequality of variances, particularly when the sample sizes are equal or nearly equal. Therefore, for ANOVA, we will assume population variances are approximately equal as long as the largest sample variance is less than four times as large as the smallest.[7] Under these conditions, the results of the ANOVA test will still be approximately correct. Caution should be used if sample sizes are small, or unequal, particularly if the smallest sample has the largest variance.

In the battery problem, sample sizes are equal, and the largest sample variance is only about 1.2 times the size of the smallest sample variance. In this case, we can proceed with the hypothesis test.

---

[5] Remember, $s^2 = \dfrac{\sum (x - \bar{x})^2}{n - 1}$. Refer to Chapter 3 if you need a refresher on this calculation.

[6] Thus, we will not be claiming a level of significance that is not justified.

[7] See David S. Moore and George P. McCabe, *Introduction to the Practice of Statistics* (New York: W.H. Freeman and Company, 2003). Moore and McCabe, in their "Rule for Examining Standard Deviations in ANOVA" (page 755), suggest that if the largest standard deviation is less than twice the smallest standard deviation, the results of the ANOVA approach will still be approximately correct. Since the variance is the square of the standard deviation, the rule could also be stated as it is here. Repeated simulations suggest that this rule is practical. Of course, the standard cautions about results when samples are small or sample sizes are very different apply.

What If the Conditions Are Not Met?   If the sample data are non-normal, there are non-parametric techniques available to make comparisons. The Kruskal-Wallis test is the non-parametric counterpart for the one-way ANOVA test. This technique is beyond the scope of this introductory text.

It may be possible to do a transformation of the data to solve the problem of very unequal variances (this problem is more troublesome when sample sizes are not equal). This involves applying some mathematical function (such as a logarithm or square root) to the original data, and working with the new measurements. These more advanced techniques are beyond the scope of this text.

EXAMPLE 11.1

Checking conditions for one-factor ANOVA

A large accounting firm has many branch offices and four different voicemail systems. The firm wants to use the same system in every branch, and minimize the amount of time it takes a customer to connect to the right person.

To test the speed with which a customer can navigate the systems, the company creates 25 scenarios of customer calls. A company intern simulates the customer calls, randomly selecting branch offices with each of the four voicemail systems. The number of seconds from the beginning of the call to connection with the right person is recorded (and referred to as "task completion time"). The data are available in the workbook called EXA11-1. Investigate the data to see if the required conditions are met.

EXA11-1

Since the data were collected at randomly selected times on randomly selected days, we can probably safely assume that the observations were randomly selected. We might wonder if the data are truly independent. Since the same intern did all of the calls, there is a possibility that he or she learned something about the voicemail systems, and became better at navigating them while collecting the data. The intern was instructed to listen carefully to the menu choices before navigating the systems, and we will hope that this approach resulted in independent observations.

We check the histograms of sample data for evidence of normal populations. The histograms are shown below (and on the next page) in Exhibit 11.5.

EXHIBIT 11.5

Histograms of Sample Data for Example 11.1

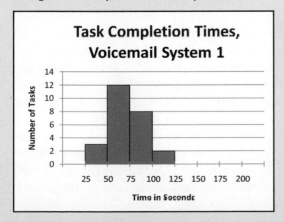

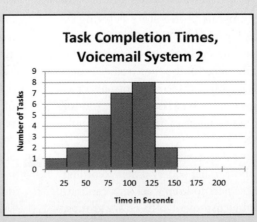

(continued)

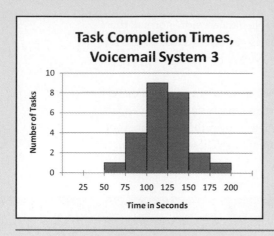

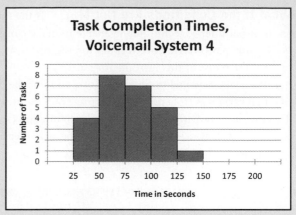

All of these histograms appear approximately normal, with some skewness in the histograms for systems 2 and 4. Remember that the ANOVA technique is not particularly affected by some skewness in the distributions, particularly for balanced designs.

The last condition we have to check is that the variances of the populations are equal. We can use the **VAR** function in Excel to do this. The results of these calculations are shown below in Exhibit 11.6.

EXHIBIT 11.6

Variances of Task Completion Times for Voicemail Systems

Voicemail System 1	Voicemail System 2	Voicemail System 3	Voicemail System 4
410.59	921.74	719.50	623.91

The largest sample variance is 921.74, which is a little over twice as large as the smallest sample variance of 410.59. Since the ratio of the largest to smallest variance is in the acceptable range (less than four), we can proceed.

DEVELOP YOUR SKILLS 11.1

1. The manager of an upscale coffee store is trying to decide which of three locations would be best for a new store. The manager currently wants to determine whether there are differences in the foot traffic at each location. The manager hires three students, and has them count the number of passersby on a random sample of days. Do these data meet the required conditions for one-way ANOVA?

DYS11-1

2. The owner of a winery is wondering whether the average purchase made by visitors to her winery differs according to age. She asks the cashiers to keep track of a random sample of purchases by customers in three age groups:

DYS11-2

under 30, 30–50, over 50. Because there is no good reason to ask a customer his or her age, the cashiers guess which age group a customer belongs to (and if they do not guess accurately, the research may not be helpful). Eventually, data from about 50 purchases made by customers in each of the age groups are collected. Do these data meet the required conditions for one-way ANOVA?

3. A college wants to compare the annual salaries of graduates of the four different streams of its Business diploma program, five years after graduation. The college randomly selects graduates from each of the streams (Marketing, Accounting, Human Resources, General

DYS11-3

Business) and, with appropriate reassurances about maintaining confidentiality, collects the data. Do these data meet the required conditions for one-way ANOVA?

4. A commuter is trying to figure out the fastest way to drive to work in the morning. She keeps track of the times (in minutes) for three different routes on a random sample of mornings. Her records are shown below in Exhibit 11.7.

EXHIBIT 11.7

Commuting Times for Three Different Routes

Commuting Times in Minutes		
Route 1	Route 2	Route 3
48	28	31
54	32	49
40	33	55
51	22	46
57	46	56
60	35	57
45	49	53
33	38	43
36	35	61
46	28	36

Do these data meet the required conditions for ANOVA?

5. Many textbooks now come with an online component for self-assessment, study, and quizzes. Teachers are experimenting with the new software components, and wondering whether they have any effect on students' final grades. A teacher who has three sections of Introductory Statistics is wondering about three variations of use of the software, as follows:

- Assigning quizzes for marks
- Creating chapter quizzes and recommending them, but not assigning any marks
- Not creating any quizzes, but relying on the sample tests built into the software (no marks assigned)

There are 45 students in each of the classes being compared. Histograms of the sample data are shown in Exhibit 11.8.

The variance of the marks of those who were assigned quizzes for marks was 212.1. The variance of the marks for those who were assigned quizzes with no marks was 225.6. The variance of the marks for those who were given sample tests only was 218.0.

EXHIBIT 11.8

Histograms of Final Grades for Different Uses of Software

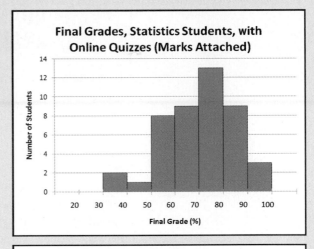

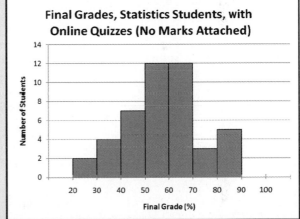

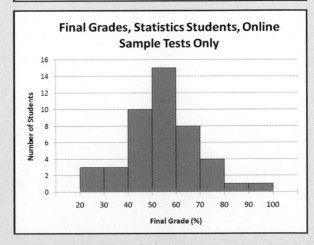

Do these data meet the required conditions for one-way ANOVA?

11.2 THE HYPOTHESIS TEST FOR INDEPENDENT SAMPLES, NORMAL QUANTITATIVE DATA—ONE-WAY ANALYSIS OF VARIANCE (ANOVA)

If the data meet the required conditions, we will conduct a test of hypothesis as follows.

$H_0: \mu_1 = \mu_2 = \mu_3$

H_1: At least one μ differs from the others.

As described in the chapter introduction, we proceed by comparing the between-sample variation (associated with different levels of the factor) to the within-sample variation (random variation). If the population means are actually equal, then the between-sample variation will be about equal to the within-sample variation. If the means are not equal, then the between-sample variation will be significantly greater than the within-sample variation.

How do we measure the between-sample and within-sample variation? We will first calculate sums of squares, which are similar to calculations of standard deviation (and variance) that you have already seen. The fundamental building block of these calculations is deviations from the mean. The deviations from the mean give us a measure of variability, that is, how widely scattered the data points are around the mean. The farther a point is from the mean, the larger the deviation from the mean will be. As usual, we square the deviations from the mean, to prevent them from cancelling out. In general, we calculate sums of squares (denoted SS) as follows:

$$\text{sum of squares} = SS = \sum (x - \bar{x})^2$$

While we would normally do these calculations with a computer, we will illustrate the arithmetic in detail here. This should help you understand what the calculations are doing, and why they help us compare the between-sample and within-sample variations so that, ultimately, we can decide whether the means are equal.

Within-Sample Sum of Squares   Let us begin with the within-sample variation, which is our measure of random variability in the data. First, calculate the mean of each sample data set. Then calculate the sum of squares for each sample. The calculations are illustrated below. The table of sample data has been repeated on the next page for ease of reference.

$$SS_{\text{Onever}} = (811 - 1{,}345.5)^2 + (942 - 1{,}345.5)^2 + (1{,}078 - 1{,}345.5)^2 + \cdots + (1{,}821 - 1{,}345.4)^2 = 991{,}854.5$$

$$SS_{\text{Durible}} = (787 - 1{,}251)^2 + (925 - 1{,}251)^2 + (935 - 1{,}251)^2 + \cdots + (1{,}666 - 1{,}251)^2 = 800{,}764.0$$

$$SS_{\text{PlusEnergy}} = (1{,}614 - 1{,}564.4)^2 + (1{,}655 - 1{,}564.4)^2 + (1{,}999 - 1{,}564.4)^2 + \cdots + (1{,}513 - 1{,}564.4)^2 = 856{,}920.4$$

EXHIBIT 11.9

Data for the Battery Example

	Battery Life in Minutes		
	Onever	Durible	PlusEnergy
	811	787	1,614
	942	925	1,655
	1,078	935	1,999
	1,263	1,134	1,321
	1,331	1,243	1,777
	1,374	1,326	970
	1,509	1,449	1,928
	1,594	1,499	1,557
	1,732	1,546	1,310
	1,821	1,666	1,513
Mean	$\bar{x}_1 = 1{,}345.5$	$\bar{x}_2 = 1{,}251$	$\bar{x}_3 = 1{,}564.4$

We add these three SS together to get SS_{within} for the entire data set.

$$SS_{within} = SS_{Onever} + SS_{Durible} + SS_{PlusEnergy} = 991{,}854.5 + 800{,}764.0 + 856{,}920.4$$
$$= 2{,}649{,}538.9$$

SS_{within} is an estimate of the overall variability in the data.

Calculation of SS_{within}

In general, the calculation of SS_{within} for k samples is as follows:

$$SS_{within} = SS_1 + SS_2 + \cdots + SS_k$$

where $SS = \sum(x - \bar{x})^2$ for each sample.

Between-Sample Sum of Squares   Now we calculate the sum of squares for the between-sample variation. We first have to calculate an overall mean for the entire data set. We will call the overall mean $\bar{\bar{x}}$. In simple terms, this is calculated by averaging all of the data points from the three samples at once. Of course, this measure can also be calculated directly from the sample means, as follows:

$$\text{Overall mean} = \bar{\bar{x}} = \frac{n_1\bar{x}_1 + n_2\bar{x}_2 + \cdots + n_k\bar{x}_k}{n_1 + n_2 + \cdots + n_k} \text{ for } k \text{ samples}$$

This calculation weights each sample mean according to the sample size. In the battery life example, we have three samples of equal size, so we can take a shortcut, and simply calculate the mean of the sample means.[8]

$$\bar{\bar{x}} = \frac{1{,}345.5 + 1{,}251.0 + 1{,}564.4}{3} = 1{,}386.967$$

---

[8] If you cannot see why the shortcut works, then notice that the 10's cancel out in the longer version of the formula. $\bar{\bar{x}} = \frac{10(1{,}345.5) + 10(1{,}251.0) + 10(1{,}564.4)}{10 + 10 + 10} = \frac{10[(1{,}345.5) + (1{,}251.0) + (1{,}564.4)]}{10(3)} = 1{,}386.967$

The overall mean is our best estimate of the true means of the populations, assuming they are all equal. We focus on the deviations of the individual sample means from this overall mean to tell us something about how much the sample means differ from the overall mean. As usual, we square the deviations.

To get the sum of squares for between-sample variation, we weight the squared deviation for each sample mean by the number of data points in the sample. In our battery example, there are 10 observations in each sample.

The individual sample means are repeated below, for ease of reference.

EXHIBIT 11.10

Summary Data about Means for the Battery Example

	Onever	Durible	PlusEnergy
Mean Battery Life in Minutes	$\bar{x}_1 = 1{,}345.5$	$\bar{x}_2 = 1{,}251.0$	$\bar{x}_3 = 1{,}564.4$
Sample Size	$n_1 = 10$	$n_2 = 10$	$n_3 = 10$
Overall Mean	$\bar{\bar{x}} = 1{,}386.967$		

The calculation of $SS_{between}$ is as follows:

$$SS_{between} = 10(1{,}345.5 - 1{,}386.967)^2 + 10(1{,}251 - 1{,}386.967)^2 + 10(1{,}574 - 1{,}386.967)^2 = 516{,}890.067$$

Calculation of $SS_{between}$

In general, the calculation of $SS_{between}$ for k samples is as follows:

$$SS_{between} = n_1(\bar{x}_1 - \bar{\bar{x}})^2 + n_2(\bar{x}_2 - \bar{\bar{x}})^2 + \cdots + n_k(\bar{x}_k - \bar{\bar{x}})^2$$

where $\bar{\bar{x}}$ denotes the overall mean of the data set, and $\bar{x}_i$ is the mean of sample i.

Total Sum of Squares   While it is not required for the hypothesis test, it is interesting to note the relationship between SS_{within}, $SS_{between}$, and the total sum of squares, which we will call SS_{total}.

The total sum of squares is a measure of the variation of all the data points from the overall mean value. The total sum of squares is calculated as:

$$SS_{total} = \Sigma(x - \bar{\bar{x}})^2$$

The relationship among the three sums of squares is as follows:

$$SS_{total} = SS_{between} + SS_{within}$$

This shows us that the total variation in the data set can be broken down into two components. The first component, $SS_{between}$, accounts for the variation between the samples, which is associated with different levels of the factor. SS_{within} accounts for the remaining or residual variation, which results from some other factor, or random variation. This residual variation is often referred to as "error," although in many cases it is simply a reflection of inherent variability in the data, with no error involved.

Mean Squares   The goal of all of these calculations is to compare the between-sample variation (associated with the different battery brands) to the within-sample variation (random variation). If the between-sample variation is significantly greater than the within-sample variation, we will have evidence that at least one of the means differs from the others.

The sums of squares we have calculated to measure this variation must be adjusted so that they are directly comparable. We do this by calculating a mean for each of the sums of squares.

You have seen this sort of calculation before. The first measure of variance we calculated (in Chapter 3) was s^2:

$$s^2 = \frac{\Sigma(x - \bar{x})^2}{n - 1}$$

Notice this is just the sum of squares divided by the degrees of freedom.

To get the mean square for within-sample variability, which we will call MS_{within}, we divide the SS_{within} by the appropriate degrees of freedom. What are they?

Remember, we calculated SS_{within} by adding the sum of squared deviations for each sample.

$$SS_{within} = SS_{Onever} + SS_{Durible} + SS_{PlusEnergy}$$

The sum of squares for each sample has $n_i - 1$ degrees of freedom, and so the appropriate degrees of freedom for MS_{within} are:

$$(n_1 - 1) + (n_2 - 1) + (n_3 - 1) = n_1 + n_2 + n_3 - 1 - 1 - 1 = n_T - 3$$

In general, the degrees of freedom for MS_{within} is $(n_T - k)$, where n_T is the total number of observations in the data set, and k is the number of samples.

So, we calculate MS_{within} as follows:

$$MS_{within} = \frac{SS_{within}}{n_T - k} = \frac{2,649,538.9}{30 - 3} = 98,131.07$$

Calculation of MS_{within}

The mean square for within-sample variation is calculated as:

$$MS_{within} = \frac{SS_{within}}{n_T - k} = \frac{SS_1 + SS_2 + \cdots + SS_k}{n_T - k}$$

where n_T is the total number of observations in the entire data set, and k is the number of samples (and also the number of levels of the factor). As usual, $SS_i = \Sigma(x - \bar{x}_i)^2$ for each sample.

To get the mean square for between-sample variability, which we will call $MS_{between}$, we divide the $SS_{between}$ by the appropriate degrees of freedom. What are they?

In the battery example, $SS_{between}$ was calculated based on the three sample means, so the degrees of freedom are $(3 - 1)$. In general, the degrees of freedom for $SS_{between}$ are $(k - 1)$ when there are k samples (and k levels of the factor).

So, we calculate $MS_{between}$ as follows:

$$MS_{between} = \frac{SS_{between}}{k-1} = \frac{516{,}890.067}{3-1} = 258{,}445.03$$

Calculation of $MS_{between}$

The mean square for between-sample variation is calculated as:

$$MS_{between} = \frac{SS_{between}}{k-1} = \frac{n_1(\bar{x}_1 - \bar{\bar{x}})^2 + n_2(\bar{x}_2 - \bar{\bar{x}})^2 + \cdots + n_k(\bar{x}_k - \bar{\bar{x}})^2}{k-1}$$

Let us summarize our work so far.

$$MS_{within} = 98{,}131.07$$

$$MS_{between} = 258{,}445.03$$

MS_{within} is the standard against which we measure $MS_{between}$. For these sample data, the between-sample variability (associated with different levels of the factor) is greater than the within-sample variability (random variation). This gives us some indication that average battery life is not the same for all batteries. But is the between-sample variability significantly greater than the within-sample variability, or is the difference just a result of sampling variability? As usual, we need a sampling distribution to help us answer this question.

The F Distribution

The usual approach is to focus on the ratio of the two mean squares. We will use a new distribution called the F distribution to assess the ratio.

$$F = \frac{MS_{between}}{MS_{within}} = \frac{258{,}445.03}{98{,}131.07} = 2.634$$

When the null hypothesis is true, and all the population means are equal, the between-sample variability will be about the same as the within-sample variability, and the F ratio will be about equal to 1 (or less). However, when one of the population means differs from the others, then the between-sample variability (associated with different levels of the factor) will be greater than the within-sample variability (random variation), and the F ratio will be greater than 1. How much greater than 1 is enough to indicate a significant difference?

Of course, the answer depends on the sampling variability that applies in each case. The F statistic, like the other sample statistics we have calculated, has a range of possible values. As usual, we have to refer to the sampling distribution of the F statistic to decide whether any specific F statistic is unusual enough for us to reject the null hypothesis. The sampling distribution of the F statistic depends on the number of samples and the number of observations. There are many F distributions, each one identified by two different degrees of freedom, one for the numerator, and one for the denominator of the F statistic. The relevant degrees of freedom come directly from our earlier calculations.

$$F = \frac{MS_{between}}{MS_{within}} = \frac{\dfrac{SS_{between}}{degrees\ of\ freedom}}{\dfrac{SS_{within}}{degrees\ of\ freedom}} = \frac{\dfrac{SS_{between}}{k-1}}{\dfrac{SS_{within}}{n_T - k}}$$

The test statistic (assuming equality of the population means) is distributed according to the F distribution with $(k-1)$, $(n_T - k)$ degrees of freedom. The F distribution with $(3 - 1 = 2)$, $(30 - 3 = 27)$ degrees of freedom applies to the battery example, that is, $F_{2,27}$.

The Sampling Distribution of $\dfrac{MS_{between}}{MS_{within}}$ with Two or More Independent Samples

The sampling distribution of $\dfrac{MS_{between}}{MS_{within}}$ follows the F distribution, with $(k-1)$, $(n_T - k)$ degrees of freedom, where n_T is the total number of observations in the data set, and k is the number of samples (and levels of the factor). The notation for the F distribution is $F_{(k-1)(n_T - k)}$.

What does an F distribution look like? The answer depends on the degrees of freedom. Exhibit 11.11 below shows three possible F distributions.

EXHIBIT 11.11

Three F Distrubutions

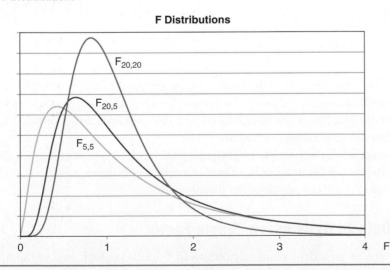

All F distributions are continuous, and positively skewed. The F distribution cannot be negative, and this is not surprising, since the test statistic cannot be negative (it is a ratio of two positive numbers).

We are interested in determining if the test statistic is significantly greater than 1, so it is always a *large* value of the test statistic that will lead to rejection of the null hypothesis. There is no such thing as a *left-tailed* test here. There is only one (right-tailed) test: whether the sample means are significantly different. And it is always relatively large values of the F statistic that lead us to conclude that they are. The *p*-value is always calculated as $P(F \geq \text{calculated F-value})$.

Because there are so many F distributions, printed tables of critical values are quite limited, and it is best to use the computer to calculate the *p*-value for our hypothesis test. First, we will recap the results of all of our calculations in an ANOVA table. See Exhibit 11.12 below.

EXHIBIT 11.12

Summary of ANOVA Calculations for Battery Brands

Summary of ANOVA Calculations				
Battery Brand	*Count(n_i)*	*Sum*	*Average ($\bar{x}$)*	*Variance (s^2)*
Onever	10	13,455	1,345.5	110,206.056
Durible	10	12,510	1,251	88,973.778
PlusEnergy	10	15,644	1,564.4	95,213.378

Source of Variation	*SS*	*Degrees of Freedom*	*MS*	*F*
Between Groups	516,890.067	2	258,445.03	2.634
Within Groups	2,649,538.900	27	98,131.07	
Total	3,166,428.967	29		

Now, we proceed with the hypothesis test.

$H_0: \mu_1 = \mu_2 = \mu_3$

H_1: At least one μ differs from the others.

$$F = \frac{MS_{between}}{MS_{within}} = \frac{258,445.03}{98,131.07} = 2.634$$

The Excel function called **FDIST** will calculate the *p*-value, which is 0.0901. That is, if the population means are equal, the probability of getting an F statistic as high as 2.634 is about 9%. This is not unusual, and so it does not appear that different battery brands have different average battery lives.

Although we did not set a level of significance for the hypothesis test, with such a high *p*-value we will fail to reject H_0. There is insufficient evidence to suggest that there are differences in the average life of the three batteries.

Using Data Analysis Anova: Single Factor

At this point, we have done many calculations to illustrate the logic behind the ANOVA test. However, we would not normally do all of the arithmetic by hand. Excel has a built-in **Data Analysis** tool that supports one-way ANOVA. It can be used with the sample data from the populations being compared. Exhibit 11.13 below shows the **Data Analysis** menu. The correct choice is highlighted: **Anova: Single Factor**.

EXHIBIT 11.13

Data Analysis Anova: Single Factor

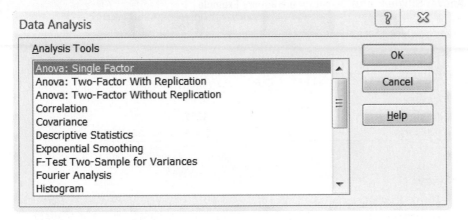

Clicking on this option leads to another dialogue box, illustrated below in Exhibit 11.14.

EXHIBIT 11.14

Anova: Single Factor Dialogue Box

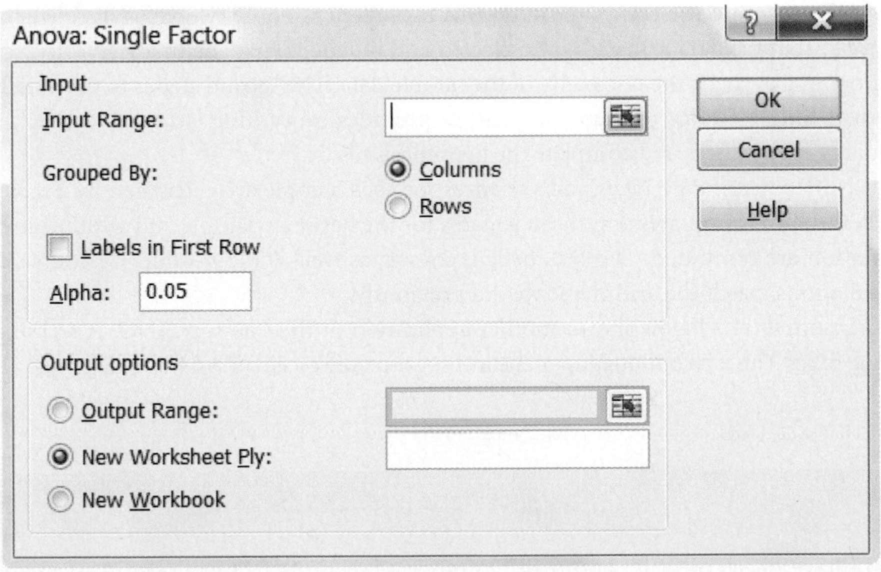

The dialogue box requires you to indicate where the sample data are stored, and whether they are stored as columns or rows (**Input Range:**). It is recommended that you include labels with your data (it will make the output much easier to read), and if you do you must tick the appropriate box to indicate that you have done so. You can also specify an output location, and sometimes it is handy to have the output in the same worksheet as the data sets.

The Excel output for the battery example is shown below in Exhibit 11.15.

EXHIBIT 11.15

Anova: Single Factor Output for the Battery Example

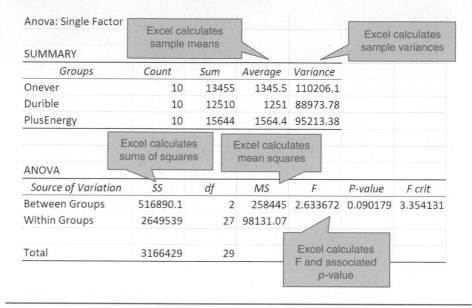

Anova: Single Factor

SUMMARY

Groups	Count	Sum	Average	Variance
Onever	10	13455	1345.5	110206.1
Durible	10	12510	1251	88973.78
PlusEnergy	10	15644	1564.4	95213.38

ANOVA

Source of Variation	SS	df	MS	F	P-value	F crit
Between Groups	516890.1	2	258445	2.633672	0.090179	3.354131
Within Groups	2649539	27	98131.07			
Total	3166429	29				

When we use the computer to do this test, there are only two steps once we have decided that the data are randomly selected and independent. The first step is to create histograms to check the normality of the sample data. The second step is to produce the **Anova: Single Factor** output. This output provides everything we need to check for equality of variances and complete the hypothesis test.

Notice that the averages and variances for each sample are calculated by Excel. As well, the sums of squares and mean squares for the between-sample and within-sample variation are computed. The F statistic is shown, as well as the p-value. Of course, the calculations match the arithmetic we did previously.

Example 11.2 below shows another application of the one-way ANOVA technique using Excel. This is a continuation of the investigation of voicemail systems in Example 11.1.

EXAMPLE 11.2

One-factor ANOVA

EXA11-2

Data have been collected about the number of seconds from the beginning of the call to connection with the right person. The data are recorded and referred to as "task completion time." The firm has decided to use a 5% level of significance to determine whether there is a difference in the speed with which customers can navigate the voicemail systems.

In Example 11.1, we established that the data meet the required conditions. Note that the output of the **Anova: Single Factor** tool from **Data Analysis** calculates the variances for each sample.

The **Anova: Single Factor** output is shown below in Exhibit 11.16.

EXHIBIT 11.16

Excel Anova: Single Factor Output for Example 11.2

Anova: Single Factor

SUMMARY

Groups	Count	Sum	Average	Variance
Voicemail System 1	25	1811	72.44	410.59
Voicemail System 2	25	2166	86.64	921.74
Voicemail System 3	25	3010	120.4	719.5
Voicemail System 4	25	1934	77.36	623.9067

ANOVA

Source of Variation	SS	df	MS	F	P-value	F crit
Between Groups	35026.91	3	11675.64	17.45409	4.02E-09	2.699393
Within Groups	64217.68	96	668.9342			
Total	99244.59	99				

$H_0: \mu_1 = \mu_2 = \mu_3 = \mu_4$

H_1: At least one μ differs from the others.

$\alpha = 0.05$

$F = 17.45$ (from the Excel output)

$p\text{-value} = 4.02 \times 10^{-9} = 0.00000000402$

This tells us that the probability of getting an F statistic as high as 17.45 if the population means are equal is practically zero. Since we did get such an F statistic, we have evidence that at least one of the means differs from the others. We reject H_0. It appears that at least one of the voicemail systems is associated with a different mean time for a customer to connect with the right person.

Now we will have to figure out which mean differs, and a technique to do this is covered in Section 11.3.

Using the F Table of Critical Values   Because there are so many possible F distributions, it is not possible to provide comprehensive tables of critical values. However, there are some tables of F distribution critical values in Appendix 6 at the back of this text, starting at page 584. The tables are organized according to the degrees of freedom and the tail probability. For each combination of degrees of freedom in the table, critical values for tail areas of 0.05, 0.025, and 0.01 are shown, because these are the most commonly used levels of significance. Of course, the tables can show only a few of the possible combinations of degrees of freedom.

Remember when you are reading the tables that a larger F-value will always correspond to a smaller *p*-value (and vice versa). For example, suppose we refer to the table for the decision about the batteries, which we examined at the beginning of this section. The degrees of freedom in the numerator were 2, and the degrees of freedom in the denominator were 27. The calculated F statistic was 2.63. Right away, we can see the limitations of the tables. The closest we can find to the degrees of freedom we want are 2 for the numerator and 25 for the denominator. An excerpt from the table is shown below in Exhibit 11.17.

EXHIBIT 11.17

Excerpt from F Table of Critical Values for $F_{2,27}$

Degrees of Freedom in the Numerator

	p-value	F = 2.63	2	3	4	5
25	0.050		3.39	2.99	2.76	2.60
	0.025	5.69	4.29	3.69	3.35	3.13
	0.010	7.77	5.57	4.68	4.18	3.85
30	0.050	4.17	3.32	2.92	2.69	2.53
	0.025	5.57	4.18	3.59	3.25	3.03
	0.010	7.56	5.39	4.51	4.02	3.70

Degrees of Freedom in the Denominator

As usual, we estimate the *p*-value by noting where our calculated test statistic would belong, if it were in the table. We can see that our F statistic of 2.63 is less than 3.39, the critical value for a 5% *p*-value. Therefore, we know the *p*-value must be more than 5%. In fact, Excel revealed that the actual *p*-value was 0.090.

Let's also use the tables to confirm the work we did in Example 11.2. There, the degrees of freedom for the F statistic were 3 for the numerator and 96 for the denominator. Again, we see the limitations of any printed table. We can identify the column for 3 degrees of freedom in the numerator, but we have to choose between 80 and 120 for degrees of freedom for the denominator, as shown in Exhibit 11.18 opposite.

Since 80 degrees of freedom is closer to 96 than 120, we will look at that section of the table. The F statistic was 17.45, and it is clear that such a large value indicates a *p*-value of less than 1%. In fact, Excel revealed that the actual *p*-value was 4.02×10^{-9}, or 0.00000000402.

EXHIBIT 11.18

Excerpt from F Table of Critical Values for $F_{3,96}$

Degrees of Freedom in the Numerator

		p-value	1	2	3	4	5
Degrees of Freedom in the Denominator	**80**	*0.050*	3.96	3.11	2.72	2.49	2.33
		0.025	5.22	3.86	3.28	2.95	2.73
		0.010	6.96	4.88	4.04	3.56	3.26
				$F = 17.45 \Rightarrow$			
	120	*0.050*	3.92	3.07	2.68	2.45	2.29
		0.025	5.15	3.80	3.23	2.89	2.67
		0.010	6.85	4.79	3.95	3.48	3.17

GUIDE TO DECISION MAKING

Three or More Independent Samples, Normal Quantitative Data—One-Way ANOVA to Decide About the Equality of Population Means

When:

- there are normal quantitative data, *k* independent samples
- trying to make a decision about whether *k* population means differ, on the basis of the sample means
- can also be understood as trying to determine whether different levels of a factor are causing variation in a response variable
- variances are equal

Steps:

1. Specify H_0, the null hypothesis, which will be

$$H_0: \mu_1 = \mu_2 = \cdots = \mu_k$$

2. Specify H_1, the alternative hypothesis, which will be

$$H_1: \text{At least one } \mu \text{ differs from the others.}$$

3. Determine or identify α, the significance level.

4. Collect or identify the sample data. Identify or calculate
- the total number of observations, n_T, and the number of observations in each sample, n_i
- the number of populations (levels of the factor), *k*
- the sample means, $\bar{x}_i$
- the sample variances, s_i^2

- the overall mean, $\bar{\bar{x}}$
- $SS_{between} = n_1(\bar{x}_1 - \bar{\bar{x}})^2 + n_2(\bar{x}_2 - \bar{\bar{x}})^2 + \cdots + n_k(\bar{x}_k - \bar{\bar{x}})^2$
- $SS_{within} = SS_1 + SS_2 + \cdots + SS_k$, where $SS_i = \sum(x - \bar{x}_i)^2$ for each sample.

5. Check for normality of populations with histograms of the sample data. ANOVA can be used with somewhat skewed data, particularly when sample sizes are large. It is best if sample sizes are equal, or nearly equal.

6. Check for equality of variances. If the ratio of the largest sample variance to the smallest is less than 4, proceed. Be cautious if sample sizes differ, particularly if the smallest sample has the largest variance.

7. *If* the samples appear to be normally distributed, with approximately equal variances, calculate the appropriate F statistic, using the following formula:

$$F = \frac{MS_{between}}{MS_{within}} = \frac{\dfrac{SS_{between}}{k-1}}{\dfrac{SS_{within}}{n_T - k}}$$

8. Use the F distribution with $(k-1)$, $(n_T - k)$ degrees of freedom to calculate (or approximate, if using tables) the appropriate p-value for the hypothesis test. In all cases, the p-value will be of the form $P(F \geq$ calculated F).

9. If p-value $\leq \alpha$, reject H_0 and conclude that there is sufficient evidence to decide in favour of H_1. If p-value $> \alpha$, fail to reject H_0 and conclude that there is insufficient evidence to decide in favour of H_1. State your conclusions in language appropriate to the problem.

See Example 11.2 on page 416.

DEVELOP YOUR SKILLS 11.2

6. The manager of an upscale coffee store is trying to decide which of three locations would be best for a new store. The manager currently wants to determine whether there are differences in the foot traffic at each location. The manager hires three students, and has them count the number of passersby on a random sample of days. At the 5% level of significance, is there evidence of a difference in foot traffic at the three locations? You should already have checked conditions in Develop Your Skills 11.1, Exercise 1.

DYS11-6

7. The owner of a winery is wondering whether the average purchase of visitors to her winery differs according to age. She asks the cashiers to keep track of a random sample of purchases by customers in three age groups: under 30, 30–50, over 50. Because there is no good reason to ask a customer his or her age, the cashiers guess which age group a customer belongs to (and if they do not guess accurately, the research may not be helpful). Eventually, data from about 50 purchases made by customers in each of the age groups are collected. The **Data Analysis** output for **Anova: Single Factor** is shown opposite in Exhibit 11.19. At the 5% level of significance, is there evidence that customers in the different ages groups make different average purchases? You should already have checked conditions in Develop Your Skills 11.1, Exercise 2.

8. A college wants to compare the annual salaries of graduates of the four different streams of its Business diploma program, five years after graduation. The college randomly selects graduates from each of the streams (Marketing, Accounting, Human Resources, General Business) and, with appropriate reassurances about maintaining confidentiality, collects the data. At the 2.5% level of significance, is there evidence of a difference in the salaries of graduates from the four different program streams? You should already have checked conditions in Develop Your Skills 11.1, Exercise 3.

DYS11-8

EXHIBIT 11.19

Anova: Single Factor Output for Winery Purchases

Anova: Single Factor					
SUMMARY					
Groups	*Count*	*Sum*	*Average*	*Variance*	
Under 30	50	3878.42	77.5684	652.9145	
30-50	50	5983.54	119.6708	555.0899	
Over 50	50	6623.37	132.4674	625.7846	
ANOVA					
Source of Variation	*SS*	*df*	*MS*	*F*	*P-value*
Between Groups	82504.42	2	41252.21	67.48684	1.61E-21
Within Groups	89855.66	147	611.263		
Total	172360.1	149			

9. A commuter is trying to figure out the fastest way to drive to work in the morning. She keeps track of the times (in minutes) for three different routes on a random sample of mornings. Her records are shown in Exhibit 11.20.

EXHIBIT 11.20

Commuting Times for Three Different Routes

Commuting Times in Minutes		
Route 1	**Route 2**	**Route 3**
48	28	31
54	32	49
40	33	55
51	22	46
57	46	56
60	35	57
45	49	53
33	38	43
36	35	61
46	28	36

Is there evidence, at the 5% significance level, of a difference in commuting times? You should have already checked conditions in Develop Your Skills 11.1, Exercise 4.

10. Many textbooks now come with an online component for self-assessment, study, and quizzes. Teachers are experimenting with the new software components, and wondering whether they have any effect on students' final grades. A teacher who has three sections of Introductory Statistics is wondering about three variations of use of the software, as follows:

a. Assigning quizzes for marks
b. Creating chapter quizzes and recommending them, but not assigning any marks
c. Not creating any quizzes, but relying on the sample tests built into the software (no marks assigned)

There are 45 students in each of the classes being compared. The **Data Analysis** output for **Anova: Single Factor** is also shown in Exhibit 11.21 on the next page.

Is there evidence, at the 5% level of significance, that differences in the use of the online software are associated with differences in final grades? Why should we be cautious in interpreting the results in this case? You should already have checked conditions in Develop Your Skills 11.1, Exercise 5.

EXHIBIT 11.21

Anova: Single Factor Output for Grades

Anova: Single Factor				
SUMMARY				
Groups	*Count*	*Sum*	*Average*	*Variance*
Assigned Quizzes for Marks	45	3155	70.11111	212.101
Quizzes, No Marks	45	2551	56.68889	226.5828
Sample Tests Only	45	2433	54.06667	218.0182
ANOVA					
Source of Variation	*SS*	*df*	*MS*	*F*	*P-value*
Between Groups	6666.844	2	3333.422	15.22801	1.12E-06
Within Groups	28894.89	132	218.9007		
Total	35561.73	134			

11.3 MAKING MULTIPLE COMPARISONS TO DECIDE WHICH MEANS DIFFER—THE TUKEY-KRAMER PROCEDURE

The one-way ANOVA test described in Section 11.2 is the first step in comparing many population means. If the result of the ANOVA test is failure to reject the null hypothesis, then we simply conclude that there is not enough evidence to think the population means differ.

But if we reject the null hypothesis, we have evidence to suggest that at least one of the population means differs from the others, and we must do some further analysis to find out which of the means differs from the others.

You might be tempted to construct confidence intervals for the difference in the various pairs of means. In Chapter 10, a confidence interval for $\mu_1 - \mu_2$ was given as:

$$(\bar{x}_1 - \bar{x}_2) \pm t\text{-score} \sqrt{\frac{s_1^2}{n_1} + \frac{s_2^2}{n_2}}$$

For the ANOVA test, the variances have to be equal, so s_1^2 and s_2^2 are replaced by the pooled estimate s^2, and the expression simplifies to:

$$(\bar{x}_1 - \bar{x}_2) \pm t\text{-score} \sqrt{s^2\left(\frac{1}{n_1} + \frac{1}{n_2}\right)}$$

where s^2 is an estimate of the variance of the pooled data set.

From our sample data, the best estimate we have of the value of s^2 is MS_{within}, so the formula could be rewritten as follows:

$$(\bar{x}_1 - \bar{x}_2) \pm t\text{-score} \sqrt{MS_{within}\left(\frac{1}{n_1} + \frac{1}{n_2}\right)}$$

The appropriate degrees of freedom are $(n_T - k)$.

How do we decide which means differ? Simply, if the confidence interval estimate does not include zero, then it appears the two means being compared are different. If the confidence interval estimate includes zero, then it does not appear that the two means being compared are different. Essentially, we are using the confidence interval to tell us about the corresponding hypothesis test of equal means (versus differing means). We first noticed this type of correspondence in Chapter 8.[9]

If we were constructing just one confidence interval estimate, that would be that. We might do this, for example, if we had a strong suspicion, before we did our analysis, about which two means differed.

However, this approach will not be reliable if we wish to make more than one comparison of means. While the approach discussed above could be used to construct (for example) a 95% confidence interval estimate for the difference in one pair of means, the 95% confidence level would not apply to a whole series of confidence interval estimates. The confidence level could be much less. Remember that over the long run, when we construct 95% confidence intervals, there is a 5% chance that the interval will not contain the parameter being estimated. If we take that 5% chance over and over, then there will be more than a 5% probability that one or more of the intervals we construct will not contain the parameter being estimated.[10]

The Tukey-Kramer procedure solves this problem. It allows us to construct 95% confidence intervals so that 95% of the time all of the confidence intervals will contain the true difference in the means being compared. Such confidence intervals are of the same general form as shown above, but the t-score is replaced with a q-score. The q-score is generally larger than the t-score would be. Essentially, the confidence intervals have to be wider to ensure that the overall level of confidence is no less than 95%.

The formula for the Tukey-Kramer confidence interval for the difference in the mean of population i and the mean of population j ($\mu_i - \mu_j$) is as follows:

$$(\bar{x}_i - \bar{x}_j) \pm q\text{-score} \sqrt{\frac{\text{MS}_{\text{within}}}{2} \left(\frac{1}{n_i} + \frac{1}{n_j} \right)}$$

Notice that for a balanced design ($n_i = n_j = n$), this formula simplifies to:

$$(\bar{x}_i - \bar{x}_j) \pm q\text{-score} \sqrt{\frac{\text{MS}_{\text{within}}}{n}}$$

There is a table of q-scores in Appendix 7 on page 586 at the back of this text.

The appropriate q-score depends not only on the desired level of confidence, but also on the number of levels of the factor (k), and the total number of data points. There is a section of the table for 95% confidence, and another for 99% confidence. The q-score has (k, $n_T - k$) degrees of freedom. The top row of the table shows various possible levels of k, and the first column shows various levels of $n_T - k$.

---

[9] See Section 8.4, page 317.

[10] Remember, this is like repeatedly skating back and forth across that frozen lake!

EXAMPLE 11.3

Using the Tukey-Kramer approach to find out which means differ

Construct 95% Tukey-Kramer confidence intervals for the data about task completion times with the four different voicemail systems, as described in Example 11.1.

From the previous example, we know that $n_1 = n_2 = n_3 = n_4 = n = 25$. As well, we know that $MS_{within} = 668.9342$. Because sample sizes are equal, we can use the simple form of the estimate:

$$(\bar{x}_i - \bar{x}_j) \pm q\text{-score}\sqrt{\frac{MS_{within}}{n}}$$

The q-score has $(k, n_T - k)$ degrees of freedom. In the example, we looked at four different voicemail systems, so $k = 4$. In total, there were four samples of 25, so $n_T = 100$, and $n_T - k = 96$. As usual, the tables are somewhat limited. We cannot identify $q_{4,96}$. The closest we can come is either $q_{4,60} = 3.74$ or $q_{4,120} = 3.68$. Fortunately, the scores are close together, and so our estimate should not be too far wrong. We will use a q-score of 3.68, as 120 degrees of freedom is the closest in the table to our desired degrees of freedom of 96.

Now it is a matter of comparing the sample means. Because the sample sizes are equal, the 95% confidence interval estimate will be of the following form.

$$(\bar{x}_i - \bar{x}_j) \pm q\text{-score}\sqrt{\frac{MS_{within}}{n}}$$

$$(\bar{x}_i - \bar{x}_j) \pm 3.68\sqrt{\frac{668.9342}{25}}$$

$$(\bar{x}_i - \bar{x}_j) \pm 19.0357$$

The most efficient way to make the comparisons is to start by creating a confidence interval based on the largest and smallest sample means. The difference in these two means is the largest for all possible pairs of means. If this confidence interval contains zero (that is, there isn't enough evidence to conclude the population means differ), we immediately know that all the other confidence intervals also contain zero. If we can't find evidence of a difference for the two samples with the largest difference in sample means, we won't find evidence of a difference for samples where the difference in sample means is smaller. If the first confidence interval does not contain zero, we proceed by creating the confidence interval for the two sample means with the second-largest difference, and so on. Note it is the absolute value of the difference that matters here.

First, recap the information about all the sample means (this information is available on the Excel output). See Exhibit 11.22.

EXHIBIT 11.22

Task Completion Times for Accounting Firm Voicemail Systems

	Sample Mean Times (Seconds)
Voicemail System 1	72.440
Voicemail System 2	86.640
Voicemail System 3	120.400
Voicemail System 4	77.360

The largest difference in sample means (in absolute value) involves voicemail systems 1 and 3, the smallest and largest sample means.

Confidence interval for $\mu_1 - \mu_3$:

$$(\bar{x}_1 - \bar{x}_3) \pm 19.0357$$

$$(72.44 - 120.4) \pm 19.0357$$

$$-47.96 \pm 19.0357$$

This results in a confidence interval estimate of $(-67.0, -28.9)$. Since this estimate does not include zero, we conclude that μ_1 and μ_3 differ.

Next, we create a confidence interval estimate for the difference in the average task completion times for voicemail systems 3 and 4, which have the second-largest difference in sample means.

Confidence interval for $\mu_3 - \mu_4$:

$$(\bar{x}_3 - \bar{x}_4) \pm 19.0357$$

$$(120.4 - 77.36) \pm 19.0357$$

$$43.04 \pm 19.0357$$

This results in a confidence interval estimate of $(24.0, 62.1)$. Since this estimate does not include zero, we conclude that μ_3 and μ_4 differ.

Next, we create a confidence interval estimate for the difference in the average task completion times for voicemail systems 3 and 2, which have the third-largest difference in sample means.

Confidence interval for $\mu_2 - \mu_3$:

$$(\bar{x}_3 - \bar{x}_4) \pm 19.0357$$

$$(86.64 - 120.4) \pm 19.0357$$

$$-33.76 \pm 19.0357$$

This results in a confidence interval estimate of $(-52.8, -14.7)$. Since this estimate does not include zero, we conclude that μ_2 and μ_3 differ.

Next, we create a confidence interval estimate for the difference in the average task completion times for voicemail systems 1 and 2, which have the fourth-largest difference in sample means.

Confidence interval for $\mu_1 - \mu_2$:

$$(\bar{x}_1 - \bar{x}_2) \pm 19.0357$$

$$(72.44 - 86.64) \pm 19.0357$$

$$-14.2 \pm 19.0357$$

This results in a confidence interval estimate of $(-33.2, 4.8)$. Since this estimate includes zero, we cannot conclude that μ_1 and μ_2 differ.

At this point, we are done. We know that all of the other confidence intervals must also contain zero, because the differences in the sample means are smaller for all the other pairs.

The net result: we have reason to believe that the average task completion time of voicemail system 3 differs from the average task completion times of all three other voicemail systems. If we examine the confidence interval estimates, we can suggest that the average task completion time is probably at least 15 seconds longer with voicemail system 3. However, there is no evidence of differences in the average task completion times of the other voicemail systems, so any one of these could be chosen as the preferred system (perhaps based on other criteria).

Using the Excel Template for the Tukey-Kramer Confidence Interval

These calculations can be done with the help of the worksheet template called "Tukey-Kramer CI," available in the workbook called "Templates". This template should be used in conjunction with Excel's ANOVA output, as that output contains almost all of the required input values. Because Excel has no built-in table of q values, you will have to input the required q-score from Appendix 7, on page 586. Exhibit 11.23 below illustrates how the template connects to the ANOVA output.

EXHIBIT 11.23

Excel Template for the Tukey-Kramer Confidence Interval and Excel ANOVA Output

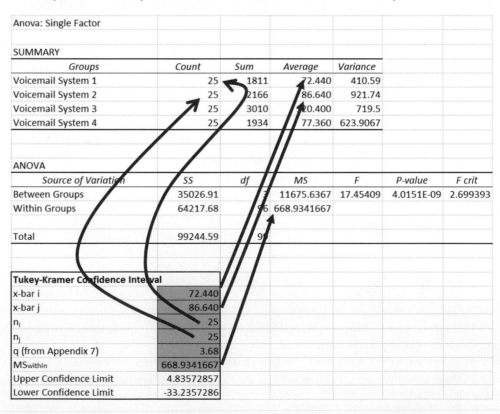

DEVELOP YOUR SKILLS 11.3

MyStatLab

Use 95% confidence intervals to answer these questions.

11. Refer to your analysis for Develop Your Skills 11.2, Exercise 6 (page 420). Which of the locations for a new upscale coffee store would be best?

12. Refer to your analysis for Develop Your Skills 11.2, Exercise 7 (page 420). Which group of customers has the highest average purchases?

13. Refer to your analysis for Develop Your Skills 11.2, Exercise 8 (page 420). How do the salaries of each stream of the Business diploma program compare, five years after graduation?

14. A commuter is trying to figure out the fastest way to drive to work in the morning. She keeps track of the times (in minutes) for three different routes on a random sample of mornings. Her records are shown in Exhibit 11.24.

You may assume the commuting times are normally distributed. Which route would you recommend to this commuter?

EXHIBIT 11.24

Commuting Times for Three Different Routes

Commuting Times in Minutes		
Route 1	Route 2	Route 3
48	28	31
54	32	49
40	33	55
51	22	46
57	46	56
60	35	57
45	49	53
33	38	43
36	35	61
46	28	36

15. Refer to your analysis for Develop Your Skills 11.2, Exercise 10 (page 421). Which method of using the online component of the textbook is associated with the best results for the students?

11.4 A BRIEF INTRODUCTION TO TWO-FACTOR ANOVA

The material in this chapter is an introduction to a kind of analysis that has many applications. So far, we have examined one-way ANOVA, looking at one factor that could be used to differentiate the populations being studied. But what if we had information about two (or more) factors?

For example, suppose we were interested in the number of defects in products made in a factory. We might be interested in whether the shift affected the number of defects. If there are three shifts, then there are three levels of this factor. At the same time, we might have data about the supplier of an important component part of the product. If there are four different suppliers of this part, then the second factor of interest is supplier, with four levels. The data set might look something like the table shown in Exhibit 11.25 on the next page.

This is a case where we could apply two-factor ANOVA. There are three questions we have to answer:

1. Does the number of defects vary from one shift to another? In other words, is the average number of defects significantly different for at least one shift?

2. Does the number of defects vary from one supplier to another? In other words, is the average number of defects significantly different for at least one supplier?

3. Does the effect of shift depend on the supplier, or do the two factors have independent effects?

EXHIBIT 11.25

Number of Defects by Shift and Supplier

	Number of Defects		
	8 A.M.–4 P.M. Shift	4 P.M.–Midnight Shift	Midnight–8 A.M. Shift
Supplier 1	8	10	9
	22	10	9
	13	4	7
	12	19	8
Supplier 2	7	12	21
	4	10	13
	5	3	2
	7	5	15
Supplier 3	15	4	5
	17	12	9
	18	15	10
	4	16	7
Supplier 4	12	8	6
	15	5	8
	17	16	18
	9	15	13

While the first two questions are familiar in form, the last question is new, because it asks about the interaction between the factors.

In general, we approach the analysis in the same way as with one-way ANOVA. We break the total variation in the data into a sum of squares for shift, a sum of squares for supplier, a sum of squares for interaction, and a residual sum of squares. F-tests are based on ratios of the associated mean squares, with the residual mean square (MS_{within}) acting as the standard against which we compare the other mean squares. Of course, the many calculations are best done on a computer.

In two-way ANOVA, the first hypothesis test should be about interaction between the two factors, because this guides the rest of the analysis. If there is evidence of interaction between the two factors, a special approach must be taken for the hypothesis tests about each individual factor. When interaction is present, F-tests about each factor should be done as one-way ANOVA tests for each separate level of the second factor. For example, we would do a one-way ANOVA on the number of defects, using the data set showing the number of defects, by shift, for only one supplier, not all four suppliers at once. In this case, it would not be helpful to use the data for all suppliers at once. If we did, and it appeared that the number of defects varied by shift, we would not be sure whether it was because of shift or because of supplier. Notice that the data requirements for this kind of analysis are more complex. Data collection must be done carefully and thoughtfully, anticipating the research questions that will be studied.

Two-way analysis of variance is not covered in detail in this introductory text. Two-way and even three-way techniques can be useful, but it is also important to think carefully about whether more complex analysis is necessary. If the only question of interest in the example above is whether there are differences in the number of defects produced with different supplier parts, then one-way ANOVA is sufficient.

One-factor ANOVA allows us to examine sample data to make conclusions about the means of three or more populations simultaneously. In general, ANOVA is used to determine whether different levels of a factor have a significant effect on the response variable. A **factor** is a qualitative explanatory characteristic that might distinguish one group or population from another. A **level** is a value or setting that the factor can take. A **response variable** is a quantitative variable that is being measured, or observed. We are interested in how this variable responds to the different levels of the factor.

The ANOVA hypothesis test compares the between-sample variation (associated with different levels of the factor) to the within-sample variation (random variation). We use the F distribution (described in Section 11.2) to determine whether the variability in the sample means is significantly greater than the random variability in the data. If it is, then we can conclude that at least one of the population means differs from the others.

Chapter Summary

11

Checking Conditions for One-Way Analysis of Variance (ANOVA)

The following conditions are required for the ANOVA test, and must be checked.

1. The data points are independent and randomly selected from each population.
2. Each population is normally distributed.
3. The populations all have the same variability. In particular, the variances are equal.

The ANOVA technique is fairly robust, in that it can safely be used with populations that are somewhat skewed, particularly when sample sizes are large. It is best if sample sizes are equal, or nearly equal.

The ANOVA test for comparing population means is not greatly affected by inequality of variances, particularly when the sample sizes are equal, or nearly equal. Therefore, for ANOVA, we will assume population variances are approximately equal as long as the largest sample variance is less than four times as large as the smallest. Under these conditions, the results of the ANOVA test will still be approximately correct. Caution should be used if sample sizes are small, or unequal, particularly if the smallest sample has the largest variance.

The Hypothesis Test for Independent Samples, Normal Quantitative Data—One-Way Analysis of Variance (ANOVA)

The form of the hypothesis test is as follows.

$H_0: \mu_1 = \mu_2 = \mu_3$

$H_1:$ At least one μ differs from the others.

The hypothesis test requires calculation of sums of squares for the between-sample variability and the within-sample variability, as follows:

$$SS_{between} = n_1(\bar{x}_1 - \bar{\bar{x}})^2 + n_2(\bar{x}_2 - \bar{\bar{x}})^2 + \cdots + n_k(\bar{x}_k - \bar{\bar{x}})^2$$
$$SS_{within} = SS_1 + SS_2 + \cdots + SS_k, \text{ where } SS_i = \sum(x - \bar{x}_i)^2 \text{ for each sample.}$$

The associated mean squares are compared in an F ratio.

$$F = \frac{MS_{between}}{MS_{within}} = \frac{\dfrac{SS_{between}}{k-1}}{\dfrac{SS_{within}}{n_T - k}}$$

The sampling distribution of $\dfrac{MS_{between}}{MS_{within}}$ follows the F distribution, with $(k-1), (n_T - k)$ degrees of freedom, where n_1 is the total number of observations in the data set, and k is the number of samples (and levels of the factor). In all cases, the p-value will be of the form $P(F \geq \text{calculated F})$.

See the Guide to Decision Making for three or more independent samples, normal quantitative data (One-Way ANOVA), on page 419.

The Excel **Data Analysis** tool used to analyze sample data is called **Anova: Single Factor**. Use of this Excel tool is described starting on page 414.

It is also possible to use a table of F critical values to do these hypothesis tests. Use of the F table is described on pages 417–418.

Making Multiple Comparisons to Decide Which Means Differ—The Tukey-Kramer Procedure

If we reject the null hypothesis that the population means are equal, we must do some further analysis to find out which means differ. The Tukey-Kramer procedure allows us to construct, for example, 95% confidence intervals, so that 95% of the time, all of the confidence intervals will contain the true difference in the means being compared.

The formula for the Tukey-Kramer confidence interval for the difference in the mean of population i and the mean of population j ($\mu_i - \mu_j$) is as follows:

$$(\bar{x}_i - \bar{x}_j) \pm q\text{-score} \sqrt{\frac{\text{MS}_{\text{within}}}{2} \left(\frac{1}{n_i} + \frac{1}{n_j} \right)}$$

When the samples are the same size ($n_i = n_j = n$), this formula simplifies to:

$$(\bar{x}_i - \bar{x}_j) \pm q\text{-score} \sqrt{\frac{\text{MS}_{\text{within}}}{n}}$$

If the confidence interval estimate does not include zero, then it appears that the two means being compared are different. If the confidence interval estimate includes zero, then it does not appear that the two means being compared are different.

There is a table of q-scores in Appendix 7 on page 586 of this text. The appropriate q-score depends not only on the desired level of confidence, but also on the number of levels of the factor (k), and the total number of data points. Use of the table is described on page 423.

There is a worksheet template called "Tukey-Kramer CI" (available in MyStatLab in the workbook called "Templates"). This template should be used in conjunction with Excel's ANOVA output, as that output contains almost all of the required input values. Because Excel has no built-in table of q values, you will have to input the required q-score from the table, on page 586. Exhibit 11.23 on page 426 illustrates how the template connects to the ANOVA output.

Go to MyStatLab at www.mathxl.com. You can practise the exercises indicated with red in the Develop Your Skills and Chapter Review Exercises as often as you want, and guided solutions will help you find answers step by step. You'll find a personalized study plan available to you too

CHAPTER REVIEW EXERCISES

WARM-UP EXERCISES

1. A student is trying to determine whether there is a difference in the average marks among three different classes. She has an idea that some professors give lower marks than others, so she wants to sign up for a class in which the average marks are higher. She manages to collect a random sample of marks in the classes. She begins by creating histograms of the marks data for each class. The histograms are shown opposite in Exhibit 11.26.

EXHIBIT 11.26

Histograms of Marks Data

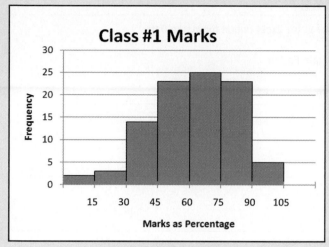

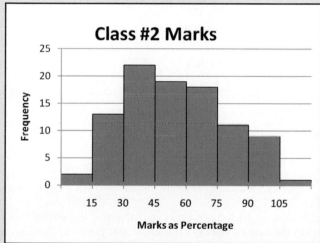

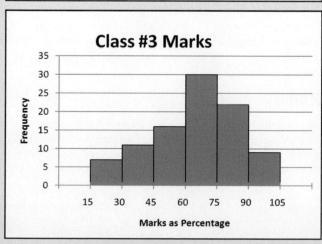

Does it appear that the normality requirements are met? Sample sizes in this case are 95.

2. The **Anova: Single Factor** output from Excel for the data set described in Exercise 1 is shown below in Exhibit 11.27 (some values are missing).

EXHIBIT 11.27

Anova: Single Factor Excel Output for Marks Data

Anova: Single Factor				
SUMMARY				
Groups	*Count*	*Sum*	*Average*	*Variance*
Class #1	95	5840		370.0179
Class #2	95	5088		590.6535
Class #3	95	6075		415.5823

ANOVA					
Source of Variation	*SS*	*df*	*MS*	*F*	*P-value*
Between Groups	5596.133				
Within Groups	129367.9				
Total	134964				

Does it appear that these data meet the requirement for equality of variances?

3. Refer to Exhibit 11.27 above. Fill in the missing values:
   - the average for each class
   - the degrees of freedom (Between Groups, Within Groups, and Total)
   - the mean squares
   - the F statistic

4. Estimate the *p*-value of the F statistic that you calculated in Exercise 3. At the 5% level of significance, do the data on class marks suggest that there are differences in the average marks of the classes?

5. Use the Tukey-Kramer procedure to identify which class or classes the student who wants a high mark should avoid, and which class or classes the student should prefer. Use a 95% confidence level. Is this method of choosing classes valid? Why or why not?

THINK AND DECIDE

CRE11-6

6. A credit card company is trying to determine whether people who own different types of credit cards typically carry different balances, on average. A random sample of people with Visa, Mastercard, and American Express cards is selected. Cardholders are enticed into revealing the balance on their most recent monthly statements with a contest that would allow them to win the amount of their most recent credit card bill.

Histograms of the sample data are shown below in Exhibit 11.28.

EXHIBIT 11.28

Histograms of Most Recent Monthly Balances of Visa, Mastercard, and American Express Owners

The output from Excel's **Anova: Single Factor** tool is shown below in Exhibit 11.29.

EXHIBIT 11.29

Excel Anova: Single Factor Output for Credit Card Monthly Balances

Anova: Single Factor						
SUMMARY						
Groups	*Count*	*Sum*	*Average*	*Variance*		
Visa	17	16,443.56	967.27	121,734.84		
Mastercard	21	24,724.35	1,177.35	91,868.65		
American Express	26	27,478.30	1,056.86	479,149.82		
ANOVA						
Source of Variation	*SS*	*df*	*MS*	*F*	*P-value*	
Between Groups	425,478.41	2	212,739.20	0.82	0.44	
Within Groups	15,763,875.75	61	258,424.19			
Total	16,189,354.16	63				

Are the conditions for ANOVA met? Are the most recent average monthly balances for the three credit cards different?

7. A telemarketing company is monitoring the performance of four newly hired employees. It is important that employees do not spend too much time on the phone with customers, particularly if the time spent does not result in a sale. A supervisor monitors a random sample of calls taken by each new employee, measuring the time spent on the call before a sale, in minutes. You may assume that the times are normally distributed. The Excel **Anova: Single Factor** output is shown below in Exhibit 11.30.

EXHIBIT 11.30

Excel Anova: Single Factor Output for Times Before Sale for New Employees of a Telemarketing Firm

Anova: Single Factor					
SUMMARY					
Groups	*Count*	*Sum*	*Average*	*Variance*	
Employee 1	35	404		6.314286	
Employee 2	37	462		14.75676	
Employee 3	32	357		10.32964	
Employee 4	42	377		13.536	
ANOVA					
Source of Variation	*SS*	*df*	*MS*	*F*	
Between Groups	264.6295				
Within Groups	1621.124				
Total	1885.753				

Does it appear that the requirement for equal variances is met?

Use the information in Exhibit 11.30 to fill in the missing values:
- the average for each employee
- the degrees of freedom (Between Groups, Within Groups, and Total)
- the mean squares
- the F statistic

8. Estimate the p-value of the F statistic you calculated in Exercise 7. At the 5% level of significance, do the data on length of calls suggest that there are differences in the average number of minutes each employee spends with a customer before making a sale?

9. Use the Tukey-Kramer procedure to identify which employees spend less time, on average, with customers before making a sale. Use a 95% confidence level.

THINK AND DECIDE USING EXCEL

10. Does the type of safety training affect the number of factory accidents? Check to see that the conditions required for one-way ANOVA are met.   CRE11-10

11. Does the type of safety training affect the number of factory accidents? Conduct a test of hypothesis at the 5% level of significance.   CRE11-11

12. Does the type of safety training affect the number of factory accidents? Use the Tukey-Kramer procedure (with 95% confidence intervals) to identify the worst training method(s).   CRE11-12

13. A semi-retired economist is thinking about retiring fully, and he finds himself checking his mutual fund portfolio daily to see how his investments are doing. He notices that the time it takes to log onto his investment account online varies widely, and he wonders whether the connection times vary by time of day. He decides to keep track of a random sample of connection times (in seconds), for five time periods: early morning, mid-day, early afternoon, late afternoon, and evening. Check whether the conditions required for one-way ANOVA are met. If they are, conduct a test of hypothesis at the 5% level of significance to determine whether the mean connection times are equal.   CRE11-13

14. A commuter is trying to decide whether there is a difference in the amount of time it takes him to drive to work, depending on departure time in the morning. He keeps track of the number of minutes his commute takes him, on a random sample of days, with three departure times: 6 A.M., 7 A.M., and 8 A.M. Check to see whether the conditions required for one-way ANOVA are met. If they are, conduct a test of hypothesis at the 5% level of significance to determine whether the mean commuting times are equal.   CRE11-14

15. A professor who hates being scheduled for 8 A.M. classes, or classes on Friday afternoons after 3 P.M., has decided to investigate whether student grades are affected by the time at which classes take place. She keeps track of the grades of students who are scheduled for class at 8 A.M. on Thursdays, 4 P.M. on Fridays, and 2 P.M. on Wednesdays. The marks of these classes are not, strictly speaking, random samples. However, if we consider the population as the marks of all students who attend the professor's classes over her entire career, we could think of particular classes as random samples. Check whether the conditions for ANOVA are met. If they are, conduct a test of hypothesis at the 1% level to see if it appears that the scheduled time for classes affects the marks. Explain why you should be cautious in interpreting these results.   CRE11-15

16. The owner of a drugstore is wondering whether the amount of a customer's purchase varies by age group. The owner runs a contest with a grand prize of a $100 gift certificate that can be used in the store. The entry ballot requires the entrant to record his/her age group, and the amount of his/her most recent purchase. The owner selects a random sample of the ballots from the contest. Does it appear that the conditions for ANOVA are met?   CRE11-16

17. Refer to Exercise 16. Does it appear that the drugstore customers' purchases vary by age group—in other words, are the mean purchases of customers in the different age groups equal? Use a 5% level of significance.   CRE11-16

CRE11-16

18. Refer to Exercise 16. Use the Tukey-Kramer procedure to identify which average purchases differ. Use a 95% level of confidence.

19. Refer to Exercise 16. Do the data represent a random sample? Explain why or why not.

20. Statistics Canada provides "microdata," based on census data for Canada. The microdata files contain representative samples of census data. You can access these data sets at the Statistics Canada website, www.statcan.ca/english/kits/microdata/2001Census/intropages.htm.

    The data sets are quite large, providing information on 43 variables. Download the data for your province. Compare the wages and salaries of the following three groups, according to their highest level of schooling:

    (04) Secondary (high) school graduation certificate
    (05) Trades certificate or diploma
    (08) College: With college certificate or diploma

    Do these data meet the requirements for ANOVA? If so, test to see whether there are differences in average wages and salaries among the three groups. Use a 5% level of significance.

TEST YOUR KNOWLEDGE

CRE11-21

21. There are many factors that affect a student's success in school. A professor is concerned that many of her students work at part-time or even full-time jobs while they are attending school. Work responsibilities leave less time available for studying. The professor selects a random sample of her students (her classes are quite large) and organizes the data according to how many hours per week each student works, on average. She then records the final marks for the Microeconomics course these students have just completed. The data are available in MyStatLab. Is there evidence, at a 5% significance level, of an association between marks and the number of hours worked per week? That is, are the mean marks equal? If there are differences in the average marks, discuss what those differences are.

CHAPTER 12

Making Decisions with Two or More Samples, Qualitative Data

INTRODUCTION

There are many situations in which two or more populations of qualitative data need to be investigated. For example, market research is often aimed at finding out whether there are differences or similarities in target market sub-groups. Markets might be segmented along lines of income, location, gender, and other customer characteristics. For example, a telecommunications company selling long-distance services might want to know whether urban and rural customers differ in their needs for long-distance plans, so it can tailor its plans accordingly. The segmentation makes sense only if real differences among the segments can be identified. The data involved are qualitative in nature, so researchers are interested in counts or proportions (or percentages) in the data.

In Chapters 9, 10, and 11, we looked at comparisons of samples with quantitative or ranked data. In Chapter 12, we will look at comparisons of two or more samples of qualitative data, which means that we will be dealing with proportions, percentages, and counts throughout. In Section 12.1, we will use two samples of qualitative data to compare two population proportions. In Section 12.2, we will compare sample data with a desired or claimed set of characteristics

LEARNING OBJECTIVES

After mastering the material in this chapter, you will be able to:

1 Choose and conduct the appropriate hypothesis test to compare two population proportions.

2 Choose and conduct the appropriate hypothesis test to compare proportions in one population with a desired distribution.

3 Choose and conduct the appropriate hypothesis test to compare proportions across many populations, and draw a conclusion about the independence of population characteristics.

by examining counts in two or more categories. The sample data will allow us to decide whether a population has a desired distribution of characteristics. In Section 12.3, we will look at several samples to see how they match up according to several characteristics, comparing counts simultaneously. This will allow us to compare many population proportions and draw conclusions about the independence of population characteristics.

12.1 COMPARING TWO PROPORTIONS—z-TEST AND CONFIDENCE INTERVAL OF $p_1 - p_2$

A company wanted to do some market research about fitness club memberships. A random sample of adult Moncton, New Brunswick, residents was surveyed. The survey results showed that out of the 153 female survey respondents, 62 had fitness club memberships. Of the 52 male survey respondents, 28 had fitness club memberships. Do the survey results suggest that males and females in Moncton have differing tendencies to have fitness club memberships?

We will refer to the data about females as sample 1, and the sample proportion as $\hat{p}_1$.

We see that $\hat{p}_1 = \dfrac{62}{153} = 0.4052$. We can calculate (for the men) $\hat{p}_2 = \dfrac{28}{52} = 0.5385$.

The proportions of males and females who have fitness club memberships are different in the samples. As always, we must ask: are the proportions *significantly* different? As in Chapter 10, when we compared population means, we will focus on the difference in the two parameters (and the corresponding sample statistics) when we make our decision. That is, we will examine $\hat{p}_1 - \hat{p}_2$ to draw a conclusion about $p_1 - p_2$. As usual, we must know what the sampling distribution of the difference in proportions looks like in order to make a decision.

Of course, the underlying probability distributions here are binomial. We count the number of *successes* in a certain number of trials. In the example, we count how many of the 153 female survey respondents had fitness club memberships ($x_1 = 62$), and how many of the 52 male respondents had fitness club memberships ($x_2 = 28$). As discussed in Chapter 6, we can convert these binomial counts into proportions, and the associated sampling distributions will be approximately normal if the sample sizes are sufficiently large. The check for the normality of the sampling distribution is that np and nq are both ≥ 10 (where p is the probability of success and q is the probability of failure). As well, n has to be large enough that no continuity correction factor is needed in the approximation of the binomial distribution with the normal distribution. Similar conditions are required for the sampling distribution of $\hat{p}_1 - \hat{p}_2$.

Sampling Distribution of $\hat{p}_1 - \hat{p}_2$

For cases where the underlying binomial distributions are sufficiently normal (n_1 and n_2 sufficiently large, and $n_1p_1, n_1q_1, n_2p_2,$ and n_2q_2 all ≥ 10), the sampling distribution of $\hat{p}_1 - \hat{p}_2$ is approximately normally distributed. Samples must be independent.

1. The standard error of $\hat{p}_1 - \hat{p}_2$ is as follows:

$$\sigma_{\hat{p}_1 - \hat{p}_2} = \sqrt{\frac{p_1q_1}{n_1} + \frac{p_2q_2}{n_2}}$$

2. The mean of $\hat{p}_1 - \hat{p}_2$ is:

$$\mu_{\hat{p}_1 - \hat{p}_2} = p_1 - p_2$$

This information about the sampling distribution cannot be directly applied, since we do not know what p_1 or p_2 (the true population proportions) are. We have to approximate p_1 and p_2 with the sample estimates, that is, $\hat{p}_1$ and $\hat{p}_2$, and we will use these values in place of the unknown population parameters in the formulas for the mean and standard error. Similarly, we check the conditions for normality using $\hat{p}_1$ and $\hat{p}_2$.

In general, the test statistic will take the usual form:

$$z = \frac{(\hat{p}_1 - \hat{p}_2) - \mu_{\hat{p}_1 - \hat{p}_2}}{\sigma_{\hat{p}_1 - \hat{p}_2}} \approx \frac{(\hat{p}_1 - \hat{p}_2) - \mu_{\hat{p}_1 - \hat{p}_2}}{s_{\hat{p}_1 - \hat{p}_2}} = \frac{(\hat{p}_1 - \hat{p}_2) - (p_1 - p_2)}{\sqrt{\frac{\hat{p}_1\hat{q}_1}{n_1} + \frac{\hat{p}_2\hat{q}_2}{n_2}}}$$

Special Case: $H_0: p_1 - p_2 = 0$

It is quite usual, in problems where population proportions are being compared, to work with the null hypothesis that $p_1 - p_2 = 0$ (that is, the two population proportions are equal). If the sample proportions are hypothesized to be equal, it makes sense to pool the data from the two samples to come up with a single estimate of the unknown population proportion.

When we pool the two samples in the fitness membership example, we find a total number of respondents of $n_1 + n_2 = 153 + 52 = 205$. Of the total 205 respondents, there were a total of $x_1 + x_2 = 62 + 28 = 90$ who had fitness club memberships. The *pooled* estimate of the proportion of those who have fitness club memberships (which we will call $\hat{p}$ with no subscript) will then be $\hat{p} = \frac{x_1 + x_2}{n_1 + n_2} = \frac{62 + 28}{153 + 52} = \frac{90}{205} = 0.439$. This means that $\hat{q} = 1 - 0.439 = 0.561$.

From the information on the sampling distribution above, we know that

$$s_{\hat{p}_1 - \hat{p}_2} = \sqrt{\frac{\hat{p}_1\hat{q}_1}{n_1} + \frac{\hat{p}_2\hat{q}_2}{n_2}}$$

Because the population proportions are supposed to be equal, we can replace $\hat{p}_1$ and $\hat{p}_2$ in the formula with our pooled estimate, "$\hat{p}$." Similarly, we will replace $\hat{q}_1$ and $\hat{q}_2$ with "$\hat{q}$". We can then take out the common factor to simplify the estimate of the standard error, as follows.

$$s_{\hat{p}_1 - \hat{p}_2} = \sqrt{\dfrac{\hat{p}_1 \hat{q}_1}{n_1} + \dfrac{\hat{p}_2 \hat{q}_2}{n_2}}$$

$$= \sqrt{\dfrac{\hat{p}\hat{q}}{n_1} + \dfrac{\hat{p}\hat{q}}{n_2}}$$

$$= \sqrt{\hat{p}\hat{q}\left(\dfrac{1}{n_1} + \dfrac{1}{n_2}\right)}$$

Here's a note about arithmetic that might be useful. In this case, we knew x_1 and x_2 (the number of successes in each sample), so we could use the formula $\hat{p} = \dfrac{x_1 + x_2}{n_1 + n_2}$ to estimate the proportion from the pooled sample data. But what if all that is given is the sample proportions and the sample sizes? The equivalent formula in this case to get the pooled sample $\hat{p}$ is

$$\hat{p} = \dfrac{\hat{p}_1(n_1) + \hat{p}_2(n_2)}{n_1 + n_2}$$

If you think about it, you will realize that $\hat{p}_1(n_1) = x_1$ and $\hat{p}_2(n_2) = x_2$, and so the formulas are equivalent. You should use whichever one matches the sample information you are given in the problem.

Now we can conduct the hypothesis test for the fitness memberships. The first step is to check for normality of the sampling distribution.

$$n_1 \hat{p}_1 = x_1 = 62 > 10$$

$$n_1 \hat{q}_1 = n_1 - x_1 = 153 - 62 = 91 > 10$$

$$n_2 \hat{p}_2 = x_2 = 28 > 10$$

$$n_2 \hat{q}_2 = n_2 - x_2 = 52 - 28 > 10$$

Sampling is done without replacement here. Remember, the binomial distribution is still appropriate as the underlying probability distribution as long as the sample is no more than 5% of the population. The target population is Moncton adults, of whom there are tens of thousands, so we can be sure that the sample is not more than 5% of the population.

- H_0: $p_1 - p_2 = 0$
- H_1: $p_1 - p_2 \neq 0$ (The question is whether males and females in Moncton *differ* in their tendencies to have fitness club memberships.)
- Use $\alpha = 0.05$.

We will compare $\hat{p}_1 - \hat{p}_2$ with its expected value. If we were required to do the exercise by hand using the normal table, we would calculate a z-score of the standard form.

$$z = \dfrac{(\hat{p}_1 - \hat{p}_2) - \mu_{\hat{p}_1 - \hat{p}_2}}{s_{\hat{p}_1 - \hat{p}_2}} = \dfrac{(\hat{p}_1 - \hat{p}_2) - 0}{\sqrt{\hat{p}\hat{q}\left(\dfrac{1}{n_1} + \dfrac{1}{n_2}\right)}} = \dfrac{(0.4052 - 0.5385) - 0}{\sqrt{(0.439)(0.561)\left(\dfrac{1}{153} + \dfrac{1}{52}\right)}}$$

$$= -1.67$$

In order to get the appropriate p-value, we first calculate $P(z \leq -1.67) = 0.0475$. Because this is a two-tailed test, the p-value $= 2(0.0475) = 0.095$. Since the p-value is greater than the α of 0.05, we fail to reject the null hypothesis. There is insufficient evidence to infer that males and females in Moncton differ in their tendencies to have fitness club memberships.

Coded Data   The data for comparison of proportions may be in coded form (for example, 1 corresponds to *yes* and 2 corresponds to *no*). In such a case, Excel's **Histogram** data analysis tool can be used to sort the data before you do any hypothesis test. We have done this before (for instance, in Example 2.3 on page 64). Example 12.1A illustrates.

EXAMPLE 12.1A

Comparing two proportions, no difference in proportions, coded data

A research officer in a public sector service organization is particularly interested in employees' perceptions of the senior manager's competence. She wants to compare the survey data collected this year and last year in response to the question, "Do you think that the senior manager is an effective leader?" The researcher is interested to see whether significantly fewer people think that the senior manager is an effective leader this year, compared with last year.

In the Excel data set, 1 corresponds to a *yes* answer, and 0 corresponds to a *no* answer.

EXA12-1a

You will be able to use Excel to organize the coded data (as we have done before). Before you do that, you should set up the hypothesis test and think about what you need to know in order to make a good decision. Suppose we refer to last year's population of responses as population 1, and this year's as population 2. We can choose to focus on either the proportion of *yes* answers or the proportion of *no* answers. In the discussion that follows, the focus is on the proportion of *yes* answers, so p_1 is the proportion of *yes* answers in population 1 (last year's responses). It is important to explicitly decide these matters before you begin, to avoid confusion. The hypothesis test will be as follows:

- $H_0: p_1 - p_2 = 0$
- $H_1: p_1 - p_2 > 0$ (If significantly fewer people think that the senior manager is an effective leader this year compared to last year then p_1 will be larger than p_2.)
- Use $\alpha = 0.025$.

Now we need to organize and summarize the data before we can proceed. One of the most straightforward ways to organize this data set is to use the **Histogram** tool in Excel, with bin numbers of 0 and 1 to calculate the frequencies of zeros and ones in the data for last year, and again for this year. It is then a fairly simple operation to create Excel formulas to calculate the percentages of *yes* and *no* answers for last year and this year.

For last year, Excel calculates that there were 25 *no* responses and 228 *yes* responses (and a total of 253 responses). For this year, Excel calculates 66 *no* responses and 246 *yes* responses (and a total of 312 responses), so $\hat{p}_1 = \frac{228}{253} = 0.9012$ and $\hat{p}_2 = \frac{246}{312} = 0.7885$.

Sampling is done without replacement, and we have no information about the total number of employees in the organization. We proceed by making an assumption that the sample size is no more than 5% of the population, and noting that our conclusions may not be correct if this assumption does not hold.

We must check for normality of the sampling distribution.

$n_1\hat{p}_1 = x_1 =$ the number of *yes* answers for last year $= 228 > 10$
$n_1\hat{q}_1 =$ the number of *no* anwers for last year $= 25 > 10$
$n_2\hat{p}_2 = x_2 =$ the number of *yes* answers this year $= 246 > 10$
$n_2\hat{q}_2 =$ the number of *no* answers this year $= 66 > 10$

Because the null hypothesis is no difference in the population proportions, we will calculate $\hat{p}$ and $\hat{q}$.

$$\hat{p} = \frac{x_1 + x_2}{n_1 + n_2} = \frac{228 + 246}{253 + 312} = \frac{474}{565} = 0.8389$$

and $\hat{q} = (1 - \hat{p}) = 1 - 0.8389 = 0.1611$.

$$z = \frac{(\hat{p}_1 - \hat{p}_2) - \mu_{\hat{p}_1-\hat{p}_2}}{s_{\hat{p}_1-\hat{p}_2}} = \frac{(\hat{p}_1 - \hat{p}_2) - 0}{\sqrt{\hat{p}\hat{q}\left(\dfrac{1}{n_1} + \dfrac{1}{n_2}\right)}} = \frac{(0.9012 - 0.7885) - 0}{\sqrt{(0.8389)(0.1611)\left(\dfrac{1}{253} + \dfrac{1}{312}\right)}} = 3.62$$

The appropriate *p*-value is P($z \geq 3.62$) $\cong 0$. There would be almost no chance of getting sample results like these if in fact there was no difference in the proportions of employees who thought that the senior manager was an effective leader last year compared to this year. With such a small *p*-value, we will reject the null hypothesis. There is sufficient evidence to infer that a smaller proportion of people think the senior manager is an effective leader this year compared to last year.

Using the Excel Template for Making Decisions About Two Population Proportions, H$_0$: $p_1 - p_2 = 0$ A worksheet called "*z*-Test of 2 Proportions" is available in the workbook called "Templates." The completed worksheet template for this example is shown opposite in Exhibit 12.1. As usual, you are required to fill in the blue-shaded boxes in the template. Also as usual, the template reminds you to check for normality of the sampling distribution, and that these conditions are met.

This is a one-tailed test, and so the appropriate *p*-value is 0.000144697, which is quite small. The template result matches our manual calculations, with more precision (as usual).

General Case: H$_0$: $p_1 - p_2 =$ Fixed Amount (Non-Zero)

It is also possible to examine qualitative data to see whether the two population proportions differ by some fixed amount. The template will also handle this situation. Example 12.1B illustrates.

EXHIBIT 12.1

Completed Excel Template, Example 12.1A

Making Decisions About Two Population Proportions	
Sample 1 Size	253
Sample 2 Size	312
Sample 1 Proportion	0.901185771
Sample 2 Proportion	0.788461538
$n_1 \bullet p_1$hat	228
$n_1 \bullet q_1$hat	25
$n_2 \bullet p_2$hat	246
$n_2 \bullet q_2$hat	66
Are np and nq >=10?	yes
Hypothesized Difference in Population Proportions, p_1-p_2 (decimal form)	0
z-Score	3.624676071
One-Tailed p-Value	0.000144662
Two-Tailed p-Value	0.000289324

EXAMPLE 12.1B

Comparing two proportions, non-zero difference in proportions

The dean of the business program is interested to see whether student satisfaction is higher for students in classes that meet every week in a classroom, compared with students who take courses completely online. Of course, there are many factors that affect student satisfaction, and past data analysis has shown that student satisfaction can vary as much as 20% between two classes in very similar circumstances. Therefore the dean wants to check to see whether there is more than a 20% difference in satisfaction levels between students with weekly classes and those enrolled online. The satisfaction level is determined by the percentage of students who answer yes to the question, "Are you generally satisfied with this class?"

A random sample of students taking face-to-face economics classes is selected, as is a random sample of students taking online economics courses. 95% of the 400 students in face-to-face classes were satisfied. 72% of the 300 students taking online courses were satisfied. Is there enough evidence to conclude that the satisfaction rate for those taking face-to-face classes is more than 20% higher than for those taking online classes?

We will refer to the satisfaction levels of those taking face-to-face classes as population 1, and of those taking online classes as population 2. The hypothesis test will be as follows:

- $H_0: p_1 - p_2 = 0.20$
- $H_1: p_1 - p_2 > 0.20$ (We want to know whether the satisfaction rate for population 1 is more than 20% higher than for population 2.)
- Use $\alpha = 0.04$.

Sampling is done without replacement. We are given no data about the total number of students in face-to-face or online classes at the college. We proceed by making the assumption that the samples are no more than 5% of the population, and noting that our conclusions may not be valid if this is not the case.

We must also check the conditions for normality of the sampling distribution.

$$n_1\hat{p}_1 = 380 > 10$$

$$n_1\hat{q}_1 = 20 > 10$$

$$n_2\hat{p}_2 = 216 > 10$$

$$n_2\hat{q}_2 = 84 > 10$$

In this case, since we are no longer hypothesizing that the two population proportions are equal, we will not pool the sample data to get an estimate of p. We will instead use $\hat{p}_1$ and $\hat{p}_2$ in our calculations, as follows:

$$z = \frac{(\hat{p}_1 - \hat{p}_2) - \mu_{\hat{p}_1 - \hat{p}_2}}{s_{\hat{p}_1 - \hat{p}_2}} = \frac{(\hat{p}_1 - \hat{p}_2) - \mu_{\hat{p}_1 - \hat{p}_2}}{\sqrt{\dfrac{\hat{p}_1\hat{q}_1}{n_1} + \dfrac{\hat{p}_2\hat{q}_2}{n_2}}}$$

$$= \frac{(0.95 - 0.72) - 0.20}{\sqrt{\dfrac{(0.95)(0.05)}{400} + \dfrac{(0.72)(0.28)}{300}}} = 1.067$$

$$p\text{-value} = P(z \geq 1.07) = 1 - 0.8577 = 0.1423$$

It would not be unusual to get sample data like these if the difference in satisfaction rates in the two student groups were only 20% (or less). Based on the data, there is not enough evidence to conclude that the satisfaction rate for those taking face-to-face classes is more than 20% higher than for those taking online classes.

Using the Excel Template for Making Decisions About the Difference in Population Proportions, H_0: $p_1 - p_2$ = Fixed Amount   As mentioned above, it is also possible to use the Excel template in this situation. Exhibit 12.2 opposite shows the completed template for Example 12.1B.

Note that the conditions for normality of the sampling distribution are checked in the template. Since this is a one-tailed test, the appropriate p-value is 0.143 (which differs slightly from our manual calculations above, because of rounding of the z-score).

Confidence Interval Estimate of $p_1 - p_2$

Following directly from the sampling distribution and the discussion of the hypothesis test, a confidence interval estimate can be constructed for the difference in population means, as follows:

(point estimate) $\pm$ (critical value) • (estimated standard error of the sample statistic)

$$(\hat{p}_1 - \hat{p}_2) \pm z\text{-score}\sqrt{\frac{\hat{p}_1\hat{q}_1}{n_1} + \frac{\hat{p}_2\hat{q}_2}{n_2}}$$

where the z-score corresponds to the desired level of confidence. Of course, the normality conditions must be met in order for this formula to be appropriate.

EXHIBIT 12.2

Completed Excel Template, Example 12.1B

Making Decisions About Two Population Proportions	
Sample 1 Size	400
Sample 2 Size	300
Sample 1 Proportion	0.95
Sample 2 Proportion	0.72
$n_1 \cdot p_1\text{hat}$	380
$n_1 \cdot q_1\text{hat}$	20
$n_2 \cdot p_2\text{hat}$	216
$n_2 \cdot q_2\text{hat}$	84
Are np and nq >=10?	yes
Hypothesized Difference in Population Proportions, p_1-p_2 (decimal form)	0.2
z-Score	1.066845806
One-Tailed p-Value	0.143020735
Two-Tailed p-Value	0.28604147

GUIDE TO DECISION MAKING

Comparing Two Population Proportions

When:

- qualitative data, independent samples
- trying to make a decision about $p_1 - p_2$ (the difference in population proportions), on the basis of $\hat{p}_1 - \hat{p}_2$ (the difference in the sample proportions)

Steps:

1. Specify H_0, the null hypothesis (usually H_0: $p_1 - p_2 = 0$).
2. Specify H_1, the alternative hypothesis.
3. Determine or identify α, the significance level.
4. Collect or identify the sample data. Identify or calculate:

   - the sample proportions, $\hat{p}_1$ and $\hat{p}_2$
   - the sample sizes, n_1 and n_2

5. If sampling is done without replacement, make sure each sample size is no more than 5% of the population, so that the binomial distribution is the appropriate underlying model.
6. Check for normality of the sampling distribution, which requires $n_1\hat{p}_1$, $n_1\hat{q}_1$, $n_2\hat{p}_2$, $n_2\hat{q}_2 \geq 10$, and n_1 and n_2 sufficiently large that no continuity correction is neccessary.

7. If the conditions are met, calculate the appropriate z-score, using the following formula for the case in which proportions differ by a fixed (non-zero) amount:

$$z = \frac{(\hat{p}_1 - \hat{p}_2) - \mu_{\hat{p}_1 - \hat{p}_2}}{s_{\hat{p}_1 - \hat{p}_2}} = \frac{(\hat{p}_1 - \hat{p}_2) - \mu_{\hat{p}_1 - \hat{p}_2}}{\sqrt{\dfrac{\hat{p}_1\hat{q}_1}{n_1} + \dfrac{\hat{p}_2\hat{q}_2}{n_2}}}$$

The most usual case is of the null hypothesis that $p_1 - p_2 = 0$, and so sample data are pooled to get a single estimate of p called $\hat{p}$. The z-score then becomes

$$z = \frac{(\hat{p}_1 - \hat{p}_2) - \mu_{\hat{p}_1 - \hat{p}_2}}{s_{\hat{p}_1 - \hat{p}_2}} = \frac{(\hat{p}_1 - \hat{p}_2) - 0}{\sqrt{\hat{p}\hat{q}\left(\dfrac{1}{n_1} + \dfrac{1}{n_2}\right)}}, \text{ where } \hat{p} = \frac{x_1 + x_2}{n_1 + n_2}$$

8. Use the normal distribution to calculate the appropriate p-value for the hypothesis test.
9. If p-value $\leq \alpha$, reject H_0 and conclude that there is sufficient evidence to decide in favour of H_1. If p-value $> \alpha$, fail to reject H_0 and conclude that there is insufficient evidence to decide in favour of H_1. State your conclusions in language appropriate to the problem.

See Example 12.1A on page 441 (no difference in proportions), and Example 12.1B on page 443 (non-zero difference in proportions).

Example 12.1C below illustrates the construction of a confidence interval for the difference in proportions of employees who thought that the senior manager was an effective leader last year compared with this year (these data are presented in Example 12.1A).

EXAMPLE 12.1C

Confidence interval for difference in proportions

As described in Example 12.1A, an organization has randomly sampled employees to understand their perceptions of the senior manager's competence. Last year, 228 out of 253 respondents thought that the senior manager was an effective leader. This year, 246 out of 312 respondents thought that the senior manager was an effective leader. Construct a 95% confidence interval estimate for the difference in proportions of employees who considered the senior manager an effective leader last year compared with this year.

First, check the conditions. As before, we assume that the samples are no more than 5% of the population, and note that our estimate may not be valid if this is not the case.

We have already checked the conditions for normality of the sampling distribution (see Example 12.1A, page 441).

As before, we know:

$$\hat{p}_1 = \frac{228}{253} = 0.9012 \text{ and } \hat{p}_2 = \frac{246}{312} = 0.7885$$

The formula for the confidence interval estimate is:

$$(\hat{p}_1 - \hat{p}_2) \pm z\text{-score}\sqrt{\frac{\hat{p}_1\hat{q}_1}{n_1} + \frac{\hat{p}_2\hat{q}_2}{n_2}}$$

$$= \left(\frac{228}{253} - \frac{246}{312} \right) \pm z\text{-score} \sqrt{ \frac{ \left(\frac{228}{253} \right) \left(\frac{253 - 228}{253} \right) }{253} + \frac{ \left(\frac{246}{312} \right) \left(\frac{312 - 246}{312} \right) }{312} }$$

$$= (0.11272) \pm (1.96)(0.029775)$$

$$= (0.0544, 0.1711)$$

Note that the proportions are left in fractional form for intermediate calculations—this is a good way to preserve accuracy.

As before, we designated p_1 as the proportion of employees who thought that the senior manager was an effective leader last year, and p_2 as the proportion who thought so this year. Since the interval is for $p_1 - p_2$, we can state our conclusion this way: With a confidence level of 95%, we believe that the interval $(0.0544, 0.1711)$ contains the true decrease in proportion of employees who considered the senior manager an effective leader this year compared with last year.

Using the Excel Template for the Confidence Interval Estimate for the Difference in Population Proportions A worksheet called "CI for diff in proportions" is available in the workbook called "Templates." It allows you to calculate confidence interval estimates for the difference in proportions. As always, you are required to fill in the blue-shaded cells in the template. A completed template for Example 12.1C is shown below in Exhibit 12.3.

The template result agrees with the calculations we did by hand.

EXHIBIT 12.3

Completed Excel Template, Example 12.1C

Confidence Interval Estimate for the Difference in Population Proportions	
Confidence Level (decimal form)	0.95
Sample 1 Proportion	0.90119
Sample 2 Proportion	0.78846
Sample 1 Size	253
Sample 2 Size	312
$n_1 \cdot p_1 hat$	228
$n_1 \cdot q_1 hat$	25
$n_2 \cdot p_2 hat$	246
$n_2 \cdot q_2 hat$	66
Are np and nq >=10?	yes
Upper Confidence Limit	0.17108
Lower Confidence Limit	0.05437

DEVELOP YOUR SKILLS 12.1

MyStatLab

1. Airline mergers are sometimes followed by a decrease in performance, as operations are rationalized and staff adjusts to new operating protocols. One measure of airline efficiency is the percentage of on-time departures. Before a recent merger, Northeast Airlines took a random sample of 100 flights, and found that 85 of them had departed on time. After the merger, a sample of 100 flights showed that 78 had departed on time. At the 4% level of significance, is there evidence that the proportion of on-time flights decreased after the merger? The airline handles thousands of flights every day.

2. In 2009, a study showed that the percentage of online Canadians with a social network profile had increased to 56%, up from 39% in a study done 18 months previously. In 2009, 824 online Canadians were surveyed (462 indicated they had a social network profile). In the previous study, 800 online Canadians were surveyed. Based on the survey results, can we conclude that the percentage of online Canadians with social network profiles has increased by more than 10% in the 18-month period before the study? Use a 5% level of significance.

3. A major bank implemented a number of policies and procedures to try to ensure that its female employees have as much opportunity for advancement as its male employees. The bank decided to check employees' perceptions of opportunity for advancement. A random sample of 240 female employees indicated that 82.5% felt that female employees had as much opportunity for advancement as male employees. A random sample of 350 male employees indicated that 94.3% of male employees thought that female employees had as much opportunity for advancement as male employees. Is there evidence, at a 5% significance level, that the proportion of female employees is more than 10% lower than the proportion of male employees? The total number of employees at the bank is over 65,000.

4. The marketing department is investigating methods of promoting the extended warranty for electronic equipment. In one method, customers are informed about the extended warranty by the cashier at the checkout. In another method, customers see a prominent display at the checkout. A random sample of customers who experienced each method of promotion is selected, and a 1 is recorded if the customer bought the extended warranty, and a 0 if the customer did not.

   DYS12-4

   At the 10% significance level, is there evidence of a difference in the proportions of customers who bought the extended warranty between the two promotion methods?

5. Create a 90% confidence interval estimate for the difference in the proportions of customers who bought the extended warranty for the two promotion methods described in Exercise 4 above. Do you expect this interval to include zero? Why or why not?

12.2 χ^2 GOODNESS-OF-FIT TESTS

So far, our decision making about qualitative data has been done in a binomial context. That is, we have been interested in the proportion of the data that corresponds to a desired characteristic (the success), and all other characteristics have been characterized as failure.

We will now move from a *binomial* context to a *multinomial* context, where the data can be classified into a number of different categories, all of which are of interest to us. It is possible to test to see whether sample data conform to a hypothesized distribution across a number of categories. For example, it is possible to test to see whether the candy produced at a factory has the right proportions of colours. We can also test to see whether the educational attainment of managers in an accounting firm has changed over the past five years. We do these tests by focusing on the counts of data in each category.

The technique that we use in such cases is called the Chi-square (χ^2) goodness-of-fit test ("chi" is pronounced "ky" to rhyme with "sky"). The approach is quite sensible. We calculate the number of data points we would expect to see in each category, assuming the distribution is as claimed, and then compare the expected counts with the observed counts. If there is a significant difference between the observed and expected values in the sample, then we conclude that the population distribution is not as we thought. Of course, we need a sampling distribution to help us make that decision. The test statistic is calculated as follows:

$$\chi^2 = \Sigma \frac{(o_i - e_i)^2}{e_i}$$

where o_i is the observed count in each category and e_i is the expected count in each category.

For each category, the difference between the observed and expected values is squared, and then divided by the expected value. The resulting terms are added up for all categories to get the χ^2 test statistic.

It is always a *large* value of the test statistic that leads to rejection of the null hypothesis, because of the way the statistic is calculated. The Chi-square test offers only a conclusion about whether the observed and expected frequencies match. Note that there is no such thing as a left-tailed test in this case. The only question is how closely the observed frequencies match the expected frequencies. There is only *one* test: that is, whether the distribution appears to be as desired or claimed. And it is always large values of the test statistic that lead us to conclude that the distribution is not as desired or claimed. The *p*-value in a Chi-square test is always $P(\chi^2 \geq$ calculated value).

How large is large enough? That depends on the Chi-square distribution, which is another distribution that has degrees of freedom. In the case of a multinomial distribution with k categories, the degrees of freedom are $k - 1$.

Sampling Distribution of χ^2

For a goodness-of-fit test, when expected values are ≥ 5, the sampling distribution of the χ^2 statistic is approximately Chi-square, with $k - 1$ degrees of freedom (where k is the number of categories in the data).

The Chi-square distribution has a shape that depends on the degrees of freedom, but it is generally skewed to the right. Exhibit 12.4 on the next page illustrates the Chi-square distribution for 8 and 16 degrees of freedom.

EXHIBIT **12.4**

Chi-Square Distribution

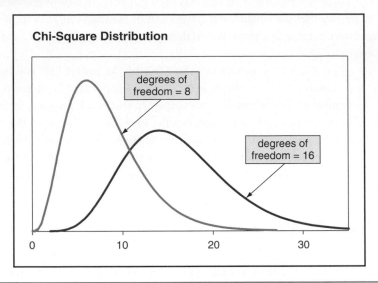

Example 12.2A below illustrates a goodness-of-fit test.

EXAMPLE **12.2A**

χ^2 goodness-of-fit test

A candy manufacturer has definite rules about the colour mixture of its candy-coated peanuts. Currently, the manufacturing process is set up to produce candies according to the distribution shown in Exhibit 12.5.

EXHIBIT **12.5**

Candy Colours Desired Proportions

Red	Green	Blue	Yellow
40%	30%	20%	10%

The company wants to be sure it is still achieving this colour balance after a recent reorganization of the production process at one of its plants. A random sample of candies is selected. The breakdown of colours is as shown in Exhibit 12.6.

EXHIBIT **12.6**

Candy Colours Count from Sample

Red	Green	Blue	Yellow
305	265	201	96

Is the company still achieving the desired colour balance at the plant after reorganizing the production process?

We begin by comparing the actual counts of the candies of each colour with the expected counts. There are 867 candies in the sample, in total. 40% of them should be red, so the expected number of red candies is 40% of 867 = 346.8. Now, of course we wouldn't expect the company to produce 0.8 of a red candy, so you might be tempted to round this number to the nearest whole number. Don't! For the purposes of this test, we will keep the numbers as calculated. Continuing on, we can calculate

- the expected number of green candies = $0.30 \cdot 867 = 260.1$
- the expected number of blue candies = $0.20 \cdot 867 = 173.4$
- the expected number of yellow candies = $0.10 \cdot 867 = 86.7$

Exhibit 12.7 below summarizes the calculations.

EXHIBIT 12.7

Candy Colours

	Red	Green	Blue	Yellow	Total
Observed sample values (o_i)	305	265	201	96	867
Expected percentage of values	40%	30%	20%	10%	
Expected values (e_i)	$- 0.40 \cdot 867 = 346.8$	260.1	173.4	86.7	867

Now, we can see by looking at the table that the observed and expected values differ. But is this normal sampling variability, or is it a significant difference? In order to decide, we have to calculate the Chi-square test statistic.

The χ^2 test statistic is based on the differences between the observed and expected values. If we merely added up these differences, they would sum to zero,[1] which would not be helpful. We will deal with the problem of the cancelling out of differences as we always have, by squaring the differences. We also standardize by dividing each squared difference by its expected value.

$$\chi^2 = \Sigma \frac{(o_i - e_i)^2}{e_i}$$

Exhibit 12.8 below illustrates the calculations for the example.

EXHIBIT 12.8

Candy Colours Chi-Square Test Statistic Calculations

	Red	Green	Blue	Yellow	Total
Observed sample values (o_i)	305	265	201	96	867
Expected values (e_i)	346.8	260.1	173.4	86.7	867
($o_i - e_i$)	−41.8	4.9	27.6	9.3	
($o_i - e_i$)^2	1,747.24	24.01	761.76	86.49	
$\dfrac{(o_i - e_i)^2}{e_i}$	5.03818	0.09231	4.39308	0.99758	10.5211457

---

[1] If you're not sure about this, try it for the candy colours in Exhibit 12.7.

There are some things you should notice about these calculations.

1. A good check that you've calculated expected values correctly is to sum them. They should sum up to the sample size (867 in the case of the example).
2. The χ^2 test statistic will always be a positive number, because we square the differences between the observed and expected values.
3. The further apart are the observed and expected values, the larger the χ^2 test statistic will be. This gives us a clue about how we will decide whether there is a significant difference between observed and expected values. If the χ^2 test statistic is *large*, we will conclude that the sample evidence suggests that the data do not fit the hypothesized distribution across categories.

Remember, it is always a *large* value of the test statistic that leads to rejection of the null hypothesis, because of the way the statistic is calculated. In the example, the number of candies is larger than expected for some colours (for example, green), and for other colours, the number of candies is smaller than expected (red). The Chi-square test offers us no guidance on whether these individual category counts are too large or too small. It only offers a conclusion about whether the numbers match, that is, whether the distribution is as claimed or desired.

In the example, there are four categories, so the degrees of freedom are $4 - 1 = 3$. The *p*-value in this case is $P(\chi^2 \geq 4.53)$, with three degrees of freedom. When we are doing a problem by hand, we will use the χ^2 table in Appendix 8 page 590 to approximate this *p*-value. The relevant row from the table is shown below in Exhibit 12.9. This table is set up in a similar fashion to the *t*-distribution tables we have used before.

EXHIBIT 12.9

χ^2 Distribution Critical Values

Degrees of Freedom	$\chi^2_{.100}$	$\chi^2_{.050}$	$\chi^2_{.025}$	$\chi^2_{.010}$	$\chi^2_{.005}$
3	6.251	7.815	9.348	11.345	12.838

10.5211

From the table, we can see that $0.010 < p\text{-value} < 0.025$. This means that the observed values in the sample are significantly different from the expected values. It would be highly unusual to get sample results like ours if the distribution of candy colours actually does match the distribution of colours desired by the manufacturer.

Let's recap all of this in standard hypothesis testing format.

- H_0: the distribution of candy colours is as desired by the manufacturer: 40% red, 30% green, 20% blue, and 10% yellow
- H_1: the distribution of candy colours is not as desired by the manufacturer (this means that at least two of the category percentages differ)
- $\alpha = 0.05$ (given)
- $\chi^2 = \sum \dfrac{(o_i - e_i)^2}{e_i} = 10.5211$, degrees of freedom $= k - 1 = 4 - 1 = 3$
- *p*-value $= P(\chi^2 \geq 10.5211) < 0.025$

Reject H_0. There is sufficient evidence to infer that the distribution of candy colours differs from the distribution desired by the manufacturer.

This result tells us that the production reorganization has not been completely successful in terms of candy colours, and some adjustments must be made. The Chi-square test itself does not give us any information about how the sampled distribution differs from the desired distribution. More analysis will be required to see what is wrong. For example, we could calculate the percentages of colour in the sample, and compare them with the desired percentages. We might even draw a bar graph to illustrate. These results are shown in Exhibit 12.10 below. The bar graph allows us to see that the problems are most pronounced with the red and blue colours.

EXHIBIT 12.10

Candy Colours

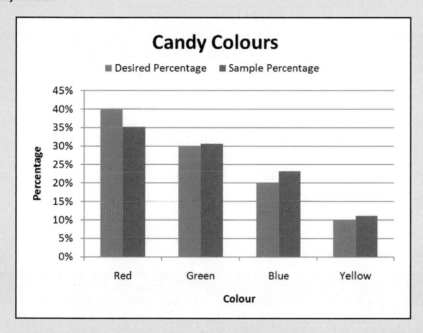

The information about the sampling distribution provided above indicated that all of the expected values must be at least 5. This leads to a question: what if they are not? Usually there is some way to combine categories so that the test is still useful, and the required condition is met. Example 12.2B below illustrates such a situation.

EXAMPLE 12.2B

Goodness-of-fit test, adjusting when $e_i < 5$

The human resources department at an international accounting firm claims that there has been a change in the managers' level of education during the last five years. The department presents a table of sample data showing the highest level of education achieved for managers, both five years ago and currently. Do the data support the human resources department's claim?

The data are shown in Exhibit 12.11 below.

EXHIBIT 12.11

Education Levels of Managers at Accounting Firm

Highest Level of Education	Percent of Managers Five Years Ago	Number of Managers Currently
High school diploma	15	19
College diploma	64	132
University degree	8	30
Master's degree	11	30
Higher than master's degree	2	5
Total	100	216

If there had been no change in the educational attainment of managers, the percentages of managers in each category would be about the same now as five years ago. We will proceed by calculating the expected number of managers in each category now, based on the category percentages five years ago, and then compare actual with expected numbers in each education category.

Five years ago, 15% of managers in the sample had a high school diploma as their highest level of education. The expected number of managers with a high school diploma in the sample today would be 15% of 216 = 32.4 (once again, although we obviously cannot have 0.4 of a manager [or could we?], we do not round). See the rest of the expected values in Exhibit 12.12 below.

EXHIBIT 12.12

Education Levels of Managers at Accounting Firm

Highest Level of Education	Percent of Managers Five Years Ago	Number of Managers Currently	Expected Number of Managers
High school diploma	15	19	32.4
College diploma	64	132	138.24
University degree	8	30	17.28
Master's degree	11	30	23.76
Higher than master's degree	2	5	4.32
Total	100	216	216

As always, we must check the conditions before proceeding any further. While all of the observed values in each category are 5 or more, notice that the expected number of managers with more than a master's degree is only 4.32, which is less than 5. Since the expected values have to be more than 5, we cannot proceed directly with our analysis.

Generally, the way to deal with this problem is to combine categories in a logical way. An obvious option for this data set is to combine the categories for the two highest levels of education, that is, the "master's degree" and "higher than master's degree" categories. The revised data table is shown opposite in Exhibit 12.13.

EXHIBIT 12.13

Education Levels of Managers at Accounting Firm

Highest Level of Education	Percent of Managers Five Years Ago	Number of Managers Currently	Expected Number of Managers
High school diploma	15	19	32.4
College diploma	64	132	138.24
University degree	8	30	17.28
Master's degree or higher	13	35	28.08
Total	100	216	216

The full hypothesis test is shown below.

- H_0: the distribution of managers by highest level of education is the same now as it was five years ago
- H_1: the distribution of managers by highest level of education is not the same now as it was five years ago
- $\alpha = 0.05$ (given)

- $$\chi^2 = \Sigma \frac{(o_i - e_i)^2}{e_i} = \frac{(19 - 32.4)^2}{32.4} + \frac{(132 - 138.24)^2}{138.24}$$
$$+ \frac{(30 - 17.28)^2}{17.28} + \frac{(35 - 28.08)^2}{28.08} = 16.89233$$

The revised table has four categories, so the distribution has three degrees of freedom. The relevant row from the χ^2 table in Appendix 8 on page 590 is shown in Exhibit 12.14.

EXHIBIT 12.14

χ^2 Distribution Critical Values

Degrees of Freedom	$\chi^2_{.100}$	$\chi^2_{.050}$	$\chi^2_{.025}$	$\chi^2_{.010}$	$\chi^2_{.005}$
3	6.251	7.815	9.348	11.345	12.838

16.892

We see that p-value = $P(\chi^2 \geq 16.892) < 0.005$.

Reject H_0. There is sufficient evidence to infer that the distribution of managers by education level is not the same now as it was five years ago.

Once again, a bar graph might be helpful in illustrating the differences, as Exhibit 12.15 shows. We can see from the graph that there appear to be differences in all of the categories.

EXHIBIT 12.15

Managers' Highest Levels of Education, Accounting Firm

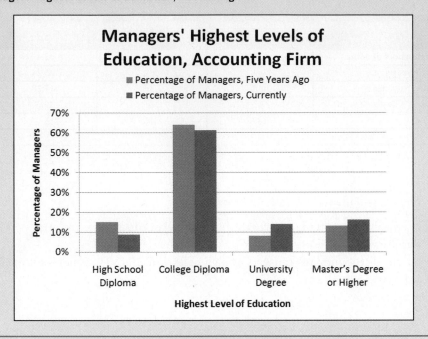

Using Excel's CHITEST Function for a χ^2 Goodness-of-Fit Test The calculations to get the expected values for a goodness-of-fit test are quite straightforward and can be done with basic Excel formulas. However, calculation of the χ^2 statistic can be quite time consuming, and it is helpful to use a computer. Once you have the expected values in a goodness-of-fit test, you can use the Excel function called **CHITEST** to get the p-value.

The dialogue box for the **CHITEST** function is shown below in Exhibit 12.16.

EXHIBIT 12.16

CHITEST Dialogue Box

Function Arguments

CHITEST

| Actual_range | | = array |
| Expected_range | | = array |

=

Returns the test for independence: the value from the chi-squared distribution for the statistic and the appropriate degrees of freedom.

Actual_range   is the range of data that contains observations to test against expected values.

Formula result =

Help on this function

OK   Cancel

The **Function Arguments** in Excel are as follows.

- **Actual_range** is the cells where the observed values are recorded.
- **Expected_range** is the cells where the expected values are recorded.

The result that is returned from the **CHITEST** function is the p-value of the χ^2 statistic. As usual, you should enter some text into an adjoining cell so that the output is labelled. Excel calculates the p-value for Example 12.2B as 0.00074, which is consistent with our estimation of the p-value from the table as being < 0.005.

GUIDE TO DECISION MAKING

χ^2 Goodness-of-Fit Test to Compare Proportions in One Population with a Desired Distribution

When:

- qualitative data, single population, with two or more categories
- trying to make a decision about the distribution across categories in the population, based on the sample distribution

Steps:

1. Specify H_0, the null hypothesis (which is that the population is distributed as claimed/desired).
2. Specify H_1, the alternative hypothesis (which is that the population is *not* as claimed/desired).
3. Determine or identify α, the significance level.
4. Collect or identify the sample data. Identify or calculate:

   - o_i, the observed frequency in each category (based on sample data)
   - e_i, the expected frequency in each category (based on the claimed/desired distribution)

5. Check that each $e_i \geq 5$, to ensure that the sampling distribution is approximately Chi-squared. If any $e_i < 5$, combine categories to meet this condition.
6. If the conditions are met, calculate the appropriate test statistic, using the following formula:

$$\chi^2 = \sum \frac{(o_i - e_i)^2}{e_i}$$

7. Use the Chi-square distribution with $k - 1$ degrees of freedom to calculate (or approximate, if using tables) the appropriate p-value for the hypothesis test, which will be $P(\chi^2 \geq$ calculated value), where k is the number of categories.
8. If p-value $\leq \alpha$, reject H_0 and conclude that there is sufficient evidence to decide in favour of H_1. If p-value $> \alpha$, fail to reject H_0 and conclude that there is insufficient evidence to decide in favour of H_1. State your conclusions in language appropriate to the problem.

See Example 12.2A on page 450, and Example 12.2B on page 453 (adjusting when $e_i < 5$).

DEVELOP YOUR SKILLS 12.2

MyStatLab

6. A furniture store has a number of payment options available to customers. Some customers pay immediately. Others delay payment for six months, with no interest and no financing charges. Others delay payment for a year, but with interest and financing charges. In the past, 26% of customers paid immediately, 37% delayed payment for six months, and 37% delayed payment for a year. The store manager is wondering whether current customers have changed their payment selections from the past. The manager takes a random survey of 75 store customers, and asks them to indicate which payment plan they would prefer. Of the 75, 23 would pay immediately, 32 would delay payment for six months, and the rest would delay payment for a year. At the 5% significance level, is there evidence of a change in customers' preferences for the different payment plans?

7. A new manager has been hired to run the campus student pub. The pub sells a limited selection of brands of beer. The past manager indicated that the brand preferences of the pub's customers were as shown in Exhibit 12.17 below.

EXHIBIT 12.17

Brand Preferences of Customers at Campus Pub

Labatt Blue	Labatt Blue Light	Molson Canadian	Kokanee	Rickard's Honey Brown
33%	8%	25%	19%	15%

The new manager wants to check on customer preferences so that he can order the correct quantities of each brand of beer. In a random sample of 85 customers, 29 preferred Labatt Blue, 6 preferred Labatt Blue Light, 21 preferred Molson Canadian, 16 preferred Kokanee, and the remainder preferred Rickard's Honey Brown. Is there evidence, at the 5% level of significance, that customers' brand preferences are different from what the previous manager thought?

8. John is a small businessman who gets in over his head, incurring debts he cannot pay. In desperation, he turns to the local motorcycle gang to borrow some money to keep his business afloat. He hopes to solve his money problems at the local casino. At first he does well, winning regularly, and then he makes a huge bet and loses it all. He is left alone, despondent, drinking bad Scotch and staring at one of the dice that let him down. He decides to check whether the die is fair. He rolls it repeatedly, recording how many times each side comes up. The results are shown in Exhibit 12.18 below. Is the die fair? (Will Mary ever forgive him?) Use $\alpha = 0.025$.

EXHIBIT 12.18

Observations from Repeated Tosses of a Die

1 Spot	2 Spot	3 Spot	4 Spot	5 Spot	6 Spot
18	24	17	25	16	25

9. A travel agency collects data on the proportion of its customers who want to travel to popular destinations. Historically, the customer preferences have been as indicated in Exhibit 12.19.

EXHIBIT 12.19

Customer Preferences at a Travel Agency

Canada	U.S.	Caribbean	Europe	Asia	Australia/ New Zealand	Other
28%	32%	22%	12%	2%	3%	1%

A random sample of 54 customers revealed that:
- 22 wanted to travel in Canada
- 14 wanted to travel to the U.S.
- 8 wanted to travel to the Caribbean
- 8 wanted to travel to Europe
- 2 wanted to travel to Australia/New Zealand
- no one wanted to travel to another destination

At the 4% level of significance, is there evidence of a change in the customer preferences at this travel agency?

10. A financial services company conducted a survey of a random sample of its customers. One of the items on the survey was, "The staff at my local branch can provide me with good advice on my financial affairs."

Customers responded as follows: 10 strongly agreed, 57 agreed, 32 neither agreed nor disagreed, 15 disagreed, and 9 strongly disagreed. The company has national benchmarks of 20% for "strongly agree," 50% for "agree," 15% for "neither agree nor disagree," 10% for "disagree," and 5% for "strongly disagree," Is there evidence, at the 2.5% level of significance, that the distribution of responses to the survey at the local branch differs from the national benchmarks?

12.3 COMPARING MANY POPULATION PROPORTIONS OR TESTING INDEPENDENCE—χ^2 TEST OF A CONTINGENCY TABLE

We first encountered contingency tables in Chapter 4. Such tables are a good means of summarizing qualitative characteristics for a number of different populations or subpopulations. For example, in Chapter 4 we used a contingency table to describe GeorgeConn's customers, according to whether they were urban or rural, and satisfied or not satisfied with GeorgeConn's service.

Comparing Many Population Proportions

Suppose a survey of customers from stores A, B, C, and D recorded the method of payment by customers. The sample results are shown in Exhibit 12.20 below.

EXHIBIT 12.20

Customer Payment Method

	Store A	Store B	Store C	Store D	Total
Cash/debit card	40	65	20	25	150
Credit card	30	80	30	40	180
Cheque	30	55	50	35	170
Total	100	200	100	100	500

With this data set, we could do a number of different analyses. We have sampled from four populations (the types of customer payments at the four locations). We could, for example, compare the proportions of cash/debit card sales at the four locations. Notice that this is an extension of the comparison of two proportions (discussed in Section 12.1) to comparison of four proportions in four populations. However, the Chi-square analysis allows us to go beyond this. It is possible to do a comparison of the proportions of all three payment types at the four locations (that is, in all four populations simultaneously). As before, the Chi-square test focuses on counts. Example 12.3A illustrates.

EXAMPLE 12.3A

Contingency table test, comparing many populations

Are the proportions of payment types the same for Stores A, B, C, and D? In other words, are the distributions of payment types the same for all four stores?

The approach is still based on comparing observed and expected values. Expected values are calculated based on the null hypothesis that the proportion of payments of each type is the same for all four locations. As we did for tests of whether two proportions are equal, we will pool the sample data to get the expected proportion of each type of payment. The original table including all of the data categories is repeated in Exhibit 12.21, for ease of reference.

EXHIBIT 12.21

Customer Payment Method

	Store A	Store B	Store C	Store D	Total
Cash/debit card	40	65	20	25	150
Credit card	30	80	30	40	180
Cheque	30	55	50	35	170
Total	100	200	100	100	500

For example, we see from the table that out of the 500 payments included in all four samples, 150 were cash (or debit card payments, which transfer the money immediately to the store's bank account, so we'll refer to cash and debit card payments jointly as simply *cash*). This includes 40 cash payments from store A, 65 from store B, 20 from store C, and 25 from store D. Therefore:

$$\bullet \ \hat{p}_{cash} = \frac{150}{500} = 0.3$$

$$\bullet \ \hat{p}_{credit \ card} = \frac{180}{500} = 0.36$$

$$\bullet \ \hat{p}_{cheque} = \frac{170}{500} = 0.34$$

To calculate expected values, we simply apply these proportions to each of the four samples. This is quite easy to do in this example, because three of the sample sizes are 100. If the expected proportion of cash payments is 0.3, then the expected number of cash payments for store A $= \hat{p}_{cash} \cdot n_A = 0.3 \cdot 100 = 30$. Similarly, the expected number of cash payments for store B $= \hat{p}_{cash} \cdot n_B = 0.3 \cdot 200 = 60$. Exhibit 12.22 opposite shows the calculations of expected values. As you go through the calculations, you will see that they rely on row and column totals in the table. In fact, you can summarize the calculation of the expected value as follows:

$$\text{expected value} = \frac{(\text{row total})(\text{column total})}{(\text{grand total})}$$

EXHIBIT 12.22

Customer Payment Method

	Store A	Store B	Store C	Store D	Total
Cash (observed)	40	65	20	25	150
Cash (expected)	$0.3 \cdot 100 = 30$	$0.3 \cdot 200 = 60$	$0.3 \cdot 100 = 30$	$0.3 \cdot 100 = 30$	$\hat{p}_{cash} = \dfrac{150}{500} = 0.3$
Credit card (observed)	30	80	30	40	180
Credit card (expected)	$0.36 \cdot 100 = 36$	$0.36 \cdot 200 = 72$	$0.36 \cdot 100 = 36$	$0.36 \cdot 100 = 36$	$\hat{p}_{credit\ card} = \dfrac{180}{500} = 0.36$
Cheque (observed)	30	55	50	35	170
Cheque (expected)	34	68	34	34	$\hat{p}_{cheque} = \dfrac{170}{500} = 0.34$
Total	100	200	100	100	500

Calculation of the χ^2 statistic is the same as before:

$$\chi^2 = \Sigma \frac{(o_i - e_i)^2}{e_i}$$

If you are doing this by hand, the calculation will be as follows:

$$\chi^2 = \Sigma \frac{(o_i - e_i)^2}{e_i}$$

$$= \frac{(40 - 30)^2}{30} + \frac{(30 - 36)^2}{36} + \frac{(30 - 34)^2}{34}$$

$$+ \frac{(65 - 60)^2}{60} + \frac{(80 - 72)^2}{72} + \frac{(55 - 68)^2}{68}$$

$$+ \frac{(20 - 30)^2}{30} + \frac{(30 - 36)^2}{36} + \frac{(50 - 34)^2}{34}$$

$$+ \frac{(25 - 30)^2}{30} + \frac{(40 - 36)^2}{36} + \frac{(35 - 34)^2}{34}$$

$$= 21.7647$$

The degrees of freedom for the Chi-square distribution for a contingency table are equal to $(r - 1)(c - 1)$, where r is the number of rows in the table, and c is the number of columns (not including the totals). In this case, there are three rows and four columns, so the degrees of freedom are $(3 - 1)(4 - 1) = 2(3) = 6$. Exhibit 12.23 below shows the appropriate row from the Chi-square table in Appendix 8.

EXHIBIT 12.23

χ^2 Distribution Critical Values

Degrees of Freedom	$\chi^2_{.100}$	$\chi^2_{.050}$	$\chi^2_{.025}$	$\chi^2_{.010}$	$\chi^2_{.005}$
6	10.645	12.592	14.449	16.812	18.548

21.7647

From the table, we can see that the p-value < 0.005. It would be highly unlikely that we would obtain a sample result such as this one if the proportions of payment types were the same at all four store locations. Therefore we will conclude that the proportions of payment types are *not* the same at all four store locations.

To summarize, let's recap all of this in standard hypothesis testing format.

- H_0: the proportions of payment types are the same at all four store locations
- H_1: the proportions of payment types are not equal at all four store locations
- $\chi^2 = \sum \dfrac{(o_i - e_i)^2}{e_i} = 21.7647$, degrees of freedom $= 6$
- all $e_i \geq 5$
- p-value $= P(\chi^2 \geq 21.7647) < 0.005$

Reject H_0. There is sufficient evidence to infer that the proportions of payment types differ at the four store locations.

Using Excel Add-in for Chi-Square Expected Values Calculations
Doing the calculations for the χ^2 statistic for a contingency table can be quite time-consuming, and it is helpful to use a computer. Unfortunately, there is no **Data Analysis** tool in Excel to allow you to calculate expected values easily. One of the Excel add-ins in **Non-Parametric Tools** allows you to quickly and easily calculate expected values and the Chi-square statistic. Once the add-ins are installed, click on the **Add-Ins** tab, click on **Non-Parametric Tools**, and then choose **Chi-Squared Expected Values Calculations**.

The dialogue box for the **Chi-Squared Expected Values Calculations** is shown below in Exhibit 12.24.

EXHIBIT 12.24

Chi-Squared Expected Values Calculations Dialogue Box

Chi-Squared Expected Values Calculations

Range: [   ]   Help
                          Cancel
"The selection must be numbers and one row and one
column of labels—no formulas and no totals."   OK

Output Options   Use:
  ○ Output Range [   ]   Chi-Squared Expected
                            Values Calculations, for
  ● New Worksheet   a two by two (or more)
                            data table.

You must indicate the range where the observed values are located. Note that you should include one row and one column of titles in your selection. You should *not* include totals in your selection. As well, the add-in will not work if any of the cells contain formulas. If they do, you should copy your table of observed values and **Paste Values**. Then use the add-in with this copy of the table.

The output produced by the add-in for the data in Example 12.3A are shown below in Exhibit 12.25.

EXHIBIT 12.25

Chi-Squared Expected Values for Example 12.3A

Chi-Squared Expected Values Calculations

Chi-squared test statistic	21.76471
# of expected values <5	0
p-value	0.001336

	Store A	Store B	Store C	Store D
Cash	30	60	30	30
Credit Card	36	72	36	36
Cheque	34	68	34	34

The output produces a table of expected values. It also provides the Chi-square test statistic, and the associated *p*-value. The output also indicates the number of expected values less than 5. Any expected values less than 5 will be highlighted in yellow in the output. Of course, you should not rely on the test statistic or *p*-value if there are any expected values less than 5. You should combine categories as necessary, and re-do the calculations.

Testing for Independence

For the examination of payment types above, samples were selected from four populations of payment types, one for each store. The χ^2 test allowed us to draw a conclusion about the distribution of payment types across all four populations simultaneously.

The same test can be used to test for independence of characteristics in a single population. Suppose the data shown in Exhibit 12.20 were the result of sampling 500 payments from the single population of payment types, keeping track of payment type by store. The information could then be cross-classified and put into the contingency table.[2] The data are repeated on the next page in Exhibit 12.26 for ease of reference.

In this case, we are in a position to test whether there is a relationship between payment type and store. If there is, the proportions of payment types will vary from

---

[2] It is unlikely that the resulting column totals would be such nice round numbers, but this slight departure from reality does not affect the discussion.

EXHIBIT 12.26

Customer Payment Method

Customer Payment Method					
	Store A	Store B	Store C	Store D	Total
Cash/debit card	40	65	20	25	**150**
Credit card	30	80	30	40	**180**
Cheque	30	55	50	35	**170**
Total	**100**	**200**	100	100	500

store to store. Another way to ask the question: is payment type independent of store location?

Tests for independence were discussed in Chapter 4. You may remember that we examined independence in samples, with contingency tables (see page 162), but you were also warned that you would need the statistical tools presented in this chapter to draw conclusions for an entire population. Nevertheless, there is a correspondence between the calculations you did in Chapter 4 and the expected value calculations we do for the Chi-square analysis.

We learned in Chapter 4 that when events A and B are independent

$$P(A \text{ and } B) = P(A) \cdot P(B)$$

Let's apply this to the example above. If, for example, "store A" and "credit card" were independent events, then P(store A and credit card) should equal P(store A) · P(credit card). From the table, we can see that:

- $P(\text{store A}) = \dfrac{100}{500} = 0.2$

- $P(\text{credit card}) = \dfrac{180}{500} = 0.36$

If the events are independent, then

$P(\text{store A and credit card})$

$= P(\text{store A}) \cdot P(\text{credit card})$

$= 0.2(0.36)$

$= 0.072$

If "store A" and "credit card" are independent, we would expect that $0.072 \cdot 500 = 36$ of the payments at store A would have been made by credit card. Notice that this exactly matches the expected value we calculated for the Chi-square analysis in Example 12.3A. All of the *expected* values are the values we would get if the factors listed in the table were independent.

The calculations for the Chi-square test for independence are the same as the test for comparing many population proportions. Example 12.3B illustrates.

EXAMPLE 12.3B

Contingency table test for independence

A manufacturing plant runs three eight-hour shifts every day. A quality control inspector is interested to see whether the number of product defects varies with the shift. A random sample of 1,160 items is collected, and the defects and the shift during which the items were produced are recorded. The results are summarized in Exhibit 12.27 below.

EXHIBIT 12.27

Quality Control, Observed Values

Shift	Items with No Apparent Defects	Items with One Minor Defect	Items with More than One Minor Defect
8:00 A.M. –4:00 P.M.	342	34	15
4:00 P.M. –midnight	336	26	7
midnight–8:00 A.M.	344	40	16

Expected values are calculated as before. The output for the **Chi-Squared Expected Values Calculations** add-in is shown below in Exhibit 12.28.

EXHIBIT 12.28

Chi-Squared Expected Values for Example 12.3B

Chi-Squared Expected Values Calculations			
Chi-squared test statistic	5.68750207		
# of expected values <5	0		
p-value	0.223732908		

Shift	Items With No Apparent Defect	Items With One Minor Defect	Items With More Than One Minor Defect
8 AM to 4 PM	344.4844828	33.70689655	12.80862069
4 PM to Midnight	325.1017241	31.81034483	12.08793103
Midnight to 8 AM	352.4137931	34.48275862	13.10344828

All of the expected values are ≥ 5, so the necessary conditions are met.

- H_0: the number of product defects is independent of the shift
- H_1: the number of product defects is related to the shift
- $\chi^2 = \sum \frac{(o_i - e_i)^2}{e_i} = 5.68750207$, degrees of freedom = $(r - 1)(c - 1)$

$$= (3 - 1)(3 - 1) = 4$$

- p-value = $P(\chi^2 \geq 5.68750207) = 0.223732908$, according to the output in Exhibit 12.28.

Fail to reject H_0. There is insufficient evidence to infer that the number of defects is related to the shift.

Notice that even if we had rejected the null hypothesis, the conclusion of this hypothesis test would *not* be "the number of defects depends on the shift." While there might be a relationship, these data do not tell us anything about *why* the relationship occurs. For example, suppose the true cause of the difference in defect rates is the behaviour of the supervisors on each shift. It would not be correct to say that the number of

GUIDE TO DECISION MAKING

Contingency Table Tests to Compare Proportions Across Many Populations, or Decide About the Independence of Population Characteristics

When:

- qualitative data, many populations, with two or more categories or one population with cross-classifications
- trying to make a decision about whether populations differ across categories, or trying to decide if category characteristics are independent

Steps:

1. Specify H_0, the null hypothesis (which is that the populations have the same distributions, or that category characteristics are independent).
2. Specify H_1, the alternative hypothesis (which is that the populations do not have the same distributions, or that category characteristics are related).
3. Determine or identify α, the significance level.
4. Collect or identify the sample data. Identify or calculate:

   - o_i, the observed frequency in each category (based on sample data)
   - e_i, the expected frequency in each category (based on pooling the sample data across all characteristics)

   Generally, for a contingency table:

   $$\text{expected value} = \frac{(\text{row total})(\text{column total})}{(\text{grand total})}$$

5. Check that each $e_i \geq 5$, to ensure that the sampling distribution is approximately chi-squared. If any $e_i < 5$, combine categories to meet this condition.
6. If the conditions are met, calculate the appropriate test statistic using the following formula:

   $$\chi^2 = \sum \frac{(o_i - e_i)^2}{e_i}$$

7. Use the Chi-square distribution with $(r - 1)(c - 1)$ degrees of freedom to calculate (or approximate, if using tables) the appropriate p-value for the hypothesis test, which will be $P(\chi^2 \geq \text{calculated value})$.
8. If p-value $\leq \alpha$, reject H_0 and conclude that there is sufficient evidence to decide in favour of H_1. If p-value $> \alpha$, fail to reject H_0 and conclude that there is insufficient evidence to decide in favour of H_1. State your conclusions in language appropriate to the problem.

See Example 12.3A on page 460 (comparing many populations), and Example 12.3B on page 465 (test for independence).

defects depends on the shift. Instead, the number of defects depends on the supervisor. As always, you should be careful about drawing causality conclusions.

Correspondence Between z-Test and χ^2 Test   A two-tailed z-test of $p_1 - p_2$ with a null hypothesis that $p_1 - p_2 = 0$ and the χ^2 test of a contingency table are equivalent when we are dealing with two categories in two populations. In fact, the χ^2 statistic is equal to z^2. We can demonstrate this by returning to the example of fitness club memberships discussed at the beginning of the chapter, in Section 12.1.

The survey results showed that of the 153 female survey respondents, 62 had fitness club memberships. Of the 52 male survey respondents, 28 had fitness club memberships. The question asked was, Do the survey results suggest that males and females in Moncton have differing tendencies to have fitness club memberships? We went on to test if the proportions of those belonging to fitness clubs were equal for males and females. Another way to put this would be, is there a relationship between gender and the tendency to have a fitness club membership? If the proportions of those belonging to fitness clubs are equal for both genders, there is no relationship. If the proportions are different, there is a relationship.

We can summarize the sample data in a contingency table, as shown below in Exhibit 12.29, and then test for evidence of a relationship with a χ^2 test.

EXHIBIT 12.29

Fitness Memberships Among Moncton Adults

	Yes	No	Totals
Male	28	24	52
Female	62	91	153
Totals	90	115	205

An excerpt of the output for the Excel add-in for **Chi-Squared Expected Values Calculations** is shown below in Exhibit 12.30.

EXHIBIT 12.30

Chi-Square Test Results

Chi-Squared Expected Values Calculations	
Chi-squared test statistic	2.797245
# of expected values <5	0
p-value	0.094426

The completed template for Making Decisions About Two Population Proportions, Qualitative Data, for this data set is also shown in Exhibit 12.31 on the next page.

Notice that the p-value for the two-tailed test of $p_1 - p_2$ is exactly the same as the p-value for the χ^2 test. Notice also that $z^2 = 1.6724966^2 = 2.797245 = \chi^2$.

Of course, if you want to do a one-tailed test of $p_1 - p_2$, you will have to use the z-score approach. Remember, the χ^2 test tells us only whether there is a relationship. It tells us nothing about the character of the relationship.

EXHIBIT 12.31

Completed Excel Template

Making Decisions About Two Population Proportions	
Sample 1 Size	52
Sample 2 Size	153
Sample 1 Proportion	0.538461538
Sample 2 Proportion	0.405228758
$n_1 \cdot p_1hat$	28
$n_1 \cdot q_1hat$	24
$n_2 \cdot p_2hat$	62
$n_2 \cdot q_2hat$	91
Are np and nq >=10?	yes
Hypothesized Difference in Population Proportions, p_1-p_2 (decimal form)	0
z-Score	1.672496562
One-Tailed p-Value	0.047213223
Two-Tailed p-Value	0.094426445

DEVELOP YOUR SKILLS 12.3

11. A random sample of the employees of a large organization were surveyed about their views of a proposed change in the company's health benefits. The results of the survey are shown in Exhibit 12.32. Is there evidence, at the 1% level of significance, that there is a relationship between the views on the proposed health benefits changes and the type of job held in the organization?

EXHIBIT 12.32

Views on Proposed Changes to Health Benefits

	In Favour	Opposed	Undecided
Management	10	18	13
Professional, salaried	56	43	15
Clerical, hourly paid	49	32	8

12. A company that sells sunscreen products wants to know whether there is a relationship between people's hair colour and their tendency to apply sunscreen before going outside. For example, it may be that redheads and blondes are more sensitive to the sun, and are therefore more likely to use sunscreen. A random sample of adults was selected, and their hair colour and tendency to use sunscreen was recorded, with the results shown in Exhibit 12.33.

EXHIBIT 12.33

Do you use sunscreen when going outside?

Hair Colour	Always	Usually	Once in a While	Never
Red	26	20	10	10
Blonde	37	24	9	18
Brown	35	34	8	7
Black	23	46	20	21

At the 5% level of significance, is there evidence of a relationship between hair colour and tendency to use sunscreen?

13. A newspaper was trying to determine whether there was a relationship between household income and the

EXHIBIT 12.34

Which section of the newspaper do you read most closely?

Household Income	National and World News	Business	Sports	Arts	Lifestyle
Under $40,000	55	26	72	10	13
$40,000 to $70,000	56	45	43	20	25
Over $70,000	32	48	21	26	22

sections of the newspaper that were most closely read. A random survey of households revealed the results shown in Exhibit 12.34.

At the 2.5% level of significance, is there evidence that income is related to the section of the newspaper read most closely?

14. A random sample of 100 students was taken from four large schools in Montreal. The first language of the students was recorded. The results are shown in Exhibit 12.35 below. Is there evidence, at the 5% significance level, of a difference in the proportions of students whose first language is English, French, or something else in these four schools?

EXHIBIT 12.35

Survey of Montreal Schools

First Language	School #1	School #2	School #3	School #4
English	44	40	50	43
French	42	50	45	40
Other	14	10	5	17

15. The marketing department of a college wanted to know whether there was a difference in the proportions of students drawn from inside and outside the college catchment area by program. A random sample of students from each of the Business, Technology, and Nursing programs revealed the results shown in Exhibit 12.36. Is there evidence, at the 2.5% level of significance, that the proportions of students drawn from inside and outside the local area are the same for all three programs?

EXHIBIT 12.36

Origin of Students in College Programs

	Business	Technology	Nursing
From local area	65	45	68
Not from local area	85	55	72

Chapter Summary

The techniques in this chapter apply when you have two or more samples of qualitative data. In some cases, the focus is on proportions; in other cases, the focus is on counts.

Comparing Two Proportions

The hypothesis test for comparing two proportions often assumes equal proportions (that is, $H_0: p_1 - p_2 = 0$). In such a case, the sample data are pooled to get an estimate of the population proportion $\hat{p} = \dfrac{x_1 + x_2}{n_1 + n_2}$. The sample size must be large enough that no continuity correction is required, and the sampling distribution is approximately normal ($n_1\hat{p}_1, n_1\hat{q}_1, n_2\hat{p}_2, n_2\hat{q}_2 \geq 10$, and n_1 and n_2 are fairly large). As well, if sampling is done without replacement, the samples should be no more than 5% of the population.

If the conditions are met, the hypothesis test can be conducted with a z-score as follows:

$$z = \frac{(\hat{p}_1 - \hat{p}_2) - \mu_{\hat{p}_1 - \hat{p}_2}}{s_{\hat{p}_1 - \hat{p}_2}} = \frac{(\hat{p}_1 - \hat{p}_2) - 0}{\sqrt{\hat{p}\hat{q}\left(\dfrac{1}{n_1} + \dfrac{1}{n_2}\right)}}$$

Excel's **Data Analysis Histogram** tool can be used to organize coded data to get frequencies (as Example 12.1A on page 441 illustrates). There is an Excel template for making decisions about two population proportions (see page 442).

It is also possible to make a decision about whether two population proportions differ by some fixed non-zero amount, as Example 12.1B on page 443 illustrates. In this case, the z-score calculation is:

$$z = \frac{(\hat{p}_1 - \hat{p}_2) - \mu_{\hat{p}_1 - \hat{p}_2}}{s_{\hat{p}_1 - \hat{p}_2}} = \frac{(\hat{p}_1 - \hat{p}_2) - \mu_{\hat{p}_1 - \hat{p}_2}}{\sqrt{\dfrac{\hat{p}_1\hat{q}_1}{n_1} + \dfrac{\hat{p}_2\hat{q}_2}{n_2}}}$$

The Guide to Decision Making for comparing two proportions is on page 445.

A confidence interval estimate for $p_1 - p_2$ can be constructed using the following formula:

$$(\hat{p}_1 - \hat{p}_2) \pm z\text{-score}\sqrt{\frac{\hat{p}_1\hat{q}_1}{n_1} + \frac{\hat{p}_2\hat{q}_2}{n_2}}$$

where the z-score corresponds to the desired level of confidence. Again, this formula is valid only if the normality conditions are met.

An Excel template is available for confidence interval estimates for the difference in two proportions (see page 447).

χ^2 Goodness-of-Fit Tests

It is possible to test whether sample data conform to a hypothesized distribution across a number of categories. The technique is the Chi-square goodness-of-fit test, which is based on comparison of observed sample frequencies to expected frequencies. The test statistic is

$$\chi^2 = \Sigma \frac{(o_i - e_i)^2}{e_i}$$

The null hypothesis is always that the population is as claimed/desired, and the alternative hypothesis is always that the population is not as claimed or desired. The p-value is always calculated as $P(\chi^2 \geq$ the calculated sample test statistic), where the related Chi-square distribution has $k - 1$ degrees of freedom (k is the number of categories in the data). A requirement for using the Chi-square sampling distribution is that all expected frequencies should be at least 5. If they are not, you must combine categories in some logical way before proceeding. Example 12.2B on page 453 illustrates.

Calculation of expected values for a goodness-of-fit test is fairly straightforward in Excel, using formulas. The **CHITEST** function of Excel reports the p-value of the hypothesis test based on observed and expected frequencies. The use of the **CHITEST** function is described on page 456.

The Guide to Decision Making for a goodness-of-fit test is on page 457.

Comparing Many Population Proportions and Test of Independence— χ^2 Test of a Contingency Table

The Chi-square distribution can be used to compare multiple populations across multiple categories (see Example 12.3A on page 460). It can also be used to test the independence of the categories or characteristics of the sample data (see Example 12.3B on page 465).

The test statistic is

$$\chi^2 = \Sigma \frac{(o_i - e_i)^2}{e_i}$$

where expected values are calculated as follows:

$$\text{expected value} = \frac{(\text{row total})(\text{column total})}{(\text{grand total})}$$

As with the goodness-of-fit test, the χ^2 test statistic should be used only if all expected frequencies are at least 5. If they are not, categories should be combined. The degrees of freedom for the Chi-square distribution are $(r - 1)(c - 1)$, where r is the number of rows in the contingency table, and c is the number of columns (not including totals).

An Excel add-in (see page 462) is available to do calculations of expected value, the χ^2 statistic, and the p-value.

The Guide to Decision Making for contingency table tests is on page 466.

Go to MyStatLab at www.mathxl.com. You can practise the exercises indicated with red in the Develop Your Skills and Chapter Review Exercises as often as you want, and guided solutions will help you find answers step by step. You'll find a personalized study plan available to you too!

CHAPTER REVIEW EXERCISES

WARM-UP EXERCISES

1. Why would it be incorrect to pool the sample data to get an estimate of $\hat{p}$ when the null hypothesis is $p_1 - p_2 = 0.05$?

2. Why don't we pool sample data when we are constructing a confidence interval estimate of $p_1 - p_2$?

3. A student who is taking Statistics for the second time (for the fun of it!) wants to compare the proportion of students who pass the course at his college using *Analyzing Data and Making Decisions* as their text, compared to last year, when a competitor text was used. The student believes the proportion of those who pass will be more than 10% higher than last year. What is the appropriate alternative hypothesis? (Use subscript "1" for last year, and "2" for this year.)

4. Why is there no such thing as a left-tailed χ^2 goodness-of-fit test?

5. Suppose you wanted to compare the proportions of customers from three different stores who bought the extended warranty plan when they bought new computers. Your friend tells you that you should do three hypothesis tests to compare proportions, that is, $p_1 - p_2 = 0$, $p_1 - p_3 = 0$, and $p_2 - p_3 = 0$. Is your friend correct? What would you do?

THINK AND DECIDE

6. A random sample of new members of a large downtown fitness club was selected, and tracked over six months. Of the 60 members who joined the club to participate in fitness classes, 38 were still working out regularly six months after joining. Of the 80 members who joined to work out with a personal trainer, 60 were still working out regularly six months after joining. At the 2.5% level of significance, is there evidence of a difference in the proportion of new members still working out regularly six months after joining the club when comparing those who attend fitness classes and those who work out with a personal trainer?

7. Re-do Exercise 6 above as a Chi-square test. Did you get the same answer? Did you expect to?

8. A large mail order company is trying to decide between two delivery services: Canada Post and a private courier. The mail order company selects a random sample of 100 deliveries for the private courier, and another sample of 75 for Canada Post. The proportion of deliveries that were on time or early when sent by the private courier was 0.89. The proportion of deliveries that were on time or early when sent by Canada Post was 0.80. The mail order company has decided it will pay the higher cost of the private courier, if its on-time or early percentage is more than 5% higher than Canada Post's. Should the mail order company hire the private courier? Use $\alpha = 2.5\%$.

9. Colleges work hard to convert offers of admission into acceptances. One college has been experimenting with phone calls from program faculty to prospective students to encourage students to accept offers of admission. In a random sample of 278 students who were called by program faculty, 234 sent acceptances. In a random sample of 302 students who were not called but received a package in the mail, 232 sent acceptances. Is there evidence that the proportion of prospective students who send acceptances is higher when they get calls from program faculty? Use $\alpha = 2.5\%$.

10. Construct a 95% confidence interval estimate for the difference in proportions of students who send acceptances after receiving offers of admission, comparing those who receive

phone calls from program faculty to those who receive only packages in the mail. (See Exercise 9 above.)

11. The human resources (HR) department is concerned that managers are resistant to the conflict resolution training mandated by the company. A random sample of 50 managers who have taken the training is selected. Of these, 36 declare the training to have been a total waste of time. A random sample of 76 non-managerial employees who have taken the training is also selected. Of these, 38 say the training was a total waste of time. Is there evidence of a difference in the proportions of managers and non-managers who think the conflict resolution training was a waste of time? Use $\alpha = 2.5\%$.

12. Consider the conflict resolution training described in Exercise 11 above. If you were the manager of the HR department, would you continue the training? Why or why not? (Your answer must be supported by the data.)

13. A quality control inspector wants to test that the proportion of defective items in three shipments of components from different manufacturers is equal. A random sample of 125 items is selected from each shipment. The first sample has 36 defective items, the second has 30, and the third has 38. Test to see whether there is evidence of a difference in proportions of defective items, with $\alpha = 0.05$.

14. A company operates two large plants. In one plant, a random sample of 150 employees revealed that 23 had had workplace accidents during the past year. In the other plant, a random sample of 125 employees revealed that 23 had had workplace accidents during the past year. At the 5% level of significance, is there evidence of a difference in the proportions of employees who have accidents at the two plants?

15. Re-do Exercise 14 above as a Chi-square test. Is the p-value the same for both tests? Did you expect it to be?

THINK AND DECIDE USING EXCEL

16. A large international company often gives its managers opportunities to work in foreign countries, and is interested to see if the willingness to accept a foreign posting is related to the family status of the individual being offered the opportunity. A random sample of 190 individuals who had been offered foreign postings in the last year was gathered, as was information about whether they accepted the post, and what their family status was. (Information about family status was freely volunteered by employees.) The results are shown in Exhibit 12.37 below.

CRE12-16

EXHIBIT 12.37

Foreign Postings and Family Status

Random Sample of Individuals Offered Foreign Postings in the Last Year		
Family Status	Accepted Foreign Posting	Declined Foreign Posting
Single, no Children	50	8
Single with Children	22	10
Partnered, no Children	40	8
Partnered with Children	38	14

Is there evidence of a relationship between an individual's family status and his/her willingness to accept a foreign posting? Use $\alpha = 5\%$.

CRE12-17

17. A car parts plant is concerned that some of its employees are more likely to call in sick on Fridays or Mondays (the plant operates only five days a week). An analyst randomly selects one week, and records the number of absences each day. The data are shown below in Exhibit 12.38.

Based on these sample data, is there evidence that absences differ over the days of the week? Use α = 5%.

EXHIBIT 12.38

Absences at a Car Plant

Number of Absences, Randomly Selected Week at a Car Parts Plant				
Monday	Tuesday	Wednesday	Thursday	Friday
15	6	4	7	16

CRE12-18

18. A random sample of people who regularly attend movies in St. John's is selected. Each is asked which of several types of movies is his or her favourite. The answers were categorized according to the gender of the survey respondent. The results are shown in Exhibit 12.39 below.

EXHIBIT 12.39

Preferences of Moviegoers

Random Sample of St. John's Moviegoers		
Favourite Movie Type	Male	Female
Action/Adventure	32	32
Comedy	12	19
Drama	16	31
Fantasy	18	18
Horror	23	22
Romance	15	26
Thriller	26	15

Is there evidence of a relationship between gender and preferred movie type? Use α = 0.04.

CRE12-19

19. A random sample of 78 employees at a large computer software firm was polled to determine method of travel to work. A random sample of 80 employees of an accounting firm in the same office complex was also polled. The results are shown in Exhibit 12.40 below. Is there evidence that the proportions of workers who travel to work via the different methods are different between the two firms? Use α = 5%.

EXHIBIT 12.40

Method of Travel to Work

Employees' Methods of Travel to Work				
	By Transit	In Car	On Bicycle	On Foot
Software Firm	51	8	16	3
Accounting Firm	52	23	4	1

20. A restaurant is interested in whether there is difference in the tendency to drink beer, wine, and other alcoholic drinks, by gender. A survey of a random sample of customers who bought alcoholic beverages revealed the data shown in Exhibit 12.41

CRE12-20

EXHIBIT **12.41**

Sample of Restaurant Customers Ordering Alcoholic Drinks

Sample of Restaurant Customers Ordering Alcoholic Drinks			
	Beer	Wine	Other Alcoholic Drinks
Male	42	36	22
Female	63	54	33

Is the distribution of preferences for beer, wine, and other alcoholic drinks independent of the gender of the customer? Why is the test statistic equal to zero in this case? What does the *p*-value tell you?

TEST YOUR KNOWLEDGE

21. A quality control inspector is checking to see whether the proportions of different kinds of nuts included in a mixed-nuts package meet specifications. She randomly selects one of the bags of nuts off the line, and counts how many nuts of each type are included. The results are shown in Exhibit 12.42 below.

EXHIBIT **12.42**

Mixed Nuts for Company A

Company A's Mixed Nuts Package					
	Almonds	Peanuts	Hazelnuts	Cashews	Pecans
Desired Percentage	22%	48%	10%	10%	10%
Observed Number	80	190	36	31	37

Does this sample provide any evidence that the proportions of mixed nuts are not as they should be? Use $\alpha = 2.5\%$.

22. The company that produces the mixed nuts described in Exercise 21 claims that the percentage of peanuts in the mixed-nuts package is no more than 50%. Does this sample provide evidence that there are more than 50% peanuts in the mixed nuts packages? Use $\alpha = 2.5\%$.

23. A randomly selected package from a competing company producing mixed nuts provides the information shown in Exhibit 12.43.

EXHIBIT **12.43**

Mixed Nuts for Company B

Company B's Mixed Nuts Package					
	Almonds	Peanuts	Hazelnuts	Cashews	Pecans
Observed Number	163	375	65	75	60

Is there evidence of a difference in the proportion of types of nuts for the two companies? Use $\alpha = 5\%$.

24. Based on the sample evidence in Exhibits 12.42 and 12.43 in Exercises 21 and 23, is there evidence of a difference in the proportions of peanuts in the mixed-nuts packages of the two companies? Use $\alpha = 5\%$.

25. Construct a 90% confidence interval estimate of the difference in proportion of peanuts in the mixed-nuts packages described in the previous exercises. Do you expect this confidence interval to contain zero? Why or why not?

26. Suppose you wanted to investigate the proportion of different types of nuts in bags of mixed nuts. You are feeling too lazy to count the number of each type of nut, so you hit upon the idea of weighing the nuts by type. Will you be able to use the information on weights and the Chi-square test to analyze the nuts? Explain fully and think carefully.

CHAPTER 13

Analyzing Linear Relationships, Two Quantitative Variables

INTRODUCTION

Woodbon, a company that produces a limited line of high-quality wooden furniture, has enjoyed remarkable sales growth since its inception in 1980. Woodbon's owner, Kate Cameron, is looking back over the company's years of operation, and is trying to plan for the future. She would like to ensure continued growth in sales, but she's not sure just why sales have grown so steadily. There are a number of factors that have probably affected sales during this time. Were the advertising campaigns effective? Were the price discounts important? Or is the company's success closely tied to housing construction in the area? Or to the incomes of residents?

Answering these questions might help Kate plan for the future. With the necessary data, she will be able to build a mathematical model to estimate the relationship between sales and the various factors affecting sales. Kate will be able to use this model to assess how strongly sales seem to depend on these factors, and possibly even to make predictions for the future. Excel, and other computer software, makes this mathematical modelling easy to do.

However, Kate must be thoughtful as she analyzes the relationship between sales and various factors affecting sales. All the data in

LEARNING OBJECTIVES

After mastering the material in this chapter, you will be able to:

1 Create a scatter diagram and estimate the least-squares regression line for a sample of x–y quantitative data.

2 Check the conditions required for use of the regression model in hypothesis testing and prediction.

3 Conduct a hypothesis test to determine if there is evidence of a significant linear relationship between x and y.

4 Produce (with Excel) and interpret the coefficient of determination for the regression relationship.

5 Use the regression relationship (if appropriate) to make predictions about an individual y-value and an average y-value, given a particular x-value.

the world cannot *prove* that there is a cause-and-effect relationship between furniture sales and housing starts, for example. Even if the number of housing starts seems to be highly related to furniture sales, the true root cause may be overall economic conditions or consumer confidence. As well, if local economic conditions are changing at a rapid rate, using yesterday's data to predict the future can be unreliable.

While analyzing relationships can be very helpful to decision making, as usual, there is no substitute for careful thinking. The estimated relationships are based on a number of requirements that must be checked carefully before any predictions are made.

Chapter 13 provides an introduction to the analysis of linear relationships between variables. In this chapter, we will explore simple linear regression models with only one explanatory variable. These mathematical models are used to understand how a variable behaves when one other related variable changes. Any analysis of this kind should start with a graph, as described in Section 13.1. A method called *least-squares regression* is used to estimate the mathematical relationship, and this is also described in Section 13.1. In Section 13.2, you will learn how to assess the sample's compliance with the required conditions for hypothesis testing and prediction. In Section 13.3, you will learn how to test to see whether there is evidence of a significant linear relationship between the variables. In Section 13.4, you will see how the coefficient of determination is used to assess the strength of the regression relationship. Finally, in Section 13.5, you will learn how to use the model (and how not to use the model) to make predictions.

13.1 CREATING A GRAPH AND DETERMINING THE RELATIONSHIP—SIMPLE LINEAR REGRESSION

Kate Cameron, Woodbon's owner, understands that many factors could be affecting her company's sales. Many of these factors (e.g., economic conditions, mortgage interest rates, and housing starts) are beyond her control. She decides to focus on just one factor, a factor she can control: advertising. Kate has always been uncertain about how to set her advertising budget, so she decides to examine the relationship between sales and advertising. Kate decides to start with a simple model of this nature. It may turn out that advertising alone is the biggest explanatory factor for sales. If this is the case, then Kate may be able to predict sales on the basis of advertising, without worrying very much about other related factors. In Chapter 14, we will extend our analysis to include more than one explanatory variable.

Kate collects the annual advertising and sales figures for the last several years, and realizes that she could make a number of choices about the data. She might look at quarterly or monthly figures instead of annual ones, for instance. However, she decides that annual figures make sense, since sales are fairly steady throughout the year, and the advertising plan is set only once a year. Kate might also choose to break down her advertising spending by categories, such as spending on newspaper ads or flyers. However, the mix of advertising media used by the company has been similar in every year of operation, so Kate decides that total advertising spending is a good measure of advertising effort.

An excerpt of Kate's data is shown in Exhibit 13.1 on the next page.

EXHIBIT 13.1

Excerpt of Woodbon Sales and Advertising Data

| Woodbon Sales and Advertising Data | | |
Year	Annual Advertising Expenditure	Annual Sales
1980	$500	$26,345
1981	$695	$31,987
1982	$765	$21,334
⋮	⋮	⋮
2004	$2,500	$101,760
2005	$2,700	$95,400
2006	$3,500	$115,320
2007	$3,200	$108,550

Creating a Graph of the Relationship

The first thing Kate does is create a graph. As discussed in Chapter 2, the usual approach is to put the response variable on the y-axis. Kate is examining how sales respond to changes in advertising. As a result, Woodbon's annual sales will be plotted on the y-axis of the graph, with advertising spending on the x-axis. A scatter diagram of the data is shown in Exhibit 13.2 below.

At first glance, it seems that there is a fairly strong positive relationship between sales and advertising. The relationship is described as positive because the variables

EXHIBIT 13.2

Woodbon Sales and Advertising Scatter Graph

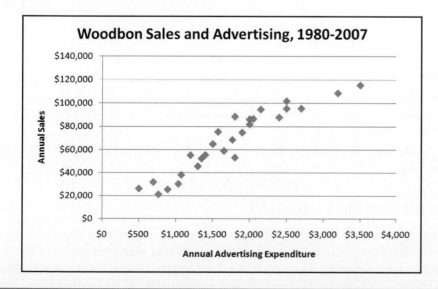

increase or decrease together. In the years when advertising spending is higher, sales are higher. The points on the graph present a fairly pronounced pattern.

We notice a couple of other things about this graphical picture of the relationship.

1. First, the relationship appears to be linear. The data points line up in a relatively straight line. There is no obvious curve in the pattern of points. Because the relationship appears to be linear, the methods discussed in this chapter can be applied.
2. While the data points do not line up in exactly a straight-line fashion, the points are clustered fairly tightly together. This is usually a good sign, but keep in mind that how a graph looks depends very much on how it is set up (misleading graphs were discussed in Chapter 3).

This point is illustrated by Exhibit 13.3 below, which shows the Woodbon data, but with the *x*- and *y*-axes scaled differently. In this graph, the points appear to be much closer together, which seems to indicate that there is a stronger relationship between the *x*- and *y*-variables; but of course the relationship is exactly the same as shown in Exhibit 13.2. Exhibit 13.3 is provided to reinforce your understanding that the eyeball test is not necessarily reliable for assessing the strength of a relationship.

EXHIBIT 13.3

Woodbon Sales and Advertising, Scatter Graph Re-Scaled

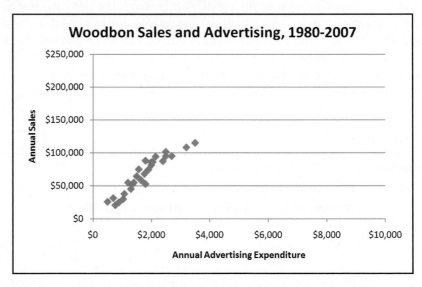

Misleading graphs aside, the graph of the Woodbon data (Exhibit 13.2) looks promising.

Determining the Relationship

It appears from Exhibit 13.2 that there is a positive relationship between Woodbon's annual sales and its annual advertising spending. The question is, what is the nature of this relationship? We can examine the data that Woodbon's owner collected, and use them to arrive at a mathematical estimate of the relationship between sales and advertising for Woodbon.

The data that we have are sample data. Even if Kate Cameron has collected *all* of the data available for sales and advertising at Woodbon, we still treat it as sample data. This is because the theoretical model (discussed in more detail below) assumes that there is a range of possible sales values for every specific level of advertising. The Woodbon sample data are only a subset of this theoretical distribution of values.

We need to come up with the equation of a straight line that best fits the points in the scatter diagram of sample data. We want to set up a straight line because it is the simplest relationship we can specify (and it seems appropriate here, because the points line up in a fairly straight-line fashion). In order to develop the equation of the straight line, we need to estimate two things: the slope and the y-intercept. The equation for the straight line will be:

annual sales $= y$-intercept $+$ slope $\cdot$ annual advertising

In this case, the slope of the line will give us an estimate of how much annual sales increase when annual advertising increases by \$1. The y-intercept is an estimate of what the annual sales will be when annual advertising is zero. However, this estimate is not likely to be reliable. As you will see in Section 13.5, it is dangerous to make predictions outside the range of the sample data. Since all the years in the sample data have an advertising budget of at least \$500, we should not use these data to predict sales with \$0 advertising. However, we still need the y-intercept to fully specify the mathematical relationship between sales and advertising.

We will use some general notation (and some Greek letters, as usual) to describe the theoretical relationship between annual sales and advertising in the population. (The Greek letter β is beta, pronounced "*bay*-tuh." The Greek letter ε is epsilon.)

annual sales $= y$-intercept $+$ slope $\cdot$ annual advertising $+$ unexplained error

annual sales $= \beta_0 + \beta_1 \cdot$ annual advertising $+ \varepsilon$

or, more generally,

$y = \beta_0 + \beta_1 x + \varepsilon$

The ε is included in the equation to remind us that we do not expect the model to be perfect. Remember, there is a range of possible sales values for every specific level of advertising, so our model has to take this variability into account.

Of course, we do not know exactly what this theoretical true model is, because we have only sample data to work with. The corresponding notation for the relationship based on sample data is

$\hat{y} = b_0 + b_1 x$

The notation $\hat{y}$ is read as "y-hat", and is used for the predicted value of y (sales), given a specific x (advertising expenditure). But how do we come up with estimates for the slope and the y-intercept (b_1 and b_0) for the equation of the straight-line relationship between annual sales and advertising?

Chances are that if five different people were asked to draw the line that *best* fits the points in the scatter diagram in Exhibit 13.1, they would draw five different lines. We need some way to decide on a single *best* line, on which everyone can agree.

We do this by focusing on what are called *residuals*. A **residual** is the difference between the observed value of y for a specific x, and the predicted value of y for that x. Residuals are also sometimes referred to as the *error term*.

Residual The difference between the observed value of y for a specific x, and the predicted value of y for that x.

For example, in the Woodbon data, advertising expenditure was $2,500 in 2004, and sales were $101,760. To put this in more general language, the observed value of y (sales) was $101,760 for a specific value of x (advertising expenditure) of $2,500. If the best-fitting line predicts sales ($\hat{y}$) of $94,208 for advertising expenditure of $2,500, the residual is (actual sales − predicted sales) = $(y - \hat{y})$ = $101,760 − $94,208 = $7,552. The prediction is "off" by $7,552 (the predicted value is below the actual value). Since we do not generally expect the predictions to exactly match the actual values, this is expected.

Exhibit 13.4, below, illustrates.

EXHIBIT 13.4

Residuals

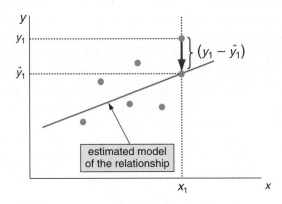

In general terms, if we pick a specific value of x and call it x_1, then the corresponding observed value of y would be called y_1. The predicted value of y, given the model of the relationship, is $\hat{y}_1$. The residual is the difference between the observed y-value (y_1) and the predicted y-value ($\hat{y}_1$), or $y_1 - \hat{y}_1$. This difference is represented by the red arrow in the graph above. Of course, there is a residual for every observed pair of x–y data. The residual is equal to zero any time the estimated line passes through an observed sample data point.

If the line that we create fits the points well, then the residuals will be small because the line will be close to all of the points. We could get a score of how well the line fits the points by summing the residuals. However, some of the residuals are positive (observed points are *above* the line) and some are negative (observed points are *below* the line). In order to prevent cancelling out, the residuals are first squared and then added up (you should be familiar with this technique to prevent cancelling out, as we have used it before). The sum of the squared residuals, $\sum(y_i - \hat{y}_i)^2$, will be small when the line fits the points well. The best-fitting line, called the **least-squares line** (or the *least-squares regression line*), is the one that has the smallest possible sum of the squared residuals.

Least-squares line The line that has the smallest possible sum of the squared residuals.

Some calculus is required to arrive at the equations for the slope and the y-intercept of the least-squares line (you may be relieved to know that the actual derivations are beyond the scope of this text). The resulting estimates for the y-intercept and the slope of the least-squares line are as follows.

$$b_1 = \frac{\Sigma(x - \bar{x})(y - \bar{y})}{\Sigma(x - \bar{x})^2} \quad \text{and} \quad b_0 = \bar{y} - b_1\bar{x}$$

where $\bar{x}$ and $\bar{y}$ are the averages of all of the x-values and all of the y-values in the sample data set.

While it is possible (particularly with variations of these formulas) to do the arithmetic involved by hand, there is no real reason to do this. Excel provides two tools that can be used to estimate the slope and the y-intercept of the least-squares line. Perhaps the easiest way to use Excel to calculate the regression line is to right-click on the points in the scatter diagram created from the data. One of the choices that comes up is **Add Trendline . . . .** If you click on this choice, the dialogue box shown in Exhibit 13.5 will appear.

EXHIBIT **13.5**

Format Trendline Dialogue Box

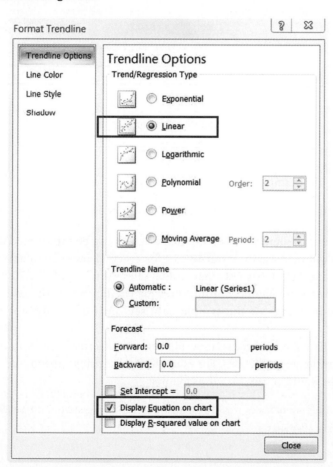

Make sure that the **Linear** choice is highlighted, and then tick the box beside **Display Equation on chart**. Excel will then insert the least-squares line into the scatter diagram, and produce the equation of that line. The result for the Woodbon example is shown in Exhibit 13.6 on the next page.

EXHIBIT 13.6

Woodbon Sales and Advertising, Least-Squares Line

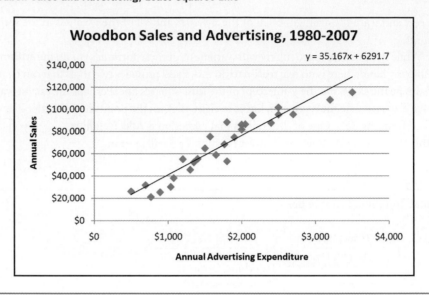

From the output, you can see that the relationship is

$$\hat{y} = 35.167x + 6291.7$$

or, in terms of the example,

predicted annual sales = 35.167(annual advertising expenditure) + $6,291.7

The slope of the line is 35.167. In this case, this can be interpreted to mean that annual sales will increase by about $35.17 for every $1 increase in advertising. The y-intercept of $6,291.70 suggests that annual sales would be $6,291.70 if advertising were $0. However, we should not interpret the coefficients of the regression equation outside the range of the sample data set, and so we will not rely on this prediction.

Once we have specified the relationship between advertising and sales, we can use it to make approximate predictions. For example, if advertising expenditure were $1,800, predicted sales would be $69,591.75, as follows:

predicted annual sales = 35.167(annual advertising expenditure) + $6,291.70

= 35.167($1,800) + $6,291.70

= $69,592.30

A word of caution is in order here. No matter how well the model fits the data, it would be wildly optimistic (and quite wrong) to think that this arithmetic suggests that spending $1,800 on advertising will lead to exactly $69,592.30 in sales. Remember, the regression line equation is based on *sample* data. It is more useful and realistic to take an interval estimation approach to predicting sales, which we will do in Section 13.5.

The second way to get the equation of the least-squares line is to use the **Regression** tool available in **Data Analysis** (under the **Data** tab). The choice is highlighted in Exhibit 13.7 below.

EXHIBIT 13.7

Data Analysis Dialogue Box

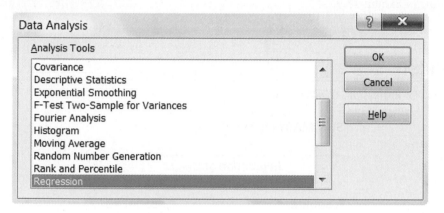

If you click **OK** here, the next dialogue box is as shown in Exhibit 13.8 below.

EXHIBIT 13.8

Regression Dialogue Box

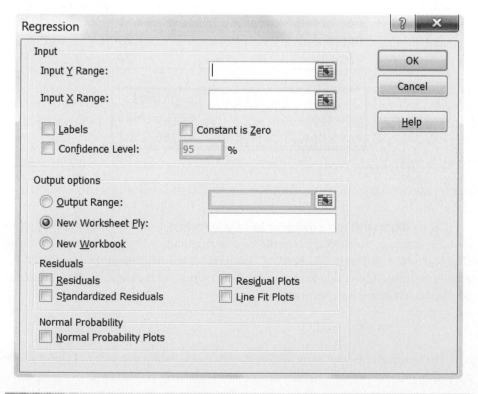

You must use this dialogue box, at a minimum, to specify where the *x*- and *y*-data are (**Input Y Range:** and **Input X Range:**), and where the output should go (**Output Range:**). It is recommended that you select labels with the input data, so be sure to tick the box beside **Labels** and include the labels at the top of your columns of data. If you tick **Line Fit Plots**, Excel will also produce a scatter diagram with the least-squares line shown. An excerpt of the output for the Woodbon data set is shown below in Exhibit 13.9.

EXHIBIT 13.9

Output for Regression, Woodbon Data

SUMMARY OUTPUT	
Regression Statistics	
Multiple R	0.941192016
R Square	0.885842412
Adjusted R Square	0.881451735
Standard Error	9370.081561
Observations	28

ANOVA	
	df
Regression	1
Residual	26
Total	27

	Coefficients
Intercept	6291.657683
Advertising Expenditure	35.16671582

Excel's **Regression** tool produces a lot of information, and we will refer to only some of it. In particular, the coefficients of the least-squares line are highlighted in Exhibit 13.9 (but will not be, in Excel). The heading "Intercept" is the estimate of the *y*-intercept, b_0, and the heading "Advertising Expenditure" is the estimate of the slope, b_1. Once again, we see that the estimated least-squares line is

$$\hat{y} = 35.167x + 6{,}291.7$$

The line fit plot produced by the **Regression** tool is shown opposite in Exhibit 13.10. Note that you will probably have to re-size the graph to see it clearly.

EXHIBIT **13.10**

Excel Line Fit Plot for Woodbon Data

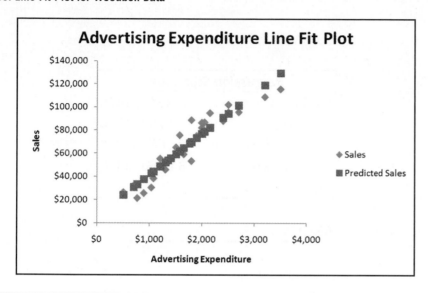

DEVELOP YOUR SKILLS **13.1**

1. The Hendrick Software Sales Company has collected data on the number of contacts made by its sales staff, and the software sales, for a random sample of months. Create an appropriate scatter diagram for these data. What is the least-squares regression line? Interpret it.

   DYS13-1

2. Data on monthly income and monthly spending on restaurant meals was collected for a random sample of households in Vancouver. An excerpt of Excel's Regression output is shown on the next page in Exhibit 13.11. What is the equation of the least-squares regression line? Interpret it.

3. Smith and Klein Manufacturing have data on annual sales and the annual amount spent on promotions. Create an appropriate scatter diagram for these data. What is the least-squares regression line? Interpret it.

   DYS13-3

4. A college professor has collected data for a random sample of 43 of her students. She has their final semester average marks, and the total number of hours each spent working during the semester. The professor has hired one of her students to help her analyze the data, and the student has estimated the regression equation to be $y = 0.1535x + 90.241$. Why is the professor sure that the student has made a mistake?

5. The Top 25 global research organizations include companies such as The Neilsen Company, the Ipsos Group, and Harris Interactive. Data about global research revenues (in US$ millions) and the number of full-time employees have been collected for 2007.[1] The question that interests the researcher is this: Do research companies with more employees have larger revenues? In this data set, which is the response variable and which is the explanatory variable? Create a scatter diagram, estimate the least-squares regression equation, and interpret it.

   DYS13-5

---

[1] *Source*: "Top 25 Global Research Organizations," *Research World* 1 (September 2008), p. 34.

EXHIBIT 13.11

Excel Regression Output for Restaurant Spending

SUMMARY OUTPUT

Regression Statistics	
Multiple R	0.420433426
R Square	0.176764266
Adjusted R Square	0.168363901
Standard Error	34.89859335
Observations	100

ANOVA	
	df
Regression	1
Residual	98
Total	99

	Coefficients
Intercept	44.90252645
Monthly Income	0.024144331

13.2 ASSESSING THE MODEL

The Theoretical Model

Woodbon's owner has already speculated that many factors could be affecting company sales. Because of this, it would not be reasonable to expect a perfectly linear relationship between sales and advertising spending. For any particular value of advertising spending, there are many different possible levels of sales. These possible sales levels arise because of variations in the other factors affecting sales (economic conditions, etc.), and also because of random variability. In the theoretical model, there is a distribution of possible sales values for each level of advertising. Ideally, these distributions are normal.

Exhibit 13.12 illustrates just two of these theoretical normal distributions of possible sales values, for two particular levels of advertising, $800 and $1,700. (These two advertising levels were picked randomly, for illustration.) As you have already seen in Exhibit 13.2, the sales for an advertising expenditure of $1,700 are higher than for an advertising expenditure of only $800. This is reflected in the different locations of the two distributions shown in Exhibit 13.12 below.

EXHIBIT **13.12**

The Theoretical Model, Woodbon Data

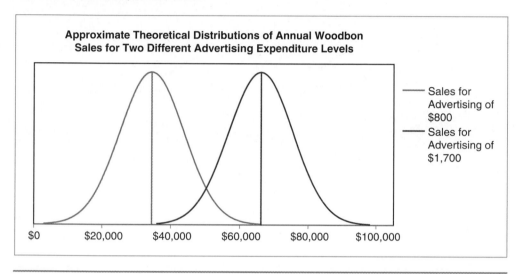

To recap: there is a theoretical distribution of sales values for every possible level of advertising expenditure (only two are shown above). The least-squares regression line focuses on the mean value of sales (μ_y) for each value of advertising expenditure.

$$\mu_y = \beta_0 + \beta_1 x$$

You have to try to see the graph on the next page (Exhibit 13.13) in three dimensions to grasp this.

Of course, we will never know what this true straight line looks like. We can only estimate it from the sample data set. Each sample will yield a slightly different estimate of the true theoretical relationship.

Checking the Required Conditions

We have already discussed *residuals,* that is, the differences between the actual y and the predicted y for each x. In the theoretical population model, this residual is ε. As usual, we use a corresponding letter, e, to denote the residuals observed in the sample data.

Remember that $\hat{y}$ is the notation we use to denote the predicted value of y for a given x. In general, residuals can be calculated as

$$e_i = y_i - \hat{y}_i$$

for each observation in the sample data set.

EXHIBIT 13.13

The Model for Predicting Sales from Advertising Expenditure

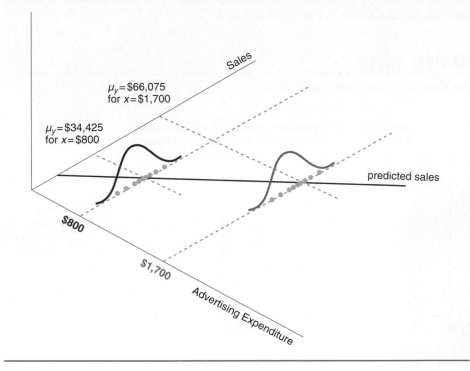

For example, we previously calculated that the regression line predicts sales of $69,592.30 ($\hat{y}$) when the advertising expenditure (x) is $1,800. From the sample data set, we can see that there are two years where advertising expenditure was $1,800: 1989 and 1998. In 1998, actual sales were $88,441. For the 1998 observation, the residual calculation is

$$e_i = y_i - \hat{y}_i$$
$$= \$88{,}441 - \$69{,}592.30$$
$$= \$18{,}848.70$$

We can picture this in the scatter diagram for the Woodbon data, as shown in Exhibit 13.14 opposite. Note that the graph has been scaled to focus on the area of interest. The residual value of $18,849 is shown by the red arrow.

Residuals can be calculated in a similar way for all of the data points in the sample. Examples of these calculations are shown in Exhibit 13.15 opposite.

The residuals are important because they allow us to check whether the sample data appear to conform to the requirements of the least-squares regression model. We can legitimately make predictions with the regression model—or do hypothesis tests to see whether there is a significant relationship between the x- and y-variables—only if these requirements are met.

EXHIBIT 13.14

Woodbon Sales and Advertising, Calculation of a Residual

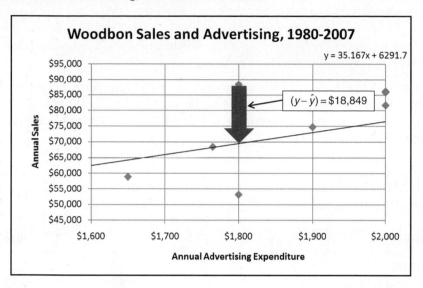

EXHIBIT 13.15

Excerpt of Residuals for Woodbon Data

Annual Advertising Expenditure	Annual Sales, y	Predicted Sales, $\hat{y}$	Residuals $e = y - \hat{y}$
$500	$26,345	$23,875.02	$2,469.98
$695	$31,987	$30,732.53	$1,254.47
$765	$21,334	$33,194.20	$-11,860.20
⋮	⋮	⋮	⋮
$2,500	$101,760	$94,208.45	$7,551.55
$2,700	$95,400	$101,241.79	$-5,841.79
$3,500	$115,320	$129,375.16	$-14,055.16
$3,200	$108,550	$118,825.15	$-10,275.15

Requirements for Predictions or Hypothesis Tests About the Linear Regression Relationship

1. For any given value of x, there are many possible values of y, and therefore, many possible values of ε (the residual, or *error* term). The distribution of the ε-values for any given x must be normal. This means that the actual y-values will be scattered in a normal fashion around the regression line, as pictured in Exhibit 13.13 (page 490).

2. The normal distributions of ε must have a mean of 0. This means that the actual y-values will have an expected value, or mean, that is equal to the predicted y from the regression line (again, this is pictured in Exhibit 13.13).

3. The standard deviation of ε, which we will refer to as σ_ε, is the same for every value of x. This means that the actual y-values will be distributed with the same variability around the regression line, all along the line.

4. The ε-values for different data points are not related to each other (another way to say this is that the ε-values for different data points are independent).

Fortunately, it is easy to calculate the residuals with Excel. When you use the **Data Analysis** tool called **Regression**, you will see the dialogue box shown in Exhibit 13.16 below. Under the heading for **Residuals**, tick **R̲esiduals**, **S̲tandardized Residuals**, and **Resid̲ual Plots** to get Excel's residual analysis.

EXHIBIT 13.16

Regression Dialogue Box

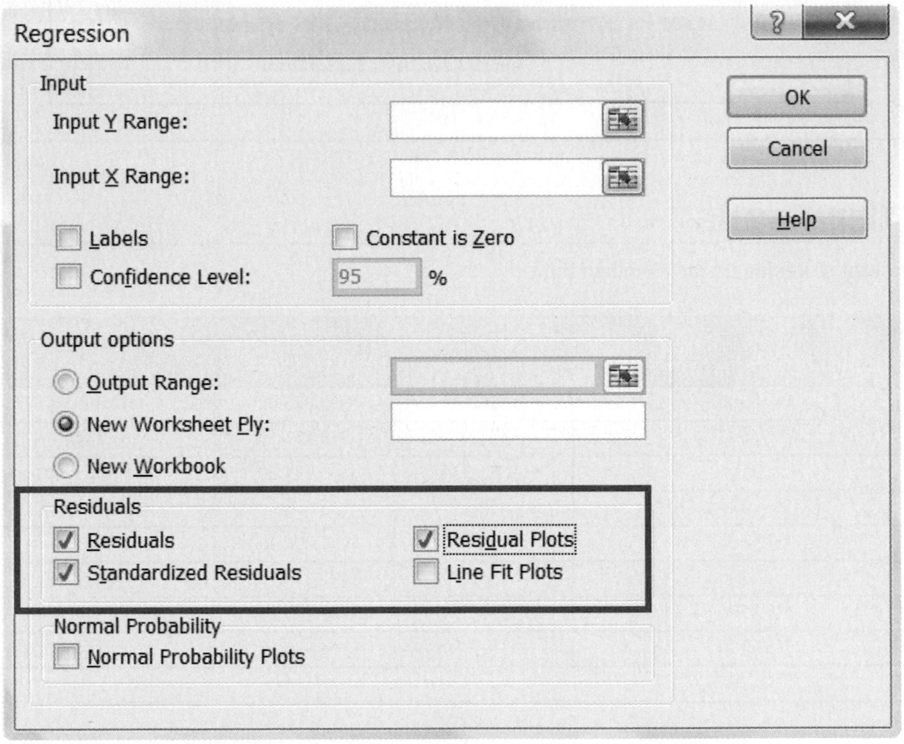

Variation in the Residuals Is Constant   The graph that is created when you tick the **Resid̲ual Plots** option in Excel's **Regression** tool in **Data Analysis** is a plot of the residuals against x. Exhibit 13.17 shows this residual plot for the Woodbon data. The graph has been re-sized so we can see it clearly.

This plot should be checked to see whether the residuals have the same amount of variation for all values of x (requirement #3 says that the residuals all have the same standard deviation).

We are looking for a residual plot showing a horizontal band, centred vertically on zero. Does this plot meet the requirements? This is a judgment call. In particular, you

EXHIBIT **13.17**

Regression Residual Plot for Woodbon Data

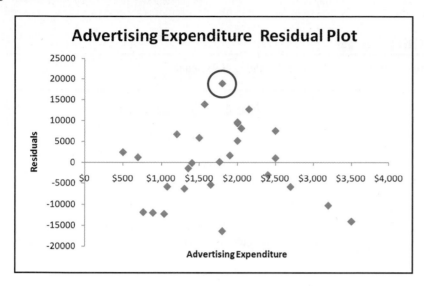

might be concerned about the point circled in red on the diagram. If it weren't there, we might be more comfortable thinking that the error terms all have the same standard deviation. We will come back to a discussion of the circled point later in the chapter.

A scatter diagram that does not meet the requirement for constant variability in the residuals is shown in Exhibit 13.18 below. In this scatter diagram, the *y*-values are scattered more and more widely as the *x*-values increase. The dotted red lines on the graph draw attention to this pattern. The increasing variability is also clearly seen in the residual plot

EXHIBIT **13.18**

Scatter Diagram with Non-Constant Variability of Residuals

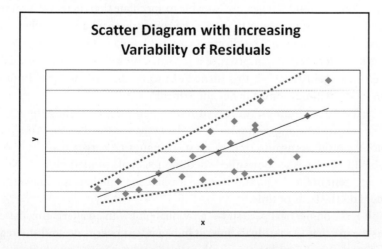

produced by Excel for this data set, shown in Exhibit 13.19. Again, dotted red lines have been drawn to reinforce this point.

EXHIBIT 13.19

Residual Plot with Non-Constant Variability of Residuals

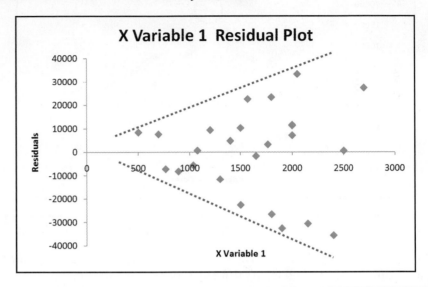

In this case, because the residual analysis indicates that σ_ε is probably not constant, we should not use the linear regression model to make predictions.

Independence of Error Terms   One of the requirements (#4) of the data is that the error terms, or residuals, are independent of one another. It can be difficult to check the independence of the error terms, since this involves imagining all of the ways in which they could be related. In the Woodbon example, it is possible that the residuals are related over time. It would not be unreasonable to speculate that there was a carryover in the effect of advertising from year to year. If the company spent a lot on advertising one year, the expenditure might still be affecting sales in the following year, even if that year's budget were smaller. This might produce a recognizable pattern in the residuals when they are plotted against time. If this turned out to be the case, we could not use the regression model without some further adjustment.

One of the most common sources of non-independence among the residuals is time. When you are working with time-series data (such as the data for Woodbon), you should plot the residuals against time to see if any pattern emerges.

Exhibit 13.20 opposite shows the Woodbon residuals plotted by year. No regular pattern is apparent in the graph, and so it is reasonable to conclude that the residuals are independent on the basis of time.

Exhibit 13.21 on the next page shows a residual plot with an alternating pattern over time. This means that the residuals are *not* independent over time, and the regression model is not reliable. When there are such regular patterns in the graph, it could be an indication that time should be added to the model as an explanatory variable. Multiple regression models (with more than one explanatory variable) are discussed in Chapter 14.

EXHIBIT **13.20**

Woodbon Residuals Over Time

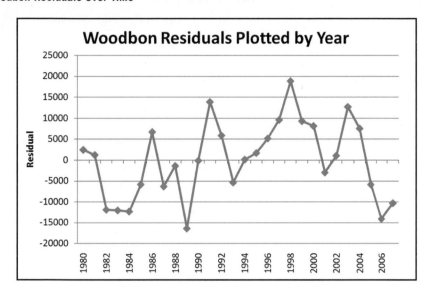

EXHIBIT **13.21**

Residuals Not Independent Over Time

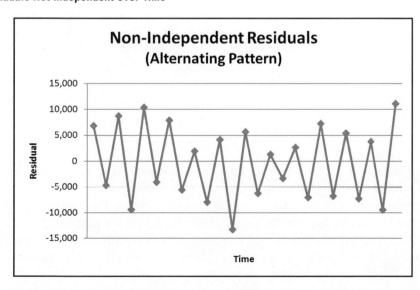

Exhibit 13.22 shows a residual plot with a decreasing pattern over time. Such a residual plot would indicate that the residuals are not independent, but are related

EXHIBIT 13.22

Residuals Not Independent Over Time

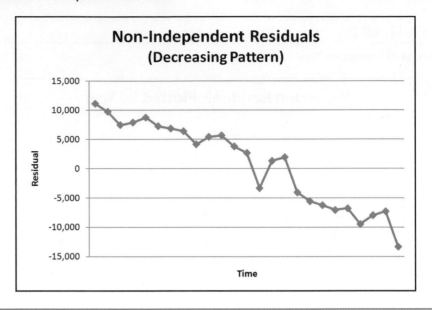

through time. Without further work, the regression relationship should not be relied upon for prediction.

Normality of Residuals We check for normality of the residuals (requirement #1) the way we generally have—with a histogram. Since we usually do not have enough sample data to create a histogram of residuals for each individual value of *x,* we create a histogram of the residuals from all of the sample data. However, we should not do this unless we first establish that the residuals are independent and the variances of the residuals are equal. If these checks have been made and the conditions are met, then we create one histogram of all the residuals.

As long as this overall histogram looks approximately normal, it is reasonably safe to assume that the requirement for normality of residuals is met. If the histogram of the residuals is severely skewed, then the current regression model is not appropriate, and it should not be used to make predictions.

A histogram of the residuals for the Woodbon data is shown opposite in Exhibit 13.23.

While graphing the residuals is one way to check for normality,[2] you can also sometimes see it (or, more importantly, see departures from it) in the scatter diagram. In the Woodbon data set, the data points are scattered fairly equally above and below the regression line, with relatively more points closer to the line. This is consistent with a normal distribution of residuals.

---

[2] Excel contains an option for a "Normal Probability Plot" in the Regression tool. Unfortunately, it is not what is generally recognized as a normal probability plot and does not, in fact, provide any guidance about the normality of residuals.

EXHIBIT **13.23**

Histogram of Residuals for Woodbon Data

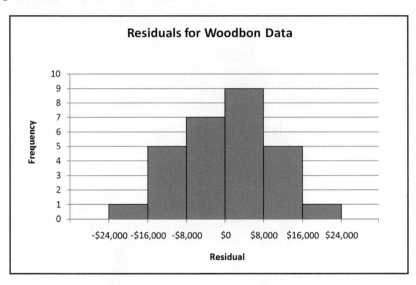

Exhibits 13.24 (below) and 13.25 (on the next page) show a scatter diagram and histogram of residuals where the requirement for normality of the residuals is not met. You should be able to see the correspondence between the two types of graphs.

EXHIBIT **13.24**

Scatter Diagram with Non-Normal Residuals

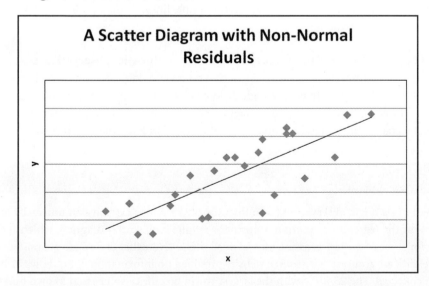

In the scatter diagram shown above in Exhibit 13.24, the spread of data points below the regression line is much wider than above the regression line. This means that there will be several points (below the line) where the observed y-values are significantly below the predicted *y*-values, leading to large negative residuals. The points above the line are much closer to the line, so the positive residuals will not be as large as the negative residual.

The corresponding histogram of the residuals, shown in Exhibit 13.25, reveals this quite clearly. The histogram is skewed to the left because of the larger size of the negative residuals.

EXHIBIT 13.25

Histogram of Non-Normal Residuals

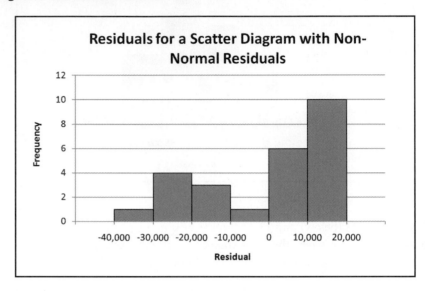

If the scatter diagram of residuals for any model was as skewed (and non-normal) as the graph shown in Exhibit 13.25, then the simple linear regression model should not be used to make predictions.

Influential observation A single observation that has an extreme effect on the regression equation.

Outliers and Influential Observations   An **influential observation** is a single observation that has an extreme effect on the regression equation. Influential observations are usually points that have high or low values of the independent (*x*-) variable, and can often be seen in the scatter diagram. Removing an influential observation will radically change the regression equation, as illustrated in Example 13.2 below.

EXAMPLE 13.2

Influential observations

Sometimes a single observation (an influential observation) can have an unusually large effect on the regression equation. Consider the following scatter diagram, which shows data for some of the top-grossing movies of all time.[3] (Note that there is no guarantee that these data are accurate. The source website provided no information about how the data were collected. The 25 films with the largest world box office values and known budgets were included in the data set (no budget was reported for The Lion King, ranked 24)).

---

[3] *Source*: "Top Grossing Films Ever—June 10, 2009," *The Movie Times*, **www.the-movie-times.com/thrsdir/alltime.mv?domestic1ByDG**, accessed June 23, 2009.

The first graph, in Exhibit 13.26, shows the regression equation as $y = 0.8759x + 796.79$ (the units are millions of U.S. dollars). In other words, it is estimated that every $1 in a movie budget returns about 88¢ in box office sales worldwide.

EXHIBIT 13.26

Scatter Diagram for Cost and Gross of Top Movies

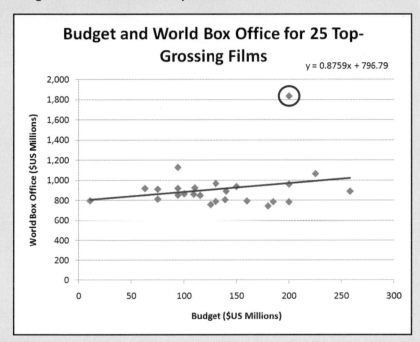

Notice the circled data point on the graph: it is clearly an outlier. This point corresponds to the movie called *Titanic*. When it was made, it was sometimes referred to as "the biggest movie of all time." As you can see from the scatter diagram, this movie enjoyed enormous worldwide success.

Not only is this data point an outlier, but it is also very influential. To see this, look at the data set and the regression relationship that results when the *Titanic* data point is removed, as shown in Exhibit 13.27 on the next page. The original regression line is shown in red, and the new regression line (without the *Titanic* data) is shown in black.

When the *Titanic* data point is removed, the regression relationship is very different. It is now $y = 0.0659x + 867.55$ (the units are millions of U.S. dollars). In other words, the amended regression relationship suggests that every $1 spent on making a movie returns about only 7¢ in box office sales worldwide. This is significantly less than the 88¢ from the original regression equation. Removing just this one observation made a huge difference.

Note that the effect of this one point can also be clearly seen in the histogram of residuals for the movie data, shown in Exhibit 13.28 on the next page.

The influential observation also shows up quite clearly in the residual plot produced by Excel, as shown in Exhibit 13.29 on page 501, although influential observations will not always reveal themselves so easily.

EXHIBIT 13.27

Scatter Diagram for Cost and Gross of Top Movies, *Titanic* Removed

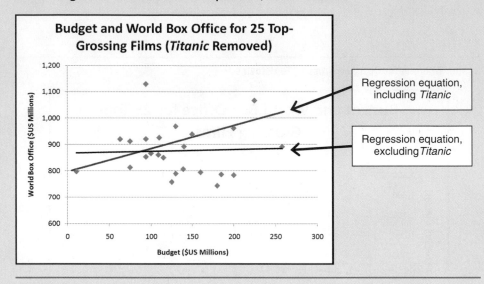

EXHIBIT 13.28

Histogram of Residuals for Cost and Gross of Top Movies

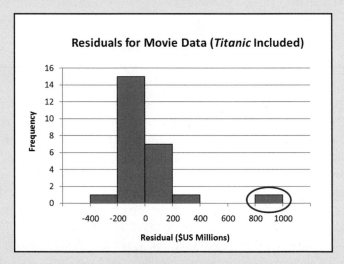

The movie data example is included to illustrate how important it is to examine the data carefully. Any influential observations should be investigated closely. Because such data points have such a great effect on the regression model, they should be checked for accuracy. You should also investigate whether there is something about this one data point that makes it significantly different from the rest of the observations. If there is, you might consider whether a model without the point would be more useful. However, you should not simply discard a data point just because you don't like it! It may be telling you something important.

An influential observation is usually an outlier in the data set, and any outliers should be investigated. An outlier can be the most important data point in the

EXHIBIT **13.29**

Residual Plot for Cost and Gross of Top Movies

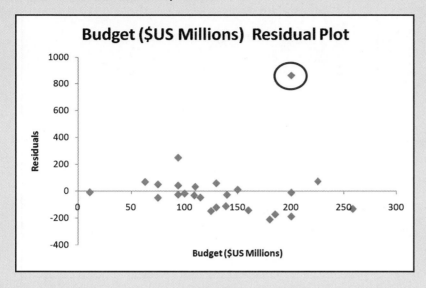

sample data set. It is also possible that an outlier is the result of an error in collecting or recording the data.

Sometimes an outlier is the only indication you have that the true relationship between the variables is not linear. For example, in the scatter diagram in Exhibit 13.30 on the next page, the circled observation is an outlier. It looks as if it does not belong with the rest of the data.

However, what if the true relationship between the variables is actually as shown in Exhibit 13.31? In this case, it is the outlier that gave us a clue that the true relationship is non-linear.

So far in our discussions, we have defined an outlier as a data point that is unusually far from the rest of the data. In the case of regression analysis, we can be a little more precise about what "unusually far" means. We will highlight any data points that have a standardized residual that is ≥ 2 or ≤ -2 (Excel produces these standardized residuals if you tick the appropriate box in the Regression dialogue box—see page 492). The standardized residuals are the residuals divided by s_ε, the sample estimate of the standard deviation of the error terms (residuals) in the model. This standard error for linear regression is calculated by Excel, and is reported beside the label that says "Standard Error" in the Excel output. It is calculated from the sample data, according to the formula shown below.

$$s_\varepsilon = \sqrt{\frac{\sum(y - \hat{y})^2}{n - 2}}$$

In normal distributions, a distance of two or more standard deviations is fairly far from the mean, and so standardized residuals ≥ 2 or ≤ -2 (and the corresponding observations) should be checked for accuracy. Of course, these values contribute to higher variability in the residuals, making the model less precise than desired.

EXHIBIT 13.30

Sample Scatter Diagram with Outlier

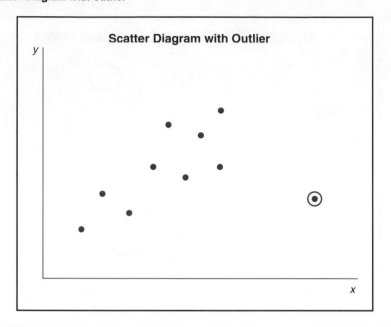

EXHIBIT 13.31

Population Scatter Diagram

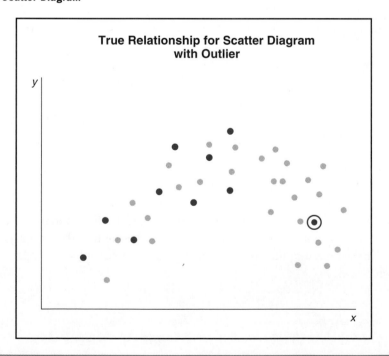

When we examine the standardized residuals for the Woodbon data, we see that there is one point with an unusually large residual. The observation is shown in

Exhibit 13.32a. Notice that this output describes the data point as observation 19. If you number the observations in the original data set from 1 to n (use Excel's Autofill feature), you will be able to identify the corresponding original data point which occurred in 1998. The result is shown in Exhibit 13.32b.

EXHIBIT 13.32

a) Excerpt from Excel's Residual Output

Observation	Predicted Sales	Residuals	Standard Residuals
19	69591.74616	18849.25384	2.049962893

b) Outlier for the Woodbon Data

Year	Advertising Expenditure	Sales	
1998	$1,800	$88,441	19

The outlier shows up more clearly on the residual plot than on the scatter diagram (see Exhibit 13.33 below). This is the point we already noticed in Exhibit 13.17 on page 493, which is reproduced in Exhibit 13.34 on the next page.

Woodbon's owner should investigate to make sure that the data were recorded properly, and that nothing unusual was happening at the company in 1998. If Kate Cameron, Woodbon's owner, can uncover truly unusual circumstances that explain why this observation is so different from the others, and these circumstances are not the norm, it could be reasonable to remove it from the data set and respecify the regression equation. However, this should not be done without real justification. If Kate cannot identify anything unusual, the point should be left in the data set.

EXHIBIT 13.33

Woodbon Scatter Diagram with Outlier Identified

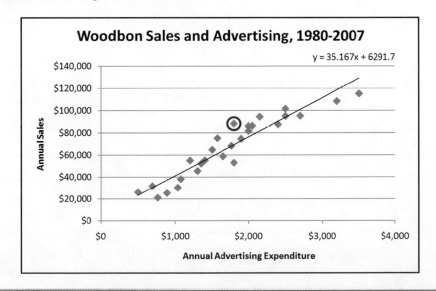

EXHIBIT 13.34

Woodbon Residual Plot with Outlier Identified

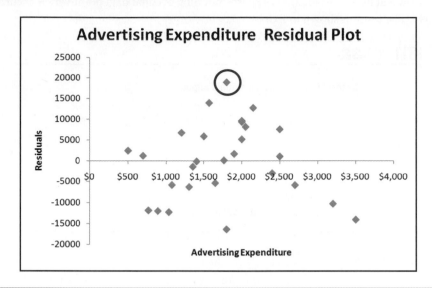

Checking Requirements for the Linear Regression Model

When:

- before performing a hypothesis test or using the regression relationship to make predictions
- using sample data to assess whether the relationship conforms to requirements

Steps:

1. Produce a scatter diagram, with a least-squares regression line. Check to see that the relationship appears linear (no pronounced curvature). Check to see that the spread of the data points on either side of the regression line is about the same, with consistent variability.
2. Use Excel's **Regression** tool to produce the **Residuals**, **Standardized Residuals**, and **Residual Plots**.
3. Examine the residual plot created by Excel. The residuals should be randomly distributed in a horizontal band, centred vertically on zero, with the same variability for all *x*-values.
4. Check for the independence of the error terms. With time-series data, plot the residuals against time. There should be no discernible pattern to the plot.
5. Create a histogram of the residuals. This should be approximately normal.
6. Check for outliers and influential observations. These will usually be visible on the scatter diagram, the histogram of residuals, and the residual plot. Check the standardized residuals, and investigate any with values $\geq +2$ or ≤ -2.

Note: If these investigations indicate problems, you should not proceed with a hypothesis test of the regression relationship, and you should not create confidence or prediction intervals. These difficulties can sometimes be solved by more advanced techniques.

What If the Requirements Are Not Met?   It may still be possible to proceed with your analysis. One possibility may be to transform the data, and the techniques for doing this are available in more advanced texts on model-building. Another possibility is to go back to the beginning, and perhaps choose another explanatory variable from your data. Adding another explanatory variable may also help for multiple regression (discussed in Chapter 14). However, most importantly, you should realize that you should not rely on the regression model if the requirements are not met.

DEVELOP YOUR SKILLS 13.2

These exercises refer to the data sets for which you created scatter diagrams in Develop Your Skills 13.1.

6. Check that the requirements for the theoretical model are met for the data from the Hendrick Software Sales Company. Are there any outliers? Are there any influential observations?

DYS13-6

7. Check that the requirements for the theoretical model are met for the data on monthly incomes and monthly spending on restaurant meals. Are there any outliers? Are there any influential observations?

DYS13-7

8. Check that the requirements for the theoretical model are met for the data on sales and promotion spending for Smith and Klein Manufacturing.

DYS13-8

9. Check that the requirements for the theoretical model are met for the data on semester average marks

DYS13-9

and hours spent working. When the professor checked the data, she noticed that there were two unusually low marks: a 22 and a 28. When she investigated further, she realized that the students with these low marks had withdrawn from the course (all of the other students completed the course). As a result, these two data points should not be included in the data set. Reassess the data, with these two erroneous data points removed.

10. Check that the requirements for the theoretical model are met for the data on the number of employees and revenues for the top 25 global research organizations. Are there any outliers? Are there any influential observations?

DYS13-10

13.3   HYPOTHESIS TEST ABOUT THE REGRESSION RELATIONSHIP

So far, we have focused on estimating the regression relationship and examining the data set to see if it conforms to required conditions for further analysis. Once we have assured ourselves that the required conditions are met, we are finally in a position to test to see whether there is a statistically significant relationship between the x- and y-variables.

The least-squares regression line is the best straight line to fit the points, but there may be *no* true linear relationship between the x- and y-variables. There is always a possibility that the sample data do not realistically represent the population data. Exhibits 13.35 and 13.36 on the next page illustrate this possibility.

Exhibit 13.36 also illustrates that when there is no relationship between the two variables, the slope of the regression line is zero. The hypothesis test for the significance of the relationship is a hypothesis test of the slope of the regression line. Essentially, the test asks the question: given this sample data set, is there sufficient evidence to conclude that the

EXHIBIT 13.35

Sample Data Suggest a Positive Relationship

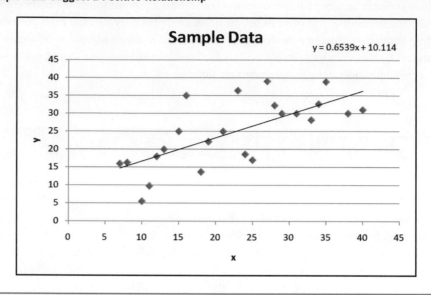

EXHIBIT 13.36

Population Data Reveal No Relationship

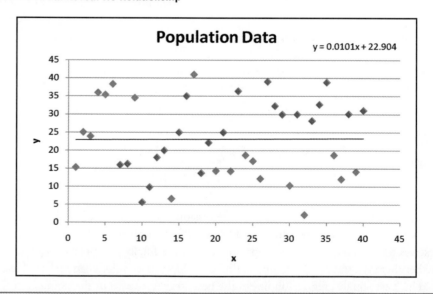

slope of the population regression line is different from zero? The null hypothesis is always that $\beta_1 = 0$. Usually we want to find sufficient evidence to *reject* the null hypothesis and conclude that there *is* evidence of a linear relationship between the variables.

Of course, in order to do a hypothesis test about β_1, the slope, we must have some information about the sampling distribution of b_1.

Sampling Distribution of b_1 (for Least-Squares Regression Equation)

If the required conditions of the distribution of residuals (normality, mean of zero, and constant variance) are met, and the residuals are independent, then the sampling distribution of b_1 will be approximately normal and can be described as follows.

1. The standard error of the sampling distribution is:

$$\sigma_{b_1} = \frac{\sigma_\varepsilon}{\sqrt{\sum (x - \bar{x})^2}}$$

where σ_ε is the (population) standard error of ε, the residuals.

2. The mean of the sampling distribution is β_1.

As usual, we cannot apply the information about the sampling distribution directly. For example, we do not know σ_ε, and so we do not know σ_{b_1}. However, we can estimate σ_{b_1} from sample data (using s_ε to estimate σ_ε). Using the standard conventions about notation, we will call the standard error of the sampling distribution s_{b_1}.

The appropriate test statistic follows a t-distribution, with $n - 2$ degrees of freedom:

$$t = \frac{b_1 - \beta_1}{s_{b_1}}$$

Of course, since the null hypothesis is always that $\beta_1 = 0$ (that is, there is no linear relationship between the variables), the test statistic effectively becomes

$$t = \frac{b_1}{s_{b_1}}$$

There exist variations on these formulas that make manual calculations easier to do, but such calculations are tedious and would not normally be done by hand. Once again, we can turn to Excel's **Regression** tool for help. Exhibit 13.37 on the next page illustrates an excerpt from the output for the Woodbon data.

Three cells are highlighted in Exhibit 13.37 to make it easy for you to see them (they will not be highlighted in Excel's output, so note exactly where they are located).

The cell outlined in green, with the heading "Standard Error" in the row called "Advertising Expenditure" is s_{b_1}, the standard error of the sampling distribution of b_1. The cell outlined in yellow with the heading "t Stat" is the t-statistic required for the hypothesis test of the slope, namely:

$$t = \frac{b_1}{s_{b_1}}$$

The cell outlined in blue, with the heading "P-value," shows the p-value of the *two-tailed* version of the hypothesis test. Now that we have the Excel output, we can proceed with the hypothesis test of the slope for the Woodbon data.

- H_0: $\beta_1 = 0$ (that is, there is no linear relationship between advertising and sales)
- H_1: $\beta_1 \neq 0$ (that is, there is a linear relationship between advertising and sales)
- Use $\alpha = 0.05$.
- From the Excel output, we see that $t - 14.204$

EXHIBIT 13.37

Output for Regression, Woodbon Data

SUMMARY OUTPUT				
Regression Statistics				
Multiple R	0.941192016			
R Square	0.885842412			
Adjusted R Square	0.881451735			
Standard Error	9370.081561			
Observations	28			
ANOVA				
	df	*SS*	*MS*	*F*
Regression	1	17713801540	17713801540	201.755337
Residual	26	2282759140	87798428.46	
Total	27	19996560680		
	Coefficients	*Standard Error*	*t Stat*	*P-value*
Intercept	6291.657683	4696.546154	1.339635016	0.19195671
Advertising Expenditure	35.16671582	2.475821305	14.20406059	9.1661E-14

- The p-value is 9.1661×10^{-14}, or 0.000000000000091661. In other words, there is almost no chance of getting sample results like the ones we got here if, in fact, there is no linear relationship between advertising and sales. Therefore, we can (with confidence) reject the null hypothesis and conclude that there is evidence of a linear relationship between advertising and sales data for Woodbon.

Of course, it is also possible to test whether there is a *positive* linear relationship between the variables (with the alternative hypothesis of $\beta_1 > 0$), or if there is a *negative* linear relationship (with the alternative hypothesis of $\beta_1 < 0$). In these cases, the p-value shown on the Excel output must be divided by 2. Example 13.3 below illustrates.

EXAMPLE 13.3

Hypothesis test of β_1 with Excel

A professor is concerned that her students' success is being hampered by the amount of time they spend working at their part-time jobs. She randomly selects 30 of her students, and polls them about how many hours per week they worked during the semester. She also records their final mark in her Statistics course. A portion of the Excel output for the regression analysis is shown opposite in **Exhibit 13.38**.

At the 5% level of significance, is there evidence of a negative relationship between the hours spent working and the mark in Statistics? You may assume that the professor checked the necessary conditions, and has concluded that a hypothesis test will be valid.

EXHIBIT 13.38

Output for Regression, Student Hours and Marks

SUMMARY OUTPUT					
Regression Statistics					
Multiple R	0.883932765				
R Square	0.781337133				
Adjusted R Square	0.773527745				
Standard Error	4.924458062				
Observations	30				
ANOVA					
	df	*SS*	*MS*	*F*	*Significance F*
Regression	1	2426.265625	2426.266	100.0510058	9.5708E-11
Residual	28	679.0080418	24.25029		
Total	29	3105.273667			
	Coefficients	*Standard Error*	*t Stat*	*P-value*	*Lower 95%*
Intercept	89.24656753	2.299501076	38.81127	6.84895E-26	84.53625317
Weekly Hours Spent at Work During the Semester	-1.392756636	0.139240158	-10.0025	9.5708E-11	-1.677977166

- $H_0: \beta_1 = 0$ (that is, there is no linear relationship between hours spent working and the statistics mark)
- $H_1: \beta_1 < 0$ (that is, there is a negative linear relationship between hours spent working and the statistics mark)
- $\alpha = 0.05$
- From the Excel output, we see that $t = -10.00$.
- The p-value shown on the output is 9.57E–11, or 0.0000000000957. This is the p-value for a two-tailed test, so we have to divide by 2 to get the p-value for this hypothesis test. The p-value will be $\frac{0.0000000000957}{2} = 0.00000000004785$, which is still extremely small, and certainly less than the α of 5%.

Reject H_0. There is strong evidence of a negative relationship between hours spent working and the statistics mark.

GUIDE TO DECISION MAKING

Testing the Slope of the Regression Line for Evidence of a Linear Relationship

When:

- two quantitative variables
- trying to decide whether there is evidence of a linear relationship between x and y, based on b_1, the slope of the least-squares regression line

Steps:

1. Check that the required conditions are met (see the "Checking Requirements for the Linear Regression Model" Guide to Technique, on page 504).
2. Specify H_0, the null hypothesis, which is always that $\beta_1 = 0$ (that is, there is no linear relationship between the variables).
3. Specify H_1, the alternative hypothesis, with three possibilities: $\beta_1 \neq 0$, $\beta_1 > 0$ (testing for a positive slope), or $\beta_1 < 0$ (testing for a negative slope).
4. Determine or identify α, the significance level.
5. Collect or identify the sample data. Identify or calculate:
   - b_1, the slope of the least-squares regression line based on the sample data
   - s_{b_1}, the standard error of b_1
   - n, the number of observations in the sample data set
6. Calculate (or locate in Excel output) the appropriate t-score, using the following formula:

$$t = \frac{b_1}{s_{b_1}}$$

7. Use the t-distribution with $n - 2$ degrees of freedom to identify or calculate (or approximate, if using tables) the appropriate p-value for the hypothesis test, keeping in mind that the p-value shown in the Excel output is based on a two-tailed test.
8. If p-value $\leq \alpha$, reject H_0 and conclude that there is sufficient evidence to decide in favour of H_1. If p-value $> \alpha$, fail to reject H_0 and conclude that there is insufficient evidence to decide in favour of H_1. State your conclusions in language appropriate to the context.

See Example 13.3 on page 508.

DEVELOP YOUR SKILLS 13.3

MyStatLab

11. If appropriate, test to see whether there is evidence of a positive relationship between the number of sales contacts and sales for the Hendrick Software Sales Company. Use $\alpha = 0.05$.
DYS13-11

12. If appropriate, test to see whether there is evidence of a positive relationship between monthly income and monthly spending on restaurant meals for the data collected for households in Vancouver. Use $\alpha = 0.04$.
DYS13-12

13. If appropriate, test to see whether there is evidence of a positive relationship between sales and the amount spent
DYS13-13

on promotions for Smith and Klein Manufacturing. Use $\alpha = 0.03$.

14. If appropriate, test to see whether there is evidence of a negative relationship between semester average marks and hours spent working. Use $\alpha = 0.05$.
DYS13-14

15. If appropriate, test to see whether there is evidence of a positive relationship between total number of employees and total sales for the top 25 global research organization. Use $\alpha = 0.02$.
DYS13-15

13.4 HOW GOOD IS THE REGRESSION?

In Chapter 3, you were introduced to the correlation coefficient (the Pearson r), which was a measure of the degree of association between x- and y-variables. (You may wish to revisit this material, on page 132, to remind yourself of this.)

There is another (related) measure of the strength of the association between x and y, called the coefficient of determination. **The coefficient of determination, R^2**, measures the percentage of variation in the y-variable that is explained by changes in the x-variable.

R^2 is equal to the correlation coefficient squared (or, more succinctly, $R^2 = r^2$). The regression output produced by Excel also shows the coefficient of determination. It is highlighted in the excerpt from the Excel data for Woodbon, shown in Exhibit 13.39 below. Since r can take on values from -1 to $+1$, R^2 can take on values from 0 to $+1$.

Coefficient of determination, R^2
A value that measures the percentage of variation in the y-variable that is explained by changes in the x-variable.

EXHIBIT **13.39**

Excerpt of Output for **Regression for Woodbon Data**

SUMMARY OUTPUT

Regression Statistics	
Multiple R	0.941192016
R Square	0.885842412
Adjusted R Square	0.881451735
Standard Error	9370.081561
Observations	28

In order to see why the R^2-value can be interpreted as it is, we must divide the difference between the observed y and the average y into two portions. This division is illustrated in Exhibit 13.40 below.

EXHIBIT **13.40**

The Change in y Is Explained by the Change in x

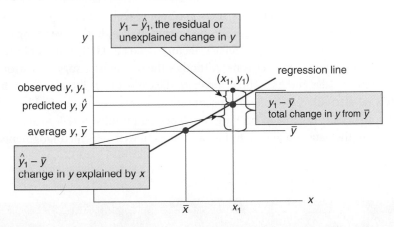

The question is, why does y vary? If there were no variation in y, then y would simply equal its average, or $\bar{y}$. But y does vary, and at the point (x_1, y_1) shown on the graph, y has increased from $\bar{y}$ to y_1. The change in y is shown as $y_1 - \bar{y}$, the total change from the average y. This total change can be divided into two parts, also illustrated on the graph.

1. Part of the change in y is explained by the change in x (from $\bar{x}$ to x_1).
2. The unexplained part of the change in y (which we have called the residual) is the difference between the predicted $\hat{y}$ and the observed y_1.

We can write this mathematically as follows:

$$(y_1 - \bar{y}) = (\hat{y}_1 - \bar{y}) + (y_1 - \hat{y}_1)$$

In words, we could say

total change in y from average $\bar{y}$	=	change in y explained by regression	+	residual (or error)

Of course, this is true for all points in the data set. A related expression, which concerns the sum of the squares of the explained and unexplained deviations, is also true.

$$\Sigma(y - \bar{y})^2 = \Sigma(\hat{y} - \bar{y})^2 + \Sigma(y - \hat{y})^2$$

total sum of squares for change in y from average $\bar{y}$	=	sum of squares for change in y explained by the regression	+	sum of squares for error (residual)

It is usual to refer to these elements with sum of squares notation, as shown below.

$$SST = SSR + SSE$$

It can be shown that $R^2 = \dfrac{SSR}{SST}$. The R^2-value therefore tells us the percentage of the total variation in y that is explained by the regression.

If your regression relationship has an R^2 above 0.8, it is considered quite good. On the other hand, if R^2 is less than 0.50, this means that less than half of the variation in the y-values is explained by changes in the x-values, and such an R^2 is an indication that your model needs more work.

In the case of the Woodbon data, about 89% of the variation in the sales data is explained by variations in advertising. It is important to realize that "explained by" is *not* the same as "caused by." For example, in the Woodbon data, both advertising and sales increase over time. As well, several related factors—such as GDP, household incomes, and prices—have increased over time. Although the data might suggest a strong relationship between sales and household incomes, the cause of the increase in both might ultimately be attributed to a booming economy, perhaps best measured by GDP. No computer analysis is capable of proving this. There is no substitute for understanding the context of the data you are analyzing, and making well-informed judgments about causality.

EXAMPLE 13.4

Interpreting R^2

Jack runs a convenience store, and he has been experimenting with the price of the freshly baked cookies he sells there. Jack has collected data for a random sample of days, with a number of different prices. Jack has used Excel to analyze his small data set, and it reports a coefficient of determination of 0.77. What does this mean?

About 77% of the variation in the number of cookies sold is explained by the price. This suggests that price is an important explanatory factor for Jack's cookie sales. This is not surprising to anyone acquainted with the law of demand.

DEVELOP YOUR SKILLS 13.4

MyStatLab

16. Interpret the coefficient of determination for the data set from the Hendrick Software Sales Company. Given this number, can you conclude that the way to increase sales is to increase the number of sales contacts made by the staff?

   DYS13-16

17. The coefficient of determination for the data collected on monthly income and monthly spending on restaurant meals in Vancouver is 0.18. What does this mean?

   DYS13-17

18. The R^2 for the data on sales and promotional spending for Smith and Klein Manufacturing is 0.83, which is a relatively high value. Does this mean that the least-squares regression line is a good model in this case?

   DYS13-18

19. Interpret the coefficient of determination for the data set on semester average marks. Given this number, can you conclude that the way to increase student marks is to keep students from working while they are studying?

   DYS13-19

20. Interpret the coefficient of determination for the data set of total revenues and total numbers of employees for the top 25 global research organizations. Given this number, can you conclude that the way to increase revenues is to increase the number of employees at a company?

   DYS13-20

13.5 MAKING PREDICTIONS

One of the uses of regression analysis is prediction. For example, suppose Kate Cameron wants to predict what annual sales will be if she sets her advertising budget at $1,800.

We can get a point estimate of predicted sales by plugging an advertising value of $1,800 into the estimated regression relationship, as we did in Section 13.1 (see page 484).

   Predicted sales

   $= 35.167(\$1{,}800) + \$6{,}291.70$

   $= \$69{,}592.30$

This point estimate is not necessarily accurate, and so an interval estimate is preferred, as it was when we estimated means and proportions.

There are two sources of error in the prediction of sales, based on a specific level of advertising.

1. The first source of error is the sampling error that results when we estimate the true population relationship between sales and advertising from sample data. The regression line we create from the sample data may not match the true population regression line. Remember, the population regression line is $\mu_y = \beta_0 + \beta_1 x$, and the estimate of $\hat{y} = b_0 + b_1 x$ is unlikely to match it exactly.

2. The second source of error is the variation of the points around the regression line. Remember, we assumed a normal distribution of possible sales values for each level of advertising (see Exhibit 13.13 on page 490), with a standard deviation of σ_ε.

If the regression model fits the data fairly well and the required conditions are met, we can use the regression model to make two kinds of predictions. A **regression prediction interval** predicts a particular value of y (sales) for a specific value of x

Regression prediction interval
Interval that predicts a particular value of y for a specific value of x.

Regression confidence interval
Interval that predicts the average y for a specific value of x.

(advertising of $1,800 in the example above). A **regression confidence interval** predicts the average y (sales) for a specific value of x (advertising of $1,800 in the example above). This is essentially an estimate of the location of one point on the true regression line. As first discussed in Chapter 8, interval estimates have a general form, as follows:

(point estimate) $\pm$ (critical value) $\cdot$ (estimated standard error of the sample statistic)

The interval estimates based on the regression model follow this same format.

The formula for a prediction interval for y, given a particular x (call it x_0) is:

$$\hat{y} \pm (t\text{-score})s_\varepsilon \sqrt{1 + \frac{1}{n} + \frac{(x_0 - \bar{x})^2}{\Sigma(x - \bar{x})^2}}, \text{ where the } t\text{-distribution has } n - 2 \text{ degrees of freedom}$$

The formula for a confidence interval for μ_y, given a particular x (call it x_0) is:

$$\hat{y} \pm (t\text{-score})s_\varepsilon \sqrt{\frac{1}{n} + \frac{(x_0 - \bar{x})^2}{\Sigma(x - \bar{x})^2}}, \text{ where the } t\text{-distribution has } n - 2 \text{ degrees of freedom}$$

There is no built-in **Data Analysis** function in Excel to calculate these interval estimates for you.

The Excel add-in called **Multiple Regression Tools** will do the calculations for you.[4] Once the add-ins are installed (see page xxx for instructions about installing Excel add-ins), you can access these tools through the **Add-Ins** tab in Excel. Before you do this, you should type the specific value of the explanatory variable that is the basis of your intervals into a cell in the spreadsheet containing the sample data. For example, if you want to create confidence and prediction interval estimates for Woodbon sales when advertising is $1,800, you will have to type the specific advertising value of $1,800 into a cell in the spreadsheet. While you can type the specific value anywhere you like in the spreadsheet,

EXHIBIT 13.41

Typing in Specific Value of Explanatory Variable as Basis for Intervals

	A	B	C	D	E	F	G
1	Woodbon						
2	Year	Advertising Expenditure	Sales				
3	1980	$500	$26,345	1			
4	1981	$695	$31,987	2			
5	1982	$765	$21,334	3			
6	1983	$890	$25,584	4			
27	2004	$2,500	$101,760	25			
28	2005	$2,700	$95,400	26			
29	2006	$3,500	$115,320	27			
30	2007	$3,200	$108,550	28			
31		$1,800		Specific Value of Advertising for Intervals			

[4] The Multiple Regression Tools add-in was first designed to supplement Excel for Chapter 14, which covers multiple regression, and this explains the name. The Confidence and Predictions Intervals Tool also works with simple linear regression.

it is a good habit to type it at the bottom of the column of explanatory variable data, with an appropriate label. Exhibit 13.41 illustrates (note that some of the rows of data have been hidden in the worksheet).

When you click on **Multiple Regression Tools**, under the **Add-Ins** Tab, you will see the window shown in Exhibit 13.42.

EXHIBIT **13.42**

Multiple Regression Tools Add-In

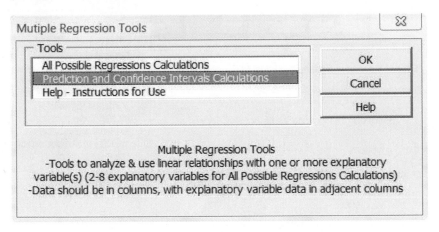

In the exhibit, the correct choice has been highlighted: **Prediction and Confidence Intervals Calculations**. When you select it and click **OK**, the dialogue box shown in Exhibit 13.43 on the next page will be activated.

You are required to:

1. Input the locations of the response (y) and explanatory (x) variable labels (Sales for the response variable for the Woodbon data, and Advertising Expenditure for the explanatory variable).
2. Input the locations of the response (y) and explanatory (x) variable values.
3. Input the location of the specific value of the explanatory (x) variable value(s) on which you want to base the confidence and interval estimates. Note that you can input several specific values (e.g., $1,800 and $2,000) if you wish. The specific values must be in a column, and it is a good habit to type them at the bottom of the column of explanatory variable data, with an appropriate label, as shown in Exhibit 13.41.
4. Choose a confidence level (% format).
5. Specify an output range (the default is a new worksheet).

Once you fill in the details, and click **OK**, the output will be as shown in Exhibit 13.44 (note that columns have been resized for visibility).

From the output we see that the prediction interval is ($49,989.12, $89,194.37). We have 95% confidence that this interval contains the sales level that corresponds to an advertising budget of $1,800. This interval is quite wide, and probably too wide to be very useful. The width of the interval is not very surprising, because we already observed a fair amount of variability in the data.

The output also shows the confidence interval limits for the average value of sales, given advertising of $1,800.

EXHIBIT 13.43

Prediction and Confidence Intervals—Calculations Dialogue Box

Prediction and Confidence Intervals for Regession Calculations   ✕

Response Variable Label (one) | ▭

Explanatory Variable Label(s) ▭

Help
Cancel
OK

Response Variable Values ▭

Explanatory Variable Values ▭

Specific Value(s) of Explanatory Variable(s)

Location of Specific Value(s) ▭

Prediction and Confidence Level (%) [95]

Use:
Generates prediction & confidence intervals, given specific values for the explanatory variables in a particular regression model. Type specific explanatory variable value(s) at the bottom of the column(s) of explanatory variable data. You may use 1-8 explanatory variables.

Output Options

○ Output Range ▭

● New Worksheet

EXHIBIT 13.44

Prediction and Confidence Intervals–Calculations Result for Woodbon Data

Confidence Interval and Prediction Intervals - Calculations					
Point	95% = Confidence Level (%)	Prediction Interval		Confidence Interval	
Number	Advertising Expenditure	Lower limit	Upper limit	Lower limit	Upper limit
1	1800	49989.12445	89194.3679	65945.27475	73238.2176

We have 95% confidence that the interval ($65,945.27, $73,238.22) contains the average sales when advertising is $1,800.

There are a couple of things to note about prediction intervals and confidence intervals:

1. Prediction intervals for y given a particular x are always wider (less precise) than confidence intervals for the average y given a particular x. The interval has to be wider to account for the distribution of y-values around the regression line in the population model (see Exhibit 13.13 on page 490).
2. Both intervals are narrowest at the $(\bar{x}, \bar{y})$ point on the regression line. Both intervals get wider for x-values that are farther from $\bar{x}$. This is illustrated in Exhibit 13.45 opposite.

It is disappointing to have done all of the work involved in analyzing the Woodbon data, only to find that the prediction interval is so wide that it is not

EXHIBIT 13.45

Confidence and Prediction Intervals

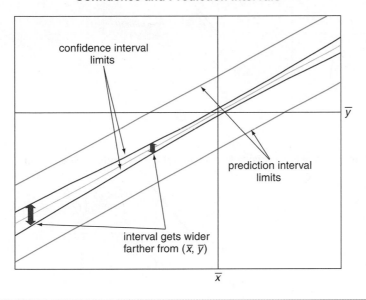

Confidence and Prediction Intervals

particularly useful. This can happen in regression analysis. The initial assessment of the data looked promising. The hypothesis test supported a conclusion that there is a linear relationship between advertising and sales. As well, the R^2-value was 0.88, which is fairly high. However, the amount of variability in the data is large, and so the predictions are not precise. The standard error was $9,370, which is fairly large, for this data set.

One further point should be made about prediction and confidence intervals based on regression analysis.

> **Caution About Making Predictions with Regression Models**
>
> It is not legitimate to make predictions with a regression model for x-values outside the range of the sample data.

Even a powerful regression relationship with a high coefficient of determination and low standard error should not be relied on outside the range of the sample data. Exhibits 13.46a and b illustrate why this is so.

The regression equation shown in the graphs could be quite useful for the range of data from the original sample, even though the true relationship is not a straight-line relationship. The error arises when the regression relationship is used for an x-value outside this range; as illustrated, the error can be quite large.

EXHIBIT 13.46

a) Sample Data and Regression Equation

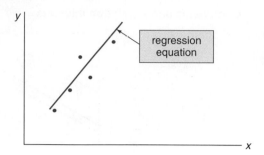

b) Population Data and Error Arising from Incorrect Use of Regression Equation

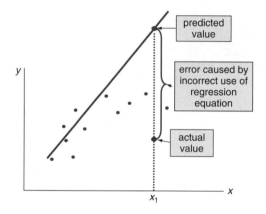

EXAMPLE 13.5

Calculating a confidence interval
estimate for an average *y*, given *x*

EXA13-5

Calculate a 98% confidence interval estimate for the average number of cookies Jack would sell at his convenience store if he set the cookie price at 75¢.

Before this confidence interval estimate is calculated, we must first check that the required conditions are met.

A scatter diagram of the data looks fairly linear. The residual plot produced by Excel indicates reasonably constant variability in the residuals, although there is one unusually negative residual. The observations were collected over time, but the dates are not available, so we cannot check for independence against time. There are no standardized residuals $\geq +2$ or ≤ -2, and there are no obvious influential observations. There are too few data points to create a histogram of residuals, but if we sort the residuals, we get the result shown in Exhibit 13.47 opposite.

It is always difficult to judge normality for a small data set. However, this one appears to be skewed to the left, with one unusually negative residual (-4.44961), and a "clump" of three residuals above but fairly close to 2.

In this case, it appears that the sample data do not meet the requirements of the theoretical model. Therefore, we will not produce a confidence interval, since it would not be reliable.

EXHIBIT **13.47**

Ordered Residuals for Data on Cookies at Jack's Convenience Store

−4.44961
−2.12403
−1.76357
−0.1124
−0.08915
1.53876
2.213178
2.224806
2.562016

DEVELOP YOUR SKILLS **13.5**

21. If appropriate, create a 98% confidence interval for the average sales at the Hendrick Software Sales Company, for 10 sales contacts.
DYS13-21

22. If appropriate, create a 95% prediction interval for the amount of monthly spending on restaurant meals, based on a monthly income of $6,000.
DYS13-22

23. If appropriate, create a 90% confidence interval for average sales when promotion spending is $10,000.
DYS13-23

24. If appropriate, create a 95% confidence interval for the average semester average mark, for students who work 200 hours during the semester.
DYS13-24

25. If appropriate, create a 99% prediction interval for the total revenue of a global research company with 10,000 employees.
DYS13-25

Chapter Summary

13

Creating a Graph and Determining the Relationship

The first step in analyzing a relationship between two variables is to create a scatter diagram, with the dependent (response) variable plotted on the y-axis, and the independent (explanatory) variable plotted on the x-axis.

The equation of a straight line that best fits the points on the scatter diagram is of the form $\hat{y} = b_0 + b_1 x$. The coefficients b_0 and b_1 result from minimizing the sum of the squared residuals for the line. A residual is the difference between the observed value of y for a given x and the predicted value of y for that x ($e_i = y_i - \hat{y}_i$). The coefficients of the least-squares line can be determined with Excel, either with the **Add Trendline** tool (see page 483) or the **Regression** tool of **Data Analysis** (see page 485).

Assessing the Model

Theoretically, there is a normal distribution of possible y-values for every x. The population relationship in which we are interested is the average y for every x, as follows:

$$\mu_y = \beta_0 + \beta_1 x$$

We cannot reliably make predictions with the regression equation, or conduct a hypothesis test to see if there is a significant relationship between the x- and y-variables, unless certain conditions are met (these are summarized in the box on page 491). We check these conditions by focusing on the residuals in the sample data set. See the Guide to Technique on page 504 for checking the requirements for the regression model.

Hypothesis Test About the Regression Relationship

Once we have assured ourselves that the required conditions are met, we can test to see whether there is a significant linear relationship between the x- and y-variables. This is done with a test of the slope of the line, β_1. The null hypothesis of no relationship ($\beta_1 = 0$) is tested against one of three possible alternatives:

- $\beta_1 \neq 0$ (there is some relationship between x and y)
- $\beta_1 > 0$ (there is a positive relationship between x and y)
- $\beta_1 < 0$ (there is a negative relationship between x and y)

The output of Excel's **Data Analysis** tool called **Regression** provides the t-score and p-value for the two-tailed version of this test. See page 507 for instructions on how to read the output.

The Guide to Decision Making for testing the slope of the regression line is shown on page 509.

How Good Is the Regression?

The Pearson r, the correlation coefficient, can be used to measure the degree of linear association between the x- and y-variables, as discussed in Chapter 3 (see page 132).

Another related measure is the coefficient of determination, or R^2. The coefficient of determination measures the percentage of variation in the y-variable that is explained by changes in the x-variable. The coefficient of determination is produced in Excel's **Regression** output (see page 511 for instructions on how to read the output). It is important to recognize that "explained by" is not the same as "caused by." Even though the R^2 may be high, the true causal relationship can only be judged on the basis of an understanding of the context of the data.

Making Predictions

Two types of predictions can be made, if the requirements are met. A regression prediction interval predicts a particular value of y for a given value of x. A regression confidence interval predicts the average y for a given value of x.

The formula for a prediction interval for y, given a particular x (call it x_0) is:

$$\hat{y} \pm (t\text{-score})s_\varepsilon \sqrt{1 + \frac{1}{n} + \frac{(x_0 - \bar{x})^2}{\Sigma(x - \bar{x})^2}}$$

The formula for a confidence interval for μ_y, given a particular x (call it x_0) is:

$$\hat{y} \pm (t\text{-score})s_\varepsilon \sqrt{\frac{1}{n} + \frac{(x_0 - \bar{x})^2}{\Sigma(x - \bar{x})^2}}$$

There is no built-in **Data Analysis** function in Excel to calculate these interval estimates. The Excel add-in called **Multiple Regression Tools** contains a tool called **Prediction and Confidence Intervals Calculations**, which creates confidence and prediction intervals based on a specific value (or values) of the explanatory variable. See the Excel instructions on page 514. Always remember that it is not legitimate to make predictions outside the range of the sample data.

Go to MyStatLab at www.mathxl.com. You can practise the exercises indicated with red in the Develop Your Skills and Chapter Review Exercises as often as you want, and guided solutions will help you find answers step by step. You'll find a personalized study plan available to you too!

CHAPTER REVIEW EXERCISES

WARM-UP EXERCISES

1. Why is it necessary to check conditions *before* conducting a hypothesis test about the regression relationship?

2. Why are regression prediction intervals wider than confidence intervals?

3. Why is a lower standard error (s_ε) preferred?

4. Why is it not recommended to make predictions outside the range of the sample data on which the regression relationship is based?

5. Why should you think carefully about any obvious outlier in the sample data set for a regression relationship, rather than simply removing it?

THINK AND DECIDE USING EXCEL

6. What determines the price of a used car? One of the factors is the odometer reading. A data set of the number of kilometres on the odometer and the asking price for a 2006 small sedan with an automatic transmission is available. Create a scatter diagram for the data set, and describe the relationship between the two variables, both generally and mathematically.

CRE13-6

7. For the data set of odometer readings and asking price of used cars described in Exercise 6, check the requirements for regression. Would it be appropriate to use the odometer reading to predict the asking price for these used cars? If so, predict the asking price for one of these cars that has 50,000 kilometres on the odometer (with 95% confidence).

8. The Standard and Poor's Toronto Stock Exchange Composite Price Index (TSX) measures the performance of the broad Canadian stock market. The Dow Jones Industrial Average (DJI) tracks the performance of the U.S. stock market. Are the values of the two indexes

CRE13-8

related? A data set of the values of the two indexes for the period from January 2nd to June 26th, 2009, is available.[5] Create a scatter diagram of these data, and estimate the relationship.

9. What is the coefficient of determination for the data set of the TSX and the DJI described in Exercise 8? Interpret it.

10. Check the requirements for regression for the data set of the TSX and the DJI described in Exercise 8. Is this data set a random sample?

CRE13-11

11. A Statistics professor wants to know whether a student's mark on the second Statistics test is a good indicator of the student's mark on the final exam. She records the two marks for a random sample of students. Create a scatter diagram, and estimate and interpret the relationship between the two variables.

12. Check the requirements for regression for the data set of student marks on the second test and the final exam in a Statistics course, described in Exercise 11.

13. An excerpt from Excel's regression output for the data set of student marks on the second test and the final exam in a Statistics course, described in Exercise 11, is shown below in Exhibit 13.48. Using the output, test for evidence of a positive slope between the two variables, with $\alpha = 5\%$.

EXHIBIT 13.48

Excel Regression Output, Student Marks

SUMMARY OUTPUT

Regression Statistics	
Multiple R	0.960374126
R Square	0.922318462
Adjusted R Square	0.918941003
Standard Error	5.190203209
Observations	25

ANOVA

	df	SS	MS	F
Regression	1	7356.303585	7356.304	273.0806
Residual	23	619.578815	26.93821	
Total	24	7975.8824		

	Coefficients	Standard Error	t Stat	P-value
Intercept	0.446442941	3.590600937	0.124337	0.902129
Mark on Test #2	0.958643709	0.058011189	16.52515	2.96E-14

14. a. If appropriate, construct a 95% confidence interval estimate for the average exam mark of students who had a mark of 65% on the second test of a Statistics course (using the data set described in Exercise 11).
    b. If appropriate, construct a 95% interval estimate for the exam mark of a student who received 65% on the second test of a Statistics course (using the data set described in Exercise 11). How does this compare with the estimate for the average exam mark of students who had a mark of 65% on the second test (your answer to Exercise 14a)? Why is there a difference?

CRE13-15

15. Aries Car Parts maintains inventory of a wide array of car parts. The owner is old-fashioned, and has not allowed computers to be used in the business, so records are kept manually. An

---

[5] *Source*: Yahoo! Finance Canada, "Dow Jones Industrial Average (^DJI) Historical Prices, June 29, 2009," **http://ca.finance.yahoo.com/q/hp?s5%5EDJI**, accessed June 29, 2009, and "S&P/TSX Composite Index (Interi (^GSPTSE) Historical Prices, June 29, 2009," **http://ca.finance.yahoo.com/q/hp?s5% 5EGSPTSE**, accessed June 29, 2009.

auditor has calculated the actual value of inventory for a random sample of car parts, and has compared this with the recorded value. Create a scatter diagram, and estimate and interpret the relationship between the two variables. If the inventory records are generally accurate, what would you expect the slope of the line to be?

16. Check the requirements for regression for the data set of actual and recorded inventory values for Aries Car Parts from Exercise 15. When the auditor examined the relationship, he noticed two outliers, for observations 1 and 25 (why are these outliers?). Careful double-checking made the auditor realize that he had misread the written records for both data points. The recorded parts inventory for observation 1 is actually $446.23, and for observation 25 is $584.04. Amend the data set accordingly, and repeat your analysis.

17. If appropriate, test for evidence of a linear relationship between the actual and recorded inventory values for Aries Car Parts (using the amended data set from Exercise 16). Use $\alpha = 0.05$.

18. Interpret the coefficient of determination for the data on actual and recorded inventory values for Aries Car Parts (using the amended data set from Exercise 16). Does this give you confidence in the recorded inventory values?

19. What is the relationship between revenue and profit? A random sample of the top 1,000 Canadian companies was selected, and revenue and profit for 2008 were recorded.[6] Create a scatter diagram, and comment on the relationship. What is the coefficient of determination for this data set? Does the high value mean that a linear relationship is a good model in this case? CRE13-19

20. A large company has developed a written test to screen applicants, and the mark on this test has been a good predictor of employee suitability for the graduates that are hired. Because administering the test is time-consuming and costly, the company is wondering if it is worthwhile. One cheaper option is to rely on the overall average mark of the graduate as an indicator of suitability. An analyst has collected data on the overall average mark of a number of interviewees, and their scores (out of 70) on the company test. Create a scatter diagram for the data. Does it appear that there is a relationship between the two variables? Describe it, generally and mathematically. CRE13-20

21. Check the requirements for regression for the data set of overall average marks and company test scores from Exercise 20.

22. An excerpt of the Excel Regression output for the data set in Exercise 20 is shown in Exhibit 13.49 on the next page. If appropriate, use the output to test for evidence of a positive relationship between overall average marks and company test scores for this data set.

23. If appropriate, create a 98% confidence interval estimate for the average test score of graduates with an overall average mark of 75, based on the data set described in Exercise 20.

24. If appropriate, create a 98% interval estimate to predict the test score of a student with an overall average mark of 75, based on the data set describe in Exercise 20. Do you think the company should continue to administer its own test in interviewing graduates?

25. Exhibit 13.50 on the next page shows the residual plot for a data set on package weight in kilograms and shipping cost. Do you think it is appropriate to use package weight as a predictor of shipping cost? CRE13-25

TEST YOUR KNOWLEDGE

26. It is often suggested that the Canadian stock market is very closely tied to the price of oil. Now you will get a chance to test whether this is true. A data set containing weekly values of the Toronto Stock Exchange Composite Index and the Canadian spot price of oil, in dollars per barrel, is available.[7] CRE13-26

[6] *Source*: "Rankings by Profit," *The Globe and Mail, Report on Business,* July/August 2009, pp. 64–78.
[7] *Source*: Energy Information Administration, "World Crude Oil Prices (Dollars per Barrel, June 24, 2009," **http://tonto.eia.doe.gov/dnav/pet/pet_pri_wco_k_w.htm**, accessed June 29, 2009. Yahoo! Finance Canada, "S&P/TSX Composite Index (Interi (^GSPTSE) Historical Prices, June 29, 2009," **http://ca. finance.yahoo.com/q/hp?s5%5EGSPTSE**, accessed June 29, 2009.

EXHIBIT 13.49

Excel Regression Output, Screening Test

SUMMARY OUTPUT		
Regression Statistics		
Multiple R	0.893821487	
R Square	0.798916851	
Adjusted R Square	0.791735309	
Standard Error	3.644976125	
Observations	30	
ANOVA		
	df	*SS*
Regression	1	1477.996173
Residual	28	372.0038266
Total	29	1850
	Coefficients	*Standard Error*
Intercept	4.977460601	4.695268235
Final Average Mark	0.642104515	0.060878474

EXHIBIT 13.50

Residuals for Shipping Cost and Package Weight

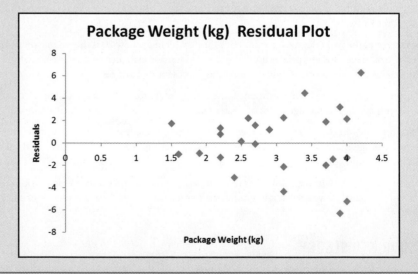

Do a complete analysis of the relationship between these two variables. Check the conditions and, if appropriate, predict the average TSX Composite Index for an oil price of $65 per barrel. Write a short report summarizing your findings, and comment on whether the data support the idea that the Canadian stock market is closely tied to the price of oil.

CHAPTER 14

Analyzing Linear Relationships, Two or More Variables

INTRODUCTION

In the previous chapter, we introduced Kate Cameron, the owner of Woodbon, a company that produces high-quality wooden furniture. Kate wanted to understand why sales have grown steadily over recent years, with an eye to planning for the future. After carefully checking required conditions for the analysis, Kate created a mathematical model of the relationship between Woodbon's sales and advertising. While there did seem to be a significant relationship between the two variables, the variability in the predictions meant that the model was not that useful for predicting sales.

The discussion in the previous chapter was a useful introduction to analyzing relationships between two variables. However, a more realistic process would begin with Kate analyzing the relationship between Woodbon's sales and a number of possible explanatory variables. Some that have already been mentioned are housing starts and mortgage rates. Kate would likely examine a number of possible explanatory variables, with the aim of developing a model that is economical (that is, has reasonable data requirements) and works well (that is, makes useful predictions).

LEARNING OBJECTIVES

After mastering the material in this chapter, you will be able to:

1 Estimate the linear relationship between a quantitative response variable and one or more explanatory variables.

2 Check the conditions required for use of the regression model in hypothesis testing and prediction.

3 Assess the regression relationship, using appropriate hypothesis tests and a coefficient of determination.

4 Make predictions using the regression relationship.

5 Understand the considerations involved in choosing the "best" regression model, and the challenges presented by multicollinearity.

6 Use indicator variables to model qualitative explanatory variables.

Section 14.1 builds on the discussion in Chapter 13, to extend the mathematical model to include more than one explanatory variable. A reasonable way to start is with some careful thinking about what other factors could most reasonably be expected to affect Woodbon's sales. For more complex models, it is crucial to have computer software to do the calculations, and you will see how to use Excel to build the mathematical model.

Section 14.2 extends the theoretical model from the last chapter to include more explanatory variables, revisiting the discussion about least-squares models. As before, we will use Excel to check the required conditions for the regression model.

Section 14.3 introduces hypothesis tests about the significance of the overall model, and the individual explanatory variables. We will also discuss a measure of the strength of the relationship between the explanatory variables and the response variables, the adjusted coefficient of determination (adjusted R^2).

Section 14.4 describes an Excel add-in that you can use to make predictions of average and individual response variables, given specific values of the explanatory variables in the model.

In Section 14.5, we will discuss an approach to selecting the best explanatory variables for our regression model. Kate will want to develop a model of sales that makes good predictions, but the simplest model that does a good job will be preferred. Selecting the appropriate explanatory variables is an art as well as a science. An Excel add-in that produces a summary of all possible models will be introduced.

In Section 14.5, we will look at ways to assess and deal with a new problem that may arise when there is more than one explanatory variable. This problem is usually referred to as "multicollinearity," and it occurs when one of the explanatory variables is related to one or more of the other explanatory variables.

It is possible to include qualitative explanatory variables in regression models, and Section 14.6 illustrates the use of indicator variables to accomplish this.

Section 14.7 refers briefly to more advanced models, so that you can get a sense of the wide variety of mathematical modelling possibilities.

 14.1

DETERMINING THE RELATIONSHIP—MULTIPLE LINEAR REGRESSION

In Chapter 13, Kate Cameron examined the relationship between advertising spending and sales. This simple linear regression model served as an introduction to the techniques of linear regression modelling.

It seems reasonable to think that there is a cause-and-effect relationship between advertising and sales. Kate is also wondering if sales are significantly affected by other explanatory variables. In particular, she is wondering about three others:

- Mortgage rates may affect a household's ability to buy furniture. Kate expects the relationship to be negative, that is, when mortgage rates are higher, she would expect a household to have less income available to buy wooden furniture.

- Housing starts may also be related to sales. When more houses are being built, more households might buy Woodbon's furniture. There is a fairly long lead time for a customer to take delivery of Woodbon's furniture, so housing starts may be a useful explanatory variable.
- Kate has been exploring Statistics Canada data, and has discovered a series of "leading indicators." In particular, she has identified a leading indicator for retail trade in furniture and appliances. Although the indicator is for Canada as a whole, Kate is wondering if it can give her some insight into Woodbon's sales.

Creating Graphs to Examine the Relationships Between the Response Variable and the Explanatory Variables

Kate begins by collecting data for the three additional (potential) explanatory variables. She finds Statistics Canada data for housing starts in New Brunswick[1] (Woodbon is located in Saint John, and delivers throughout the province). The data are available on a quarterly basis. Kate decides to add up the quarterly numbers so she can relate annual housing starts to annual sales.

Statistics Canada provides data on a variety of mortgage interest rates, and Kate decides to work with mortgage rates for five-year conventional mortgages at chartered banks. Statistics Canada provides data about monthly mortgage rates[2] (based on the last Wednesday of the month). Kate could simply use the mortgage rate for one month of the year to represent mortgage rates for that year (e.g., the January or June mortgage rates). In general, it is simplest to use the available data in raw form to build models. In this case, Kate decides to compute a simple average of the monthly rates to create a data series of annual average mortgage rates.

An excerpt of the data set, including data on sales and advertising, is shown on the next page in Exhibit 14.1. The complete data set is available in an Excel file called SEC14-2.

 SEC14-2

Initially, it can be useful to create scatter diagrams to explore the relationship between sales and each one of the potential explanatory variables. The four scatter diagrams are shown in Exhibit 14.2.

We have already established (in Chapter 13) that there is a positive association between Woodbon's advertising expenditure and sales. From the scatter diagrams we can see that there is a negative relationship between Woodbon sales and mortgage interest rates, as expected. There appears to be a positive relationship between Woodbon sales and the Canada-wide leading indicator for retail trade in furniture and appliances, although it may not be linear. There is a somewhat curved appearance to the plot, which flattens out for higher levels of the leading indicator.[3] There does not appear to be much of a relationship between Woodbon sales and housing starts in New Brunswick. However, this does not necessarily mean that housing starts will not be useful in the regression model. This variable, in conjunction with others, could still potentially improve the model's predictions.

---

[1] Statistics Canada, "CMHC, Housing Starts, under Construction and Completions, All Areas; New Brunswick; Housing Starts; Total Units; Unadjusted (units) [J15005]," CANSIM Table 027-0008, **www.statcan.gc.ca**, accessed October 13, 2008.

[2] Statistics Canada, "Financial Market Statistics, Last Wednesday Unless Otherwise Stated, Monthly (percent)(1), Bank of Canada – 7502 Rates (Percent) Chartered Bank – Conventional Mortgage: 5 year," CANSIM Table 176-0043, **www.statcan.gc.ca**, accessed October 13, 2008.

[3] It is possible to model non-linear relationships, but this is a more advanced topic.

EXHIBIT 14.1

Woodbon Sales and Explanatory Variable Data

				Leading Indicator (Retail Trade, Furniture and Appliances, Canada)	
Year	Mortgage Rates	Housing Starts (New Brunswick)	Advertising Expenditure		Sales
1980	14.52083	2,646	$ 500	599	$ 26,345
1981	18.37500	2,188	$ 695	639	$ 31,987
1982	18.04167	1,680	$ 765	577	$ 21,334
⋮	⋮	⋮	⋮	⋮	⋮
2004	6.23333	3,947	$2,500	2,014	$101,760
2005	5.99167	3,959	$2,700	2,195	$ 95,400
2006	6.66250	4,085	$3,500	2,515	$115,320
2007	7.07083	4,242	$3,200	2,648	$108,550

Table header: Woodbon Mortgage Rates, Housing Starts, Advertising Expenditure, Leading Indicator, and Sales, 1980–2007

EXHIBIT 14.2

Scatter Diagrams for Woodbon Sales and Explanatory Variable Data

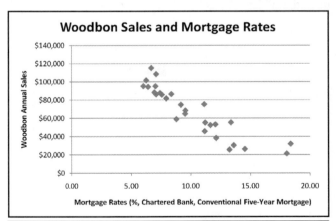

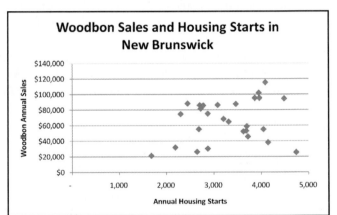

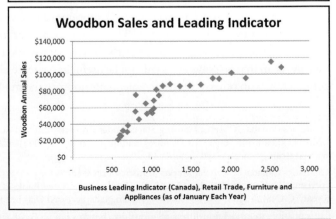

Determining the Relationship Between the Response Variable and the Explanatory Variables

We will begin our analysis by adding all of the new explanatory variables to create a new multiple regression model. The model is built using Excel's **Data Analysis Regression** tool, as illustrated in Chapter 13. The only difference is that more than one explanatory variable will be selected for **Input _X_ Range:**. It is highly recommended that you include labels when selecting the data in Excel, because it will make the output much easier to read. Exhibit 14.3 illustrates.

EXHIBIT 14.3

Excel Regression Dialogue Box

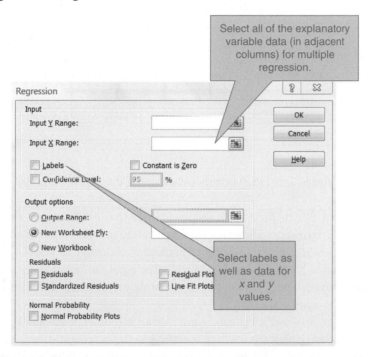

The Woodbon output for the regression model is shown on the next page in Exhibit 14.4. At first glance, this model looks promising. The R^2 value is 0.955. The mathematical relationship from the regression model is as follows:

$$\text{Woodbon annual sales} = \$89,159.92 - \$3,814.57 \text{ (mortgage rate)} - \$6.40 \text{ (housing starts)} + \$14.71 \text{ (advertising expenditure)} + \$10.44 \text{ (leading indicator)}$$

How do we interpret this mathematical model?

1. The intercept $89,159.92 is an estimate of average Woodbon sales when all of the explanatory variables have a value of zero. This number does not have a practical interpretation, because it is highly unlikely, for example, that mortgage rates would ever be zero. Additionally, a regression model should never be applied for values of the explanatory variables that are outside of the ranges in the data set used to build

EXHIBIT 14.4

Excel Regression Output for Woodbon Sales and Explanatory Variable Data (All Variables Included)

Regression Statistics					
Multiple R	0.977269651				
R Square	0.955055971				
Adjusted R Square	0.947239618				
Standard Error	6251.003405				
Observations	28				

ANOVA					
	df	SS	MS	F	Significance F
Regression	4	19097834678	4774458670	122.186906	3.83971E-15
Residual	23	898726002.1	39075043.57		
Total	27	19996560680			

	Coefficients	Standard Error	t Stat	P-value	Lower 95%	Upper 95%
Intercept	89159.92438	14444.22871	6.172702342	2.6863E-06	59279.7609	119040.0879
Mortgage Rates	-3814.56869	690.1923678	-5.52681958	1.275E-05	-5242.340378	-2386.79701
Housing Starts	-6.39732635	1.837777835	-3.48101181	0.00201934	-10.19905943	-2.59559327
Advertising Expenditure	14.71076331	6.518471372	2.256781148	0.03382727	1.226277974	28.19524865
Leading Indicator	10.44591571	6.900630411	1.513762524	0.14370781	-3.829125824	24.72095724

the model, and none of the variable values in the data set for Woodbon was even close to zero.

2. The mortgage rate coefficient can be interpreted as follows. If all values of the other variables are fixed at specific levels, there would be a decrease in Woodbon's average sales by $3,814.57 for each 1% increase in the conventional five-year mortgage rates at the chartered banks. It seems reasonable that higher mortgage rates would leave less money available to households for spending on furniture, and so the negative relationship makes sense.

3. The housing starts coefficient can be interpreted as follows. If all values of the other explanatory variables are fixed at specific levels, there would be a decrease in Woodbon's average sales by $6.40 for each additional housing start in New Brunswick. We would have expected that furniture spending would increase, not decrease, with additional housing starts. However, it is important to recognize that this coefficient applies only when all of the other explanatory variables are included in the model. There may be some interaction between housing starts and one or more of the other explanatory variables that results in a coefficient of the "wrong" sign. Remember, there did not appear to be a strong relationship between Woodbon's sales and housing starts in the first place. The fact that the sign on the coefficient is "wrong" increases our suspicion that this "explanatory" variable may not actually explain very much about Woodbon's sales.

4. The advertising expenditure coefficient indicates that each additional dollar in advertising spending results in an increase of $14.71 in Woodbon's annual sales, when all other variables held the same. Note that this coefficient is different from the $35.17 value in the regression model based on advertising expenditure alone (see Chapter 13 page 484).

It appears that the "all-in" model has some difficulties. Normally, we might stop and rethink at this point. However, we will continue analyzing this model, because it will give us the opportunity to discuss relationships which both do and do not meet the required conditions of the theoretical linear regression model.

DEVELOP YOUR SKILLS 14.1

The Develop Your Skills exercises in this chapter frequently refer to a data set called "Salaries."

1. For the Salaries data set, create scatter diagrams showing the relationship between each possible explanatory variable and salaries. Are there any obvious problems? Are there some variables that seem particularly strong as candidates for explanatory variables?

2. For the Salaries data set, create a multiple regression model that includes all the possible explanatory variables. Interpret this model. Are there any obvious difficulties with this model?

3. Create a scatter diagram showing the relationship between age and years of experience. Does it seem sensible to include both of these explanatory variables in the model?

4. Create a multiple regression model for the Salaries data set that includes years of postsecondary education and age as explanatory variables. Interpret the model.

5. Create a multiple regression model for the Salaries data set that includes years of postsecondary education and years of experience as explanatory variables. Interpret the model.

14.2   CHECKING THE REQUIRED CONDITIONS

The Theoretical Model

In Chapter 13, we described how the least-squares line was created, as a best fit between the explanatory and response variables. The theoretical relationship was

$$y = \beta_0 + \beta_1 x + \varepsilon$$

This indicated that the y-value could be predicted from x. The ε term reminds us that we do not expect the prediction to be perfect. There may be some unexplained or random variation in the y-values that cannot be predicted from the x-values.

The corresponding notation for the regression relationship based on sample data is

$$\hat{y} = b_0 + b_1 x$$

The coefficients b_0 and b_1 were arrived at by minimizing the sum of the squared residuals for the data set, that is

$$\text{SSE} = \sum (y_i - \hat{y}_i)^2$$

Now we extend the model so that it includes more explanatory variables:

$$y = \beta_0 + \beta_1 x_1 + \beta_2 x_2 + \cdots + \beta_k x_k + \varepsilon$$

The corresponding notation for the relationship based on sample data is

$$\hat{y} = b_0 + b_1 x_1 + b_2 x_2 + \cdots + b_k x_k$$

Again, the coefficients are estimated by minimizing the sum of squared residuals, for all of the data points in the data set. This requires the use of advanced algebra, but the idea is the same as in Chapter 13. Essentially, this creates a multiple regression model where the predicted values are simultaneously as close as possible to the observed values.

When the model has one response variable and one explanatory variable, as in Chapter 13, we can think of the relationship as a line, because we are operating in two dimensions (x and y). When we have one response variable and k explanatory variables, we are operating in $k+1$ dimensions. With two explanatory variables, we can imagine a plane as the regression surface. With more than two explanatory variables, there is no way to picture the regression relationship.

Examining the Residuals

In Chapter 13, we saw that analysis of the residuals $(y_i - \hat{y}_i)$ was required to check whether the sample data appear to conform to the requirements of the least-squares regression model. As before, we can legitimately make predictions with the model, or perform hypothesis tests about the relationship between the y- and x-variables, only if these requirements are met.

Requirements for Predictions or Hypothesis Tests About the Multiple Regression Relationship

1. For any specific combination of the x-values, there are many possible values of y and the residual (or "error term") ε. The distribution of these ε-values must be normal for any specific combination of x-values. This means that the actual y-values will be normally distributed around the predicted y-values from the regression relationship, for every specific combination of x-values.

2. These normal distributions of ε-values must have a mean of zero. The actual y-values will have expected values, or means, that are equal to the predicted y-values from the regression relationship.

3. The standard deviation of the ε-values, which we refer to as σ_ε, is the same for every combination of x-values. The normal distributions of actual y-values around the predicted y-values from the regression relationship will have the same variability for every specific combination of x-values.

4. The ε-values for different combinations of the x-values are not related to each other. The value of the error term ε is statistically independent of any other value of ε.

As in Chapter 13, we create a number of residual plots to check these requirements. If they appear to be met in the sample data, we will assume they are met in the population. As usual, Excel is a great help in creating the required graphs. As before, in the **Regression** dialogue box, you should tick **Residuals**, **Standardized Residuals**, and **Residual Plots**. As in Chapter 13, you should create a histogram of the residuals, and you should plot the residuals against time if you have time-series data.

Variation in the Residuals Is Constant   A plot of the residuals against the predicted values from the model can give us an indication of whether the variability of the error term is constant. Such a plot can be created from the information created by Excel in the **Residual Output**, an excerpt of which is shown below in Exhibit 14.5 (note that some of the rows of data have been hidden in the worksheet).

EXHIBIT **14.5**

Excerpt of Excel Regression Output for Woodbon, Showing Residuals

RESIDUAL OUTPUT			
Observation	*Predicted Sales*	*Residuals*	*Standard Residuals*
1	30454.36781	-4109.37	-0.712267688
2	21968.79525	10018.2	1.736433405
3	26872.26659	-5538.27	-0.959935572
12	59828.247	15556.8	2.696417798
13	63476.35725	1449.64	0.251263391
25	97947.18162	3812.82	0.660867428
26	103625.1312	-8225.13	-1.425643909
27	115371.4319	-51.4319	-0.008914583
28	109785.5139	-1235.51	-0.214148915

The plot of residuals against predicted values is shown below in Exhibit 14.6. In Excel 2007, it is quite easy to produce this scatter diagram. Simply highlight the two adjacent columns (Predicted Sales and Residuals, in this case), and **Insert** a **Scatter** diagram.

EXHIBIT **14.6**

Plot of Residuals Against Predicted Sales, Woodbon

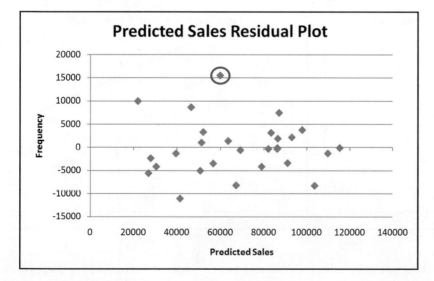

The requirement is that the variability of the error term is constant, so a residual plot with constant variability (a horizontal band, centred on zero vertically) is ideal. This residual plot does not show any particular pattern, and appears as a horizontal band. There is one residual that is unusually high (it is circled on the plot). This point corresponds to the data point for 1991.

It can also be helpful to plot the residuals against each individual *x*-variable, particularly if there appears to be a problem with the plot of the residuals against the predicted values. The additional plots can indicate which explanatory variables might be the source of any problem.

When **Residual Plots** is ticked as an option in Excel's **Data Analysis** tool for **Regression**, graphs are automatically created to show residuals against every *x*-variable in the model. The graphs for the Woodbon model are shown in Exhibit 14.7 below. Note that the graphs have been resized for visibility.

EXHIBIT 14.7

Residual Plots for Woodbon Multiple Regression Model

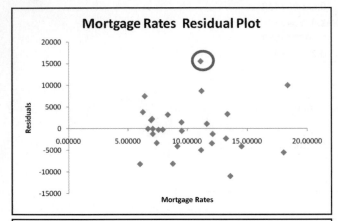

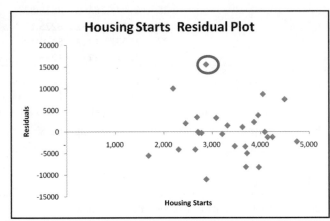

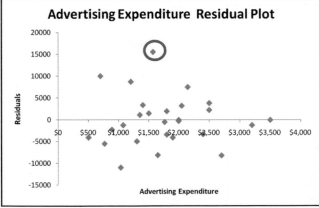

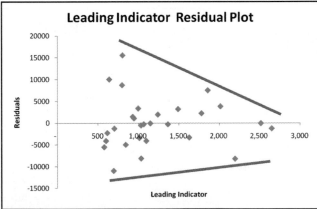

The mortgage rates residual plot has the desired horizontal band appearance, although there is one point (circled on the plot) where a residual seems unusually high. This is the data point for 1991, the same point that stood out in Exhibit 14.6.

The housing starts residual plot exhibits fairly constant variability in the residuals, although again there is one point (circled) that gives an unusually high residual. Again, this is the data point from 1991.

The advertising expenditure residual plot has something of a horizontal band appearance, although there does not seem to be as much variability in the residuals when the advertising expenditure is higher. Again, the data point for 1991 shows an unusually high residual.

The leading indicator residual plot gives the greatest cause for concern. This plot shows reduced variability in the error term for higher values of the leading indicator, and the pattern is more pronounced than for the advertising expenditure residual plot, although it is also affected by the 1991 data point. Remember that the scatter plot of sales against the leading indicator looked non-linear. The residual plot is consistent with the curved scatter diagram that we saw earlier. Since we are trying to build a linear multiple regression model, we may not be able to use this variable in its present form.

Independence of Error Terms   Plotting the residuals in the time order in which the data occurred allows us to check if the error terms are related over time. The Woodbon data set was arranged by year, so the residuals are also arranged by year.

A plot of the residuals over time is shown in Exhibit 14.8 below.

EXHIBIT 14.8

Plot of Residuals Over Time, Woodbon Model

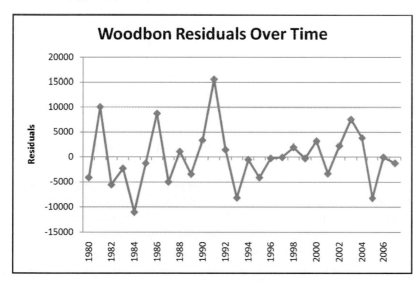

There does not appear to be any particular pattern in the residuals over time, and so it is reasonable to conclude that the residuals are independent over time.

Normality of Residuals   A histogram is created for the residuals, to check for normality. The histogram for the initial Woodbon model is shown on the next page in Exhibit 14.9.

The histogram appears to be approximately normal, although it is somewhat skewed to the right. As well, the histogram appears to be centred approximately around zero, which is desirable.

Outliers and Influential Observations   Outliers, that is, observations that are far from other observations, should always be investigated. Such points may be the result of

EXHIBIT 14.9

Histogram of Residuals for Woodbon Multiple Regression Model

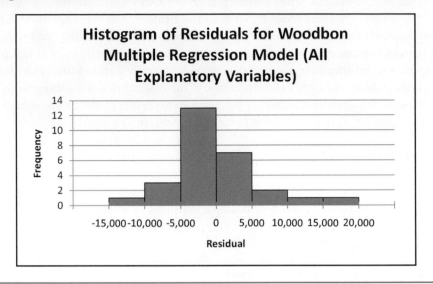

an error in observing or recording the data. If that is the case, and they are not corrected or removed, the result will be a model that is less correct than it could be. As before, a general rule is to investigate any observation with a standardized residual that is $\geq +2$ or ≤ -2. If you examine the **Residual Output** for the Woodbon model (see Exhibit 14.5 on page 533), you will see that there is one point that would be identified as an outlier, that is, observation 12. It is no surprise that data point 12 is the observation for 1991, given how often it has shown up as an unusual point in the residual plots. This data point is accurately recorded. There is no obvious reason why it does not belong in the data set. Therefore, we will not discard it.

An influential observation is one that has an extreme effect on the regression model. In the simple linear regression model discussed in Chapter 13, we could use scatter plots to identify such values. Influential observations are more difficult to locate in the multiple regression model, because the influence might come from just one *x*-variable, or a combination of them. There are several techniques available to help identify influential observations, and they can be found in more advanced texts. If you suspect that an observation is having an undue influence on the regression model, one way to check is to recalculate the model without the suspect observation. If the regression coefficients change significantly (a judgment call), then the observation is influential.

What If the Required Conditions Are Not Met?   The hypothesis tests and confidence intervals that will be described in Sections 14.3 and 14.5 are valid only if the data appear to meet the requirements for the linear regression model. If they do not, further work must be done before hypothesis tests are done or confidence intervals are calculated.

There exist more advanced techniques that could be used to solve some of the problems that arise. For example, it may be possible to transform the data by applying some mathematical function (such as a logarithm or square root) to the original data, and work with the new measurements. It may also be possible to build a useful model without including the variables that are responsible for the conditions not being met. It may be necessary to start over, to try to find explanatory variables that meet the requirements. It may also be useful to proceed, if the violation of the required conditions is not too pronounced. If the resulting model provides useful predictions, it may be the best we can do.

Before we proceed with our regression analysis, we will remove the leading indicator as an explanatory variable, as it does not meet the requirements for linear regression in its present form. In particular, the variability in the residuals is not constant. Especially when we are just beginning our analysis of a model, we should not necessarily discard explanatory variables that do not meet the requirements of a linear regression model, especially when they seem to be reasonable choices. As mentioned above, we may be able to transform the leading indicator data so that the model does meet the requirements for linear regression. However, the leading indicator data also presents other difficulties (see Section 14.5), so we will drop it now to streamline the discussion. As we will see later, choosing the best explanatory variables for any model is an art.

Once we use Excel to create a new regression model, we will see that the model better meets the required conditions for linear regression. Example 14.2 illustrates.

EXAMPLE **14.2**

Checking conditions for linear multiple regression

Use Excel to re-specify the multiple regression relationship between Woodbon sales and mortgage rates, housing starts, and advertising expenditure. Check to see that the new model meets the required conditions for hypothesis tests and confidence intervals.

The regression output for the new model is shown in Exhibit 14.10 below.

EXHIBIT **14.10**

Regression Output for Woodbon Model, with Mortgage Rates, Housing Starts, and Advertising Expenditure as Explanatory Variables

SUMMARY OUTPUT

Regression Statistics	
Multiple R	0.974976011
R Square	0.950578223
Adjusted R Square	0.944400501
Standard Error	6416.987757
Observations	28

ANOVA

	df	SS	MS	F	Significance F
Regression	3	19008295115	6336098372	153.871961	8.35857E-16
Residual	24	988265564.9	41177731.9		
Total	27	19996560680			

	Coefficients	Standard Error	t Stat	P-value	Lower 95%	Upper 95%	Lower 95.0%	Upper 95.0%
Intercept	80640.56739	13655.93989	5.9051642	4.3041E-06	52456.09289	108825.0419	52456.09289	108825.0419
Mortgage Rates	-3521.91472	680.1559808	-5.1780986	2.649E-05	-4925.68766	-2118.14178	-4925.68766	-2118.14178
Housing Starts	-5.47726	1.780411941	-3.0763977	0.00517198	-9.151844821	-1.80266558	-9.15184482	-1.80266558
Advertising Expenditure	23.41351	3.153796991	7.42391066	1.1541E-07	16.90439008	29.92262413	16.90439008	29.92262413

From the output, we can see that the regression relationship has become (approximately):

Woodbon annual sales = $80,640.57 − $3,521.91 (mortgage rate)
− $5.48 (housing starts) + $23.41 (advertising expenditure)

The various residual plots for the revised model all appear to conform to the required conditions. Exhibit 14.11 shows the revised predicted sales residual plot, which appears to have the desirable horizontal band of points.

EXHIBIT **14.11**

Predicted Sales Residual Plot for Woodbon Model, with Mortgage Rates, Housing Starts, and Advertising Expenditure as Explanatory Variables

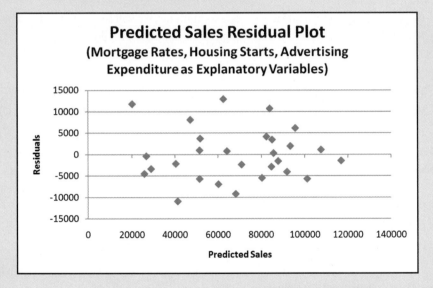

As well, none of the residual plots for the three explanatory variables give an indication of violation of the required conditions. Exhibit 14.12 opposite shows these residual plots.

The plot of the residuals over time does not exhibit any particular pattern, so we can conclude that the residuals are independent over time. Exhibit 14.13 illustrates.

Finally, the histogram of residuals for the new Woodbon model appears fairly normal, although there is some right-skewness. Exhibit 14.14 on page 540 illustrates.

A check of the standardized residuals reveals one data point that could be classified as an outlier. This is the data point that corresponds to 1991 (notice that this point also attracted our attention when we examined the residual plots for the original model). Since the data are correct, we will leave the point in the data set. It appears that 1991 was not a typical year for Woodbon.

EXHIBIT 14.12

Residual Plots for Woodbon Multiple Regression Model (Mortgage Rates, Housing Starts, Advertising Expenditure as Explanatory Variables)

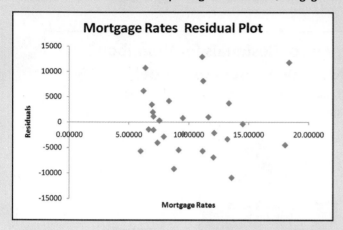

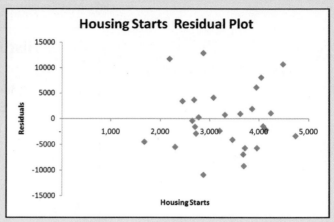

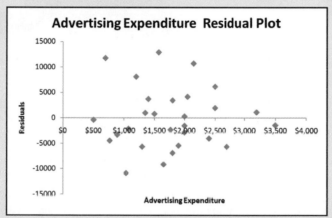

EXHIBIT 14.13

Plot of Residuals Over Time, Woodbon Model (Mortgage Rates, Housing Starts, Advertising Expenditure as Explanatory Variables)

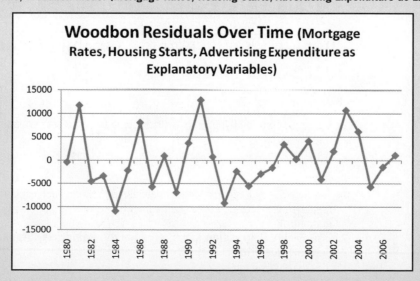

EXHIBIT 14.14

Histogram of Residuals for Woodbon Model (Mortgage Rates, Housing Starts, Advertising Expenditure as Explanatory Variables)

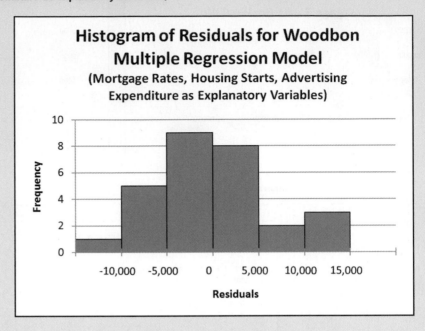

The new Woodbon model appears to meet all of the required conditions for the linear regression model. However, it still does not meet the test of common sense, in that the coefficient for housing starts is negative when we would expect it to be positive. We will say more about this difficulty in Section 14.5, when we discuss criteria for selecting explanatory variables.

GUIDE TO TECHNIQUE

Checking Requirements for the Linear Multiple Regression Model

When:

- before performing hypothesis tests or using the regression relationship to create confidence or prediction intervals
- using sample data to assess whether the relationship conforms to requirements

Steps:

1. Produce scatter diagrams for the relationship between each explanatory variable and the response variable. Check to see that each relationship appears linear (no pronounced curvature).
2. Use Excel's **Regression** tool to produce the **Residuals**, **Standardized Residuals**, and **Residual Plots**.

3. Create a plot of the residuals versus the predicted *y*-values. The residuals should be randomly distributed around zero, with the same variability throughout.
4. Examine the plots of residuals versus each explanatory variable. Again, the residuals should be randomly distributed around zero, with the same variability (a random horizontal band appearance is desirable).
5. Check time-series data by plotting the residuals in time order. There should be no discernible pattern to the plot.
6. Create a histogram of the residuals. This should be approximately normal, and centred on zero.
7. Check for outliers and influential observations. Carefully check any data point with a standardized residual $\geq +2$ or ≤ -2.

Note: If these investigations indicate significant problems, you should not proceed with a hypothesis test of the significance of the model, and you should not create confidence intervals or prediction intervals with the model in its current form.

DEVELOP YOUR SKILLS 14.2   *MyStatLab*

The Develop Your Skills exercises in this chapter frequently refer to a data set called "Salaries."

6. Examine the residual plots produced by Excel for the Salaries multiple regression model that you built for Develop Your Skills 14.1, Exercise 2, which included all possible explanatory variables. Are these residual plots consistent with the required conditions? Create a plot of the residuals versus predicted salaries. Does this plot meet the required conditions?

7. Examine the residual plots produced by Excel for the Salaries multiple regression model that you built for Develop Your Skills 14.2, Exercise 4, which included years of postsecondary education and age as explanatory variables. Are these residual plots consistent with the required conditions? Create a plot of the residuals versus predicted salaries. Does this plot meet the required conditions?

8. Examine the residual plots produced by Excel for the Salaries multiple regression model that you built for Develop Your Skills 14.2, Exercise 5, which included years of postsecondary education and years of experience as explanatory variables. Are these residual plots consistent with the required conditions? Create a plot of the residuals versus predicted salaries. Does this plot meet the required conditions?

9. Create histograms of the residuals for the models discussed in Exercises 6, 7, and 8 above. Do these histograms appear to be at least approximately normal?

10. Check the Excel output for the models created in Exercises 6, 7, and 8 above for outliers. If you had access to the original records for this data set, what would you do?

14.3   HOW GOOD IS THE REGRESSION?

Because the new Woodbon model appears to meet the required conditions, we can now conduct hypothesis tests about the overall model, and about the individual explanatory variables. We begin by testing whether the regression model is significant. Given this sample data set, is there evidence that there is a population regression relationship between sales and at least one of the explanatory variables?

Is the Regression Model Significant?—The F-Test

In the discussion of simple linear regression (Chapter 13), we performed a test of hypothesis about the slope of the regression line.

In multiple regression, we test the model as a whole.

$$H_0: \beta_1 = \beta_2 = \cdots = \beta_k = 0$$

H_1: At least one of the β_i's is not zero.

If the null hypothesis is true, then the y-variable is not related to any of the x-variables. If the alternative hypothesis is true, then the y-variable is related to at least one of the x-variables. As in Chapter 13, we hope to reject the null hypothesis, so that we can conclude there is a significant relationship between the response variable and at least one of the explanatory variables.

We conduct the hypothesis test by examining how much of the variation in the y-variable is explained by the regression relationship. Remember from Chapter 13 that the total variation in the y-values can be broken down into two parts: the variation that is explained by the regression relationship, and the variation that is left unexplained.

$$\Sigma(y - \bar{y})^2 = \Sigma(\hat{y} - \bar{y})^2 + \Sigma(y - \hat{y})^2$$

It is usual to describe this relationship as follows:

$$SST = SSR + SSE$$

The total sum of squares (SST) is equal to the sum of squares explained by the regression (SSR) plus the residual (or error) sum of squares (SSE).

When the response variable (y) is related to the explanatory variables, then SSR will be relatively large, and SSE will be relatively small. Before we can compare SSR and SSE, we must adjust them so they are directly comparable. This is accomplished by dividing each by its degrees of freedom to calculate the associated mean square value.[4]

The degrees of freedom for the error sum of squares are $n - (k + 1)$, because we estimate k coefficients plus an intercept from n data points. The degrees of freedom for the total variation are $(n - 1)$. This leaves k degrees of freedom for the regression sum of squares.

The test statistic is the ratio of the mean squares, and is an F statistic. The F distribution is described on pages 412–419 in Chapter 11.

$$F = \frac{\dfrac{SSR}{k}}{\dfrac{SSE}{n - (k + 1)}} = \frac{MSR}{MSE}$$

[4] If this seems familiar, it should. We made the same adjustment to compare mean squares in Chapter 11. See page 411.

When the null hypothesis is true, and the response variable is not related to any of the explanatory variables, the mean square for the regression (MSR) will not be significantly larger than the mean square for error (MSE), and the F statistic will be relatively small. However, when the response variable is related to at least one of the explanatory variables, the MSR will be significantly larger than the MSE, and the F statistic will be relatively large. The question is, how large does the F statistic have to be to provide evidence of a significant relationship?

Of course, the answer depends on sampling variability. As usual, we have to refer to the sampling distribution of the F statistic to decide whether any specific F statistic is unusual enough for us to reject the null hypothesis. The sampling distribution of the F statistic depends on the number of data points and the number of explanatory variables.

The Sampling Distribution of $\frac{MSR}{MSE}$ in Linear Multiple Regression Models

The sampling distribution of $\frac{MSR}{MSE}$ follows the F distribution, with $(k, n - (k + 1))$ degrees of freedom, where n is the number of observed data points and k is the number of explanatory variables in the model.

Fortunately, the Excel output not only calculates the F statistic for the hypothesis test of the regression model, it also calculates the associated p-value.

EXAMPLE 14.3A

Hypothesis test of significance of regression model

Complete the hypothesis test for the significance of the Woodbon model based on mortgage rates, housing starts, and advertising expenditure. Use a 5% level of significance.

$H_0: \beta_1 = \beta_2 = \cdots = \beta_k = 0$

H_1: At least one of the β_i's is not zero.

$\alpha = 0.05$

The Excel output of the regression model is reproduced on the next page in Exhibit 14.15, for ease of reference.

From the output, we see that F = 153.9 and the p-value is 0.000000000000000836. Since the p-value is less than the level of significance, we reject H_0. There is strong evidence to infer that there is a significant relationship between Woodbon sales and at least one of the explanatory variables. As always, we remember that a significant relationship is not necessarily a cause-and-effect relationship. Some other factor may be the cause of associated changes in sales and the explanatory variables.

EXHIBIT 14.15

Excel Regression Output for Woodbon Model, with Mortgage Rates, Housing Starts, and Advertising Expenditure as Explanatory Variables

SUMMARY OUTPUT

Regression Statistics	
Multiple R	0.974976011
R Square	0.950578223
Adjusted R Square	0.944400501
Standard Error	6416.987757
Observations	28

ANOVA

	df	SS	MS	F	Significance F
Regression	3	19008295115	6336098372	153.8719615	8.35857E-16
Residual	24	988265564.9	41177731.87		
Total	27	19996560680			

	Coefficients	Standard Error	t Stat	P-value	Lower 95%
Intercept	80640.56739	13655.93989	5.905164203	4.30411E-06	52456.09289
Mortgage Rates	-3521.91472	680.1559808	-5.178098581	2.64897E-05	-4925.68766
Housing Starts	-5.47726	1.780411941	-3.076397702	0.005171979	-9.151844821
Advertising Expenditure	23.41351	3.153796991	7.423910661	1.15414E-07	16.90439008

Are the Explanatory Variables Significant?—The *t*-Test

If the hypothesis test of the overall regression model indicates a significant relationship between the response variable and at least one of the explanatory variables, the next step is to figure out which of the explanatory variables is significant.

We conducted a *t*-test about the slope of the regression line in Chapter 13. We test the individual coefficients in the multiple regression model in a similar fashion. The test of the coefficient of explanatory variable *i* is conducted as follows.

$$H_0: \beta_i = 0$$

$$H_1: \beta_i \neq 0$$

The test statistic is $t = \dfrac{b_i}{s_{b_i}}$, with $(n - (k + 1))$ degrees of freedom.

It is important to realize that this *t*-test for the significance of each explanatory variable assumes that all the other explanatory variables are included in the model. The *p*-values for the individual coefficients do give us some indication of how important each explanatory variable is. Those with small *p*-values are likely more strongly related to the response variable. However, we cannot just eliminate an explanatory variable with a p-value greater than the level of significance. If we decide to eliminate any explanatory variable, we must rerun the regression analysis and examine the new model and the new p-values for the coefficients.

Remember that the t-tests for the individual coefficients should only be conducted if the F-test of the overall model shows that it is significant. We can control the Type I error rate on a single t-test with the level of significance (α), but the error rate becomes larger with repeated tests based on the same data set.[5] Therefore, the individual t-tests should only be performed when the overall Type I error rate is controlled, through the F-test.

EXAMPLE **14.3B**

Hypothesis tests of individual coefficients in regression model

Conduct hypothesis tests about the significance of the individual coefficients in the Woodbon model.

As in the simple linear regression case, the Excel output contains the p-values for the two-tailed tests of significance for the individual coefficients. An excerpt from the Excel output is shown below in Exhibit 14.16.

EXHIBIT **14.16**

Excerpt from the Excel Regression Output for Woodbon Model, with Mortgage Rates, Housing Starts, and Advertising Expenditure as Explanatory Variables

	Coefficients	Standard Error	t Stat	P-value
Intercept	80640.56739	13655.93989	5.9051642	4.3041E-06
Mortgage Rates	-3521.91472	680.1559808	-5.1780986	2.649E-05
Housing Starts	-5.47726	1.780411941	-3.0763977	0.00517198
Advertising Expenditure	23.41351	3.153796991	7.42391066	1.1541E-07

For convenience, we will refer to the mortgage rates as explanatory variable 1, housing starts as explanatory variable 2, and advertising expenditure as explanatory variable 3.

Hypothesis test for mortgage rates:

$$H_0: \beta_1 = 0$$

$$H_1: \beta_1 \neq 0$$

$$t = \frac{b_1}{s_{b_1}} = -5.18 \text{ (from Excel output)}$$

The p-value is 0.000026, so we reject H_0. There is strong evidence that mortgage rates are a significant explanatory variable for Woodbon annual sales, when housing starts and advertising expenditure are included in the model.

---

[5] This problem was discussed in Chapters 10 and 11—be careful when you are skating back and forth across the frozen lake!

Hypothesis test for housing starts:

$H_0: \beta_2 = 0$

$H_1: \beta_2 \neq 0$

$t = \dfrac{b_2}{s_{b_2}} = -3.08$ (from Excel output)

The p-value is 0.005, so we reject H_0. There is strong evidence that housing starts are a significant explanatory variable for Woodbon annual sales, when mortgage rates and advertising expenditure are included in the model.

Hypothesis test for advertising expenditure:

$H_0: \beta_3 = 0$

$H_1: \beta_3 \neq 0$

$t = \dfrac{b_3}{s_{b_3}} = 7.42$ (from Excel output)

The p-value is 0.0000001, so we reject H_0. There is strong evidence that advertising expenditure is a significant explanatory variable for Woodbon annual sales, when mortgage rates and housing starts are included in the model.

As always, while we can conclude that mortgage rates, housing starts, and advertising expenditure are significant explanatory variables for Woodbon annual sales, this does not mean that we can conclude that changes in these variables have caused the changes in sales.

Adjusted Multiple Coefficient of Determination

In Chapter 13, we used the coefficient of determination, or R^2, as an indication of how well the x-variable explained the variations in the y-variable. Remember, that

$$R^2 = \frac{SSR}{SST}$$

Adding more explanatory variables to the regression model will never reduce the R^2 value, and generally will tend to increase it. In fact, if you have n data points, it is always possible to develop a model that will fit the data perfectly, with $n - 1$ explanatory variables. However, this model is not likely to yield good predictions, because it is only the result of a lot of arithmetic instead of good thinking about the relationships between the response and explanatory variables. Such a model is usually described as "overfitted." It is possible to adjust the R^2 value to compensate for this tendency of R^2 to increase when another explanatory variable is added to the model.

It is easiest to see the relationship between the R^2 and the adjusted R^2 if we start with a restatement of R^2. We know $SST = SSR + SSE$, so $SSR = SST - SSE$. Substituting this into the formula for R^2 yields the following:

$$R^2 = \frac{SSR}{SST} = \frac{SST - SSE}{SST} = 1 - \frac{SSE}{SST}$$

The adjusted R^2 is calculated as follows:

$$\text{Adjusted } R^2 = 1 - \frac{\dfrac{SSE}{n - (k + 1)}}{\dfrac{SST}{n - 1}}$$

The adjusted R^2 is calculated by Excel as part of the **Regression** output.

The adjusted R^2 value will generally be smaller than the unadjusted R^2 value. As well, because the formula takes into account the number of explanatory variables being used (k), the adjusted R^2 will not necessarily increase when another variable is added to the model.

Excel's **Regression** output provides the adjusted R^2 value. For the Woodbon model, it is 0.944, as shown below in Exhibit 14.17. Notice that the adjusted R^2 value, at 0.944, is less than the R^2 value of 0.951.

EXHIBIT **14.17**

Excel Regression Statistics for Woodbon Model, with Mortgage Rates, Housing Starts, and Advertising Expenditure as Explanatory Variables

SUMMARY OUTPUT	
Regression Statistics	
Multiple R	0.974976011
R Square	0.950578223
Adjusted R Square	0.944400501
Standard Error	6416.987757
Observations	28

The Develop Your Skills exercises in this chapter frequently refer to a data set called "Salaries."

11. Apply the formula for the adjusted R^2 to verify the value shown in Exhibit 14.17. Note that the SSE and SALARIES SST are shown in the Excel **Regression** output.

12. Conduct a test of the significance of the overall model for the salaries model which includes all explanatory variables. Test the significance of the individual explanatory variables. What does this tell you?

13. Conduct a test of the significance of the overall model for the salaries model that includes years of postsecondary education and age as explanatory variables. Test the significance of the individual explanatory variables. What does this tell you?

14. Conduct a test of the significance of the overall model for the salaries model that includes years of postsecondary education and years of experience as explanatory variables. Test the significance of the individual explanatory variables. What does this tell you?

15. Compare the adjusted R^2 values for the three models of salary from Exercises 12, 13, and 14 above. Based on the adjusted R^2, which model does not seem worth considering at this point?

14.4 MAKING PREDICTIONS

One of the reasons for building a multiple regression model for Woodbon annual sales was to allow Kate Cameron, Woodbon's owner, to make sales predictions. Of course, the only explanatory variable in the present model that Kate can control is advertising expenditure. Kate will have to guess at the values of the other variables (mortgage rates and housing starts) if she wants to predict sales for the coming year. Suppose Kate plans to spend $3,000 on advertising next year, and she expects that five-year mortgage rates will be around 7% and that housing starts for the province will be 3,800.

By substituting these specific values into the regression equation, Kate arrives at a point estimate for Woodbon annual sales.

Woodbon annual sales = $80,640.56739 − $3,521.91472 (mortgage rate) − $5. 47726 (housing starts) + $23.41351(advertising expenditure)

= $80,640.56739 − $3,521.91472 (7) − $5.47726 (3,800) + $23.41351 (3,000)

= $105,414.11

In Chapter 13, we also created prediction and confidence intervals from regression relationships. Remember, a regression prediction interval predicts a particular value of y (sales) for a set of specific values of the x-variables (in this case, mortgage rate, housing starts, and advertising expenditure). A regression confidence interval predicts the average y for a set of specific values of the x-variables.

While the formulas for prediction and confidence intervals were fairly simple to understand when there was only one explanatory variable (with a given value of x_0), they become more complicated with two or more explanatory variables. Constructing these intervals for multiple regression requires the use of matrix algebra. An Excel add-in (**Multiple Regression Tools**) has been created to do these calculations. This add-in was first introduced in Chapter 13 (see page 514).

You should type the specific values of the explanatory variables that will be the basis of your intervals into adjacent columns in the spreadsheet containing the sample data. It is easiest to input the values in the correct order if they are typed at the bottom of the columns of explanatory variable data. Exhibit 14.18 illustrates (note that some of the rows of data have been hidden in the worksheet).

EXHIBIT 14.18

Typing in Specific Values of Explanatory Variables as Basis for Intervals

	A	B	C	D	E	F	G	H
1	Woodbon							
2	Year	Mortgage Rates	Housing Starts	Advertising Expenditure	Sales			
3	1980	14.52083	2,646	$500	$26,345			
4	1981	18.37500	2,188	$695	$31,987			
5	1982	18.04167	1,680	$765	$21,334			
6	1983	13.22917	4,742	$890	$25,584			
27	2004	6.23333	3,947	$2,500	$101,760			
28	2005	5.99167	3,959	$2,700	$95,400			
29	2006	6.66250	4,085	$3,500	$115,320			
30	2007	7.07083	4,242	$3,200	$108,550			
31		7.00000	3,800	$3,000	Specific Values of Explanatory Variables for Intervals			

As before, the **Confidence Interval and Prediction Intervals – Calculations** tool in **Multiple Regression Tools** requires you to indicate the locations of the labels and values of the variables, the location of the specific values of the explanatory variables on which you want to base your intervals, a level of confidence (percentage form), and an output range. Example 14.4 below provides the results.

EXAMPLE 14.4

Calculating confidence and prediction intervals with Excel

Use Excel to create a prediction interval for Woodbon sales, when mortgage rates are 7%, housing starts are 3,800, and advertising expenditure is $3,000.

Once these specific values are typed into the spreadsheet, the **Multiple Regression Tools** add-in is used to create the following output (note that columns have been resized for visibility).

EXHIBIT 14.19

Confidence Interval and Prediction Intervals – Calculations Result for Woodbon Data

Confidence Interval and Prediction Intervals - Calculations								
Point		95 = Confidence Level(%)				Prediction Interval		Confidence Interval	
Number	Mortgage Rates	Housing Starts		Advertising Expenditure		Lower limit	Upper limit	Lower limit	Upper limit
1	7	3800		3000		91016.42	119811.8113	99767.012	111061.2202

A 95% prediction interval for Woodbon sales when mortgage rates are 7%, housing starts are 3,800, and advertising expenditure is $3,000, is ($91,016.42, $119,811.81). Notice that even though we have added explanatory variables to the model, and the fit is better than it was in the simple linear regression model, the prediction interval is still quite wide.

Remember, it is not legitimate to make predictions from the regression model for values of the explanatory variables that are outside the range of the values in the data set on which the model is based. So, for example, Kate should not rely on the model to make predictions for an advertising budget of $5,000, because Woodbon has never spent more than $3,500 on advertising in the past.

DEVELOP YOUR SKILLS 14.4

MyStatLab

The Develop Your Skills exercises in this chapter frequently refer to a data set called "Salaries."

16. Use Excel to create a 95% confidence interval of average Woodbon sales, when mortgage rates are 6%, housing starts are 3,500, and advertising expenditure is $3,500. Interpret the interval.

17. Would it be appropriate to use the Woodbon model to make a prediction for mortgage rates of 6%, housing starts of 2,500, and advertising expenditure of $4,000? Explain why or why not.

18. Use the salaries model based on years of postsecondary education and age to make a 95% prediction interval estimate of the salary of an individual who is 35 years old and has five years of postsecondary education.

SALARIES

19. Use the salaries model based on years of postsecondary education and age to make a 95% confidence interval estimate of the average salary for individuals who are 35 years old and have five years of postsecondary education. Do you expect this confidence interval to be wider or narrower than the prediction interval estimate from Exercise 18? Why?

20. Use the salaries model based on years of postsecondary education and years of experience to make a 95% prediction interval estimate of the salary of an individual who has five years of postsecondary education and 10 years of experience.

14.5 SELECTING THE APPROPRIATE EXPLANATORY VARIABLES

Let us recap the steps we have followed to build the Woodbon sales model.

1. We began by thinking carefully about what explanatory variables might reasonably be expected to have an impact on Woodbon's sales, and we examined the relationship between each of these variables and sales.

2. We used Excel to estimate the multiple regression relationship between Woodbon sales and mortgage rates, housing starts, and a leading indicator for retail trade in furniture and appliances. We noted that the initial model had a negative coefficient for housing starts, the opposite of what we expected.

3. We used Excel to check whether the regression model met the required conditions. We examined plots of residuals against predicted sales, and residuals against each of the explanatory variables. We noted that the residual plot for the leading indicator did not exhibit the desired horizontal band shape. We also examined a plot of residuals over time, which did not exhibit any particular time-related pattern. We created a histogram of the residuals, and it appeared normal. We identified one outlier in the data set.

4. The model that included the leading indicator did not conform to the required conditions for linear regression (the variability in the residuals was not constant). For this and other reasons, we eliminated the leading indicator as an explanatory variable and recalculated the model. Again, we checked the required conditions, and this time did not identify any obvious violations of the required conditions. We identified one potential outlier, but because the associated data point was correct, we left it in the model.

5. We conducted an F-test of the significance of the overall model, and we were able to conclude there was a significant relationship between Woodbon sales and at least one of the remaining explanatory variables (mortgage rates, housing starts, and advertising expenditure).

6. We then conducted hypothesis tests about the coefficients for each explanatory variable. In each case, we concluded that there was evidence that each of the explanatory variables was significant, assuming the other explanatory variables were included in the model.

7. We examined the adjusted R^2 value, which was 0.94, indicating that the regression model explained a significant portion of the variability in Woodbon sales.

At this point, it might seem that we have done enough work and that we have the best possible model for Woodbon's sales, based on these explanatory variables. However, we must reflect carefully before we settle for the new model. More complicated models are not necessarily better. We should realize that the adjusted R^2 value for the new model, at 0.94, is not that much higher than the adjusted R^2 of 0.88 for the model based on advertising expenditure alone. This might not be enough of an improvement to justify the extra data required.

As well, it is possible for the adjusted R^2 value to be high for a model that does not predict well. Ultimately, a model that does not provide useful predictions of future sales for Woodbon will not be worth maintaining.

Building a good regression model is a process that requires many steps, as we have seen. Fortunately, computers do the calculations easily and quickly, and so we can look at a number of possible models before choosing the "best" one. It is not always easy to determine which is the best regression model, but these are some goals to keep in mind.

> ### Goals for Regression Models
> 1. The model should be easy to use. It should be reasonably easy to acquire data for the model's explanatory variables.
> 2. The model should be reasonable. The coefficients should represent a reasonable cause-and-effect relationship between the response variable and the explanatory variables.
> 3. The model should make useful and reliable predictions. Prediction and confidence intervals should be reasonably narrow.
> 4. The model should be stable. It should not be significantly affected by small changes in explanatory variable data.

One method of finding the "best" possible regression model is to create regressions for all possible combinations of the explanatory variables being considered. For the Woodbon data set, this would entail creating a regression model for each of the following:

1. sales and mortgage rates
2. sales and housing starts
3. sales and advertising expenditure
4. sales and housing starts and mortgage rates
5. sales and mortgage rates and advertising expenditure
6. sales and housing starts and advertising expenditure
7. sales and housing starts and mortgage rates and advertising expenditure.

The resulting models can be assessed according to the criteria above. Some values that may be useful to compare models are as follows:

1. The adjusted R^2 values provide a measure of the strength of the relationship between the explanatory variables and the response variable.
2. The standard error (s_ε) gives some indication of how wide the confidence and prediction intervals would be. As discussed in Chapter 13, s_ε is the sample estimate of the standard deviation of the error terms (residuals) in the model. A model with less variability in the error terms will produce narrower and therefore more useful confidence and prediction intervals.
3. The number of explanatory variables gives some indication of the data requirements of the model. Adding an explanatory variable may reduce the width of confidence and prediction intervals, if it reduces s_ε. However, adding an explanatory variable will also decrease the degrees of freedom for the t-score ($n - (k + 1)$) used in the confidence and prediction intervals (each additional variable increases k by 1), and t-scores with smaller degrees of freedom are larger (look at the table of t-scores in Appendix 3 on page 581 if you are not sure of this). The larger t-score may at least partially offset any reduction in s_ε that results from adding an explanatory variable.

The **Multiple Regression Tools** add-in allows you to easily create all possible regression models from a data set. Exhibit 14.20 opposite shows the **Multiple Regression Tools** dialogue box, with the correct choice highlighted: **All Possible Regressions Calculations**.

EXHIBIT **14.20**

Multiple Regression Tools Add-In, All Possible Regressions Calculations

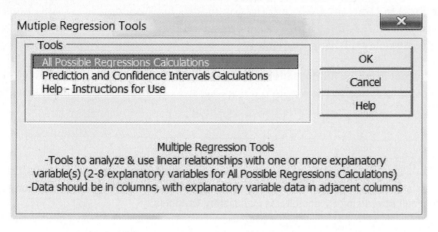

With this choice selected, click **OK**, and the next dialogue box will be as shown in Exhibit 14.21.

EXHIBIT **14.21**

All Possible Regressions Dialogue Box

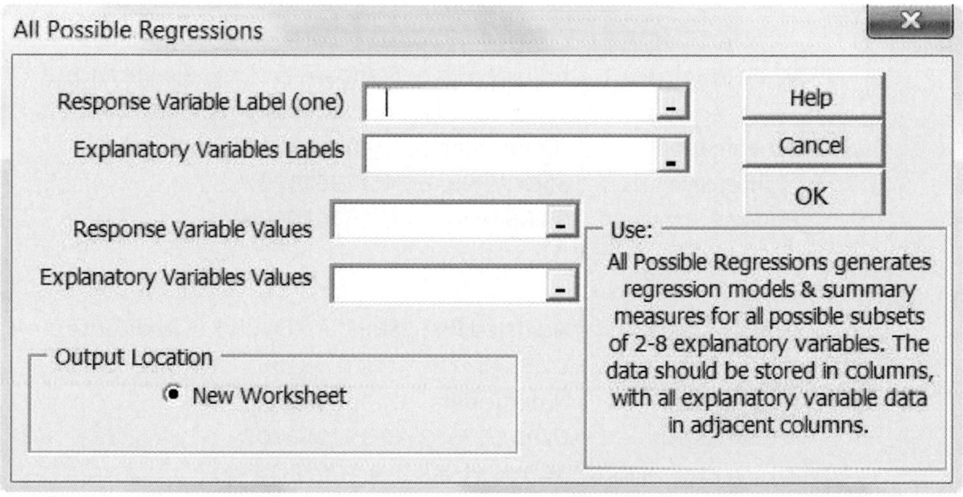

You are required to:

1. Input the locations of the response (y) and explanatory (x) variable labels (Sales for the response variable for the Woodbon data, and Mortgage Rates, Housing Starts, and Advertising Expenditure for the explanatory variables).
2. Input the locations of the response (y) and explanatory (x) variable values.

The output is illustrated in Example 14.5A on the next page.

EXAMPLE 14.5A

Assess all possible regressions

Use Excel to create all possible regression models for Woodbon sales, using housing starts (which we will refer to as x_1), mortgage rates (x_2), and advertising expenditure (x_3) as possible explanatory variables.

The output from the **All Possible Regressions Calculations** results are shown below in Exhibits 14.22a and b. The output is quite long, and when you are working in Excel, you will have to scroll up and down to see everything.

EXHIBIT 14.22

Results of All Possible Regressions for Woodbon Sales Model, with Housing Starts, Mortgage Rates, and Advertising Expenditure as Explanatory Variables.

a)

Multiple Regression Tools-All Possible Models - Calculations

Model Number	Adjusted R^2	Standard Error	K	Significance F
1	0.816696238	11651.4898	1	2.73738E-11
Variable Labels	Coefficients	p-value		
Intercept	140617.432	1.92382E-17		
Mortgage Rates	-7201.80514	2.73738E-11		

Model Number	Adjusted R^2	Standard Error	K	Significance F
2	0.038514112	26685.00127	1	0.161030209
Variable Labels	Coefficients	p-value		
Intercept	35847.59546	0.129611207		
Housing Starts	9.686480483	0.161030209		

Model Number	Adjusted R^2	Standard Error	K	Significance F
3	0.881451735	9370.081561	1	9.1661E-14
Variable Labels	Coefficients	p-value		
Intercept	6291.657683	0.191956707		
Advertising Expenditure	35.16671582	9.1661E-14		

Model Number	Adjusted R^2	Standard Error	K	Significance F
4	0.824051049	11415.34684	2	1.41103E-10
Variable Labels	Coefficients	p-value		
Intercept	160079.6411	9.65112E-11		
Mortgage Rates	-7626.20345	6.38131E-11		
Housing Starts	-4.56439049	0.160992622		

b)

Model Number	Adjusted R^2	Standard Error	K	Significance F
5	0.925576239	7424.23274	2	3.01022E-15
Variable Labels	Coefficients	p-value		
Intercept	59670.88304	0.000196457		
Mortgage Rates	-3132.530105	0.000433979		
Advertising Expenditure	22.74342288	1.54935E-06		

Model Number	Adjusted R^2	Standard Error	K	Significance F
6	0.886993562	9148.446728	2	5.57177E-13
Variable Labels	Coefficients	p-value		
Intercept	16136.21269	0.053896821		
Housing Starts	-3.761645082	0.144006697		
Advertising Expenditure	36.68747295	2.43629E-13		

Model Number	Adjusted R^2	Standard Error	K	Significance F
7	0.944400501	6416.987757	3	8.35857E-16
Variable Labels	Coefficients	p-value		
Intercept	80640.56739	4.30411E-06		
Mortgage Rates	-3521.914719	2.64897E-05		
Housing Starts	-5.477255203	0.005171979		
Advertising Expenditure	23.41350711	1.15414E-07		

So which model is best? While the results shown in Exhibit 14.22[6] can help us assess the various regression models, these values cannot tell the whole story. There is a trade-off when variables are added to the model. While the model may have more explanatory power, it will also be more complicated, and more difficult to maintain.

If we look at Exhibit 14.22, we see that the model with all three explanatory variables has the highest adjusted R^2 and the lowest standard error. However, the model has a negative coefficient for housing starts, which does not seem reasonable. As well, adding the housing starts variable only slightly improves it from the model with just advertising expenditure and mortgage rates.

Whichever model we choose, it is important to check that it meets the required conditions described in Section 14.2. An F-test of the significance of the model should also be conducted. While it would be disappointing if the "best" model from all of the possible regressions did not meet the required conditions, it would not be legitimate to use the model for prediction or confidence intervals if it did not.

By now you can see that building a multiple regression model is an iterative process. It can take some time to build, assess, and ultimately decide on the preferred model. Fortunately, it is fairly easy to explore the possibilities with software such as Excel.

There is one more consideration that is important as we build multiple regression models. Whenever we use more than one explanatory variable, we have to consider that there may be interactions among these variables.

---

[6] If your output for Model 5 does not match what is shown in this exhibit, see the note called "Excel's Floating Point Problem" at the end of the chapter, after the Chapter Review Exercises.

A New Consideration: Multicollinearity

Collinearity occurs when two of the explanatory variables are related to each other. Multicollinearity occurs when more than two of the explanatory variables are related to each other. Generally, this potential problem with multiple regression is referred to as "multicollinearity."

Multicollinearity may cause one or more of the following problems:

1. The adjusted R^2 is large and the F-test shows the overall model is significant, but one or more of the estimated regression coefficients are statistically insignificant.
2. The estimated regression coefficients are not stable. The values change significantly when explanatory variables are added to the regression relationship.
3. The estimated regression coefficients do not make sense. They are larger or smaller than would seem appropriate, or they have an unexpected sign.

Because of these problems, it is important to consider multicollinearity when building a multiple regression model. Some degree of multicollinearity is present in almost every multiple regression model.

The first method of guarding against multicollinearity is to choose the explanatory variables carefully. If mortgage rates, for instance, are being considered as an explanatory variable in the Woodbon model, it would not make sense to include prime rates or another mortgage rate in the model. Because such variables are likely highly correlated with each other, most of the explanatory power is gained when the first variable is introduced. The second variable will not likely tell us more about the response variable.

There are various methods aimed at identifying collinear variables if the relationship between them is not immediately obvious. One of these is to create a scatter diagram of the relationship of every explanatory variable with every other explanatory variable.

In the Woodbon model, if we are thinking of choosing the model with advertising expenditure and mortgage rates, we could create a scatter diagram of advertising expenditure and mortgage rates. Such a scatter diagram is illustrated in Exhibit 14.23 opposite. It appears there is a fairly strong negative correlation between the two variables.

Another method of assessing the correlation between the explanatory variables is to create a correlation matrix for the variables. This is easy to do with Excel, using the **Correlation** tool of **Data Analysis**. If you select the adjacent columns of data, Excel will produce a correlation matrix such as the one shown for the Woodbon problem in Exhibit 14.24. Note that it is helpful to select the labels along with the data when using this Excel tool.

The correlation coefficients tell us something about how the variables are related as pairs. Of course, it is also possible that one explanatory variable could be simultaneously related to two other explanatory variables, and neither the scatter diagrams nor the correlation matrix will reveal this. The scatter diagrams and the correlation matrix will help identify obvious pair-wise correlations between variables, but other harder-to-identify sources of multicollinearity may also be present.

Whenever the correlation coefficients are close to 1 or −1, there are potential problems with multicollinearity. For example, in Exhibit 14.24 opposite, we see a correlation coefficient of 0.946 between advertising expenditure and the leading indicator. If we had not already eliminated the leading indicator as a potential explanatory variable, we would probably have eliminated it because of its high correlation with advertising expenditure.

EXHIBIT **14.23**

Scatter Diagram of Mortgage Rates and Advertising Expenditure

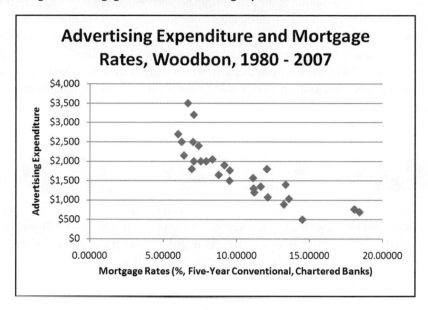

EXHIBIT **14.24**

Correlation Matrix for Woodbon Variables

	Mortgage Rates	Housing Starts	Advertising Expenditure	Leading Indicator	Sales
Mortgage Rates	1.0000				
Housing Starts	-0.4168	1.0000			
Advertising Expenditure	-0.8424	0.3850	1.0000		
Leading Indicator	-0.7598	0.4473	0.9460	1.0000	
Sales	-0.9075	0.2723	0.9412	0.8811	1.0000

Including the leading indicator variable in the model would have robbed advertising expenditure of its explanatory power.

The collinearity between advertising expenditure and the leading indicator is unexpected. There is no obvious reason for the two variables being connected. However, the mathematical connection is clear, and because of it we should not include both variables in the model.

The correlation coefficient between mortgage rates and advertising expenditure is −0.8424, confirming what we saw in the scatter diagram: there is a fairly strong negative relationship between the two variables. Does this mean we should reject this regression model?

The answer depends on how Kate Cameron intends to use the model. Because of the collinearity between mortgage rates and advertising expenditure, she should be careful interpreting the regression coefficients. In the Woodbon sales model that includes mortgage rates and advertising expenditure, $y = \$59{,}670.88 - \$3{,}132.53x_2 + 22.74x_3$, the x_3 coefficient is 22.74. Normally, we would interpret this coefficient as follows: for a given mortgage rate, each additional dollar spent on advertising increases Woodbon sales by $22.74. However, because of the collinearity, such an interpretation is not reliable. If Kate wants to know the true nature of the relationship between Woodbon sales and advertising, she should not rely on a model that includes both advertising expenditure and mortgage rates. However, if Kate's only purpose is to predict Woodbon's sales, this model is still probably the best, because it has a high adjusted R^2 and a fairly low standard error.

Example 14.5B below discusses a case in which there is strong collinearity between explanatory variables, and suggests a way to deal with the problem to improve the regression model.

EXAMPLE **14.5B**

Multiple regression, dealing with collinearity

EXA14-5b

A sales manager is trying to build a model to predict sales by region. He has data on population and total income in each region. The manager begins by creating a regression model including both total income and population as explanatory variables. An excerpt from the Excel output is shown below in Exhibit 14.25. Examine the output and explain the results.

EXHIBIT **14.25**

Regression Output for Example 14.5B

SUMMARY OUTPUT					
Regression Statistics					
Multiple R	0.722				
R Square	0.521				
Adjusted R Square	0.485				
Standard Error	686.664				
Observations	30				
ANOVA					
	df	*SS*	*MS*	*F*	*Significance F*
Regression	2	13833194.713	6916597.356	14.669	0.000
Residual	27	12730684.665	471506.839		
Total	29	26563879.378			
	Coefficients	*Standard Error*	*t Stat*	*P-value*	*Lower 95%*
Intercept	26453.443	582.730	45.396	0.000	25257.781
Total Income (Millions)	0.592	0.783	0.757	0.456	-1.014
Population	0.040	0.034	1.174	0.251	-0.030

The regression model has an adjusted R^2 value of 0.485. The model is significant, according to the F-test (the *p*-value is approximately zero). However, the *p*-values for each of the explanatory variables are quite large, indicating that none of them is significant. Since these are the only variables in the model, this does not make sense.

Total income for a region will of course be closely related to the population of the region. Regions with larger populations will have greater total incomes. In this data set, the correlation coefficient between total income and population is 0.936. If the sales manager wants to investigate the effect of income on sales, he should take out the population effect by working with per capita income. Adjusting the income data and exploring the new regression model are left to the reader as an exercise (see Develop Your Skills 14.5, Exercise 22).

DEVELOP YOUR SKILLS 14.5 **MyStatLab**

The Develop Your Skills exercises in this chapter frequently refer to a data set called "Salaries."

21. Does the Woodbon model that includes mortgage rates and advertising expenditure meet the required conditions for regression? If so, conduct an F-test on the significance of the model.

SEC14-2

22. Adjust the total income data for Example 14.5B, and analyze the new regression model that includes both per capita income and population. Is the model significant? Are both explanatory variables significant? Continue your analysis of the data and decide on the best regression model for this data set.

CXA14-5b

23. Create a correlation matrix for the variables in the Salaries data set. Discuss which explanatory variables

SALARIES

should not be used simultaneously, and which look most promising to explain salaries.

24. Create all other possible regression models for the Salaries data. The models will be based on the following explanatory variables:

a. years of postsecondary education alone
b. years of experience alone
c. age alone
d. age and years of experience

25. Compare all possible models for the Salaries data, and select the "best" regression model.

14.6 USING INDICATOR VARIABLES IN MULTIPLE REGRESSION

The regression analysis discussed so far has investigated quantitative explanatory variables. Sometimes we are interested in the effect that a qualitative characteristic might have on a response variable (for example, male/female, urban/rural). It is possible to include such information in regression analysis with the use of indicator variables (sometimes called "dummy" variables). If the qualitative variable we are interested in is binary, that is, it has only two categories, then we can represent it with a single indicator variable (for example, "0" for male, "1" for female).

Indicator Variables for Qualitative Explanatory Variables with Only Two Categories   Once the qualitative variable is coded, it can be treated like any other variable in the regression analysis. For example, suppose we have data on the income and gender of the head of household for a random sample of credit card holders, as well as the monthly credit card bill.

SEC14-6

The Excel **Regression** output for the data set, with both explanatory variables, is shown on the next page in Exhibit 14.26.

EXHIBIT 14.26

Excel Regression Output for Credit Card Data Set

SUMMARY OUTPUT

Regression Statistics	
Multiple R	0.6793385
R Square	0.46150079
Adjusted R Square	0.42784459
Standard Error	394.818505
Observations	35

ANOVA

	df	SS	MS	F	Significance F
Regression	2	4274963.023	2137482	13.7122	4.9999E-05
Residual	32	4988212.862	155882		
Total	34	9263175.886			

	Coefficients	Standard Error	t Stat	P-value	Lower 95%
Intercept	581.641159	427.1660441	1.36163	0.18283	-288.467596
Income (000)	18.6627831	5.319860768	3.50813	0.00136	7.82658133
Gender of Head of Household (0=Male, 1=Female)	-341.71492	142.7877078	-2.39317	0.02274	-632.563965

From the F statistic and the associated p-value, we can see that the model is significant. There appears to be a relationship between the monthly credit card bill and at least one of income and the gender of the head of household. As well, the p-value for the t-test of the significance of the gender variable is 0.023, indicating that it is significant in the model (for a significance level of 0.05, for instance).

The regression relationship is as follows (with some rounding of the coefficients):

Monthly credit card bill = \$582 + \$19 (income in \$000) − \$342 (gender variable)

Notice that this means the following:

- If the credit card holder is male (gender variable = 0), the regression relationship is:

Monthly credit card bill = \$582 + \$19 (income in \$000)

- If the credit card holder is female (gender variable = 1), the regression relationship is:

Monthly credit card bill = \$582 + \$19 (income in \$000) − \$342

= (\$582 − \$342) + \$19 (income in \$000)

= \$240 + \$19 (income in \$000)

A binary indicator variable is sometimes called a "shift" variable, because it shifts the y-intercept while leaving the slope unchanged. The two regression relationships are shown in Exhibit 14.27 opposite. The regression relationship predicting monthly credit card bills for

EXHIBIT **14.27**

Effect of Gender Variable on Credit Card–Income Relationship

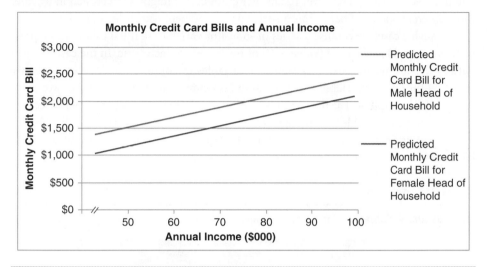

male heads of household (the blue line in the graph) is $342 higher than the regression relationship predicting monthly credit card bills for female heads of household (the red line).

Another way to think of the binary variable is as an on-off switch. When the switch is on (gender variable = 1), we are estimating the monthly credit card bills of female heads of household. When the switch is off (gender variable = 0), we are estimating the monthly credit card bills of male heads of household.

Adding gender to the regression model improves it over the model with income alone (in Develop Your Skills 14.6, Exercise 26, you will get a chance to explore this). However, we should not automatically conclude that gender is the cause of the difference in monthly credit card bills. Other factors such as wealth and the number of people in the household may be the cause of the differences we have observed in the credit card bills of male and female heads of household.

Since the end result of this regression analysis is two regression lines, one for each gender, you might wonder if it would be reasonable to skip the indicator variable, and instead build two regression models, one for male heads of household and one for female heads of household. The advantage of using the indicator variable approach is straightforward. Using the indicator variable in the model allows us to test whether gender has a significant effect on the credit card bills. If we simply build two models, we cannot conduct this statistical test. As well, pooling all of the data together allows us to make better estimates of the coefficients.

Another question you might have is this: is it possible to do regression analysis with only indicator variables, and no quantitative explanatory variables? The answer is yes, and the equivalent procedure is covered in Chapter 11. There, we tested to see if a quantitative response variable (such as battery life) varied according to levels of a qualitative explanatory factor (such as battery brand). The equivalence between the ANOVA procedures in Chapter 11 and regression with indicator variables is illustrated on the next page in Example 14.6. Since our ANOVA analysis considered factors with more than two levels, we will first consider regression using qualitative explanatory variables with more than two categories.

Indicator Variables for Qualitative Explanatory Variables with More Than Two Categories Sometimes the qualitative variable we are interested in has more than two possible (mutually exclusive) results. For example, we might be interested in whether three different brands of battery are associated with different battery life in minutes.

In such a case, we can use a series of indicator variables that tell us about the presence (value = 1) or absence (value = 0) of the brand characteristic. In the case of three battery brands, we will use two indicator variables in combination. For example, we could set the Onever variable = 1 if the brand is Onever, and 0 otherwise. We would set the Durible variable = 1 if the brand is Durible, 0 otherwise. This is sufficient, because if both indicator variables are equal to zero, this necessarily means that the third brand category (PlusEnergy) must apply. Exhibit 14.28 below illustrates. Note that we could have used any of the possible categories as the "missing" one.

EXHIBIT 14.28

Two Indicator Variables for Three Battery Brands

Two Indicator Variables (in Combination) to Convey Three Battery Brands		
Onever	1	0
Durible	0	1
PlusEnergy	0	0

It is important to use one fewer indicator variables than categories, to avoid problems with the regression analysis. We know that the value of the PlusEnergy indicator variable would be equal to (1 − sum of the values of the indicator variables for the other battery brands). Including a third indicator variable in the model would violate the requirement for independence of the explanatory variables. In addition, it would cause an error in Excel.

Recognize that some common sense is required when introducing qualitative variables into regression analysis. If a qualitative variable has many possible categories, requiring the use of several indicator variables, and if more than one qualitative variable is being considered, the number of explanatory variables can quickly get very high, perhaps too high to be reasonable for small data sets. As always, think carefully before you introduce a qualitative variable (or any variable) into the analysis.

Example 14.6 below illustrates the use of indicator variables for a qualitative explanatory variable with more than two possible categories.

EXAMPLE 14.6

Regression with a qualitative explanatory variable

EXA14-6

The owner of a winery is wondering whether the average purchase of visitors to her winery differs according to age. She asks the cashiers to keep track of a random sample of purchases by customers in three age groups: under 30, 30–50, over 50. Because there is no good reason to ask a customer his or her age, the cashiers guess which age group a customer belongs to (and if they do not guess accurately, the research may not be helpful). Eventually, data from about 50 purchases made by customers in each of the age groups is collected. Does it appear that there is a relationship between customer age and the value of the winery purchase?

First, the winery data must be arranged with all purchases in one column, and the indicator variables set up to indicate age group. Exhibit 14.29 below provides an excerpt from an Excel spreadsheet where the data are set up as required.

EXHIBIT 14.29

Excerpt of Winery Purchase Data Set with Indicator Variables for Age Group

Winery Purchase	1 = Under 30, 0 = Not Under 30	1 = 30-50, 0 = Not 30-50
$ 100.97	1	0
$ 97.55	1	0
$ 134.32	1	0
⋮		
$ 101.96	0	1
$ 75.96	0	1
$ 125.86	0	1
$ 155.44	0	1
$ 125.70	0	1
⋮		
$ 101.79	0	0
$ 168.45	0	0
$ 124.84	0	0

Next, run Excel's **Regression** tool on the data set. The output is as shown in Exhibit 14.30 on the next page.

How do we interpret the regression equation?

- When the "under 30" indicator variable = 1, then:

    Winery purchase for customers under 30 = $132.47 − $54.90 (1) − $12.80 (0) = $77.57

- When the "30–50" indicator variable = 1, then:

    Winery purchase for customers aged 30–50 = $132.47 − $54.90 (0) − $12.80 (1) = $119.67

- When the "under 30" indicator variable = 0, and the "30–50" indicator variable = 0, then the age group is "over 50."

    Winery purchase for customers over 50 = $132.47 − $54.90 (0) − $12.80 (0) = $132.47

Notice that a hypothesis test about the overall regression would report an F statistic of 67.49, with a very low significance level. Thus we can conclude that there is evidence of a relationship between winery purchase and age group. As well, each of the indicator variables included in the regression is significant (at the 5% level of significance).

For comparison, the Excel output for **Anova: Single Factor** is shown in Exhibit 14.31 on the next page.

The F-statistic for the hypothesis test about equality of population means is also 67.49, with the same significance level as in the **Regression** output. Notice that both procedures analyze the data in a similar way. In the regression analysis, the total variation in the y-variable (winery purchases) is partitioned into the portion that can be explained by the x-variable (the age groups), and the portion that is unexplained (the residuals, or errors). In the

EXHIBIT 14.30

Regression Output for Winery Purchase Data Set

SUMMARY OUTPUT

Regression Statistics	
Multiple R	0.69186325
R Square	0.47867476
Adjusted R Square	0.4715819
Standard Error	24.7237335
Observations	150

ANOVA

	df	SS	MS	F	Significance F
Regression	2	82504.42097	41252.2	67.4868	1.6125E-21
Residual	147	89855.6606	611.263		
Total	149	172360.0816			

	Coefficients	Standard Error	t Stat	P-value	Lower 95%
Intercept	132.4674	3.49646392	37.8861	9.7E-78	125.557572
1 = Under 30, 0 = Not Under 30	-54.899	4.944746696	-11.1025	3.5E-21	-64.670973
1 = 30-50, 0 = Not 30-50	-12.7966	4.944746696	-2.58792	0.01062	-22.568573

EXHIBIT 14.31

Anova: Single Factor Excel Output for Winery Purchase Data Set

Anova: Single Factor

SUMMARY

Groups	Count	Sum	Average	Variance
Under 30	50	3878.42	77.5684	652.9145
30-50	50	5983.54	119.6708	555.0899
Over 50	50	6623.37	132.4674	625.7846

ANOVA

Source of Variation	SS	df	MS	F	P-value	F crit
Between Groups	82504.42	2	41252.21	67.48684	1.61248E-21	3.057621
Within Groups	89855.66	147	611.263			
Total	172360.1	149				

analysis of variance, the F statistic compares the variation associated with the age groups (the "between groups" variation) with the unexplained variation ("within groups"). Of course, the sums of squares and the mean squares are exactly the same for the two procedures, because they are accomplishing the same tasks. This explains why some of the regression output has the "ANOVA" heading. The Regression sum of squares (SS) in the **Regression** output is the same as the Between Groups SS in the ANOVA output. The Residual SS in the **Regression** output is the same as the Within Groups SS in the ANOVA output.

DEVELOP YOUR SKILLS 14.6

26. Examine the data set for credit card bills. Create a regression model for credit card bills based on income. Compare this with the regression model for credit card bills based on income and the gender of the head of household. Does adding the gender variable improve the model significantly?
SEC14-6

27. Build a regression model, with indicator variables for battery brand, to assess whether there is a significant relationship between battery life in minutes and battery brand. This revisits the battery example in Chapter 11.
DYS14-27

28. A sales manager is trying to build a sales forecasting model based on number of sales contacts and region. Is region a significant explanatory variable in this model?
DYS14-28

29. A production manager has collected data on the number of units produced and the number of employees at
DYS14-29

work, for the day shift and the night shift. Is shift a significant explanatory variable for the number of units produced?

30. Statistics Canada collects census data about Canadians every five years. The department provides data files that contain a representative sample of anonymous individual responses to census surveys. A subset of these data is provided in the file DYS14-30. There is information on Canadians from Alberta and Ontario. Age and wages and salaries are shown for individuals who had non-zero wages and salaries in the data set.[7] Use an indicator variable for province, and build a regression model for wages and salaries, based on age and province. Is province a significant explanatory variable in this model?
DYS14-30

14.7   MORE ADVANCED MODELLING

This chapter has been an introduction to building mathematical models of linear relationships between quantitative response variables and two or more explanatory variables. Within the chapter we have seen many modelling possibilities.

You should be aware that more advanced mathematical modelling techniques exist, which are beyond the scope of this text. It is possible to build models that are polynomial, to account for curvature in the relationships. There are special techniques for time-series trend analysis. With the appropriate training and good computer software, it is possible to build complex and sophisticated models of relationships. However, complex models are not necessarily the "best" models. The simplest model that provides useful predictions is preferred.

Finally, always remember that mathematical models generally cannot prove cause and effect, and we should always be careful in interpreting the results of model building. Even if a model appears to work very well, the true cause-and-effect relationship may not have been revealed.

---

[7] Data for this exercise are a subset of the data available in the StatsCan microfile. Only age, wages, and salaries for those with non-zero wages and salaries data are used, for only Alberta and Ontario.

Chapter Summary

Determining the Relationship

Begin by thinking carefully about the explanatory variables that might reasonably be expected to affect the response variable. Create scatter plots to examine the relationship between the response variable and each explanatory variable. Use Excel's **Regression** tool to estimate the coefficients of the multiple regression relationship.

Checking the Required Conditions

Theoretically, there is a normal distribution of possible y-values for every combination of x-values. The population relationship we are trying to model is as follows:

$$y = \beta_0 + \beta_1 x_1 + \beta_2 x_2 + \cdots + \beta_k x_k + \varepsilon$$

We cannot reliably make predictions with the regression equation, or conduct a hypothesis test about the significance of the regression relationship, unless certain conditions are met (these are summarized in the box on page 532). The Guide to Technique: Checking Requirements for the Linear Multiple Regression Model on page 540 outlines a process for checking the required conditions for the regression model.

How Good Is the Regression?

If the required conditions are met, conduct an F-test of the significance of the relationship. This will be of the form:

$H_0: \beta_1 = \beta_2 = \cdots = \beta_k = 0$

$H_1:$ At least one of the β_i's is not zero.

The F statistic is

$$F = \frac{\dfrac{SSR}{k}}{\dfrac{SSE}{n - (k + 1)}} = \frac{MSR}{MSE}$$

with $(k, n - (k + 1))$ degrees of freedom, where n is the number of observed data points and k is the number of explanatory variables in the model. When the response variable is related to at least one of the explanatory variables, MSR will be significantly larger than MSE.

The output of Excel's **Regression** tool provides the F statistic and the p-value for this test. See page 544 for instructions on how to read the output.

If the results of the F-test show that the model is significant, t-tests of the significance of the individual explanatory variables can be conducted. The test of the coefficient of explanatory variable i is conducted as follows.

$H_0: \beta_i = 0$

$H_1: \beta_i \neq 0$

The test statistic is $t = \dfrac{b_i}{s_{b_i}}$, with $(n - (k + 1))$ degrees of freedom.

The output of Excel's **Regression** tool provides the p-values for the two-tailed tests of significance for the individual coefficients. See page 545 for instructions on how to read the output.

The adjusted R^2 value is a measure of the strength of the relationship between the explanatory variables and the response variable.

$$\text{Adjusted } R^2 = 1 - \frac{\dfrac{SSE}{n - (k + 1)}}{\dfrac{SST}{n - 1}}$$

The adjusted R^2 is calculated by Excel as part of the **Regression** output.

Making Predictions

Two types of estimation intervals can be created if the requirements are met. A regression prediction interval predicts a particular value of y, given a specific set of x-values. A regression confidence interval predicts the average y, given a specific set of x-values. The **Multiple Regression Tools** Excel add-in (**Prediction and Confidence Intervals Calculations**) calculates these intervals (see page 548). Always remember that it is not legitimate to make predictions outside the range of the sample data.

Selecting the Appropriate Explanatory Variables

The goals of a good regression model include the following:

1. The model should be easy to use. It should be reasonably easy to acquire data for the model's explanatory variables.
2. The model should be reasonable. The coefficients should represent a reasonable cause-and-effect relationship between the response variable and the explanatory variables.
3. The model should make useful and reliable predictions. Prediction and confidence intervals should be reasonably narrow.
4. The model should be stable. It should not be significantly affected by small changes in explanatory variable data.

Use Excel to create all possible regression models for all combinations of possible explanatory variables. The **Multiple Regression Tools** Excel add-in (**All Possible Regressions Calculations**) makes this easy to do. The add-in produces a summary report which shows each regression model, the adjusted R^2 value, the standard error (s_ε), and the number of variables (k) for each model. Use these measures to select a "best" model. Be sure to check the model chosen to see that it meets the required conditions. Review the appropriate p-values to ensure that the overall model is significant, and that the individual explanatory variables are significant.

Multicollinearity occurs when one of the explanatory variables is highly correlated with one or more of the other explanatory variables. This can result in unstable or inaccurate regression coefficients. To guard against this problem, choose explanatory variables carefully. Create scatter diagrams of explanatory variable pairs, and create a correlation matrix for all the variables in the model. If there is a pronounced pattern visible in the scatter diagram or a high correlation for a pair of variables, consider including only one of them in the final model.

Using Indicator Variables in Multiple Regression

The effect of a qualitative characteristic on a response variable (for example, male/female, urban/rural) can be modelled with indicator variables (sometimes called "dummy" variables). If the qualitative variable we are interested in is binary, we can represent it with a single indicator variable (for example, "0" for male, "1" for female). If the qualitative variable has more than two possible (mutually exclusive) results, we can use a series of indicator variables that tell us about the presence (value = 1) or absence (value = 0) of the qualitative characteristic. It is important to use one fewer indicator variables than categories, to avoid problems with the regression analysis.

Go to MyStatLab at www.mathxl.com. You can practise the exercises indicated with red in the Develop Your Skills and Chapter Review Exercises as often as you want, and guided solutions will help you find answers step by step. You'll find a personalized study plan available to you too!

CHAPTER REVIEW EXERCISES

CREDIT CARD

MARKS

The Chapter Review Exercises allow you to explore two major data sets. One, called "Credit Card," contains data about credit card balances and possible explanatory variables such as income and number of people in the household. Another data set, called "Marks," contains data about the final exam mark and marks on evaluations done during the semester (assignments, tests, and quizzes).

WARM-UP EXERCISES

1. The multiple regression model for monthly credit card balances and the age of the head of household, income (in thousands of dollars), and the value of the home (in thousands of dollars) is described in the Excel output shown below in Exhibit 14.32. Interpret the model.

EXHIBIT 14.32

Excel Output for Monthly Credit Card Balances, Income in Thousands, and the Number of People in the Household

SUMMARY OUTPUT				
Regression Statistics				
Multiple R	0.604771472			
R Square	0.365748533			
Adjusted R Square	0.304369359			
Standard Error	435.3412786			
Observations	35			
ANOVA				
	df	*SS*	*MS*	*F*
Regression	3	3387992.99	1129330.997	5.958837626
Residual	31	5875182.895	189522.0289	
Total	34	9263175.886		
	Coefficients	*Standard Error*	*t Stat*	*P-value*
Intercept	38.35751156	539.3083936	0.07112352	0.94375632
Age of Head of Household	0.992027023	11.58540256	0.085627324	0.932313329
Income (000)	22.03697173	8.899239591	2.47627581	0.018939953
Value of Home (000)	0.375387927	3.933953149	0.095422572	0.924593365

2. Refer to the Excel output shown in Exhibit 14.32 above. Is the overall model significant? You will have to estimate the *p*-value from the tables at the back of the text. Use a 5% level of significance.

3. Refer to the Excel output shown in Exhibit 14.32 above. Test the individual coefficients for significance. Use a 5% level of significance.

4. Given your answers to Exercises 2 and 3, what concerns do you have about the model? A correlation matrix for the values in the model is shown below in Exhibit 14.33 below.

EXHIBIT 14.33

Correlation Matrix for Credit Card Data Set

	Age of Head of Household	Income (000)	Number of People in Household	Value of Home (000)	Monthly Credit Card Bill (Annual Average)
Age of Head of Household	1				
Income (000)	0.781920213	1			
Number of People in Household	0.044761895	0.144977942	1		
Value of Home (000)	0.713556435	0.623129703	0.022990811	1	
Monthly Credit Card Bill (Annual Average)	0.48555699	0.604253286	0.618354542	0.393600727	1

THINK AND DECIDE

5. Consider the Marks data set, where the goal is to predict the final exam mark. Possible explanatory variables are the marks on Assignments 1 and 2, Tests 1 and 2, and Quiz marks. The tests and the final exam are written in a classroom, with all computations done manually with a calculator. The quizzes are done with online testing software, and the calculations can be done manually with a calculator or with Excel. Students can attempt the quizzes as many times as they wish before the due date (the quizzes are similar but not the same). The assignments are Excel-based and include a written report on the Excel analysis. Based on this information, which of the evaluations do you think would be the best predictor of the final exam mark, and why?

6. Exhibit 14.34 below shows the correlation matrix for the Marks data set. Is there any concern about multicollinearity? Which explanatory variables seem the most promising?

EXHIBIT 14.34

Correlation Matrix for Marks Data Set

	Assignment #1	Test #1	Assignment #2	Test#2	Quizzes	Final Exam Mark
Assignment #1	1.0000					
Test #1	0.2453	1.0000				
Assignment #2	0.4619	0.3719	1.0000			
Test#2	0.2970	0.5147	0.3514	1.0000		
Quizzes	0.3254	0.3247	0.4117	0.5865	1.0000	
Final Exam Mark	0.3898	0.5195	0.4914	0.7167	0.4992	1.000

7. Exhibit 14.35 on the next page shows the output of the **All Possible Models Calculations** tool in **Multiple Regression Tools** for all of the Marks models with one explanatory variable. Given these results, is there one model that you would choose as better than the rest? If so, explain why.

EXHIBIT 14.35

All Possible Models Calculations Output for Marks Models with One Explanatory Variable

Multiple Regression Tools-All Possible Models - Calculations				
Model Number	Adjusted R^2	Standard Error	K	Significance F
1	0.14285023	18.87369279	1	9.42336E-05
Variable Labels	Coefficients	p-value		
Intercept	41.9078595	9.25152E-11		
Assignment #1	0.39827912	9.42336E-05		
Model Number	Adjusted R^2	Standard Error	K	Significance F
2	0.26205943	17.51213989	1	6.85999E-08
Variable Labels	Coefficients	p-value		
Intercept	30.1007124	2.93098E-06		
Test #1	0.55058773	6.85999E-08		
Model Number	Adjusted R^2	Standard Error	K	Significance F
3	0.23330345	17.85008461	1	4.27328E-07
Variable Labels	Coefficients	p-value		
Intercept	47.5765866	1.19338E-23		
Assignment #2	0.33971697	4.27328E-07		
Model Number	Adjusted R^2	Standard Error	K	Significance F
4	0.50836095	14.29393191	1	3.18098E-16
Variable Labels	Coefficients	p-value		
Intercept	31.7519266	4.18575E-14		
Test#2	0.60113345	3.18098E-16		
Model Number	Adjusted R^2	Standard Error	K	Significance F
5	0.2411435	17.75858482	1	2.6112E-07
Variable Labels	Coefficients	p-value		
Intercept	49.3510102	2.14567E-27		
Quizzes	0.37275646	2.6112E-07		

THINK AND DECIDE USING EXCEL

CREDIT CARD

8. Use the model for credit card balances illustrated in Exhibit 14.32 to create a 95% prediction interval for the monthly credit card balance of a credit card holder where the age of the head of household is 45, income is $65,000, and the value of the home is $175,000. Do you think this regression model is useful?

MARKS

9. Use Excel to create all possible Marks models, and then consider those that have two explanatory variables. Note that there are 10 such models. Which of these models is best, and why? Is this model a real improvement on the best single-variable model? Explain.

10. Check that the best model you selected in Exercise 9 meets the required conditions.

11. For the Marks data set, create and examine all models with three explanatory variables that include the mark on Test 2. Note that there will be six of these models. Does any of these represent a real improvement on the best two-variable model you selected in Exercise 9? Explain.

12. Create a regression model for the Marks data using all of the explanatory variables. In light of the work you did in Exercises 9, 10, and 11, is this the best model? Explain.

13. Use the model you decided was best for the Marks data to predict the final exam mark of a student who received a mark of 55 on Assignment 1, 60 on Test 1, 65 on Assignment 2, 70 on Test 2, and 95 on the quizzes.

14. A researcher has collected a random sample of data about Honda Accords for sale in Ontario. The data indicate year of the car, number of kilometres, and list price. Create and analyze all possible regression models for these data. Be sure to check that the required conditions are met. Is your model useful in terms of predicting the list price of used Honda Accords?

CRE14-14

15. Think about your analysis in Exercise 14. Is the year of the car a quantitative variable? Create an indicator variable for the year of the car, and rebuild the model. Describe the models, and choose the best one.

16. A chain of retail outlets famous for their delicious (if unhealthy) doughnuts is looking for a new location. The company is trying to use data on local median income, population in the local area, and traffic flows by a proposed location to decide where to open a new store. The company has collected data for a number of existing stores. Investigate these data, and make a recommendation to the company about how to proceed.

CRE14-16

17. A researcher has discovered some extra data for the doughnut store location decision described in Exercise 16 above. Information was collected about whether each location was within a five-minute drive of a major highway (1 = within a five-minute drive of a major highway, 0 = otherwise). Re-analyze the data, including this extra information.

CRE14-17

18. An MBA (Master of Business Administration) student decides to see if he can predict the Standard and Poor's Toronto Stock Exchange Composite Index from the price of one or more share prices of Canadian companies.
    a. The student collects monthly historical price data (November 2002 to November 2008) for stocks from some important Canadian sectors[8]:
       • Rona Incorporated, the largest Canadian distributor and retailer of hardware, home renovation, and gardening products
       • Royal Bank of Canada, a major Canadian bank
       • Petro Canada, a Canadian oil and gas company with international interests
       • Potash Corporation of Saskatchewan, an integrated producer of fertilizer, industrial, and animal feed products

       Do any of these stocks (or a combination of these stocks) provide a good predictor of the TXS Composite Index?
    b. During the fall of 2008, the world economy experienced an unprecedented crisis and stock markets around the world gyrated wildly. Is there evidence of this in the data you examined in part a of this question? Would it be wise to try to build a model to predict the TSX Composite Index using data from this period? Explain.

CRE14-18

19. Statistics is a course with a bad reputation. Students tend to expect that they will have difficulty with the course, even when they do not know exactly what the course is about. A student decides that he wants to place Statistics in a proper context, and he collects data on a random sample of students studying in their third semester (the beginning of second year).

CRE14-19

---

[8] Yahoo! Finance Canada, "Potash Corp Sask Com NPV (POT.TO), Royal Bk of Canada Com NPV (RY.TO), S&P/TSX Composite index (Interi ∧GSPTSE), Rona Inc Com NPV (RON.TO), Petro Canada Com NPV (PCA.TO), Historical Prices, November 20, 2008," **http://ca.finance.yahoo.com**, accessed November 20, 2008.

The student attempts to predict the Statistics mark from the marks in other courses. Help him by deciding which of the possible models is best.

20. Check the required conditions of the model you chose in Exercise 19. If the required conditions are not met, do some further analysis and develop a model that will predict the Statistics mark and meets the required conditions.

21. Use the best model you created in Exercise 20 to predict the Statistics mark of a student who received 65 in all of the other courses.

TEST YOUR KNOWLEDGE

CRE14-22

22. Marcharpex is a company selling specialized software products to a select number of manufacturing companies. The company relies on senior salespeople to make contacts, sell the product, and provide a company contact for after-sales support. The company is wondering if its sales model is effective, and it has collected some data on

    • the years of experience of the salesperson
    • the monthly travel and entertainment budget of the salesperson
    • the local advertising budget (monthly) for the salesperson's area
    • the sales in the area

    Analyze the data, and select the best model to predict sales. Be sure to check the required conditions. Once you select the best model, create a 95% prediction interval (approximate) of the sales for a salesperson who has 15 years of experience, a monthly travel and entertainment budget of $2,000, and a local advertising budget of $4,000.

A NOTE ABOUT EXCEL'S FLOATING POINT PROBLEM

Depending on your computer, you may have seen a different result in your output for the Woodbon model with mortgage rates and advertising expenditure. The model might have been $y = \$10.31 - \$0.87x_2 + 0.01x_3$, with an adjusted R^2 of 0.948, and a standard error of only $2! The first time the author ran the regression in Excel (on an older computer) this was the result. However, if we examine this model, we see that it does not make any sense. If advertising expenditure were $3,000 and mortgage rates were 7%, this model predicts that Woodbon's sales would be $\$10.31 - \$0.87(7) + 0.01(\$3,000) = \$34.22$. This prediction is clearly unreasonable. This is a good lesson in using some common sense, and not relying too much on measures such as R^2 to choose a regression model. But what went wrong?

Excel has a "floating point" problem that sometimes produces inaccurate results when the data used to calculate the model are on significantly different scales. Advertising expenditures range from $500 to $3,500 and sales range from $21,334 to $115,320. In contrast, mortgage rates range from 5.99 to 18.38. Because mortgage rates vary only by units (as these rates are expressed), and the other variables vary by hundreds or thousands, the scales are not the same general order of magnitude. The alternate model shown above does not make sense, because Excel and an older computer did not successfully handle the situation. While such a problem does not arise often, it can be a good idea to scale your input data to the same order of magnitude. As well, if Excel produces nonsensical results, you should check the scale of your input data and re-scale if necessary.

Fortunately, the fix is easy. If this happened to you, simply change the scale of the mortgage rates by multiplying by 100, for example. A mortgage rate data point of 14.52083 becomes 1452.083, which is effectively $100x_2$. Then the mortgage rate data points will vary by hundreds, and will be on a similar scale with the other explanatory variable in the model. The multiple regression model that includes these adjusted mortgage rate data points and advertising expenditure is:

$$y = \$59,670.88 - \$31.3253 (100x_2) + 22.74x_3.$$

This can of course be rewritten as

$$y = \$59,670.88 - \$3,132.53x_2 + 22.74x_3.$$

This model matches the output in Exhibit 14.22.

APPENDIX 1 Cumulative Binomial Tables

Table value = P($x \leq$ number of successes)

Cumulative Binomial Probabilities for $n = 5$

no. of successes \ P	0.01	0.05	0.10	0.20	0.25	0.30	0.40	0.50	0.60	0.70	0.75	0.80	0.90	0.95	0.99
0	0.951	0.774	0.590	0.328	0.237	0.168	0.078	0.031	0.010	0.002	0.001	0.000	0.000	0.000	0.000
1	0.999	0.977	0.919	0.737	0.633	0.528	0.337	0.188	0.087	0.031	0.016	0.007	0.000	0.000	0.000
2	1.000	0.999	0.991	0.942	0.896	0.837	0.683	0.500	0.317	0.163	0.104	0.058	0.009	0.001	0.000
3	1.000	1.000	1.000	0.993	0.984	0.969	0.913	0.813	0.663	0.472	0.367	0.263	0.081	0.023	0.001
4	1.000	1.000	1.000	1.000	0.999	0.998	0.990	0.969	0.922	0.832	0.763	0.672	0.410	0.226	0.049

Table value = P($x \leq$ number of successes)

Cumulative Binomial Probabilities for $n = 6$

no. of successes \ P	0.01	0.05	0.10	0.20	0.25	0.30	0.40	0.50	0.60	0.70	0.75	0.80	0.90	0.95	0.99
0	0.941	0.735	0.531	0.262	0.178	0.118	0.047	0.016	0.004	0.001	0.000	0.000	0.000	0.000	0.000
1	0.999	0.967	0.886	0.655	0.534	0.420	0.233	0.109	0.041	0.011	0.005	0.002	0.000	0.000	0.000
2	1.000	0.998	0.984	0.901	0.831	0.744	0.544	0.344	0.179	0.070	0.038	0.017	0.001	0.000	0.000
3	1.000	1.000	0.999	0.983	0.962	0.930	0.821	0.656	0.456	0.256	0.169	0.099	0.016	0.002	0.000
4	1.000	1.000	1.000	0.998	0.995	0.989	0.959	0.891	0.767	0.580	0.466	0.345	0.114	0.033	0.001
5	1.000	1.000	1.000	1.000	1.000	0.999	0.996	0.984	0.953	0.882	0.822	0.738	0.469	0.265	0.059

Table value = P($x \leq$ number of successes)

Cumulative Binomial Probabilities for $n = 7$

no. of successes \ P	0.01	0.05	0.10	0.20	0.25	0.30	0.40	0.50	0.60	0.70	0.75	0.80	0.90	0.95	0.99
0	0.932	0.698	0.478	0.210	0.133	0.082	0.028	0.008	0.002	0.000	0.000	0.000	0.000	0.000	0.000
1	0.998	0.956	0.850	0.577	0.445	0.329	0.159	0.063	0.019	0.004	0.001	0.000	0.000	0.000	0.000
2	1.000	0.996	0.974	0.852	0.756	0.647	0.420	0.227	0.096	0.029	0.013	0.005	0.000	0.000	0.000
3	1.000	1.000	0.997	0.967	0.929	0.874	0.710	0.500	0.290	0.126	0.071	0.033	0.003	0.000	0.000
4	1.000	1.000	1.000	0.995	0.987	0.971	0.904	0.773	0.580	0.353	0.244	0.148	0.026	0.004	0.000
5	1.000	1.000	1.000	1.000	0.999	0.996	0.981	0.938	0.841	0.671	0.555	0.423	0.150	0.044	0.002
6	1.000	1.000	1.000	1.000	1.000	1.000	0.998	0.992	0.972	0.918	0.867	0.790	0.522	0.302	0.068

Table value = P($x \le$ number of successes)

no. of successes	P 0.01	0.05	0.10	0.20	0.25	0.30	0.40	0.50	0.60	0.70	0.75	0.80	0.90	0.95	0.99

Cumulative Binomial Probabilities for $n = 8$

no. of successes	0.01	0.05	0.10	0.20	0.25	0.30	0.40	0.50	0.60	0.70	0.75	0.80	0.90	0.95	0.99
0	0.923	0.663	0.430	0.168	0.100	0.058	0.017	0.004	0.001	0.000	0.000	0.000	0.000	0.000	0.000
1	0.997	0.943	0.813	0.503	0.367	0.255	0.106	0.035	0.009	0.001	0.000	0.000	0.000	0.000	0.000
2	1.000	0.994	0.962	0.797	0.679	0.552	0.315	0.145	0.050	0.011	0.004	0.001	0.000	0.000	0.000
3	1.000	1.000	0.995	0.944	0.886	0.806	0.594	0.363	0.174	0.058	0.027	0.010	0.000	0.000	0.000
4	1.000	1.000	1.000	0.990	0.973	0.942	0.826	0.637	0.406	0.194	0.114	0.056	0.005	0.000	0.000
5	1.000	1.000	1.000	0.999	0.996	0.989	0.950	0.855	0.685	0.448	0.321	0.203	0.038	0.006	0.000
6	1.000	1.000	1.000	1.000	1.000	0.999	0.991	0.965	0.894	0.745	0.633	0.497	0.187	0.057	0.003
7	1.000	1.000	1.000	1.000	1.000	1.000	0.999	0.996	0.983	0.942	0.900	0.832	0.570	0.337	0.077

Table value = P($x \le$ number of successes)

Cumulative Binomial Probabilities for $n = 9$

no. of successes	0.01	0.05	0.10	0.20	0.25	0.30	0.40	0.50	0.60	0.70	0.75	0.80	0.90	0.95	0.99
0	0.914	0.630	0.387	0.134	0.075	0.040	0.010	0.002	0.000	0.000	0.000	0.000	0.000	0.000	0.000
1	0.997	0.929	0.775	0.436	0.300	0.196	0.071	0.020	0.004	0.000	0.000	0.000	0.000	0.000	0.000
2	1.000	0.992	0.947	0.738	0.601	0.463	0.232	0.090	0.025	0.004	0.001	0.000	0.000	0.000	0.000
3	1.000	0.999	0.992	0.914	0.834	0.730	0.483	0.254	0.099	0.025	0.010	0.003	0.000	0.000	0.000
4	1.000	1.000	0.999	0.980	0.951	0.901	0.733	0.500	0.267	0.099	0.049	0.020	0.001	0.000	0.000
5	1.000	1.000	1.000	0.997	0.990	0.975	0.901	0.746	0.517	0.270	0.166	0.086	0.008	0.001	0.000
6	1.000	1.000	1.000	1.000	0.999	0.996	0.975	0.910	0.768	0.537	0.399	0.262	0.053	0.008	0.000
7	1.000	1.000	1.000	1.000	1.000	1.000	0.996	0.980	0.929	0.804	0.700	0.564	0.225	0.071	0.003
8	1.000	1.000	1.000	1.000	1.000	1.000	1.000	0.998	0.990	0.960	0.925	0.866	0.613	0.370	0.086

Table value = P($x \le$ number of successes)

Cumulative Binomial Probabilities for $n = 10$

no. of successes	0.01	0.05	0.10	0.20	0.25	0.30	0.40	0.50	0.60	0.70	0.75	0.80	0.90	0.95	0.99
0	0.904	0.599	0.349	0.107	0.056	0.028	0.006	0.001	0.000	0.000	0.000	0.000	0.000	0.000	0.000
1	0.996	0.914	0.736	0.376	0.244	0.149	0.046	0.011	0.002	0.000	0.000	0.000	0.000	0.000	0.000
2	1.000	0.988	0.930	0.678	0.526	0.383	0.167	0.055	0.012	0.002	0.000	0.000	0.000	0.000	0.000
3	1.000	0.999	0.987	0.879	0.776	0.650	0.382	0.172	0.055	0.011	0.004	0.001	0.000	0.000	0.000
4	1.000	1.000	0.998	0.967	0.922	0.850	0.633	0.377	0.166	0.047	0.020	0.006	0.000	0.000	0.000
5	1.000	1.000	1.000	0.994	0.980	0.953	0.834	0.623	0.367	0.150	0.078	0.033	0.002	0.000	0.000
6	1.000	1.000	1.000	0.999	0.996	0.989	0.945	0.828	0.618	0.350	0.224	0.121	0.013	0.001	0.000
7	1.000	1.000	1.000	1.000	1.000	0.998	0.988	0.945	0.833	0.617	0.474	0.322	0.070	0.012	0.000
8	1.000	1.000	1.000	1.000	1.000	1.000	0.998	0.989	0.954	0.851	0.756	0.624	0.264	0.086	0.004
9	1.000	1.000	1.000	1.000	1.000	1.000	1.000	0.999	0.994	0.972	0.944	0.893	0.651	0.401	0.096

Table value = P($x \leq$ number of successes)

Cumulative Binomial Probabilities for $n = 15$

no. of successes \ P	0.01	0.05	0.10	0.20	0.25	0.30	0.40	0.50	0.60	0.70	0.75	0.80	0.90	0.95	0.99
0	0.860	0.463	0.206	0.035	0.013	0.005	0.000	0.000	0.000	0.000	0.000	0.000	0.000	0.000	0.000
1	0.990	0.829	0.549	0.167	0.080	0.035	0.005	0.000	0.000	0.000	0.000	0.000	0.000	0.000	0.000
2	1.000	0.964	0.816	0.398	0.236	0.127	0.027	0.004	0.000	0.000	0.000	0.000	0.000	0.000	0.000
3	1.000	0.995	0.944	0.648	0.461	0.297	0.091	0.018	0.002	0.000	0.000	0.000	0.000	0.000	0.000
4	1.000	0.999	0.987	0.836	0.686	0.515	0.217	0.059	0.009	0.001	0.000	0.000	0.000	0.000	0.000
5	1.000	1.000	0.998	0.939	0.852	0.722	0.403	0.151	0.034	0.004	0.001	0.000	0.000	0.000	0.000
6	1.000	1.000	1.000	0.982	0.943	0.869	0.610	0.304	0.095	0.015	0.004	0.001	0.000	0.000	0.000
7	1.000	1.000	1.000	0.996	0.983	0.950	0.787	0.500	0.213	0.050	0.017	0.004	0.000	0.000	0.000
8	1.000	1.000	1.000	0.999	0.996	0.985	0.905	0.696	0.390	0.131	0.057	0.018	0.000	0.000	0.000
9	1.000	1.000	1.000	1.000	0.999	0.996	0.966	0.849	0.597	0.278	0.148	0.061	0.002	0.000	0.000
10	1.000	1.000	1.000	1.000	1.000	0.999	0.991	0.941	0.783	0.485	0.314	0.164	0.013	0.001	0.000
11	1.000	1.000	1.000	1.000	1.000	1.000	0.998	0.982	0.909	0.703	0.539	0.352	0.056	0.005	0.000
12	1.000	1.000	1.000	1.000	1.000	1.000	1.000	0.996	0.973	0.873	0.764	0.602	0.184	0.036	0.000
13	1.000	1.000	1.000	1.000	1.000	1.000	1.000	1.000	0.995	0.965	0.920	0.833	0.451	0.171	0.010
14	1.000	1.000	1.000	1.000	1.000	1.000	1.000	1.000	1.000	0.995	0.987	0.965	0.794	0.537	0.140

Table value = P($x \leq$ number of successes)

Cumulative Binomial Probabilities for $n = 20$

no. of successes \ P	0.01	0.05	0.10	0.20	0.25	0.30	0.40	0.50	0.60	0.70	0.75	0.80	0.90	0.95	0.99
0	0.818	0.358	0.122	0.012	0.003	0.001	0.000	0.000	0.000	0.000	0.000	0.000	0.000	0.000	0.000
1	0.983	0.736	0.392	0.069	0.024	0.008	0.001	0.000	0.000	0.000	0.000	0.000	0.000	0.000	0.000
2	0.999	0.925	0.677	0.206	0.091	0.035	0.004	0.000	0.000	0.000	0.000	0.000	0.000	0.000	0.000
3	1.000	0.984	0.867	0.411	0.225	0.107	0.016	0.001	0.000	0.000	0.000	0.000	0.000	0.000	0.000
4	1.000	0.997	0.957	0.630	0.415	0.238	0.051	0.006	0.000	0.000	0.000	0.000	0.000	0.000	0.000
5	1.000	1.000	0.989	0.804	0.617	0.416	0.126	0.021	0.002	0.000	0.000	0.000	0.000	0.000	0.000
6	1.000	1.000	0.998	0.913	0.786	0.608	0.250	0.058	0.006	0.000	0.000	0.000	0.000	0.000	0.000
7	1.000	1.000	1.000	0.968	0.898	0.772	0.416	0.132	0.021	0.001	0.000	0.000	0.000	0.000	0.000
8	1.000	1.000	1.000	0.990	0.959	0.887	0.596	0.252	0.057	0.005	0.001	0.000	0.000	0.000	0.000
9	1.000	1.000	1.000	0.997	0.986	0.952	0.755	0.412	0.128	0.017	0.004	0.001	0.000	0.000	0.000
10	1.000	1.000	1.000	0.999	0.996	0.983	0.872	0.588	0.245	0.048	0.014	0.003	0.000	0.000	0.000
11	1.000	1.000	1.000	1.000	0.999	0.995	0.943	0.748	0.404	0.113	0.041	0.010	0.000	0.000	0.000
12	1.000	1.000	1.000	1.000	1.000	0.999	0.979	0.868	0.584	0.228	0.102	0.032	0.000	0.000	0.000
13	1.000	1.000	1.000	1.000	1.000	1.000	0.994	0.942	0.750	0.392	0.214	0.087	0.002	0.000	0.000
14	1.000	1.000	1.000	1.000	1.000	1.000	0.998	0.979	0.874	0.584	0.383	0.196	0.011	0.000	0.000
15	1.000	1.000	1.000	1.000	1.000	1.000	1.000	0.994	0.949	0.762	0.585	0.370	0.043	0.003	0.000
16	1.000	1.000	1.000	1.000	1.000	1.000	1.000	0.999	0.984	0.893	0.775	0.589	0.133	0.016	0.000
17	1.000	1.000	1.000	1.000	1.000	1.000	1.000	1.000	0.996	0.965	0.909	0.794	0.323	0.075	0.001
18	1.000	1.000	1.000	1.000	1.000	1.000	1.000	1.000	0.999	0.992	0.976	0.931	0.608	0.264	0.017
19	1.000	1.000	1.000	1.000	1.000	1.000	1.000	1.000	1.000	0.999	0.997	0.988	0.878	0.642	0.182

Table value = P(x ≤ number of successes)

Cumulative Binomial Probabilities for $n = 25$														
no. of successes \ P	0.01	0.05	0.10	0.20	0.25	0.30	0.40	0.50	0.60	0.70	0.75	0.80	0.90	0.95	0.99
0	0.778	0.277	0.072	0.004	0.001	0.000	0.000	0.000	0.000	0.000	0.000	0.000	0.000	0.000	0.000
1	0.974	0.642	0.271	0.027	0.007	0.002	0.000	0.000	0.000	0.000	0.000	0.000	0.000	0.000	0.000
2	0.998	0.873	0.537	0.098	0.032	0.009	0.000	0.000	0.000	0.000	0.000	0.000	0.000	0.000	0.000
3	1.000	0.966	0.764	0.234	0.096	0.033	0.002	0.000	0.000	0.000	0.000	0.000	0.000	0.000	0.000
4	1.000	0.993	0.902	0.421	0.214	0.090	0.009	0.000	0.000	0.000	0.000	0.000	0.000	0.000	0.000
5	1.000	0.999	0.967	0.617	0.378	0.193	0.029	0.002	0.000	0.000	0.000	0.000	0.000	0.000	0.000
6	1.000	1.000	0.991	0.780	0.561	0.341	0.074	0.007	0.000	0.000	0.000	0.000	0.000	0.000	0.000
7	1.000	1.000	0.998	0.891	0.727	0.512	0.154	0.022	0.001	0.000	0.000	0.000	0.000	0.000	0.000
8	1.000	1.000	1.000	0.953	0.851	0.677	0.274	0.054	0.004	0.000	0.000	0.000	0.000	0.000	0.000
9	1.000	1.000	1.000	0.983	0.929	0.811	0.425	0.115	0.013	0.000	0.000	0.000	0.000	0.000	0.000
10	1.000	1.000	1.000	0.994	0.970	0.902	0.586	0.212	0.034	0.002	0.000	0.000	0.000	0.000	0.000
11	1.000	1.000	1.000	0.998	0.989	0.956	0.732	0.345	0.078	0.006	0.001	0.000	0.000	0.000	0.000
12	1.000	1.000	1.000	1.000	0.997	0.983	0.846	0.500	0.154	0.017	0.003	0.000	0.000	0.000	0.000
13	1.000	1.000	1.000	1.000	0.999	0.994	0.922	0.655	0.268	0.044	0.011	0.002	0.000	0.000	0.000
14	1.000	1.000	1.000	1.000	1.000	0.998	0.966	0.788	0.414	0.098	0.030	0.006	0.000	0.000	0.000
15	1.000	1.000	1.000	1.000	1.000	1.000	0.987	0.885	0.575	0.189	0.071	0.017	0.000	0.000	0.000
16	1.000	1.000	1.000	1.000	1.000	1.000	0.996	0.946	0.726	0.323	0.149	0.047	0.000	0.000	0.000
17	1.000	1.000	1.000	1.000	1.000	1.000	0.999	0.978	0.846	0.488	0.273	0.109	0.002	0.000	0.000
18	1.000	1.000	1.000	1.000	1.000	1.000	1.000	0.993	0.926	0.659	0.439	0.220	0.009	0.000	0.000
19	1.000	1.000	1.000	1.000	1.000	1.000	1.000	0.998	0.971	0.807	0.622	0.383	0.033	0.001	0.000
20	1.000	1.000	1.000	1.000	1.000	1.000	1.000	1.000	0.991	0.910	0.786	0.579	0.098	0.007	0.000
21	1.000	1.000	1.000	1.000	1.000	1.000	1.000	1.000	0.998	0.967	0.904	0.766	0.236	0.034	0.000
22	1.000	1.000	1.000	1.000	1.000	1.000	1.000	1.000	1.000	0.991	0.968	0.902	0.463	0.127	0.002
23	1.000	1.000	1.000	1.000	1.000	1.000	1.000	1.000	1.000	0.998	0.993	0.973	0.729	0.358	0.026
24	1.000	1.000	1.000	1.000	1.000	1.000	1.000	1.000	1.000	1.000	0.999	0.996	0.928	0.723	0.222

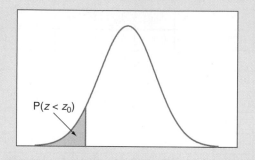

$P(z < z_0)$

z	0.00	0.01	0.02	0.03	0.04	0.05	0.06	0.07	0.08	0.09
−3.9	0.0000	0.0000	0.0000	0.0000	0.0000	0.0000	0.0000	0.0000	0.0000	0.0000
−3.8	0.0001	0.0001	0.0001	0.0001	0.0001	0.0001	0.0001	0.0001	0.0001	0.0001
−3.7	0.0001	0.0001	0.0001	0.0001	0.0001	0.0001	0.0001	0.0001	0.0001	0.0001
−3.6	0.0002	0.0002	0.0001	0.0001	0.0001	0.0001	0.0001	0.0001	0.0001	0.0001
−3.5	0.0002	0.0002	0.0002	0.0002	0.0002	0.0002	0.0002	0.0002	0.0002	0.0002
−3.4	0.0003	0.0003	0.0003	0.0003	0.0003	0.0003	0.0003	0.0003	0.0003	0.0002
−3.3	0.0005	0.0005	0.0005	0.0004	0.0004	0.0004	0.0004	0.0004	0.0004	0.0003
−3.2	0.0007	0.0007	0.0006	0.0006	0.0006	0.0006	0.0006	0.0005	0.0005	0.0005
−3.1	0.0010	0.0009	0.0009	0.0009	0.0008	0.0008	0.0008	0.0008	0.0007	0.0007
−3.0	0.0013	0.0013	0.0013	0.0012	0.0012	0.0011	0.0011	0.0011	0.0010	0.0010
−2.9	0.0019	0.0018	0.0018	0.0017	0.0016	0.0016	0.0015	0.0015	0.0014	0.0014
−2.8	0.0026	0.0025	0.0024	0.0023	0.0023	0.0022	0.0021	0.0021	0.0020	0.0019
−2.7	0.0035	0.0034	0.0033	0.0032	0.0031	0.0030	0.0029	0.0028	0.0027	0.0026
−2.6	0.0047	0.0045	0.0044	0.0043	0.0041	0.0040	0.0039	0.0038	0.0037	0.0036
−2.5	0.0062	0.0060	0.0059	0.0057	0.0055	0.0054	0.0052	0.0051	0.0049	0.0048
−2.4	0.0082	0.0080	0.0078	0.0075	0.0073	0.0071	0.0069	0.0068	0.0066	0.0064
−2.3	0.0107	0.0104	0.0102	0.0099	0.0096	0.0094	0.0091	0.0089	0.0087	0.0084
−2.2	0.0139	0.0136	0.0132	0.0129	0.0125	0.0122	0.0119	0.0116	0.0113	0.0110
−2.1	0.0179	0.0174	0.0170	0.0166	0.0162	0.0158	0.0154	0.0150	0.0146	0.0143
−2.0	0.0228	0.0222	0.0217	0.0212	0.0207	0.0202	0.0197	0.0192	0.0188	0.0183
−1.9	0.0287	0.0281	0.0274	0.0268	0.0262	0.0256	0.0250	0.0244	0.0239	0.0233
−1.8	0.0359	0.0351	0.0344	0.0336	0.0329	0.0322	0.0314	0.0307	0.0301	0.0294
−1.7	0.0446	0.0436	0.0427	0.0418	0.0409	0.0401	0.0392	0.0384	0.0375	0.0367
−1.6	0.0548	0.0537	0.0526	0.0516	0.0505	0.0495	0.0485	0.0475	0.0465	0.0455
−1.5	0.0668	0.0655	0.0643	0.0630	0.0618	0.0606	0.0594	0.0582	0.0571	0.0559
−1.4	0.0808	0.0793	0.0778	0.0764	0.0749	0.0735	0.0721	0.0708	0.0694	0.0681
−1.3	0.0968	0.0951	0.0934	0.0918	0.0901	0.0885	0.0869	0.0853	0.0838	0.0823
−1.2	0.1151	0.1131	0.1112	0.1093	0.1075	0.1056	0.1038	0.1020	0.1003	0.0985
−1.1	0.1357	0.1335	0.1314	0.1292	0.1271	0.1251	0.1230	0.1210	0.1190	0.1170
−1.0	0.1587	0.1562	0.1539	0.1515	0.1492	0.1469	0.1446	0.1423	0.1401	0.1379
−0.9	0.1841	0.1814	0.1788	0.1762	0.1736	0.1711	0.1685	0.1660	0.1635	0.1611
−0.8	0.2119	0.2090	0.2061	0.2033	0.2005	0.1977	0.1949	0.1922	0.1894	0.1867
−0.7	0.2420	0.2389	0.2358	0.2327	0.2296	0.2266	0.2236	0.2206	0.2177	0.2148
−0.6	0.2743	0.2709	0.2676	0.2643	0.2611	0.2578	0.2546	0.2514	0.2483	0.2451
−0.5	0.3085	0.3050	0.3015	0.2981	0.2946	0.2912	0.2877	0.2843	0.2810	0.2776
−0.4	0.3446	0.3409	0.3372	0.3336	0.3300	0.3264	0.3228	0.3192	0.3156	0.3121
−0.3	0.3821	0.3783	0.3745	0.3707	0.3669	0.3632	0.3594	0.3557	0.3520	0.3483

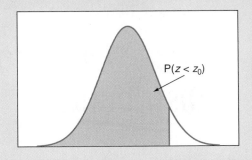

z	0.00	0.01	0.02	0.03	0.04	0.05	0.06	0.07	0.08	0.09
−0.2	0.4207	0.4168	0.4129	0.4090	0.4052	0.4013	0.3974	0.3936	0.3897	0.3859
−0.1	0.4602	0.4562	0.4522	0.4483	0.4443	0.4404	0.4364	0.4325	0.4286	0.4247
−0.0	0.5000	0.4960	0.4920	0.4880	0.4840	0.4801	0.4761	0.4721	0.4681	0.4641
0.0	0.5000	0.5040	0.5080	0.5120	0.5160	0.5199	0.5239	0.5279	0.5319	0.5359
0.1	0.5398	0.5438	0.5478	0.5517	0.5557	0.5596	0.5636	0.5675	0.5714	0.5753
0.2	0.5793	0.5832	0.5871	0.5910	0.5948	0.5987	0.6026	0.6064	0.6103	0.6141
0.3	0.6179	0.6217	0.6255	0.6293	0.6331	0.6368	0.6406	0.6443	0.6480	0.6517
0.4	0.6554	0.6591	0.6628	0.6664	0.6700	0.6736	0.6772	0.6808	0.6844	0.6879
0.5	0.6915	0.6950	0.6985	0.7019	0.7054	0.7088	0.7123	0.7157	0.7190	0.7224
0.6	0.7257	0.7291	0.7324	0.7357	0.7389	0.7422	0.7454	0.7486	0.7517	0.7549
0.7	0.7580	0.7611	0.7642	0.7673	0.7704	0.7734	0.7764	0.7794	0.7823	0.7852
0.8	0.7881	0.7910	0.7939	0.7967	0.7995	0.8023	0.8051	0.8078	0.8106	0.8133
0.9	0.8159	0.8186	0.8212	0.8238	0.8264	0.8289	0.8315	0.8340	0.8365	0.8389
1.0	0.8413	0.8438	0.8461	0.8485	0.8508	0.8531	0.8554	0.8577	0.8599	0.8621
1.1	0.8643	0.8665	0.8686	0.8708	0.8729	0.8749	0.8770	0.8790	0.8810	0.8830
1.2	0.8849	0.8869	0.8888	0.8907	0.8925	0.8944	0.8962	0.8980	0.8997	0.9015
1.3	0.9032	0.9049	0.9066	0.9082	0.9099	0.9115	0.9131	0.9147	0.9162	0.9177
1.4	0.9192	0.9207	0.9222	0.9236	0.9251	0.9265	0.9279	0.9292	0.9306	0.9319
1.5	0.9332	0.9345	0.9357	0.9370	0.9382	0.9394	0.9406	0.9418	0.9429	0.9441
1.6	0.9452	0.9463	0.9474	0.9484	0.9495	0.9505	0.9515	0.9525	0.9535	0.9545
1.7	0.9554	0.9564	0.9573	0.9582	0.9591	0.9599	0.9608	0.9616	0.9625	0.9633
1.8	0.9641	0.9649	0.9656	0.9664	0.9671	0.9678	0.9686	0.9693	0.9699	0.9706
1.9	0.9713	0.9719	0.9726	0.9732	0.9738	0.9744	0.9750	0.9756	0.9761	0.9767
2.0	0.9772	0.9778	0.9783	0.9788	0.9793	0.9798	0.9803	0.9808	0.9812	0.9817
2.1	0.9821	0.9826	0.9830	0.9834	0.9838	0.9842	0.9846	0.9850	0.9854	0.9857
2.2	0.9861	0.9864	0.9868	0.9871	0.9875	0.9878	0.9881	0.9884	0.9887	0.9890
2.3	0.9893	0.9896	0.9898	0.9901	0.9904	0.9906	0.9909	0.9911	0.9913	0.9916
2.4	0.9918	0.9920	0.9922	0.9925	0.9927	0.9929	0.9931	0.9932	0.9934	0.9936
2.5	0.9938	0.9940	0.9941	0.9943	0.9945	0.9946	0.9948	0.9949	0.9951	0.9952
2.6	0.9953	0.9955	0.9956	0.9957	0.9959	0.9960	0.9961	0.9962	0.9963	0.9964
2.7	0.9965	0.9966	0.9967	0.9968	0.9969	0.9970	0.9971	0.9972	0.9973	0.9974
2.8	0.9974	0.9975	0.9976	0.9977	0.9977	0.9978	0.9979	0.9979	0.9980	0.9981
2.9	0.9981	0.9982	0.9982	0.9983	0.9984	0.9984	0.9985	0.9985	0.9986	0.9986
3.0	0.9987	0.9987	0.9987	0.9988	0.9988	0.9989	0.9989	0.9989	0.9990	0.9990
3.1	0.9990	0.9991	0.9991	0.9991	0.9992	0.9992	0.9992	0.9992	0.9993	0.9993
3.2	0.9993	0.9993	0.9994	0.9994	0.9994	0.9994	0.9994	0.9995	0.9995	0.9995
3.3	0.9995	0.9995	0.9995	0.9996	0.9996	0.9996	0.9996	0.9996	0.9996	0.9997
3.4	0.9997	0.9997	0.9997	0.9997	0.9997	0.9997	0.9997	0.9997	0.9997	0.9998
3.5	0.9998	0.9998	0.9998	0.9998	0.9998	0.9998	0.9998	0.9998	0.9998	0.9998
3.6	0.9998	0.9998	0.9999	0.9999	0.9999	0.9999	0.9999	0.9999	0.9999	0.9999
3.7	0.9999	0.9999	0.9999	0.9999	0.9999	0.9999	0.9999	0.9999	0.9999	0.9999
3.8	0.9999	0.9999	0.9999	0.9999	0.9999	0.9999	0.9999	0.9999	0.9999	0.9999
3.9	1.0000	1.0000	1.0000	1.0000	1.0000	1.0000	1.0000	1.0000	1.0000	1.0000

Critical Values for the *t*-Distribution

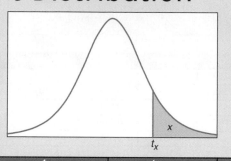

t_x

Degrees of Freedom	$t_{.100}$	$t_{.050}$	$t_{.025}$	$t_{.010}$	$t_{.005}$
1	3.078	6.314	12.706	31.821	63.656
2	1.886	2.920	4.303	6.965	9.925
3	1.638	2.353	3.182	4.541	5.841
4	1.533	2.132	2.776	3.747	4.604
5	1.476	2.015	2.571	3.365	4.032
6	1.440	1.943	2.447	3.143	3.707
7	1.415	1.895	2.365	2.998	3.499
8	1.397	1.860	2.306	2.896	3.355
9	1.383	1.833	2.262	2.821	3.250
10	1.372	1.812	2.228	2.764	3.169
11	1.363	1.796	2.201	2.718	3.106
12	1.356	1.782	2.179	2.681	3.055
13	1.350	1.771	2.160	2.650	3.012
14	1.345	1.761	2.145	2.624	2.977
15	1.341	1.753	2.131	2.602	2.947
16	1.337	1.746	2.120	2.583	2.921
17	1.333	1.740	2.110	2.567	2.898
18	1.330	1.734	2.101	2.552	2.878
19	1.328	1.729	2.093	2.539	2.861
20	1.325	1.725	2.086	2.528	2.845
21	1.323	1.721	2.080	2.518	2.831
22	1.321	1.717	2.074	2.508	2.819
23	1.319	1.714	2.069	2.500	2.807
24	1.318	1.711	2.064	2.492	2.797
25	1.316	1.708	2.060	2.485	2.787
26	1.315	1.706	2.056	2.479	2.779
27	1.314	1.703	2.052	2.473	2.771
28	1.313	1.701	2.048	2.467	2.763
29	1.311	1.699	2.045	2.462	2.756
30	1.310	1.697	2.042	2.457	2.750
35	1.306	1.690	2.030	2.438	2.724
40	1.303	1.684	2.021	2.423	2.704
45	1.301	1.679	2.014	2.412	2.690
50	1.299	1.676	2.009	2.403	2.678
60	1.296	1.671	2.000	2.390	2.660
70	1.294	1.667	1.994	2.381	2.648
80	1.292	1.664	1.990	2.374	2.639
90	1.291	1.662	1.987	2.368	2.632
100	1.290	1.660	1.984	2.364	2.626
150	1.287	1.655	1.976	2.351	2.609
200	1.286	1.653	1.972	2.345	2.601
∞	1.282	1.645	1.960	2.326	2.576

APPENDIX 4

Wilcoxon Signed Rank Sum Test Table, Critical Values and p-Values

n	W_L	W_U	$P(W \le W_L) = P(W \ge W_U)$
4	0	10	0.062
	1	9	0.125
5	0	15	0.031
	1	14	0.062
6	0	21	0.016
	1	20	0.031
	2	19	0.047
	3	18	0.078
7	0	28	0.008
	1	27	0.016
	2	26	0.023
	3	25	0.039
	4	24	0.055
8	1	35	0.008
	2	34	0.012
	3	33	0.020
	4	32	0.027
	5	31	0.039
	6	30	0.055
9	3	42	0.010
	5	40	0.020
	6	39	0.027
	8	37	0.049
	9	36	0.064
10	5	50	0.010
	8	47	0.024
	9	46	0.032
	10	45	0.042
	11	44	0.053
11	7	59	0.010
	10	56	0.021
	11	55	0.027
	13	53	0.042
	14	52	0.051
12	9	69	0.008
	10	68	0.011
	13	65	0.021
	14	64	0.026
	17	61	0.046
	18	60	0.055
13	12	79	0.009
	13	78	0.011
	17	74	0.024
	18	73	0.029
	21	70	0.047
	22	69	0.055
14	16	89	0.010
	21	84	0.025
	25	80	0.045
	26	79	0.052

n	W_L	W_U	$P(W \le W_L) = P(W \ge W_U)$
15	19	101	0.009
	20	100	0.011
	25	95	0.024
	26	94	0.028
	30	90	0.047
	31	89	0.054
16	23	113	0.009
	24	112	0.011
	30	106	0.025
	35	101	0.047
	36	100	0.052
17	28	125	0.010
	35	118	0.025
	41	112	0.049
	42	111	0.054
18	33	138	0.010
	40	131	0.024
	41	130	0.027
	47	124	0.049
	48	123	0.054
19	38	152	0.010
	46	144	0.025
	53	137	0.048
	54	136	0.052
20	43	167	0.010
	52	158	0.024
	53	157	0.027
	60	150	0.049
	61	149	0.053
21	49	182	0.010
	59	172	0.025
	67	164	0.048
	68	163	0.052
22	56	197	0.010
	66	187	0.025
	75	178	0.049
	76	177	0.053
23	62	214	0.010
	73	203	0.024
	74	202	0.026
	83	193	0.049
	84	192	0.052
24	69	231	0.010
	81	219	0.025
	91	209	0.048
	92	208	0.051
25	77	248	0.010
	89	236	0.024
	90	235	0.026
	100	225	0.048
	101	224	0.051

Source: Data extracted from C.H. Kraft and C. van Eeden, *A Nonparametric Introduction to Statistics* (New York: Macmillan, 1968). Used with permission.

APPENDIX 5 Wilcoxon Rank Sum Test Table, Critical Values

n_1	n_2	W_L	W_U	$P(W_1 \leq W_L) = P(W_1 \geq W_U)$
4	4	12	24	0.057
		11	29	0.029
		1	26	0.014
4	5	13	27	0.056
		12	28	0.032
		11	29	0.016
		10	30	0.008
4	6	14	30	0.057
		13	31	0.033
		12	32	0.019
		11	33	0.010
4	7	15	33	0.055
		14	34	0.036
		13	35	0.021
		12	36	0.012
		11	37	0.006
4	8	16	36	0.055
		14	38	0.024
		13	39	0.014
		12	40	0.008
4	9	17	39	0.053
		15	41	0.025
		13	43	0.010
4	10	18	42	0.053
		16	44	0.027
		15	45	0.018
		14	46	0.012
		13	47	0.007
5	5	19	36	0.048
		18	37	0.028
		17	38	0.016
		16	39	0.008
5	6	21	39	0.063
		20	40	0.041
		19	41	0.026
		18	42	0.015
		17	43	0.009
5	7	22	43	0.053
		21	44	0.037
		20	45	0.024
		19	46	0.015
		18	47	0.009
5	8	23	47	0.047
		22	48	0.033
		21	49	0.023
		20	50	0.015
		19	51	0.009
5	9	25	50	0.056
		23	52	0.030
		22	53	0.021
		21	54	0.014
		20	55	0.009

n_1	n_2	W_L	W_U	$P(W_1 \leq W_L) = P(W_1 \geq W_U)$
5	10	26	54	0.050
		24	56	0.028
		23	57	0.020
		22	58	0.014
		21	59	0.010
6	6	28	50	0.047
		27	51	0.032
		26	52	0.021
		25	53	0.013
		24	54	0.008
6	7	30	54	0.051
		28	56	0.026
		26	58	0.011
		25	59	0.007
6	8	32	54	0.054
		30	60	0.030
		29	61	0.021
		27	63	0.010
6	9	34	62	0.057
		31	65	0.025
		29	67	0.013
		28	68	0.009
6	10	36	66	0.059
		35	67	0.047
		33	69	0.028
		32	70	0.021
		30	72	0.011
		29	73	0.008
7	7	39	66	0.049
		37	68	0.027
		36	69	0.019
		35	70	0.013
		34	71	0.009
7	8	41	71	0.047
		39	73	0.027
		38	74	0.020
		36	76	0.010
7	9	44	75	0.057
		41	78	0.027
		40	79	0.021
		38	81	0.011
		37	82	0.008
7	10	46	80	0.054
		45	81	0.044
		43	83	0.028
		42	84	0.022
		40	86	0.011
		39	87	0.009
8	8	52	84	0.052
		49	87	0.025
		46	90	0.010

(Continued)

n_1	n_2	W_L	W_U	$P(W_1 \leq W_L) = P(W_1 \geq W_U)$
8	9	55	89	0.057
		54	90	0.046
		52	92	0.030
		51	93	0.023
		48	96	0.010
8	10	57	95	0.051
		54	98	0.027
		53	99	0.022
		50	102	0.010
9	9	67	104	0.057
		66	105	0.047
		63	108	0.025
		60	111	0.012
		59	112	0.009

n_1	n_2	W_L	W_U	$P(W_1 \leq W_L) = P(W_1 \geq W_U)$
9	10	70	110	0.056
		69	111	0.047
		66	114	0.027
		65	115	0.022
		62	118	0.011
		61	119	0.009
10	10	83	127	0.053
		82	128	0.045
		79	131	0.026
		78	132	0.022
		75	135	0.012
		74	136	0.009

Source: Data taken from the Wilcoxon Signed Rank Sum Test Table as prepared by Dr. Richard Darlington at
http://comp9.psych.cornell.edu/Darlington/wilcoxon/wilcox.5.htm. Used with the permission of Dr. Richard Darlington.

APPENDIX 6 — *F*-Distribution, Critical Values

Degrees of Freedom in the Numerator

df (denom)	p-value	1	2	3	4	5	6	7	8	9	10	15	20	25	30	40	50	80	120
1	0.050	161.45	199.50	215.71	224.58	230.16	233.99	236.77	238.88	240.54	241.88	245.95	248.01	249.26	250.10	251.14	251.77	252.72	253.25
	0.025	647.79	799.50	864.16	899.58	921.85	937.11	948.22	956.66	963.28	968.63	984.87	993.10	998.08	1001.41	1005.60	1008.12	1011.91	1014.02
	0.010	4052.18	4999.50	5403.35	5624.58	5763.65	5858.99	5928.36	5981.07	6022.47	6055.85	6157.28	6208.73	6239.83	6260.65	6286.78	6302.52	6326.20	6339.39
2	0.050	18.51	19.00	19.16	19.25	19.30	19.33	19.35	19.37	19.38	19.40	19.43	19.45	19.46	19.46	19.47	19.48	19.48	19.49
	0.025	38.51	39.00	39.17	39.25	39.30	39.33	39.36	39.37	39.39	39.40	39.43	39.45	39.46	39.46	39.47	39.48	39.49	39.49
	0.010	98.50	99.00	99.17	99.25	99.30	99.33	99.36	99.37	99.39	99.40	99.43	99.45	99.46	99.47	99.47	99.48	99.49	99.49
3	0.050	10.13	9.55	9.28	9.12	9.01	8.94	8.89	8.85	8.81	8.79	8.70	8.66	8.63	8.62	8.59	8.58	8.56	8.55
	0.025	17.44	16.04	15.44	15.10	14.88	14.73	14.62	14.54	14.47	14.42	14.25	14.17	14.12	14.08	14.04	14.01	13.97	13.95
	0.010	34.12	30.82	29.46	28.71	28.24	27.91	27.67	27.49	27.35	27.23	26.87	26.69	26.58	26.50	26.41	26.35	26.27	26.22
4	0.050	7.71	6.94	6.59	6.39	6.26	6.16	6.09	6.04	6.00	5.96	5.86	5.80	5.77	5.75	5.72	5.70	5.67	5.66
	0.025	12.22	10.65	9.98	9.60	9.36	9.20	9.07	8.98	8.90	8.84	8.66	8.56	8.50	8.46	8.41	8.38	8.33	8.31
	0.010	21.20	18.00	16.69	15.98	15.52	15.21	14.98	14.80	14.66	14.55	14.20	14.02	13.91	13.84	13.75	13.69	13.61	13.56
5	0.050	6.61	5.79	5.41	5.19	5.05	4.95	4.88	4.82	4.77	4.74	4.62	4.56	4.52	4.50	4.46	4.44	4.41	4.40
	0.025	10.01	8.43	7.76	7.39	7.15	6.98	6.85	6.76	6.68	6.62	6.43	6.33	6.27	6.23	6.18	6.14	6.10	6.07
	0.010	16.26	13.27	12.06	11.39	10.97	10.67	10.46	10.29	10.16	10.05	9.72	9.55	9.45	9.38	9.29	9.24	9.16	9.11
6	0.050	5.99	5.14	4.76	4.53	4.39	4.28	4.21	4.15	4.10	4.06	3.94	3.87	3.83	3.81	3.77	3.75	3.72	3.70
	0.025	8.81	7.26	6.60	6.23	5.99	5.82	5.70	5.60	5.52	5.46	5.27	5.17	5.11	5.07	5.01	4.98	4.93	4.90
	0.010	13.75	10.92	9.78	9.15	8.75	8.47	8.26	8.10	7.98	7.87	7.56	7.40	7.30	7.23	7.14	7.09	7.01	6.97
7	0.050	5.59	4.74	4.35	4.12	3.97	3.87	3.79	3.73	3.68	3.64	3.51	3.44	3.40	3.38	3.34	3.32	3.29	3.27
	0.025	8.07	6.54	5.89	5.52	5.29	5.12	4.99	4.90	4.82	4.76	4.57	4.47	4.40	4.36	4.31	4.28	4.23	4.20
	0.010	12.25	9.55	8.45	7.85	7.46	7.19	6.99	6.84	6.72	6.62	6.31	6.16	6.06	5.99	5.91	5.86	5.78	5.74
8	0.050	5.32	4.46	4.07	3.84	3.69	3.58	3.50	3.44	3.39	3.35	3.22	3.15	3.11	3.08	3.04	3.02	2.99	2.97
	0.025	7.57	6.06	5.42	5.05	4.82	4.65	4.53	4.43	4.36	4.30	4.10	4.00	3.94	3.89	3.84	3.81	3.76	3.73
	0.010	11.26	8.65	7.59	7.01	6.63	6.37	6.18	6.03	5.91	5.81	5.52	5.36	5.26	5.20	5.12	5.07	4.99	4.95
9	0.050	5.12	4.26	3.86	3.63	3.48	3.37	3.29	3.23	3.18	3.14	3.01	2.94	2.89	2.86	2.83	2.80	2.77	2.75
	0.025	7.21	5.71	5.08	4.72	4.48	4.32	4.20	4.10	4.03	3.96	3.77	3.67	3.60	3.56	3.51	3.47	3.42	3.39
	0.010	10.56	8.02	6.99	6.42	6.06	5.80	5.61	5.47	5.35	5.26	4.96	4.81	4.71	4.65	4.57	4.52	4.44	4.40

Degrees of Freedom in the Denominator

Degrees of Freedom in the Numerator

Denominator df	p-value	1	2	3	4	5	6	7	8	9	10	15	20	25	30	40	50	80	120
10	0.050	4.96	4.10	3.71	3.48	3.33	3.22	3.14	3.07	3.02	2.98	2.85	2.77	2.73	2.70	2.66	2.64	2.60	2.58
	0.025	6.94	5.46	4.83	4.47	4.24	4.07	3.95	3.85	3.78	3.72	3.52	3.42	3.35	3.31	3.26	3.22	3.17	3.14
	0.010	10.04	7.56	6.55	5.99	5.64	5.39	5.20	5.06	4.54	4.85	4.56	4.41	4.31	4.25	4.17	4.12	4.04	4.00
15	0.050	4.54	3.68	3.29	3.06	2.90	2.79	2.71	2.64	2.59	2.54	2.40	2.33	2.28	2.25	2.20	2.18	2.14	2.11
	0.025	6.20	4.77	4.15	3.80	3.58	3.41	3.29	3.20	3.12	3.06	2.86	2.76	2.69	2.64	2.59	2.55	2.49	2.46
	0.010	8.68	6.36	5.42	4.89	4.56	4.32	4.14	4.00	3.89	3.80	3.52	3.37	3.28	3.21	3.13	3.08	3.00	2.96
20	0.050	4.35	3.49	3.10	2.87	2.71	2.60	2.51	2.45	2.39	2.35	2.20	2.12	2.07	2.04	1.99	1.97	1.92	1.90
	0.025	5.87	4.46	3.86	3.51	3.29	3.13	3.01	2.91	2.84	2.77	2.57	2.46	2.40	2.35	2.29	2.25	2.19	2.16
	0.010	8.10	5.85	4.94	4.43	4.10	3.87	3.70	3.56	3.46	3.37	3.09	2.94	2.84	2.78	2.69	2.64	2.56	2.52
25	0.050	4.24	3.39	2.99	2.76	2.60	2.49	2.40	2.34	2.28	2.24	2.09	2.01	1.96	1.92	1.87	1.84	1.80	1.77
	0.025	5.69	4.29	3.69	3.35	3.13	2.97	2.85	2.75	2.68	2.61	2.41	2.30	2.23	2.18	2.12	2.08	2.02	1.98
	0.010	7.77	5.57	4.68	4.18	3.85	3.63	3.46	3.32	3.22	3.13	2.85	2.70	2.60	2.54	2.45	2.40	2.32	2.27
30	0.050	4.17	3.32	2.92	2.69	2.53	2.42	2.33	2.27	2.21	2.16	2.01	1.93	1.88	1.84	1.79	1.76	1.71	1.68
	0.025	5.57	4.18	3.59	3.25	3.03	2.87	2.75	2.65	2.57	2.51	2.31	2.20	2.12	2.07	2.01	1.97	1.90	1.87
	0.010	7.56	5.39	4.51	4.02	3.70	3.47	3.30	3.17	3.07	2.98	2.70	2.55	2.45	2.39	2.30	2.25	2.16	2.11
40	0.050	4.08	3.23	2.84	2.61	2.45	2.34	2.25	2.18	2.12	2.08	1.92	1.84	1.78	1.74	1.69	1.66	1.61	1.58
	0.025	5.42	4.05	3.46	3.13	2.90	2.74	2.62	2.53	2.45	2.39	2.18	2.07	1.99	1.94	1.88	1.83	1.76	1.72
	0.010	7.31	5.18	4.31	3.83	3.51	3.29	3.12	2.99	2.89	2.80	2.52	2.37	2.27	2.20	2.11	2.06	1.97	1.92
50	0.050	4.03	3.18	2.79	2.56	2.40	2.29	2.20	2.13	2.07	2.03	1.87	1.78	1.73	1.69	1.63	1.60	1.54	1.51
	0.025	5.34	3.97	3.39	3.05	2.83	2.67	2.55	2.46	2.38	2.32	2.11	1.99	1.92	1.87	1.80	1.75	1.68	1.64
	0.010	7.17	5.06	4.20	3.72	3.41	3.19	3.02	2.89	2.78	2.70	2.42	2.27	2.17	2.10	2.01	1.95	1.86	1.80
80	0.050	3.96	3.11	2.72	2.49	2.33	2.21	2.13	2.06	2.00	1.95	1.79	1.70	1.64	1.60	1.54	1.51	1.45	1.41
	0.025	5.22	3.86	3.28	2.95	2.73	2.57	2.45	2.35	2.28	2.21	2.00	1.88	1.81	1.75	1.68	1.63	1.55	1.51
	0.010	6.96	4.88	4.04	3.56	3.26	3.04	2.87	2.74	2.64	2.55	2.27	2.12	2.01	1.94	1.85	1.79	1.69	1.63
120	0.050	3.92	3.07	2.68	2.45	2.29	2.18	2.09	2.02	1.96	1.91	1.75	1.66	1.60	1.55	1.50	1.46	1.39	1.35
	0.025	5.15	3.80	3.23	2.89	2.67	2.52	2.39	2.30	2.22	2.16	1.94	1.82	1.75	1.69	1.61	1.56	1.48	1.43
	0.010	6.85	4.79	3.95	3.48	3.17	2.96	2.79	2.66	2.56	2.47	2.19	2.03	1.93	1.86	1.76	1.70	1.60	1.53

Degrees of Freedom in the Denominator

APPENDIX 7 Critical Values of q

$n_T - k$ \ k	2	3	4	5	6	7	8	9	10
Confidence Level = 0.95									
1	17.97	26.98	32.82	37.08	40.41	43.12	45.40	47.36	49.07
2	6.08	8.33	9.80	10.88	11.74	12.44	13.03	13.54	13.99
3	4.50	5.91	6.82	7.50	8.04	8.48	8.85	9.18	9.46
4	3.93	5.04	5.76	6.29	6.71	7.05	7.35	7.60	7.83
5	3.64	4.60	5.22	5.67	6.03	6.33	6.58	6.80	6.99
6	3.46	4.34	4.90	5.30	5.63	5.90	6.12	6.32	6.49
7	3.34	4.16	4.68	5.06	5.36	5.61	5.82	6.00	6.16
8	3.26	4.04	4.53	4.89	5.17	5.40	5.60	5.77	5.92
9	3.20	3.95	4.41	4.76	5.02	5.24	5.43	5.59	5.74
10	3.15	3.88	4.33	4.65	4.91	5.12	5.30	5.46	5.60
11	3.11	3.82	4.26	4.57	4.82	5.03	5.20	5.35	5.49
12	3.08	3.77	4.20	4.51	4.75	4.95	5.12	5.27	5.39
13	3.06	3.73	4.15	4.45	4.69	4.88	5.05	5.19	5.32
14	3.03	3.70	4.11	4.41	4.64	4.83	4.99	5.13	5.25
15	3.01	3.67	4.08	4.37	4.59	4.78	4.94	5.08	5.20
16	3.00	3.65	4.05	4.33	4.56	4.74	4.90	5.03	5.15
17	2.98	3.63	4.02	4.30	4.52	4.70	4.86	4.99	5.11
18	2.97	3.61	4.00	4.28	4.49	4.67	4.82	4.96	5.07
19	2.96	3.59	3.98	4.25	4.47	4.65	4.79	4.92	5.04
20	2.95	3.58	3.96	4.23	4.45	4.62	4.77	4.90	5.01
24	2.92	3.53	3.90	4.17	4.37	4.54	4.68	4.81	4.92
30	2.89	3.49	3.85	4.10	4.30	4.46	4.60	4.72	4.82
40	2.86	3.44	3.79	4.04	4.23	4.39	4.52	4.63	4.73
60	2.83	3.40	3.74	3.98	4.16	4.31	4.44	4.55	4.65
120	2.80	3.36	3.68	3.92	4.10	4.24	4.36	4.47	4.56
∞	2.77	3.31	3.63	3.86	4.03	4.17	4.29	4.39	4.47

Confidence Level = 0.95									
k $n_T - k$	11	12	13	14	15	16	17	18	19	20
1	50.59	51.96	53.20	54.33	55.36	56.32	57.22	58.04	58.83	59.56
2	14.39	14.75	15.08	15.38	15.65	15.91	16.14	16.37	16.57	16.77
3	9.72	9.95	10.15	10.35	10.52	10.69	10.84	10.98	11.11	11.24
4	8.03	8.21	8.37	8.52	8.66	8.79	8.91	9.03	9.13	9.23
5	7.17	7.32	7.47	7.60	7.72	7.83	7.93	8.03	8.12	8.21
6	6.65	6.79	6.92	7.03	7.14	7.24	7.34	7.43	7.51	7.59
7	6.30	6.43	6.55	6.66	6.76	6.85	6.94	7.02	7.10	7.17
8	6.05	6.18	6.29	6.39	6.48	6.57	6.65	6.73	6.80	6.87
9	5.87	5.98	6.09	6.19	6.28	6.36	6.44	6.51	6.58	6.64
10	5.72	5.83	5.93	6.03	6.11	6.19	6.27	6.34	6.40	6.47
11	5.61	5.71	5.81	5.90	5.98	6.06	6.13	6.20	6.27	6.33
12	5.51	5.61	5.71	5.80	5.88	5.95	6.02	6.09	6.15	6.21
13	5.43	5.53	5.63	5.71	5.79	5.86	5.93	5.99	6.05	6.11
14	5.36	5.46	5.55	5.64	5.71	5.79	5.85	5.91	5.97	6.03
15	5.31	5.40	5.49	5.57	5.65	5.72	5.78	5.85	5.90	5.96
16	5.26	5.35	5.44	5.52	5.59	5.66	5.73	5.79	5.84	5.90
17	5.21	5.31	5.39	5.47	5.54	5.61	5.67	5.73	5.79	5.84
18	5.17	5.27	5.35	5.43	5.50	5.57	5.63	5.69	5.74	5.79
19	5.14	5.23	5.31	5.39	5.46	5.53	5.59	5.65	5.70	5.75
20	5.11	5.20	5.28	5.36	5.43	5.49	5.55	5.61	5.66	5.71
24	5.01	5.10	5.18	5.25	5.32	5.38	5.44	5.49	5.55	5.59
30	4.92	5.00	5.08	5.15	5.21	5.27	5.33	5.38	5.43	5.47
40	4.82	4.90	4.98	5.04	5.11	5.16	5.22	5.27	5.31	5.36
60	4.73	4.81	4.88	4.94	5.00	5.06	5.11	5.15	5.20	5.24
120	4.64	4.71	4.78	4.84	4.90	4.95	5.00	5.04	5.09	5.13
∞	4.55	4.62	4.68	4.74	4.80	4.85	4.89	4.93	4.97	5.01

Confidence Level = 0.99									
$n_T - k$ \ k	2	3	4	5	6	7	8	9	10
1	90.03	135.0	164.3	185.6	202.2	215.8	227.2	237.0	245.6
2	14.04	19.02	22.29	24.72	26.63	28.20	29.53	30.68	31.69
3	8.26	10.62	12.17	13.33	14.24	15.00	15.64	16.20	16.69
4	6.51	8.12	9.17	9.96	10.58	11.10	11.55	11.93	12.27
5	5.70	6.98	7.80	8.42	8.91	9.32	9.67	9.97	10.24
6	5.24	6.33	7.03	7.56	7.97	8.32	8.61	8.87	9.10
7	4.95	5.92	6.54	7.01	7.37	7.68	7.94	8.17	8.37
8	4.75	5.64	6.20	6.62	6.96	7.24	7.47	7.68	7.86
9	4.60	5.43	5.96	6.35	6.66	6.91	7.13	7.33	7.49
10	4.48	5.27	5.77	6.14	6.43	6.67	6.87	7.05	7.21
11	4.39	5.15	5.62	5.97	6.25	6.48	6.67	6.84	6.99
12	4.32	5.05	5.50	5.84	6.10	6.32	6.51	6.67	6.81
13	4.26	4.96	5.40	5.73	5.98	6.19	6.37	6.53	6.67
14	4.21	4.89	5.32	5.63	5.88	6.08	6.26	6.41	6.54
15	4.17	4.84	5.25	5.56	5.80	5.99	6.16	6.31	6.44
16	4.13	4.79	5.19	5.49	5.72	5.92	6.08	6.22	6.35
17	4.10	4.74	5.14	5.43	5.66	5.85	6.01	6.15	6.27
18	4.07	4.70	5.09	5.38	5.60	5.79	5.94	6.08	6.20
19	4.05	4.67	5.05	5.33	5.55	5.73	5.89	6.02	6.14
20	4.02	4.64	5.02	5.29	5.51	5.69	5.84	5.97	6.09
24	3.96	4.55	4.91	5.17	5.37	5.54	5.69	5.81	5.92
30	3.89	4.45	4.80	5.05	5.24	5.40	5.54	5.65	5.76
40	3.82	4.37	4.70	4.93	5.11	5.26	5.39	5.50	5.60
60	3.76	4.28	4.59	4.82	4.99	5.13	5.25	5.36	5.45
120	3.70	4.20	4.50	4.71	4.87	5.01	5.12	5.21	5.30
∞	3.64	4.12	4.40	4.60	4.76	4.88	4.99	5.08	5.16

Confidence Level = 0.99										
$n_T - k$ \\ k	11	12	13	14	15	16	17	18	19	20
1	253.2	260.0	266.2	271.8	277.0	281.8	286.3	290.4	294.3	298.0
2	32.59	33.40	34.13	34.81	35.43	36.00	36.53	37.03	37.50	37.95
3	17.13	17.53	17.89	18.22	18.52	18.81	19.07	19.32	19.55	19.77
4	12.57	12.84	13.09	13.32	13.53	13.73	13.91	14.08	14.24	14.40
5	10.48	10.70	10.89	11.08	11.24	11.40	11.55	11.68	11.81	11.93
6	9.30	9.48	9.65	9.81	9.95	10.08	10.21	10.32	10.43	10.54
7	8.55	8.71	8.86	9.00	9.12	9.24	9.35	9.46	9.55	9.65
8	8.03	8.18	8.31	8.44	8.55	8.66	8.76	8.85	8.94	9.03
9	7.65	7.78	7.91	8.03	8.13	8.23	8.33	8.41	8.49	8.57
10	7.36	7.49	7.60	7.71	7.81	7.91	7.99	8.08	8.15	8.23
11	7.13	7.25	7.36	7.46	7.56	7.65	7.73	7.81	7.88	7.95
12	6.94	7.06	7.17	7.26	7.36	7.44	7.52	7.59	7.66	7.73
13	6.79	6.90	7.01	7.10	7.19	7.27	7.35	7.42	7.48	7.55
14	6.66	6.77	6.87	6.96	7.05	7.13	7.20	7.27	7.33	7.39
15	6.55	6.66	6.76	6.84	6.93	7.00	7.07	7.14	7.20	7.26
16	6.46	6.56	6.66	6.74	6.82	6.90	6.97	7.03	7.09	7.15
17	6.38	6.48	6.57	6.66	6.73	6.81	6.87	6.94	7.00	7.05
18	6.31	6.41	6.50	6.58	6.65	6.73	6.79	6.85	6.91	6.97
19	6.25	6.34	6.43	6.51	6.58	6.65	6.72	6.78	6.84	6.89
20	6.19	6.28	6.37	6.45	6.52	6.59	6.65	6.71	6.77	6.82
24	6.02	6.11	6.19	6.26	6.33	6.39	6.45	6.51	6.56	6.61
30	5.85	5.93	6.01	6.08	6.14	6.20	6.26	6.31	6.36	6.41
40	5.69	5.76	5.83	5.90	5.96	6.02	6.07	6.12	6.16	6.21
60	5.53	5.60	5.67	5.73	5.78	5.84	5.89	5.93	5.97	6.01
120	5.37	5.44	5.50	5.56	5.61	5.66	5.71	5.75	5.79	5.83
∞	5.23	5.28	5.35	5.40	5.45	5.49	5.54	5.57	5.61	5.65

Source: Reprinted with permission from E. S. Pearson and H. O. Hartley, *Biometrika Tables for Statisticians* (New York: Cambridge University Press, 1954).

APPENDIX 8

Critical Values for the χ^2-Distribution

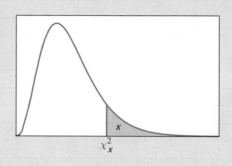

Degrees of Freedom	$\chi^2_{.100}$	$\chi^2_{.050}$	$\chi^2_{.025}$	$\chi^2_{.010}$	$\chi^2_{.005}$
1	2.706	3.841	5.024	6.635	7.879
2	4.605	5.991	7.378	9.210	10.597
3	6.251	7.815	9.348	11.345	12.838
4	7.779	9.488	11.143	13.277	14.860
5	9.236	11.070	12.832	15.086	16.750
6	10.645	12.592	14.449	16.812	18.548
7	12.017	14.067	16.013	18.475	20.278
8	13.362	15.507	17.535	20.090	21.955
9	14.684	16.919	19.023	21.666	23.589
10	15.987	18.307	20.483	23.209	25.188
11	17.275	19.675	21.920	24.725	26.757
12	18.549	21.026	23.337	26.217	28.300
13	19.812	22.362	24.736	27.688	29.819
14	21.064	23.685	26.119	29.141	31.319
15	22.307	24.996	27.488	30.578	32.801
16	23.542	26.296	28.845	32.000	34.267
17	24.769	27.587	30.191	33.409	35.718
18	25.989	28.869	31.526	34.805	37.156
19	27.204	30.144	32.852	36.191	38.582
20	28.412	31.410	34.170	37.566	39.997
21	29.615	32.671	35.479	38.932	41.401
22	30.813	33.924	36.781	40.289	42.796
23	32.007	35.172	38.076	41.638	44.181
24	33.196	36.415	39.364	42.980	45.558
25	34.382	37.652	40.646	44.314	46.928
26	35.563	38.885	41.923	45.642	48.290
27	36.741	40.113	43.195	46.963	49.645
28	37.916	41.337	44.461	48.278	50.994
29	39.087	42.557	45.722	49.588	52.335
30	40.256	43.773	46.979	50.892	53.672
35	46.059	49.802	53.203	57.342	60.275
40	51.805	55.758	59.342	63.691	66.766
45	57.505	61.656	65.410	69.957	73.166
50	63.167	67.505	71.420	76.154	79.490
60	74.397	79.082	83.298	88.379	91.952
70	85.527	90.531	95.023	100.425	104.215
80	96.578	101.879	106.629	112.329	116.321
90	107.565	113.145	118.136	124.116	128.299
100	118.498	124.342	129.561	135.807	140.170

Glossary

1st quartile – Quartile usually denoted Q_1; is the 25th percentile. p. 129

3rd quartile – Quartile usually denoted Q_3; is the 75th percentile. p. 129

A

Alternative hypothesis – What you are going to believe about the population when there is strong evidence against the null hypothesis. p. 260

C

Classical definition of probability – If there are n equally likely possible outcomes of an experiment, and m of them correspond to the event you are interested in, then the probability of the event is $\frac{m}{n}$. p. 153

Coefficient of determination, R^2 – A value that measures the percentage of variation in the y-variable that is explained by changes in the x-variable. p. 511

Complement of an event A – Everything in the sample space that is not A. p. 172

Conditional probability – The probability of an event A given that another event B has already occurred; the usual notation is $P(A|B)$, read *the probability of* A, *given* B. p. 160

Confidence interval estimate – A range of numbers of the form (a, b) that is thought to enclose the parameter of interest, with a given level of probability. p. 298

Continuous random variable – A random variable that can take on any value from a continuous range. p. 185

Continuous variable – A measurement variable that can take *any* possible value on a number line (possibly within upper and lower limits). p. 28

Coverage errors – Errors that arise because of inaccuracy or duplication in the survey frame. p. 11

Cross-sectional data – Data that are all collected in the same time period. p. 29

D

Descriptive statistics – A set of techniques to organize and summarize raw data. p. 14

Deviation from the mean – The distance of the point from the mean value for each data point. p. 106

Discrete random variable – A random variable that can take on any value from a list of distinct possible values. p. 185

Discrete variable – A variable that can take on only certain identifiable values on a number line (possibly within upper and lower limits). p. 28

E

Estimation errors – Errors that arise because of incorrect use of statistical techniques, or calculation errors. p. 12

Event – One or more outcomes of an experiment. p. 153

Excel bin number – The upper included limit of a class. p. 40

Experiment – Any activity with an uncertain outcome. p. 153

Experimental study – The researcher designs the study so that conclusions about causation can be drawn. p. 16

Explanatory variable – Variable observed (and sometimes controlled) by the researcher, which is the apparent cause of the change in the response variable. p. 76

F

Factor – A qualitative explanatory characteristic that might distinguish one group or population from another. p. 400

Frame – A list of the elements in a population. p. 7

Frequency distribution – A summary table that divides quantitative data into classes, and records the count (or frequency) of data points in each class. p. 31

H

Histogram – A graph of a frequency distribution, with lower class limits shown along the x-axis, and class frequencies shown along the y-axis. p. 32

I

Independent events – Two events A and B are independent if the probability of one of the events is unaffected by whether the other event has occurred; $P(A|B) = P(A)$ and $P(B|A) = P(B)$. p. 162

Inferential statistics – A set of techniques that allow reliable conclusions to be drawn about population data, on the basis of sample data. p. 7

Influential observation – A single observation that has an extreme effect on the regression equation. p. 498

Interquartile range (IQR) – $Q_3 - Q_1$; it measures the range of the middle 50% of the data values. p. 129

L

Least-squares line – The line that has the smallest possible sum of the squared residuals. p. 482

Level – A value or setting that the factor can take. p. 400

M

Mean – A measure of central tendency calculated by adding up all the numbers in the data set, and then dividing by the number of numbers. p. 105

Median – The middle value (if there is a unique middle value), or the average of the two middle values (when there is not a unique middle value) in an ordered data set. p. 108

Mode – The most frequently occurring value in the data set. p. 111

Mutually exclusive events – Events that cannot happen simultaneously; if two events A and B are mutually exclusive, then $P(A \text{ and } B) = 0$. p. 171

N

Negative (inverse) relationship – Increases in the explanatory variable correspond to decreases in the response variable. p. 77

Nonresponse error – Error that arises when data cannot be collected for some elements of the sample. p. 11

Nonsampling errors – Other kinds of errors that can arise in the process of sampling a population. p. 11

Nonstatistical sampling – The elements of the population are chosen for the sample by convenience, or according to the researcher's judgment; there is no way to estimate the probability that any particular element from the population will be chosen for the sample. p. 5

Null hypothesis – What you are going to believe about the population unless the sample gives you strongly contradictory evidence. p. 260

O

Observational study – The researcher observes what is already taking place. p. 16

Outlier – A data point that is unusually far from the rest of the data. p. 55

P

Parameter – A summary measure of the population data. p. 7

Pearson correlation coefficient – A numerical measure that indicates the strength and direction of the linear relationship between two quantitative variables. p. 133

Point estimate – A single-number estimate of a population parameter that is based on sample data. p. 298

Population data – The complete collection of *all* of the data of interest. p. 5

Positive (direct) relationship – Increases in the explanatory variable correspond to increases in the response variable. p. 77

Primary data – Data that are collected for your specific purpose. p. 3

Probability distribution for a discrete random variable – A list of all the possible values of the random variable, and their associated probabilities. p. 185

Probability distribution of a continuous random variable – A graph or a mathematical formula describing the probabilities in a continuous range p. 185

Probability – A measure of the likelihood of an event. p. 153

Processing errors – Errors that occur when the data are being prepared for analysis. p. 12

P^{th} percentile – X_p, the data point that is above P% of the data points. p. 128

p-value – In a hypothesis test, the probability of getting a sample result at least as extreme as the observed sample result; the probability calculation is based on the sampling distribution that would exist if the null hypothesis were true. p. 265

Q

Qualitative data – Data containing descriptive information, which may be recorded in words or numbers (the numbers represent codes for the associated words; arithmetical operations such as averaging are not meaningful in this case). p. 27

Quantitative data – Data containing numerical information, for which arithmetical operations such as averaging are meaningful. p. 27

R

Random variable – A variable whose value is determined by the outcome of a random experiment. p. 185

Range – A number that is calculated as the difference between the maximum and minimum values in the data set. p. 115

Ranked data – Qualitative data that can be ordered according to size or quality. p. 29

Regression confidence interval – Interval that predicts the average y for a specific value of x. p. 514

Regression prediction interval – Interval that predicts a particular value of y for a specific value of x. p. 513

Relative frequency – The percentage of total observations that fall into a particular class. p. 55

Relative frequency approach to probability – Probability is the relative frequency of an event over a large number of repeated trials of an experiment. p. 153

Residual – The difference between the observed value of y for a specific x, and the predicted value of y for that x. p. 481

Response errors – Errors that arise because of problems with the survey collection instrument (e.g., the questionnaire), the interviewer (e.g., bias), the respondent (e.g., faulty memory), or the survey process (e.g., not ensuring that the respondent fits into the target group). p. 12

Response variable – Variable that changes when the explanatory variable changes. p. 76

Response variable – A quantitative variable that is being measured or observed. We are interested in how this variable responds to the different levels of the factor. p. 400

S

Sample data – A subset of population data. p. 5

Sample space – A complete list or representation of all of the possible outcomes of an experiment. p. 153

Sample statistic – A summary measure of the sample data. p. 7

Sampling distribution – The probability distribution of all possible sample results for a given sample size. p. 225

Sampling error – The difference between the true value of the population parameter and the value of the corresponding sample statistic. p. 11

Scatter diagram – Displays paired x-y data points of the form (x, y). p. 76

Secondary data – Data that were previously collected, not for your specific purpose. p. 3

Significance level – The maximum allowable probability of a Type I error in a hypothesis test. p. 263

Simple random sampling – A sampling process that ensures that each element of the population is equally likely to be selected. p. 7

Six Sigma – BMO Financial Group appears to know the value of using statistical methods in business. The company first adopted **Six Sigma** methods in its Product Operations Group in 2005, resulting in fewer errors, less waste, and expected savings of $86 million over a five-year period. ("Six Sigma & Business Improvement Deployment Leader of the Year: Richard Lam, BMO Financial Group." The Global Six Sigma & Business Improvement Awards. **www.tgssa.com**.). p. 3

Skewed to the left (or negatively skewed) distribution – A distribution in which some unusually small values in the data set destroy the symmetry. p. 53

Skewed to the right (or positively skewed) distribution – A distribution in which some unusually high values in the data set destroy the symmetry. p. 52

Spearman rank correlation coefficient – A numerical measure that indicates the strength and direction of the relationship (linear or non-linear) for two variables, one or both of which may be ranked. p. 139

Standard deviation – A measure of variability in a data set that is based on deviations from the mean. p. 117

Statistical sampling – The elements of the population are chosen for the sample in a random fashion, with a known probability of inclusion. p. 7

Symmetric distribution – The right half of the distribution is a mirror image of the left half. p. 52

T

Time-series data – Data that are collected over successive points in time. p. 29

Type I error – Error that arises when we mistakenly reject the null hypothesis when it is in fact true. p. 263

Type II error – Error that arises when we mistakenly fail to reject the null hypothesis when it is in fact false. p. 263

V

Variable – A characteristic or quantity that can vary. p. 26

Index

CHAPTER 9

Test statistic for the hypothesis test of the mean difference in matched pairs (p. 335)

$$t = \frac{\bar{x}_D - \mu_D}{s_D/\sqrt{n_D}}$$

Constructing a confidence interval estimate for the mean difference in matched pairs (p. 335)

$$\bar{x}_D \pm \text{critical } t\text{-score} \left(\frac{s_D}{\sqrt{n_D}}\right)$$

Test statistic for W, in the Wilcoxon Signed Rank Sum Test, $n \geq 25$ (p. 353)

$$z = \frac{W - \mu_W}{\sigma_W}$$

$$= \frac{W - \left(\frac{n_W(n_W + 1)}{4}\right)}{\sqrt{\frac{n_W(n_W + 1)(2n_W + 1)}{24}}}$$

Test statistic for the sign test (p. 361)

$$z = \frac{\hat{p} - p}{\sigma_{\hat{p}}} = \frac{\hat{p} - p}{\sqrt{\frac{pq}{n_{ST}}}}$$

CHAPTER 10

Test statistic for the hypothesis test of the difference in means, independent samples, unequal variances, p. 380

$$t = \frac{(\bar{x}_1 - \bar{x}_2) - (\mu_1 - \mu_2)}{\sqrt{\frac{s_1^2}{n_1} + \frac{s_2^2}{n_2}}}$$

Constructing a confidence interval estimate for the difference in population means, independent samples, unequal variances (p. 381)

$$(\bar{x}_1 - \bar{x}_2) \pm t\text{-score}\sqrt{\frac{s_1^2}{n_1} + \frac{s_2^2}{n_2}}$$

Test statistic for W_1, in the Wilcoxon Rank Sum Test, $n_i \geq 10$ (p. 391)

$$z = \frac{W_1 - \mu_{W_1}}{\sigma_{W_1}}$$

$$= \frac{W_1 - \frac{n_1(n_1 + n_2 + 1)}{2}}{\sqrt{\frac{n_1 n_2(n_1 + n_2 + 1)}{12}}}$$

CHAPTER 11

Calculating the mean square for within-sample variation (p. 411)

$$MS_{within} = \frac{SS_{within}}{n_T - k}$$

$$= \frac{SS_1 + SS_2 + \cdots + SS_k}{n_T - k}$$

Calculating the mean square for between-sample variation (p. 412)

$$MS_{between} = \frac{SS_{between}}{k - 1}$$

$$= \frac{n_1(\bar{x}_1 - \bar{\bar{x}})^2 + n_2(\bar{x}_2 - \bar{\bar{x}})^2 + \cdots + n_k(\bar{x}_k - \bar{\bar{x}})^2}{k - 1}$$

Calculating the test statistic for one-factor ANOVA (p. 419)

$$F = \frac{MS_{between}}{MS_{within}}$$

Calculating the Tukey-Kramer confidence interval for $(\mu_i - \mu_j)$ (p. 423)

$$(\bar{x}_i - \bar{x}_j) \pm q\text{-score} \sqrt{\frac{MS_{within}}{2}\left(\frac{1}{n_i} + \frac{1}{n_j}\right)}$$

CHAPTER 12

Calculating the pooled proportion for the hypothesis test of two proportions, with proportions hypothesized to be equal (p. 439)

$$\hat{p} = \frac{x_1 + x_2}{n_1 + n_2}$$

Test statistic for the hypothesis test of two proportions, proportions hypothesized to be equal (p. 445)

$$z = \frac{(\hat{p}_1 - \hat{p}_2) - \mu_{\hat{p}_1 - \hat{p}_2}}{S_{\hat{p}_1 - \hat{p}_2}}$$

$$= \frac{(\hat{p}_1 - \hat{p}_2) - 0}{\sqrt{\hat{p}\hat{q}\left(\frac{1}{n_1} + \frac{1}{n_2}\right)}}$$

Test statistic for the hypothesis test of two proportions, proportions hypothesized to differ by a fixed amount (non-zero) (p. 446)

$$z = \frac{(\hat{p}_1 - \hat{p}_2) - \mu_{\hat{p}_1 - \hat{p}_2}}{S_{\hat{p}_1 - \hat{p}_2}}$$

$$= \frac{(\hat{p}_1 - \hat{p}_2) - \mu_{\hat{p}_1 - \hat{p}_2}}{\sqrt{\frac{\hat{p}_1\hat{q}_1}{n_1} + \frac{\hat{p}_2\hat{q}_2}{n_2}}}$$

Constructing a confidence interval estimate for the difference in population proportions (p. 444)

$$(\hat{p}_1 - \hat{p}_2) \pm z\text{-score} \sqrt{\frac{\hat{p}_1\hat{q}_1}{n_1} + \frac{\hat{p}_2\hat{q}_2}{n_2}}$$

Calculating Chi-square test statistic (pp. 449, 461)

$$\chi^2 = \Sigma \frac{(o_i - e_i)^2}{e_i}$$

Calculating expected values for a contingency table (p. 460)

$$\text{expected value} = \frac{(\text{row total})(\text{column total})}{(\text{grand total})}$$

CHAPTER 13

Calculating the residual for a least-squares line (p. 489)

$$e_i = y_i - \hat{y}_i$$

Test statistic for a hypothesis test about the slope of the regression line (p. 509)

$$t = \frac{b_1}{s_{b_1}}$$

CHAPTER 14

Calculating the test statistic for hypothesis test of overall regression model (p. 542)

$$F = \frac{\frac{SSR}{k}}{\frac{SSE}{n - (k + 1)}} = \frac{MSR}{MSE}$$

A Guide to the Descriptive and Inferential Te

Type of Investigation	Type of Data	
What are the characteristics of this distribution of quantitative data?	Single-variable quantitative data • Organize in a frequency distribution	• Histogram • Comment on shap

Compare two or more distributions of quantitative data	Two or more sets of single-variable quantitative data
	• Organize in frequency distributions
	  (use relative frequencies where appropriate)
		• Two or more histogr comparison
		  • Comment on shap
		• See Guide to Techni on page 60

What are the characteristics of the qualitative categories?	Collection of data with one qualitative characteristic, with two or more levels • Organize in a simple table	Bar graph (or pie char few categories and sha
Compare two or more distributions of qualitative data • What are the characteristics of the qualitative categories? • Are these qualitative categories related?	Collection of data with two (or more) qualitative characteristics, each with two or more levels • Organize in a contingency table (at least a 2×2 table)	Bar graph with two or category
What are the trends over time? • Compare trends over time for two or more variables	Time-series data (generally quantitative)	• Line graph, with tim • Multiple lines on the are being compared
Are these variables related/associated and, if so, how?	• Paired data, quantitative or ranked, of the form $(x_1, y_1), (x_2, y_2), \ldots, (x_n, y_n)$	Scatter diagram for qu • Explanatory variable • Response variable on
	• Quantitative response (y) variable, with quantitative or qualitative explanatory variables (more than one)	

chniques of *Analyzing Data and Making Decisions*

Graph	Numerical Measure(s)	Inferential Techniques
e and skewness	• Measure of central tendency and measure of variability • See Guide to Decision Making: Choosing a Measure of Central Tendency on page 114 • See Guide to Decision Making: Choosing a Measure of Variability on page 131	• Hypothesis tests about μ (Chapter 7) • Confidence intervals about μ (Chapter 8)
ms set up for easy and skewness ue: Comparing Histograms	• Measures of central tendency and measures of variability • See Guide to Decision Making: Choosing a Measure of Central Tendency on page 114 • See Guide to Decision Making: Choosing a Measure of Variability on page 131	Matched Pairs • Hypothesis tests about μ_D (Chapter 9) • Confidence intervals about μ_D (Chapter 9) • Wilcoxon Signed Rank Sum Test (Chapter 9) Independent Samples • t-test of $\mu_1 - \mu_2$ (Chapter 10) • Confidence intervals about $\mu_1 - \mu_2$ (Chapter 10) • Wilcoxon Rank Sum Test (Chapter 10) • ANOVA (Chapter 11)
, if there are relatively e of the total is important)	Frequencies or relative frequencies of categories	• Hypothesis test about p (Chapter 7) • Confidence intervals about p (Chapter 8) • χ^2 hypothesis test about goodness of fit (Chapter 12)
nore bars in each	Frequencies or relative frequencies of categories	• Hypothesis test about difference in matched pairs of ranked data, Sign Test (Chapter 9) • Hypothesis test about locations of populations of independent ranked data, Wilcoxon Rank Sum Test (Chapter 10) • Hypothesis test about $p_1 - p_2$ (Chapter 12) • Confidence intervals about $p_1 - p_2$ (Chapter 12) • χ^2 hypothesis test for testing many proportions, or testing for independence (Chapter 12)
e on the x-axis graph if time series	Absolute change or percentage change over time • Significant increases or decreases noted, citing specific values • Significant changes in trend noted, citing specific values	
ntitative data on the x-axis the y-axis	• Pearson r or Spearman r • Coefficient of determination, R^2 • See Guide to Decision Making: Choosing a Measure of Association on page 142 - • Adjusted R^2	• Hypothesis test about the regression relationship (Chapters 13 & 14) – Regression confidence and prediction intervals (Chapters 13 & 14)

CHAPTER 2

Calculating class width (p. 35)

$$\text{Class width} = \frac{\text{maximum value} - \text{minimum value}}{\sqrt{n}}$$

CHAPTER 3

Calculating the sample mean (p. 105)

$$\bar{x} = \frac{\sum x}{n}$$

Calculating the location of the median (p. 109)

$$0.5(n + 1)$$

Calculating the sample standard deviation with the computational formula (p. 119)

$$s = \sqrt{\frac{\sum x^2 - \frac{(\sum x)^2}{n}}{n - 1}}$$

Calculating the interquartile range (p. 129)

$$\text{Location of } Q_1 = 0.25(n + 1)$$
$$\text{Location of } Q_3 = 0.73(n + 1)$$
$$IQR = Q_3 - Q_1$$

CHAPTER 4

If two events are independent, then (p. 162)

$$P(A|B) = P(A) \text{ and}$$
$$P(B|A) = P(B)$$

Calculating the conditional probability of A given B (p. 166)

$$P(A|B) = \frac{P(A \text{ and } B)}{P(B)}$$

Calculating the probability of A and B (p. 167)

$$P(A \text{ and } B) = P(A) \cdot P(B|A)$$

Calculating the probability of A and B when A and B are independent events (p. 169)

$$P(A \text{ and } B) = P(A) \cdot P(B)$$

Calculating the probability of A or B (p. 170)

$$P(A \text{ or } B) = P(A) + P(B) - P(A \text{ and } B)$$

Calculating the probability of A or B when A and B are mutually exclusive (p. 171)

$$P(A \text{ or } B) = P(A) + P(B)$$

Calculating the probability of an event A using the complement rule (p. 172)

$$P(A) = 1 - P(A^C)$$

CHAPTER 5

Calculating the mean of a discrete probability distribution (p. 187)

$$\mu = \sum(x \cdot P(x))$$

Calculating the standard deviation of a discrete probability distribution using the computational formula (p. 187)

$$\sigma = \sqrt{\sum x^2 P(x) - \mu^2}$$

Calculating the mean and standard deviation of a binomial random variable (p. 190)

$$\mu = np$$
$$\sigma = \sqrt{npq}$$

Calculating the probability of x successes in binomial experiment with n trials and probability of success p (p. 194)

$$P(x \text{ successes}) = \binom{n}{x} p^x q^{n-x}$$

Calculating the z-score to standardize a normal random variable (p. 212)

$$z = \frac{x - \mu}{\sigma}$$

Calculating the x-value that corresponds to a particular normal probability (p. 214)

$$x = \mu + z \cdot \sigma$$

CHAPTER 6

Calculating the mean and standard error of the sampling distribution of sample means (p. 233)

$$\mu_{\bar{x}} = \mu$$
$$\sigma_{\bar{x}} = \frac{\sigma}{\sqrt{n}}$$

Calculating the mean and standard error of the sampling distribution of sample proportions (p. 248)

$$\sigma_{\hat{p}} = \sqrt{\frac{pq}{n}}$$
$$\mu_{\hat{p}} = p$$

Conditions required for the normality of the sampling distribution of the sample proportions (p. 248)

$$np \geq 10 \text{ and } nq \geq 10$$

CHAPTER 7

Test statistic for the hypothesis test of a proportion (p. 274)

$$z = \frac{\hat{p} - \mu_{\hat{p}}}{\sigma_{\hat{p}}} = \frac{\hat{p} - p}{\sqrt{\frac{pq}{n}}}$$

Test statistic for the hypothesis test of the mean (p. 276)

$$t = \frac{\bar{x} - \mu_{\bar{x}}}{s_{\bar{x}}} = \frac{\bar{x} - \mu}{s/\sqrt{n}}$$

CHAPTER 8

Constructing the confidence interval estimate for p (p. 304)

$$\hat{p} \pm (\text{critical } z\text{-score})\sqrt{\frac{\hat{p}\hat{q}}{n}}$$

Constructing the confidence interval estimate for μ (p. 309)

$$\bar{x} \pm (\text{critical } t\text{-score})\left(\frac{s}{\sqrt{n}}\right)$$

Calculating the sample size required for an estimate of μ (p. 314)

$$n = \left(\frac{(z\text{-score})(s)}{\text{HW}}\right)^2$$

Calculating sample size required for an estimate of p (p. 316)

$$n = \hat{p}\hat{q}\left(\frac{z\text{-score}}{\text{HW}}\right)^2$$